TOIL, ENDURE, BELIEVE

Coloured map of the Kingdom of Sikkim and the Chumbi Valley, Tibet, from the survey of the 1903/4 Younghusband Expedition to Lhasa. This map covers all the main routes taken by George and Doreen during their 1942/3/4 treks in the foothills of the Himalayas.

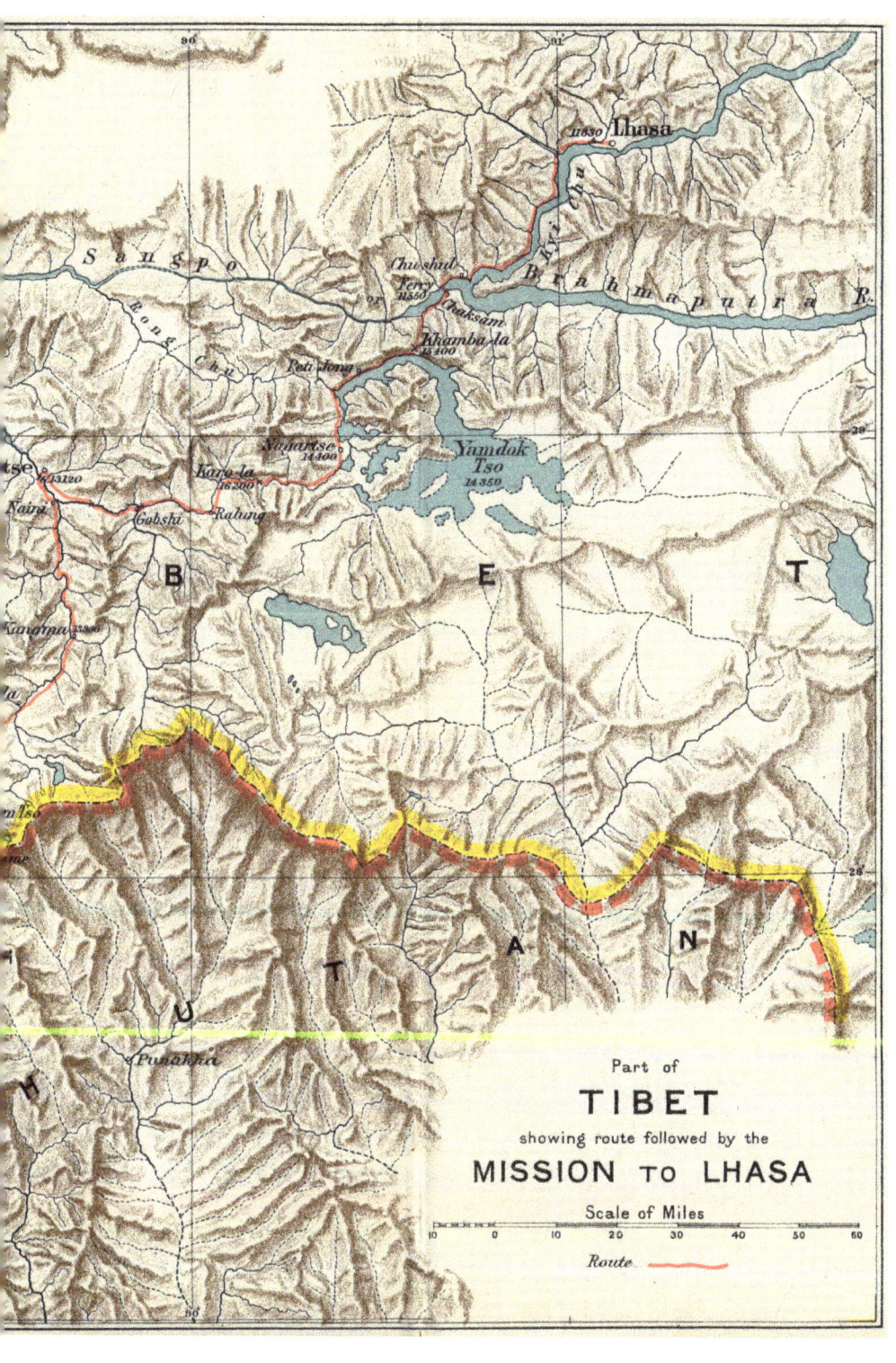

Part of

TIBET

showing route followed by the

MISSION TO LHASA

Scale of Miles

Route

TOIL, ENDURE, BELIEVE

The biography of Sir George Morton, OBE, MC his war on the Somme, a career as a leading businessman and banker in India in WW2, & member of the Economic Mission to Greece 1946-7

To Brian,

with every best wish

from John

JOHN MORTON

Christmas 2022.

In honour of George and Doreen, and in memory of Jean and Jen

Our children are like music,
    like the notes of a song,
We've scarcely begun to take them in,
    before they're gone.

Our parents are a story,
    like a book we've not read.
We've scarcely begun on chapter one,
    before they're dead.

*(by kind permission of the reverend Dom Paul Brown
O.S.B., Ampleforth Abbey)*

George at sea . . . probably taken by Doreen on their way back to Bombay from Marseilles after their honeymoon in Paris October 1929

First paperback edition 2022

978-1-80227-315-1 (Paperback)
978-1-80227-316-8 (Hardback)
978-1-80227-317-5 (eBook)

CONTENTS

ILLUSTRATIONS

Endpaper. Coloured map of the Kingdom of Sikkim and the Chumbi valley Tibet from the survey of the 1903/4 Younghusband expedition to Tibet. This map covers all the main routes taken by George and Doreen during their 1942/43/44 treks in the foothills of the Himalayas.

Frontespiece. George at sea . . . probably taken by Doreen on their way back to Bombay from Marseilles after their honeymoon in Paris October 1929.

(Note the illustrations 10,11,12,13 above are all sourced from 'The Battle of Boom Ravine' by the late Trevor Pidgeon)

A collection of illustrations with a group placment between Part 1 and 2 (all Morton Archive)

Part 2 Magical India – A new start in new life (note all illustrations Morton Archive)

Part 3 Magical India – Marriage and children – "the three J's" – Separations and a hazardous sea voyage back to India

A selection of coloured illustrations (Morton Archive and other anonimous sources)

Authors note to illustrations 71-76. Doreen was a keen ornothologist, and particularly knowwledgable of Himalayan Birds and in this she was encouraged and supported by Sir Paul Benthall, who lived just few yards away from us in Rajasantosh Road at that time. Sir Paul himself was a well repected authority both as a botanist and ornothologist in the great traditon of Kingdom Ward, Ludlow, George Sheriff and others. Doreens birdbooks have survived, and contain two illustrations by Sir Paul as well as a number of her own, and a selection of these follow and are grouped together.

Authors note to Illustrations 77-82 & 84. These are from a rare set of 1944 Christmas cards printed on locally made paper by the Kalimpong Industries. This was a charity established by Norman and Bunty Odling to support local employment particularly of the disabled and the blind. George was a director and auditor, and Bunty one of three daughters of the founder of the Homes, Dr Graham of the Church of Scotland.

The Kalimpong Homes London Association held a Christmas Bazar every November in the crypt of St Colombas Church Pont Street to raise funds for the Homes; the authors late sister Jean a former pupil was a member of the committee before her death and this family tradition has been carried on by her daughter Caroline.

Papermaking in the Far East originated with the Chinese 2000 years ago, who made it from the finest fibres of jute stalks; examples still survive. But Jute does not grow on the high Tibetan Plateau, so the Tibetans used the fibrous root of the Rijac plant instead. This was boiled in water, pulped and the fibres filtered out and used to make paper. The plant is poisonous and so the paper is largely impervious to insect attack and survives almost indefinitely.

These rare cards are block printed in colour on this fine fibrous light tan paper, as paper was rationed and in very short supply during the war. The scenes depicted are evocative of the lives of the hill people amongst whom George and Doreen travelled and where the author lived and spent his happy childhood.

In the writers conversations with the late Sir David Goodhall he recalled as High Comissioner to India visiting the school to present the prizes. He was a distinguished artist and we are particularly grateful for the families permission to reprint his sketch of the Victoria Memorial which was opened on 28th December 1922 almost exactly 100 years ago, by HRH Edward the Prince of Wales. The authors Grandfather attended the opening as a member of the Prince,s Tour Party and George was a Trustee from 1939–42.

(Note the illustrations 89-91 are all illustrated by Robert Morton 'German storm troopers on a counter offensive')

Part 4 Our new home in Kalimpong, Georges leadership role in an unlovely and forgotten war (October 6ᵗʰ 1940 – June 1945)

A second selected group of illustrations

Part Five George retires, buys Rectory House, packs up India (Spring 1946) joins British Economic Mission to Greece (Winter 1946–7) and realises his farming dream. June 1945-13.04 1954)

ACKNOWLEDGEMENTS

The initial research for this book started in 1998. I was anxious to find out more about my fathers first world war record, and so went to the National Archive at Kew to see whether they had his details. I was able to access the full file and ordered copies. I also found Trevor Pidgeon's book of the Battle of Boom Ravine in which George was seriously wounded, and wrote to Trevor. I had a charming letter back enclosing the relevant extracts of the history of the 18th Division. Unusually there was also a history of the 54th Infantry Division and he sent me copies from this source as well. There the matter rested until I retired in 2015.

My first act was to access the family archive collected and left to my mother by my uncle, James O'Kinealy and a search of the material led me to research my first book "Family of the Raj" I had strong support from my late wife Jane to whom this first book is dedicated as well as help from many other folk. Jane and I went to Ireland to begin the research into the origins of the O'Kinealy family. But the record and story of my father's life represented unfinished business. So my first thanks go to Jane for encouraging me to write and the late Trevor Pidgeon for his kindness.

At the beginning of June 2018 in order to start the story of the 11th Fusiliers, I made a date to see the archivist at the Fusilier Regimental HQ in the Tower of London to see whether they had the war diaries of the various Fusiliers battalions of the first world war. It was a trip down memory lane as I had last been there when we mounted the Tower picquet from Chelsea barracks in 1956. We took part in the Ceremony of the Keys at sunset in the roadway opposite the Governor's House . . . "who goes there???" . . . "The Keys" . . . " Whose Keys???" . . . "The Queens Keys".

The HQ is in the Museum building next to what used to be the officers mess. So my thanks to Stephanie Killingbrook–Turner for her help and so promptly sending me the 1915-1918 11th Battalion fully digitised diaries. This enabled me to contrast what George was writing to his sister with what was actually happening on the ground, and to piece together my fathers activities from the diaries, his trench book and other records and photographs that he and his sister, Alice, kept.

Early contact was made with Richard Benthall through the hospitality of Jim and Carol Devlin at Lindridge. Richard and I swapped books of mutual interest ; it was he that gave me the last copy of the Birds Heilger private history written in 1964. This coupled with Richards knowledge of the company for whom he had worked, (as did my father) his knowledge of India, and advice and unstinting support for the project has all been of great help in putting together a cogent account of the companys activities in which my father played his part. Richard and I and his twin brother James were contemporaries in India in the early 1960s. His father Sir Paul Benthall and George worked together for many years as fellow partners in Birds Heilgers, and Sir Paul went on to serve as senior partner of the firm and also twice as President of the Bengal Chamber. I am most grateful to Richard for his unstinting help and for agreeing to write the foreword to this book.

I have incorporated my own research into the massive educational and progressive professional development programme of the second half of the 19th and early 20th century as Indians grasped all aspects of international business and self-government. I have illustrated this from my notes of the hisrory of the astonishing development of Western Medicine after the British Government took over the Colonial Management of the country in 1858. This enabled me to put together a picture of the environment in which my father worked which complemented the account from his letters to "Sis" of his experiences when he arrived in India in late November 1919. Here I have also drawn on the family records of my grandfather's life as a doctor in the Indian Medical Service. Thank you Richard and Stella for your kindness and hospitality It was Richard who directed me to the Cambridge Institute for South Asiatic Studies when I attempted to locate the Benthall archive of his uncle Sir Edward in the British Library; this substantial archive of some 34 boxes did not contain any references to my father, but contained important and as yet unpublished references to various meetings of the Round Table Conferences leading up to the 1935 Government of India Act. My interest in this stemmed from my fathers Directorship of the Imperial Bank which up to 1937, when the Reserve bank was opened, had performed many of the functions of a reserve Bank. This Act also established in 1937 the new and quite independent Reserve Bank of India also in Bombay.

This led to the discovery of an account of Sir Edward's various meetings with Mahatma Ghandi which because of it's importance is reproduced in full as an appendix to the book; his account includes new insights into the decision by the Viceroys council to arrest Ghandi and his followers after the launch of the quit India movement in late 1942. I have also included here the letters written by Ruth, his wife and my godmother, to my mother from home in 1940-42.

Thank you too, to Dr Kevin Greenbank the archivist of the Camebridge Institute, who not only directed me to the various sections of the Benthall archive but also arranged for me to stay at Wolfson College, close to the Institute. When I came to research the appointment of my father as Chairman of the Calcutta Evacuees Committee he directed me to the Macrell archive which contained a mass of relevant information (including Ritchie Gardiner's diary account) of the evacuation itself. I was able to show him the family copy of Ritchie Gardiner' diary. I know of only one other copy which is in he Imperial War museum. It was through Kevin also that I was introduced to *Flight by Elephant* by *Andrew Martin* the astonishing story of the rescue by Giles Macrell and his elephants, of the 200 or so members of Sir John Rowland's party attempting to escape to India from Burma over the 8,500 ft Chukan pass during the monsoon.

I would also like to thank Hedley Sutton and the staff at the Africa and Asia section of the British Library. It was they who located the report of the Bengal Chamber, 1941, presented to the members on 26th February 1942 by my father, and also the digitised elements of the Times of India including the August 1945 report of Netaji Subbhas Bose's death, as well as Sir Reginald Dorman – Smith's report on The Civil Evacuation of Burma (1943), and other official reports.

My thanks are also due to Dorothy Hunter who succeeded in obtaining a copy of Dr. Ahanasios Lykogiannis's PHD thesis written in 1999 while at the London School of Economics and Political Sciences (UK) entitled *Britain and the Greek economic crisis 1944-1947 From Liberation to the Truman Doctrine* which has been central to this section of the book.

Thanks also to Fr Paul for his permission to use his poignant poem as a part of the dedication on this book.

My thanks to John and Jean Mackie for their hospitality and loan of many books, and also to my old friends Richard Brasher, Richard Penfold, and Caro Burmaster as well as Richard Benthall for their most valuable help with the draft manuscript. Caro has been through the manuscript of the book several times and also suggested the title as well as helping with the interpretation and translation of Genevieve's prayer given to my father in 1916. Thanks too to David Jenkins for his loan of the Imperial Airlines pre-war international map of their air routes reproduced in colour in the book. David must have been one of the last unaccompanied boys to travel out with Imperial before it became B.O.A.C. to join his parents in Rangoon after the war. And thanks to my many friends particularly Garry Reynolds and Caroline Shaw of Courtiers for their encouragement in writing this book, and last but not least my children Janetta, May, Robert and James, and my eldest grand-daughter Zoe for their patience help and encouragement to their father.

Special thanks to Robert a talented illustrator for his coloured sketches of German stormtroopers.

Thanks also to Patrick, Sophie, Alexander, Ben and Karl. The brilliant team at Publishing Push in guiding me through the production process and putting up with my endless questions.

January 1st 2022

INTRODUCTION

Writing this book has been something of a pilgrimage to get to know my father. George died when I was just seventeen, and so I was unable to have an adult relationship with him. During the first few years we as a family were in India, our parents working flat out in Calcutta in a life that was dominated by the Far Eastern War; we children were in Kalimpong in the hills of the Himalayas near Darjeeling for nine months of the year. Their desire was to protect us from the consequences of the pressures of war and the harsh summer Calcutta climate, and so we missed out on parental contact and the close relationship with our parents that normally forms as a result. Not that we thought of this as anything odd, because it was the situation that most families there experienced. In spite of this, mine was an extraordinarily happy childhood. It is only now through the writing of this book that I realise what astonishing people both parents were, and the courage and dedication of their lives to their childen, their friends, and their more public duties, and the rich friendships that developed.

The backbone of the book is a collection of family letters, photographs and artifacts. Around this I have attempted to flesh out the relevant history of their time through study and research. Some content relies on memory; my only regret is that none of my immediate family are around to add their own story. Naturally being the youngest family member my memory is that of a young child growing up. The historical research has been structured around the events with which they were closely involved, and which to some extent shaped the decisions that they made, and the thinking that generated them. I have also have had the benefit of living and working in India during the early 1960s for the Tata organisation, and so have both a direct and personal adult experience of living there, and speaking the languages, and can relate as a result to my parents life experiences.

I am lucky to have inherited a large collection of books on India, to which I have added throughout my own life. Some of these are almost unique, for example Ritchie Gardiner's personal diary of his escape from Burma over the 8500ft Chukan Pass in the monsoon – I know of only one other copy which is in the Imperial War Museum. My interest as a part of the story is from my parents friendship with him following his escape from Burma over the 8500 ft Chukan pass through the monsoon, and his recuperation at our home in Calcutta. My father's was working at the time amongst his many other responsibilities as Chairman of the Calcutta Evacuees Committee, which fielded close on half a million refugees to Calcutta from Burma during the first nine months of 1942.

George was born in the last decade of Queen Victoria's reign, that sixty two year period characterised by the growth and concepts of Empire. His parents were of humble origin, his father William listed as a labourer on their marriage certificate. George was the middle child with two siblings, his elder brother William an accountant; he then, as an artilliaryman was to die from wounds suffered in July 1917. His younger sister Alice was the lynchpin for both brothers, which came to the fore with her support for them during the war. The family grew up in Balham, the children privately educated. William had developed a dairy and grocery business and prospered. The immediate family were largely self made individuals with a shrewd Scottish streak in their make-up. His mother died and father William now a widower sought to enhance the family fortunes through a disastrous investment in Canada; returning he committed suicide in early 1915.

George left school aged sixteen and joined Deloitte Plender and Griffiths as a trainee accountant. He joined the Inns of Court in 1913, and then enlisted as a volunteer in the 11th Royal Fusiliers at the onset of war. He was commissioned, and after a period of training in Wiltshire the Battalion joined the 54th Infantry Brigade (part of the 18th Division). The British Expeditionary force had by now expanded into Kitchiners second army plugging the line between the Begians to the North and the French to the South who extended to the Swiss border. Between August 1915 and the onset of the Somme battles they were mostly in the Albert trenches, their lives consisting of ten day spells in the front line followed by ten days in reserve. Their life experiences were of shelling, snipers, mines, saps, rats, and trench life with its mud cold and rain, and with it's constant drip feed of casualties from sniping and shelling. They fought at Pommiers Redout, Trones Wood and the final battles of the Somme to take the village of Thiepval and the Schwaben Redout. . The battalion war diaries do not mention the casualties of the main battles, but some idea is indicated by the very substantial numbers of the new drafts of soldiers posted to the Battalion to replace dead and wounded. The histories of the 54th Infantry Brigade and 18th Division were researched at the Imperial War Museum.

George survived for nineteen months in the front line when the average life expectancy of a young officer was measured in weeks. He was severely wounded losing half his right foot at the little known and bloody Battle of Boom Ravine. He convalesced staying with his sister for the rest of the next two and a half years, in and out of hospital, and in between times worked in the Ministry of Pensions. After the death of his brother William on 22nd July 1917, just George and Sis of the original family survived. I have ended this part of his story on the first Armistice day 1919 which was celebrated on board ship on his way out to India. He could now walk about a mile using sticks.

Through an introduction from his Uncle Tom he had been offered a job with Bird Heilgers and Company Calcutta, a managing agency and then the largest company in India employing over 100,000 people. The letters to his sister provide a fascinating account of life there through the fresh eyes of a newcomer, and these continue thoughout 1920 and 1921. There is then a gap in the correspondence which I have completed with an account of the historical events surrounding his life there and the story of Bird Heilgers activities in which he was closely involved. This was a formative and difficult period with the great depression, and Indian agitation for independence, and the watershed Government of India Act of 1935.

Marriage and children formed an important part of his life in the 1930s, and again his letters to my mother give a detailed insight to his life and work. Here I have also relied heavily on the copy of the firms private history kindly given to me by Richard Benthall, who himself worked in the company with his father Sir Paul and alongside his twin brother James after the second world war. The Benthall archives of Richard's uncle Sir Edward Benthall in the Cambridge Institute for South Asiatic Studies gave fresh insights into the political developments leading to the 1935 Government of India Act which affected all businesses and particularly Birds of which George was now a partner. Sir Edward's lively notes of the second Round Table Conference, while representing the interests of European business, of his various discussions with Mahatma Ghandi are published in full, as are his wife Ruth's letters of 1940-2 to my mother describing war-time life in England. She was a daughter of Baron Cable, who was the inspiration behind the Bird and Company business. I have also had the benefit of a copy of the private history of Grindlays Bank given to me by the Bank during the early 1960s.

My mother had been born and brought up in India, the daughter of an IMS surgeon, who had had a distinguished career and some of the earlier research surrounding my first book *Family of the Raj* has been used in the account of her part and that of her family in the family story,

Their later letters leading up to and during the first year of the war illustrate the difficulties experienced by separated familiies struggling with the problems of separation as well the educational needs of their children at a time of global conflict. Above all regular letter writing was the lifeblood of a strong relationship, and the first half of the twentieth century was truly a golden age of letter writing and the introduction of airmail the lubricant of their more speedy delivery.

The central part of his life was a balance between his many responsibilities as a leader, not just of Birds, but in the many other responsibilities thrust upon him during the war as well as the demands of family life. The discovery of his annual 1941 report of 26th February 1942 as President of the Bengal and Associated Chambers of Commerce on the occasion of the AGM and his address to the members sent a shiver down my spine His was a prophetic statement that "India would now have to rely on home produced food".

The Government files in the British Library enabled me to take a fresh look at the inbalance between the decline in local production of rice and a rising consumption because of the rise in population over the ten previous years. This was a major and principle cause of the Bengal famine of 1943 when top-up supplies of rice from Burma were cut off after the Japanese invasion and production dropped dramatically in the 1942/3 season as a result not just of the severe cyclone in Bengal, but as a result of drought in the Cauvery river delta near Madras and tidal waves in Southern India too.

1942 was also the year of the mass exodus from Burma in the face of the Japanese invasion. George was closely involved as Chairman of the Calcutta Evacuees Committee in co-ordinating the response of the diverse Calcutta ethnic and religious communities to the developing crisis of fielding, feeding, clothing and housing upwards of 400,000 refugees over a short period of nine months. Again the research carried out at the Cambridge centre with the Macrell Archive and the official reports in the British Library of Sir Reginald Dorman-Smith and others enabled a fairly detailed account to be given of these largely forgotten aspects of the Far Eastern war. I have included also a section on the activities of the behind the lines activities of Force 136 because of my parents friendship with Ritchie Gardiner.

George throughout this time was the senior partner of Birds, responsible for the daily activities of a complex series of companies, many of whom had switched their activities and production to the needs of the war effort. Here I have largely relied on the Birds history and my personal knowledge of some of the industries involved (for example iron and steel making). Birds made a very substantial contribution to the war effort, and George was also involved in many of the committees set up to co-ordinate the war supplies procurement programme, for both the Burma and European sectors.

I became fascinated by the story of the Indian Liberation Army, and although there is no evidence that I was able to find of any family connection except perhaps indirectly through his membership and regular meetings of the National Defence Council in Delhi,and I felt that a section ought to be devoted to this aspect of the war. The activities of Netaji Subbhas Chandra Bose read like an adventure story, and his death remains a mystery. He is regarded as a great hero in contemporary India and his influence in the Indian Independence movement, particularly amongst the young, was immense.

Family time largely found place during the winter months in Calcutta, and also in the parental visits to us children in Kalimpong and their local leaves. During these times my parents also organised treks to explore Sikkim and Tibet and the foothills of the mountains of the Himalayas. I have used some of the many photographs of these treks to illustrate the book. Again apart from these photographs there is virtually no written material apart from diary outlines and birdwatching notes of the places visited. I have therefore used some of Spencer Chapman's magical descriptions of the Chumbi Valley from his book *Lhasa the Holy City* to give the reader an impression of what they saw and experienced. Spencer Chapman had been retained as Secretary to the 1936 diplomatic mission with a special responsibility for plant collections and bird observations.

And so the end of the European war came, and we sailed home with George following shortly afterwards. Initially the family home was in Sussex but then we moved to near Marlborough in Wiktshire to be near other family. George was recalled to join the Greek Economic Mission and the family tradition is that he was recruited by the Foreign Office to head the commercial activities of the mission during the final wind down from November 1946 to April 1947, when the Americans took over. George returned to India in early 1946 and his letters paint a poignant and nostalgic picture of India after the war with Independence looming.

In the archive there is an astonishing letter from Betty Sheriff wife of the intrepid explorer botanist and ornithologist George Sheriff written from South Eastern Tibet while on an expedition to collect samples for the British Museum. This 6 anna (about 4p in modern currency) airmail letter was taken by runner to Lhasa, a six week journey, to be stamped in the post ofice there, and then travelled the 250 mile journey onwards by pony to Gantok. Then, descending to the head of the mountain railway along the Teesta valley to Siliguri it went from there to Calcutta, and on by air to London Croydon, before ending up delivered to our home in Wiltshire. Such was the astonishing traditional efficiency of the Indian postal system in delivering mail to and from remote locations.

Later George bought an adjoining farm, and built up a herd of pedigree Ayrshire cattle while continuing to hold directorships in London and enjoying retirement, and the life of a country gentleman. Shooting and fishing were a serious part of this. He died in April 1954 and is buried with my mother in the village churchyard.

He lived in extraordinary times and one can gain an understanding of aspects of his character from his life. First he was a person of quite extraordinary courage, not just evidenced from his war record, but also in his determination not to let his wounds interfere with his life. He became a good golfer an excellent shot and took serious exercise playing tennis, golf, and riding in Calcutta. In his letter of 1st May 1921 he describes walking twelve miles to a neighbouring bungalow to catch up with a shooting party – this in northern Assam in one of the hotter pre – monsoon months – he was therefore very fit despite only having half a foot. He was also very determined and did not suffer fools gladly and could be stern and frightening. He was a stickler for good English, almost a fettish.

He was perceptive of others, intelligent and a fine administrator as again shown in the letters with a wicked sense of humour. He was known as a safe pair of hands. He adored my mother but at the same time respected her judgement despite an age difference of 12 years. As a father he was remote, but that was probably a result of the circumstances of wartime. He spent his last months waiting for death in the West Middlesex hospital suffering from cancer of the liver – a friend commented that "he wished he had courage like his" and he died in early April 1954, just a few months short of their silver wedding.

His life is probably best reflected in the family motto he chose for himself "Toil, Endure Believe"

FOREWORD

George Morton was a man of considerable strength of character and he had a career which was rewarded by the possession of a loving family, public recognition and honour, and finally retirement to the ownership of a farm which he had always dreamed about. His son John has been able to put together this biography of the man largely because he was a prolific letter-writer, first to his sister and then to his wife, both of whom preserved his letters. We can therefore read of the detailed life of a young officer in the trenches of the First World War, until he was severely wounded and partially disabled, and then his adventure into a new career in India, with a clear picture of the life in Calcutta of an expatriate in the 20s and 30s. Then the agonising anxieties at the start of the Second World War when his family was stuck in England and it was uncertain whether they would be reunited. Fortunately his family joined him in India and was able to support him during the war years when he took on great responsibilities as the Senior Partner of the Birds Heilgers group of companies and as a leading representative of the business community.

My father, Paul Benthall, joined Birds shortly after George, worked alongside him until George's retirement, and followed him as senior partner and in the important public positions. Our house in Rajasantosh Road was only about a hundred yards from theirs, but whereas John and his sisters spent the war years in Kalimpong, I spent those years with my brothers in Darjeeling. So we children did not know each other well and it was only when we met again in Calcutta in the early 60s and, later still, after I had returned to live at Lindridge, that we have become friends. However, our respective parents knew each other so well, and our paths have crossed so often that I have read this biography of George with great interest and was flattered to be invited to add this simple foreword. I am sure this book will be prized by John's family and will be read with interest by others for whom one man's career can throw light on a period of history.

Richard Benthall

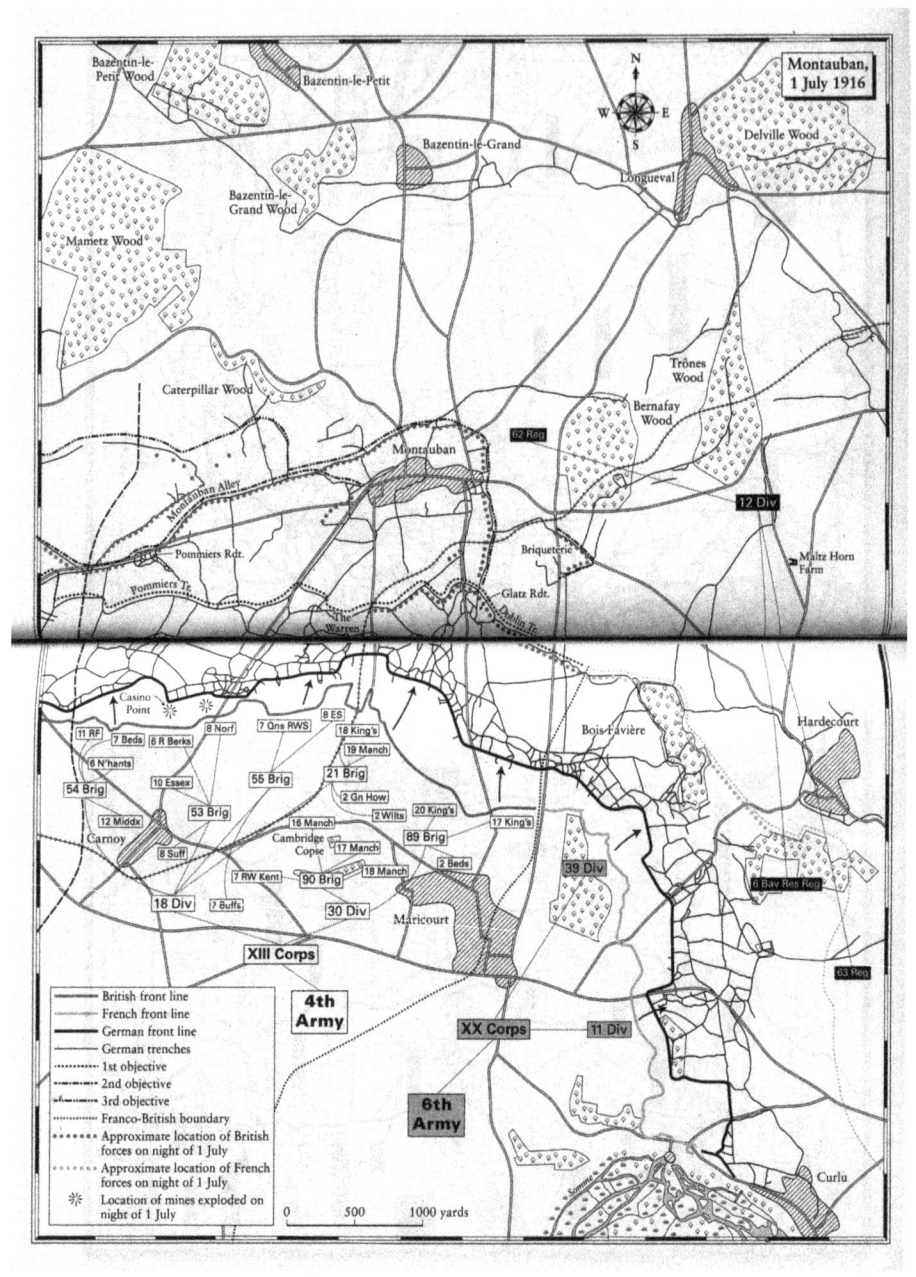

Map 1 *The general advance of 4ᵗʰ Army – 11ᵗʰ Fusiliers on extreem left attacking Pommiers Redout. See also the location of Trones Wood upper right where the Battalion was also engaged.*

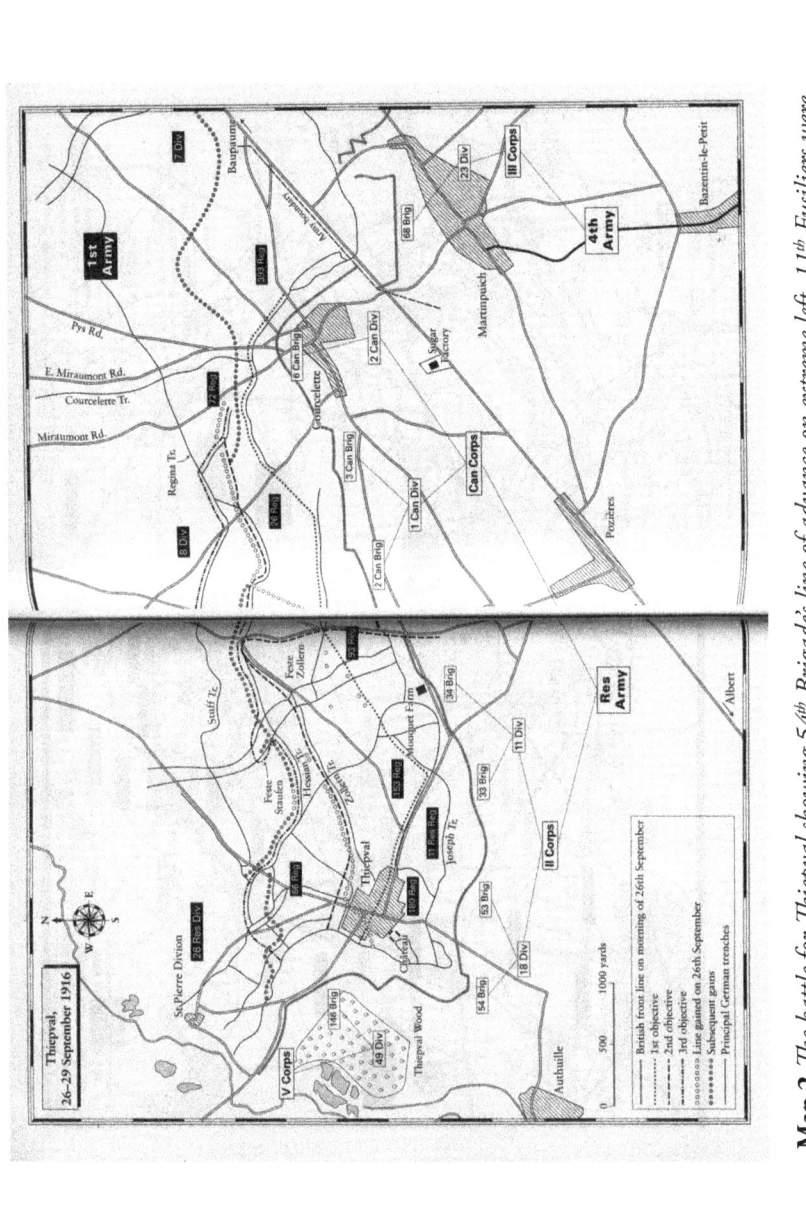

Map 2 *The battle for Thiepval showing 54th Brigade's line of advance on extreme left. 11th Fusiliers were the left hand Battalion of the Reserve Army within 54th Brigade. Regina Trench on the line of the 3rd Objective was to be the trench line for the advance to Oxford Circus the start line for the Battalion attack into Boom Ravine and battle that followed on 17th February 1917, where George was seriously wounded.*

PART ONE

From Balham and Boom Ravine to Bengal
(13.02.1893 to 11.11.19)

George was born on 13th February 1893, the second child of William and Alice Morton. They had married in 1890, William, a Scot born in Ayrshire aged 39, she, Alice Cattel, aged 24 from North Devon. On the marriage certificate, he is listed as a labourer. The Mortons were an Ayrshire clan of farmers, becoming in the 19th century wealthy milliners, linen and lace makers. Their eldest child William had been born on 13th February 1891, and a third child, Alice, followed in April 1895. Initially, the family lived in East Dulwich.

In the 1901 census, they are listed as living at 76 High Road, Balham, William aged 50, Alice aged 35, children William 9, George 8 and Alice 6, with the household completed with a Chambermaid and a Cook. Balham at that time was a rapidly growing town south of London. In the latter half of the 19th century, it had become an expanding new town with the developing railway network linking villages and small towns across the whole of the south-east of the country to the capital, London.

1 l to r George, Alice and William in the parlour at 87 Balham Road London circa 1901 census (Morton Archive)

The boys were privately educated at Balham School. We suspect that at this stage, my grandmother or grandfather may have inherited family money; certainly, the household and the sons' private education suggests that they had come up in the world. Both boys were academically very bright; George left school at age 16 and became articled as an accountant to Deloitte, Plender and Griffiths. William is also listed as an accountant on his application to the Inns of Court (Artists Rifles) in October 1914. By then, William would have been fully qualified.

At that time, it was necessary to make a financial deposit to become articled, which was then paid back with salary. My father's finals were interrupted by the war although he had over four years' articled service before entering full-time military training, and going off to war in the final year of his studies.

1

2 *Grandfather William county bowler (Morton Archive)*

My grandfather was a county bowler and there are photos of him bowling, as well as silver captions of trophies that he won, in the family archive. George was a keen rugby player and joined the Harlequins, playing alongside the famous England fly-half, Adrian Stoop.

While at Oxford in 1958, I wrote to the then Sir Adrian to ask whether I might be considered for a trial with the club, and had a charming letter back, in which he remembered my father, inviting me for a trial. He told me that he would have had a trial for England had the First World War not intervened. Sadly, Sir Adrian died three weeks later but I was later accepted into the Harlequin Rugby Football Club.

3 *Grandparents William and Alice with Sis (Jan Archibald's mother) at the turn of the century (Morton Archive)*

It appears to have been a very happy childhood for the three children, with relatives and friends from both sides of the family, including Uncle Tom Morton who was to be a formative influence on George after my grandfather suddenly died in February 1915. He was at that stage a widower and had returned from a disastrous speculative business adventure in Canada. By this stage, war had broken out and both boys had joined Kitchener's second 1915 army, William in C battery of the 282 Army Brigade Royal Field Artillery and George in the 11th Battalion Royal Fusiliers.

"Oh what a lovely war" – letters from the trenches – the reality of the horrors

This controversial musical brought a mixture of tears and laughter to audiences as well as rave reviews after its first performance at the Theatre Royal East Stratford on 19th March 1963. Its success was guaranteed following Princess Margaret's endorsement to the Lord Chamberlain and the show's move to the West End that followed. However, the reality of the war was far from funny.

The origins of the First World War are well charted. A whole series of interlocking and mutual support treaties had been formed with Russia committed to supporting Serbia, along with Bulgaria and Romania, against the Austro-Hungarian central alliance with Germany. Her stated objective was to support Austria, but the natural enemy was France, the strongest European military power.

A German military plan called the "Schlieffen" plan existed for the invasion of France, modified for invasion via Belgium. A bilateral treaty between France and Russia also existed and Britain had treaties of mutual support with France and Belgium. War was declared between Serbia and the Central Powers of Germany and Austria after the assassination of Crown Prince Ferdinand in Sarajevo. This in itself was probably insufficient as a *"causus bellum"*, but Russia moved to support Serbia. France then declared war on Germany; the conquest of France probably represented unfinished business to Germany after the short six-month campaign of the Franco-Prussian war of the 1870s. And now, following the invasion of Belgium by the German armies, Britain declared war on Germany at the beginning of August. Thus, the Central Powers of Germany and Austria were ranged against Russia in the East and France, Belgium and England in the West.

A front was later to be opened against Italy who joined the Allies; later, Turkey joined the Central Powers to strike against Mesopotamia, threatening Egypt and the British possessions of the Middle East. This was to be countered by the campaign of the Indian Army in the disastrous siege of Kut, and the successful campaign by General Allenby's advance to Damascus in 1917 supported by Feisal and Lawrence's Arab Revolt in the South West from Aqaba. Oil was becoming of increasing importance to the western allies. This was now truly a world war.

The Belgian armies were swept aside initially by an open war as seven German armies entered Belgium and France. A line of defence was quickly established in the North around the Ypres Salient by the Belgian armies and in the south, around Rheims up to the Swiss border, by the French. Britain initially sent an expeditionary force of around 70,000 regular soldiers supported by artillery brigades. The Belgian armies in the North stiffened resistance around Ypres, and the water sluices to the West of the town were opened flooding the plains in front of the German advance. This slowed the advance; both armies dug in and created an extensive system of defensive trenches. The water in the low-lying plains between the two armies became a sea of glutinous mud, pockmarked with shell holes.

Further to the South, the British held about 50 miles of the line between Ypres and the Belgians to the North and the French armies to the South. The line of the Somme River, but more particularly the north eastern tributary of the Ancre, represented a part of the British and Commonwealth sector. From this moment onwards, the war became a more static one between opposing and increasingly elaborate trench systems, and was to be dominated by artillery. This decimated the ground and woods around and between the trenches. In the Somme sector, the initial German advance was halted north east of Amiens in the centre of the line and the British Albert trench system.

This then was the developing background to William and George's early manhood in 1914 . . . George was now 21 and William 23, rising 24; both had promising civilian careers opening out ahead. George, bar his finals, was now almost fully qualified as an accountant after over 5 years' training, and William fully qualified. But, along with so many others of their generation, it was the world of war that was opening up before them in the second half of the year 1914.

The popular view was that it would only last a few months and be over by Christmas. After all, the Austro–Prussian war of 1866 had lasted only seven weeks, and the French in the Franco-Prussian war of the 1870s had held out for just six months; the American Civil War and the Boer War were not thought to be reliable indicators of what might happen in Europe. But the First World War was to last a terrible four years and three months.

William and George had joined the Inns of Court, by then a territorial series of regiments largely for the training of officers. George passed his medical board on 24th January 1913 at Lincoln's Inn as a territorial private following a proposal for membership on 28th November the previous year. This represented part-time training in drill, musketry, bombing in trench warfare, field exercises in open warfare covering a whole series of subjects from sanitation through tactics, map reading and the history of warfare. He was obviously a good shot because he received a prize for musketry. He was promoted to the rank of lance corporal on 5th May 1914 and sergeant on 4th August in the same year. From then on, things moved quickly as he was appointed to a commission in the 11th Service Battalion of the Royal Fusiliers on 3rd September 1914. This now

4 George seated and William standing as cadets at the Inns of Court (Morton Archive)

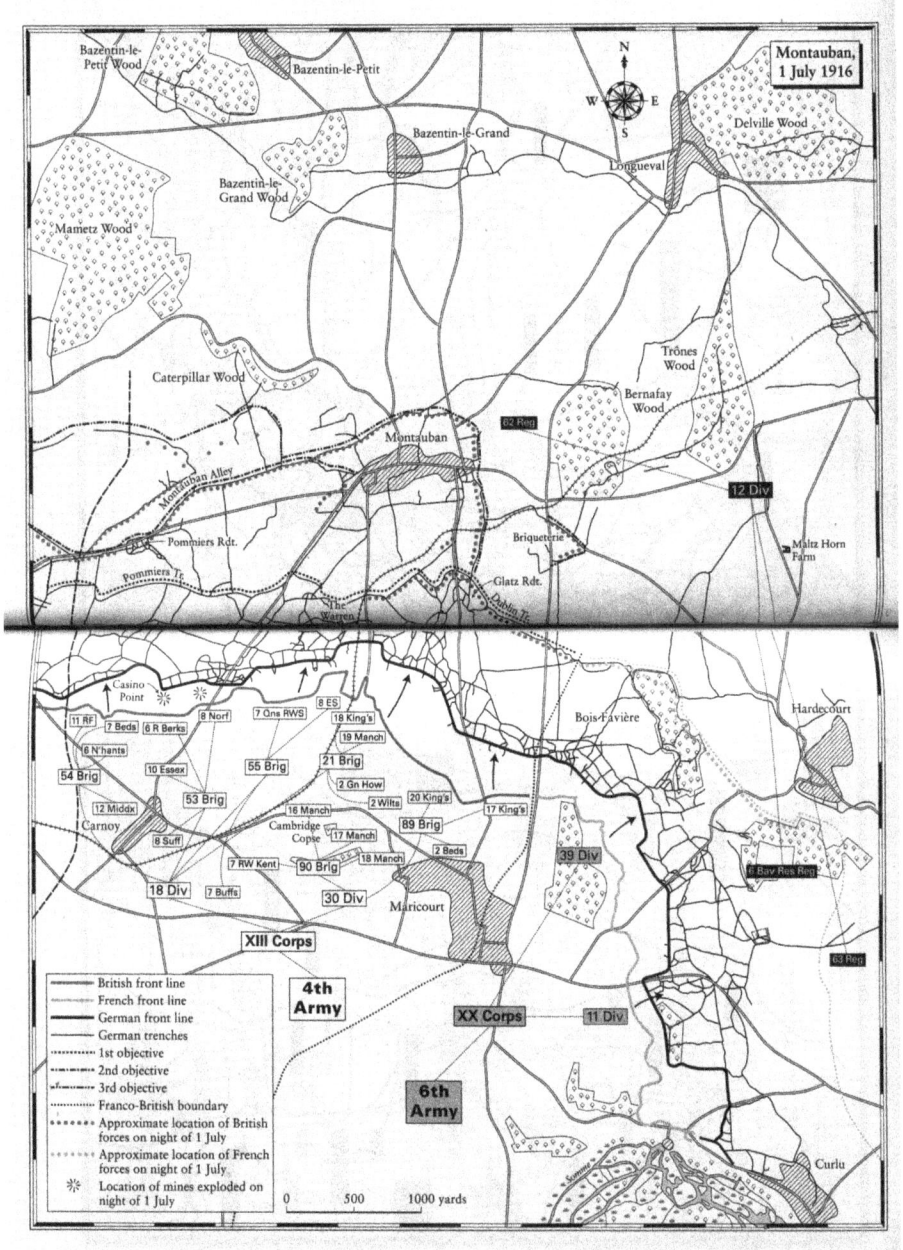

5 Map of opening Somme battles July 1916 see 4th Army on right of line with 18th division on left of 4th Army and 54th Infantry Brigade on left with 11th Fusiliers extreem left heading to their objective of Pommiers Redout..note also Trones Wood in top right corner (source Hugh Sebag-Montefiore's Somme)

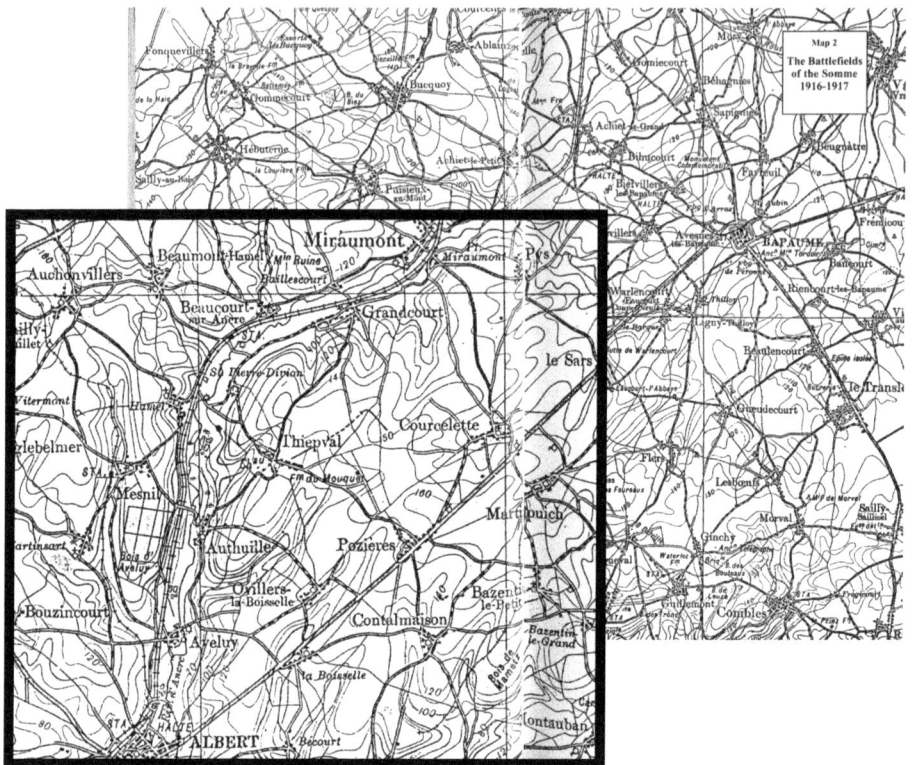

6 *A general map of the place names of the Somme battlefields, with the expanded left hand lower quadrant showing the main area of the actions of 18th Division, between their arrival in France and end February 1917, when George was wounded.*

involved full-time training as an officer for this newly formed battalion, at the officers' training school at Berkhamsted. The records show that 13 miles of linear trenches were dug here, partly as fitness training, partly as a part of the Northern defences of London, and partly as training for more senior officers in the design and layout of trench systems. Reportedly, fragments of the trench system survive to this day in a field behind the castle, and are owned by Berkhamsted School.

The training would have taken several months before his commission was confirmed and he passed out back into the Royal Fusiliers. The battalion was destined to be a part of the 54th Infantry Brigade in the 18th Infantry Division, commanded by Brigadier General Maxse, now within Kitchener's second army of 1915. Within the brigade were the 6th Northants, 12th Middlesex and also the 2nd Bedfordshires.

The Inns of Court Yeomanry have a history going back to the Middle Ages when judges helped to form militias for the protection of London and to fight in the King's wars. In the early 1800s, a review of the Regiment by George 3rd prompted the monarch to ask whether they were all lawyers. "They are all lawyers, Sire," replied Erskine, the commanding Lieutenant-Colonel. "What, what" exclaimed the King. "Call them the Devil's own, call them the Devil's own . . ." and so this is what they were called. In 1859, they were formally renamed the 23rd Middlesex (Inns of Court) Rifle Volunteer Corps, becoming, almost immediately, the Inns of Court Officer Training Corps (I.C.O.T.C.) and then a territorial unit in 1908.

The basis of the membership were the gentlemen of the four Inns of Court: Gray's Inn to the North, and the Inner and Middle Temples clustered around Lincoln's Inn and the Chancery Bar on the north bank of the Thames. (Lincoln's Inn incidentally also provided the examination base for membership of the Indian bar. Calcutta was where both my great-grandfather James O'Kinealy, judge of the Bengal Judiciary, and his younger brother Peter, Attorney General, had practised in the late 1800s.) A number of other professions were enrolled amongst their ranks, including accountants.

William's military records are much less complete than George's. He is recorded as signing on as a private in the 28th County of London (reserve) Battalion, the London Regiment (Artists Rifles) on 9th September 1914, taking his oath on that day, six days after George, but it is not clear whether this is full-time or part-time territorial service. He is recommended, after interview by the Brigadier Royal Field Artillery (RFA) of the territorial force on 16th November, for a commission in the 3rd London Brigade. Now, after 97 days' service as a territorial, he is accepted for a commission as a second lieutenant on 27th November 1914, which is confirmed by the Brigadier commanding 282 Army Brigade of the RFA.

He was to remain within this brigade, (C battery), until his death on 22nd July 1917 from wounds received in action. On his application, he nominates his sister Alice as next of kin at 89 Redcliffe Gardens, London, reflecting perhaps the departure of his father on a business venture to Canada. (Within the family archive, there is a rather battered $1 Canadian note.) There are a few more useful details on the file – his address given as the family home at 76 High Road, Balham, his education at Balham School, and his profession as "Chartered Accountant". It would appear that Alice, now just eighteen, had already moved out of the family home; George and she lived for nearly two years in a little flat in Redcliffe Gardens after he was wounded at the Battle of Boom Ravine in February 1917. On the file, there is a copy of the letter notifying Alice of William's death.

So now, George and William's war started with George as an infantryman at the Somme and William in the artillery about 20/25 miles further north, close to the Ypres Salient. Both were to write regularly to Alice and luckily most of these letters to her survive. We do also have George's trench notebook containing his reports from 20th August 1915 to April 18th 1916. A large later section of it covering January, February and March 1917 has been cut out. These reports do, however, give a detailed picture of this period of his life in the trenches.

The 11th Fusiliers war diary opens with the report of the movement of the battalion to France . . . *"July 25th CODFORD-FRANCE Left Codford on 25.7.1915 – half left at 3.30 am and remainder at 4.45 pm Arrived at Folkestone 10.30 pm and embarked on*

St Ceriol; proceeded to Boulogne arriving there at 1.30 am. Marched to camp at Adstronove situated about 2 miles from landing stage. The Bn left Boulogne at 8.30 pm on 28.7 and on-trained and arrived at Fiesselles at 4 am, detrained and marched to Taimas where the Bn was billeted."

Codford is in Wiltshire just off the A36 north of the A303, and the battalion had been working up over the previous eight months with drafts of new recruits being trained by a core of regular soldiers, including fieldwork and field firing, on the Salisbury Plain ranges. Over and over again, they would practise section, platoon, company and battalion formations in attack and defence. The men were largely Cockneys from the East End of London, resilient and cheerful in adversity. George was commanding No 1 platoon in 'A' Company. A military camp is still there.

An infantry battalion consisted of four infantry companies of four platoons, each commanded by a lieutenant or second lieutenant, with a company headquarters whose staffing consisted of the company commander, generally a major or captain, a company sergeant major, a company quartermaster sergeant with one or two stores men, and a batman who doubled as a runner. Each platoon had a platoon sergeant, a batman runner and a Stokes mortar section. There were four sections in each platoon with maybe a dozen men commanded by a corporal with a light machine gun section with one or two Lewis guns in each section. Each company would have a strength of around 180 men. In addition, the battalion had a machine gun company, with the water-cooled Vickers machine gun, although this was sometimes detached to Brigade, a Stokes heavy 4" mortar company and a transport company. In all, at full strength, a battalion would number close to 1000 men. Each brigade consisted of a minimum of three battalions with a headquarters commanded by a Brigadier General. A division comprised three brigades and was commanded by a Lieutenant General or Major General.

On 26th July, George writes from Codford St. Mary on smart 11th Fusilier notepaper.

"My dear Sis,

I have sent you a small handbag (by rail) with a few of my things in it. I also send you today photos that I had forgotten about. They want cleaning up a bit but are alright otherwise.

I sent my large kitbag by rail to Aunt Edie's. (She is Uncle Tom's wife.) Don't throw away anything in it, as I have destroyed everything I don't want, and sold other things that were useless. If you are down there, unpack it, as there are some clothes, socks etc in it.

We are off this afternoon, and I am really glad as it is rather dull hanging around waiting.

I will write to you as soon as I can when I arrive. As you can guess, we are frightfully busy. I sent Sybil Johnson a button, and hope she receives it all right. Well, Sis, I will close. I hope that you are well, also all at Benrig. Love to all, and don't worry about me, I shall be all serene. Take care of yourself. Your loving brother George."

He gives his address as 'A' Company, 11th Royal Fusiliers, 54th Infantry Brigade, 18th Division, Brit Exped Force, France.

Meanwhile, the battalion was moving up towards the trenches, arriving at Bonnay on the 9th where they were billeted for a few days. George writes again on 4th August.

"My dear Sis,

Many thanks for your letter. The vest is just the thing and one every fortnight would be excellent. We are quite cheery here. Our grub has been most excellent up to now. We are messing by companies and I am in charge of our company mess. We get boxes of "extras" from Fortnum and Masons of Piccadilly once a week. They contain all sorts of stuff; butter, sausages, soup tablets, candles, tinned meats and potted meals, tinned milk, coffee, cocoa, Quaker oats, chocolates, fruit (dried and tinned). Everything in the box can be kept for ages, over a year I believe, as it is all in sealed tins. This box is not to be used exclusively for we get rations in the ordinary way, which are very good, & the Fortnum boxes only supplement our rations. Cigarettes and tobacco are issued as rations.

I had a letter from Eileen Sharp, also one from Mrs Johnson. Aunt Edie sent me a most excellent little writing case. It is very compact indeed. The weather here has been very good until the last few days when it has rained like the dickens. I am glad you enjoyed the Holbrook trip. They should be nice to you, there is absolutely no reason why they shouldn't be, however, everyone has peculiarities which one must allow for. No one is perfect you know, Sis, it is impossible to please everyone.

Remember me to all. I cannot let you know everything of what is happening in the military line; we have strict orders against writing anything that might possibly be used. I don't know if the orders will become less strict later.

Write again soon. Hope Dolly, Duncan and Sheila are well, your loving brother George."

The vests were butter muslin ones worn next to the skin to deter lice and George wore them for a fortnight, and after that, he gave them to his platoon sergeant who wore them for a fortnight longer! Lice were a constant problem, laying their eggs in the seams of the clothing, which could only be dealt with by ironing the seams with a hot iron.

The Battalion now moves up to Bray and 'A' and 'D' Companies move into the trenches in 'A' sector for training, 'A' Company by 1st Devon Regiment, and 'D' Company by the 2nd Battalion the Manchester Regiment. Here, 'A' Company suffered two casualties. They were relieved by 'B' and 'C' Companies when a further casualty, Major Hudson, was wounded. A bombing attack on the German trenches was carried out.

It is perhaps worth recording that the life of a subaltern was measured in weeks in the trenches in 1915/16. George was to survive for 19 months before being seriously wounded.

Meanwhile, George was unwell and obviously missing his sister from whom he hadn't heard for a little while. Perhaps Alice was a little miffed at the somewhat peremptory nature of the instructions in his previous letter . . . as his letter of Monday 9th August reveals.

"My dear Sis,

I haven't heard from you for some days. Have you received my letters? I think that I have written five. I have had two letters from you, the last I received you wrote at Chislehurst on the Friday. Has my large bag arrived at Chislehurst? We are still quite serene. I have had violent diarrhoea; it is a beastly nuisance. We had to march many miles yesterday – for about five and a half hours, so you will gather that we have moved. Yesterday was one of the hottest days I have ever known, and as I was not very fit, I felt it rather, but stuck it out all serene.

The country we passed through was lovely. The crops are all ripe & the whole country is scattered about with beautiful woods. Long rows of magnificent poplars are very frequent & an occasional old chateau looking very peaceful in the woods. It is difficult to realise that war is going on in the midst of all this, and it is only the absence of all the men of fighting age that makes one think. The flies trouble us a lot; there are millions of them about.

We are not in the trenches yet, so all is well in that direction!

Let Will know that I am well etc. I enclose a list of things that I would like sent out. Have them packed in a thin strong wooden box if possible and send by Parcel post, as any other way takes three weeks to get here, other than letter post. I am enclosing a cheque for £2.0.0. Let me know if it is enough. Well, I will close. I have heard from Dorrie twice. Much love, hope you are well. Your loving brother George. Better registered parcel."

Life began in the trenches with 'A' & 'D' Companies working with the 1st Devons. Philip Gibbs, the war correspondent to the Telegraph and London Chronicle, commented that this was the moment that the young officer was introduced to the real world of saps, mines, bombing, patrols & repairing revetements in the trenches as well as the living conditions in the trenches themselves. George's trench notebook opens with a report of a patrol.

"To the adjutant 1st Devons. August 20th 1915

Sir, I have the honour to report that I went out from left sub-sector A near the listening post last night at 10.30 pm in charge of a patrol consisting of one lance corporal and two men. When we were about thirty yards from the enemy's trench, we heard sounds of digging and earth being beaten down which I concluded was a party of the enemy working on their fire trench and parapet. We were unable to see the party who were a little to the right of where the patrol had halted. There were no signs of a protective screen or any patrol. The sounds heard continued until we returned at 11.45 pm. I have the honour to be, sir, your obedient servant, Geo B Morton, Lieut OC no 1 platoon 11th Royal Fusiliers."

Interestingly, he signs himself off as Lieut, clearly a promotion. He tells the story of the patrol in his letter to Sis of the 29th August, now out of the trenches and in reserve.

My dear Sis,

I received the tobacco all serene yesterday, and I received your welcome letter with the rest, and chocolate for which many thanks. The chocolate has been consumed already I may say.

I thought that Turner would write you. He is organising the supply of comforts for the Battalion. I should get a few people to work, who will continue to make things for some time. It is best to get someone who already makes things and direct the articles into the channel leading to the 11th RF!!!

I already have two pairs of hose tops, but things are always welcome and anything that is sent will either be used by myself or other officers here or the men; we all share in where necessary. If you have to supply your working party with wool, let me know the cost. Woollen articles will be very useful later on when it gets cold. If you let me know who to send articles, I will write them if possible.

We usually spend ten days in the trenches at a time and then rest for ten, but our last stay was for four days. We go in sometime this week again. This is a new sector for us (11th RF); we have had a few moves since we have been here. Up till now, they have been getting us used to the trench life, quite a long time for our turn.

It is not frightfully exciting as a general rule; of course, there are times when the excitement is more than intense. Our friends the Germans have many ways of keeping us interested! Their snipers are always at work of course and they have many varieties of shells and bombs. The men we lost were all on account of rifle grenades, but of course, we do the same; the real scrap is who has the crater. This may sound bad, but it is not as bad as it sounds really. The last time that we were in, the Germans were 60 to 150 yards from us. I had a little mild excitement one night. I took out a personally conducted tour (consisting of one NCO and two men) out in front reconnoitering. We got within about 25 yards of the Germans' trench. It was quite dark (we could see about 40 yards fairly clearly for night-time; it is never absolutely dark at this time of year), and we were out for about an hour.

I am still second in command of 'A' Company & will most likely remain so now, though I don't think it means promotion. About tobacco. There is a cheaper way of sending it. If you can get a firm who will send it out of bond, it saves the duty. I will try and find out about it & get the name of a firm. I haven't heard from Will lately. I don't know if he has his leave, but if he has, he should drop down and see you.

I don't expect that we shall get any leave for a long time yet, but I shall, of course, take the opportunity of getting leave when it offers itself. We may have to wait quite a long time for our turn. . . . soon, all being well. Well, Sis, I will close. I hope you are fit, old thing; I am very well at present. Love to all. I will write again soon all being well, your loving brother George.

PS We had a group photo taken just before we left Codford. I have asked them (Elliot and Fry) to send the copies direct to you. If they send the a/c to you, send it on to me. Keep the photos for me." (The photos have survived.)

The battalion diary records two casualties from 'A' Company. The rifle grenade is fired through an adaptor to the standard rifle with a range of about 150 yards. The grenade is designed to fragment into shrapnel and is about half the size of a really small pineapple.

This exchange of letters emphasises the importance to soldiers of letters from home. Sis was the link between the world they had known and left to go to war and the terrible conditions and experiences in the trenches and of the battles that were to follow.

On 24th August, the whole battalion moved to Dernancourt with 'B' Company seconded to Becordel-Becourt where two platoons were detached to assist 178th Tunnelling Company Royal Engineers. These specialist companies comprised ex-miners who were put to work digging tunnels under the German trenches. This was hazardous work, the Germans countermining with fights often taking place underground. The tunnels were packed with explosives, generally, guncotton or amatol, which was then exploded under the German trenches, leaving a shocked enemy and a large crater. The trench line was then advanced to the forward edge of the crater. It was during this rest period that the above letter was written because, on 4th September, there commenced an extensive period of trench operations as the Battalion took over sector D1 of the line. 'A' & 'D' Companies were initially in the trenches with 'B' & 'C' Companies in reserve.

It is perhaps worth describing a typical trench system. It was, in fact, a double trench system with the front line a fire trench and the support trench providing accommodation in the form of dugouts, first aid stations and stores, including ammunition. Short communication trenches linked the fire and support trench systems. The trenches were arranged in tight zig-zags to minimise the effects of bombing or artillery bursts. The trenches themselves were lined with duckboards to provide, in theory at least, a raised surface above the mud. In practice, water and mud often seeped above the duckboards. The fire trench had a fire step and a parapet often of beaten earth and sandbags. The fronts of the trenches were revetted with corrugated iron held back against the surfaces by posts. Sometimes timber brushwood was used for the purpose. Communication trenches ran back to the secondary and reserve trench systems. It was off these communication trenches that the latrines were dug and re-dug. Some communication trenches were shallow and here, those using them had to crawl on hands and knees to avoid appearing above ground and becoming exposed to sniper fire. Soldiers lived in their clothes and officers wrote reports in candlelight . . . most of George's reports were written in the early hours of the morning in his dugout. The fire trenches were manned on a shift system, being generally fully manned at first and last light, the times when enemy attacks were most likely. In front of the fire trenches, there was further protection in the form of barbed wire often arranged in coils. Tripwires with tins were also used, the tins rattling to give a warning of a hostile approach. Saps were sometimes dug out towards the enemy trenches to give access to forward listening posts or provide protected exit routes for patrols. Apart from the lice, rats were also the soldiers' constant companions.

Trench foot was a serious problem resulting from boots and puttees being constantly immersed in water. Waders were issued but there were not enough to go around everybody, and so their issue was restricted to officers and NCOs whose duties consisted of walking the trenches and inspection and supervision of the constant work of repair and improvement. Spare socks would be sent up with the rations and soldiers would throw the old ones away. Frostbite was also a problem in winter.

A story told by George about this time was when he asked the quartermaster sergeant how many sheets of toilet paper should be ordered per man . . . a typical question from an accountant. The sergeant paused for a moment before answering, "Three sheets, Sorr, one up, one down, one polish, Sorr!"

Communications were by field telephone; miles and miles of wire were laid, but the system was regularly interrupted by artillery fire and connections were broken until repaired. Runners were used as well as pigeons. The history of the 54th Brigade contains an amusing report of an intelligence officer reporting the sighting of a pigeon, over the German lines at Fricourt, "behaving suspiciously!"

Such was the life of the First World War soldier in the trenches. It was a static war, almost one of siege warfare broken by often violent individual actions. The front-line troops were encouraged to take out not just reconnaissance patrols at night, but also fighting patrols, and to capture prisoners for interrogation. There was a constant drip-feed of casualties, as is evidenced by the war diaries, from sniper and shell fire.

'A' and 'D' Companies were relieved on 8th September by 'B' and 'C' Companies who had been helping the 178th Tunnelling Company. A tunnel was normally started with a vertical shaft some 20 to 30 feet down and the forward tunnel dug towards the German trench line using compass bearings. As soon as this was reached, trenches were dug at right angles and packed with explosives, detonators inserted and wires run back to the rear. The explosives were packed in with soil spoil. Spoil from the tunnels was taken back and used to either fill sandbags or improve the trench system.

On 7th September, the night before 'A' Company's relief, a successful operation was carried out and a mine exploded in front of the Fusilier position. The Fusiliers quickly advanced and occupied the front lip of the crater and dug in, effectively occupying and holding the enemy trench system in front of them. They were congratulated on the efficiency of this manoeuvre but it was not without casualties as the letter from Brigadier General Heneker commanding 54th Infantry Brigade recognises:

> "*Dear Carr,* *
>
> *I wish you to let all ranks of the 11th Bn Royal Fusiliers know how pleased I am with their demeanour and with the work that they have done while in D1. The little operation of occupying the crater opposite 77 was well managed and carried out with excellent spirit. I have told General Maxse and also Sir T. Harland about it and the latter has specially expressed his appreciation.*
>
> *I am so sorry that you have suffered so many casualties, but the majority of this was pure bad luck, and not because proper arrangements were not made.*
>
> *You must be proud now, after a trying time, to find such excellent spirit and tone in your Battn, and I congratulate you. Yours sincerely, etc.*"

*Lt Col C.C. Carr commanding 11th Fusiliers.

Between the period 04.09 and 09.09.1915, the Bn suffered 5 killed, 22 wounded and one gassed by the fumes of the explosion, and on 19th September, the Bn received a draft of 50 NCOs and men from base depot to replace the casualties in August and September. The Bn was now relieved by the 6th Northants which gave George the time to write a short letter to Sis.

"9th September 2015

My dear Sis,

Many thanks for your letters received all serene. We get very little time for writing letters these days, any spare time being spent resting in dugouts. I am writing this letter from the trenches in the "officers' mess"; some mess too I tell you!

It is quite a warm corner here and the trenches of our friends Fritz are very close to ours, only about fifteen yards in places, so you will see that sleep is a thing to be snatched whenever possible for a short time.

We must look rather fine after being here for a few days, as washing and shaving is a luxury only to be indulged in at rare intervals. I was lucky to get to shave and wash (in about a pint and a half of water) after three days. We don't get as dirty as you might think though.

We don't remove our boots from the time we come in to the time we go out as a rule, unless just to change socks that are wet through, and then the boots are only off for a few minutes. I put my boots and clothes on on Saturday last & haven't had them off since!

All this might sound bad, but it isn't really – not half bad. Of course, it could be much worse! We very soon shake down, and get quite used to the life here. I expect that it will be worse in winter for those in for very long periods, but even then, I don't believe it is half as bad as people would have us believe.

I am glad you saw Will. I had a letter from him a few days ago. I hear from Dorrie regularly, Ida and Eileen have both written me and Eileen (Sharp) sent me some cigarettes. Well, Sis, I will close.

Hoping you are very fit. Love to Duncan, Dolly, & Sheila. Your loving brother George. P.S. I am writing Will all being well. Don't put Brigade and Divn on your letters, just the regiment."

Tellingly, the letter says nothing about the action after the mine or the casualties. It is written to reassure rather than inform what was going on.

The battalion returned to the trenches on 16th September and on 22nd, the artillery commenced bombarding the German trenches. The battalion came out again on the 25th having suffered 6 killed and 6 wounded.

George writes again on September 16th. There are the usual social references but also the more serious matter of their father's estate. He had died "suddenly" in February of that year . . . the family tradition is that he took his own life after a disastrous investment in Canada.

"I don't know what to think about taking over the estate. What Mr. Davies suggests is certainly very sound, but no doubt you can see what he is getting at. I will write Will on the subject and see what his opinions are."

The letter continues with a reference to the return of his wounded company commander;

"You will be surprised to hear that Neale is back again. He is quite fit again but has a nasty scar running from the centre of his forehead to his left temple, and his eyes are not quite the same as before, but very little different. He is the sort of stuff we want. Our new officers are nothing like the old ones.

We are down behind the old spot again, not exactly the place we were before, but nearly. We are midway between where Will was & where I was some months ago. I believe Will is in our old spot now, having a busy time. I should like to see him, but have to stop here, as we may be wanted at short notice. (The reference is probably to the second battle of Ypres – JMM) *Great news has just come in; old Fritzy is getting hell now, as he now knows what it means to be outclassed with artillery. You will hear no doubt by the time you get this letter."*

This action was confirmed in the battalion war diary of 22nd September.

Artillery was a Divisional resource with four Artillery brigades within each division. Each brigade consisted of four batteries, generally of four to six guns and commanded by a Major. Three of the brigades comprised eighteen pounders firing an integrated single-piece shell and cartridge and capable of firing six to eight rounds per minute. These eighteen pounders had a range of around 6000 yards but with a low trajectory from a maximum elevation of 16 degrees. So, it was a fast-firing flat trajectory gun with its principal use to break up infantry attacks, exploding on impact with shrapnel. But it was also used against static targets such as trenches where ball bearings within the shell could cause widespread casualties. So, the Divisional artillery resource consisted of about 72 guns.

The fourth brigade was mostly a heavy artillery one, generally with 9.2" Howitzers. These guns had a more vertical elevation and a range of 9000 yards with plunging fire, again, an anti-trench weapon. The practice of providing a creeping barrage in support of and ahead of infantry attacks became a tactical development and deployment used increasingly as the war developed. The guns were moved with teams of horses which also brought up the ammunition limbers to the guns.

The trench reports reflect the monotony of trench warfare. The reports of 5th – 8th September contain details of repairs and improvements to the trenches – the building up of parapets and revetements, clearing up stores left by the Northants, constructing loopholes, making dugouts, and general repairs to the trenches. All reports are timed in the very early hours of the morning, and one can picture him writing them by candlelight in his dugout, perhaps with the eyes of the rats and mice pinpointed in the candle's reflection. The reports contain requests for materials including sandbags and iron loopholes. The latter were inserted into the loophole construction to protect the rifleman or snipers from counter rifle fire. There is further detail of trench conditions in George's letter to brother Will of 13th September.

"Dear Will, Many thanks for your letters and cutting. It should be a good thing to get a regular commission & if I were you, I should worry until your C.O. lets you go in for it. Gunners out here have a soft thing; they pinch all the good billets while we are in the trenches & when we come out in reserve to rest, we have to take what is left!!!

I don't think that I shall apply yet as it would mean starting all over again for me. If there is a chance at the end of the war, one might go in then.

Am glad you had a good time on leave. I heard you were down from Sis. I have not yet sent the paper I got from T.M. Have been too busy.

We came out of the trenches (when I mention "trenches" it always means the front-line fire trenches) a few days ago. We had a week in, & are now in Brigade reserve, and hope to go back to rest soon now. We have more casualties this trip. Pure bad luck though, mainly from high explosive shells (equivalent to our 6" size) & a few snipers. In parts of this sector that we are running, the Germans are only 20 to 30 yards away; we are separated by deep mine craters. Our Company have the worst bit, & are the nearest of anyone in the Brigade. The excitement starts when a mine goes up to get to the edge of the crater and consolidate it (unless it is one of Fritzy's & blows in our parapet.) The chief problem in the trenches is the lack of sleep; one is on the go all day and night, & we have to get an hour when we can. Of course, we haven't usually any water to wash in. I had one wash during our last stay. When I find time, I will write the people you mention.

Write as often as you can, as it is fine to hear from people. No more news at present. Cheer up.

Your affect. brother George."

T.M. is a reference to Uncle Tom Morton.

His letter of September 25th to Sis also describes in some detail the ongoing conditions in the trenches.

"My dear Sis,

Many thanks for your letters and the vest & chocolate.

We have been having a busy time of it lately. I haven't had my clothes off since Sept 3rd, but we hope to get out for a rest soon. We have either been in reserve or in the trenches all the time. It has rained for the last two or three days & the trenches are filthy. We came out of the front trenches yesterday & are a few hundred yards behind in dugouts. There are hundreds of rats and mice about. The rats are the finest specimens I have ever seen & they eat anything from the human to the human's leather equipment.

I heard that the Zepps have been over London. It must have caused some excitement. It is a pity you didn't see the shelling of the brutes, as shelling aircraft is quite a sight, unless you happen to be immediately under where the shells are bursting, & then it hasn't the same attraction, as the falling pieces of shrapnel can cause some trouble."

The letter continues to enquire about friends and relatives and to report letters and parcels received. He then comments about the vests; *"The vests you send me are a little too small. I don't know if I have swollen around the chest(!) but they get tight to the skin. Another six inches would be better. They are doing their job quite well. My servant usually has a careful search every few days when I wash. It would amuse you to see the thoroughness of the hunt."* He then asks her to send out the spare strap for his "Sam Brown", the one that goes over the shoulder, and from the comment earlier, it would seem that rats have destroyed the one that he has with him. At this time, the trench reports also reveal that he is the intelligence officer for the Company alongside his other duties.

The reference to "servant" was a common colloquialism for his batman, part of whose responsibility was to look after his officer's clothes.

Mention is also made of the rats. Bodies would be left in "no man's land" between the trenches, and the smell must have been appalling, while providing a feast for the local rodent population. . . . imagine knowing that a friend was lying out there.

There is a reference in the Battalion diary of Oct 5th to a Lieut. Sharp who was killed while going out to see some bombers he had posted out while a trench parapet was repaired after a German mine had exploded – *"L/Cpl Warner, D Company, acted with conspicuous bravery and recovered Lieut Sharp's body from within 15 yards of the German trenches."*

Such was the example and commitment of an ordinary soldier to fallen colleagues.

In a letter to the proprietor of the Hotel du Rhin in Amiens, he asks him to direct an orderly to the best shop to purchase two rugby balls and footballs of good quality, together with laces and lacing awls!! Amiens was the nearest big town and place of relaxation and recreation for the front-line troops with bars and restaurants. Later on, he plays rugby for the Division.

The pattern of trench warfare established in September was to continue for the rest of the year, with the constant attrition of casualties through mines, raids, and sniper fire recorded in George's letters, his trench reports, and the Battalion war diary. He writes to Sis immediately on the Battalion retiring from the trenches on 25th September.

> *"My dear Sis,*
>
> *Many thanks for the letter and vest. I have been fairly lucky up to date, have only fourteen "bugs" (lice) in my shirt. Some have found dozens. Will you include some bug destroyer in the parcel?"*

He continues with a comment about her weekend at the Johnsons. Will hadn't written for a while and he hopes that he is alright, and then comments on Sis's reports of dissension in the tennis club.

> *"It really is amusing to hear of the little storms at the tennis club. Some people are never happy unless they are scrapping. Why don't some of 'em come out here? They wouldn't then worry about washing up, and would think themselves damned lucky if they had enough water to wash up in."*

He asks Sis what she thought of the photos and particularly drew her attention to the fact that they were wearing shorts. The nights were closing in and it was getting colder. *"It's getting a bit parky for them now but I expect that we shall continue wearing them. We are known in the Division as the "Codford Scottish". The other night, we passed another regiment in the division* (probably the 6th Northants) *& I heard a voice from that regiment saying, "oo are you" and another voice replied "can't you see it's the old Codford Highlanders" and the chat began! We are great pals with all the other regiments, chiefly because our fellows are mostly frightfully cheerful Cockneys, always ready with the reply!!"* And then *"I think that it is an excellent idea to try to get into some war department, that is if you are competent yet. Is fifty words sufficient?* (Sis was clearly after secretarial work and the reference is to her typing speed.)

At present, we are resting. It is quite a pleasure to take one's clothes off once more (first time since 4th September). As usual (and to be expected) we lost a few men last trip. Well, I will close. Love to all, Your loving bro George"

The battalion had lost 12 – 6 killed, 6 wounded.

October and November continue with spells in the front line with more casualties; his trench reports give a vivid and fascinating insight into trench life . . . German mines being exploded, sniper fire, and the wet and cold.

He gives an account in his report of 8th October of an aerial torpedo, which he first thought was a star light which had failed to ignite properly . . . it had sparks like a rocket and struck a house adjoining the graveyard near the Bedford Regiment lines . . . it appeared to be fired from near Fricourt. There is an account on 9th October of missing trench tools, shovels and picks, from a visiting work party that had left them behind, and further accounts of rifle grenades being fired at the German trenches, and incoming sniper fire from the German second line. There are reports of the improvement of the trench parapets and the use of plates to protect sentries and snipers, and the extension of the trench system and saps towards the German lines to provide listening posts. Bombers protect the listening posts. . . . these bombers are grenade throwers; there are also detailed instructions for defence in the event of patrols being sighted. Another report tells of three men being seen carrying sandbags who, when fired upon, fell into the German trench. There is a detailed account of work done sector by sector in the 'A' Company trenches with platoon dugouts being built with RE labour being supplied by the Fusiliers. Another report of 20th October tells of mortar bombs ("sausages") being fired from Fricourt and landing behind the front line, and a "friendly" 18 pounder shell landing just in front of their trench system. There are also reports of German artillery fire preceded by green very lights, and a report of a German work party being fired upon by snipers and several being hit.

The reports from November seem to be written now to the Battalion intelligence officer and he signs himself as Captain G.B. Morton, O.C. 'A' Company, an obvious promotion. It was, however, temporary in the absence of the company commander. He was later to take over command permanently.

His next surviving letter is of November 13th.

"I am a careless devil not to write but will mend my ways. Davidson told me that he had seen you. Did he give you any news? He is a first-rate old chap . . . a real good sort. He seemed very amused by your asking if I was getting enough food.

Tell Will any news you have . . . I have an idea that he is near Doullens, but it's only a surmise. I can understand him not wanting these vests as the artillery birds have a comparatively good time. If he gets lousy as I did, he will want the vests right enough!

We have been in billets a couple of days. The trenches were filthy, mud and water everywhere, but we are all cheery and not in the least "damped" in spirit however damp our feet and clothes may have been. The men are extraordinary; they are cheerful through everything. It makes one proud of the blighters sometimes to hear them ragging one another. Several men get a kind of frostbite through prolonged standing in water. (This was to become a real problem as the winter progressed – JMM) *I was in command of the company last time in the trenches as our coy commander wasn't there. Glad to hear you were at Johnsons, & hope that they are all well and fit.*

I hope to be going on leave in about a fortnight's time. What ho!

Well, Sis, I will close. Hope you're very fit; am glad you saw Dorrie. Write soon, yours lovingly, George.

PS I have been asked to play rugger for the Division. Will you send out (1) My white flannel shorts – the largest pair in my kit bag (2) Fusilier shirt (3) Fusilier stockings. I should like these things as soon as possible. Yours, George."

The battalion had again retired to billets at Morlancourt on the 10th after another tour in the trenches when it suffered 2 killed, 11 wounded and 17 cases of "trench foot" caused by continuous immersion in water. It was from here that he wrote the letter above to Sis. The next day he writes again;

"Just a few lines to let you know that all being well I expect to arrive in London on 24th of this month. I know where Will is now, he is only 17 to 20 miles from me. We hope to meet sometime. I shan't be able to do it this trip as we are going up into the trenches again very soon now.

Excuse paper, have just been working on matters military. I have raised this pen & ink from Lord knows where! It has been snowing for the last few days. The country looks fine but it is cold."

He is back in the trenches but writes again on the 23rd.

7 George in rugby kit note Harlequin stockings

19

"Thank you for your letters received all serene . . . I was to have gone on leave today but was prevented, & had to take command of the company. We are in the trenches and I am writing this in my "dugout" by the side of a coke brazier which seems very doubtful whether it has decided it will light up and warm me, or merely go out!

I hope to start on leave sometime early next month & if everything goes well, I should be in London by the 4th or 5th.

I heard from Will today and got his letter about 2 a.m. He is very fit and working hard. I may be able to see him sometime if we can arrange it. It has been freezing hard for some time here now and as you can imagine, the trenches are somewhat cold but with one blessing – that the mud is all frozen & we manage to keep our feet dry.

I have not thought much about where I shall stay if I get on leave but expect that I shall be dodging about."

There is now a gap of three weeks in the trench reports and his letters start again in December after he returns from leave. In his next letter, he gives an account of his journey back and the rugger game.

"16.12.15 My dear Sis,

Many apologies for not having written sooner. We did not go into the trenches last Sunday as expected; it was put off for a few days. Anyway, here we are now back to mud land. The mud and water everywhere is well over the ankles & many places up to our thighs. I am lucky being fairly tall as the deepest place just comes below the tops of my waders.

Last Sunday, we played the A.S.C. at rugger. We drew, but should have won. They scored one goal and a drop goal – 9 pts to our three tries. It was a topping game. I was surprised at myself that I was fairly fit & scored one of the tries! We had a hefty pack, most of them (6 out of eight) averaging close to 13 stone or perhaps a little over." (Contrast that with now where forwards average over 16 stone.) "I was one of the lightest of the six. (He was 12 stone 8lbs and played hooker.) The two others were small (flank forwards). We were not well together though, & the A.S.C. had played together quite a lot. Young Nield (Peggy!) was wounded yesterday – lucky one too!

Mrs Hawkins sent me a parcel for Neate, Ashmole & myself; jolly good of her. It was here when I arrived back. It is a top-hole sweater & fits me A1! She has done it jolly quickly, I am wearing it now. I had quite a good journey here or rather to billets of course. I "catted" going over, it was very rough but unlike my usual, I was quite alright previous to the "catting" & afterwards the trouble being over in about five minutes! I am going to write to Will by this post. His bill was £6.5.00 Well, cheer oh! Write soon. Yours lovingly, George."

The battalion war diary reports that the trenches at the beginning of the month of December were in a "very bad condition owing to incessant rain" and that there was great difficulty carrying out the relief by the Northampton Regiment on the 4th when the battalion went into billets at Morlancourt. The trenches had drains at the rear below the duckboards but these became blocked and choked with mud.

But George was on leave and he would have had the opportunity to catch up with Sis. According to Will, he was a great theatre-goer and the London Christmas season would have been in full swing.

George's December trench reports make particularly interesting reading. On 16th December, he reports going out on a reconnaissance patrol into "no man's land":

To intelligence officer 11th RF

Sir, I have the honour to report that I took out a patrol of three grenadiers last night at about 10.20 p.m. We went out from the listening post dividing the left sub-sector from the right sub-sector of point 88/89 listening post known as Birdcage Walk.

We went along a sunk road as far as a low barricade about 100 yards from our lines & waited & listened. We could hear very faintly an engine wailing. We crossed the barrier and passed a cart which appeared to be a two-wheeled ammunition cart with the remains of two horses harnessed in. Another sunk road runs at right angles to the one we went along and in the left part, there are some shelters fallen in. We went about twenty yards beyond the cart and listened. We could distinctly hear an engine working. It sounded like a small gas or oil engine, and was a long way off, probably in Fricourt half right from where we had halted. The German lines were about 50 to 100 yards away. We heard no sounds of digging or drilling and I do not think the engine was working a drill. Sniping was going on in front of us, from the German front line as far as we could judge.

The night was rather light and the roadway showed up clearly in front of us. We returned about 11.10 p.m. I have the honour to be Capt. Geo. B Morton I.O.11th. RF 09.45 a.m.

On the same day, he reports again to:

Adjutant 11th. R.F. Sir, I have the honour to report that yesterday morning about 11.15 a.m., Lt Neild reported to Capt. H.O. Drew-Mercer that no 1282 Sgt. D Gunn was in his (Lt. Neild's) dugout.

I went round to arrange about accommodation and called Sgt. Gunn out.

He took some time to come out, and when he spoke to me from the dugout, I noticed that he was speaking with difficulty, He eventually came out without any equipment on. When he got out, my opinion was confirmed – he was drunk.

I placed him in close arrest & sent him back to the dugout, & reported what I had done to Capt. Drew-Mercer. I have the honour to be, Sir, Your obedient Servant. George Morton Capt. O.C. 1 platoon 'A' comp.

Shortly after this incident, he writes to Sis, saying that Mercer has reported sick and that he is back in command of the company again.

"BEF France Dec 23rd/15 My dear Sis,

Have just received your letter (and pen which I am writing with now); it is top-hole & very many thanks. I enclose a cheque for you to get yourself something. Will you send baby Hawkins & the Johnson kiddie something small out of it?

I got a Christmas card from Will and he says he is writing. I also got a card from Nellie Crawford.

I am glad that you are going to Chislehurst for Christmas. Give my love to them all. I am sorry that Dorrie is not looking so fit. I wonder if she will be able to stand the strain. I had a cheery letter from her the other day.

What a good time we had together on my leave. It seems ages ago now. Never mind, with any luck I shall be back again in February.

I am sorry to hear that Will isn't cheery. Rain and mud are depressing at times unless one is over the knees and then it becomes less depressing somehow!! Inverse ratio or something like that comes in, I think.

I don't suppose that you will get this letter before Christmas but never mind. We are in reserve at present, & everywhere is mud and water. We shall be in billets for Christmas, and I expect to have a jolly time. I have had a very busy time this turn in. Mercer has gone down to the base ill and I am in command.

Bill McNaught must have been funny on the subject of Duncan and Dolly. Bill is a jolly good fellow.

I expected the play would have been good; it must have been enjoyable to see the kiddies.

It won't matter not sending the Hawkins & the Johnsons presents until after Christmas. Don't spend much; small things are just as good as big. I didn't know what to get you & thought you would know best.

With kindest regards to the Gillesons and anyone who may be interested in me. Hoping you have a very merry Christmas & will have a happy new year, yours lovingly, George.

Again, many thanks for the pen; it is topping."

They were to be in the trenches until Christmas Eve and then in billets at Morlancourt over Christmas until New Year's Day. Casualties were heavy over the pre-Christmas period due to trench mortar and shell fire with 7 other ranks killed plus Lt W.H.E Nield, 7 wounded and one evacuated with trench foot. Over the Christmas period, the battalion received a draft of 59 men to replace casualties, a total of 109 during the period August through December.

11th Fusiliers in The Battles of the Somme

1916 was the year of the great Battles of the Somme fought between July 1st and the end of November. It was to be followed in 1917 by the battles to the East along the Ancre river and particularly, the Battle of Boom Ravine, in which George was to be severely wounded on 17th February 1917. This bloody two-Division battle, in which 25,000 British soldiers fought at the end of the general Somme and Ancre campaigns, gets little mention in the history books.

Strangely, detail of the Somme offensive, and its commencement date was an open secret, known well in advance to the Germans as well as to the English public. Around a quarter of a million Commonwealth soldiers took part and there were a similar number in reserve. The logistics of the preparations for the battle were huge. Roads and railways had to be built, trenches and fortifications constructed and stores accumulated, particularly shells, of which enormous quantities were fired by both sides.

The Germans strongly fortified their lines with "redoubts" or underground store and accommodation rooms and hospitals built into the chalk and providing safe and shellproof facilities for the stormtroopers lining their trenches. The 11th Fusiliers, part of the 54th Infantry Brigade, and General Maxse's 18th Division were to be in the thick of it as a part of the British 4th Army.

Only five letters from George survive from this year, the first three months of which were to be spent in the same trenches as in the thick of winter. Imagine living in what was effectively a hole in the open ground, with the uncertainty of life over death from artillery or sniper fire and the bitter cold.

It may have been around this time that he was given a copy of a prayer in a letter from a French girl who signs herself Genevieve. The circumstances of their meeting are not clear but there is an air of innocence and strong faith about the letter, as well as an obvious concern about his safety, and a gentle affection in the way she signs herself. Written in French, an approximate translation is as follows.

"Prayer in honour of God for the health of the world. Lord Jesus Christ, Son of the living God, have mercy on us. Saviour of the world, help us I pray. Help me at the hour of my soul departing my body. Intercede with your dear son, my saviour, that he will vouchsafe to pardon me my sins. Amen. Jesus, Mary, and Joseph, have pity on me. Queen of the Angels and Martyrs, support of the weak, Mother of souls, fountain of mercy, tabernacle of the spirit, Paradise of Martyrs and of Confessors, through this help me, and through your mercy now and at the hour of my death, so that one day, I may enjoy eternal glory. Amen."

She continues . . .

"A very special protection is promised to anyone who reads, or hears this being read or carries with him this prayer, found in the Sepulchre in 1909. A priest, after saying Mass, found this prayer wrapped in a cloth in the Sepulchre. Anyone who carries it with him will fear no misfortune nor fear death, nor fall into the hands of enemies, nor will be attacked by poisonous creatures, nor die in battle or in any evil encounter." She concludes, *"With good memories and good luck, Genevieve."*

The author found this letter in an old leather wallet, which would have been carried in his tunic. There is no supporting information about it, but soldiers from the front did get a few days' leave on occasions and the nearest big town to the battlefields would have been Amiens. Sources refer to this town as being a place where units were given local leave. But whatever may have been the circumstances, the fact remains that George survived, and the letter has also survived and has been found over 100 years later.

George's letter of 4th January to Sis dwells on Christmas memories following his December leave.

"My dear Sis,

Many thanks for the letters and rest. I am sorry not to have written sooner, but have had lots of work. I am at present commanding the company, as Mercer has gone away very ill. He is now in England. I don't know if I shall continue in command of the company as there are several men only 2nd in command of other Coys who are senior to me. We have filled up again with new officers.

Howard has not come back yet, and I don't know if he will now; he might get some soft job in England, though I hope that he does return.

We are in the trenches again now. It is not as bad as it was, although it is not quite like Piccadilly yet!!

I heard from Will. All his parcels I sent off hadn't arrived when he wrote, but they might have done by now. Has his sergeant been on leave yet? He told me that he had moved north and was in quite a jolly place!

I am glad that you went to Holbrook. I was very amused at what you mentioned re Harold. He is a "howl" (joke doesn't quite meet the case) and many times I haven't known whether to raise my fist in anger or to laugh hard. Now young Tom is different as you know. He is a man of the world! He is the type the men would go anywhere with. There are several types that appeal to the men out here and he is one of the few." (George was always fairly scathing about Harold. They were cousins . . . Tress Morton was Harold's younger brother and both brothers were involved in Morton Brothers, the family firm of Stockbrokers in the city. Harold won an MC which George always said was for "marching the band to Paris"!)

"I didn't know what to send you for Christmas, so thought it best to let you choose for yourself. It is the lazy way of doing things really, but much more satisfactory. You seem to have had quite a lot of presents at Christmas. I did quite well also. Mostly grub!!

There were only two officers and one from another Coy (who was attached as we were so short in A Coy) in the Coy at Christmas (we were in billets on Christmas Day) so we joined with another Coy and had our Christmas dinner all together. We had a most cheery dinner; we had soup (packets!) salmon (tinned), turkey (sent from England), Christmas pudding, fig, sherry, etc, nuts, crackers and everything complete.

The men had quite a cheery time too. They were to have had roast beef, but when the day arrived, we found that most of the beef was not of the roasting kind and would have to be stewed. Well, the men have stew almost every day, so we decided it was to be different if possible. One of the officers who could speak French was sent off with a private (who was a butcher and slaughterer of animals) by myself to prospect for meat. They soon arrived back with a live sheep tied onto a hand barrow. They had bought the sheep for 50 francs from the mayor of the village. The sheep was in the oven within three-quarters of an hour after it arrived at the billets!! It was jolly nice too; I tasted a bit. The men, therefore, had roast beef or mutton, Christmas pudding, bar, oranges, smokes, almonds and raisins, and each man had a parcel with a muffler, pipe, mug, and other useful articles. After the dinner at 6 pm, there were a few words and then we left them and they had a concert, and "some" concert it was too from what I can hear! So, everyone was cheery, as far as possible.

Well, Sis, there isn't much more. Everything goes on much the same as usual. Give my kindest regards to all, Yours lovingly, George"

Trench life was to dominate in January when the Battalion alternated with the 6th Northants, a fellow regiment in 54th Brigade. The months were quiet on the whole with just sporadic small arms fire.

The relief of troops on the front line was generally carried out at night. Those being relieved "stood too" (a general practice anyway at dusk and dawn). Each incoming platoon came up the communication trenches and took up position, man for man, replacing the outgoing platoon in the fire trench. Strict march discipline was maintained, with no lights or smoking permitted. The company commander took over the stores and ammunition and signed for them, although this generally happened before the formal handover. Thus the fire trench was continually manned during the relief.

In February, the Battalion was placed into Divisional reserve and there is just one entry in the Battalion war diary . . . "*. . . while the Bn was in Divisional reserve, the time was spent in resting and getting rid of trench staleness. For training, the Bn practised bombing, musketry, practice with gas helmets, attacks in the open and attacks from trenches. For recreation, inter-Battn. and platoon competitions were held in boxing, football, shooting, etc.*"

At the beginning of March, the Battalion progressively moved to new billets at Bronfay Farm and Billon Wood before deploying to sector A1 NE of Carnoy, relieving the 12th Middlesex in the trenches, also a fellow battalion within 54th Brigade. On the whole, the month was a quiet one, but again with constant attrition through casualties.

George meanwhile managed to get leave and a letter from Will indicates that George was in London at the beginning of the month.

April continues with the battalion alternating with the 12th Middlesex in the same sector. Sis had her 21st birthday, acknowledged in George's letter to her of 9th April.

"My dear Sis,

Apologies for lateness. Very many happy returns of your birthday. A little present will no doubt arrive in due course.

Well, Sis, I am not going to write a long epistle for your coming of age. The event might have happened under better circumstances so that Will or I had been home on leave when we would have celebrated the birthday in the best manner.

I am sure that the coming years will bring you happiness so cheer up! The times we have had the last few years can't go on. We have had our share of bad luck, but not so bad as many & not worse than most. I hope the time is not too distant when you and Will & I shall be able to settle down together again, when we shall make up for it.

I got back all serene. We were held up at the port in England for one night and a day, but were not allowed off the boat. It was very dull work when one might have been in Town.

The weather here is delightful, spring seems to have come to stay at last. We go into the trenches in a few days.

I found a letter from Will awaiting me when I returned. He seems very fit and cheery. Dolly sent me some socks & Mrs Hawkins some cigarettes.

There is nothing fresh here. I hope that you have a very merry holiday. I enclose a little to help with the expenses.

Well, give my kind regards to the Gillisons. Write soon, ever yours, lovingly George."

The month of April was full of activity with artillery fire being exchanged as well as trench mortars in action. The battalion's machine guns, accompanied by rifle fire, concentrated upon enemy wiring parties. The Vickers machine guns, with a range of well over 1000 yards, were particularly effective firing on fixed lines and laying a devastating curtain of fire on predetermined targets both by day and night.

The British Army was preparing for a new offensive, which General Haig, the commander of British forces, expected to lead to a complete breakthrough of the German lines and an early victory with his French and Belgian allies. General Rawlinson (of Indian C.I.G.S. fame) was more cautious preferring a "bite and hold" policy and the progressive attrition of the German positions.

As part of this preparation, a massive programme of road-building was started, the building also of new rail networks leading to the front with small gauge tracks and trollies to bring up supplies to the front and bring back casualties to the forward dressing and field hospitals. A massive extension in accommodation and billets for troops behind the front line was now also underway. Production of shells was stepped up in British factories and brought up into the artillery batteries stationed behind the front line to supply the guns for the great artillery barrage that was to precede the attacks on July 1st. The Battle of the Somme was about to start.

The artillery bombardment, which started on 24th June, was planned to last five days with the final two days allocated for a "hurricane" bombardment all along the 26 miles of the assault. The artillery programme was in two parts – the 18 pounders and 2" Stokes mortars objectives were to degrade the wire in front of the German positions, with the heavies, the massive 9.5" mortars, 8" guns and 4" Stokes mortars directing their fire on the German first and second trench positions and villages, with the objective of destroying and degrading the trench system and any deeply dug emplacements. Over a million shells were fired by the Royal Artillery in this initial bombardment.

The German trench system had three lines of trenches, and the infantry objective was to capture and hold the first two. German tactics were to degrade the British assault and then immediately counter-attack using fresh stormtroopers held in reserve. And so, initial British gains were often lost on counter-attack as the individual battles ebbed to and fro.

In the preparation phase, the battalion diary records that the 11th Fusiliers, during virtually the whole of May, were occupied in assisting the Civil Engineering 13th Corps in hut-building, road-making and quarrying, and at the beginning of June, employed on Royal Engineer fatigues on unloading barges and road-making. From here at Chipilly, the Battalion marched on 3rd June to Beaumesnil and commenced building practice trenches at Ailly-sur-Somme. Following this, the Battalion marched to Picquigny, and, for the next 11 days, practised the "attack" in the training area near Ailly-sur-Somme, moving to Bray towards the end of the month, and then to Carnoy in preparation for the commencement of the offensive on 1st July.

George, meanwhile, had managed a leave at the beginning of June as his letter of June 16th relates . . .

"My dear Sis,

Very sorry I haven't written before, but have been absolutely 'up to the eyes' in work. We don't get a moment from the time we get up until after dinner at night, then it is usually bed and sleep in a very few minutes! We are not in the trenches but have moved from the place we were in when I came home on leave. We are in a village now – fairly comfortable.

I had quite a good journey back here – managed to get a berth on the boat with two others. I slept most of the time on the boat.

I think that last leave was the best I have had. I thoroughly enjoyed myself – though when I shall get another leave I should not like to say!!!!

I can't tell you what work we are doing at present, though if I could, it would be interesting. Anyhow, my face is nearly raw with the sunburn so quite justify my nickname 'Tomato'.

I shall write Will when I find enough time, probably tomorrow – also Dorrie, then I think I shall not write anyone for a week! I should like to have spent that Saturday afternoon and evening with you and Dorrie; we might have gone to Daly's. It was quite an oversight to have missed that show as it was probably the only one that was left to see!

Well, I will chuck it. Write soon. Love to the Gillisons. Yours lovingly, George."

The battalion diary not only records the wait at Carnoy pending the offensive and the British bombardment going on overhead but also the significant casualties from German counter artillery, with 6 killed, 8 died from their wounds, 46 wounded of whom 6 returned to duty . . . .and this, of course, was before the attack even commenced.

The 4th Army had been allocated the Southern and right-hand sector of the British line next to the French 6th Army, the main objective being to break through the German lines up to Montauban and beyond. Intelligence from two German deserters indicated that much of the German trench system had been degraded and troops exhausted from the continuous artillery bombardment. The 18th Division had been allocated the left centre of the 4th Army with the 54th Infantry Brigade on the left of the Divisional line, with the 11th Fusiliers as the left-hand Battalion next to the 22nd

Manchester Regiment, their objective being the trench system beyond the German front line known as Pommiers Trench in front of the Pommiers Redoubt.

The battle formation had 'A' and 'B' companies as the front attack troops, followed by 'C' and 'D' companies. The attack started at 7.30 a.m., just after first light and about a minute later, an enormous mine exploded under the German stronghold position at Casino Point. The explosion should have been timed to coincide exactly with the start time and, as a result, the minute or so delay caused significant casualties in the 53rd Brigade to the right of the Fusiliers.

As a result of the hurricane bombardment, Fusilier casualties were initially few with the front German line offering little resistance, but resistance stiffened with the advance to Pommiers Trench and fierce fighting took place before the Redoubt itself was captured. The Battalion then consolidated its position and parties from the dumps brought up wire, stakes, bombs, ammunition, and water.

'A' Company was commanded by a Major Hudson, but George, much to his disappointment, was left behind in reserve as second in command, as his letter of July 7th to Sis reveals.

> *"Thank you for your letter received all serene. I had a letter yesterday from Mrs Hawkins acknowledging the pin. She seems very pleased with it.*
>
> *Well, as you will have seen by the papers, we are pushing at last. The Battn were in the first line over the top & did splendidly. The men were wonderful, fought like tigers. Only a certain proportion of officers were allowed to go over the top, & I was one of those who had to remain behind, but hope to be in the next show. Quite a lot had to remain behind. The Colonel sent for me to go up after the scrap started, but the General would not let me go. The Colonel asked for two others as well, but none of us were allowed to go. The General says that we shall get our bellies full of fighting before we have done!! I don't want to indulge in heroics, but I was damn sick at staying behind.*
>
> *Young Howard did jolly well. Before the show (a day or two before) he took a raiding party over to the German lines. He could not find any Boches in the front line so he went to the second line; not finding any there went to the third line, and finding plenty of Boches there proceeded to scrap them outnumbered by about ten to one. He and his party used all of their bombs & then came away without losing a man. bringing back many souvenirs with them, & gaining much valuable information. Howard did splendidly and should get at least a Military Cross out of it.*
>
> *The paper's description of the battle is quite amusing. Some of the correspondents are quite funny in their descriptions and criticisms, more often than not getting the wrong end of the stick! Although the Daily Mail man was quite near the show, he is one of the most amusing.*
>
> *Well, I will chuck it. Love to all. Yours lovingly, George."*

The policy of not allowing all of the officers to go into battle is an interesting one. Officer casualty rates were significantly higher than other ranks principally because they were so obvious in their attack leadership role. Many did not carry a rifle but a revolver as a personal weapon, and therefore stood out as a target to sniper fire. . . . and hence the policy of reducing officer numbers going into the attack. Despite this, the battalion officer casualties were significantly higher than the overall casualty numbers judging by the drafts of replacements, as casualties were not listed in the diary battle reports by Colonel Carr commanding the 11th RF.

The Battalion was relieved on 2nd July by the 12th Middlesex which had been held in reserve within 54th Brigade and retired to reserve in order to regroup.

Elsewhere, the battle was not going so well and was characterised by massive and shocking casualties, particularly in front of the ridge on which the Theipval village and chateau stood. Some 16,000 men died on that first day. While the barrage had proved effective in parts of the line, here, the deep German dugouts and redoubts provided shelter to the German defenders who simply re-emerged once the barrage had lifted, manning machine-gun posts and pouring devastating fire on the attack as it faltered. The more spectacular territorial gains were made on the flanks, particularly in the southern 4th Army sector.

In this sector, Montauban had been captured and overrun and held with a territorial gain of over 3,000 yards, enabling the British to swing North and, over a period, to capture Thiepval village and the surrounding redoubts at the end of November.

The 18th Division was next to be involved in the capture of Trônes Wood. A number of attempts had been made but repulsed by German troops in the wood itself. 18th Division was ordered forward; the 11th Fusiliers, now in Trigger Valley and the Maricourt trenches, were ordered out at 2 a.m. on 14th July. It advanced in full fighting order to the base of the wood where it occupied the captured German first-line trenches and remained in reserve. One platoon was detached to reinforce the 12th Middlesex and the wood was taken and completely cleared. The Germans put up a very heavy barrage, and one Fusilier officer was wounded with 1 OR killed, 17 wounded and 1 shell shock casualty.

During much of July, the Battalion remained in defensive positions in and around Trônes Wood, suffering very heavy shell fire and sustaining further casualties before moving out on the 18th into Bois des Tailles to clean up and bathe. George's next letter recalls the fighting:

"B.E.F. France July 24th My dear Sis,

Thanks for your letter received all right. We are now away from the scrap for a short while I hope. The men need a rest badly. We have spent several days travelling, & have had some pretty stiff marching to do, but we have been one night here now. We are a long way South of where Will is, in fact, we are North of young Tom.

I'm glad Aunt Edie called on you & hope you had a good weekend. The weather here was delightful over the weekend.

I am sorry not to have written but as you can guess, we have been pretty busy – although, as I told you, the first part of the attack I was kept in reserve. The Division did jolly well, & were in the fight up to our present forward position. Our Battn. got further forward than anyone on 1st July.

There is little news to tell you really. Howard got his Military Cross, & jolly well deserved it.

I expect that you will miss Dorrie now she has gone off to Devonshire. I am glad that Charlie was amusing over dinner.

Well, old girl, I will chuck it. Regards to Gillisons, Yours lovingly, George."

There followed a number of moves, some by rail, ending up at Serous where the Battalion was inspected by the Divisional Commander, Major General Maxse, before refitting at Lynde, and re-joining the rest of the brigade at Wallon-Cappel. July ended with a further short period of training. The Battalion had been involved in two major battles but remained in good shape. Not much was heard from George during this very active period. In early August, the Battalion moved to billets between Erquinghem and Armentieres before occupying trenches at sector B1 at Bois Grenier, where much improvement was carried out to the trench defences. Intermittent shell and machine-gun fire was experienced before the Battalion was relieved by the 12th Middlesex in the middle of the month. Further training was carried out particularly with the Lewis gunners. Towards the end of the month, a further move was made to the training grounds near Orlencourt at the Monchy Breton training area, with 9 days of training with snipers and Lewis gunners on the ranges, while others practised bayonet fighting, rapid loading, practices in wood fighting, extended order drill and consolidating trenches with attacking drills in bombing. Meanwhile, the Battalion was reinforced with three drafts of 70, 50, and 55 other ranks. There are no records of casualties for the major battle at Pommiers, but these draft figures give the indication that they were substantial.

The month of September was largely spent in refitting in preparation for the attack on Theipval and the ridge commanding the battlefields to the West, East and South leading to the Schwaben Redoubt. This included night attacks, musketry, running and physical drills, with the Battalion moving to a number of different training areas up into Flanders with integrated training within the whole of 54th Brigade.

Meanwhile, the 4th Army, building on the success at Mametz and Montauban, took the villages of Orvilliers and La Boisselle and made further progress with the capture of the south-eastern trench of the Hindenburg line and part of Limberg trench, opening up the possibility of taking the Pozieres Ridge, on which Thiepval stood, from the south. On 24th September, after completion of training, the Battalion moved up to the support trenches in the Leipzig sector in preparation for the attack on the ridge.

Once again, 18th Division was given the centre of the line with 54th Brigade on the left with the line of advance through the village of Thiepval itself, to the Schwaben trench and Redoubt. Eight tanks were made available. A preliminary bombardment lasted three days, the Divisional guns reinforced by the allocation of the artillery of 25th and 49th Divisions, firing 60,000 rounds of field artillery and 45,000 rounds of heavier shell.

The Battalion war diary takes up the story; the initial assault was led by 'D' and 'C' Companies with 'A' Company led by Major Hudson, and 'B' Company following

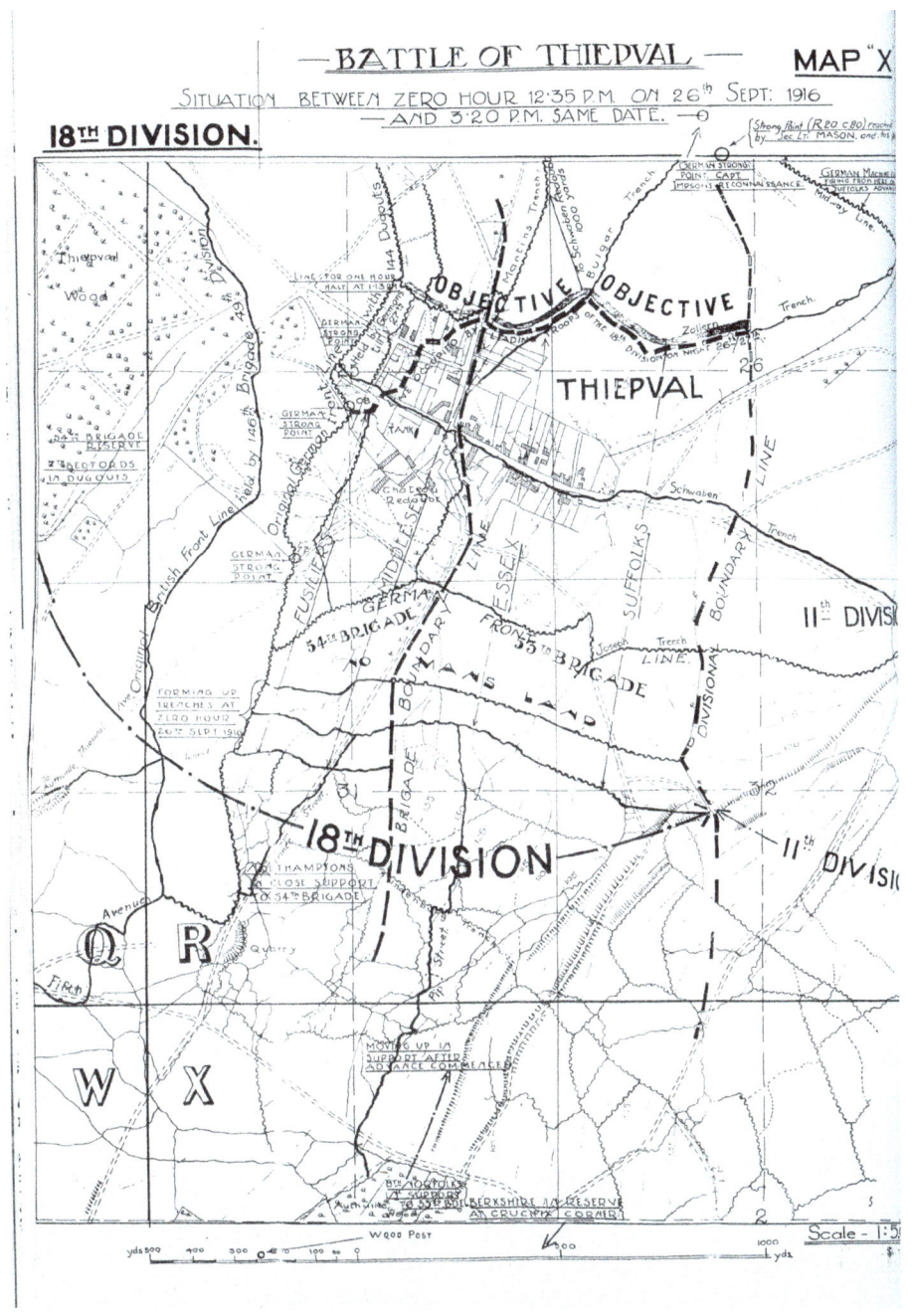

8 General Manxe's 18th Division map showing the line of advance to Thiepval Village. Note 11th Fusiliers again on left of the line. (Source Thiepval Somme – by Michael Stedman)

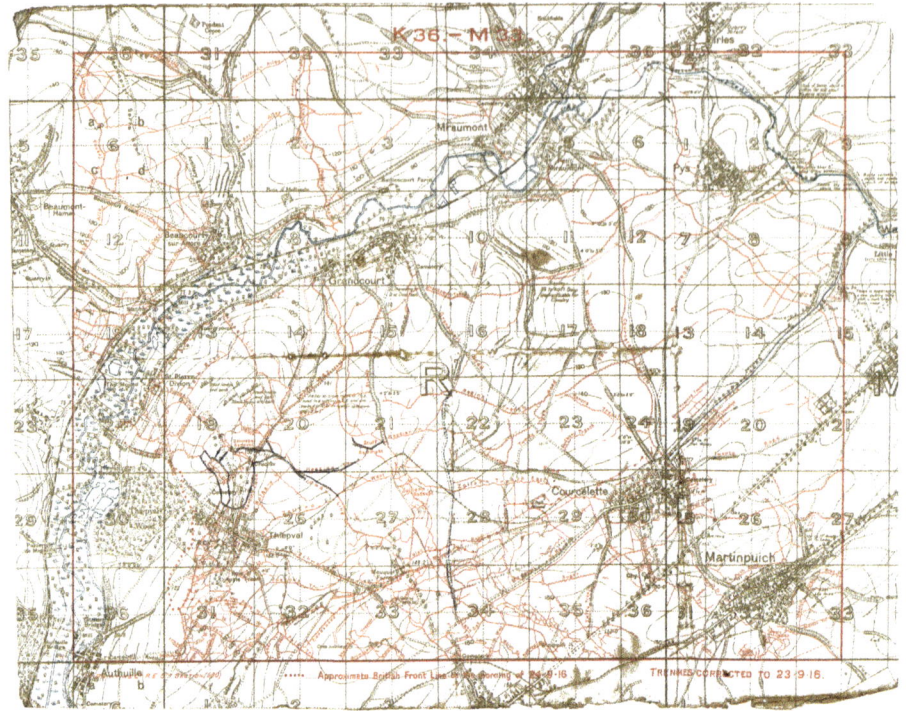

*9 Georges trench map showing attack on Theipval and Schwaben redout
marked in pencil map sections 19/20 and 25/26 also Boom Ravine
battle area 10/11 and 16/17 (Morton archive)*

behind, with the 12th Middlesex also accompanying the Fusiliers. The fighting was bitter; a hand-to-hand battle ensued as the Germans were pushed back. Colonel Carr and his adjutant Lieut Cumberledge had been wounded about half an hour into the fight and the Battalion was now being led by Captain Johnson of 'C' Company.

One of the tanks reached the village; another stuck on the approach, and with the village captured, the Battalion moved onto the second objective, and it was at this point that Major Hudson was wounded and George took over command of 'A' Coy. Trenches were dug north of the village, and in the evening, the Battalion was relieved by the Bedfordshires, before retiring to Bois de Martinsart and then to billets at Maillet Wood to rest, re-equip and refit.

The casualties of 54th Brigade were particularly heavy but the taking of Thiepval Village is largely credited to the 11th Fusiliers and 12th Middlesex. It was, however, not until 5th October that most of the Schwaben Redoubt was captured by the 18th Division, by which time the Division had fought itself to a standstill, with casualties of 80 officers and 1910 other ranks.

During the first half of October, the Battalion received drafts of 252 other ranks and 5 officers were attached from 12th Middlesex which gives a further indication of the casualties suffered by the Battalion in the taking of Thiepval. The commander in chief visited them and expressed his thanks for what they had achieved.

Once again, they were to return to the trenches at Albert on 24th October after a period of retraining and integrating the drafts within the Battalion. This was a very active tour with appalling conditions of wet and mud and artillery exchanges resulting in the death of Captain Hoare with 12 other ranks killed, another 23 wounded and 3 missing. This was a short tour; coming out on 26th, the rest of the month was spent in training. In November, another tour in the trenches was undertaken, again a short tour of three days but again with heavy casualties of 7 killed, 15 wounded and 1 shell shock. Another trench tour started on the 14th, this time for 4 days close to Orvilliers, also with significant casualties from gas and shelling; and then, on the 21st, the Battalion started a seven-day march ending at Drucat in billets. There then began another period of training including intensive trench digging with the rest of the month spent training with a day off for Christmas.

George managed leave in December as his letter of 26th December confirms.

"My dear Sis,

After much journeying & hanging about, I have arrived all serene. We were kept all day at the English port and remained there for the night. We spent another night en route on this side and after a lot of trouble, got here on Christmas afternoon, and in time for the men's dinners.

All the officers dined together in the evening. I have got the menu signed by all who were there – the card was done by Little. The menu was strictly adhered to so you will see that we had a jolly good dinner & plenty of bubbly! I found a letter from you waiting for me written on the 7th, so you will see the posts have been somewhat late. The pudding that Aunt Edie sent me has not yet arrived.

Well, Sis, I had a jolly good leave only it was too short. Give my love to Mrs Macpherson and kind regards to all at 59.

I hope you had a good Christmas, Yours lovingly, George.

PS. I enclose menu & Xmas cards – one signed by Brigadier was done by Little. The menu reads "Oysters, Oxtail Soup, Fried Soles, Roast Turkey, Xmas Pudding, Mince pies, Savoury . . . January 3rd."

At the turn of the year, the Battalion was once again in training with the 54th Brigade. Sir Ivor Maxse KCB CVO DSO had vast experience as a former Army Training General with advanced battle plans and formations, and so the whole division was at a state of readiness with his methods through regular training designed to reduce casualties and to initiate and train new drafts in these procedures. January was very cold and snow and ice were to continue for most of February as well.

Sir Ivor's letter of farewell on promotion is as follows:

"I cannot relinquish command of the 18th Division without expressing to every officer, N.C.O. and man my admiration for the indomitable spirit and my confidence in their

ability to beat the enemy. Having seen the Division grow from untrained civilians in October 1914 into veterans in January 1917, I part with them with extreme regret. Ivor Maxse, Lieut-General commanding 18th Division."

On 19th January, the Bn was in the trenches, but 'A' Coy was detached to act as a fatigue company to the 6th Northants, possibly in anticipation of the coy making a fighting patrol in early February. Instructions were issued to rub the men's feet with whale oil and to allow socks to be pulled over trousers rather than puttees to help prevent frostbite. After a spell on fatigues, the Bn returned to trenches in mid-February for a short spell. During this time, the trenches were frozen over, the men using their helmets to play curling on the ice.

'A' Coy now made a night attack on a German strongpoint on 10th February, which was rushed and captured. Significant casualties were, however, incurred as the Germans mounted heavy machine-gun and rifle fire. Reserves were sent out to reinforce this two-platoon attack but the company was forced to retire after suffering 1 officer and 5 other ranks killed, 17 wounded and 6 missing. George would have been commanding the company, although this is not mentioned in the Bn war diary.

George's last surviving letter from the field was written on 5th February, just twelve days before he was wounded . . .

"My dear Sis,

I got your letters all right. I am glad the late work has now stopped. Yes, it was good of Margaret and Fergus to take you out. I hope you had a very cheery time. I wish I could have been there. I haven't seen Fergus since Aug 1914. I had a letter from Aunt Edie a few days ago and a pair of socks from May – a jolly good pair too. Ida Cole wrote me a letter too. I expect that Willie Morton is already a Major if he is on that course. It is a very pleasant rest to get three months in England.

I don't know how you can have seen the Battle of the Ancre on the films as the attack took place at dawn – and at the time, it was thick mist & very dark. We were in the line at that time and not a hundred miles away. What you must have seen was probably another attack (if you actually saw the men 'over the top' but why they should call it the Battle of the Ancre I can't see.) Films of gunners in action can be got at any time & may easily have been the actual guns that were firing on that particular front at the time, but taken after or before the show. You may have seen some of the casualties coming down as they were probably some of the late ones who got back after dawn – when it was light and clear, but you can take it from me that the actual attack you did not see as it was very dark & very misty at the time, & the objective was gained before photography was possible (without artificial light). Will wasn't near the place at the time, he was further south. I don't know where he is now, but I don't think that he was near that place when he was last in action. I think that he is resting now but I am not certain.

Aunt Martha is a dear old soul. She is one of those large-hearted people who are so scarce these days. I must write her soon. If you hear Arthur's address in the meantime,

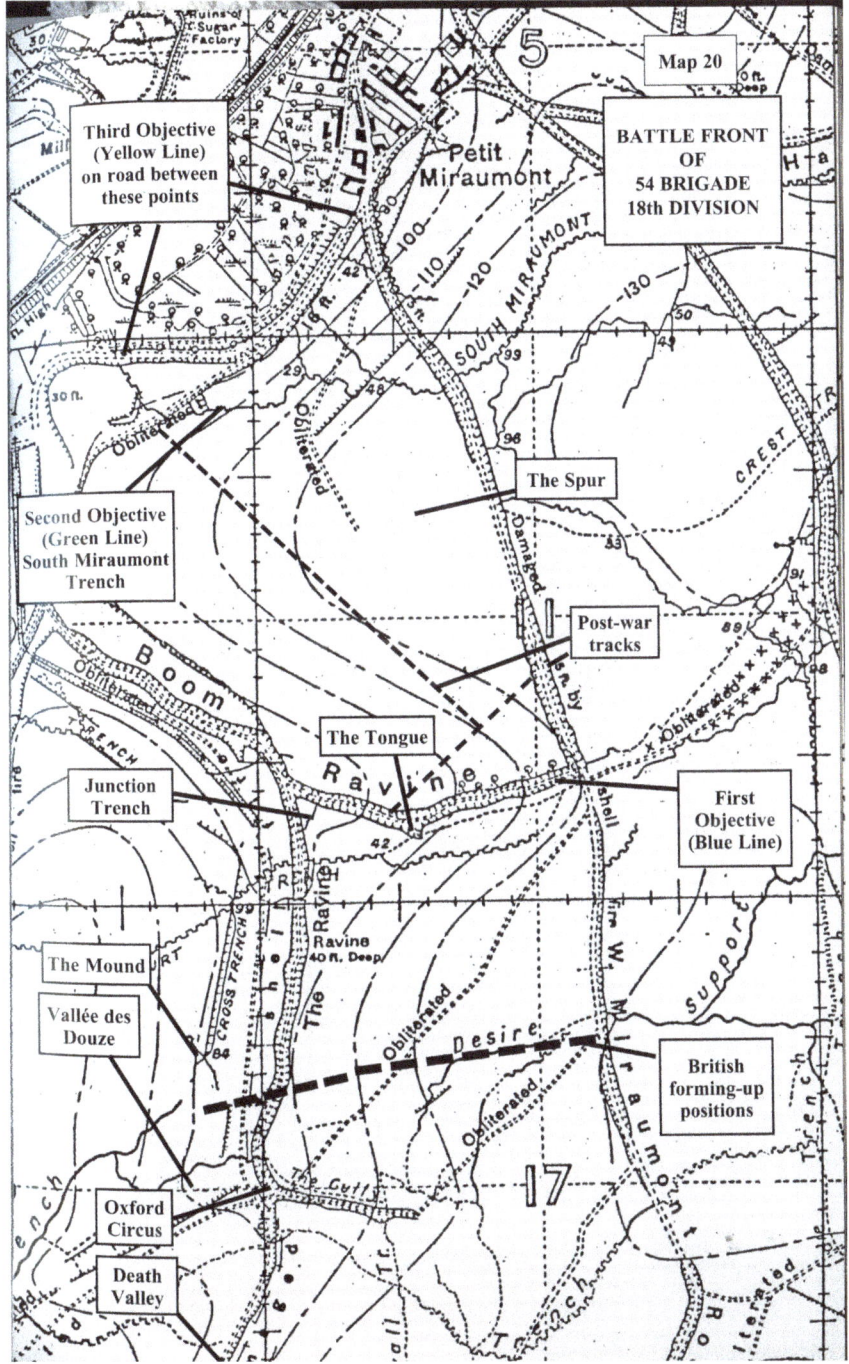

10 *Map of the area of Boom Ravine. It is likely that George fell seriously wounded going over the Mound to the left of the Ravine*

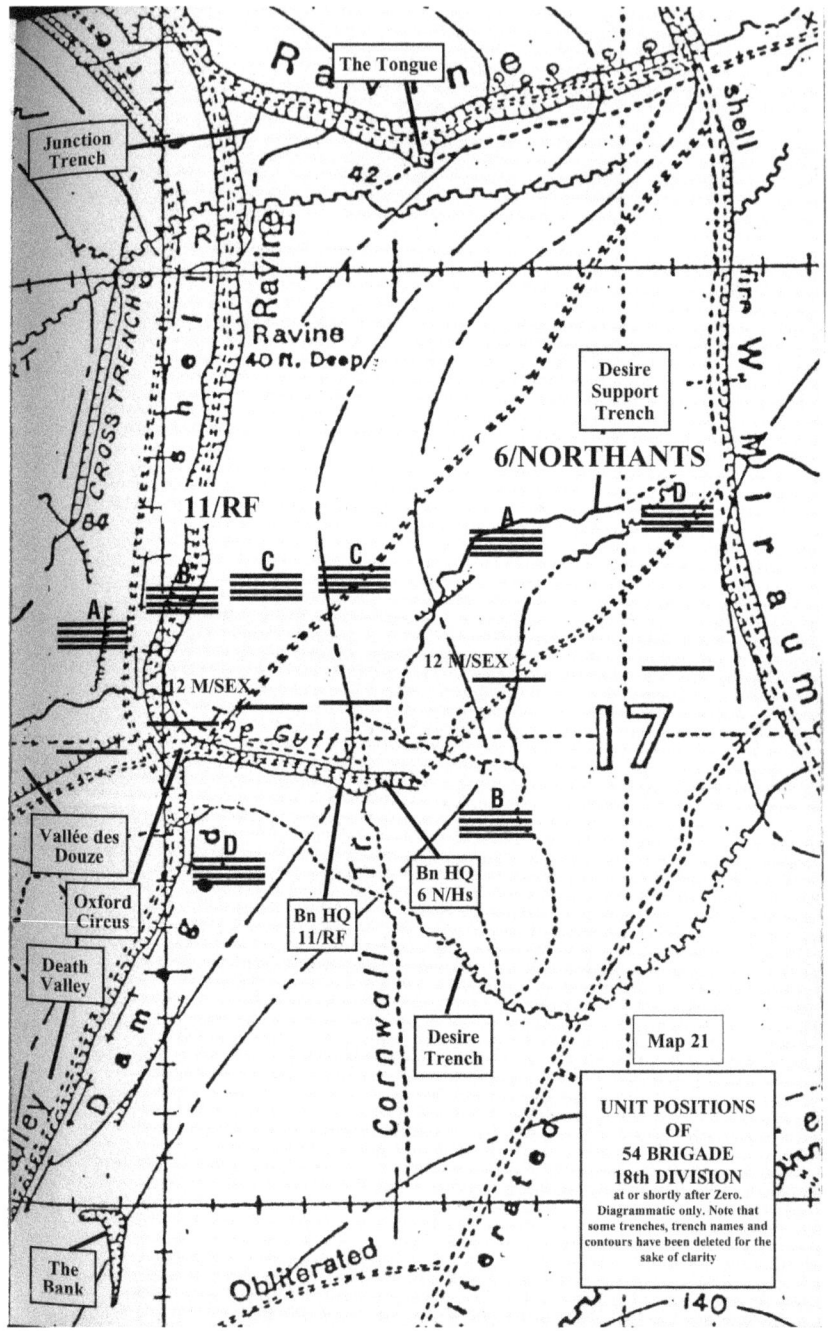

11 *Attack formation of 54th Infantry Brigade – 11th Fusiliers and 6th Northants – at the Battle of Boom Ravine. Note 'A' company 11th RF with George in command on the left of the Ravine*

you might let me know. I had to think for some time before I could remember who 'John Willie' was but I got him at last. I am glad to hear that he is so much better.

The frost still holds & my chief difficulty is to keep warm, but we manage to scramble along somehow.

Well, Sis, I will close. I hope that you are very fit. I have a cold but it is much better now. Yours lovingly, George."

This letter is a bit of a puzzle. Fergus and his sister May were first cousins. Fergus was a barrister in the Chancery Bar who went on to become a King's Council, High Court Judge and Lord of Appeal. May married and her son George Millar was in the SOE during the Second World War and wrote a number of books afterwards. There were, in fact, a number of major actions North and South of the Ancre, a tributary of the Somme. These actions cleared out the area North and South-East of the river of the exhausted German Army, in what modern historians call the first and second battles of the Ancre.

The 11th Fusiliers were to occupy Regina Trench in preparation for the attack on Grandcourt Trench and the town of Miraumont beyond. Almost the last battle before the Germans retreated to the Hindenburg Line, this action, named the Battle of Boom Ravine, was a two-division attack on 17th February 1917.

This was to be one of the final and bloodiest battles of the Somme campaign, and yet it hardly receives a mention in the history books. It was a 'two-division' affair (around 25000 troops) with troops of the 2nd and 18th Divisions supplemented by Royal Marines and Naval gunners from the 198th Brigade of the Naval Division. The Naval Division was an idea of Winston Churchill due to substantial numbers of sailors and marines being surplus from a shortage of ships, and three battalions were allocated to hold and advance the left of the line.

The 54th Infantry Brigade was in the centre of the line with the 11th Fusiliers attacking astride the ravine itself and, as it turned at right angles, directly to the front of it. The objective was the capture of Grandcourt trench behind the ravine and the town of Miraumont behind that. The ravine was a sunken roadway, 30/40 feet deep in places and heavily fortified with dugouts and machine-gun emplacements. The German positions had, however, been softened up with a heavy artillery barrage before the attack.

The Germans knew the battle plan, thought to have been revealed to them by deserters, and so when the troops advanced to the forming-up position, they were shelled and fired upon by small arms, machine gun and mortar and artillery fire, particularly up a shallow valley named Death Valley and at the assembly point known as Oxford Circus where the 11th Fusiliers and their right-hand sister battalion, the 6th Northants formed up.

Detailed orders had been issued for moving up the night before in preparation for a dawn attack, with 'A' & 'B' Companies in the front attack line followed by 'C' & 'D' Companies. George was commanding 'A' Company. By the time the battalion formed up on the start line, all the officers had either been killed or wounded except George and the company commander of 'B' Company. The winter of 1917 was the coldest of the whole war, but it was now beginning to thaw and mud was beginning to thaw out in the advance trenches. Soldiers were slipping and sliding as they advanced. It was here that George won his MC in getting the soldiers up and into the attack and leading it despite the heavy enemy fire.

The Germans knew exactly the line of advance and heavy enemy fire caused significant casualties before the men even formed up on the start line. The full and graphic account of the battle was given by Philip Gibbs, the noted war correspondent, in an account syndicated in the Daily Chronicle and the Telegraph of Monday 26th February 1917.

"Boom Ravine Battle In The Fog – A Grim Struggle"
By Philip Gibbs, War Correspondent British headquarters France, the Telegraph, 26th February 1917 George's Military Cross

In a broad outline, I have already described the heavy fighting which took place last Saturday morning (Feb 17th) across a deep gully called Boom Ravine and up the slopes towards Miraumont. The history of this attack needs to be told more fully. In difficulty, in grim human courage, in all its drama of fog, and darkness, and shell fire, and death, it seems to me to hold more of what this war means to individual men – all that can be asked of them in such hours. Some of the young officers who went through and beyond Boom Ravine – and had the luck to come back again – described their adventures as though they were but a nightmare from which they had awakened, laughing.

It was very dark – pitch black before dawn and heavy in fog when daylight failed to come. The thaw had just set in, and the ground was soppy, which was bad luck. In spite of the thaw, it was horribly damply cold, but the men had been given a good meal before forming up for the attack, and the officers brought up the rum ration in bottles so that the men could attack with some warmth in them. In the utter darkness, unable to make any glimmer of light lest the enemy should see, the brigades had to get into line. Two companies lost themselves but got into touch again in time. A great fire of high explosives burst over our assembly lines. The darkness was lit up by the red flashes of these bursting shells. Men fell, wounded and dead. One battalion was particularly tried, and their brigadier wondered whether they would have the spirit to get up and attack when the hour arrived."

This battalion was the 11th Fusiliers. The short citation of George's Military Cross reads;

"He succeeded in forming up his company and launching them in the attack in spite of very hostile fire. He set a splendid example throughout. He was severely wounded."

The article continues . . .

"But when the moment came, they rose and went forward, and fought through to the last goal – splendid and wonderful! They were the first to get to Grandcourt Trench, which lay between them and the Boom Ravine. The wire was not cut, and there was the hammering of machine-guns and the swish of machine-gun bullets.

12 The battle for the Ravine with trees blasted by shellfire

Lost All Its Officers

The battalion had already lost all the officers, who had gone forward gallantly, leading their men and meeting the bullets first. A sergeant – major took command, shouted to his men to keep steady, and found a gap through the wire." This was Company Sergeant Major Fritterer of 'B' coy. His company commander, Captain Collis-Sandes of 'B' Company, had been killed, shot through the neck 200 yards from the start line. A little further on, George fell, shot through the left and right sides, which I guess knocked him flat. As he lay wounded, bursting shell fragments took off half his right foot with shell fragments in the left leg and foot as well. He was the last officer to fall. Company Sergeant Major Fitterer of 'B' coy, although himself wounded in the buttock, regrouped and took over command of the battalion and led it to take the objective. (See his letter to Lieut Colthorp below). The account continues. . . .

"They forced their way through, passed Grandcourt Trench, and, with other men, dropped into Boom Ravine. That place is a deep gully almost parallel with Grandcourt

Trench, and with South Miraumont Trench beyond. It was a ravine of death. Our shell fire had smashed down all the trees and their tall trunks lay at the bottom of the gully, and their branches were flung about. The banks had been opened out by shell craters, and several of the German dugouts, built into the sides of them, were upheaved or choked. Dead bodies or human fragments lay among the branches and broken woodwork. A shell of ours had entered one dugout and blown six men out of its doorway. Inside were six other dead. From dugouts not blown up or choked came groups of German soldiers, pallid and nerve broken, who gave themselves up quickly enough. One man was talkative. He said in perfect English that he had been coachman to an English Earl, and he cursed our artillery and said that if he could get at our blinking gunners he would wring their blighted necks – or words to that effect. Another man was an ex-waiter in the Trocadero, and after the battle, was kept for making coffee, which he did as though he loved it.

Germans sham death

But the battle was not over yet. It had only just begun. While Boom Ravine was being cleared of its living inhabitants by the first wave of English soldiers (they were men of London and the Southern Counties), other waves were coming up, or rather, not waves, but odd groups of men, trudging over the shell craters, and hunting as they went for German snipers; some lay in shell holes firing until they were pinned by bayonet points. Their bodies lie there now, curled up. One of them lay still, with his face in the moist earth. "See that man is properly dead," said an officer and a soldier with him pricked the man. He sprang up with a scream and ran hard away . . . towards our lines. Six prisoners came trudging back from the Ravine with a slightly wounded man as an escort. On the way back, they found themselves very lonely with him and passed some rifles lying in their way. They seized the rifles and became fighting men again until a little Welsh officer met them and killed every one of them with a revolver.

Behind the troops who went up to the Boom Ravine was a colonel and a young lieutenant with a whimsical way of hiding his courage. "We'd better get up to Grandcourt Trench," said the colonel. "I feel a bit anxious." They went up, picking their way amongst the dead. "There is a lot of machine-gun firing," said the young adjutant, whose ears since Loos were trained to the sound of it. "We had better get down." "I want to see what's going on, eh," said the colonel. He did not see much because presently, he was hit by a bullet and dropped. The adjutant went up with an intelligence officer, who afterwards, led an attack on a German strongpoint. On the way, this intelligence officer, with six men of a machine gun team, lay in a shell hole to escape a scythe of bullets. When it seemed time to get out and get on again, all the six men fell, and only the intelligence officer escaped. He took command of another party, attacked the strongpoint, and captured it with rifle grenades.

A Defensive Flank

The young adjutant made himself busy in the Ravine (this would have been Capt. G.F.J. Cumberledge Adjutant 11th RF). *There was a mixed crowd here, and he got them together and started forward for South Miraumont trench. The Sergeant Major, who had reorganised the first wave, had gone on ahead with ten men and pushed out to within 80 yards of that ditch, where he was joined by the adjutant and supporting troops. The intelligence officer was working up with another group on the left. Machine-gun fire was sweeping down from high ground near Petit Miraumont, and by this time it was lighter, so that the enemy could see our men coming over the slope. Outside South Miraumont Trench, the wire was still solid and uncut but here and there the enemy had left a gap for working parties and on the left, the intelligence officer had got through with six men while a little to the right, the adjutant rushed in with twenty men. Between them were Germans. It was a dangerous situation anyhow. It became enormously dangerous when, owing to German counter-attacks, troops were forced to fall back on the extreme right of the attack, leaving the adjutant and his men naked and exposed on this side. He is just a boy, this adjutant, although he would not like one to say so. But he thought quickly and remembered tactical lectures from his Divisional General on the subject of defensive flanks: "A defensive flank sounds alright," said the adjutant, and he proceeded to make one with 300 men – "a party of sorts" – along the West Miraumont Road. It seemed just the place, with a high bank, good as a parapet.*

13 *The evacuation of the wounded on light railway trollies. George was taken from the battlefield by stretcher and then trollied back to the advance dressing station*

The defensive flank, with their rifles over the bank, felt safe and easy until after a while, they found bullets coming from behind. Several men were hit in the back of the head and fell. The others began to feel white around the eyes. "Pineapple bombs" were exploding behind them. "This defensive flank seems to have been played out," said the adjutant, and he decided to withdraw his men and form them up at right angles to the West Miraumont road, on a line parallel to the Boom Ravine. It would have been easy to swing them into their new position by the ordinary movement but for the machine-gun fire and he had to withdraw them down from shell crater to shell crater and then let them crawl out in the same way by the left. Later in the day, a retirement was made to the Boom Ravine, but after reorganisation, the line was advanced again to the reverse side of the last slope, with snipers shooting down into South Miraumont Trench, and supported now by strong bodies of men on the right and left, so that they were in a good defensive position. The intelligence officer, who had done so gallantly as a leader of men, was one of those who did not come back, though all day long, stretcher-bearers went searching for the wounded. This is the story of the Battle for Boom Ravine."

The 11th Fusiliers were relieved in the line that evening by the brigade reserve battalion, the 12th Middlesex. It had suffered severe casualties with two officers killed and one died of wounds, 11 officers wounded, 36 other ranks killed and 6 died of wounds, 162 other ranks wounded, 69 other ranks missing, a total casualty list of 297 or more than a quarter of the battalion. Of the missing, some were taken prisoner to be repatriated after the war, but others were either blown up by shellfire or were buried, or died in the bottom of mud-filled shell craters. The huge total war numbers of British and Commonwealth missing are commemorated on the Theipval Memorial, designed by the architect, Lutyens, with over 72,000 names of British and Commonwealth soldiers. A further 54,900 of those missing between 4th August 1914 and 15th August 1917 are inscribed on the Menin Gate in Ypres, plus a further 34,888 inscribed on Sir Herbert Baker's memorial at Tyne Cot Cemetery, as there wasn't enough room on the Menin Gate for all their names.

George was stretchered back to the light railhead some 2700 yards behind the line by a German stretcher party consisting of prisoners who had been organised into stretcher parties by the Battalion medical officer, Major J.C. Sale They succeeded in dropping him at least once. He was then trollied back a further two miles or so to an advance dressing station before travelling to a field hospital, from where he went by hospital train to a Red Cross hospital in Rouen. Here, he had all his toes except the little toe amputated on his right foot and other wounds to his chest and left leg attended to and dressed. It was all just after his 23rd birthday on 13th February. He was able to write to Sis on Feb 19th.

Casualty, Convalescence and a new adventure

British Red Cross and Order of St John. No2 Red Cross Hospital, Public Schools Wards

A.P.O.2 B.W.F My dear Sis,

I am at the above hospital with wounds – not serious. I got "the little lot" in the show on 17ᵗʰ inst. I hope to be in England soon now. A Padre friend of mine met me on the way down & promised to drop you a P.C. I don't know if he did. Well, old girl, there isn't much to say. Hope that you are fit. Yours lovingly, George."

On 25ᵗʰ February, he was evacuated back to England on the hospital ship, St David, arriving two days later at Southampton, and then moving on to London. Other correspondence survives. A fellow wounded officer, Lieut Colthorp of 'B' Coy, wrote on 13th March when George was recovering and convalescing in hospital at The Princess Christian Hospital for Officers at no 6 Grosvenor Place. George was now close to Sis who was living at 59 Radcliffe Gardens, not far from the hospital.

Hatchford Park Cobham, Surrey 13/3/17.

"My dear Morton, I find by personal experience that I am rather more of a fool than I thought I was and I will now tell you why. You remember I came round to show you Fitterer's letter, and could not find it – well I had it all the time in my pocket case. However, I have recovered since and here it is as I thought you would like to read it yourself. Please let me have it back when you have finished with it. How are you getting on? I hope that the foot is not giving you any pain now – I have heard twice from Captain Neate since I came here. Can you imagine old Neate a Capt.? I hope they will keep him within 'B' Company. He says that 2 new officers are with 'B' Company so I expect that all Coys have got some too. This is a jolly nice place; Sir Henry and Lady Samuelson's. They are most awfully good to us, but things are rather boring especially as the weather is so rotten. "Uncle" Haslett is here – he came the day after I did – I was so glad to see him down here. His knee is not right yet and keeps going out so I expect he will be some time. It is his left knee, mine is my right leg – so we have wonderful duets on the pianola. There is a lovely billiard table here but as I am no earthly use at billiards, I don't derive much benefit. However, I am coming on and hope in the near future to be able to hit balls rather more frequently than I do at present. Well, there is really no news here except that the sun came out this morning. O! In case you have not heard from France the last few days, they have found Collis's grave and are putting up a decent cross. They are now in tents on the battlefield making railroads and having their tents blown down periodically.

I don't expect I shall get away from here till at least the end of next week. I will look you up whenever I possibly can. Cheers! And hurry up and get fit.

Yours ever, A.G. Calthrop

P.S. I hope you will get something from the CO's recommendation – I'm sure you jolly well deserve it!

C.S.M. Fitterer received praise from everyone for his bravery and leadership in taking command of the battalion. He later received the M.C., an unusual step and honour, as did George, and Capt. Collis-Sandes. A letter from the C.S.M. to Lieut Colthorp was passed on to George and follows.

"7479 P.J. Fitterer 28.2.17.

In reply to your very welcome letter of the 24th.

I am most happy to say that I am still very much alive and kicking and so old Fritz found on the morning of the 17th. You ask me if I can tell anything about Capt. Collis-Sandes. Well, he only got about 100 yards when he was shot through the neck and died; he was brought back and buried in the Gully the next day. You will be very surprised to hear that I had to take command of the Battalion in the field, 50 yards before Grandcourt Trench. I managed to steady them and take them through to their objective where I discovered that we had suffered a lot more casualties than we had at first expected to, and if you can get hold of the Chronicle of the 26th you will see an account of a Sgt. Major as Battalion Commander. Mr Neate is now CCB (Company Commander 'B') and I should very much like to save 7 Platoon for you, so please hurry up and come back to us. I am so very sorry you missed the show after seeing all the first stages of the Battle.

14 Will in waders in a forward trench

I myself have been shot through the thigh but have managed to hang on and help Mr. Neate as much as I can.

Poor old Sgt. Bailey was a nasty knock for me for he and I were very old friends and I miss him very much. Should you see any of the other Officers of the XI RF, will you please give them my very best regards for a speedy and complete recovery and please accept my very best regards yourself and as I have said, hurry up and come out to us again. I must now close, trusting to hear from you again very soon.

Yours very sincerely, P.J. Fitterer"

George was to receive another letter from a W.S. Minchin on 24.02.17:

"My dear Morton, I was jolly glad to see your last letter to Sal and to know that you were so cheery, in spite of the loss of 4 members. There were all sorts of rumours, more or less sanguine, with regard to your condition. We also heard that the carrying party dropped you at least once.

We are now recovering in the village at the back of the front and expect very soon to go back to the line. Reinforcements are expected, but our chief handicap now is the loss of so many Officers.

No one quite realises that dear old Collis has gone.

Your kit has been forwarded in the usual way to DWART Boulogne from which place I understand it is either sent to your hospital or, if you have proceeded home, to Cox & Co. If you are likely to remain a few days in this country, send a line to that address and ask for the kit to be sent to you.

Your remark in Sal's letter was no doubt "very kindly meant". Special care was made with all your belongings and I sincerely hope that you will have no cause for a "grouse".

The sum of 3 francs 85 cents was found with your kit. This has been sent to Cox & Co with a request for an acknowledgement and also that they advise you. QMS (Quartermaster Sergeant JMM) Trump has or had some money you entrusted to him. This may be company money but nothing has been handed to me.

I had a line from Hawkins. On 22ⁿᵈ he was in No2 BRC Hospital Rouen. Is this identical with your hospital? He said that you were somewhere in R but he did not think that you were in his hospital. Should much like to hear how you are getting on sometime. Always yours sincerely, W.S. Minchin"

Now that he was in hospital in England, George's main priority was to recover and learn to walk again once his wounds had healed. As a wounded military officer, he was subject to regular Medical Boards to determine whether he was fit for duty. During 1917, the Medical Boards were under considerable pressure to return as many wounded as possible to front line duty because of the huge British casualty list incurred around Ypres and in the battles of the Somme and the need for soldier replacements was acute. There are numerous copies of the various medical boards on his file and at one stage, he was recommended to go back to his battalion for active duty. He appealed against this decision on the grounds of his limited mobility being only able "to walk at his own pace

15 *Wills last leave June 1917*

for about one and a half miles with the aid of a stick." The decision was reversed. He was to be in and out of hospital for the next eighteen months or so and, at one stage, his foot went septic which set him back.

Will managed to spend a leave with George in late June/early July 1917 and there is a photograph of the two brothers sitting together in a garden, possibly at a family gathering with Aunt Edie and Uncle Tom. There is a poignant message on the back of the photograph – "Will's last leave".

Shortly afterwards, they heard the sickening news that Will had been killed on return to France. The circumstances are described in a letter of 22nd July from one of Will's fellow officers to his wife.

> *"My darling precious, I have the saddest news for you; poor Morton was badly hit at about 11 o'clock this morning and died of wounds about 4 o'clock this afternoon. He was on the way up to the O.P* (Observation post – JMM) *with Barker (an officer with 'A' battery who you may perhaps remember was on leave at the same time that I was, a tall man) and going up a communication trench a shell burst right on top of them killing one of their signallers outright and wounding Barker and another signaller as well as Morton. It is too terrible for anything; old Morton was one of my best friends and one of the few remaining of the old lot. The bravest man I have wit. Please, if you*

are in London, go and see both his brother and sister and if you like, show them this letter. There is very little information I can let them have. Major Havis was about 20 yards away when they were hit and did all he could for Morton. He gave him morphia to relieve the pain and he told me he never saw anyone so brave and when he sent them away on stretchers, Morton was fit enough to shake hands with him and say goodbye. It is very, very sad and I feel too depressed for words. Do all you can for Miss Morton and her poor brother; they are left all alone now. I need hardly add that he died as only a brave man could nowadays, by fighting for his country. All my love, darling girl. Your loving and very sad Harry."

In 2005, my sister Jen visited his grave at Lijssenthoek Military Cemetery (grave XIII B 29) in Belgium and made notes and took photographs.

George and Sis were now living in a flat at 59 Redcliffe Gardens and George, while retaining full pay, was seconded to the Ministry of Pensions where he worked. He later described this work period as "licking on stamps at the Ministry of Pensions" and was thoroughly bored. But at least Sis and he were together in their grief, having lost their father and mother and now Will as well.

In September 1917, he appears to have consulted a Harley Street specialist and there is a medical report that his little toe had been pulled inwards, and that while something might "be done" about that, it is not clear whether further surgery took place. The medical board of 15th August '17 reports that "the foot is still raw and tender and that he is unable to wear an ordinary boot." Regular medical examinations were carried out at Caxton Hall, South London. He was then transferred to a convalescent hospital at Rose Mount, Eastbourne and it was here the report from Caxton Hall stating that he was fit for duty was quashed.

As a boy, I can remember going into his dressing room at Rectory House in Ogbourne St George, Wiltshire (to where we had moved after the war), and he showed me his wounds. His shoes were specially made for him by Peels of London and shaped around his right foot to accommodate it. He had a pad of felt underneath which had a small hole cut in it to relieve the pressure from the remains of the ball under his big toe and a remaining spike of bone. The shoe was a normal shape despite the shortness of his foot with the toe padded out, and this

16 *Alice relaxing now aged 21*

extension gave him balance. So far as I remember, the little toe was gone and had been surgically removed. His chest wounds had small puckered scars and had obviously healed cleanly; that on his left side had just missed the thorax. He was lucky, as a few inches or so to right or left would have meant that one or other of the bullets would have struck his heart and killed him outright, so perhaps Genevieve's prayer saved him.

Medical Boards continued in 1918, and we know from letters that he was back in hospital in November 1918. In December 1918, there is acknowledgement that George is permanently unfit for duty, but by this stage, the war was over. He has meanwhile had his rank of Captain made substantive and he was granted a severe wound gratuity of £62 per annum. It was recommended also that George be gazetted out, and this was agreed together with the award of a lump sum wound pension of £250. He wrote to the Secretary of State on 14th July 1919 confirming this and asking for payment as he was due to go to India in August. This appointment was to Bird and Co, Calcutta, then the largest company in India employing over 100,000 people. He attended the Victory parade in London on July 5th, and he was discharged from service.

The job had originally been offered to his cousin Harold Morton who turned it down, the job opportunity coming through connections of Uncle Tom. There were further delays in settling payment of his wound gratuity and pension, the subject of bitter letters to the War Office, but eventually, the matter was settled and he was on his way out to India in November 1919. He left the pension moneys for Sis.

At long last, he was on his way to a new life and the voyage gave him time to reflect, in two letters written to Sis, the first on 6th November and the second on the first anniversary of the Armistice.

"SS Loyalty, 6th November 1919.

My dear Sis,

I will start off with myself as usual. I was down with mal-de-mer on Saturday night, quite fit on Sunday & Monday & then down again on Tuesday and yesterday. Today we are passing through the Straits of Gibraltar, and should reach that spot in about ¾ of an hour. I am sitting on deck looking southwards towards Africa. The sun is shining, the air is warm and the sea is calm and a distant coast is shrouded in mist. Altogether the morning is lovely. Up to today, the weather has been bad & the decks wet and slippery. My cabin mates aren't bad fellows. Last night, as we were feeling a little off colour, we cracked a bottle of Pol Roger so you will see that life is not too bad at present.

The ship is not all it might be being dirty and badly managed below decks. The passengers are not all they might be, & in many cases, I have no doubt that they are also dirty below decks. The first few days after I left good old London, I was very miserable; by the way, the ship didn't sail until about 5.00 p.m. on Saturday. I hated leaving you, & wished you could have been with me. I do hope that you will be happy. As you know, it is my greatest wish to see you happy, and there is nothing that I wouldn't do to make you so. Often, I have thought that you must have thought that I had a queer way of showing my affection but I always was a funny-tempered devil and my old hoof doesn't help at times.

I have been very happy in our little flat, and am very glad you will always have it as a home until you come out to me or until I come home – whichever happens first. When I feel my feet out in Calcutta, I will let you know, & you can come along if you wish it but I don't want you to come out until I can give you the kind of time I want you to have. But who knows, in a few years I may be home again for good. It's a bad plan to try and arrange things too far ahead. In the meantime, have as good a time as you can & don't worry, everything will pan out all right.

How did you enjoy the weekend with Broome's friends? I hope you thoroughly enjoyed yourself. I expect that by the time you get this, you will be having a much-needed rest away from London. Don't overdo the work, old girl. There comes a time when a rest is essential, and if taken, you will start work again feeling all the better for it.

Re finances . . . I forget if I paid Mrs Jones for the week I left, and also if I settled with you for the lamp and Betty's wedding present. In any case, let me know when you send your statement. I think that I settled for the lamp etc., but I am not sure of the debt to Mrs Jones. Don't forget to let me know. Well then, old Sis, I will chuck it & will write again in a few days. Love to all my friends. Yours lovingly, George."

The parting must have been tough. They had been through so much together . . . the death of their mother, the suicide of their father, the death of Will, and George's trauma of wounds and the gradual recovery back to health. Alice had friends and family for support, but George had left all that behind, off to a new and unfamiliar country and a new career. But within a year, George had established himself in a new and promising career, and Alice had found Dick Tonge and was engaged to be married, with two children, Bill and Janet, to follow before George came home on leave in 1922.

The tide of misfortune was about to turn.

George wrote again when they were about to get to Port Said on 11th Nov.

"My dear Sis,

Here we are again on the anniversary of Armistice. I shall not forget my last year's experiences on this day – in that beastly hospital. I remember so well lying in bed reading the paper when the signal guns were fired. The sisters and nurses came dancing up the ward full of excitement. At my corner where the men near me were serenely reading the papers, the sisters stopped & tried to infuse a little of their excitement into us, but all they got were denials that it could possibly be armistice and that in all possibility it was another daylight raid. I hate to think what looks & words of reproach we got, but I have to say that I felt anything but happy, though I suppose that inside there must have been a deep feeling of thankfulness that probably the future would contain no more of those long casualty lists. I think that with armistice came the first realisation of all that had passed, and from living only in the present & immediate past, I permitted myself the first real glimpse of the future – and I didn't like it- it meant starting again in every way, including re-making old friends and making new ones and today I am feeling more content than I was a year ago, and less hungry!

Since my last letter, we have had perfect weather, lovely sunny days and cold nights. I am writing this at 8 a.m. (we rise early – 6.30 a.m.) on deck looking out over a perfect sea of wonderful blue with the sun shining, but not too hot as it is early yet. One of these days, we will have a trip around the Mediterranean, if possible, about this time of the year.

We passed Gibraltar but not very near, & I cannot say that I felt anything but vague disappointment at my first view of the key to the Mediterranean; the atmosphere was not very clear, and the rock was shrouded in mist. We sailed along the coast of Africa and passed Algiers which looks a delightful spot. We also passed Tunis, but I didn't see it. We kept quite close to the coast of Africa for several days and could make out little villages all the way. Our next place of interest was Malta and we passed very close. Valetta, the capital, looked very interesting but we didn't call there, unfortunately. Since leaving Malta (on Sunday), we haven't seen land. We hope to reach Port Said tomorrow morning, when we hope to land for a few hours.

Today, by order of the King, all work is to cease for two minutes; the engines are to stop, and complete silence, & as far as possible, stillness are to be maintained, a very simple but fitting ceremonial. This afternoon we are having a sports meeting & tonight there is to be a dance.

I have seen Lady & Miss Procter quite often; they both seem to be most charming, especially Lady Procter. There are several nice people on board, and of course, there are others!

I wonder how you and all are in old London. I hope you are very fit. Have the Land Tax people stumped up? Let me know. Don't forget my photographs of Will & you & the various little things you were going to send out to me.

How you will love this trip when you make it! Remember me to all my friends, Much love, Yours lovingly, George."

Both George and Sis as brother and sister had been through a great deal over the past years since the outbreak of war. Sis had been the link between normality and the horrors of a terrible war in which George and Will had lost friends and fellow officers and men. He had seen and experienced things that no young person on the threshold of adulthood should have seen or experienced. But he was a survivor and of great courage. When the average life of a subaltern in the trenches was to be measured in weeks, he had survived for 19 months, but more importantly, it had only scarred him physically but strengthened his inner fibre. Although seriously wounded, he was determined to lead as normal a life as possible. The letters home from India speak of golf and tennis, of a very active life, and of making new friends. Effectively, he knew very few to start with and was going out to a completely new and unknown environment, one that was climatically harsh and difficult.

But it was to be a new start to a new life, and a new beginning, and he was to make a great success of it, and rise to the heights of business life, ending up with a knighthood in recognition of his considerable achievements, leading to the appointment to a leadership role in the Economic Mission to Greece after the end of the Second World War.

17 *The full Bn 11th Royal Fusilers in open order at Codford camp prior to embarkation to France July 1915*

*18 Officers of 11th RF prior to embarkation for France July 1915
(George seated fourth from left)*

19 George's no 1 platoon 'A' company prior to embarkation for France July 1915

20 *Mini playing cards used in the trenches*

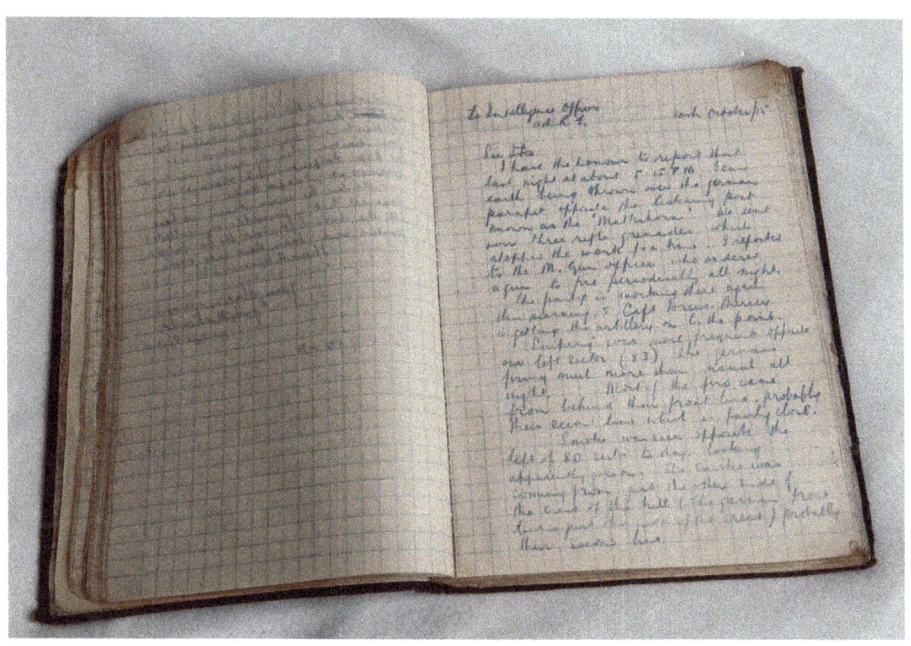

21 *George's trench book*

22 George's wallet, and Genevieve's letter and prayer

23 *Signed Christmas menu 1916*

24 *Christmas 1917 Roll call of medals won by 11th RF 1915-17*

25 The 'Codford Highlanders' on the march!

26 Will in uniform as Lieut on the Royal Artillery and his Royal Artillery cap badge

HE whom this scroll commemorates was numbered among those who, at the call of King and Country, left all that was dear to them, endured hardness, faced danger, and finally passed out of the sight of men by the path of duty and self-sacrifice, giving up their own lives that others might live in freedom. Let those who come after see to it that his name be not forgotten.

Lieut. William Cattell Morton
Royal Field Artillery.

27 *Commemorative scroll from HM George V honouring*
the sacrifice of Uncle Will's life

H M.H.S. ST. DAVID.

*28 HMHS St David on which George was taken across the
channel back to hospital in England*

*29 Scroll issued on the occasion of the victory march in the City of London
by the London regiments on July 5th 1919*

30 *Rowley, George's great friend referred frequently in letters and best man at his wedding*

31 George in full dress uniform prior to his discharge on medical grounds. Note his medals and the resting of his weight on his left leg rather than his wounded right foot

PART TWO

Magical India – A new start in a new life – (12.11.1919 – 26.09.1929)

Arrival in Bombay and travel to Calcutta – his letters

George's next letter is written from the Indian Ocean a few days short of their arrival in Bombay. The relationship with the Procter mother and daughter was obviously developing well.

"SS Loyalty 19/11/19

My dear Sis,

The last time I wrote you was from Port Said – a postcard. Port Said was our first stop and the first real glimpse of the East. It was all very wonderful. We first sighted a town or lighthouse – I wasn't sure which, but I was told that it was a lighthouse at Port Said. The sea was dead calm – not even a ripple. I have never seen anything like it away from the Serpentine. As we got nearer, we could make out the houses and the statue of Dr Lesseps, the engineer who designed the canal, & incidentally died a disappointed man. Outside of the harbour & entrance to the canal, one can see four or five wrecks (results of Fritzy and his U boats) with their masts above water. When we got in, the boat was moored, and about a dozen natives swam out & proceeded to dive for coins. Some of them made quite a lot of money – which was put into their mouths! We landed about 12.00, & were immediately surrounded by a chattering mob of vendors of everything imaginable from filthy postcards to foreign stamps. I got a few of the best for Doug & sent them to him. I got them 'cheap' after a lot of hard bargaining. The 'gent' finished by saying, "You are very hard and business is bad." I countered with "I am very poor & the business does not interest me." In the end, he came down to my price which was between a third and a half of what he had originally asked.

We had an excellent lunch at the Casino Hotel & went shopping in the afternoon buying delicious Turkish Delight & various other things. We got back to the ship in time for dinner, accompanied by a diminutive boy carrying a basket of purchases as big as himself almost!

We left Port Said about 10.00 at night and as we had had a dance the night before, I didn't wait up very long, although it was a wonderful moon & starlit night. In order to go through the canal, a powerful light (searchlight almost) was erected just under the bowsprit. In the morning when I woke up, I looked out of the port & saw a wall about

20 yards away! It was the bank of the canal. The land on either side is not very thrilling, but it has a distinct attraction, & it was most fascinating to see (through glasses) the people onshore working cultivating the soil. An aeroplane came very low over the ship & the men waved to us.

There are most attractive little stations on the banks with palm trees etc., but it must be devilish dull to live there. We reached Suez about midday and started down the Red Sea. This was the hottest part of the journey, but we managed it quite O.K.

We are now out in the Indian Ocean seeing flying fish, etc. Last night, we had a fancy-dress dance. I went as the Red Sea – the main object being coolness dressed in white with a large red C on my back. Some of the costumes were wonderfully good. I had about half the programme with Miss Procter who dances 'divinely'. The previous dance I had all but two, and tomorrow, when there is another dance, we are trying to have most of the programme together. I think that Lady & Miss Procter are most charming people and very cheery. Lady Procter has been simply delightful, and I have an invitation to dinner the night we arrive in Bombay.

Today we have had a sports meeting, a most excellent show. I have taken quite a lot of photos, which I will send to you if any are successful.

Well & how goes it with you? How did Mme. Roy's wedding go off? Tell her that I will write to her one of these days and give her a little talk as one married woman to another; for the sake of her blushes, I will refrain so that when she sees my writing, she need have no qualms about what she is going to read!

20/11/19 As the light was failing last night I had to close, & am off once more just after breakfast, which, as you know, is the time when all the world seems bright & even the cat is a friend of mine!! Breakfast on this ship is not exactly a happy meal, or rather the choice of dishes cannot be described as happy. For example, this morning the menu read as follows (the bracketed remarks are mine)

Porridge (musty, with rather offensive tinned milk)
Kippered herring (tinned)
Steak and onions (shades of Mrs Lockhart)
Liver and bacon (to have eaten the former would have been adding fuel to an already roaring furnace)
Preserves

I had herring, black coffee, & got out with the greatest possible speed!

We hope to land in Bombay on Sunday but I don't expect we shall get our luggage from the hold until Monday. In any case, Sunday is a dull day to land and try and get things done as all the places are shut.

I wonder how you are going on? I suppose you have had a good rest, & have started in on a job of work again. It does seem strange not to hear how everything is going, but soon one will have got over the three weeks delay & before long it will seem quite normal not to hear about things until they are about a month old.

Will write you when I get to Calcutta. Look after yourself, & have a good time. Love to all. I hope Mrs Jones is fit. Yours lovingly, George. "

The SS Loyalty was formerly the SS Empress of India and had been bought by a consortium of Indian millionaires who formed the Scindia Steam Navigation Company. She was a comfortable and quite fast ship making the voyage out in 22 days.

His next letter from Calcutta, at the end of the week after landing in Bombay, comes from temporary accommodation in the Great Eastern Hotel. In the early 1960s, the hotel was owned by Bilimoria, a colourful character known affectionately as "Billy". He was the auctioneer for the scrap tube coming from Tata's Indian Tube Company, my employers. Billy was kind enough to buy my golf clubs from me when I left India.

The letter is full of excitement at meeting new friends, some of them with connections from the war. This was to be a common occurrence since he was of a generation who had had wartime experience and many former servicemen had gone out to the colonies to escape the post-war depression. The comment about the delay of three to four weeks in receipt of letters relates to sea mail, but airmail was to begin with Imperial Airlines starting an airmail service by the end of the 1920s using Handley Page converted bombers and Sunderland flying boats. This shortened the time for post to arrive to about five to six days. Cables were used for particularly urgent messages but were expensive.

"Great Eastern Hotel, 27th November 1919.

My dear Sis,

Here we are at last after quite a good journey. Since I wrote to you, we had the dance on board, & a very excellent show it was. I had most of the programme with Miss Procter. She is a topping dancer, & an awful good sort. I simply can't understand the May Edwards episode & can only conclude there is more in it than we know. Anyhow, we arrived in Bombay on Sunday at about 11.00 a.m. which is very good time – 22 days – I received a wireless message from Mike that he would meet me, & when we got close enough, I saw a familiar figure limping along the quay with another man – who curiously enough turned out to be Sir Henry Procter, to whom Mike had a letter of introduction. It was curious because Lady Procter had told me to come up to tea on Sunday & bring the man who was meeting me if he had nothing better to do. Anyway, old Mike met me & was splendid. Most people slept on floors etc. but I had a bed in Mike's room at the Hotel Majestic. I didn't worry about luggage but just cleared out of the howling mob and went off to Mike's hotel, where we had cooling drinks. Later in the day we went back & got my luggage all serene. We went out to tea at the Procters as arranged. A third man had lunch with us on the Sunday & he was an ex-Lieut. Colonel D.S.O. – quite young and an excellent fellow. In the course of conversation, I told him I had been in the 18th Div. He then said, "You must know Chute". Then we got busy for Chute was a great pal of mine in Brigade Headquarters, a great rugger man, & one of the original Colchester officers. The Lieut. Colonel, Chute and Mike came out on the same boat, & a fourth man called Churchill – who was once loaned to my company for a month! He had served in the Middlesex under Phuston, & having been in my Coy for a month, he naturally knew me!! The result was that Mike, Lockwood (the Lieut. Col.), Chute and I dined together & the same four, with the addition of Churchill, lunched together on Monday. It was quite a gathering of the clans! I only missed Cumberledge by a few days, but hope to see him here before long. On the Monday, I shopped and called on the Bombay office to arrange about my ticket to Calcutta etc. We had lunch as I have told you, & at four, I went up to the Procters to be shown around Bombay. We motored round (Lady Procter, Miss & self) to Government House, then to the Yacht Club where we picked up another man & then went shopping & finally collected Sir Henry at his office. We then went to the Willingdon Club for tea. The club is most delightfully situated, & they play golf, tennis, polo, & everything else. Whilst we were having tea, we discovered (much to our joy) that there was dancing every evening. We had a couple or three dances & then went back with seven or eight people who made up the party on board. On the Tuesday at one-thirty, I bade a sorrowful farewell to Bombay! For in spite of most kind invitations which would have meant another night in Bombay, I couldn't let myself forget that I had come to India in the first place to work! Before leaving the Procters, I should like you to be under no illusion concerning them. Lady Procter is one of the kindest, most charming & best women it has been my pleasure to meet. What little I saw of Sir Henry left the impression that he was an absolute white man, & what more can one say. Miss Procter (in spite of adverse circumstances) is a thorough sportsman and is lucky enough to possess a very keenly developed sense of the ridiculous. The adverse circumstances I mentioned are many. No doubt Mme. has had a tremendous lot of court paid her by my romantic (!) sex, for she is most attractive and just the girl that many men would do anything for. She is the daughter of a very wealthy man, & naturally does not want for much. The remainder of the adverse circumstances I leave to your imagination. Whether or not she found me amusing I can't say, but if she did it was because of the total absence of romance in my case – except to rag her and all I can say is that I found her a most charming companion as full of mischief as a load of monkeys!!

The journey across India was novel and quite comfortable. We had four in the compartment, which was at least twice as large as the ordinary compartment at home. There is no corridor so a little room is gained thereby. We had some meals at stations where we stopped for some time, & some (most) on the train. We got out of our compartment & into the dining car at one station and back again at the next. The journey took two days and two nights, & I got quite a few snaps on the way.

The country is full of interest for the newcomer, & everything is most attractive. Some of the colouring is lovely. The average group of native women, even the low caste, is a lesson in colour. I saw three women in Bombay carrying baskets on their heads wearing drapery of different shades of mauve and violet & I must say one would have had to go a long way to find such blending of shades. Everywhere one goes & everything one's eyes light upon is strange and interesting.

I arrived here today and went and saw Slater. He arranged for me to stay here for a few days, & then I go into a 'chummery' I hope. I start work tomorrow morning, for which Allah be praised! as I am fed up with doing no work, though travelling has undeniable attractions.

By the time you get this, it will probably be Christmas. If it is, I wish you the very best of times, a very happy Christmas & an extraordinarily prosperous new year, & I wish we were together to enjoy it. This seems to have lengthened out somewhat, so will close. Best love to all my friends & all for yourself. I will send along a small Xmas gift later, yours lovingly, George."

As the next letter reveals, he was to move into No 14 Harrington Mansions, a company property that was to be his home for almost the next ten years. The property is described in some detail in his next letter. The chummery system worked well. Small groups of bachelors clubbed together in shared accommodation with both individual and common servants serving the household.

For the first four months of my stay in India (winter 1961/2), I was in the Dover Street Chummery, a large house shared by four of us: Barnes (who had witnessed as a small child the murder of his father in the Punjab), Simon Maxwell Scott with whom I had been at prep school, and who worked at Birds, and one other whose name I no longer remember.

Now perhaps is the moment to introduce the reader to Bird and Company, Calcutta, and the managing agency system, which was almost unique to India, and which was the basis of George's career as an accountant there. The day after his letter to Sis was written, i.e., 28th November, he could perhaps have walked the short distance in the morning from The Great Eastern Hotel to join Birds at the Chartered Bank Building close to the corner of what was then Clive Street and Dalhousie Square.

The founders of Bird and Company were two brothers, Samuel and Paul Bird. Originally from a Suffolk family, they were seafarers and ship's captains. Tradition has it that they salvaged a schooner loaded with sandalwood and sold the cargo and their ship for a good profit in Madras.

The company history records that Sam was working in Calcutta for The Indian Steam Navigation Company in 1858. They were shipping materials upriver to Allahabad for the building of a bridge by the East Indian Railway Company to replace the pontoon bridge across the Ganges below the confluence of the Jumna and Ganges. The bridge was to carry the extension of the railway from Calcutta to Delhi. Sam spotted the opportunity to arrange a labour *(coolie)* contract to carry wheat across the river while the bridge was being built, and he then arranged a similar contract with the railway company to load and unload their wagons at the Jumna.

Bird and Company was now born, and labour contracts were to form the bedrock of the company's operations for the rest of the century and beyond. Further labour contracts were negotiated with East Indian Railways in 1864 and with The Eastern Bengal Railway in 1872. A bullock cart train service from Sahibgunge was initiated to carry cargo the 188 miles up 7500 ft to the Darjeeling hill station, and this continued for some time even after the narrow-gauge mountain railway system was developed from Siliguri to Darjeeling. A branch line was later extended up the river Teesta to the road bridge to provide rail and road links to Kalimpong and Gangtok, the capital of the Kingdom of Sikkim.

In 1870, Sam Bird moved to Calcutta, and the firm was expanding. A nephew-in-law, Henry Kinnaird York designed and developed a successful cotton baling press which was widely taken up, with Birds taking a royalty on every machine sold. The great famines of the late 1860s led to the importation of rice in 1873, mainly from Burma, and Birds obtained the labour contract taking over The Calcutta Loading and Shipping Company in the process.

But now there was a setback. Birds lost the renewal of the East Indian Railways contract. Sam had, however, made sufficient money to survive and there ensued a changeover of personnel. Enter the young Ernest Cable in 1881, aged just 21. He was increasingly to become the driving force behind the expansion of the company over the next four decades.

Birds now embarked on a number of managing agency contracts in jute and coal. These were contracts between an operating company and a managing agent, who would provide a number of services for the company in exchange for fees, and, in the process, take a percentage of profits. The services ranged from the selection and appointment of executives, accountancy services, specialist services such as selection of machinery, and marketing and sales through specialist departments. Sometimes Birds would be the originating company of the operation itself, raising capital through the flotation of public companies, with the directors taking a shareholding themselves and Birds subscribing a minority, generally around 20% of the equity. In this way, all parties had an interest in the success and profitability of the business.

The Oriental Jute Manufacturing Company had been founded in 1874 with an American, Macallister, as managing agent, but the company faltered and, by 1880, was heavily in debt to the Agra Bank. Initially, Birds took on the managing agency, but then a year later, formed the Union Jute Company, which then acquired the shares of Oriental Jute.

The jute industry was in the process of evolving from a cottage industry to full mechanisation with looms being set up all along the river Hooghly. Jute is a natural fibre that grows rapidly with stalks up to three metres high. It is harvested and then soaked in water, enabling the fibres to be separated out and then dried. Known as the 'golden crop', the fibres vary in density, the finest making a fine cloth or used in papermaking. Chinese paper made over 1700 years ago from jute fibres still exists. Uses of jute are varied, ranging from hessian backing for carpets to sandbags. One of George's letters just before the Second World War tells of an order for five million sandbags. Most of the jute was grown in East Bengal, now modern Bangladesh. The main processing location in the UK, from bales of raw jute shipped from India, was Dundee on Scotland's East coast. W.B. Colville, a technical expert, was appointed manager of the jute department, which, over the next seventy years or so, was to provide a very significant element of Bird's operations and profit.

The next venture was into coal. In 1862, massive coal fields had been found around Assensole, which had been progressively opened up. Birds secured the managing agency of the Burrakur Coal Company, which had been languishing under the same managing agent, Macallister, as had Oriental Jute. Within two years, Birds had increased raisings from the Kumardhubi mine from 20,000 to 80,000 tons a year, and restored the company to profit. The next step was to change the operation of the mine from a shallow underground mine to open cast by stripping away the overburden. But the deposit had a limited future life, and so, in 1880, Birds secured the purchase of the Lot Olipur property. The name was changed to the Alipore Coal Company, and other concessions and purchases were to follow. With industrialisation and the rapid development of the railways and shipping, the future of coal was bright.

Meanwhile, Sam Bird retired and his brother Paul died of pneumonia; and so, a new partnership was formed from the rising younger generation in which Ernest Cable was the lead player. Birds survived the early 1890 recession and emerged stronger afterwards through securing fresh labour contracts in the Calcutta ports. A Birds company called Bull's Patent Brick Kiln Ltd had been formed around Bull's brick kiln inventions in 1883, and in the same year, Birds were also appointed managing agents of the Bengal Barragunda Copper Company. Early assays of ore sent to England showed an astonishing 27-28% copper. Another Birds venture was an investment into tea in the Terai, which never produced a profit, and the agency was released back to Williamson Magor and Company eleven years later. Birds were to avoid any future involvement in the growing of tea.

A number of changes of office had taken place, which was to conclude with the move to the Chartered Bank offices in Clive Street in 1908.

In 1897, Cable was elected President of the Indian Mining Association and then in 1903, President of the Bengal Chamber of Commerce, and in the following year was knighted. Cable had married in 1888, his bride being the sister of Herbert Sparkes, the junior partner of the solicitor Sylvester Dignam, with whom the firm had had a long association. He was to have three children, a son tragically killed in the First World War, and two daughters. One of these, Ruth, was to marry Tom Benthall. She was to become my godmother, and he the senior partner of Birds. In the 1930s, he became President of the Bengal Chamber and was later knighted.

The greatest growth of the business before the First World War was to come from these three departments; labour, jute and coal. By 1897, Birds coal sales were 400,000 tons a year and, within the next twelve years, more than doubled again. Sales considerably exceeded output, the difference being maintained by buying in coal. Under Colville's leadership, Birds jute looms rose from 200 to 2000. The labour business expanded through contracts with the two Calcutta railway companies, and now many of the leading shipping companies.

In August 1907, the Tata Iron and Steel Company was formed, with an integrated steelworks built at Jamshedpur by Dorabji Tata, fulfilling the vision of his father,

Jamshedji Tata. The works was named after him. Products needed for iron and steelmaking include fireclay and silicon bricks for lining furnaces, including blast furnaces, and ladles, as well as coke ovens; previously, Tata had imported coke from England. In 1914, a plan was devised to manufacture refractory bricks in India.

After initial development work, Birds formed the Kumardhubi Fireclay and Silica Works Ltd which went into full production after initial trials. The manufacture of coke was also started by Birds with the registration of the Loyabad Coke Manufacturing Company in the same year, supplying coke to the blast furnaces at Jamshedpur.

Birds quickly recognised the potential business opportunities in other minerals needed for iron and steelmaking as well. The Bisra Stone Lime Company held extensive leases in Chota Nagpur for deposits of dolomite and limestone. In 1914, F.W. Heilgers resigned the managing agency and Birds took it on. A mining engineer was taken on to prospect for new sources and found vast deposits of both minerals at Raipura; the necessary leases were signed in 1917 while a battery of kilns was built and railway lines constructed, with the Bengal – Nagpur railway building the bridges.

The development of all these projects spurred on Birds interest in finding iron ore. A certain Mr A Dundas Whiffin had obtained a licence to prospect over large areas in the Keonjhar State and Singhbhum in Orissa and found 'mountains' of high-quality haematite. He and Duff, together with Joseph Zobel, the owner of Bisra, took their find to Birds. The Orissa Minerals Development company was formed and took over all licences and leases owned by the syndicate. The area was thoroughly surveyed and mining development started.

Towards the end of the war, other ventures were started. Interests in timber, graphite and leather were taken with mixed results. One of these was to survive – Assam Saw Mills and Timber, making three-ply boxes, with the tea industry a major customer.

The developments of the previous years had created the need for Birds to have their own research department with a staff of geologists, chemists and mining engineers; the department was formed in 1918. But it was the next master stroke, the acquisition of Heilgers, completed by Cable, that was to establish Birds as the largest company in India, employing over 100,000 people.

F.W. Heilgers & Company were established in Calcutta in 1872. For a long time, all the partners and staff were German, but gradually, more and more English employees joined. Heilgers held an important complementary trading position in both coal and jute, through a number of agencies and investments, as well as ventures which provided diversification to the new joint enterprise. The deal was completed in a remarkably short time on 1st January 1918, just two years before George joined. There were now seven coal companies, and interestingly, a paper company, Titaghur Paper Mills Company Ltd. Some agencies did not survive the war. Both companies occupied adjoining floors in the Chartered Bank buildings and knew each other well. The Heilgers name was retained and continued, but naturally, some operations were combined and reshaped as the merger process progressed in the inter-war period.

A company was started in East Africa; a fledgling Insurance business also began to flourish, as well as a timber company in Rangoon supplying wood and bamboo for pulping and paper production.

We would today call Birds a conglomerate. As the above account shows, it comprised a complex structure of interlinking shareholdings supporting managing and other agency contracts.

Each legal entity had its own management board responsible to shareholders, often within the structure of a publicly owned company. Some shares were also held by specific charitable trusts established by the Cable family and later the Benthall family. Other shares were sometimes allocated to Birds staff, often providing the opportunity for profit-taking once trading opened on the stock market.

It is also clear that a high degree of financial and accountancy skill was required to provide effective management information of the very diverse company that Birds had become; it was this skill that George was increasingly to be called upon to provide. Above all, it required a high degree of technical accountancy ability and tact in dealing with often sensitive inter-partner and family issues. He was also to be involved in the restructuring and business planning of individual businesses after the First World War, evident from his letters home.

His first tour – Letters to Sis – 1919/20/21.

The correspondence between George and Sis throughout 1920 reflects their very close relationship, but this relationship alters when Sis gets married at the end of the year. However, first, George is adapting to his new job, the environment within the cold weather and the Calcutta Christmas social season, as his initial letters describe.

"14 Harrington Mansions, Calcutta 4-12-19.

My dear Sis,

Since writing my last long epistle, I have been working and settling down here.

I stayed at an hotel until Monday this week when I came to this place. This is a most delightful flat consisting of a dining room, drawing room, a billiard room, and three bedrooms. At present, there are four men sharing (including myself) but one is going in the next few days. The firm arranged it & when we are settled, I expect there will be three of us – all from Birds. The flat is in a delightful neighbourhood, but it will be quite reasonable to run as a chummery. The three living rooms are all very big – any of them would hold a billiard table (full size of course) and the bedrooms are also very big & each one has its own bathroom. There is one extra bathroom off the billiard room so altogether there are four bathrooms. I think that it is going to be very comfortable. The furniture is very nice & there are plenty of settees & comfortable armchairs. We have a pianola – a very good one. All the floors are of a red polished composition with a surface like marble. The bathrooms are all tiled (real tiles) with squares of marble (about a foot square) for floors. If one could bring a block of these flats to London, only multi-millionaires could afford to live in them!!!

I went out and played golf this morning; it was delightful, about the same temperature as home. In fact, it reminded me very much of the days when I used to get up & golf before breakfast. When I say the same temperature as home, I mean summer or autumn temperatures with just a nip in the air.

I have an invitation to dinner with the Governor's secretary on Dec 9th and to go to a dance at Government House. I went to the races last Saturday with Bond; I forget if I told you, but my first night in Calcutta, I met a man who was in Deloitte's before the war, & who was also in Harold's regiment. He is now in the same company as Freddy Limpenny and his name is Bond. It was the merest chance he happened to be living at the same hotel, but what a bit of luck for me! He arranged for the members' stand at the races & we went to a cinema in the evening.

I have some photos which I will send to you next mail. In the meantime, have a merry Christmas & a happy new year & best of luck. In haste to catch mail. Much love, Yours lovingly, George."

The mail always went on a Thursday . . . sea mail to start with, then a choice of airmail when the service started up in the later 1920s. So, Thursdays were always rushed days in office life to make sure that the mail got away. Fridays were what we would now call a "dress down" day, and sometimes Saturday mornings would involve an hour or two in the office to prepare for the following week. This traditional pattern of working life was still being followed 40 years later in the early 60s, even after the advent of daily airmail which landed home within 24 hours. George's letters are full of references, generally at the end of letters, of the need to finish the letter to make sure that it caught the post, as these letters were invariably written and then posted on a Thursday.

George was by now settling into a life with servants. The Calcutta Christmas season was in full swing as his next two letters describe:

"18th Dec 1919

My dear Sis,

I got your first letter all serene, and am glad you are having a good time. The news of Jimmy's death came as a great shock to me. I had hoped for the sake of the kiddies that he would have recovered his normal state of health. It is rotten luck to have come through the war safely to be knocked out when one thought that the risks were once again normal. It is lucky that Arthur is at hand, as he will look after things better than anyone could in view of his associations with Begg Johnston's. I expect that Aunt Martha & Uncle Duncan will be very much shaken up, & I wish one could do something, but of course, it is impossible – in fact, I rather think it would be better if I didn't write them a letter, but left it until later, when I can refer to it in an ordinary letter. I wrote Beatrice a few lines; she is having a poor time with first her mother's trouble & then Jimmy. Thank goodness she has lots of character.

Since my last letter, I have been having a good time. Plenty of work and play. I like my job here & later, when I am more settled down, I expect that there will be lots of chances of doing things. At first, one has to go steady & stick to things. If one does that, I am certain that good things will follow. Everyone here is very kind, and they all do anything to help a newcomer. Of course, Calcutta isn't real India; it might be London except for the weather, though just now, the evenings are quite chilly & the other evening I was dining with a man at the Bengal Club where a good log fire was blazing away. Later I hope to go upcountry, but I am not anxious to do too much until I speak more of the language.

Of course, this place is full of strange sights & smells & wonderful colours and everything new, but in Calcutta itself, things have been adapted to European ideas. The golf course is a good deal better than Ealing, for instance, and the race course is quite the prettiest I have seen, & I am told it is second to only one in the whole world, and that is in Australia.

One is waited on hand and foot – literally, not metaphorically. I never put on my own shoes or slippers, & am practically dressed by my bearer who is my personal servant (and who systematically robs me!) He buys me things on which he takes his commission, but even with his commission, his price is less than I could get the articles for! We have an excellent cook at the flat, with an assistant who washes dishes (a 'misalchi' – author), also we have a kitmaghar who is a sort of butler who waits at table (actually the word means a table servant) & who dispenses drinks. We have a sweeper who, like his name, sweeps floors & dusts things. In addition, there are three personal servants who wait at table also. All these servants for three Europeans!! Their total wages – including the personal servants – amounts to Rs 140 per month (which is about £14 at the present rate of exchange). Out of this, they have to feed themselves & find lodging (most of them occupy a large room we have in the servants' quarters). So, you will see that it isn't very expensive to keep servants.

On 9ᵗʰ Dec, I dined with people called Gourlay. He is the Governor's secretary, & quite a big man in Calcutta. We went on to a dance at Government House, & I had about half the programme with a Miss Pavitt, a great good sort who was a V.A.D. in France during the war and who is a very good dancer. These people were on the boat, and are very kind. Of course, it was through Miss Pavitt (who is staying at Government House with the Gourlays) that I got my invitation to the dance. I have an invitation for another dance at Govt. House on 26ᵗʰ inst. at which the Viceroy is to be present. It should be quite amusing. Monday and Tuesday were holidays this week – peace celebrations. Cumberledge turned up in Calcutta last week and I have seen quite a lot of him. On Saturday, we went to the races, I dined with him in the evening & we went to see Marie Tempest in 'Penelope'. On Sunday, Cumberledge lunched with us & went on to the Peace Exhibition. On Monday, I went to a tennis party at Slater's (the chief accountant) house, & in the evening dined at the Bengal Club with one of the men to whom Willie gave me an invitation. He is an excellent fellow named Gatherall, a very clever man & a very good sort and the best golfer in India. On Tuesday we all went to the races & had another topping day; Cumberledge dined with us that night.

Last night I went to bed at about 9.45, & tonight, being Cumberledge's last night in Calcutta, we are going out to the theatre.

I cannot find anything that I like for your Christmas present, and if nothing is found by next mail, I will send you a small cheque to get what you most need. I have an idea that you may be needing furs fairly soon, so if you let me know what kind, shape, etc., I will try and get some for your birthday. I know that one can get almost every kind of fox here, & of course things like leopards, etc. can also be got though I don't suppose that you wish to be quite so conspicuous with leopard's skin!! Anyhow, let me know your ideas & don't be disappointed if that kind of skin doesn't grow here!

Love to all my friends; look after yourself. Yours lovingly, George."

George's next letter was written on New Year's Day 1920.

"My dear Sis, I got your letter (second) written at Hall Place, and I am glad you received the first consignment of my mail. Needless to say, I am in a much happier frame of mind than when they were written – at any rate the first! I could see by your letter that your visit to Hall Place was not giving you the maximum amount of peace & contentment as one might imagine it should – but never mind, they mean awfully well and it is good for all of us to get disciplined occasionally, though it may be deemed unpleasant at the time!

I am enclosing a draft for a fiver for a Christmas present. I tried hard to find you something, but anything that I wanted was a fabulous price, as Calcutta is the place at the moment, it being the height of the season with the Viceroy in residence. Later on, I may be able to get things more or less reasonably cheap – especially if I go upcountry, & then I will send you some things.

Well, I have had a very pleasant Christmas and I hope you have had ditto. Had a very good dance at Govt. Hse. on Boxing Night, & on Saturday, Ferrier (one of the men in the flat – Teasdale is the other) & I joined a river party of about 20 people. Our host is the Medical Officer for Health for the Port. We had two topping launches & went down the river. We then turned and landed at the botanical gardens – a wonderful place, & had a picnic. After an excellent lunch, some wandered round the gardens & some went on the river. I did the latter & thoroughly enjoyed every minute of the day. Yesterday, being the last day of the old year Teasdale motored Ferrier & I & one Campbell out to the botanical gardens where we quietly loafed round had a very pleasant lunch, did more loafing round & came quietly home. We spent a very peaceful day, just the four of us. After dinner, we went to a picture house & saw some very good pictures. We then went to Campbell's flat & exchanged reminiscences (!) & had a whisky & soda & then about 1.30 rolled quietly home. Today I am going to the races, & dance at the Viceroy's tonight. I think that I shall do less dancing – I have had about four since I came to Calcutta, but am getting a little tired of it. It isn't quite the same as it is in England. Music not so good & partners not so good either, though most of them are very charming!

Well, once more we have broken a new year. May this be a good one for you, old bean. I have a sort of feeling that one has shaken off the old life & war & everything, & this 1920 will bring the beginning of new things & happy times. The past has been a very happy one, but I think you will have a better time yet. Anyway, keep your heart up & don't worry – think of the jolly time you will have when you have the trip out here! I expect that you are having the time of your young life now – don't miss a moment of it.

If and when you send parcels to me, always register them, & if they are valuable, insure them also, as theft is quite common here. I haven't received any parcels from you yet, but they always take very much longer than letters so there is nothing to worry about yet.

Love to all. Very best wishes for 1920, Yours lovingly, George."

There is much mention of Government House. This was located on the north side of the Maidan, that great open space in the middle of the city surrounding Fort William. Government House was the former residence of the Viceroy and his staff before 1911. The decision announced at the Delhi Durbar to move the seat of government to Delhi changed that. Completed in 1803, it was designed after the seat of the Curzon family home, Kedleston Hall; Lord Curzon himself was to become Viceroy and resident there in the final year of the century, as was my grandfather, as surgeon to the Viceroy in 1911. It was now the residence of the Governor of Bengal and his staff.

The botanical gardens to the south of the city contained a magnificent collection of trees, shrubs and plants from all over the sub-continent. I remember a magnificent banyan tree with a forest of branch tendrils stretching down and rooted around the main trunk.

It had been a momentous year. George had been welcomed with the traditional and generous hospitality of the East. He had come through the transition with flying colours, and was now becoming firmly established. During this process, he had found that many of his generation in India had had a common war experience, and this initial empathy was to give a basis for real and lasting friendships over the next 25 years.

It is perhaps worth reflecting on events in India at this time. India had given generously of both its treasure and blood during the First World War and was expecting more movement towards independent self-government. In this, it was to be bitterly disappointed.

Over the sixty or so years since the uprising of 1857, India had been under direct rule from Great Britain, which had progressively taken over the institutions established by the East India Company. 2/5th of the country was administered by the princes, those hereditary rulers who collected taxes and established the infrastructure of government of their states, for which they were responsible. A Viceroy was appointed, the direct representative of the British Monarchy, but effectively responding to the dictats of the India office in London and the Secretary of State for India in London. The princes, royalty in their own right, had, therefore, an indirect relationship with the Monarchy. This relationship was exercised through the Viceroy with local residents, almost in an ambassadorial role within each state, building on the treaties established under East India Company rule.

The rest of the country was administered by a cadre of members of the Indian Civil Service through a district organisation of officials collecting tax, and administering justice according to a developing system of law, including a new penal code of 1861 administered through a structured system of local, district, and national courts.

The Indian army was organised on British military lines reinforcing the Indian regiments originally established under Company rule but now reorganised within a national structure under a commander in chief and a divisional organisation throughout the country, also incorporating British regiments of infantry and cavalry. These regiments were organised within a brigade structure incorporating two Indian to one British regiment.

These Indian regiments had fought in every theatre of the First World War in which well over a million Indian members of the Indian armed forces took part. They were volunteers, unlike the British who were conscripted after 1915. Mahatma Gandhi himself had volunteered for service amongst a spontaneous outpouring of support for Empire. But the Indian army had now returned from the war with many demobilised; those who had fought in Mesopotamia and had been captured and interned by the Turks at Kut had also been returned, having been treated abominably, and the local reputation of the Indian army for invincibility was somewhat tarnished.

The political situation was a rapidly developing one against the background of an increasingly well-educated Indian middle class, with the aristocracy and princes leading the way with European standards of modern democratic institutions and infrastructure, including hygiene, roads, schools and public buildings. The Indian National Congress, founded in 1885 at the initiative of a retired British Indian Civil Service (ICS) officer, Allan Octavian Hume, had developed into a national organisation, spearheading the move to independence. Mahatma Gandhi had returned to India from South Africa in 1915, and, in 1920, became President of the Congress which backed his programme of civil passive disobedience. But ever since its origins, there had been a divide between the Hindu and Muslim elements of the Congress. Due to the overwhelming Hindu influence, the Muslims felt seriously disadvantaged as a result.

The All-India Muslim League was originally founded as a literary organisation in Dacca in 1906, but now increasingly took on the political causes of the Muslim population, with Muhammad Ali Jinnah, co-founder and leader, taking a leading role. This political divide was to have the most serious consequences on Indian independence in 1947, and the partition of the country which resulted.

Following the Delhi Durbar of 1911 (at which my grandfather was present as Surgeon to the then Viceroy Lord Hardinge, with my grandmother Mabel), Delhi was now the designated capital of India, the new city rising in magnificent new red sandstone buildings designed by Edward Lutyens. The Viceroy, Lord Chelmsford, whom George had now met at least at the Boxing Day dance at Government House, had been in post as Viceroy since 1916. He had been the co-sponsor with Edwin Montagu, the then Secretary of State for India, for what became known as the Montagu-Chelmsford reforms.

Their report, prepared in 1918, formed the basis of the recommendations for the Government of India Act of 1919. Montagu had put forward proposals for the development of free institutions with a view to self-government. However, this emphasis was altered at the intervention of Lord Curzon, now foreign secretary and himself a former Viceroy and traveller throughout India. The emphasis in the act was the intention to involve Indians in every branch of government with the gradual development of self-governing institutions as an integral part of the British Empire, and this is what went forward in the Act itself. Many Indians, who now wanted full independence from the British, were deeply disappointed at this change of emphasis.

Montagu was to remain a most unpopular figure amongst most of the British in India, as my grandfather's diaries reveal, after his resignation in late December 1921.

There were two further events in 1919 which deserve mention, and the first of these was the Jallianwala Bagh massacre of 13th April in Amritsar. The insurrection occurred around the Sikh festival of Baisakhi-Baisakhi marking the Sikh new year and followed the implementation of the Rowlatt Act and the arrest and deportation of two national leaders. In the previous days, rioting crowds had murdered British bank officials in the city and a crowd of thousands had assembled in the walled Jallianwala gardens. Sensing further trouble, a curfew had been instituted and all meetings banned, with martial law and a curfew declared. Brigadier-General Dyer, the officer commanding 2-9th Gurkhas, 54th Sikhs and 54th Sind Rifles of the 45th Infantry Brigade, sensing further trouble, ordered troops to fire on the crowd to disperse it. In the resulting fusillade, 379 people were killed and approximately 1,100 wounded. There was an immediate reaction to this appalling event, and, following an inquiry, General Dyer was suspended and later retired. Reaction at the time was mixed evidenced by a collection of some £23,000 for the benefit of the retired General, a sum well into the millions in today's money. Historians regard this as the principal turning point in the moves to Indian independence.

The third major event was what historians call the Third Afghan War, which started just three weeks after the Amritsar massacre on 3rd May 1919. Unlike the first and second Afghan wars which lasted years, this was largely all over in four weeks. It had been stimulated by the declaration of Jihad by the Imam of Turkey at the commencement of the War and the subversion of Indian prisoners of war of the Muslim Afridi tribal regiments as part of the German and Turkish moves to undermine Muslim troops. German diplomatic missions were spearheaded by former troops of the Afridi Regiments in Afghanistan. The long-running dispute over the redrawing of the border – the new Durand line – between India and Afghanistan – was a main *causus bellum*.

It all started with an invasion across the border by the Afghan army and cavalry, numbering some 50,000, a mixed irregular force of indeterminate quality. The British moved quickly, the first step being to snuff out a potential insurrection in Peshawar by surrounding the town with troops and threatening to cut off the water supply. The British had overwhelmingly superior troops. The headquarters of the North-East Frontier Province military command was based at Rawalpindi. There were two infantry divisions and two cavalry brigades supported by artillery and two squadrons of RAF at hand supported by local militias. The initial actions, which took place progressively, degraded the Afghan forces. The key actions were around the forts at Thal, and Landi Kotal and Rana in Waziristan, culminating in the commitment of the reserves from Rawalpindi to finish the war. It is worth noting here the actions of the 45th Infantry Brigade under the same Brigadier-General Dyer (the General in charge at Amritsar) in the battle and in forcing the relief of the garrison at Thal. By the beginning of June, the Amir of Afghanistan had had enough, and following an armistice, a peace treaty was concluded at the beginning of August 1919.

This war had consequences. First, the political relationship with Afghanistan changed with the country now recognised as an independent nation, able to direct its own foreign policy. Second, the contentious border issue was more settled with the Durand line now agreed as the formal border between India and Afghanistan. So, it was something of a "draw" with advantageous outcomes on both sides.

At the initiative of successive Viceroys, the Indian railway system had been extensively developed under the Raj. By 1920, some 30,000 miles of track had been laid, often across challenging country, with bridges over formidable obstacles and rivers. There were a number of private rail operators which created a problem since some operated broad gauge and others metre gauge, so freight had to be loaded and unloaded to change over from one rail system to another. This was to be a challenging issue to Birds in opening up major mineral concessions in the 1920s. And so, George was arriving in a politically unsettled atmosphere where independence was to become an increasingly dominant issue.

George had experienced the rail journey right across the continent from Bombay to Calcutta, and had now settled into his new life and the social scene in Calcutta around the Christmas season. The 1920 letters make fascinating reading, fresh with the discovery and eyes of the newcomer, and full of good humour, and, at the same time, very supportive of his sister who was given to bouts of depression and loneliness. His letter of 8th January carries more of the same Calcutta social round, and he mentions mail day so we know that this was a Thursday.

"My dear Sis,

Mail day once more. I didn't get a letter from you last mail, but received two very welcome parcels. What a topping flask you have given me! It is absolutely the thing – in fact, I couldn't have chosen better myself (ahem!). After showing it to several of my friends and hearing their praise of the good taste of the chooser, I took it to a jeweller's here & am having my initials engraved on it. I am having plain block capitals written diagonally across the corner. Many, many thanks. I sent you a Christmas present last mail in the shape of a cheque & hope it arrived all serene. It is hard to get silver articles here made and finished like the home article, though at some work, the native is very, very good; he carves ivory very well & when I can get upcountry, I hope to get some good examples of Indian work. It is very expensive in Calcutta at present, as I think I told you before, so I am not buying any of their work.

Well, nothing much has happened since I wrote you last. I went to the usual Saturday race meeting, and on Sunday, played tennis at the house of one of the men here. The lawns are delightful – absolutely flat & most carefully tended. The top of the net is of red tape, and at the end of the courts are large screens of blue fabric – all the courts are similar. There are small boys who pick up balls at each end of the court & also at the net; in fact, tennis out here is absolute luxury – such a thing as stooping to pick up a ball from the ground isn't done!!! I play golf (more or less badly) each morning before breakfast, & have been elected a member of the Royal Calcutta Golf Club. There is to be a State Ball on 15th January to which I have an invitation. I had an excellent time at the Viceroy's dance on 1st Jan (which was a general holiday) & met several new 'young women' who could dance.

I will send you some photos by next mail if possible. I have got some very good ones. Well, how goes it with you? Have you got your return of income tax yet?

Was vaccinated yesterday – a doctor comes round to the office periodically, so thought I may as well get it done again! Much love to all. Hope that you are 'in the pink', yours lovingly, George."

One of the features of the Calcutta winter season was the arrival of the 'fishing fleet' – young unattached ladies arriving for the round of dances, tea parties, governor's camps and parties of all types. It was a sort of marriage market, both eligible bachelors and young ladies looking for a partner. Many liaisons were established with marriages arranged, the ladies often thrust into a society in a strange country, not knowing the local languages, and having children in what became a harsh climate from March to October and particularly in the monsoon season from June onwards. The three-week journey out was sufficiently short to make up to a three-month stay possible. Those returning without having arranged anything were rather cruelly referred to as 'returned empties'. Many of those coming out to India had spent childhoods there and were both familiar with the country and spoke the languages, and so these had a head start over those coming for the first time. George was in his first tour and would have been discouraged from marrying probably until after the age of 30 as a condition of his contract, but this didn't stop him from enjoying himself. George's next letter is full of amusing incidents; –

"15. 01. 1920

My dear Sis,

I received your letter last Sunday which you wrote at Cheniston. Am glad they are all well, & that you had a nice time down there. They are good sorts, labouring under terrible handicaps, & I feel very sorry for all of them, specially your chum. Well, I have nothing fresh to tell you. I have been working fairly hard, & find I am getting more & more to do every week.

The work is interesting, though it is difficult at times owing to my inability to speak the language. I am mastering that difficulty though, & hope soon to be able to yarn away quite well in Hindustani. I have a very decent old teacher (a "moonchie" in Hindi – JMM). He tells me all about the habits and customs of the high and low caste Indians. He is a high caste Hindu himself, & is a gentleman in spite of the darkness of his skin. He also appreciates decent treatment, & when I made a tentative suggestion that he should tell me all about caste & religion, he said he would and proceeded to tell me a little, withholding the main part until later. I told him I hadn't asked any Indian any questions at all about religion, etc., as I was afraid of hurting his feelings by saying the wrong thing. He immediately said, "Of course, being a gentleman, you didn't refer to these matters at all, but I will give you a lecture later on & tell you all the details so you can talk freely without fear of hurting anyone." They are extraordinary people, & intensely interesting, and most of them have a very keen sense of humour. This morning at golf, Ferrier's caddy said he wanted a decent job in an office (as a messenger) & he tried to find out what work I did, & asked Ferrier "Is he in the Government service?" Ferrier – "No", Caddy – "Is he in a bank?" Ferrier "No", Caddy – "Where does he work then?" Ferrier – "In the zoo!!" I started giggling & was just putting, but on looking round & finding that the caddy had a broad grin of amusement on his face which he was trying to conceal, I burst out laughing, much to his amusement. The whole situation was so full of humour that it took some time to regain our gravity!!

Another time we were shopping in the New Market & had the usual coolie who has a large basket which he carries on his head, & in which he places one's parcels. His fee is two annas, but he expects a little extra. We had only two annas between us, so when we got into the taxi, Ferrier waited until the taxi had actually started, & then thrust the two annas into the coolie's hand, and as we were well under way, realising that he had been defeated, was making the best of it by laughing heartily! And yet some people say that the Indian has no sense of humour!!

I already have a pal in the New Market. The man in question has a fruit stall & is a Parthan, (who are the most warlike & treacherous of all the tribes, but who make topping soldiers). One day, he was singing to himself as we went by, & on sighting a rather nice-looking dark girl, he started singing louder. I was rather amused & showed it, I suppose, for he beckoned Ferrier & I over & gave us walnuts which he cracked & we ate. Every time we pass, he greets us and we go and join him with a walnut, or rather, he doesn't eat but he cracks the nuts and he hands them to us. Last Sunday, Teasdale (the 3rd man in the flat), who speaks several dialects in India, came with us and was also regaled with several nuts. He was rather tickled as the man told him we were 'pals of his'.

Well, how goes it with you? I hope that you are finding plenty to do & that some kind of job has turned up. Don't be afraid to worry T.M. You asked in your last letter if you might take the money realised in the sale of my clothes. My dear old girl, have just what you want so long as it is there. I mean to pay for the various things you mention – couch, etc. If you are short, draw on me at Rowley's.

Has your return of income tax come in yet? Let me know how things go, & what you do re cash. Much love, & look after yourself, Yours lovingly, George."

The New Market, very much still operating to this day, is just behind Chowringhee, the main thoroughfare in Calcutta. the 'Piccadilly', as it were, of the city. Here, one could buy just about anything – clothing, cloth, fruit, food, household items, furniture, household stores, jewellery and cut stones. Not far away was the "chore bazaar", the thieves' market, where just about anything could be bought. The Royal Calcutta was a fine golf course, but had been overtaken in popularity by the Tollygunge Club in the 1960s, a country club with a golf and race course, swimming pools, tennis and squash courts and a magnificent club house built around an old indigo planter's house.

George's next letter to Sis is wonderfully supportive, as she was going through a difficult time on her own.

29ᵗʰ January 1920

My dear Sis,

I got your letter all serene, and am so sorry that you have been feeling lonely and unhappy. Of course, one must have fits of depression occasionally, but it doesn't do to worry too much, for worrying only produces grey hairs and wrinkled faces, and we do not want those before our time! My dear old girl, anyone would think that you had something to reproach yourself about so far as I am concerned, which is perfectly ridiculous. Naturally, one hates parting, though mine was perhaps the easier as I go amongst things and faces new, & start a new life with no old friends, whilst you remain behind to continue on the old paths. The times I had at the little flat were the happiest I have known, so you can set your mind at rest on that score, and they were only disturbed by the ever-present feeling that I should sooner or later be off to some far corner of this old world. Try as I would, the feeling was there, and I was quite relieved when I first came out here because I couldn't imagine any future for me at home; in fact, any future at all. My only concern was yourself, and you have strength and plenty of mother wit (and a small income) and we discussed things so I knew that you would settle down to wait until my position was such that I could see you were comfortable and had all the material wants and kept the home fires burning, so to speak. With any luck, it will not be long.

Life at best, you know, Sis, is a dreary kind of business unless we make it otherwise, & to do this requires the best in us, and is easier said than done. When one can hold up one's head, look one's troubles in the face & laugh at them, most of them vanish, as they are imaginary ghosts of the future that we have gone out to seek. If one allows them the mastery, they become hard taskmasters. You know my views on people living alone, so I will not repeat them except to say that you might find it a great help if you find a girl you like to live with you. To have to give and take is good for all of us & human companionship helps to keep problems at their normal level.

How are the classes going? I hope that you are finding it fairly easy to get back to your former level. Remember that the better you are at any job, the more valuable your services are & the more pleasant the job becomes. Don't look on work as a kind of horrible drudgery, but as a means of spending a few months, or at most, a very few years until we fix something much better which will enable you to do much as you please. I have no doubt you will find some very pleasant job – there are lots going and even if you don't get the right kind just at first, it is easier once you are doing some kind of job.

Well, things still progress here. Morton Steven called at the office last week, but as he had to leave early the same night. he couldn't dine with me so I called at his club after I left the office and we had a quiet drink and a yarn.

He is getting quite big and broad and is looking very fit; the life out here seems to suit him very well. He tells me he has a couple of horses, & one of these days, I am going to spend a few days with him. I had a cheery letter from Roy, & one from Rowley written on the day he had you all with the kiddies round for tea. It must have been a good show, & I bet the kiddies loved it. Rowley is a topper, & his letter was 'great' – just typical of him. I had sent him a long screed sometime previously so our letters crossed. I wrote Bell & Arthur McNaught the last two mails. I hadn't the heart to do it before, but wrote them at fair length.

I went to see the Bengal Tennis championship last Saturday. It was quite good & we saw some fairly good games On Sunday, I played tennis and on Monday (which was a holiday,) I played golf before breakfast, dropped off at the office for a couple of hours after breakfast, went to bed after lunch, had tea brought to me in bed, got up and played golf until about 6.00 pm, had a bath, changed, dined and went for a motor run. I still play golf most mornings and also spend a fair amount of time studying Hindustani.

Well, I will chuck it. Life here is good up to the present – long may it remain so, & hope you find that things adjust themselves to the new conditions & that you settle down to happiness, for as you know, it counts much to know that you aren't being worried, and are happy.

Much love, Yours lovingly, George. "

This letter and the advice he gives to Sis epitomises his own developing approach to his life; perhaps it was easier for him to have left everything behind with the journey out to India, and in his own words, out to a "new life with no old friends", whereas Sis was still following the "old paths". He was later to sum this up in the family motto of "toil, endure, believe" which he composed on his knighthood some 25 years later, and on retirement from India. We children thought that this motto was something of a serious joke, but later life experiences have taught us otherwise.

At this time, there were no Indian partners or directors in British business houses and few Indian assistants either; most of the clubs were closed to Indians also. The notable exception was the Saturday club, opened in 1907, whose charter and membership were specifically designed to promote understanding between peoples of all races.

Many Englishmen did not take the trouble to learn a language, but it is a measure of George's open approach to his new life that he was studying Hindustani and George was looking forward to mastering the language so that he could take a fuller part in office, business and social life. Birds were ahead of their time in encouraging a study of Hindustani, Bengali and Urdu, with a clause in their agreement that new assistants coming out to India had to study and learn a language and pass an examination within two years of arrival, and with success, they were given a generous honorarium of Rs 500, a very significant sum of money then.

George's approach to his *moonchie's* religious sensibilities is also quite unusual and sensitive. It would have also given him an understanding of the various religious festivals and holidays.

These attitudes of the business community, or *box wallahs* as they were known, were in stark contrast to those of the eighteenth and early nineteenth century when a much more integrated social approach to Indian society was in place, particularly in the early period of the East India Company; although, in the Indian Civil Service, which operated to the highest standards, a knowledge of local custom, law and language was essential. A strong structure of Indian magistrates, judges, doctors, and officials was already in place by the 1920s.

Birds were going through a difficult period in the immediate post-war period. The war years had been good for the company, with high demand for jute, coal and minerals brought about by the needs of war. During this period, a number of new ventures were started but many of them failed because of a number of factors; probably principal amongst these was the lack of experienced people, many of whom had gone off to the war. A post-war depression set in and the newly created Baron Cable, now elevated to the House of Lords, and the Birds partners, were engaged in a programme of consolidation and reorganisation with the closure of many of the hitherto unprofitable business ventures newly established at the time George joined the company.

Lord Cable had spent the war years in England. In 1915, he bought Lindridge House, a Palladian mansion, and its accompanying 1,400-acre estate for a reputed £75,000, but later, he made it over to his new son-in-law and daughter, Ruth and Tom Benthall. It was here that we were to stay in the early days of the Second World War as guests of Ruth and Tom. Tragically, Lord Cable lost his only son killed in the early part of the war.

George's advice to Sis bore fruit as his letter of 14th February relates. He had missed the post the week before, but the turn-around of letters home and a reply was taking six weeks by sea mail, and this suggests that she had already taken steps to address her problems before his letter arrived.

"14 Harrington Mansions 14/02/20

My dear Sis,

I was very glad to hear in your last letter that you were starting at the Foreign Office. You couldn't have done better, and though at first the work will probably be dull in the registry, you may very easily get on to very interesting work. I should swot up shorthand and typing in case you can get a chance of a really good confidential job – which might turn out to be very interesting and quite worth the trouble. Am also delighted to hear that in all probability, Ag'n and you are going to live together. I shall feel quite happy about everything if you and she fix up together either at No 59 or a better place if you can get it. By better, I mean more healthy, as I am wondering if Longridge Road will suit Ag'n.

You and she will judge for yourselves, however, and I shall be interested to hear whether you do fix up together and if so, where & all about it. Your letter cheered me up no end, as lately, I have been wondering how you would fix things.

Am glad old Tonge has been to town again, and that you dined together. He is a cheery 'cove' and a jolly good sort; proper also. He is a topper, quite unspoilt with that rare gift of taking pleasure in giving other people a good time. I wish that I could have been with you all, or better still, that you could have all been here. We had a great dinner party at the flat a couple of nights ago. I think that we shall all become famous for the excellence of our dinners, as we have a really first-class cook (man, of course) who would make a fortune as a chef in London at some of the smaller restaurants. I am getting quite good at suggesting things, which the old cook makes like a good 'un. There is no shortage of food here, I can assure you.

I had a letter from Les, and another from Doug & one from Margaret by last mail, I must write Doug and Margaret; they are good souls, & I have had another letter previously from Marg.

Am glad to hear about Mrs Beves. If you see Arthur, ask him to give her my love and tell her that I hope that she will soon be dancing again, though not too soon of course!!!

Last week I went to the races & had a very pleasant day, & went out to a bachelor dinner afterwards. On Sunday I loafed.

Well, old bean. I must stop as the mail will not wait. Everything goes along well here & I am very pleased with life in general. Will write more next week. Yours lovingly, George."

This is the first mention of Dick Tonge; Sis and he were to get engaged at the beginning of May and to marry at the end of the year. Sis is now much recovered as George's letter relates.

"14 Harrington Gardens

26ᵗʰ February 1920

My Dear Sis, I missed the mail last week so you didn't get the usual letter. I had one from you last week, and am glad to hear that things are going strong. I am sorry that the work at the F.O. is so tiring but I expect that you will get used to it, especially if you take exercise. A half-mile run before breakfast, besides giving you an appetite like nothing on earth and promoting the growth of a couple of calves like young Indian clubs, would no doubt be a very beneficial effort. Exercise, my boy, that's what you want (said he being almost Uncle Tommish!) As a matter of cold hard fact (always unpleasant!), you never did like anything requiring physical energy. No fault of yours, just a fact!! Please don't misread this info as a suggestion that you should like standing about all day just for the sake of the physical exercise. I can't think of anything more dull, but had you been more fond of exercise, the standing about might not have come so hard. To be serious for a moment, don't over-tax your strength; it isn't worth it.

How is Ag'n? I suppose she has started work by now! Are you living together, or are you still alone?

Everything goes well here. I have been in bed with a poisoned leg from a mosquito bite that I scratched. One has to be devilish careful out here, and the bite was on my dud leg so it fell an easier victim to poisoning as it must be predisposed. It is better now, thank goodness.

Last Saturday, I did the last five holes in a total of 20 shots averaging fours which wasn't bad.

Owing to this rotten leg, I missed Lady Procter last weekend. She came to Calcutta alone on business, and had she known that I was in bed on the days she was here, no doubt she would have called. I will not be able to join them all at Agra on Monday – there is much too much to do. I should have liked to take the trip with them; they are all so cheery.

The weather is beginning to warm up now, and in a few weeks, I expect that we shall be melting with heat. I have ordered my thin clothes; thank goodness I didn't get more than were absolutely necessary at home, as one can get things most excellently made very cheaply here. I recently had some shirts made, and they cost me about half or less what they would have cost in a shop at home before the war. I got a native tailor and gave him one of my shirts as a pattern & he turned out a couple of shirts that might have been made in Bond Street.

Will you send out my leather looking glass, Sis? It wants a new glass which I shall be glad if you will have it put in. Also, will you get me, or ask Bill McNaught to get me if you like, 30 yards of material for shirts and pyjamas. I don't know but I believe it is called Zeyphar (cotton of course). I can get material out here but it is not as fine as I want. I want something very, very fine in texture. If you can get it, can you send 20 yards plain white and 10 yards very pale blue – just a blue tint, in fact? I have no doubt that Bill McN will do it if he can. Let me know the cost and I will send you a cheque.

Well, old bean, I must chuck it. Much love. Hope that you are fit. Wish you were here. Yours lovingly, George.

P.S. I have pinned on a sample of the type of material I want so far as texture goes."

Towards the end of February, the weather heats up in Calcutta, and although relatively dry until the monsoon breaks in the middle of the year, there are often sharp storms with short bursts of torrential rain, and as the city is low lying and with a river running through, it can become very humid. Temperatures over 40 degrees centigrade with relative humidity over 90 degrees are common. Thin clothes are essential and a *durzi* (tailor) would run up clothes e.g., thin trousers of cloth twill and cotton shirts, often bringing his Singer sewing machine, scissors and thread onto the verandah to make up and fit the clothes in situ. There was no air-conditioning in the 1920s . . . Birds Chartered Bank offices were not air-conditioned until 1937. Constantly going in and out of air-conditioning was not necessarily conducive to good health as it could lead to congestion of the sinuses and bronchial passages. Mats of *cuscus (*a coarse grass) would sometimes cover windows and be drenched with water, the evaporation providing a cooling effect; spinning *punkas* (overhead fans) also assisted air-circulation.

George, in his next letter, describes a visit from a *'box wallah'* to the flat, a travelling merchant with silks and decorated tableware, carpets and sometimes jewellery for sale. This was the somewhat derogatory nickname given to anyone in 'trade'.

14 Harrington Mansions 3/3/20

My dear Sis,

I didn't get any mail from you last week so that there is nothing to answer.

I spent most of last week in bed with a poisoned leg arising from a mosquito bite that I had scratched!! It is better now and I have been back at the office since Monday. Tomorrow is a holiday and I hope to go to the races. I haven't got your photos yet but I suppose that they will be arriving one of these days. Parcels take much longer than letters – usually at least twice the time. You remember my request for material in my last letter? Well, if Bill McD doesn't get the stuff, & I know he is busy and may forget all about it, do you mind buying it for me? Heron may be able to tell you the best place, or even get it for me. I shall want the stuff by May or beginning of June if possible.

As I told you in my last letter, the Procters wanted me to join them at Agra but it couldn't be done. Agra is full of interest for the tourist as there are many relics of the old kings and their regime. Bad luck as I would have liked to have gone. The great thing at Agra is a beautiful place known as the Taj Mahal, a beautifully proportioned marble building with a huge dome.

The building is in beautiful surroundings beside the river. The intention of the bloke that built it was to build one on the other side of the river, but made of dead black marble. His project never materialised however & he was captured and imprisoned, & I believe his prison windows permitted him to see in the distance the palace that he had built!! (The 'bloke' who built the Taj was the Emperor Shah Jahan, as a mausoleum for his beloved wife Mumtaz, and he was indeed later put under house arrest by his son Aurangzeb in the fort at Agra where he spent eight years before he died. JMM) I believe the fort at Agra is noted, & there are many beautiful old buildings. If I live long enough, I shall see it all, I hope. Northern India is full of beautiful things. Since writing the foregoing, your photos have arrived. They are topping, & I am jolly glad to have them. I think I like the head best, but both are good. I think that you had a proof of the figure one before I left? It is a topping present. Many thanks.

Everything goes on much the same here. It is a life of luxury these days. There is no rationing orders here, & our cook is an artist, so if I get frightfully fat, you will know the causes!! Also, one is waited on hand and foot.

Have been busy getting summer clothes. The other night we had an ancient old bird in the flat selling beautiful silks & Kashmiri work & hand-embroidered silk tablecloths, etc. I bought some tussore silk for suits, topping thick silk. The old man was a pukka merchant, and arrived with many huge bundles of merchandise carried by coolies. He squatted on the floor and proceeded. We entertained each other for about 1,1/2 hours, and finally, I tossed him whether I paid him my price or the price he had come down to. Of course, he won, though at the price I bought the silk, I did very well, & one couldn't buy it as cheaply in the Calcutta market; in fact, I haven't seen stuff of that quality in Calcutta.

I wanted to buy a lovely silk embroidered tea cloth with wonderfully worked silk peacocks round the edge, but he wanted too much for it, and up in the north where the work is done, they are a little cheaper, & the very finest work is to be got. I hope to go up north one of these days & will then get some things for you. He had some topping scarves, table cloths (fancy), dressing table covers, etc. but the price was too great. I have no doubt that I shall have him as a constant visitor now, and perhaps he will come down to my price in time!! These merchants are extraordinary gentlemanly old men, and they are always very respectful. It is topping the way one jokes & rags with them without the slightest familiarity or anything but the deepest respect. The Hill men are a much finer type than the Bengali, who is rather a 'gutless' individual.

How you would love it all with the colours, the luxury and everything!

Well, how is everyone? It all seems very far away, as indeed it is & it would be great if one could only exchange visits with a few of one's friends occasionally! I had a great letter from Doug the other day. He is a great sportsman.

How is Dorrie and how are the kiddies? I hope the measles disappeared all serene!

Give my regards to Charlie when you see him. Kind remembrances to all of my friends. Yours lovingly, George."

These travelling merchants were a breed apart . . . I particularly remember Mooni Lal, who had a wonderful collection of jewellery for sale, well beyond the scope of my purse, and who knew my parents. He had his son with him and showed us a lovely pear-shaped pale blue sapphire pendant.

In the next letters, George describes a visit upcountry, and his plans to take an Easter holiday with a visit to Puri, a resort by the sea due south of Calcutta, a very popular spot, with bungalows by the sea shore, often owned by the main business houses for the use of their British staff. He also is now a member of the Royal Calcutta Golf Club.

"14 Harrington Mansions 24th March

My dear Sis,

I enclose a small table cloth and a cheque for your birthday with best wishes and many happy returns. I have been very busy for some time, and I am afraid that I didn't write by last mail. I got your letter, and am glad to hear that things are still going strong; any luck with returned income tax yet?

Last weekend I went upcountry. I left on Saturday at about 6.00 pm and arrived at about 11.00 at Assensole where I was met by car & driven about fifteen or sixteen miles to the Works (engineering). I went to bed & got up about 6.05. From up to about 2.00 pm, I worked at figures & accounts with the chief engineer & then had lunch. At about 4.00 pm, we had tea & then went for a tour round, finishing at the small club where we had a drink and wandered back to his bungalow. We dined a little before nine & at 10.30 pm I left by car & got the train at Assensole at 11.40 pm. The train was a very slow one & I arrived in Calcutta at about 8.30 am. I had a good sleep in the train so was fit, & having had a bath & breakfast, proceeded to the office for another day's work.

I hope to go to a seaside place called Puri for Easter. It should be good fun & a rest and a change. It is about fourteen hours' journey from Calcutta, but we travel at night, & travelling here is very different to home. All the first-class carriages have sleeping berths & bathrooms, & food can always be got either on the train as at home or at stations where a long halt of ¾ of an hour may be made.

I had a topping letter from Rowley by last mail, and one from May Morton (Hall place) by the previous mail. They all seem to be going strong. I played golf and tennis the Sunday before last but was not in very good form! I still play golf most mornings and sometimes accomplish quite a respectable score.

Well, old bean, no more now. I don't seem to get time to breathe these days. I am going to write you a long letter soon, enclosing some photographs I have taken.

Hope you are very fit. Remember me to jolly old Tonge. Much love, Yours lovingly, George. Good luck on 11ᵗʰ April."

George was to become a very fine amateur photographer. In the archive, there are a number of albums of his photos, masses of loose photos and some 16 mm reels of film. Sadly, these latter have not responded well to transcription to disc with the exception of one spool. Henley Regatta features on this as well as children playing in the gardens of Remenham House, Sis's family home after her marriage to Dick Tonge. These children are probably Janet and her brother Bill and a guestimate suggests the summer of 1926. There are some particularly fine pictures of trekking in the Chumbi Valley in Tibet, and the Kanchenjunga massif, as well as friends at Shimmerali, the weekend snipe-shooting camp north of Calcutta. A selection is included in this book. His camera equipment consisted in the mid-1950s of a fine plate camera, a 35mm Leica, a 16mm cine camera, and Zeiss Super Iconta, a bellows camera taking 618 film (almost quarter plate).

Over the past 40 odd years, Birds had invested substantially in the development of the massive coal deposits in the North of West Bengal. The trip to Assensole was probably to the Engineering works established by Birds in 1909 near the Kumardhubi coal deposit, north of the Damodar river. Called the Kumardhubi Engineering Works, it was floated as a separate company in 1915. The company history records an over-stocked position in the company which had to be resolved in 1920, and possibly this was part of the reason for the visit. It was unusual that this visit took place over a weekend, which suggests a confidential investigation.

Kumardhubi was owned by the Burrakur Coal Company, representing the original excursion by Birds into coal when they took over the managing agency in 1878 and later acquired a proportion of the shares. Coal mining in India had begun in 1774 when two prospectors, John Sumner and Suetonius Healy of the East India Company, began commercial exploitation of the Ranigunge coalfield along the Western bank of the Damodar river. Discovery of further massive deposits in the Assensole region of North-Western Bengal in 1862 led to the development of the coal industry exploited by firms such as Andrew Yule and Balmer Lawrie and others. The coal concessions established and managed by Birds led the company to a commanding position with raisings increased to 950,000 tons by 1909.

In 1919-20, all of the Birds coal companies, with the exception of one, Budrochuk, were consolidated under the Burrakur name. Coal supported the massive development of the railways, as well as coaling for river traffic and shipping from the port of Calcutta, but demand had dropped substantially in the slump after the war due to the almost complete loss of export markets. The engineering works supported the maintenance and engineering requirements of the Birds collieries as well as other collieries in the area, and it also had a small foundry.

George's next letter is a most descriptive one, announcing his election as a full member of the Royal Calcutta Golf Club, his meeting with the senior partner, and an amusing description of office life.

"14 Harrington Mansions 31/3/20

My dear Sis,

I have just received your letter telling me that you had been seedy. You know that we are a bronchial lot so be careful of colds, etc. I do hope that you are better again; I hate to think of your being seedy, and I can't say how glad I am to hear that Dorrie and Betty have been calling around every day. It is when you are ill that I get worried about you, though it is of little use, but I shall be glad when you can make a better arrangement re having someone living in my little room. I shall be glad when I can allow you enough to allow you to do as you like. Never mind, old bean, I suspect that you are in the 'pink' again by now; anyway, I hope so.

I enclose some snaps I have taken at various times. I had written a few notes on the backs to assist. Some of them are quite good, in fact, all except those of the people in fancy dress are good I think. I have enlarged one or two and they are wonderfully good. If you will take the prints to Kodak's and get them to mount them in a suitable album, I will pay the damage. It is jolly hard to mount them properly so if you do it at all, take them to Kodak & let me know the cost. By the way, how much do I owe you? I don't know if it is anything, but do let me know.

Last Saturday I played tennis at the house of one of the partners, & on Sunday played golf. I am now a full member of the golf club, and jolly lucky I am to be a full member, as I expect it will take some time for some of the men who have gone up lately, even years to become full members.

Our senior partner took me for a ride round in his car the other evening after office, and came to the flat afterwards for a drink & stayed for about an hour & a half yarning with us. He is a jolly good fellow, & I think he enjoys having a yarn with some of the new younger members of his staff!

I had a long letter from young Macdonald by last mail. (Perhaps you remember him – he saw me off on 1ˢᵗ Nov). He is in Germany having a pretty miserable time by what I can read between the lines! He is a good-hearted youngster, & has his head screwed on the right way. He tells me that Germany is a bad spot to be in these days, and from the news, I should think that he is right.

I go off to Puri tomorrow for Easter. It should be good fun. I will let you know how things go.

Life here is just the same – the Babus (our Indian clerks) are amusing blokes, though mostly as lazy as the very devil. I was put on to be in charge of the most 'difficult' of the lot, a man who had hitherto defeated anyone who was put over him. I set my teeth & sat down to it, with the result that he fired in his resignation saying that "he found it impossible to please Mr Morton". Little did he think that it would be accepted!! However, he is still here, and is much more amenable, and has at last realised what the difference is between an order and a request. It is not often that one has to 'order', but when one does, it has to be obeyed. The Indian clerk is an amusing devil as a rule. One sportsman wrote a most flowery epistle the other day asking for an increase in pay as "owing to the considerable increase in his family, he found it impossible to manage on his present pay" From the way he put it, anyone would have thought that the "considerable increase in his family" was due to the firm. They are mostly very well-educated and some of them are absolute gentlemen and very clever fellows too. Am glad that the shares in the club have been sold. I shall be glad to have all the various accounts in order that I may see some kind of record. I note that you have had a bit of a skirmish with Uncle Tom. He means well but he does write offensive letters at times!! Never mind, old bean, it isn't worth letting out! Life is too short, and one of these days you will not need assistance over the estate, as it seems to be clearing up very nicely.

I love your photos. The more I look at the head the more I like it. It is absolutely you looking out of it. I haven't yet found a frame worthy of it but I live in hopes!

Do look after yourself. Much love, yours lovingly, George. PS Hope that you liked the table cloth. How does it look on the oak stool? Does the blue match?"

The senior partner was B.A. White. He had originally come out to Calcutta with C.S. Cox as his secretary; Cox was a very close associate of Ernest Cable. Cox had his own firm in Calcutta and Birds shared offices with them in London. Cox was particularly well connected with the financial world and he and Cable worked together on a number of joint business ventures. The two London companies were to merge. When Birds took over the agency for R.S. Steel and Co, they also took on White who had joined Birds jute department. After retirement, White was to provide a detailed chronicle about Birds, an invaluable source of information for future historians.

White was to look after the Calcutta end of Bird's coal business while another recruit, William Ironside, was also to join Birds. In 1906, he took over responsibility for reorganising and improving the quality of coal from Birds collieries. White became a partner in 1915 and Chairman of the Indian Mining Association the following year. Ironside had, meanwhile, been appointed head of the firm, becoming Chairman of the Bengal Chamber of Commerce, a member of The Imperial Legislative Council and Director of the Bank of Bengal, but he succumbed to cholera in early 1919 and died.

B.A. White then took over as senior partner. He took over from Ironside as Director of the Bank of Bengal, and also became a member of the Legislative Council, and Local Director of the Imperial Bank of India. He went back to England in the summer of 1920, but on his return, his health broke and he cabled Cable to come out. On return to England, he attached himself to Birds London becoming Chairman during the Second World War. He died in 1960 at Exmouth at the age of 80. He was to become a very close associate of George, particularly during the Second World War.

When White sailed back to India in the autumn of 1920 in the Kaisar-i-Hind, he travelled with Edward Benthall (always known as Tom), his wife Ruth (daughter of Ernest Cable) and their new son Michael, just eighteen months old. Having lost his own son during the war, Cable now had a real successor in his new son-in-law. After Cable's death in 1929, George was to work very closely with Tom Benthall in unscrambling the Cable shareholdings and transferring them to Tom and also in the tax planning needed to enable the continuity of the firm to be maintained. Tom was no mean intellect, a King's scholar at Eton, and a scholar at King's College Cambridge. He was a Cambridge rugby blue and reserve second row for England. He had been in India during the First World War with the 1st/4th Devons and loved India and was a keen ornithologist. He had fought his war in Mesopotamia with the Devons and had spent some time, before joining Birds, working for the White Star Line. His younger brother Paul joined Birds later and his twin sons Richard and James were contemporaries in the early 60s, also working for Birds.

George was now a member of the Royal Calcutta Golf Club. He played there nearly every morning, just a few holes to exercise before going to the office. I used to do the same at Tollygunge, getting up at six for an hour's golf, and then back to breakfast at eight and to the office before nine. George's exercise regime of golf and tennis is all the more remarkable in view of the loss of half his right foot; he was determined to keep fit and also to prove to himself that he could 'do it'.

Calcutta club life and long weekends at Puri, Gaya, and Jessore

In the next letter, there is a description of the Easter trip to Puri.

"14 Harrington Gardens Calcutta 8th April 1920

My dear Sis,

Back once more to purrich & auld claes. Have had a topping holiday at Puri and am feeling very fit. Had a hell of a rush on Thursday, and managed to bust off from office at about 5.45 p.m. Got home, superintended packing and then left in two cars – first car containing myself and Ferrier and the second, two servants and piles of luggage. On the way, picked up one Campbell, and arrived at the station at about 7.30 p.m. We proceeded to the platform where we deposited our servants and luggage. We had booked berths so all was well. We then had dinner at the station restaurant, and immediately afterwards, climbed into our carriage where our beds had been made up, undressed and went to sleep. Up at 6.00 a.m. next morning, hot to roast & wash shave & arrival at Puri station at about 7.30 a.m. on Good Friday. Went to a hotel and changed, ate a roaring good breakfast and then retired for another nap! Woke in time for lunch & then had another nap! Played golf after tea, and then had a delightful bathe amongst fierce breakers. It was lovely. There are fishermen in strangely shaped straw hats (& a little cloth about the middle!) who act as attendants. The first bathe they came in with me (we had two each) but afterwards, they used to sit on the shore watching and enjoying the fun, ready to join in if anything went wrong. The waves were very fierce, and most of the people who are indifferent swimmers have one of the fishermen holding each hand all the time. The hotel had a tennis court attached so we had a little tennis, a little golf on a very poor golf course, a lot of bathing and a tremendous lot of sleep. The reason that we had so much sleep is that it is pretty hot from about 10.00 a.m. until 3.30 p.m. and it is only asking for headaches to wander about in the sun during the period between these times. Puri itself consists of many and scattered typically eastern houses spread over a large area. Most of the houses are single-storey bungalows. I have taken some photographs which have come out fairly well. I will send you prints when I get them. We left Puri on Monday evening after dinner, had breakfast at the flat here and went to office. Travelling out here is very pleasant, for one gets a real sleep between sheets, clothes off and everything O.K. The carriages are usually made without a corridor with a door either side of the compartment, bunks on either side and a bathroom at one end with a separate "thunder box" in its own compartment with a window. As you will see from the drawing, they are very comfortable. (His drawing is out of proportion as there is too much space between the bunks! – JMM).

Well, old bean, I wonder what you did over the holiday. I hope that you had a good time. How is the cold? I hope that it is better, and that you are quite fit again now.

Last Thursday, Slater, the chief accountant and financial expert under whom I work, said to me whilst we were discussing some point of principle in the words, "By the way, Morton, we have issued small bonuses to some of the people for last year, but we haven't included you as you were only here for a month last year – I know you are underpaid as well as you do, but there is no need to worry as we will make it up in the form of a handsome bonus at the end of the year."!! I was surprised, & it seemed to amuse him that I was underpaid. He repeated the phrase and told me that White, the senior partner, also realised that I was not getting as much as I should. Of course, I told him that I was not worrying about it. I am a vain devil as you know, and it made me feel quite 'nice like' to think that they appreciated the fact that I was doing my best. The end of the year is a long way off, but I may get a decent increase and then it will be good!

Well, Sis, I will chuck it. I have told you about finance because I want you to know that I am not standing still at present whilst not placing the pursuit of the elusive coin before health etc. Things are beginning to look good, if I can continue to keep going as hitherto.

I had a letter from Richard by last mail. He is in Switzerland with Gladys who is in a sanatorium there. Tuberculosis, I believe, but she is improving. Richard is out looking after her, and is, I believe, very fit. Much love, look after yourself, yours lovingly, George."

Campbell was probably Toby Campbell, later married to Gladys. They retired to Scotland after the Second World War. They lived at Urrard House just north of Killiecrankie, the site of the Battle of Killiecrankie, fought on 27th July 1689 between the Jacobite Catholic supporters of James 7th of Scotland and the forces of the protestant Dutch King William 3rd. It ended in defeat for the Scots. Further down the glen towards Pitlochry, is the famous Soldier's Leap where a fleeing Scot escaped his pursuers by jumping the narrow gorge over the river Garry.

It was here that I spent a holiday shortly after the death of my father in the summer of 1954. Staying in the cottage were Gill and Bertie Sinclair with their three small children . . . Gill was Barney Shuttleworth's sister; he was to be my future brother-in-law, marrying my eldest sister, Jean. Also part of the party were Pitts Squarey (author's godfather) and his new wife Francis. Pitts was a great friend of my father. A keen fisherman, Bertie was working for Balmer Lawrie in Calcutta. We shot grouse in the hills above the house in August during a memorable holiday.

Some mention should be made of the Indian railway system. The main trunk routes were mainly broad gauge but some of the lines were metre gauge and the rolling stock was not interchangeable. At that time, there were no corridors between compartments. There were sometimes interlinking doors between compartments and later corridors e.g., on the Royal Train, as described in my O'Kinealy grandfather's diaries of the Prince of Wales's visit of 1920/21 (see "Family of the Raj p 156) In very hot weather, blocks of ice were placed in special wells in the floor of the first-class compartments to provide cooling.

Meals taken on board in a restaurant car meant that the transfer to the car and return to the compartment would take place at a station stop. Sometimes a stop also would be made for about three-quarters of an hour to enable a meal to be taken at a station restaurant; hence the comment that travel on Indian railways was a leisurely business.

"14 Harrington Gardens Calcutta 14/04/1920

My dear Sis,

Mail once more; time seems to fairly fly these days. Last weekend I did the usual exercise stunt. On Saturday I played tennis at the house of one of the partners – Kirkpatrick. Two other partners were there including the chief. They are a very nice cheery lot, and much less stiff than heads of firms at home. We had some topping good tennis. In the evening I went to the theatre and saw a real London company 'the Luaints' who are a most excellent company of Pierrots. On Sunday I played golf at the 'Jodhpur Club' with a very cheery lad; we started at about 8.00 a.m. & got back to the club for breakfast at about 11.00 after having a bath and a change. We joined up with two others and breakfasted. After that, we played a four-ball until about 3.00. I then returned here, changed into tennis gear & went out to a tennis party where I played five sets right off. On Monday we had the women to dinner and had a little dance afterwards; it was a most excellent show, & we went for a moonlight drive afterwards at about 2.00 a.m. – it didn't matter because

Tuesday was a holiday! On Tuesday I again played golf, at the Royal Calcutta this time – of which I am now a full member, great luck. On Tuesday evening we dined with another chummery & went to the theatre again. Last night I went to a tea dance at the Saturday Club from about 6.30 p.m. to 8.00 p.m. and went to bed about 9.30 p.m. I am going to quieten down now for a day or two, as I am working each day like ten thousand devils, or nine thousand anyway! The excuse for our recent bust was Tuesday's holiday. Everything goes along slowly. I lead a very quiet life in the ordinary way, and still don't smoke, and drink practically nothing. I am joining the Jodhpur Club if possible as it is a jolly place and has a nice little golf course and about a dozen tennis courts, and a very nice club house. It is outside Calcutta, and in nice jungle. It is a club for both men and women and as far as golf is concerned is not quite so keen and difficult as the Royal Calcutta, which is useful as far as the women are concerned. Women are not often seen on the latter club until after the rush of the day. Wait till you come out – you will have the time of your life.

Am finishing this in the office, and am just off to catch the mail. I haven't got your last letter by me, but I know there is something that I have to answer in one of your recent letters. I will answer by next mail.

Much love, & I hope that you are quite fit again. Yours lovingly, George."

The partner, Kirkpatrick, had joined Birds with the Heilgers purchase. The Jodhpur club (now Jodhpur Park in south Calcutta) was as he stated it, not in any way rivalling Tollygunge club, which he was to join eventually as well as the Bengal Club. In his next letter, he again amusingly charts his progress in the office in dealings with staff and his work.

"14 Harrington Gardens 21ˢᵗ April 1920.

My dear Sis,

Before I forget, the address of the place to get notepaper is Wodderspoons Parliament Street. There are several receipted bills from them, including one for making a die which I believe I left amongst the household bills in the bureau – second drawer from the top. I was glad to hear that you had gone down to the Cross's. They are ripping good sorts, and I expect that your visit did you no end of good. I love the place, don't you? I think that they are simply topping. I like the lovely meadows there and the horses and cattle. The weekend I spent there made a deep impression on me; everyone was so kind, and everything was so nice & peaceful- unlike other places we know of. It made me realise how nice country life with a couple of hunky and a car would be, and alas, how impossible it would be for me unless – y'never know, y'know, and one of these days, when you have married a millionaire, I shall be rolling up at your house with the usual eastern liver (and thirst!) and habits, and teach you how to run everything!!!

I am glad that you have someone with you at last and do hope that you are both happy and not too hearty before or after breakfast! How does Miss Steadman like my little room? I hope that she doesn't find it too small. It's all very well for a small feller like me, but I wonder how one of the opposite sex manages to manage? Anyhow, there is always your room I suppose. I haven't forgotten the furs either, but have not yet had an opportunity of finding the best kind at a more or less reasonable cost. I will send you some before next winter if possible.

I have shown your photographs to a few people here and they are all unanimous in voting them topping. One rude bloke said, "That your sister? What an ugly devil like you!"

Life goes on in the same way. It is a little trying at times as regards one's understrappers; they are so thoroughly unreliable at times. I am constantly asking for old correspondence regarding various things and I am often met by a blank stare and protestation that such things have never happened or been received. I have a fairly good memory (touch wood!) and up till now have been able to supply details etc. and have insisted & insisted until I have got what I wanted; it is then that I get going with a few stingers. The half breed or quarter or eighth breed here is a perfect devil at times, and is without exception the most barefaced liar that it has been my misfortune to meet. We are getting down to it slowly – I think they had an idea that I was 'mother's boy' when I arrived as I was inclined to be polite (!!) Like the breed, they immediately tried to take advantage of it. It was then the fun started, and now things are very much better, and I think we are beginning to "understand one another".

I like the life immensely, and there is a lot to do, as we are getting on towards the hot weather, but I do not mind it yet (again, touch wood!) I suppose the old place is beginning to take on a little green and days are commencing to be liveable with sunshine & rain and the jolly old puddly roads and pavements. How is my friend, Mrs Jones? I hope that she is fit and flourishing and not too hard-worked. Give her my kind regards. You remember little Martin that we met at the Alan Ironsides? He sent his remembrances to you a week or two ago, and was asking when you are coming out.

Well, old bean, I will chuck it. I often wonder how things are going in London. One doesn't realise how changed things are until one gets to a place like this where there is plenty of everything. I hope three years will see things back to normal in the old country. It would be topping to get back on leave & find conditions almost as before the war! Love to everyone, George."

In today's world, George's comments about staff would have been considered racist, but they are as written a hundred years ago. English was a foreign language to Indian staff, only anxious to please, and often, from a grammatical point of view, came out strangely. In Hindustani, the verb is generally at the end of a sentence, and thus grammatically, quite different from English. Office work required a knowledge of Hindi and Bengali, the script of the latter peculiar to the language, as was the third language, Urdu, a mix of Hindi and Persian. So, it was hardly surprising that communication was a complex affair. As a child, I spoke Nepali Hindustani and English in that order, with some Tibetan thrown in for good measure. At one stage, our Nepalese ayah forbade me from playing with her son Jonghi, because I swore and used bad Tibetan words, not that I understood them! They had been picked up in the bazaar. On return to India in 1961 to work for Tatas, I re-learnt Hindustani, like George, and the language which I had spoken as a child came back very quickly.

George's dream of country living was to be realised with the rental of Walstead House near Lingfield in Sussex while on leave in the thirties; it perhaps also explains the purchase of Rectory Farm in Ogbourne St. George, Wiltshire, which became our permanent family home after the war, and his life as a farmer after he retired. But things at home changed dramatically as he now receives a cable from Sis saying that she is engaged to Richard Tonge!

"14 Harrington Mansions 6th May 1920

My Dear Sis,

I haven't got over the wire yet. What can I say, dear old thing? I congratulate you both. I wouldn't wish for anyone I like more than jolly old Tonge, and as for yourself, you know that it is my constant wish that you may be happy, and I have often thought & wished that you might find someone you would be fond of.

I am jumping to know all about it – curiosity killed the cat! Must 'a bin a bit sudden like! I do wish that I were at home, but it's no use worrying for it is impossible. I hope T.M. will look after things. Let me know all about everything, and exactly what you want. I am not going to say any more about it at present, but I am awfully pleased, and I know that you will both be very happy.

Last Saturday, I had some topping tennis at the Jodhpur Club and got back to dinner here where two men dined. We had arranged a moonlight picnic, and after dinner, we collected the five young women & had a small dance at the flat until 10.30 p.m. & then left Calcutta in three motors and arrived at the scene of the picnic at about 11.30 p.m. We had sent servants and grub & gramophone on in advance. We had a topping supper & dance in the moonlight on the balcony of a disued bungalow; a great evening. We arrived home after 4.00 a.m., & at 6.00 a.m. were up again & off to golf. Ferrier and I played together in a four-ball at the Jodhpur club. We fairly smote our opponents, & felt so strong that after a drink, we played a second eighteen holes, got back to flat about 11.30 a.m. & had a roaring good breakfast with lashings of beer and food. Bed until 4.30 & then another topping tennis party. I felt jolly fit on Monday, and since then have been working like smoke. I find I am getting more and more to do thank goodness, and most of the work is very interesting. I am getting a fair amount of Income Tax work, appeals & very technical and complicated cases to fight the authorities over. I took over Rs 30,000 out of the Income Tax authorities over one case, & was frightfully bucked about it. The other work consists of getting things straightened out after five years of war – very interesting work. Thank goodness I had five well-spent years in Deloitte's; I find my experience is invaluable, & am hoping that the powers that be will appreciate my efforts!!

Well, old bean, I have just heard that I have missed the mail, damn! Best love to you and Richard. Wish I were with you. Yours lovingly, George."

As he had missed the post, he sent a postscript on the 13th May;

"My dear Sis,

Having missed last mail, I didn't post this epistle so am adding a few words. Nothing fresh has happened since I wrote last. I received the packet of accounts of the Imperial Property last mail but didn't get a letter from you!!! I haven't had time to look into them yet but hope to get a little time soon! Last weekend we had the usual topping good time – tennis, theatre, golf, etc.

Last night the tennis finals (office) were played at a partner's house which was given over to Mr White, the head of B & Co, who held an at home. He is a ripping good sort & nothing if not very cheery! The result was a most excellent evening from about 5.15 to 8.00 p.m. We then went home & made Ferrier take us out to the theatre! Tonight, we are dining out with the Shrosbrees. He is one of our head people and a topping good sort. Mrs Shrosbree is delightful & is a wonderful hostess. They are going home within the next few weeks – I must try and get them to look you up if they can. I know you would like them; you couldn't help it.

Well, till next time. Hope you are as fit as ever. Much love to you and Tonge, Yours lovingly, George."

The comment about his work is revealing. The income tax work was almost certainly on behalf of the partnership and individual partners. The figure of Rs 30,000 was equivalent to low thousands in sterling terms then, and is equivalent to a six-figure sum today. It is indicative of the level of partners' income at that time, even after taking into account that the rebate may have accrued over more than one year.

As mentioned already, Birds at that time had entered a consolidation phase, and this was probably a part of George's "interesting work". The post-war period was characterised by a slump in trade, and the rationalisation of Birds business activities was a major part of B.A. White's task as senior partner. He had moved now into 37 Ballygunge Park, described in the Birds history as the "Chequers" of the firm, and this is most probably where the firm's tennis finals took place. This had been the residence of Lord Cable, but he had spent the war years in England, and at Lindridge during the war.

The core of Birds business and profit lay in the firms under their management involved in jute and coal, now reinforced by those acquired with the purchase of Heilgers. Paper was a new venture through Titagur and processes using pulped bamboo were going to be developed by the new research department, reducing the dependence on pulped wood from the Burmese and North Indian forests. This was to be particularly important during the Far Eastern War.

Birds labour contracts continued to operate profitably, despite the post-war slump. Everything else was subject to financial and business analysis to establish viability. Where Birds operated as managing agents, protective shareholdings, generally above 20%, had been secured as a part of the managing agency deal, so there was a major exercise of reconstruction and reappraisal being undertaken.

B.A. White was to return to the UK in the middle of the year, returning before the cold weather. Slater, the head of finance, also returned to the UK at much the same time on business, as George was to report in subsequent correspondence. White's health was to break under the strain by the end of 1920, when Lord Cable returned to India to finalise the reconstruction.

In the end, White reckoned that the total cost of the clean-up was about £1¼ million. Companies were ruthlessly pruned and to finance the reconstruction, some of the coal concessions held by Birds were sold as well as a selection of Cable's own shareholdings. Many of the so-called "war babies" were closed down, and the shareholdings of many major investors such as Messrs Kinneson & McGowan held firm in expectation of the turnaround, a strong endorsement of Cable's capability. The effective pruning action by Cable and others was timely, the recovery of Birds illustrating the very strong potential of the business based on the underlying profitability of the core businesses. George was obviously playing his role in getting things "straightened out after five years of war".

His next letter concentrates on his social activities and describes the entertainment of a group of exiled Russian seamen in the flat.

"Calcutta 20ᵗʰ May 1920

My dear Sis,

I got your letter all serene, and am glad you liked the birthday presents. Am glad to hear that you are enjoying life, and that all sorts of pals are turning up. I had a letter from Rowley by last mail. He is cheery as ever and he told me he had seen you recently.

I am amused to hear about Jules. Were Fergus and Margaret being sporting and pretending not to see you, or didn't they see you? It is very easy not to see people in a restaurant especially if one is with a party. Talking about Harris whom you met at the Grafton Galleries, funnily enough, I was talking about him with a man who knew him in Eastbourne – Douetil by name – and shortly afterwards, I got your letter.

I went to a before-dinner dance yesterday at the Saturday Club and had quite a cheery time. We had a dinner party afterwards with two men & their wives from the office – the men, not the wives! They were all four good topping sorts & we had a ripping evening; everyone was most cheery. We have a famous game we play – 'billiards skittles' It is played on the billiard table & gets very noisy at times, but is very cheery.

Last weekend I went to a topping party out at Jodhpur – given by one of the men in the office. Had some tennis. I wish you could see some of these places; they are delightful. In the evening we had two young women to dinner – quite a good party. On Sunday morning I played golf with one of our chief men & his wife & had breakfast (– or it was more like a lunch) at about 10.30. Went home and went to bed until 4.00 p.m. More tennis and then a quiet dinner at home. After dinner, we entertained a Russian Captain & three of his officers from a large training ship which escaped from Russian waters & is touring the world. They were topping men and very musical. One of them sat down at the piano and the others sat round & they sang part songs. It was topping though most of the songs they sang were a bit wistful; some of the songs were rolling songs of the sea, but one song in particular which they called the Volga Boatman's Song was delightful. Poor devils. No country worth a cuss, people mostly murdered or worse; property, money all gone. I imagine they were about the pick of the Russian Navy. One of them had been a kind of King over part of the coast, which was all upset. He had been in command of a destroyer, & landed and took charge of a large part of the country until some months afterwards, a bomb was thrown at him and he "had to go". It was a good evening & the free and happy way we mixed up, – we were all twelve of us either soldiers or sailors, – was good – in spite of the fact that nobody was very great at the other man's lingo. I think that this war has done more to promote kinship than anything that has happened before.

Tell Dorrie when you see her that I know that I don't deserve ever to hear from her again for not having written a line. I make no excuses, but tell her that if she thinks she is going to escape hearing from me she is quite wrong, as I am going to write quite soon, and then if I don't get a reply, I shall write again & so on until I get leave in 1999 & & then . . . I shall call at No 50 B & holler through the letter box until somebody comes along and says how d'y do!! I have intended writing to Fender and several others but especially Fender. I am glad you gave the old bean the photos to have a look at. I will write him quite soon. I will write Uncle Tom and Gerish regarding the estate. It is my wish that you should have the whole of the estate – it is small enough in all conscience. I should like to have some of the things we had at No 59, but you won't find me unreasonable in my demands! The only things I am likely to be interested in are articles of silver (cups, etc., not cutlery or spoons!) and books. We had a jolly time at No 59. Anyway, you are not likely to be getting rid of much of the contents of No 59 yet awhile.

Mr and Mrs Shrosbree (SHROSBREE) are going on leave next week, and Mrs Shrosbree will get you out to lunch or something if you drop her a line. I have given her your address. Mrs Shrosbree is simply topping & is a wonderful hostess. You will like her no end, she is most awfully kind & is very interested in you – she has seen your 'mug' as portrayed by Cecil. Mr Shrosbree is a very cheery individual of good fun and kindness. He is a rising man here and quite brilliantly clever.

Much love, old bean. Love to Richard, Yours lovingly, George."

This letter illustrates the very lively social round in Calcutta and the closely knit nature of the British business community. Weekends were devoted to a round of exercise, golf and tennis to which squash was added later (often played with a professional 'marker' whose job was to make the sahib sweat and lose weight), swimming and riding. During the Prince of Wales's visit the following year, squash featured strongly, (the battle cruiser 'Renown' which carried him and his staff had a squash court specially built for the Prince on board). To the great concern of the medical staff for his safety, the Prince played endless chukkas of polo and rode a variety of horses in local races. George later bought a "topping" horse and, despite his foot, joined the Calcutta Light Horse. Members were trained in cavalry drills by professional soldiers and took part in paper-chases over jumps in south Calcutta most weekends. George was determined to take part and keep up with his contemporaries despite his disability.

George now writes to Uncle Tom about the estate.

"14 Harrington Mansions, Calcutta 23rd July 1920.

My Dear Uncle Tom,

At last, I am writing to you to talk business and to tell you about myself & how things are going on.

First of all, I will get over the business part. Sis told me some time ago that you wanted my views with regards to the 'estate' in order that the final settlement might be arrived at. It is my wish that the whole of the estate shall be handed over to Sis. I understand that there is now no liability attached to taking over the assets as the mortgages have all been cleared. It must be clear to even the most cautious solicitor that it can be nothing but to the advantage of Sis to take over the assets! The only proviso I make is that I want the various silver cups, etc., to be kept in order that Sis and I may divide them between us at a future date. Sis is engaged to be married and I want everything to be done as it would be done if I were in England. I know Dick Tonge very well and had I set out to choose the best fellow I knew, I couldn't have passed Tonge by. You have met him so know a little, perhaps, of the good fellow he is. I hate worrying you over these matters, but I remember you saying to me that I hadn't to worry about Alice as she would be looked after in my absence. As you know, Sis is more to me than anyone I know at the moment, & it is my chief wish that she shall be happily settled down. I am not a wealthy man (yet!) but am prepared to "stand up to" the expense of seeing Sis married (always hoping that it will not ruin me!!). With yourself standing by as the representative of the family, I feel quite happy, and you know that Sis's wishes are mine.

Having got that off my chest, I will tell you how things are over here. I expect you have heard from the family how I am progressing, and I am still going strong.

Financially, I am quite well off, having recently been given an increase which gives me considerably more now than I should have been getting at the conclusion of my agreement, had they adhered to the terms of the agreement. Everything is very expensive here but I am saving a little and manage to enjoy myself pretty well. There are several excellent golf courses near Calcutta, and I belong to two courses; one is the championship course with no women members (for 'liver' days!!) and the other is a delightful little club with tennis courts, stables, a golf course, and a topping club house (a sort of miniature Ranelagh). There is a great deal of tennis played at private houses; it is great fun and the courts are all of grass and are usually very fine as labour is so cheap and it is not difficult to have them well kept. There is a race course and we have some excellent racing with everything done in a very luxurious manner.

There is some of the finest snipe shooting in the world within thirty miles of Calcutta, & though there is a fair amount of shooting done, one can always find snipe to shoot in the season. The beauty of it is that there is no such thing as preserved snipe shooting, The first man on the ground has the right to shoot, even if the King came along!

Upcountry, big game shooting is different, as most of the best shooting is on some of the estates belonging to the Indian Princes, although several of the companies own or rent ground containing quite a lot of Tiger, Panther, Leopard, Bear, Deer, etc. I already have several invitations for October and hope to go to a place called Gaya to the estate of the Maharaja Tikari. I went up there about two months ago & had an excellent time for about five days. If you ever come to Calcutta, & I seriously hope that some of you will visit me some cold weather (from October to March), I can get you some great shooting.

Business goes strong; I am delighted to be at it again. The work is very interesting. The work consists of managing and running dozens of Companies, & naturally, with new flotations & general business, there is a great deal of accountancy and financial work to be done. I do most of the income tax now. The finance work here is enormous, and the factor of ever-changing rates of exchange makes it all the more difficult, and interesting. There is a great deal of money to be made here, and the firm are jolly good to us. They have been simply splendid in my own case. If I can only keep going long enough, there should be great chances later on, if I don't spoil my chances by making big mistakes which I hope I shall not do.

Well, I expect you have heard enough about it all for the time being. Before I close, I want to ask you if Harold still has that pair of 12 bore hammerless ejectors for sale, and if so, what is the price? I want a good hammerless ejector, (or a pair if they aren't too ruinous) 12 bore by one of the best makers, and if you should know of any second-hand, I shall be glad if you will let me know. I want something good and reliable as one uses ball sometimes against Tiger, Leopard, etc., and one doesn't want to be 'let down'.

Best love to Aunt Elsie & the girls & I hope Tom & Tress are as lean and fit as ever!! Tell them to drop me a line sometimes, and if you can spare the time, I should like to hear from you.

Hoping all are well. Yours affectionately, George."

Uncle Tom confirms on 7th December 1920 all the arrangements for the transfer of the estate to Sis.

"My dear George, I acknowledge receipt of your letter of 23rd July, and thank you for giving me your views with regards to the disposal of your father's estate. I note you wish the whole of the estate handed over to Alice, and I shall proceed as quickly as possible to have it turned over to her.

I have recently accepted, with Alice's sanction, a bid for six more houses, which leaves only one to be sold, and Mr Munro is busy trying to get a definite bid for it also. This will enable me to put the balance of the funds belonging to the estate into good Government stocks after paying off the balance of Mrs Campbell's mortgage (obviously a private mortgage – JMM).

A marriage settlement was duly prepared and signed by Tonge and Alice, the former putting up £2000 (well over £150,000 in today's terms JMM) and insuring his life, and she later binding herself to hand over the monies coming to her from the estate, which will form a fair nest egg for both of them if adversity should unexpectedly attack them in the future. I think that it is wise to tie up the bulk of the money so that Alice cannot touch it, and so far as I remember the arrangements, the money coming from your father's estate, or the bulk of them, will go to you if Alice dies without issue. Fergus and Harold act for Alice, but one of them will retire if you return to England permanently, and I think this is provided for in the deed. I shall attach a copy of this letter to your letter of 23rd July and put it away as a definite agreement that Alice is to have the whole of your Father's estate. Yours sincerely."

George and Uncle Tom had now made sure that Sis was adequately provided for, with the settlement and estate valued at a significant sum. Uncle Tom had sensibly waited until after the marriage at the end of the year to conclude things, and he personally paid for the costs of the wedding for his niece. George's letter to Uncle Tom gives an interesting insight into the complexity of his work for Birds.

George's next letter describes a trip to Jessore to take part in a big game shoot.

"14 Harrington Mansions Calcutta 9th June 1920

My dear Sis,

I got your last letter all serene and am glad you are still going strong. I bet there was a "certain liveliness" when the ring arrived! Let me know as soon as you are able when you are going to be married. Of course, you can't possibly work right up to the time you get spliced; you must chuck it a few months beforehand. Anyway, we will arrange something between us so don't worry, but let me know as soon as possible.

I wish I could see you and be with you now but what's the use of wishing? I can't get away, worst luck; you and Dick are going to be very happy, and you are in good hands. How I hope that you will come out here for a trip one cold weather. It would be topping and I know that you would love it.

Well, I have had my first big shoot upcountry. We didn't get much and I shot nothing larger than jungle fowl, which is like a large pheasant and flies like the wind. I enjoyed every moment of it though and will tell you all about it. We got leave for Friday and Monday (Saturday was a holiday) and Teasdale, Ferrier and I and three ladies left Calcutta on Thursday night. We arrived at Gaya, a distance of nearly 300 miles, at about 3.00 a.m. on Friday. We were met by Wakefield, our host, who is the agent of the Maharaja Tikari, & driven to the bungalow in an enormous six-cylinder car. Our servants and luggage followed in a lorry. We had drinks and pushed off to bed. Up at 8.00 a.m., wandered round the grounds shooting birds with a rook rifle. Had lunch at which Tikari (the Maharaja) was present. He is a good sort and was on the staff in France. At about 6.00 in the evening, we started off for the shooting box which is about 36 miles into the jungle along the grand trunk road, and consists of a topping bungalow and many outhouses. On the way there, we had our rifles & guns ready, as big and small game is constantly crossing the road, & often stands and gazes out at the lights of the car. This is a ripping form of shooting, footling along the road quite quietly, & when the game (bears, panther, deer, black buck etc.) crosses the road, stopping the car and having a bang at them. We arrived at about 10.00 p.m., had dinner & turned in. The party consisted of about fourteen people.

We got up again at about 2.00 a.m., got onto elephants and started off into the jungle. After a few miles, we came to the spot where we were to shoot & where the machans had been built (wooden platforms up trees). We left the elephants and perched ourselves up the trees & waited for dawn when the animals would be returning to the hill. We left again about 6.00 a.m., returned to the shooting box, had a light breakfast & went to bed. We did the same the following evening, and went along the road before dinner, and again after dinner, & got back about 2.00 a.m. when we changed and left again for another shooting ground perched up on huge rocks. Home again about 8.00 a.m. and more sleep. On Sunday night we returned to Gaya and on Monday went off to a place called Buah Gaya, where there is a wonderful temple of Buddha which is the spot where he is supposed to have acquired his learning and wonderful power. I got some good photos which I will send you in time. Left Gaya at about 5.00 p.m. on Monday & arrived in Calcutta at about 11.00 a.m. The whole trip was delightful; how you would have loved it. We have a standing invitation to shoot there whenever we can get away, and a special night for Christmas, which is the best time of the year for shooting.

Everything else goes along in the same old way and there is plenty of work to do. I want you to have some things packed up & sent to me . . . Wolsley Valise (green canvas & straps . . . Gun Case . . . Cartridge bag . . . Service Jacket. All of these things are in the large canvas kit bag which I think was sent to Aunt Bess. The gun case may be separate. Well, old bean, I will chuck it once more. Much love to you and Dick. Yours lovingly, George."

The practice of big game shooting was common in the colonies before the Second World War, particularly in India and Africa. Different standards and customs applied a hundred years ago. First of all, the population of India has quadrupled since 1920, creating enormous pressures on available land through the demands for land for growing food, and correspondingly, there was a very substantial reduction in jungle habitat, the natural home of these animals. The Bengal tiger, unique to India, has suffered a reduction in numbers from well over 100,000 in the 1920s to just a little over 3,000 now, as a result of hunting and poaching, largely for animal parts for aphrodisiacs and eastern medicines. Other animals, bears, elephants, deer and black buck, rhinoceros, monkeys and snakes have been hunted to the verge of extinction. All of these animals are dangerous to man in any event; two man-eating tigers killed and ate over four hundred humans before being killed by Jim Corbett, the legendary hunter, in the Kumaon district, much to the relief of terrified villagers. A man-eating leopard, hunting mainly at night, killed over four hundred. But attitudes have now completely changed as to hunting these animals for sport.

At that time, the Royal family were famously entertained by successive Kings of Nepal in the shoots in the Terai, most notably George V during his 1911 visit after the Delhi Durbar, and his son Edward, Prince of Wales, in December 1921. The author's grandfather, Colonel Frederick O'Kinealy, also attended this 1921 shoot and his diaries of the visit describe the shoot in graphic detail. So, an example was set from the very top of society, and big game hunting was the norm and regarded as nothing out of the ordinary . . ., and this continued until the end of the 1960s.

Meanwhile, the weather was heating up before the monsoon broke later in the month.

"14 Harrington mansions 17ᵗʰ June 1920

My dear Sis,

Just a short note this time as I am in the office and there is not much time left to catch the mail.

Glad to hear you & Richard went down to St. Albans. I expect they were glad. They are good sorts really and have often been very kind. It is only in certain moods that one finds them anything but charming. I am glad that T.M. (Uncle Tom Morton) and Richard hit it off. I expect that T.M. is frightfully bucked and will be only too delighted to talk farming with Richard. I don't expect that it will take much persuasion to get him to stay with you both when you marry and settle down on the farm!

Morton Steven lunched with us a few weeks ago & we hope to spend the weekend with him at Jessore. He is a sportsman & is putting up the three of us from Thursday (Friday is a holiday) to Sunday night. We are motoring out – a distance of about 80 miles. Will tell you all about it next mail.

I can't find out about Arthur Sieger, but will make further enquiries & let you know. Von Ernsthausen is closed up. Enemy firm. Well, old bean, I will chuck it. More next mail. Love to R, Yours lovingly, George.

P.S. I enclose cheque for £8 for material. Expect it will arrive shortly. G."

In his next letter, he describes the trip to Jessore.

"14 Harrington Mansions Calcutta 23ʳᵈ June 1920

My dear Sis,

Nothing from you this week, so I suppose that you are busy. I heard from Aunt Bess that she had been down to dinner with you and one of Richard's aunts. Am glad it went off well, and hope you sent them all home 'hic'ing with happiness or rather 'hic'- appiness!

Well, last week was simply topping. We arranged to leave Calcutta at 6.00 a.m. but didn't get away until 6.35 a.m. My bearer took our luggage by train & we motored. The distance is about 76 miles. It was a topping run, and we arrived at about 10.45 having spent about an hour over breakfast. On arrival, we had another breakfast, and after a yarn, we turned in for a nap. Tea at 4.00 p.m. and golf afterwards in Morton's garden. There are about 10 holes, some of them well over 200 yards, so you can guess the extent of his grounds. The house is ripping and he has two lakes and stables with two horses. Quite palatial. After golf, we loafed and then dinner out with some friends of his. On Saturday, Teasdale and I had to be in Calcutta, so we got an early morning train and got into Calcutta about 10.30 a.m. We left again about 2.50 p.m. & arrived in time to have a short chat & then change for dinner. Morton had five people in and we had bridge afterward.

On Sunday morning, Morton and I went for a ripping ride for about a couple of hours (I was very stiff afterwards – needless to say!). We returned & lugged the other two out & had breakfast & then went to the native prison which Morton inspected in his official capacity, we lending our commanding appearances to support his official visit – quite an imposing spectacle. We then started off with another party in a car to visit a man about 27 miles away to have lunch. On the way, I shot a jackal with a little .22 bore rifle – some shot! The natives were delighted & Teasdale took our photographs, myself nearly as delighted as the natives.

We had a topping run back and arrived at about ten o'clock. On the way, I shot two more jackal – more delighted natives, as the jackal eat chicken & ducks and small babies! It sounds funny but the deaths amongst children under 12 years old owing to jackal are very numerous. Total bag – jackal three, all with a .22 rifle. Two days later, Morton strolled into the flat & had breakfast with us, much to our delight. He has got a move to the secretariat in Calcutta or Darjeeling, wherever Government happens to be, so he is an under-secretary. He is a lucky old devil as these jobs are the plums of the civil service and he will be in close touch with the government. He deserves it as he is a brainy bloke for himself. I shall see him more often now, I hope. With the least amount of luck, he will make a name for himself.

Well, the rains have broken at last and we have weeping skies day after day now. This will last until September and then all will be fair and delightful. I received the shirting – it is ripping stuff. If I had searched the whole world I couldn't have got better. It does make a difference to get home material, it is so much finer & nicer, & the native tailors are very good and make things very well & are absurdly cheap.

No more now. I wish I were with Richard and you. What a time we'd have. Love to both of you. Yours lovingly, George."

George seems to have hit it off with Morton Steven, and, although there is no evidence that they were related, sharing the same family name they probably exchanged family details. The letter illustrates the life of the district officer within the Indian Civil Service (ICS). They attracted the finest of intelligent people and had a reputation for fairness, integrity and incorruptibility. Carrying big responsibilities at an early age, they were respected for their fine administrative abilities and knowledge of local languages.

Jessore is now in Bangladesh, but then was in East Bengal, administered directly from Calcutta, reversing the split administration of West and East Bengal introduced by the Viceroy, Viscount Lord Curzon, at the turn of the century. This reversal was a part of the announcement by George V at the Delhi Durbar of 1911 which also moved the central seat of Government from Calcutta to Delhi. This resulted in the building and design of New Delhi by Lutyens. Now, of course, they are two separate countries, India and Bangladesh, the one largely Hindu and the other largely Muslim. Jessore was also close to the jute-growing districts upon which Birds depended for their jute processing businesses, a fact which was to cause them significant problems at the Partition of India in 1947.

George's next letter illustrates the change in Calcutta's social activity brought about by the breaking of the monsoon.

"14 Harrington Mansions Calcutta 1ˢᵗ July 1920

My dear Sis,

I received a letter from you dated 3ʳᵈ June; I think it came the mail before last. Anyway, you were in the throes of entertaining future relations! It must be very trying, for I think nothing can be so tiring as being "on parade" before critical eyes – especially those of the gentler (!) sex. Daniel's lot would seem child's play compared with this ordeal of being engaged. I had a letter from Aunt Bess, & she described your party and said all went well, & that Gwen Steadman helped like a good 'un. You have said from time to time Gwen must be a thorough sportsman. Well, good luck to you, and I hope the luncheon party was a success!

Have done nothing for a fortnight – ever since our return from Jessore, except a little golf and an occasional motor trip and we went out after dinner & I drove the car home. I hope to be able to buy a motor coat button & then shall be well on the way to becoming the owner of a fleet of Rolls Royces!! Seriously I should be surprised if I buy a small car next year. It is essential here especially for a 'hitch and kick' member of the community. Walking very far here in the hot weather is apt to become a little (!) tiresome. Teasdale is a thorough sportsman, & most kind-hearted & though not a hitch and kick, is one of 'us', so I get the use of his car very often, & he always gives me a lift home etc.

And how is old Richard? I hope he is "in the pink as it leaves me at present". Tell him I hope to see him out here 'if and when', and maybe we shall manage to sink a pint, or maybe a pint and a half when we do meet.

I played golf this morning. Morton Steven came out to Jodhpur, and I gave him a round and he breakfasted afterwards at our flat. Morton is a good sort; I like him no end.

Well, I must chuck it. Much love & hope you are very fit. Yours lovingly, George."

Monsoon, "upcountry" business trips to Tata Jamshedpur & business development work

The golf courses were drenched with rain and tennis was limited to breaks in the rain. Squash was yet to take off, with the Calcutta Squash Club eventually established on the South side of the Maidan close to the Turf Club. The rain also closed down racing. A rugby season later opened again after World War Two playing during the monsoon to take advantage of the softer grounds. There was an "all-India" rugby tournament involving teams from the Assam tea gardens as well as the Ceylonese and Southern tea gardens, Karachi and the Mahratta police force. The local Calcutta rugby sides also were prominent. We played in 37-degree centigrade heat and 90 % relative humidity, praying that the ball was not passed so as to avoid running with it . . . "Mad dogs and Englishmen" but no midday sun!

A colleague of George's, A.S. Oliver, who was to join Birds as an accountant at the Titagur mills in 1921 (and later became a partner in 1943), was a member of the Calcutta rugby team before the war, playing in the centre. Cricket, however, was the main cold-weather team activity at the Calcutta Cricket Club in Ballygunge.

"14 Harrington Mansions Calcutta 15th July 1920

My dear Sis,

I received your letter all serene, and to get over finance at once! I have asked Rowley to transfer £50 to your a/c at the same time increasing your allowance to £8.6.8 a month. Of course you asked me for cash and why not? I should be angry if you wanted oof and didn't let me know. It is the best news that I have heard for some time to hear that you are taking a real long holiday; it is much needed and should do you no end of good if you get out of London & have a quiet time & do not worry. I have just had an increase of pay so you need not worry about my being short. I am now getting more than I should have been in my third year under the agreement, so you can guess the increase has been a good one. They are jolly good to one if one sticks in & works; the firm doesn't overlook it.

Well, I am still going strong, and have just been upcountry to Tata's engineering works. They had a large claim against us & one Roberts, a very clever engineer, & myself went up to represent the firm & arrive at a settlement. This we did and came off with colours flying. The firm was very pleased with our effort.

We (the occupants of the flat) still go out shooting now and then & hope to go out this evening. At present, I have to borrow a gun, but hope to buy one soon. I refuse to buy anything but a first-class hammerless ejector 12 bore and have not yet come across one that is reasonably priced. If you hear of anything really good below say £30 (second-hand of course) let me know by wire. In the meantime, I am trying to buy one here.

Write and let me know when and where you are going for your holiday. Much love. Excuse short letter. Love to Richard & I hope that he is fit, yours lovingly, George."

He refers to Tata's "engineering works". The claim is likely to have been against Birds for the poor quality of silica refractory bricks manufactured at Kumardhubi, and is recorded in the First World War in the Birds history and was a long-standing problem. The reference to the "engineering works" rather than the steel works suggests that the complaint could have been from the repair shop for rebricking ladles. These were used in transporting molten iron from the blast furnaces at Jamshedpur to the steel works, or alternatively used with finished molten steel poured into moulds before cropping and rolling into various shapes. Both operations carried serious safety risks; for example, moisture in the ladle or damp bricks which could cause violent explosions, and the stopper in the pouring ladle could also become jammed causing a leaking stopper or a blocked ladle. The brickwork needed to be precise, and fully dried out . . . such are the hazards of steelmaking.

George's next letter describes the effects of the monsoon.

"14 Harrington Gardens, Calcutta 28th July 1920.

My Dear Sis,

The mail is due today but having a spare few minutes, I am writing a few lines before I get your letter (I hope!). I received the shaving mirror all serene for which many thanks. There hasn't been a great deal of excitement lately. We occasionally get an evening's shooting and dinners and suppers have been fairly frequent and there was a topping dance last Saturday evening. I still get my golf fairly & now the rains are here there isn't much to do except golf & "poodle fakin'."

'The Rains' probably doesn't convey a lot to you, but it is a real thing here as the whole of the low-lying country gets flooded, and the rice fields get the requisite moisture. The air is so damp that in one day, leather etc. gets covered with mildew & boots have to be watched constantly & kept clean.

It is an amusing sight to see the Indian farmers wading about their 'paddy' (rice) fields, up to their waist in water, with the 'bullocks' well in the water also. The floods upcountry are already becoming serious in parts, and several men have been sent upcountry to take matters in hand & find out what is to be done. In one instance, one of our railways has been carried away at one point, thereby isolating one of our companies temporarily, & I expect a trolley line will have to be run out. In another case, a new bridge (costing about £50,000) has given at the base of one of the trestles and it is about three feet out of line which causes the bridge to be unsafe at the moment until it can be got at. All traffic beyond that point is temporarily suspended also, but they are hoping to get it patched up fairly soon. These incidents happen at most rains, and cause a certain amount of dislocation of traffic and therefore trade. It soon gets all serene, though, once the rains have passed (September). I am plugging along, & Slater, our chief, is going home tomorrow & I shall have a good deal more to do. The experience I hope to get should be invaluable, and if everything goes well, I don't think that it will do me any harm! I don't expect Slater will be here again until October or November, though he is only going to London on a business trip.

I am finishing this just before the mail goes. I got your letter yesterday and was very glad to hear you are still going strong & having a good time. Am glad that Richard liked Margaret and Fergus & that the like was mutual. How could it have been otherwise, knowing them all? I wonder how the visit to St Albans went off – well, I hope.

I am writing to Uncle Tom by this mail re finances & he may write & get you to take over all the assets of the estate as I have told him that you are to get it all except a few articles of silver which we can divide at some future date.

Nothing more now. Love to Richard & hope he is very fit. Yours lovingly, George."

The monsoon in India starts off on the coast of Mumbai to the West and sweeps across the Northern part of the country before returning to the South. Generally, it arrives at the back end of June in Calcutta. It brings high humidity, damp, and torrential rains. Low-lying areas, villages and dwellings flood. Cholera becomes rife; while the writer was in India in 1962, there were 200 deaths a day in Bengal from cholera and many more from snake bites as snakes were flooded out and took refuge from the water in low-lying dwellings during the particularly heavy monsoon of 1962.

Returning from a visit to the oil fields in north-west Assam, I remember flying over the Brahmaputra through dark steepling storm clouds with lightening flashing, the river below like a sea from 12,000 feet with water from horizon to horizon, a dramatic exhibition of nature at its most powerful. The first rice crop was flooded and largely destroyed by the inundation and combination of rain and meltwater from the mountains. Food shortages followed in the autumn with famine in some areas.

The concrete bridge built before the war across the Teesta River by Birds had, by 1941, been carried away by rain and meltwater from the Kanchenjunga massif, and our journey up to Kalimpong as children involved crossing the river on a temporary suspension bridge.

As mentioned, Birds were going through a consolidation and reorganisation period. The senior partner, B.A. White, accompanied by Slater, (George's chief) were going home for consultations with the London board and particularly Lord Cable concerning the restructuring of the company. Later that year, both White and Slater were to return. White's health was to break and Cable himself was to come out that winter to take charge of implementing the restructuring. During their absence, George was to take on additional departmental responsibilities as his next letter illustrates.

"14 Harrington Gardens Calcutta 12ᵗʰ August 1920

My dear Sis,

I received your last two letters all serene. I didn't write last mail as I was upcountry at our Engineering works & Pottery works the whole of last week. I didn't expect to remain there for very long – not more than two days, but when I got there, I found a week was necessary. All of these shows require a great deal of reorganisation both from the practical, & the financial, accounts & costing point of view. One Roberts, who is in charge of the engineering dept in Calcutta, also went up. We have both been banging away at these shows for months now, and at last, our efforts are beginning to bear fruit, though we are far from the end of our task yet.

It is all very interesting, and gives scope to anyone who is keen & willing to work like the devil!

Since Slater has gone home, I have been given more and more to do and it is all that I can do to keep it down. I am managing to do it all serene up to the present time, but am not sure of the future. I expect it will pan out all serene, & I can stand hard work at most times; in fact, I welcome it.

Well, I am glad to hear that you are enjoying life. You make me green with envy when you speak of the Hyde Park Club being as delightful as ever! I enjoyed the dances more than any I have been at which brings back to me Miss Sanctuary 'wot was'. Do you ever hear of or see her now she is married? She was a topping good sort & a ripping dancer, but I suppose she will have given up such frivolity now!! I think the best evening we had there was with Miss S, May Edwards, you, Cooper, Richard & myself. We have topping dances out here, but not in the same class as the Hyde Park, eh!

Am glad you like Richard's people; they sound topping. It must be strange for Richard to meet some of our people after what you say about his. I don't make any apology for them – they will not alter this side of the Jordan, & one must take them as one finds them. It is devilish hard at times, but soon we hope you will be happily paid up with your own circle of friends, & removed from the patronage of some of our dear relations, who would patronise the Almighty if he were immediately available. They have their points too you know, but thank goodness there are a few of the very best in Scotland whom Richard will meet one of these days I suppose.

I had a topping letter from Rowley by last mail. Why don't you arrange a meeting between old Richard and Rowley? Rowley is about the best man I know, and as I place Richard in the same class, I think they ought to meet. Rowley mentioned that he hadn't met Richard yet, but that he hoped to someday soon. They would like one another no end, I know.

Life is still going strong. I have had a fairly gay time lately, and have been to the theatre fairly often, & spent a weekend out at a place about forty miles down the river. We had a ripping time there, the only downbeat being the number of mosquitos. Last Sunday we went to the zoo, & went for an evening motor run after dinner. Tonight, we are going to see "Our Mr Hepplewhite" played by the Waring Company, which is just as good as many first-class London Companies.

Will you order a half dozen of my photographs from Searle? I should like three of the plain clothes and three of the uniform head and shoulders (not the full length).

Well, I will chuck it. I also have a feeling that you and Richard will visit me some day. This place is the best in the world from November to Feb or March, and the rest of India (Kashmir and the hills, not the plains) for the remainder of the year. What a time we shall all have when you do come out!

Love to Richard. I am going to write the old 'bird' soon. Hope your holiday is going strong. Yours lovingly, George.

If you know the address of the Procters, let me have it."

George's visit 'upcountry' needs some explanation. As mentioned before, Birds were going through a 'post war' restructuring brought about by the 'post-war' slump. During the war, Burrakur, Birds principal colliery operation, had spawned two new Limited Companies.

The first of these two "war babies", registered in 1915, was Kumardhubi Engineering Works Ltd. (K.E.W Ltd for short) provided engineering support to Bird's and other companies' colliery operations in the area. It was what we would call today a 'jobbing' engineering operation carrying out repairs and manufacturing steelwork. The works also incorporated a foundry producing castings for the railway operations. During the war, demand for its services had expanded to the extent that towards the end of the war, it reported an eighteen-month order book. Stocks of raw materials, particularly steel, were consequently at an all-time high and the post-war slump left it in a financially unstable and significantly over-stocked position.

The second of these twins was the Kumardhubi Fireclay and Silica Works Ltd. It was dependent almost entirely upon Tata's burgeoning steelworks at Jamshedpur. Development had started with experiments in 1914 into refractory brick production for lining furnaces and ancillary equipment (e.g., ladles) to replace imports, which were running at around Rs 250,000 per year, using indigenous raw materials. Tatas were given Rs 150,000 in shares for cash at par, and options to subscribe for 50% of any future capital, with Birds appointed as managing agents. The company also supplied the railways with refractory products, (for locomotive boilers and fire-boxes) and had its own additional production of pottery products including stoneware pipes and glazed tiles.

The production of fireclay products had got off to a poor start with quality not meeting expectations. But in spite of this, production was increased and a five-year contract signed with Tatas in 1918 for increased quantities.

Two other companies were formed around this time. The first of these was Loyabad Coke Manufacturing Co. Ltd. which, as its name implies, converted coking coal to coke for Tata's blast furnaces. The other new venture was the Sijua (Jherriah) Electric Supply Company which went into production in 1917 supplying seven companies in the area with electricity.

Another venture, The Bisra Stone Lime Company, transferred its managing agency to Birds in 1914, and prospecting by the intrepid geologist Gordon Duff at nearby Raipura revealed enormous deposits of both limestone and dolomite earmarked to be developed by Bisra. This geological development led to the discovery also of vast deposits of high-grade ironstone – haematite with an iron content of 65%, and led to the formation of The Orissa Minerals Development Company in 1918. Thus, by the end of the war, Birds had secured a commanding position in most of the ingredients for steelmaking . . . iron ore, limestone, coke and refractory bricks, but excepting manganese ore, used in making fine grain high tensile and ductile steels.

The idea then grew of Birds establishing a steelworks and negotiations with Cammell Laird were carried out with the development of project codenamed TUSCAL being worked up to establish an integrated iron and steel works. A geologist named Henry Day also identified deposits of manganese ore sufficient to supply TUSCAL with 70,000 tons a year into the future, and prospecting licences were taken out with extraction starting in 1923. TUSCAL, however, never got off the ground due to lack of sufficient demand for steel and the 1930's depression. Sales of manganese ore started although iron ore sales did not start until much later in 1930.

There were other ventures started by Birds around this time but the level of new activity was not sustainable and consolidation and restructuring were the order of the day. This was to occupy much of George's time during his first tour. To keep K.E.W. going, Birds made an interest-free loan and paid its head office expenses, as the company's engineering support operations were essential to keep the profitable collieries running, even though they were operating at a loss.

George's next letter asks Sis to find him a shotgun reflecting perhaps his growing prosperity as a result of his salary increase.

"Bird & Co, Calcutta 26th Aug 1920

My Dear Sis,

Have not heard from you for two mails but suppose you have been busy. I received your cable re gun and replied as follows "Gun fourteen and a half one and three quarters three inches." (Attached to the letter is a drawing of each dimension). I suppose it was understood. If you have already sent out the old case there will be no need to buy another and all that will be necessary will be a strong box in which to pack the gun. I suppose that T.M. has been on the job for me or did you do it yourself? I expect you have managed to get me just what I wanted in your own particular way. You always seem to get things for me which I couldn't improve on myself! I suppose it is because you know my tastes almost as well as I know them myself, and you know that I invariably go for the best, provided that I am not paying for unnecessary flourish! There is a 20% import duty on guns so don't overstate the value. Guns out here are very expensive and at £35 + £7 I shall be getting jolly good value for money, as one has to be very lucky to get anything really good at that price.

Well, I am still going strong. Lots to do work & play. I went to the Saturday Club last Friday and had a very jolly evening. Played two rounds of golf on Sunday & went out on Sunday evening. Yesterday was another holiday so played two rounds again and dined out and went to the theatre afterwards and then went on to supper with Maharajah Tikari — a thorough sportsman! We are going up to his Raj in October for a few days shooting. It should be great fun. If I shoot a tiger, I will send you one of its hairs.

The increases of pay for the staff have just been put through, & they all come up to me before going to the firm. We have several hundred babus and we get many & varied letters putting forward their claims for consideration. The enclosed is a specimen of one of the applications! The applicant has burst into verse & the enclosed is a true and faithful copy of his application.

More next week. Love to Richard. I wish you were both coming out this cold weather. Yours lovingly, George."

This is the poem:

Messrs. Bird & Co. (THROUGH G.B. MORTON ESQR.)

1
Oh "Ho": this Company is a big firm dear Sir,
I grieve for small Rs.2/- from you are my respected here
Ashu Babu who has got Rs.7/- is an outdoor Stores Sircar
Who knows not how to read and write English really Sir.

2
Regret very much "Oh Lord" if be true and kind
your poor servant of Messrs. Bird & Co. is hungry behind
Bearers, Sweepers and Methars have got paid Rs.2/- in each hand
But am I like them to get so? Oh kind, Please, do more by my own hand.

3

An increase of Rs.2/- is worth a cup of only tea
In this famine dear hard time for me;
You are very kind master; please do and help for me
If you conceive the helpless your poor servant if you see.

4

I am in want of Rs10/- for my only house rent
I do not get my sufficient food to have not been sent,
May Lord kindly accept which I am longing to have,
In this hard days of bad time if you save.

5

I pray God for our long life and sound health
I wish you success of everything and on good health
Be stately and respectable, happy and gay,
Poor I am your helpless Gopal Ch. Day (Stores Deptt.)

This is just one of a number of writings collected by George during his career in India. They have a charm of their own, grammatically written in tune with local language. George was a stickler for correct English and these letters would have appealed to his sense of humour.

George's next letter deals with family issues.

"Bird & Co Calcutta 9ᵗʰ September 1920

My Dear Sis,

I received a letter from you by last mail and am glad to hear that things are going strong. I hope Dick manages to find a suitable farm for I expect both of you want to settle down now & grow pigs 'n' things. It doesn't do to be too precipitous though & time spent in finding just the farm Dick wants will be well spent, and if delay is caused, it will be worth it eventually. Many thanks for the trouble you and Dick took over the gun; am much obliged. I suppose you received my cable all serene, & hope it is on the way to being sent off.

Well, old bean, there is not a great deal of news. I seem to have been doing less in the evenings than a short while ago & except for an occasional dance or theatre party, I spend my time working like the devil during the day and spending quiet evenings at the flat. I play golf most weekends and one day we went for a flip in the aeroplane. It was topping and Calcutta looked the quaintest little place you ever saw. The weather is now at its worst and it is the weather that makes me feel that dancing is not what it was! When the cold weather comes again, I have no doubt that my old enthusiasm will return unless I am grown too old and serious-minded!! I sometimes think that I was spoilt, as far as dancing is concerned, by the top-hole time we had in Town last year.

The 'chummery' & I hope to go upcountry this month for a bang at Black Buck. We have been promised some good sport & there is a short holiday so I think we shall go.

101

Am glad Harold and Bee did you proud. They are good sorts I suppose, & am glad the former is becoming more human. It is probably only a question of time, for I have no doubt the London Stock Exchange will teach him that there are others in the world. Life is too short to be anything but friendly towards our relations, but one can be friendly without being fast friends. If Harold has ceased to patronise his betters, then he has gone quite a considerable distance towards being tolerated by his senior cousins.

Am glad to hear that Effie is still going strong. Give her my love & tell her that one day I hope to write her a few lines. Up to the present I have written to very few people, but always hope to do more.

Give my love to Dorrie and Charlie. I am going to write quite soon.

My love to old Dick & you and here's hoping that you will be out here before I am in England! Yours lovingly, George."

Snipe shooting, the *Darshan* of Lt. Col. Maharaja Gopal Saran Narain Singh of Tikrit at Gaya, the Calcutta "season" & paper-chasing

In George's next letter, he describes going snipe shooting for the first time, and how he is now walking more freely, has chucked his sticks, and adjusted to the wounds on his feet.

"Bird & Co Calcutta 16th September 1920

My Dear Sis,

Got your long letter written from Neion which sounds a delightful spot, and am glad that you are having a jolly time. You were in need of a real long holiday & I hope you have a real rest.

Well, I have shot my first snipe and as luck would have it, the first snipe I shot at I killed. We have taken on a shikari who is now part of our establishment. He gets paid so much a month & so much for every day's shooting we do – which is an excellent arrangement. He spends his days searching for good spots for game round about Calcutta, and reports to us every few days. Last Friday he reported that he had found an excellent spot for snipe about 38 miles out. He made all arrangements and Teasdale, Ferrier & I left the flat at about 4.30 a.m. on Sunday. We motored out & started shooting about 6.30 a.m. None of us are any good with a gun at present, but we are improving rapidly. I shot four snipe which isn't too bad for a novice as they are devilish quick & hard to hit. In order to get snipe, one has to walk almost knee-deep in water through the flooded rice fields. It is topping fun, though on Sunday, we had golf shoes & stockings on so got a trifle wet! I am getting better on my pins every day & can now play 18 holes of golf without the aid of a stick. In fact, I have placed my sticks in a corner of the room where I hope that they will remain, & may the dust grow thick upon them!! Next Sunday, we are shooting hare and green pigeon and the following weekend, we hope to get Black Buck.

We are through the worst of the rains now and the drying process is on. With any luck, by the middle of next month, we shall be at the commencement of the cold weather, in fact, it is distinctly cooler now & in the early mornings & evenings, it is delightfully cool and pleasant. Soon we shall be stopping the fans and once more wearing ordinary tweed suits like summer in London, the only difference being that the winter evenings are decidedly more cool than in Europe. The winter here is rather like September at home.

I am still finding lots of work to do, and am liking my job more and more. At present, there seems to be lots of scope.

Love to Richard, and I hope that he is very fit. I will write him soon. Yours lovingly, George."

Snipe shooting was a popular cold-weather sport, and although he does not mention it, it seems as if George's gun may have arrived. Snipe are particularly difficult to shoot, flying straight while getting up to speed for 20 yards or so and then jinking. They get slower as the sun gets up. Delicious eating, they however go "off" in heat, and so needed to be brought back and eaten straight away, sometimes packed in ice or in a wide-mouthed thermos flask to keep the birds fresh. The rice fields or *jheils* were flooded at that time of year, but the footwear of golf shoes was not really suitable and it would have been better instead to wear proper snipe boots made of canvas with rubber soles. The deadly puff adder also enjoyed basking in the fields and so wearing thick stockings was important. Drier scrub and jungle ground would hold hares and green pigeon, both also good eating.

George's right foot would give him trouble all his life, and he developed a support of thick felt under his foot, with a hole cut in it to support the foot around a spike of bone which protruded under what had been his big toe. I remember his handmade shoes from Peels of London. In Calcutta, his shoes would have been specially made for him by the excellent Chinese boot and shoe makers around lasts shaped exactly to the profile of his feet, with extra depth to accommodate the felt. All his letters transmit a real determination to take a full part in all sports, and he even joined the Calcutta Light Horse for a short time later.

This was the successor regiment to Gardiner's Horse, a regular cavalry regiment, but now recruiting part-time cavalrymen, drawn from the young bloods of commerce, but drilled and trained by regular cavalry NCOs. Paper-chasing was a popular weekend sport in the fields of South Calcutta, a four or five-mile paper trail steeplechasing course set over low jumps and the ditches between fields. The acknowledgement of his letter of resignation from the Light Horse gives no reason for his decision, but no doubt the strain on his foot in the stirrup might have played a part. Golf, tennis and snipe shooting appear to have occupied most of his weekends, although later, and especially during the Second World War, when we children were in the hills, both my mother and father made extensive treks from Kalimpong into Sikkim, Tibet up into the Chumbi Valley.

There is now a gap in the letters, not I suspect for any reason other than they may have been lost, as he was writing regularly.

"14 Harrington Gardens Calcutta 1ˢᵗ November 1920.

My dear Sis,

I have just received your letter written after you had seen Uncle Tom & fixed things up for your wedding. What a happy thought for you and Dick to have the reception at Jules; many a cheery evening we have all spent there & many more may we have. T.M. is a sportsman to stand the reception. I bet friend Emile sees to it that all goes well. It seems funny but by the time that you get this letter you will be Mrs Tonge & you & old Dick will be sunning yourselves somewhere in the South of France.

Today is the anniversary of my leaving England, and, as I sit here writing, I have on my table photographs of you, Will & Rowley, three of the best pals God ever gave to any man. I remember how I hated leaving you all alone, and hoped that you might be happy. My dearest wish is that you should be happy – it always will be & I know it is Dick's. I don't know who is the luckier, you or he. May you both have every happiness. I hope to hear all about your wedding & the presents & the guests & everything so just make up your mind that you are going to write me a real long history.

At present, I am feeling rather like a small boy who has just returned to school. I had a topping time at Gaya & got a very fine head of Black Buck and one of Chinkara (a Bovine Deer). I had shots, or rather the man with me had shots at three Bears; I was too slow in spotting them as it was at night. I had shots at Sambar, an enormous stag, almost as large as a horse, but missed him; excitement I suppose. The Rajah got a Sambar with a magnificent head – almost 50-inch antlers so you can imagine the size – 51 inch is the record. I could have shot a hyena, but let him go as we were after more important game & didn't want to frighten it! I shot quite a number of hares, sand grouse, partridge, wild duck & quails. We had a wonderful time altogether. The holiday was the Indian's Poojah, similar to our Christmas, & is a great time for festivals both religious and otherwise. Whilst we were at Gaya, the Rajah asked us all to lunch at his town of Tikari which consists of an enormous fort & a regular town. We motored out about 18 miles & reached the town at about 1.30 p.m. There are no Europeans in the town & our entrance was most impressive. The place was crowded with gaily dressed Indians & children & the houses were decorated. We entered the most impressive looking fort you can imagine, just like a castle in a fairy story & after a few yards – about 150 – arrived at the foot of a long stone staircase. Here we were met by Wakefield, our host, who is the Rajah's right-hand man.

We were conducted by an armed & magnificent guard through stone-flagged passages & up & down stairs to the Rajah's private apartments where the genial sportsman met us & took us along to luncheon. We had a topping time as he is a real good sort & quite European in his ways (& stories!) and everything. I really believe that he is happier with his English friends & guests than his own people. After lunch, we stood on the top of the buildings & looked at the enormous crowds below. It was a wonderful sight. There were thousands of fine-looking men, the Rajah's vassals, who occasionally give a deep-throated roar for the health of the 'Maharajah'. They had all come to do homage and offer gifts

& to see the Rajah whom they hadn't seen for five years as he has been on the staff in France. Can you imagine the scene?

After we had stood round for a time, there was a procession of elephants, camels, Gods, Goddesses etc. etc. & the Rajah left to do some religious ceremony. He then returned & we had tea. He quietly told the few of us who were staying with Wakefield to remain & have an Indian Dinner & see an Indian Play. It was most amusing; we laughed until we didn't know whether we had tummies or not! After that we had dinner & after that, we went & saw a Nauch, or an entertainment by Indian dancing girls. It was quite good, though, by 1 a.m., we were ready to go home & proceeded to clear off. The next day we shot duck or rather shot at duck for some !!! idiot frightened them &they got up off the lake & water & flew over us just out of range. There were thousands of them & they were flying over us for over half an hour. Since my return to Calcutta, I have worked like ten thousand devils mad with rage!! I am finishing this letter in the office.

One of these days I will send you and Dick a wedding present; don't think that I have forgotten you both, but I can find nothing I like here & shall either get you something of the country or ask you what you want and send you a cheque.

Suppose that I must close. The very best love to you both and may you both have long life and prosperity in addition to my oft-repeated wish for happiness – the most important of all, & not the bovine variety!! Yours lovingly, George.

P.S. If any business crops up requiring my signature, please refer to Rowley. Don't forget gun. G."

***32** The shooting party with Maharaja Tikrit at Gaya*

33

34 *George in the middle of the line*

35 (Opposite & above) The gathering of the Rajputs below the Maharaja's palace to celebrate his return

This wonderfully descriptive letter starts with a wistful reference on the anniversary of his leaving England and the photographs of Sis and George's dead brother Will and his friend Rowley on his desk. George must have had moments of home-sickness, perhaps relieved by the so very fresh new experiences described in his letters during his first tour of India.

His host in Tikari was Lt Col Maharaja Gopal Saran Narain Singh, an honorary colonel in the British army, who was returning home after a five-year absence during the First World War. His ancestors had received the property from the Moghul Emperor Akbar. The forests between Agra and Bengal were home to dacoits and robbers who regularly plundered the Moghul caravans and so an arrangement was made with the leading dacoit for protection in exchange for the gift of the land. The Maharajah had volunteered for service at the onset of war, and went as a Lieutenant despatch rider to General Haig, making a gift of a squadron of tanks.

There was an incident at the front when the Germans complained that their concealed steel plates protecting sniper posts were being taken out with a weapon that contravened the Geneva Convention. A group of staff officers sent to investigate found the young maharaja shooting out the plates with a double-barrelled Westley-Richards .476 tiger rifle! Another version of this event has the Maharaja arriving in his gorgeous pyjamas (pantaloons after the Rajput style) bearing a gun case, requesting a loop hole, and proceeding to take out the German sniper positions.

After a quarrel with Warren Hastings in the previous century, the Tikari lands had been restored in 1911 to the Maharaja together with the original title and a 13-gun salute. The level of hospitality by the young Maharaja Tikari rivalled that given by maharajas to the British by Indian royalty in the 19th and early 20th centuries. so graphically described in George's letter (and also in my grandfather's diaries of HRH Edward, Prince of Wales's tour of India during the following winter of 1921. See "Family of the Raj"). The members of George's chummery had also survived the war, and so there was an immediate rapport in the party with the Maharaja.

Tikari is in the southern part of Bihar some 300 miles west of Calcutta. The Maharajas were a family of Rajputs, with generations of ancestors. For a time, the rulers were from the female line but it was restored to the male line through adoption in the second half of the 18th century. They were a Zamindari family, with a fief over large tracts of land, collecting taxes for the Moghul Emperors and later for the East India Company and the Government, from the *ryots* or cultivators of the land. They would have enjoyed direct cultivating rights over *khameer* land, which had fallen into their control, but the arrangement fell short of outright ownership. Nevertheless, they had rights to receive payment from the *ryots*, which formed the main revenue stream to the Maharaja and his family and state administration. During the absence of Maharaja Gopal Singh, the estates had been managed by Wakefield. George described Wakefield as the Maharaja's right-hand man.

The appearance on the rooftops of the party was called a *darshan* (literally, an "appearance"-JMM) and gave the opportunity for citizens to give homage to their ruler. The religious ceremony afterwards could have been a short *durbar* or meeting of the most senior officials, again to pay homage to the Maharaja. George was lucky to be a guest for this almost unique event at the homecoming of a royal Indian Maharaja.

The shooting programme gave the Maharaja the opportunity to provide entertainment to his guests, again a common event amongst the royal families of India to provide entertainment, not just for the British, but other persons of importance. This would horrify modern generations but it has to be remembered that big game was plentiful and that some of the animals were hostile to man, as death rates from wild animals indicate. Many districts were terrorised by man-eating tigers, for example, and increases in population had the effect of encroaching on jungle for cultivation. It is interesting to note that despite a fourfold increase in population to 1.2 billion over the last hundred years, India has only just become self-sufficient in food production, largely as a result of advanced methods of irrigation and cultivation.

There is a story about a commitment by the elder Tikari in 1925 to the retiring Governor of Bihar, Sir Henry Wheeler. They were talking about partridge shooting.

"But you know, Sir Henry, that we have one of the finest partridge shoots in India?" said the Maharaja. (In fact, there weren't any partridges). An invitation followed for the Governor to come and shoot and Tikari immediately telegraphed his son to arrange it. So, the Calcutta and Delhi markets were scoured for partridges which were bought in huge numbers. A large area of forest was set aside, corn fields sown and ash baths laid out so that when the partridges were released, they stayed there. In a four-hour shoot, thousands of cartridges were fired and about five hundred partridges picked with Sir Henry saying it was the finest shoot he had ever attended!

Black buck is now a protected species but in the 1920s, they were plentiful. An attractive antelope, it has a black/brown back and saddle with a white underbelly and is a medium-sized and graceful animal weighing around 100-150 lbs and with two barley-sugar twisted vertical antlers. They feed on grass, a typical habitat savannah with light tree covering. They can be found now in game parks but are largely extinct in the wild in India and Sri Lanka.

Sambar is a much larger species of deer, slightly smaller in size than the moose and elk, and are one of the largest in the world, between two and three times the size of our native red deer. The head and curved antlers are particularly fine. It is a forest animal found both on the plains and in the hills of India ranging up to 11,500 ft.

The chinkara is a species of gazelle about 2 ft tall weighing in at around 50 lbs. It has a reddish-brown coat which develops into white fur on the belly and throat. It is a dry forest animal found in desert country and is still plentiful. George was a particularly good rifle shot, later representing the Calcutta Small Bore Shooting Club.

Sis had by now got married and George's next letter is a request for all the wedding news.

"Bird & Co Calcutta 16th November

Today is the day and I am with you wishing I were in old London to be present at the ceremony. I know everything will go off splendidly, and this evening I shall drink to the long and happy wedded life of you and Dick. Do let me know who were at the wedding & what was said and how everyone looked & give me a real long description of the ceremony, reception, presents etc, not omitting all the little details which you all might take for granted, but a far-away hungry individual like myself will delight in hearing. I am writing to Aunt Bess by this mail – I expect she has been the perfect brick over your marriage that she has always been in the past over everything connected with you and me. I was delighted when I heard you had asked Mary to be one of your bridesmaids for you know the affection I have for all at Grange Dene. Molly Wilson's wee girl was also a very happy suggestion and I hope she was able to be there. You couldn't have made a better choice. How you always manage to think of just the right thing I can't understand. I suppose I must possess myself and wait for news.

Everything is going strong here & we are now at the commencement of the cold weather and the evenings and nights are quite chilly. From now until March, the weather here is lovely. How you & Dick will love this place when you come out to see me, for I have made up my mind that one of these days you will be turning up. How I would like to spend a couple of months touring round Kashmir with you both.

Last Saturday I had my first tennis party this season & dined out & danced in the evening. I played golf on Sunday morning & did a fairly good round for me. At 11.15 a.m. I joined a river party and eight of us went up the river in a topping steam launch arriving home at about five having had lunch on board. I then went to the pictures & dined about 8.30 & then a short read and bed. Tuesday & Wednesday (today) are holidays & I spent yesterday morning at the office & played golf in the afternoon. I have been to the office for a short while this morning & am writing this in the office where I am all alone. I am going to a tea dance at the Saturday Club this afternoon. So, you will see that when I am not hard at it in the office, I find plenty to do out of the office.

Best Love to you and Dick, Yours lovingly, George.

P.S. I had a letter from Mrs Shrosbree & she told me she had written to you but the letter had been returned 'unknown'. Do see her if you can as she is such a good sort & Shrosbree is an awfully good fellow & has been most kind to me. Sorry to worry you, old bean.

Don't forget Photographs, Cartridge bag, (pigskin in my army kit bag) straps for Wolseley valise & gun, when you have time. "

George's final two letters from 1920 mention for the first time the arrival of Tom Benthall and his wife Ruth. She was Lord Cable's daughter. His son had been killed in the war and he was left with his two daughters. The Benthalls had spent their early married life at Lindridge, a Palladian mansion in 1400 acres near Torquay in Devon and had arrived now in India with their young son Michael. Tom Benthall was joining Birds and he and George became fast friends and colleagues in the company.

"Chartered Bank Buildings Calcutta 16th Dec 1920

My dear Sis,

I got your letter written from Paris, the first after your wedding, by last mail and am glad you are going strong & so happy. I wonder where you are living now? I keep sending my letters to 59 as I know no other address & I hope our friend Mrs Jones will attend to the delivery at your new address.

I had a topping letter from Dorrie the mail before last telling me a certain amount about everything, but everyone assumes that somebody else must have written & told me about everything; result – nothing at all as far as news except airy suppositions that I know all about it, & here I am starving for a few details!!

T 'were ever thus & I suppose it must always be so. If only all you dear things would realise that once a week a mail arrives from England & once a week one can, if lucky, be with you all for a few moments whilst devouring the pages of your letters. Every apparently unimportant detail is of interest as one has nothing with which to keep touch except letters. The newspapers help, but they do not assist personal interests.

Well, having got that off my chest, I will turn to this wonderful country. It is a fascinating spot & the more I see of it the more I like it. Every time I go out of Calcutta, I find fresh interest. Last weekend, Mrs Benthall, Benthall, Ferrier & I went out shooting. It was delightful and full of interest. We picnicked of course & having trained a certain distance, got out, collected a few coolies & made for the waters of the lakes through which river and sea come. We raised a native boat & set forth after duck. We saw hundreds but couldn't get near them as they were too shy. We had lunch on the boat & spent the whole day wandering round. We landed on the other side & got a few snipe. While on the other side, we wandered into a native village & saw fish caught in a pond which they were netting. About dusk, we started back, but just missed a train and had to wait. We picnicked in the stationmaster's office, got some eggs & had a roaring good tea of boiled eggs and everything else. So, home to dinner & an early bed & another topping weekend gone. Last night I danced at the Saturday Club & am having tea there today (at 6.15 p.m.) On Saturday I shall probably go to the races, a.m., & then due out to tea & dance at the Saturday Club. Sunday Tennis & Golf.

At Christmas & the New Year, I hope to get away shooting, but will let you know more anon.

Well, I suppose I must chuck it. I am an awful blighter not having sent you a Christmas present yet, but it will come along, a bit late perhaps, but never mind!

I hope Dick is fit as ever & going strong.

Much love to you both, yours lovingly, George."

George's letter illustrates the frustrations of communications in the early part of the last century. By contrast, huge technical strides have been made since. Now it is possible to talk directly to folk on the other side of the world and at the same time to see the other speaking. The main casualty has been the quality and the frequency of letter writing and if nothing else, these letters illustrate their descriptive merits, in bringing to life events of a hundred years ago . . . truly, it was the golden age of letter writing. The final letter of the year is written just before Christmas.

"Chartered Bank Buildings, Calcutta 23.12.20.

My dear Sis,

You and Dick are dear things to have sent me such a topping Christmas present. I feel a hell of a knut when I permit myself to wear it, & thank you both very, very much. It is just the thing.

Well, nothing fresh. I am off tonight on a shooting expedition. We are going to a place near the sea & it should be topping. I am going with Mr & Mrs Benthall who have just come out both are keen on shooting & picnicking so we mean to make the best of it.

I suppose you will have settled down in some cosy flat or other in town & are probably off for Christmas, or perhaps you are spending Christmas in your new quarters!

Anyway, wherever you both are, I wish you a merry time and a bright New Year.

I have had a touch of fever for the last few days – nothing to speak of, & I expect my holiday will do me a bit of good.

More next mail. Love to Dick. I will write him in a few weeks! Yours lovingly, George."

And so ends George's first year in India. These letters give a real insight into life there just after the First World War, written through the fresh eyes of the newcomer. It was the beginning of a period of unrest in India, leading up to the momentous events of not just another war in Europe, but also a war in the Far East, and finally, to the Independence of India in August 1947.

Christmas holiday in Puri & Easter trip to Karanpura coalfields with Tom and Ruth Benthall; Visit to Assam sugar plantations

Just seven letters survive from 1921, compared with 29 in the previous year, reflecting perhaps a less frequent correspondence with Sis following her marriage to Dick, and the arrival of their children, Bill and Janet. The correspondence opens with his letter describing the holiday over Christmas with the Benthalls.

"Chartered Bank Buildings Calcutta 20.01.21

My dear Sis,

Nice day once more with a heavy day gone & little time left for my own letters. I was glad to hear all about the new flat; it sounds top-hole & your ground plan afforded me many hours (!) of innocent amusement trying to make out what all the various marks represented. I left off my letter suddenly last week so will carry on & give you a few details of Christmas and New Year. I left Calcutta on Thursday night with a retinue of servants & much baggage and went to the first halt where I bugged around from about 6.00 a.m. until nearly 10 a.m. trying to fix things up for the remainder of the journey to our destination involving a drive of about ten miles. Having fixed that, I bathed & had breakfast & the shikaris (hunting men!) having turned up, I went out for a bang at the birds. I got a few partridge & quail & a few pigeons & arrived back dog tired about 4.30 having covered about twelve miles. Bathed, changed & had tea.

The Benthalls then arrived about 5.00 and we stayed the night & pushed off at daybreak the following morning & arrived at Charanpur at about 11 a.m. I told you all about our time there. We had a delightful bungalow overlooking the sea and the peace of it all was wonderful. There were no other Europeans within miles. I travelled back on Monday night & arrived in Calcutta to have breakfast, bathe & get to the office for a hard day's work. On Tuesday night, I travelled to an Engineering works & spent Wednesday doing "Expert advice & general organisation,"

I travelled back on Wednesday night and again arrived in Calcutta in time for bath, breakfast & office. That was mail day Thursday & that night I left for Puri with the Benthalls on another shooting trip so altogether I had four nights' travelling, & four days' work. The second place was nine miles from a station so Mrs Benthall and I (having strained my knee) were carried by Palki wallahs in a palanquin (two – one each) & Benthall walked. We arrived with about thirty-five retainers including a cook, two personal servants, three shikaris, 4 bullock cart men and about 20 Palki wallahs – great fun.

We had three days there & shot eleven different kinds of duck & three buck. It was just lovely & I enjoyed every minute of it. Since then, I have been out for a quiet bang at the birds twice.

At present, Frankie & Mike are staying with me at the flat and I can't tell you how much I am enjoying their visit. Mike has a touch of fever but he will be all serene. Must stop now to catch mail. Love to Dick, Yours lovingly, George."

(A palanquin is a sort of reclining bed with curtains and pillows set on two poles and carried fore and aft by a team of four porters working in relays).

This letter illustrates the developing relationship between George and the Benthall family. Tom Benthall, Baron Cable's son-in-law, was to be a commanding figure in the Birds story, becoming a partner in 1923 and senior partner throughout the 1930s. Standing at 6ft 4, he had been a King's scholar at Eton and a scholar at King's College Cambridge. He was also a keen rugby player, Cambridge Blue and reserve for England. He had seen service in India with the 1st/4th Devons and had fallen in love with the country. The Benthalls and Cables were both Devonshire families and the two families knew each other. His younger brother Paul also later joined Birds, as did Sir Paul's two sons, James and Richard, in the late 1950s. Prior to joining Birds, Tom had been working with the White Star Line. Ernest Cable had initially rented Lindridge in Devon in 1915 and then bought it for a reputed £75,000, with its associated 1400 acres of farmland. He made it across to Ruth and Tom as a wedding gift. It became a home from home for all their friends from India; we were to spend the early war years, 1939 & 1940, there as a family before returning to India in July 1940.

George and he had much in common; rugby football, City of London experience, and military service during the war. Tom was to take a strong role in the reorganisation of Birds. He was a charismatic character and a keen ornithologist (an interest that he shared with my mother) who genuinely loved India.

George's next letter mentions the Duke of Connaught's arrival in Calcutta as well as Ernest Cable about ten days previously.

"Chartered Bank Buildings, Calcutta. 2nd February 21

I received your letter written after your visit to Hereford and am very glad that you are having such a good time. We have been having great times lately. Frankie and Mike have been staying with me & we have been seeing life for the last few days. The Duke of Connaught is in Calcutta at the moment so there are lots of social functions & for them that likes 'em. Everyone I know seems to have given a dance lately & I have been footing it more or less merrily pretty often lately. It has been topping having Frankie and Mike with us, though poor old Mike got a go of fever a day or two after his arrival. He is better now but he is not fit yet as he was running a temperature up to 104.6. Frankie remained with him most of the time & occasionally we went off together & played tennis or danced – as soon as Mike was reasonably fit & could be safely left. They arrived about ten days ago & are unfortunately leaving on Friday. We have had some great games of tennis and golf & have visited the theatres & the clubs. Frankie went to the state ball two nights ago. Yesterday we golfed & had breakfast at Jodhpur Club.

Lord Cable is here at the moment so you can imagine that we are not exactly slack in the office. He is a wonderful man with a first-class brain and has been doing lots since his arrival.

I have bought you a little present apropos of nothing but I know that you will like it. It is a cashmere shawl which can be drawn through a wedding ring it is so fine and light. I thought that it would make a nice muffler or scarf for tennis or motoring or travelling. Did you ever order the photographs for me? Perhaps you remember I asked for three (heads) for 3 of myself in plain clothes and three (heads) as a 'snolgier'. I had forgotten until now.

The weather is still cold & delightful, and everyone seems to be fresh & fit & full of beans.

I suppose that you and Dick are still looking for a farm. I hope that Dick is going strong & keeping fit & not letting you have all your own way!! Give him my love.

Give Betty and Les my love when you see them & tell Betty how sorry I am to hear of her mother's death. What bad luck it was. Yours lovingly, George."

Originally, a tour of India was planned with Edward Prince of Wales for 1920/21. In June 1920, my grandfather, Col Frederick O'Kinealy, was selected to accompany him and his party as chief medical officer and he made a visit to Simla to assess the arrangements. He had previously been surgeon to the Viceroy Lord Harding from 1910-1912 in Simla and Calcutta. He subsequently became superintendent of the Presidency General Hospital in Calcutta. A lifelong member of the Indian Medical Service as a surgeon and specialist ophthalmic and ear, nose and throat surgeon, he had a detailed knowledge and a lifetime's experience of oriental medicine. He had returned to India in late 1919 after home sick leave around the same time of George's arrival.

The Presidency General Hospital was the lead hospital in Calcutta with full surgical and pathological facilities and while it is possible that George met my grandfather (e.g., for medical attention to his foot), there is no reference to that in any of the letters. George's doctor, Stanley Nairn, was still practising in the Middleton Street surgery when I arrived in Calcutta and met him in late 1961.

In August 1920, the Prince of Wales's tour was postponed; however, since many of the arrangements had already been made, the Duke of Connaught was substituted for the Prince. The Duke was a grandson of Queen Victoria, a member of the royal family and cousin of the Prince's father George V. The Duke was, at that time, Governor-General of South Africa.

However, on March 24th 1921, Col Frederick was promoted to the post of Surgeon General of Bengal, perhaps the most senior medical post in India outside of the IMS Director General's post (General Edwards) in Simla. At that time, Frederick also became a member of the Bengal Legislative Council; so, George was in Calcutta at the same time as his future father-in-law, while my mother was a schoolgirl aged fifteen in England. Later, in 1921, the Prince of Wales's four-month tour of India and Burma was reinstated, with my grandfather now chief medical officer to the royal party. The experience gained with the Duke of Connaught's tour was to prove invaluable in the planning processes of the 1921 tour.

Lord Cable needs no further introduction. B. A. White, the senior partner, had fallen ill and was invalided home and so Cable came out to steady the ship and maintain the impetus of the reorganisation. Besides, his daughter and new son-in-law and young grandson were now in Calcutta, and this gave him the opportunity to be with them.

In George's next letter, he describes shooting a tiger!

"Bird & Co Calcutta, 31st March 1921

My Dear Sis,

I received your letter written after your return from farm hunting in Devon. How heavenly it would be to get a place in that county. Well, I have some news for you. I have shot a tiger, or to be accurate a tigress, measuring from nose to tip of tail 8ft 7ins. Naturally, I am frightfully bucked as many, many men who spend small & large fortunes & many, many years hunting do not even see the 'lord of the jungles' and very few of those who see tigers seem to kill them. I am going to have the skin set up and will then send it to you to adorn some floor in your new abode until I claim it for some floor of my own abode – if I ever have one at home! One of its ears is missing – probably disagreed with hubby at some time or other so take warning!

36 *Georges Tiger*

Well, to be more explicit, The Benthalls and I left Calcutta on the night of 22ⁿᵈ to go to a district called Karanpura where we own many square miles of country which simply 'stinks' of coal – some of the seams 60 ft. thick & really a very wonderful proposition. The place where we were going to stay consists of one large bungalow tenanted by a Major Marr D.S.O. – one of our mining Engineers; an absolute little topper – an ex-sapper. We took a train to Ranchi which is a minor hill station & then had two cars, one for ourselves & one for servants and luggage, which met us the next morning. Had breakfast in Ranchi & then motored to the bungalow & Major Marr at Bhankunda. This is about 40 miles from Ranchi & there is nothing nearer except Indian villages. We struck off the main road about 30 miles out & took to a rough private road of about 10 miles length. The motor run was delightful through the hills (varying between 2,500 & 4,500 ft high) & the road overlooked wonderful panoramas through the valleys. At Marr's bungalow, we were absolutely in the wilds and everything was delightful. The second day, we had tea with a man and his wife who had been surveying for the new railway which is going through. They had been several months drifting down that wonderful country with about twenty pack camels, & three or four horses, & chickens, goats, cows, & everything. That evening, we went out after bear but didn't get any. The local holy man is a thorough gentleman & a thorough sportsman in spite of his clothing being only about the size of a pocket handkerchief! He came with us. On the Friday, we again went out over the country & in the afternoon left for the big shoot to which we had been asked. We motored to Hazaribagh – about 40 miles – & spent the night at the bungalow of a charming old man called Eagles. Up again at 5 a.m. & another motor run of 38 miles to the scene of the shoot. We gathered at an inspection bungalow – a party of about 40. There were about a thousand beaters. There were about 25 machans each holding two people. A machan is a platform of branches tied up in a tree about 15 feet above the ground. Major Marr and I had one machan and the Benthalls another. In the morning, there was a beat in one direction & in the afternoon the beat was in the opposite direction. We swapped machans in the afternoon (the Benthalls, Marr and I) which was thoroughly sporting of the Benthalls as I had the better one (we were a long way apart; they had 18, we had 7). In the morning, nothing came through, and having had a good lunch we again went up our trees and waited. First of all, a small panther came through on Marr's side & he had a shot at it but missed, & then about half an hour later, when I was beginning to wish it were all over, I saw a tiger slink into view. I could hardly believe my eyes. The country was thick jungle & one could only see about twenty yards at most. The tiger appeared in a sandy nullah & stood looking at the next machan. I took careful aim & pressed the trigger but there was only a 'click' – misfire! Can you imagine the next few seconds – I was shooting with a .318 rifle – my favourite, which is hardly large enough for tiger but which has a terrific velocity, a magazine rifle & as I was getting another cartridge in, the idiot in the next machan shouted "tiger!" Naturally, the tiger whipped round & as she turned, I had a quick but steady shot & sent her pearling over. She got up again before I had another ready & with a 'wouf', was gone. I then sat at very high tension waiting for another glimpse & praying that she would see me before the beaters, poor devils. There was murder in my heart against my neighbouring machan! Presently, I saw a slight movement in the bushes & had another quick but steady shot & heard the bullet strike flesh, & all was still. When the beaters came up, they were persuaded to approach the spot very gingerly & presently one of the sidars (sort of leader) came running and asked for a gun. I gave him a gun loaded with ball and took my rifle & with Marr went into the jungle to find friend tigress with one bullet behind the heart and a little high & another behind the shoulder & through the heart – dead as mutton . . . joy!

We then gathered at the Bungalow & had a cup of tea & motored back to Hazaribagh to the Eagles' bungalow where we had dinner & at about 10 p.m., set off for Bhowkunda. I shall always remember the drive through the wonderful Indian night, the moon up, the stars shining with the hills in the background & with the air heavy with the scents of the trees. The beauty of an Indian night in that district is indescribable & as we went throbbing through the starlit night, I wished you and Dick could have been there. We arrived at 4.00 a.m. having had tyre trouble on the way, but at peace with all the world, away from everyone with nothing to think of but another jolly day.

On Sunday & Monday, we continued looking over the area – on Monday, we saw a village dance by the Santals, a tribe of hunters who are known to hunt tigers with bows & arrows! It was the first real dancing I have seen. On Tuesday we left for Ranchi & I went back to this spot & the Benthalls continued their tour to another place. I expect that is the last big shoot we shall get his season, worst luck.

Well, old bean, I got the photos; three only arrived, of myself in plain clothes. If they haven't done the uniform ones, do you mind cancelling the order & asking them to send three more plain clothes ones? Best love to you and Dick. Yours lovingly, George."

I remember seeing this tiger skin rug at Remenham House, Henley-on-Thames while visiting Aunt Sis after the war. Not only did it have an ear missing, but on the same side, the whiskers were missing too. We were regular visitors until she died in 1947, and I can remember the shock when hearing the news while at school in Sussex.

In 1962, we were invited to join a shooting party by Bob and Annie Wright. Bob was a partner in Andrew Yule, a leading Calcutta managing agent with substantial coal concessions in and around Ranchi. The town had developed considerably, no longer a 'minor hill station' but a large town and centre for firms with coal concessions in the fields around Assensole and surrounding areas. He had taken a 'block' and large bungalow near Manatu where we stayed having taken the overnight train from Howrah to Ranchi. We had two beats perched in machans and I remember shooting a small sambar deer with solid ball from a 16 bore as well as a peacock with BB shot. After the weekend, Bob and I had to get back to Calcutta and we drove through the night, the beauty of it echoing George's wonderful description. I left my 16 bore for Annie as there had been reports of a leopard and she was going to sit up over a tethered goat in a machan with a friend and Ramchandra, the Wright's bearer.

When they returned, Bob invited us to breakfast at their home in Ballygunge Park to hear the story. Annie and party had driven to within a mile of the machan in the evening along jungle roads. They tethered the goat and climbed up onto the machan for the night. After a wait, the leopard came, Annie fired and it slunk off, obviously seriously wounded, into nearby bushes. She decided that they couldn't wait all night and so they made their way back to the car. Halfway there, they realised that they had left the tethered goat and so turned around. With Ramchandra shaking like a leaf, they fetched the goat and drove back to the bungalow. A wounded leopard is a most dangerous animal, and they hunt at night, but fortunately, the shot had paralysed the animal, and the next morning they went back and despatched it. Bob was furious when he heard this story but recognised that all's well that ends well. And so, just over 40 years later, I followed in my father's footsteps.

Bob later retired and became secretary to the Tollygunge club, and died sixteen years ago. He was a character much-loved by Indians and Europeans alike. Belinda, their daughter, and a little girl at the time, became an internationally recognised expert in the tiger preservation movement, and continues this work north of Delhi to this day. Annie, now in her nineties, lives in Delhi.

The Karanpura concession owned by Birds was substantial and the story of its acquisition a most interesting one. Birds already had substantial coal-mining interests at Burrakur but the concession had a limited life and the coal fields were being worked out. Eyes turned to the Karanpura area. Birds were fiercely contesting rights to the Bokaro-Ramgarh field, but Cable realising that it might take years to settle the outcome agreed to give up all rights in exchange for the Karanpura area. The offer was accepted and a six-year prospecting licence obtained over 500 square miles of territory. Payment included Rs. 9 lakhs as an interest-free loan, a 'salami' of Rs. 1 lakh and an annual rental of Rs. 8000. The lease was granted just before the outbreak of WW1 but was not signed for a year, during which time, Birds had the run of the area to prospect. Two geologists worked for a year, and, by 1917, had discovered huge coal reserves in the central and southern areas of the concession. Ironside, senior partner, and Cable, personally backed the project, with Cable taking a 75% and Ironside a 25% interest. The later development of the field showed huge reserves of first-class coal.

George's description ' stinking with coal ' was a comment on the 1920 survey which confirmed 6 million tons of first-class coal and 10.5 million tons of second-class coal, with a further 200 million tons of first-class coal not proved absolutely, with seams of great depth. The surveys for Communications, and particularly railways, were going ahead with the first line started in 1922. The visit of George and the Benthalls shows the early development of the concession and the surveying of the railway route, combining business with pleasure.

The phrase "pearling" comes from the Cockney colloquialism "taking a pearler", i.e., falling over, probably coming from the wartime 11th Fusiliers, most of whom were Cockneys.

George's next letter describes a visit to the company's sugar interests in Assam.

"1ˢᵗ May 1921

Mail Day & May Day! I haven't written to you for an age I know but it hasn't been because I have been ill or depressed! I had the usual lot of work to do & in my other time I have been busy amusing myself or sleeping.

Very glad to hear you have been enjoying life & having lots of people to stay with you. It's very good for both of you – yourself as a keen attendant of race meetings, even though they are hunt meetings, amuses me – I see Mother in that! What a pity you and Dick aren't horse people. Dick would be, I know, if it weren't for his poor old tummy. Perhaps you would be too – anyhow, I have got one of the nicest little polo ponies that ever was. I have been given him for his keep as he bolts! And when he doesn't get away, he is the merriest little devil – takes a positive delight in trying to put the wind up me! Strange thing – he will stop if I lean over his head & talk to him – I don't think he bolts; he only likes an adventure sometimes and is as sure-footed as any horse I have ridden. At polo, no doubt he would be difficult, but for a scamper across country, he is great fun. Someday, I hope to hunt even if only for a day on 'hire'.

Well, I had a wonderful shoot at Easter. It was entirely my own fault that I had a shoot at all. First, my bearer "ratted" – frightened of the country and the people, I believe – anyhow, I set out alone – train left at about 4.30 p.m. & I arrived at the station next morning at 9.30. No car or lorry had turned up. I didn't wait however as there is nothing at the station but the usual small shanty – I got a bullock cart (pace 2 miles an hour) and having gone 14 miles along the worst road in India, I met the lorry broken down about 2 1/2 miles from the factory. (A sugar factory in the edge of nowhere owned by the firm.) Shortly afterwards, I met the car. The devils on the lorry had broken down about 7.00 in the morning & hadn't sent back to the factory until about 4.00 in the afternoon. It was then 5.00 and I was feeling damned hungry, not having eaten since early morning. Well, I got to the bungalow & there met one Peterson and Van Ingen, his assistant. First of all, the bungalow & the factory. They are about 8 miles from the mountains of Bhutan on the border East of Darjeeling. The Bhutanese are like the Tibetans rather & are great thieves. We are not allowed into the country. It is just range upon range of mountains – Peterson had sent out his camp about 14 ½ miles N.W of here & a few miles from his nearest neighbour (12 miles off). Peterson decided at the last minute that he couldn't come as he had a breakdown in one of his engines. Van Ingen therefore came. Next morning, we were to have started for camp but neither car nor lorry would go so having cursed them all, I set forth on foot and walked 12 miles to Peterson's neighbour where Van Ingen & I had lunch – staying at the bungalow was a man I knew in Calcutta. After lunch, Van and I left on his elephant – picked up our two elephants in our camp & went off for a short shoot before dinner to get food for the camp.

We shot a couple of deer & came back. Next day, Herriot and his hostess picked us up early & the three elephants set out. I got no luck – could have shot deer & sambar & pig but didn't want them & I was after Mithun or tiger. Mithun is a large Bison; some stand 7 ft. at the shoulder. They are devils if they are hit & charge every time. Well, having

37 Visit to Assam shooting Indian Bison from elephants.
George's howdah on the right hand & largest elephant

got 1 hog deer, 2 pig, 1 sambar, most of which got up before Herriot & Van Ingen – a magnificent Bull Mithun got up between Herriot & Van Ingen – Herriot got him first in the body & then he charged the elephant but the elephant stood & Herriot shot it in the neck about 30 yards away. It was about 6ft 10 inches at the shoulder – I enclose a photograph of the head we cut off – isn't it magnificent? Well, we got back to camp, had lunch and went out again. This time, we came upon a herd. They wouldn't let the elephants come near so we got off & stalked them over two miles. Finally, I got to within 100 yards & tried to pick up the Bull (it was difficult in failing light and deep grass). I shot it & knocked it down. When I saw the remainder of the herd move off (not in my direction fortunately), I saw the Bull climb out of a nullah behind & join the herd.

When I got up, I found that I had shot an enormous cow. Quite a good head, but a cow!!! Let it be only whispered. Anyway, I did go to within 100 yards which is more than the others would do. We didn't see them again & next day only got deer & pig. The following day, I had to leave & damned sorry I was to go. Can you imagine a camp beside a stream with woods on the opposite side and mountains towering above seeming to rise straight out of the ground ½ a mile away? – very little slope, just sudden mountains. In the morning, we could hear jungle murgi (translates to "chicken" or "cock") (really like a small game cock) crowing in the jungles & at night, the coppersmith (bird) & others

*kept us company. One evening, we heard wild elephants screaming in the mountains –
terribly eerie – that is great country though unhealthy if one isn't very, very careful. Well,
I expect you have heard enough.*

*A Kashmiri is coming at the weekend – I may get you a bedspread & curtains – am
always trying.*

Best love to you all, George."

While this sounds like purely a pleasure trip, it nevertheless enabled George to see
the sugar factory and Birds business which seems to have been located in the Terai (the
fever-infested strip of jungle between the plains and the hills stretching all along the
mountains and northern borders of India).

Assam Estates and Factories Limited had been floated in 1919 as a result of a
proposition presented to Birds by a sugar expert from Java and the investment was given
the go-ahead by both Ironside and Cable; however, what had not been mentioned was
that the acreage of cane within the plantation only produced enough to keep the factory
working for six weeks, and as mentioned above, the location was malarious, and it was
impossible to recruit labour (perhaps George's bearer had been right!) The cane fields
were also regularly raided by bears. Birds were to struggle with this investment, and
despite attempts to sell the business, it was eventually closed down in 1924.

Elephants were the standard form of transport through this country with its tall
grass, with passengers either in a howdah (a raised boxlike structure with seats inside) or
seated on pads with ropes to hang onto, on the back of the elephant. George must have
been very fit to have walked 12 miles through the heat on his partly amputated foot.

George's next letter and its commentary on a potential life in Devon also tells of
his golf and riding.

Chartered Bank Buildings Calcutta 5th May 1921

My Dear Sis,

*I got your letter all serene and am glad you and Dick are taking it quietly down in
the West Country. I envy you both being down there – it must be getting to its best now,
& I can imagine how beautiful it must be with those lovely lanes & fields. I often think
of the West Country and especially the "Lawnes", the home of the Cross's. What a topping
spot that is. I was only there once, but it made a very deep impression on me, it's all so
peaceful and delightful, with a few young horses wandering through the meadows and
everything radiating contentment. Must be a little different now without Mrs (blank!)
If I live long enough & prosper sufficiently, I hope I may be able to have such a spot to
retire to – unless I decide to retire to a couple of rooms in Jermyn Street which isn't likely!!!*

*Things are still going on here & I am playing golf & riding & studying the language
every morning. Occasionally, I do a good round of golf but nearly always just spoil it at
the end! The other morning, I went round the first nine in 44 & the first 7 of the next
nine in 27! One under bogey. I then took 7 & 8 over the last two! 86 altogether which
should have been 81. At other times, I take almost 181!!*

I am in touch with a good horse at last & I am trying him tomorrow so am hoping he is all they say! Just able to catch the mail. Yours lovingly, George."

George is clearly trying to keep up with Sis and Dick moving around because several of the envelopes are addressed to Lloyds in the Strand. The next letter to him is written from Gloucestershire.

"Chartered Bank Buildings Calcutta 19ᵗʰ May 1921

My Dear Sis,

I received your letter written from Gloucestershire wherein you told me the great news. I hope that you are feeling better now & that all is well! I can't tell you how frightfully pleased I am, and hope that it will be a boy. It seems only a short time ago you were a long-legged little tomboy up to any kind of mischief that you thought that you might be allowed to share with your hardened little scoundrels of brothers!

And now, you are going to make Dick a happy father of an enormous black-eyed ruffian and myself the uncle of the self-same gentleman (or mischievous young woman). It is all very wonderful and makes me feel very much of a back number! Never mind, I hope that I shall have the pleasure of seeing some husky young devil of a nephew run and shove and tackle like a good 'un one of these days.

I had a letter from Uncle Tom last mail. He and Aunt Edie & the girls are coming out in the cold weather. T.M. is coming out on business, but how long they will be here I don't know. Naturally, I am looking forward to their coming no end, and hope I shall arrange to give them a good time. I only wish it were going to be you & Dick, but that is a pleasure delayed.

Well, we are now sweating & grilling in an 'ell of an 'eat with fans bugging round – no sound to speak of though, and long glasses of lemon squash which almost sizzle as they go down & hit the base of one's stomach with a hiss!!! It has been particularly hot this last fortnight, & we had a record one day. I am managing to get along all serene though, (touch wood), and take things very quietly. I golf and ride many mornings from six onwards & still have lessons from the quaintest little moonchie who is an excellent little man. I go out very little at night & am in bed before 10.00 most nights. The difficult thing in this country is to strike the right amount of exercise so as not to overdo it, for if one gets at all run down or overtired, it is the very devil to pick up unless one gets a week in the hills. I am hoping to get away to the hills in October for a week's shooting – living in a camp. It should be just heavenly & peaceful & cool.

Well, I will close, best love to Dick & you and do take care of yourself. Yours lovingly, George."

Bill and Jan were twins born towards the end of the year. Bill sadly died on the ski slopes of Switzerland just after he was married. Jan became a doctor, married an orthopaedic surgeon, David Archibald, and had two sons, Michael and Christopher. Both Jan and David have died as well as Christopher. George was to spend several leaves with Dick and Sis.

George's next letter of 4th August is the last that seems to have survived of this series and in a poetic sense, marks closure of all the events that occurred in the previous seven years on this, the anniversary of the declaration of war. He and Sis were now the only survivors of the family, but both had managed now to move on and develop their own lives; Sis was now married and expecting a family, and George had a developing and interesting career in India.

"Chartered Bank Buildings Calcutta 4th August 1921

My dear Sis,

Still going strong with nothing to report except that I have just realised the date and flashed back to 7 years ago. Seven years! Seems to date from a previous existence when one thinks of the changes which have taken place during those seven years, and yet when the memories come flooding back, it seems only a month or two ago that I was tramping around Lincoln's Inn with some of the best fellows that ever existed, making the old squares and courts – usually so peaceful and out of the world – ring and echo with words of command & tramping feet. What a cheery crowd of young untroubled youngsters that was – with no shadow in their eyes and no drawn & worried faces. It was a merry hive with lots of hard work and no thought of the morrow. I often wonder where they all are now, and how wonderful it would be if we could all keep our experiences & yet throw off the load of our war experiences & all meet again in one of those delightful old halls with their coats of arms on panelled walls decorated with life-sized portraits of legal lights of the past. What a merry gathering it would be – how the old roof would ring. Sole musings, Sis, only calculated to bring realisation – though without bitterness, of the present and the spirit haunted gathering, any meeting of those who were left must be.

Everything is much the same except that I have moved from the flat temporarily and am staying at Ballygunge in the house of one of our partners who has gone home on leave. It is a delightful place & the change will probably do me good. Better send letter to me c/o Bird & Co. I haven't written anyone lately.

Sorry to worry you but do you mind getting me a pound of Elephant felt for my foot? Grey or white will do & it should be about ½ inch thick.

I hope that you are very fit, love to Dick, yours lovingly, George."

This is a haunting and poetic letter in which George calls to mind the seven previous years. The halls he recalls like a dream from a haunted past are the halls of Lincoln's Inn where the young recruits used to meet to be drilled and taught musketry by the Inns of Court instructors.

George was a survivor. He had experienced the loss of his mother, his father's suicide in early 1914, his brother killed in July 1917, and he himself had gone through 19 months in the trenches and the hell of the battles of the Somme. This at a time when the average life of a young officer was measured in weeks. The soil of France and the Low Countries was drenched in British blood . . . 744,000 British killed . . . one in ten men of the British population between the age of twenty and forty. Countless others were wounded, some crippled for life, others gassed. George had witnessed comrades dropping beside him in the horror of war. Over 1.3 million Indian Army soldiers took part with distinction alongside their British comrades. The action on the Somme where dismounted Indian cavalrymen of Gardiner's Horse fought alongside the Grenadier Guards is still remembered to this day in a joint regimental meeting. Volunteers from the Empire fought together; Australians, with massive casualties in the Dardanelles, and Canadians, who captured Vimy Ridge where a small section of French ground is granted in perpetuity to Canada and the Canadians and the numerous graveyards kept and tended by the War Graves Commission.

No other letters from George survive until 1929.

Civil reconstruction after 1858 exemplified by the development of Western medicine led by the IMS; the Indian Independence Movement

It is not the purpose of this book to give a detailed history of the various events that led to independence in India but to provide sufficient detail to enable an account to be given as a background to George's life and work with Bird and Company.

That which the historians of the first half of the 20th century called "the Mutiny", Indian historians today call the "First War of Independence"; others call it "the rebellion". I shall call it "The uprising of 1857". For this is what it was – part reaction to what was perceived as religious intolerance and insensitivity, and the potential destruction of caste, a part the fulfilment of prophesy, and a part a reaction to the overbearing and insensitive attitudes of the British as rulers towards Indians whom they largely regarded as inferior mortals. This uprising was mainly confined to the northern states around Delhi and West Bengal. The southern states of the Deccan and the Western states around Bombay and in the Mahrattas stood firm, as did, largely, the Princely States. Most of them had signed treaties of protection with the East India Company and the last thing they wanted was a major disturbance and further conflict.

It gave the British an almighty shock, and the rumours which swirled around the events, of murder and rape of women and children (killings, yes, but rape, untrue), served to inflame the reaction to the "pandies", most of whom were summarily executed either by being hanged or blown from the guns. By 1858, the uprising had been suppressed, the Charter of the East India Company withdrawn, and direct rule imposed from London. This was implemented through a new Indian Civil Service and Viceroy, the direct representative of the Crown, building on the organisation left behind by the "John Company". Many of the personnel simply transferred across, while others were recruited from the universities of Great Britain. Examples of this were the author's great-grandfather, James O'Kinealy, and his younger brother, Peter, both of whom obtained degrees in the newly formed Irish University of Galway in science and engineering, and passing, at Lincoln's Inn, the Indian Civil Service exams (reckoned to be difficult), emigrated from Ireland to India. They both later qualified with the relevant examinations in the new Indian penal code, and procedures, plus the law of succession, before becoming high court judges in the Bengal judiciary.

There followed a period of about 25 years while new structures of government were put in place. Amongst these was a new legal system. Work done by Lord Macaulay in the 1830s was consolidated into a new comprehensive Indian penal code in 1862. Previously, the courts of the East India Company presided over the British while respecting the various codes of Hindu and Muslim law These were now settled into a series of legal procedures sufficiently flexible to allow for regional variations. New acts of land tenure were passed in 1885 to address the tenure and financial relationships between the *ryots* (cultivators*), the *zamindars* (rent and tax collectors) and the government; this trinity of relationships had become financially unbalanced and was causing friction and social unrest between the *ryots* and the *zamindars & talukdars*.

India was to be divided into two administrative blocks. The first of these was the district organisation within each province. Each district was headed by a Collector, technically responsible for the collection of tax. A district might be as large as an English county. He would have at least one Assistant, a Magistrate and a small police force. India was developing rapidly particularly with the extension of the railway network, partly for strategic reasons to enable troops to be moved quickly from place to place. But it also provided a lifeblood for the transport of coal, other minerals and other supplies including food grains for India's developing infrastructure and industry. By the turn of the century, 20,000 miles of rail had been laid and by the time George arrived, a further 10,000 miles had been added. We have a description and example of district life with Georges visit to Morton Steven's district at Jessor.

The other 2/5ths of the country was ruled by the Princes. New legislation established the Princes' rights to security of tenure under the Crown as well as defining their territorial rights and areas, removing at a stroke their fears of annexation. At the same time, their royal status was recognised and a new direct relationship was established to the Monarch through the monarch's representative, the Viceroy of India, initially located in Calcutta. In each state, there was an Agent, the Viceroys representative, a sort of ambassador, and his staff. The status of each state was partly recognised by the number of gun salutes to which the maharaja was entitled, and the 500 or so princely States graded in importance. An example of this is given in George's letters of his visits to Gaya and being entertained by the Maharaja, Hon Lieut. Col. The Maharaja Gopal Saran Narain Singh of Tikari, returning home after being a member of staff throughout the First World War. The visit and homecoming of the maharaja is described above in George's letter of 1st November. 1920. Each of the major states had rights of governance over their own estates including the collection of revenue with the general proviso that not more than 10% should be allocated to the Maharaja, his family and estates, known as his privy purse.

One of the main building blocks of Direct rule was to be devoted to education. Schools were established to provide education to a new administrative cadre within the Civil Service and military.

Examples are the establishment of Mayo College in Ajmer, in Rajasthan in 1875 by Richard Bourke, Viceroy 1869-72 and the military College at Dehra Dun, modelled upon Sandhurst. Educational establishments were progressively established across the country, with much debate around the various curriculums.

Nowhere was this educational trend more marked than in the establishment of Western medicine. The origins of the Indian Medical Service (IMS) can be found in the arrival of surgeons in the four ships of the Association of English Adventurers who sailed to India and further East under charter from Queen Elizabeth 1st in 1600. Many of these early surgeons were surgeon barbers, with the skills to open and close a vein, and some became shore-based, providing early land-based medical services, often with a dual role as merchant traders, serving the local settlements. The service was popular and many of these early surgeons had dual commissions in both the Army and Civil branches with the lucrative prospect of offering medical services to Indian potentates.

There are several colourful accounts of this. One of the early surgeons, Charles Broughton, was sent from Surat to Agra at the request of the Emperor Shah Jahan to attend his daughter who had been badly burnt. He managed to cure her successfully and when asked what he would like as a reward, very patriotically asked for the concession to trade free of taxes in the Eastern Provinces. This was immediately granted thereby gaining at a stroke what Sir Thomas Rowe, the British ambassador based in Surat, had failed to achieve after many years of negotiation.

Hospitals began to be built as the settlements grew, each with their resident surgeons and supplement of assistant surgeons, and as the relationship with the Indian population grew, so also grew an appreciation of the ancient Indian medicinal traditions and practices, including Ayurveda. The techniques of this branch of Indian medicine are based on complex herbal remedies with an emphasis on a holistic approach to curing, including the mental, through meditation techniques. There were also medical links to astrology, and many of the herbal-based techniques found their way into western medicine, for example, the use of opiates in the relief of pain.

Another early and colourful coup was achieved by a certain William Hamilton in 1715. He had been dismissed from the service in Bombay but somehow found his way back to Calcutta where they had no knowledge of his previous record. As part of a diplomatic mission to Delhi, he was called upon to attend Emperor Farukh Siyar, then suffering from swellings of the groin, which he cured. Much in demand, he was prevented from leaving but was eventually released with the reward of the gift of an elephant, 5,000 rupees, a horse, 2 diamond rings, a jewelled aigrette, a set of gold buttons, and models of all his surgical instruments in gold. He died two years later in Calcutta.

Shortly after the formation of the East India Company and the growing influence of the military, a new structure for the now sizeable medical establishment was formalised with the constitution of the Indian Medical Service in Bengal by orders passed on 20th October 1763 with fixed grades and rules of promotion from grade to grade. Each Presidency followed suit with its own establishment with separate rules. There was a preference amongst Indian sepoys for Indian doctors initially using non-European medical practices, and this was reflected in the early medical establishment of both cavalry and infantry.

Another notable surgeon, John Zephaniah Holwell, appointed Zamindar of Calcutta, was present at the siege, survived the "Black Hole" incident, and wrote his account of it on his voyage home. The Holwell memorial to the dead, originally in Dalhousie Square, was rebuilt by Lord Curzon in the early 1900s and still survives to this day, now in the churchyard of St John's Church.

There was still a degree of conflict between the military and civil needs for the service. Generally, newly appointed surgeons had to spend at least two years in the military before being granted a civil commission. Apart from anything else, this enabled the newly arrived surgeon the opportunity to learn the languages. Military service, however, remained a priority at the end of the eighteenth century.

The pace of development accelerated after 1858, matching the rapid technical development of medicine itself, particularly in the use of anaesthetics and operative techniques. Many IMS surgeons established large practices as specialists, my grandfather among them as a specialist ophthalmic and ear, nose and throat specialist in the last decade of the century. The Presidency General Hospital, (of which he was to become Surgeon Superintendent in 1912) had been newly sited on the south of the maidan in Calcutta in the early 1800s, to be followed in 1835 by a new Medical College. This initiative of Lord Bentick was to provide a teaching facility for a new cadre of Indian doctors with training imparted in the vernacular. This facility replaced the medical classes at the Sanskrit college and the Madrassa and the teaching of Indian Medicine. Its purpose was to take 14 to 20 students a year, irrespective of caste. Candidates needed a reading and writing knowledge of English, a knowledge of Bengali and Hindustani and a proficiency in arithmetic. Candidates normally came from the Hindu College, the Hare School or the General Assembly institution. The course lasted from 4 to 6 years, after which they received certificates enabling them to practice as native doctors in surgery and medicine. A programme of scholarships was established and contributed to by such luminaries as Rabindranath Tagore and others. He personally funded the further training of four students to study in London with three of them gaining the coveted MRCS qualification. Later programmes included medical classes in Urdu and Hindustani with European texts translated into Bengali as well. Women were admitted to the CMC by resolution of June 29th 1893 (and long before women received the vote in England).

By the time of my grandfather's appointment as Surgeon General of Bengal in March 1921, the number of medical students at the Medical College had increased to 1030 and students now took the Cambridge Medical Board examinations. He himself was a member of the Legislative Council of Bengal and President of the Examination Board. His daughter Doreen later married George.

Other hospitals had been opened across the country; The principal ones in Calcutta were the Eden Hospital (Midwifery and Gynaecological – 110 beds) – The Campbell

Hospital (637 beds) which included the Prince of Wales Hospital and the Chuni Lal dispensary (206 beds) – The Medical Hospital group (206 beds), the Shama Charan eye infirmary – (1891 – 59 beds) The Sambu Nah Pandit Hospital (102 beds), the Howrah Hospital (129 beds), the Presidency General Hospital (235 beds), the Mayo Hospital (104 beds) and finally the Carmichael Medical College, Belgachia (230 beds). One of my sisters and I were born in the Eden Hospital in the 1930s. All of these hospitals were largely staffed by newly trained Indian doctors and specialists as a result of progressive education and training programmes from 1858, and led by the IMS. As the numbers show, there had been quite an astonishing development and progress in medicinal treatment for the ordinary individual over the previous 63 years largely at the initiative of the Raj and the IMS in cooperation with their Indian colleagues.

As my grandfather's report for Bengal in 1921 shows, there were in Calcutta 23 dispensaries, including hospitals, and a further 765 outside Calcutta in Bengal serving a population of 46.65 million people in 1920. Just under 6 million patients were treated and 280,396 operations were performed in that year according to the official statistics for 1921, again largely by Indian doctors and surgeons. The Presidency General Hospital had a pathological laboratory, with a fine record of medical research; for example, the discovery of the malarial parasite in mosquitoes by Sir Ronald Boyle for which he was awarded the Nobel Prize in December 1902. The legacy of this early programme of medical educational development is the large number of fine Indian doctors and specialists who currently serve in our NHS.

This huge educational programme extended from schooling to training in all walks of professional life including the civil service and there were now also strong political developments intended to extend to Indian self-government, but this did not satisfy a political class growing in confidence and striving for full independence. Central to the political development of the Independence movement was the Indian National Congress. It was initially established in 1875 by a retired British member of the Indian Civil Service as a forum for Indian intellectuals to meet and discuss matters of common interest. However, it quickly developed a political life of its own, becoming central to the moves towards Independence as a new Indian political party.

Initial representations broadened the scope of the Legislative Councils, the advisory bodies to the individual Provincial Governors, and this had resulted in a new Councils Act in 1892. Effectively, this changed little as the Governors still had the same reserved powers, but the Legislative Council's Indian representation expanded. This process was to continue with progressive expansion, particularly as a result of what became known as the Morley-Minto reforms, with representation and Indianisation of the regional Legislative councils reflecting the increasing drive from a now English-educated electorate. In 1915, a Prince's council was set up to act as a forum to reflect the views of the self-governing Princely States.

Just before George's arrival, two events of significance occurred. The first of these, already mentioned, was the massacre at Amritsar. This totally disproportionate action was to be a critical turning point, souring relations between the British and Indian communities.

The second event coincided with the appointment of Edwin Montagu, a Liberal, as Secretary of State for India in 1917. Following a visit to India, he published, in the summer of 1918, his *Indian Constitutional Reforms*. This suggested for the first time the belief that parliamentary democracy could work in India. The so-called Montagu-Chelmsford reforms planned to delegate powers from government to the legislatures, principally in civil administration, e.g., roads, education and schools. Finance, the military, police and railways remained the reserved responsibility of central government. While in theory, powers were to be delegated to the legislatures, in practice, control remained with the Governors who retained powers to govern and override the councils by ordinance. Montagu was not a popular Secretary of State and my grandfather's diaries record with some pleasure his resignation over New Year 1921/22.

The 1919 India Act provided for a review after ten years, and the Simon enquiry was set up early in 1927. The political structure had by now been fragmented along religious lines between the Muslim League led by M.A. Jinnah and the National Congress, the former with ambitions of a Muslim "caliphate". The nationalist movement had surfaced during the Prince of Wales's visit across the winter of 1921-22. On his arrival in November in Bombay, rioting broke out in the Byculla district of Bombay and the Royal visits across the Northern states were characterised by *hartals* (strikes) designed to limit the turnout for the Royal Prince. Gandhi's movement of non-cooperation had taken hold. As a security precaution, the railway lines along which the royal trains passed (mainly at night) were protected by soldiers spaced 200 yards apart along the whole length of the line.

When HRH arrived in Calcutta, he was greeted by the cry from the burning ghats, *"Gandhi Mahatma jai ki jai"* ("Gandhi, Great Soul, hail oh hail!!"). During the stay at Government House, despite the efforts of the police in rounding up 2,000 dissidents, crowds circled around the grounds at night chanting *"Gandhi"* which, according to my grandfather's diaries, *"put the wind up"* the young Prince. The Royal party had arrived just before Christmas, and processed over Howrah Bridge and down Clive Street into Dalhousie Square on their way to Government House. They had passed the Chartered Bank Buildings, and it is likely that George would have seen his future father-in-law in one of the open landaus of the procession as they went past. The Royal Tour had a much better reception in the Deccan; however, parts of the remaining Tour of the North had to be cancelled due to unrest.

The dominating political personality of George's time was Mahatma Gandhi with his programme, refined in South Africa, of non-cooperation with the British. His was a non-violent protest, and although violence occurred, he set an example of passivism. Frequently imprisoned, he led the movement that resulted in independence for India. But after the Government of India Act of 1935 and the new federal government elections in 1937, the independence process became irreversible.

A developing Birds Heilgers Group of
companies in the inter-war years

Much has already been written about the reorganisation of Birds of the early 1920s and the acquisition of F.W. Heilgers, as well as the accounts in George's letters about his part in this work. The events of this time are contained in a set of reflections written by Tom Benthall, quoted from the Bird Heilger history ... *"in the old companies, dividends were distributed on a fantastically high scale and insufficient sums were often put into reserves ... when the limits were reached, as much as eight percent had to be paid on debentures raised on the companies' assets ... I shall never forget the daily puzzle over the cash balance books when we used to calculate how we were going to meet the most pressing bills ... If strong action had not been taken, there might have been a catastrophe ... but Lord Cable came out ... once the badly conceived ventures were cut adrift and the drain on finances stopped, and, provided the sound business was properly managed, the recuperative powers of the firms were immense. The work of the next few years was to consolidate the business and to repair the damage caused by becoming involved in the war and post-war boom."*

This then was the story of the twenties, and it was when George made his name through his work in the company reorganisation, and afterwards, in the reorganisation of the capital structure of the firm after the death of Lord Cable.

The development of the coal fields, particularly at Karanpura, went ahead as the negotiations with the Railway Board and other railways proceeded to provide essential distribution facilities, but it was interrupted by a slump in demand for coal at the start of the great depression of the late twenties.

Jute production was controlled through an industry-wide agreement to restrict working hours in 1921, but profits were so high that it led to a rapid expansion of new mills up and down the Hooghly River. More and more raw jute was being exported to Europe, but despite this, through the combined strength of the newly combined Birds and Heilgers companies, costs were kept down and the businesses were able to increase both output and profit in the five years to 1927. 1922 was the year of the failure of Birds' old associates, Cox McEuen and Company; the takeover by Birds was completed in an afternoon, thereby avoiding an interruption in trading. With the deal came R Steel & Company, which prospered under Birds' management – particularly the Steel Baling Company whose output of jute bales progressed steadily.

Despite the loss of the Eastern Bengal State Railway contract, the labour department continued to flourish. However, the rescue operation with the Bengal Nagpur Railway in handling a sudden upsurge in demand for labour to handle seed traffic enabled Birds to secure the whole contract. In 1929, Birds were still the most prominent labour contractor.

In the Kumardhubis, the 1920s represented a difficult period, but in a fresh development, a small steel re-rolling plant was acquired, being moved bodily from Madras to Kumardubhi Engineering together with most of its workforce. This was the result of a joint deal with Best and Company. Known as the Eagle Rolling Mills, Birds took on its management after flotation. This plant was the only one in India, and it was to become of increasing importance during the Second World War.

Elsewhere, the Loyabad Coke Company held secure supplies of coking quality coal from Burrakur collieries and continued to increase supplies to the Tata Jamshedpur steelworks. The Sijua (Jherriah) power station flourished as more and more collieries went electric and output was doubled by the installation of a 4,000-kilowatt generator in 1927. Indian Patent Stone, manufacturing products from a composite formed from ironstone (e.g., paving slabs), after financial restructuring, began to move ahead profitably. And finally, The Assam Sawmills & Timber Company product range was re-cast, a new veneer box developed, with sales doubling in the five years to 1928.

Birds' mineral portfolio was expanded as a result of extensive prospecting, and the existing businesses were developed. The opening of the Bisra Stone Lime Company, and particularly from the Burnpur works, depended on the establishment of rail infrastructure. Disaster struck when during a heavy monsoon and floods, the bridge over the Koel River was carried away. With inadequate finance to repair and complete the rail links, the rail lines, bridges, and associated infrastructure were sold to the Bengal Nagpur Railway Company at a loss, but despite this setback, deliveries started. Production expanded rapidly, additional lime kilns were added, and the company was restored to regular profit.

The Tuscal project already mentioned was never completed; nevertheless, after disappointing early prospecting results in the substantial Keonjar 93-square-mile concession, a subsequent survey by Henry Day revealed mountains of high-grade haematite iron ore with an average 65% iron. But their development took several years. Henry Day was also retained to prospect for manganese ore, a key ingredient of high-grade steels. Deposits were discovered in the same area, concessions obtained, and production started in 1923, with regular production of iron ore in 1929.

Activities during the thirties represented, by and large, much of the same. The depression, which started in 1929 with the Wall Street crash, continued during the first few years of the next decade and created a worldwide depression in trade. The main effort was directed to keeping things going and controlling costs. India continued in a depressed economic state until the outbreak of the Second World War.

Coal was the early casualty of a drop in prices while the railway companies chased demand. A scheme was put to the Government to reduce output but was rejected. Burrakur suffered a disaster in 1936 at its largest mine, Loyabad, where an underground fire broke out and a fall trapped miners, including senior mining engineers. It was not until the next year that it was considered safe to re-open the pit and the remains were recovered, and to save the feelings of Indian miners, this was carried out entirely by European teams.

Jute production was also hit by the slump, but despite short-time working and a write-down in the value of jute stocks, the Birds' jute operations continued to show profit. Meanwhile, the steel companies handled exports; Becker Gray and Company, a company dealing in gunny exports, was taken over in 1930 from the Inchcape group, and it then adsorbed Birds gunny export department.

Indian Patent Stone continued to struggle, but diversified into the precast concrete

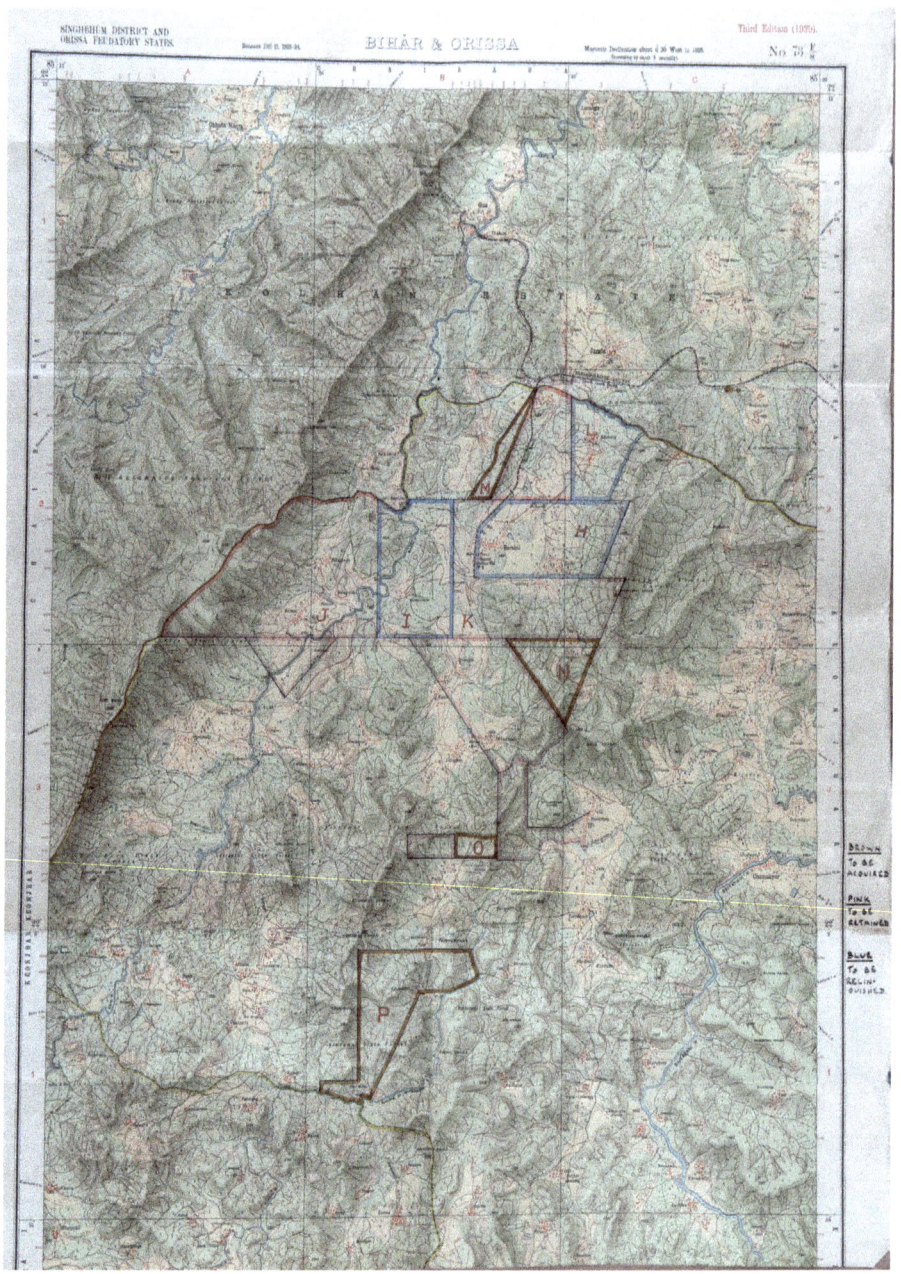

38 (Above & opposite: Maps showing Bird's haematite manganese
ore and kematite concessions in Orissa

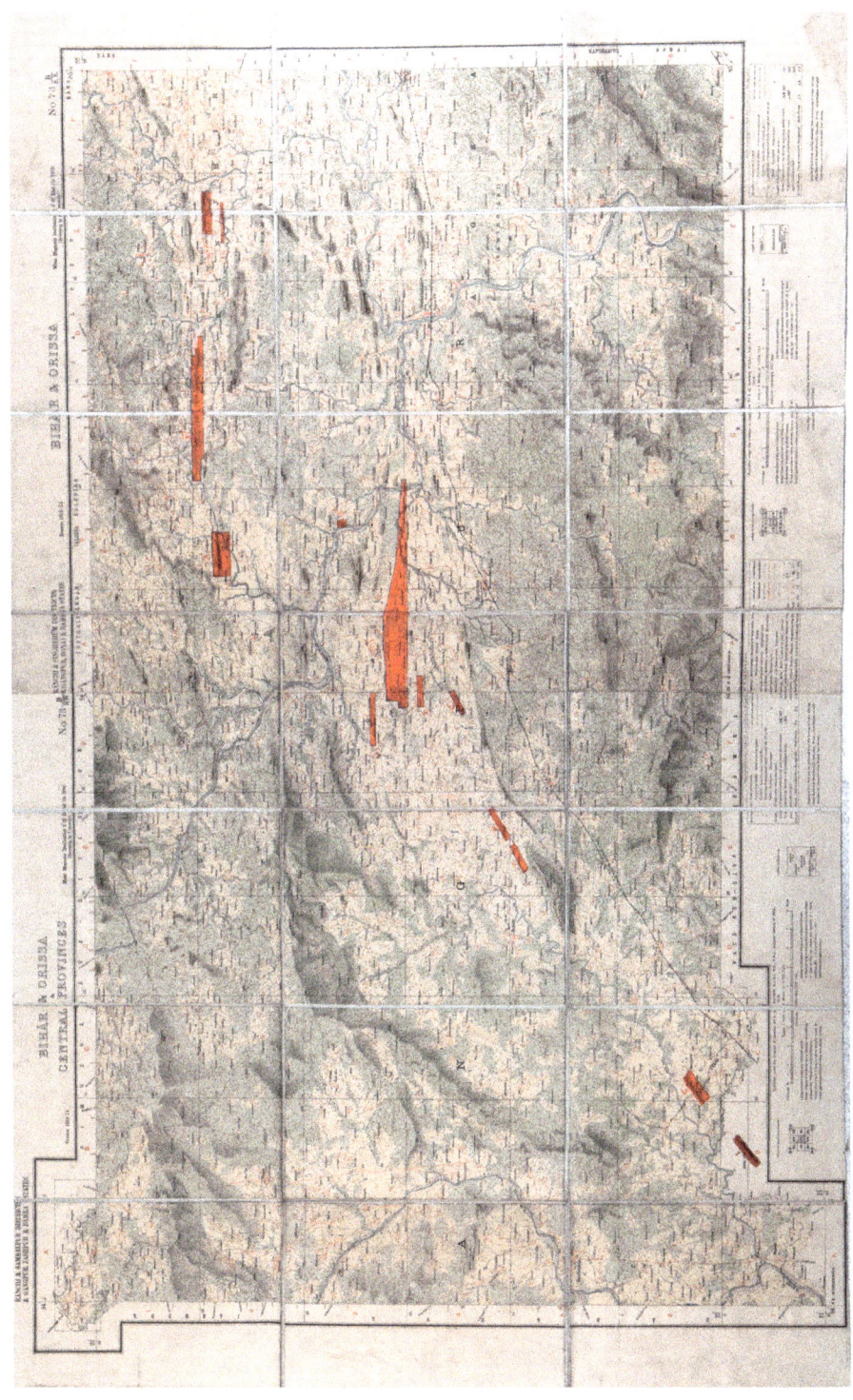

business, building a number of bridges including the beautiful Anderson Bridge across the Teesta River on the road to Kalimpong.

Kumardhubi Fireclay and Silica Works suffered particularly from the slump in steelmaking but managed to add to its product range both insulating and mullite bricks. The former are porous with low thermal conductivity and used in both high and low-temperature insulation; mullite bricks are used in glass manufacture; the composition of these involved the use of kyanite.

The story of the Birds development is interesting. A former employee, D. Lawri, had settled at Ghatsila, 115 miles west of Calcutta. He noticed a hill that had resisted the harsh weather better than the rest and reported the fact to Dr Edmondson Spencer, the head of Birds' expanding research department. The discovery turned out to be kyanite – a company called Eastern Minerals was formed and mining started. An export trade was built up and the mineral was also used in the manufacture of mullite bricks.

Eagle Rolling Mills struggled with the unnatural marriage between small-scale scrap-based and high-cost electric arc steelmaking at K.E.W. and the rolling of basic steel billets, until Tatas began to supply billets to replace those made at K.E.W. This enabled output to be tripled. Electric arc steelmaking is ideally best suited economically to making stainless steels, fully austenitic steels and smaller quantities of high tensile steels.

Orissa Minerals continued to operate, supplying around 150,000 tons a year of high-grade haematite to Indian Iron and Steel as well as manganese ore; also, mining manganese dioxide used in glassmaking.

The research department under Dr Spencer continued to flourish and there were numerous examples of mineral discoveries researched by his team, as well as other work including the development of papermaking with paper pulp from bamboo. As will be appreciated, all of this required detailed financial evaluation, much of which crossed George's desk.

As an interesting aside, Lawrence of Arabia was in India from 1928-1929. In my father's book collection was an original first edition of his "Seven Pillars of Wisdom" (of which only a very limited number of copies – around 100 – were printed with illustrations in full colour). There is also a copy of the second edition. My mother sold the first edition around 1956 and kept the second. This suggests that my father may have met Lawrence during his visit. There is also a copy of "Crusader Castles", an original thesis by Lawrence for his degree at Oxford, bound in quarto leather in the collection. Lawrence spent some time with the Waziristan Scouts on the North-West frontier to Afghanistan during his visit; the author's late father-in-law, Col R.J.F.A. Lawder was serving as a young officer with the North-West Frontier Corps at that time.

George was a very keen shikari (Hindi for hunter – JMM) and the narrative above describes some of his shooting exploits at snipe, duck and big game. There are photos of trips to Kashmir in 1928 which are probably best told through the photos themselves and duck shooting at that Christmas through extracts from his game book. Whether they had met yet or not is unclear, but Doreen was in Calcutta too at that time and attended the Governor's camp and week-long shoot at the same; this was a little time before they became unofficially engaged.

A collection of photos of Georges August/September 1928 leave to Kashmir.

39 *My houseboat at Shrinugga*

40 *Camping in the hills in Kashmir*

41 *A view from the hills of Nanga Parbat mountain*

42 *Shikkari wallas-hunters – with the monk of a sambur deer shot by George.*

43 *George with his bearer Anthony outside his tent*

TEL: CALCUTTA 3326.

11, CAMAC STREET,
CALCUTTA.

	Dec 23 Eve	24 Morn	25 Morn / Eve	26 Morn / Eve	27 Morn / Eve	28 Morn / Eve	29 Morn / Eve	30 Morn / Eve	Total
Geese		3	2	2	1	1	2		8
Pintail	2		4 6	8 1	10 1	10 1	1 1	10 2	51
Gadwall		1	5 13	4	4 1	4	1	14	56
Spotbile				1					2
Pochard Common			3 1	3			3		7
Pochard White Eye			1						6
Pochard R Crested		4	2						6
Pochard Tufted	1	4	3				1		8
Nukhta	1		3	3	3		3	1	15
Shoveller			2		2		2	1	6
Brahminy							1		1
Teal Common		1	2 1	4 2	1	3	2 5		20
Teal Gargeney		1		2	1	1	2 4		11
Teal Whistling		6	1		1				8
Teal Cotton			1	H			1		1

Christmas 1928

9 12 23 26 10 14 10 21 6 17 11 42 201

44 *Extract from George's gamebook – Christmas shooting camp 1928*

PART THREE

Marriage and children – "the three J's" – Separations and a hazardous sea voyage back to India. (26.09.1929 – 05.10.1940)

My mother was born in Darjeeling on 28th October 1905. Her father, then Major Frederick O'Kinealy, had been transferred to Darjeeling as civil surgeon on 20th June that year and this was to be her mother's (Helen Mabel – always known as Mabel) second child after James, their son, born on 27th July 1903 in London. She was baptised Doreen Elisabeth, but was always known as Dorks.

Frederick was the eldest son of Justice James O'Kinealy, who had emigrated to India as a newly qualified engineer from Galway University in Ireland in 1862, to be followed ten years afterwards by his younger brother Peter (also an engineer from Galway University). Peter, at the time of their marriage, was still in Calcutta as Attorney General and Judge.

Frederick had already seen service in the North-West frontier in the Malakand and Tirah campaigns of the 1890s and was a rising member of the Indian Medical Service. Mabel's grandfather, Andrew

45 Uncle Jim and Doreen circa 1920

Trevor, had seen service as Surgeon to Arthur, Duke of Wellington's 33rd Regiment of Foot and certified the death of the notorious Tippu Sultan at the siege of Seringapatam on 4th May 1799. Her uncle, Charles Binney Trevor, had also been a High Court Judge in the Bengal Judiciary in the second half of the 19th Century, and a brother had been killed as a young Lieutenant in the Sussex Regiment after falling down a cliff in the Punjab. There were numerous other Trevor relatives with service in India. Mabel, an only daughter, had eight brothers. Her father George was a clergyman in London, and researcher of the Trevor family tree, going back to the 5th century. Mabel's mother was born Elisabeth Tull of Peasemore, Wiltshire, granddaughter to Jethroe.

Dorks thus came from a long line of family in India as soldiers, doctors and lawyers. She spent her early years there as a child up to the First World War, and therefore, was familiar with India and spoke Hindi well (as did most children brought up there). Early years were spent in Darjeeling. The family went on leave to England in late 1908, returning to Calcutta in May 1909, with Frederick now appointed Superintendent of the Campbell Medical College, and professor of ophthalmic surgery and ophthalmic surgeon at the Medical College, both important teaching hospitals. He was by now the leading ophthalmic surgeon in Calcutta, as well as an ear, nose and throat specialist.

The families next move was to Simla, with Frederick now promoted to Lieutenant Colonel as Surgeon to the Viceroy Lord Hardinge of Penshurst, the family alternating between Government House Calcutta in the winter months, and Government House Simla in the summer. There are pictures of the children attending fancy-dress parties in Simla: this is also where Frederick's mother Harriet died and was buried.

In 1912, Frederick returned to Calcutta, as Surgeon Superintendent of the Presidency General Hospital, which was then in open country south of the *maidan,* that great open space around Fort William to the South of the city. Their home would have been the Superintendent's house between the two wings of the hospital. This was the leading general hospital in Calcutta serving the European community of the time.

Frederick was urgently recalled from leave back to Calcutta at the onset of World War 1 in August 1914 and seems to have spent the next four years there, gallantly holding the hospital together while surgeon after surgeon was recalled to front-line regimental duty, the hospital rotating thirty-six surgeons over the war years, a turnover of no less than six times. Shortly after the end of the war, Frederick returned home on sick leave exhausted after long continuous hours both operating and running the hospital. Both children were now at school, James at Wellington College and Dorks at Ravenscroft School in Eastbourne. Mabel was a talented pianist and musician, as was Dorks; and so, on leaving school, she went on to the Paris Conservatoire to study music and piano under the renowned pianist Alfred Cortot, at the same time learning French.

Frederick retired after a short period as Surgeon General of Bengal, and Chief Medical Officer to HRH Edward Prince of Wales during the winter Tour of India and Burma 1921-22. He rented a house at 18 Queen's Square, London, and this was to be the family home until Frederick's death in July 1940. He practised there with consulting rooms as a specialist and was a senior member of various medical bodies, including a council member of the British Medical Association. He also became a council member of the Oriental Club.

Jim was to return to India working for one of the managing agencies on a tea garden in Darjeeling, but he had had polio as a child and was profoundly deaf, and so, his health failing, he returned to London where he joined the Merchant Trading Company, working in the city of London.

Dorks had by now graduated from the Paris Conservatoire and so, in the autumn of 1928, it was decided that she should go out and spend the winter season in Calcutta. Now young, beautiful, talented, speaking French, Hindustani, aged just 23 and a musician of significant ability, with all the right connections, she joined the Governor-General's winter shooting camp over Christmas. From her great uncle Peter, who had died in 1913, she also inherited £2,000, a not inconsiderable sum of over £100,000 in today's terms, and no doubt her parents helped financially too.

At some stage, she must have met George. He was now a rising star in Birds, aged 35, and with Sis married and her children Bill and Janet aged eight, the time had come perhaps to settle down. When they got engaged is not clear but he was due to go on leave at the conclusion of his third tour in April 1929 and convention suggests that he would have asked Frederick's permission to marry his daughter.

There are, however, clues to their developing relationship in the one letter that survives:

"25.04.29. 11 Camac Street Calcutta

Dear Doreen,

I was very glad to get your letter from Aden and to hear that you were going strong. It must have been an amusing trip and I look forward to hearing more Pughisms later. Oscar got letters from you and Alison and as Jeff didn't get a letter, Oscar carried his two letters about all Sunday most ostentatiously, just like a small boy – he even brought them to meals – poor old Jeff! But it was funny – in the end, I told him he didn't deserve letters if that was the use to which he put them! I don't seem to have done very much since last Thursday except get a letter from you and get nearer to 20th May. Last night, Jeff, Tom & I dined with the Chief Justice – just the four of us and we had a most pleasant & amusing evening. Tom was in good form & amused Sir George vastly. Sir George was telling us about some of his days in the "Union" in Cambridge & at the end, Tom's comment was, "The only time I went to the Union was when I had lost my "square" & gown – there were always plenty hanging up there" . . . Sir G said, "But I hope you confined your depredations to men of your own college?" Tom – "No, anybody!" Tom then went on to tell how they left their bicycles outside "lectures" & when they came out, they just took anybody's bike and often kept it for weeks – it was all very amusing but

46 *Doreen at the time of her engagement 1929*

139

J.M.J.   13.6.29
Nkana Stnt

Respected Sir

I humbly and respectfully
beg to state you to following few lines
to your kind consideration.

That we are all doing well by the
grace of our almighty God. Hope to
hear the same from master and all at home
Dear sir we are getting very well on
driving. But they don't teach and
punishing work, because in the company
they have no any of special master
for the same. Anyhow as we are
attending daily to the company &
watching while the fidendoing
its work who we are helping to them.
we had no rain here this
month. Sir I am glad to inform your
honour that I am going to marrie on
September. I have heard this from
Mr Fletcher, everything going all right
in the mine. My father and his
best wishes to Bhana Sahib him Sahib

Master self
Z

I beg to remain
Sir your own most
obedient servant & Pan Roy

Please sir say my salam to mies
Patel & him Sahib. Slame to mast

47 Letter written in the bazaar for Anthony George's bearer to George 13.06. 1929

Tom suddenly grew serious and said, "But you know, we once had a visit from thieves in Cambridge . . ." We all collapsed.

I have been riding early morning & am getting fitter & less sleepy every day . . . the horse is a great success. Miss Weatherall went to Shillong last week & Liz went to Kalimpong. I haven't seen Ruth & Eileen since last Saturday week.

Well, all the time this place grows more irksome. I am beginning to appreciate deeper meanings in such phrases as "the abomination of desolation"! I didn't think that I could ever feel so starved & lonely in this place. Things that used to keep me going have lost their virtue and it is becoming more and more impressed upon me that there isn't much in this life which really matters terribly. Without you, things seem dead & meaningless and life becomes a kind of aimless meander. How little of one's capacity is taken up in this place when one leads the life that I do. There seems to be lots of work but it is all so unsatisfactory as a life. Yet there is a lot of pleasure but so unsatisfying & one just goes on – conscious of ever-increasing waste of something more valuable than all the energy & capacity utilised in everything one does---and it's all your fault, O'Kinealy!

I suppose that in one's lifetime, such a thing as happiness is rank impossibility. Lucky ones know times of happiness which nothing can take away from them and there can be no happiness like times shared with somebody else. Those times would have their dead time but never so dead as being alone, and they would surely have their periods of most wonderful happiness & contentment never possible of achievement alone. But soon I shall see you again. I was vaccinated yesterday and I am writing to be sure my sister & her two "savages" have been vaccinated also. There is, of course, no more smallpox here than usual at this time of the year & the risk is no greater than at this time in any other year but there have been cases – picked up at some of the intermediate ports possibly, so one should be done. If you haven't been done, my child, well just go and tap gently on father's consulting room door.

My next assistant went sick yesterday but he is a little better today so I hope he will be OK in a day or two. It would be dreadful if my leave were cancelled. But that thought must not be encouraged. I so look forward to seeing you & being with you. If you don't hear again from me by letter or wire, I will telephone you. In less than a week I shall be off to Bombay & then heigh-ho for the best of all. Longing to be with you, Love George."

There are lists in the archive of household things to be taken out to Calcutta and in this, she would have had the benefit of Mabel's experience, as well as, of course, their wedding presents. Four months were available to prepare for the wedding to be followed by a three-week journey out by sea to Bombay and a crossing by train to Calcutta to arrive by the end of October.

The wedding took place in the Catholic Church of St. James Spanish Place, on 26th September 1929, with Charles Trevor, a solicitor (Doreen's uncle) and Philip Ironside, a cousin by marriage, as witnesses. The wedding photograph includes Doreen's parents and Aunt Sis with Janet as bridesmaid and Bill as page boy, Bets Ironside as maid of honour and also Rowley, George's best man. An apostolic blessing was received by

48 *George and Doreen's wedding. L to r standing Rowley George Doreen*
seated Betty Ironside Bill Tonge Sis and Janet Tonge

telegram from the Pope. There is a photograph of George and Dorks (as she was always known) back now in Calcutta, garlanded with (I guess) the Birds accounts department members around them, of which he was now head.

Birds had been through a period of change as a result of Ernest Cable's death at the end of March 1927. Sir George Godfrey was, at that time, senior partner and due to retire in 1929, with Tom Benthall the obvious successor. George was to be deeply involved in the restructuring of Cable's complex share ownership, as his will had specifically directed that the firms should continue.

Tom had become a partner in 1923, and, after his father-in-law's death, had sketched out a potential scheme of arrangement to take his shareholdings. Two of Cable's trustees refused to act, but the remaining three, with considerable courage and no small personal risk, agreed to do so. The arrangement was for Tom to buy the firm's goodwill, a tremendous liability for a man with little capital of his own. Two private companies, Cable Limited and F.W. Heilgers Limited, were created to hold the ordinary shares with Tom owning the shares of the two private companies; he had to borrow the money to finance the purchases, which was to be paid off out of profits over seven years. The issue of the preference shares was solved by the trustees agreeing to take up any balances not held by others. The proprietary companies became partners in the firms, thereby ensuring their participation in their management. George is recorded as being most helpful to Tom in advising and helping facilitate the arrangement.

These events took place at the onset of the Wall Street Crash and the collapse of world trade and international recession, as well as a turbulent time in India. The Simon Commission had published its report which was rejected by Congress led by Pandit Jawaharlal Nehru. Dominion Status had been rejected, and independence demanded, with agitation becoming widespread. Gandhi was arrested, and a fresh campaign of civil disobedience started with a boycott of British goods and outbreaks of terrorism. One of the members of the Dover Street "chummery" in which I stayed, Robin Barnes, witnessed, as a young boy, his father murdered in the Punjab in the 1930s. G.F. de Montmorency, a senior member of the Prince of Wales's 1921-2 Tour and distinguished member of the Indian Civil Service, survived an assassination attempt while Governor of the Punjab – a policeman standing next to him was killed, and there were other terrorist attacks too; in Calcutta, a number of policemen were murdered.

The unrest is referred to in George's letter to Dorks, now in the hills of Shillong out of the heat as she was expecting my sister Jean.

Arrival of Jean "the bun"

"27ᵗʰ May 1930

Dorkie, my darling,

I got your last letter today in good time and as usual I was delighted to get it. I haven't been in the office so consistently before 9.30 a.m. ever since I came to India! But when I do, I work & if your letter hasn't come, I don't seem able to settle down to work until it does. Well, I went to look at the house this morning and the brickwork is now above ground level by the verandah. By the time the next photograph is due, there should be a most marked improvement to show you. Charles Stone, who is in charge of Talbots in Shrosbree's absence, is coming to dinner on Friday & I hope to get him more personally interested in gingering things up for us.

I played squash with the marker last night; there was a terrific dust & rain storm last night just as I left the office which has cooled things down a little bit but it is still very sticky. Last night, I had a typical uneasy night full of dreams. I dreamt someone was tickling me very gently – my hands – & then I really struggled to come to & of course I was soon wide awake & looking round with a big stick! I am sure you will never be able to get any sleep in the porch room – one hears every movement down to the late wayfarer clearing his throat in the road! I think that we must move into Ronnie's room when he goes – just for sleeping – or else onto the verandah. Ronnie's room would be best I think, except for the frigidaire – we talked about the date of his departure the other day & as he is leaving either on 31ˢᵗ July or early in August. We agreed it would be best for him to move out at the end of June. He has two places he can easily go to so it makes no difference to him. He has been such a brick since he has been with me. We might try the porch room first & then try the others if it is noisy.

Tonight, Liza & Joyce & Hugh are dining with us and we are going on to the gramophone concert at the Saturday Club for a bit afterwards. Poor old H.E . . . .he is such a dear "old lady" and now the poor darling is losing his nerve! Well, well, well, I suppose it is very worrying for him really & truly & he is anyhow nominally responsible but how Clive Street will snigger if he gets "nerves" and goes home. He hasn't done much since he has been out except do what he is told, which is a blessing, I suppose.

We haven't had a reply from "Ballygunge Hall" yet and we don't know whether they will accept our challenge . . . Oscar has been very full of grins & chuckles so I expect some "strafe" is brewing!!!

Ayah hasn't appeared as yet but I will ask Francis this evening; she may have come this morning. The new one sounds good – it is so much better when they will laugh!! And it will help you to get really expert at Hindustani and then you can be my interpreter most useful! I had a letter from Dad last mail on business. He wanted to see Imp. Bank about a wrong charge they are making & I saw them today & got them to agree to rectify it so that's all right. I didn't send Dad's letter on to you as it wouldn't have interested you. The more I think of them coming out, the better it seems and there seems to be only one snag & that is the possible unrest. By the time they come I expect it will be well on the way to settlement or else it will have broken out afresh so that can be left until the time is nearer.

I long to be with you, Dorkie, more every day and I only hope that old monsoon will send along & break good and well so that it will be cool for you here, and the sooner the better, sweetheart – anyhow, I am glad you are keeping amused. Surely, surely, it won't be long now before I am on my way to you. Keep fit, sweetheart & little George too. All my love to you, Dorkie Darling, always, from Geordie."

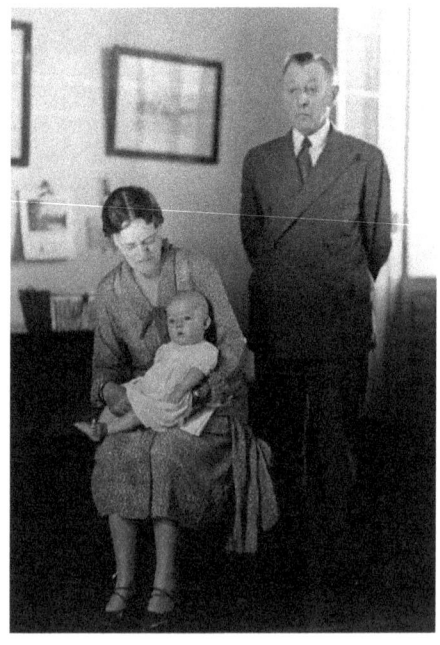

Dorkie was just over six months into her time with my eldest sister Jean and in the hills (probably Shillong) and out of the hot pre-monsoon weather. George was looking forward to the breaking of the monsoon so that he could travel up, spend a few days perhaps and then bring her back, and was also concerned about the comfort of their Calcutta sleeping arrangements. Charles Stone was still there in the early 1960s and also helped me find accommodation, & reminded me of the fact that he had helped build our home at 5 Alipore (now Raja Santosh) Road.

This was the time of Gandhi's salt tax protest, his arrest and imprisonment. It was

49 Parents Mabel and Frederick with Jean their first grandchild Calcutta 1930

144

also the time of the beginnings of the negotiations between the British Government and Congress about Dominion status for India, the cause of Churchill's resignation from the Baldwin cabinet. As an indication of the seriousness taken of the unrest in India, Tom Benthall was accompanied everywhere by a detective with a loaded revolver; a number of British in Bengal were murdered.

Amidst all this unrest, Dorkie returned to Calcutta from the hills and my eldest sister Jean was born on 3rd August 1930 at home in No.11 Camac Street. Frederick and Mabel did, after all, decide to come out that cold weather to be introduced to their new granddaughter, and there is a charming photograph of Mabel holding Jean. Their visit also provided them with an opportunity to visit old friends after eight years of retirement.

The next surviving letter is of Sunday 20th July 1931 and the inference seems to be that Dorkie and baby Jean are in the hills, probably Shillong again. . . .

"My darling Dorkie,

Your ordinary mail letter arrived safely yesterday and needless to say, it was lovely getting it. Four letters also arrived for you from the Bank of England and I am sending the four reference slips which accompanied the printed matter. I am sure you are right to convert and keep your capital in British Sterling Govt. Securities, but you should get more than £25 bonus. I had an idea that it should be £28 or more – from these slips it is clear that you have four accounts. You began with two amounts and you had the two receipts from the Bank of England showing these two amounts – then there is the interest on these two amounts which was reinvested by the Bank of England in a similar War Loan, and they may have opened two fresh accounts for this invested interest on the two original sums, and then I expect Arthur will see you get it all all right and it will be interesting to see what the total sum really is. The interest that falls due at the end of this half-year is to come & I presume this will be re-invested by the Bank in the new Conversion Loan. I should leave similar instructions with the Bank of England as before, i.e. to re-invest all interest as it is paid and then you will escape Indian Taxation – which is no small matter these days. Also, your nest egg will go on increasing which is all to the good.

Well, I am writing this before breakfast having got into bed at 2.30 this morning! But I don't feel sleepy. I dined with the Procters at the Saturday Club and Mrs Kingston, Mrs Tyson, (both husbands were away in Dacca with the Governor) Mrs Tobin, Major Murray, & G.A were there. There was a Cabaret at the Slap (slang for the Calcutta Club – JMM) in which Mrs Tobin was performing but we didn't stay for it & went to flicks instead. I never saw such a "mushy" film & you can imagine some of the comments from our own party. We had a big box. It was all about a chap who thought that he had married the wrong girl. He was an awful young stiff really and married rather a good sort. However, everyone was complaining that his wife had no babies – in fact, babies seemed to crop up every few minutes, or rather the having or not having them. You can imagine the effect on our party! One remark of the Hero, made perfectly solemnly, finished us off when he complained to his wife, "My friends are always asking me why we haven't had any children and I can't tell them"!! Then, later on, his second wife really is going to have a baby and Murray from the back of the box, in a loud sepulchral voice, said. . . . "He's done it at last!" It was funny and everyone was in great form. Mrs Procter looks fitter than I have ever seen her, I think. After the flick, Mrs Tyson went home, also G.A., and the rest of us went back to the Slap for sandwiches & a night cap. Mrs Farqueson commented that I had wanted to marry Peggy myself and have wanted to marry her for years . . .! Silly old fart. People like that give me the windies . . . as we were leaving, we saw Mrs Farqueson & sat down with the remnants of her party. She started off on me all about the wedding but I told her I really knew nothing about it except that we had asked Dorrie and Pegs to stay with us and also Dorrie after the wedding and we hoped they would do so for as long as they liked.

I was very polite to her of course as I don't want to be the cause of even the faintest feeling between two families. I'm told the boy is far and away the best of the bunch and I devoutly hope that it is true. Mrs Farqueson bucked away about all the arrangements and I must say she is working hard at it all and seems determined to make a real good show of it . . . but what a tongue! Of course, what I would like most of all would be for you to come up to Darjeeling with me but we will talk it over later as it may be too much of a sweat. It is very sticky here still and we are very short of rain, but only six inches, which can easily be made up in one good day's rain . . . Touch wood, I am very fit – have never been so fit at this time of year – long may it last. . . . there is plenty of work and I seem to get more and more drawn onto the councils of the firm. Tom has been particularly pleasant and more like his old self than I have known him for years . . . and all the time I miss you more than ever, sweetheart; every day you become more precious to me and every day I seem to find you in fresh places in my heart. . . .

Later – I am just going to spend the day at Titaghur – Khan is here beginning to work and after breakfast, Cook told me he has changed his mind about going on leave and did not now want to go – I told him to please himself so long as he didn't want to go when you returned – he assured me that he wouldn't want to go until you went on leave again – I am glad as he is the mainstay here – though touch wood again, they are a very good lot we have and Dominique is an extremely quiet and efficient lad.

I forgot to mention that last night I saw lots of people I know at the Club, which was simply packed. I saw Charles Ormond looking well and Helen & Jack looking thin but well. Jack asked me to come and see them and Helen said she had heard from you yesterday. Both seemed very cheery. Then I saw Alec Taylor who I hope is going to lunch with me next Wednesday and Ronnie who was most boisterous when we met as I was crossing the dance floor! He is a cheery bloke, Ronnie, & one is always glad to see him. I also saw Doris Birlingue but not to speak to & a whole host of others I hadn't seen before, including Coppie who was full of inquiries after you. Being S.G. (Surgeon General) seems to suit him as he is developing the complexion and figure of a country squire . . .!

I am glad the photographs of Jean are so good & I hope mine will soon come. Sweet wee souls. I do love her so, my Dorkiebus & I would much rather she was a young pickle than a nice clean ladylike wee thing!! I like to think of her all grubby & dirty & happy though I know it it's all very well for me to talk about not having to keep her tidy! I never cease being thankful for being such a lucky chap to have you – and her. Wish her many happy returns from me – I will cable too.

All my love to you, my own darling Dorkie, and to our wee Jean. Always your Geordie."

The next correspondence is from 1932. Dorks and the baby Jean (now 21 months old) had sailed home leaving Calcutta on 25th April with George due home later in the year on leave, a decision taken to enable them to avoid the hot weather and monsoon. There is discussion about an English Nanny and whether her services should be retained; she appears to have been employed in India and gone home with them. Jack and Helen Thomas were good friends. There is also reference to Oscar . . . this was Oscar Pearce of Birds, later to become a partner in the 2nd World War. The references to Ronnie are most probably Ronnie Cameron, husband of Sandy, father of Micky and Diana, good family friends also. . . . more of them later. Dorks is now at home with Jean.

Calcutta 2nd July 1931

My own darling Dorkiebus,

I have just heard that the Air Mail has been put on again, so I am writing this hoping that it will arrive with the one I wrote on Saturday 18th. Well, I got your two letters yesterday all safe & I was very glad to get them as usual! I think that you are right about the OB. It's all very well putting up with things – up to a point, but once that point has been passed, it is far better to let her go. I could never have put up with her rude ways as you have done, and now Jean is past the difficult feeding stage, I am sure you will be wise to try & get someone who is not so rude and tactless. You may not get someone with her training and experience, but I don't think that it is so necessary now & I am sure you will get somebody reliable anyhow – somebody who can be trusted to take charge of the situation in our absence. But don't let it worry you, sweetheart – you will get someone alright and it is far better to get rid of her in the autumn.

About May salary – I found a counterfoil "24th April" (the day before you sailed) Miss N. Orpen Rs48 which I suppose is her April salary which I seem to remember you did pay as an "advance". I can find nothing else that might be it, so I should pay her for May & say no more about it. It is all very muddling, leaving and paying bills, etc., & one can't possibly remember, but I quite agree about "advances". They are a mistake & she was very bad about it. As you say, she is excellent with the Bunkin but it is not good enough to feel that everything is controlled by her, and I am sure you are wise, sweetheart. I am sure you will be able to get someone good at home. I am sorry you are being worried about it but I expect that it will all work out all right.

I too hate getting rid of people – I even hated sacking that sweeper – swine though he is. I got what seems to be quite a good man (on Rs 20, the last one got 21). He is a friend of the Watty's man so it should solve godown (accommodation) *worries & perhaps they will work together. (I am writing you with my new pen – its first letter.)*

Yesterday, being Sunday, we got some more plants etc. from Titaghur including a few creepers for the fence – I haven't been able to tell the Mali (gardener) where they go but will do so this evening or tomorrow morning. I shall tell you about our ordinary doings in the ordinary mail. I like the rhyme about Gilda!! Meg's a bad lot . . .! I lunched with Tom Thomas on Saturday & Alec & Hugh Thatcher (I don't think you know him?). Hugh and Mother live at Rottingdean so I hope you meet her. Tom expects to be home from November & is going to Switzerland too D.V. We agreed it would be great fun to fetch up at the same place . . . he is such a nice person – then we played golf at Tolly. Good fun. Alec showed me some snaps of Hazel & his daughter at Rottingdean – they look so fit and happy. One of his daughters is in the pose of "the landlord of the Chequers"!! I am so looking forward to the photos of the Savoy bun, and I do hope you are enjoying it all & that the weather is being kind.

There has been a slight break in the monsoon and we have seen a bit more of the sun since Saturday. Very good growing weather for the garden. Caunas are already beginning to bloom and the colours are going to be lovely. One of the shrubs is actually blooming too. Tom Benthall is dining out tonight, apparently, and Ruth has asked herself to dinner – it will be nice having her to dinner & I like the way she just comes along! Oscar still spends a lot of his time with them, but he is very much more like his old self again & is great fun.

It is just as well I didn't try & get to Puri for the festival for I couldn't have gone, as Tom has been away every day on a Committee on Army Retrenchment which is sitting now. I might possibly go away for the Poojas (holy days – JMM) if I feel the need for it. I shall see, but, touching wood, I am very well at present except for a cold in the head which doesn't count & if I remain so (as I hope to D.V.), I think that I shall stay here & perhaps spend a couple of extra days at the new shooting camp.

I have been looking at the cane settee & chairs & I am afraid they will have to be covered before I leave as they are beginning to come to pieces. I think a deep gold would look rather nice; what do you think? If you agree, shall I get it or will you send it to me? I will find out how many yards are necessary & let you know in case you decide to send it out. Apart from that, I don't think there is anything that is wanted. No . . . we want a fire grate & I will give you measurements of the fireplace by the ordinary mail. One simply can't get them here.

Well, we shall soon be into August & then it won't seem so long!! I simply live for the mails & your letters & I spend most of my time thinking about home leave & all it means. I am always thinking of you, my darling. . . . D.V. It won't seem long before I again have you with me, and the wee Bunkin of ours, but it does seem an age since you left. Never mind; it will pass. All my love to you, Dorkie my Darling and my sweet Bunkin, always your Geordie."

The letter makes reference to air mail and ordinary mail (i.e., sea mail) and clearly suggests that there is something of a real cost difference between the two. The principal carrier was Imperial Airlines with destinations to the Far East including Australia although there were other carriers, principally KLM with services being developed throughout the Far East with destinations including the Dutch East Indies.

Imperial Airlines was formed in 1923 with headquarters at Croydon. The initial regular service flights were to Europe, established in 1925. A proving and survey fight then opened up the Capetown route. This was followed in 1927 with the Australia route. A survey flight to India was completed in January 1927 in a de Haviland 66 Hercules, taking 12 days, with a flying time of 62 hours 27 minutes. A regular route to Delhi was then established in March 1929 taking 7 days. Passengers travelled to Basle by air, by train to Genoa, by flying boat to Alexandria, by train to Cairo, then by a DH 66 flying to Karachi and then Delhi. Travel was expensive with capacity limited to around 20 passengers who stayed at comfortable hotels overnight. These flights also carried the mail between destinations. A flying boat service was later developed in 1937 to Calcutta and Rangoon with Short flying boats. My mother was to fly out and back home in May 1938 and my father also took return flights over 1939/40 using the Calcutta service, at that time, using the Cape Town via Africa service. All these flights needed staging, landing and maintenance facilities along the routes. Air mail reduced the time for letters to arrive from 3 to 4 weeks to around ten days.

George was now in a senior position in the firm and head of the accounts section, (effectively finance director). He was to become a partner in Birds in 1933. Tom's younger brother Paul had also joined the firm some years previously and also became a partner in 1934.

The history of the firm records that George had been deeply involved in the restructuring of Ernest Cable's shareholdings during this and the next tour. Following on from Ernest Cable's death at the end of 1927, and the scheme of arrangement outlined above, put in place to enable Tom to continue with Cable's shareholdings, a separate investment company had also been created to hold shares not just in Birds companies, but also in other investments. George also became involved in the Bengal Chamber's finance committee as chairman around this time and was also Chairman of the Lord Cable Trust.

George joined Dorks in England on leave towards the end of 1932. This was the end of his fourth tour. The last surviving letter of 1932 is dated Monday 14th Sept.

"My Own Darling Dorkiebus,

It was so good getting your letter yesterday especially as I had been wondering all last week how you had fared with the Bunkin (Jean, now two – JMM). *I am so glad you managed to cope alright, as I knew you would, but it is a most exhausting proceeding and I devoutly hope you didn't allow it to wear you out. Poor wee sweetheart and her big tooth! It would happen just as you took over, but never mind, and if, as you say, it has given you more confidence, that is something, though I hadn't noticed any lack of confidence between you and the Bunkin – but I do know exactly what you mean, for "coping" by oneself does give out the feeling that one can do it. I wish I could have been there, Sweetheart, but then I always wish that – whatever is going on.*

Last Friday, Hugh lunched with me at the club and before that, I had been having a real good "think" & when I faced it all up, I decided that it would be better if I stayed on here in the porch room only up to the end of October (i.e. about a fortnight) and went to the Bengal Club from 1ˢᵗ Nov until I leave in December – there are many reasons – not just the transport question – since sending the car to Walford's, I have realised how very much one misses a car – especially at this distance out – then being here in our own flat & house but not having it for oneself, although I know it would all work out perfectly well (with Joyce and Hugh especially, for I would rather they were here than most people I know). I don't feel that I should feel so comfortable about it & I am sure it is better to hand it over & get right out! Then there is the question of downstairs. I should be with Sylvia and Watty a good deal (young Charles is there too, of course) and it would mean that before they could have anyone in to dine, there would be Charles and me. Also, I think that I am too old to live in such confined quarters with a young married couple – it's not fair on them always to have somebody around. This is not so important but it does exist. I like Sylvia & Watty very much and I am grateful to them for offering (as I was careful to explain to Watty) but I am sure it is better for me to go off to the club. Both of them have been absolute bricks to me and I was very careful to put it all to Watty in a way that he would realise that I deeply appreciated their offer. Anyhow, I made my decision & told Watty & at lunch, I told Hugh. Both Watty and Hugh of course said at once that it would please them best if I did exactly as I liked . . . .it has all been without a shadow of a difficulty. . . . Hugh is coming in on 1ˢᵗ or 2ⁿᵈ October on "chummery" terms until the 15ᵗʰ when he takes over. Either Oscar or Denis will be moving out on 30ᵗʰ September to make room. Then on 15ᵗʰ· I shall move into the porch room for a fortnight & Hugh will take over. Then on 1ˢᵗ November, I shall move to the club. I can live there for Rs400 a month (including lunch and drinks) so it isn't so bad, & by the time one calculates everything, there is nothing in it as far as expense. I am sure it is best to do this. . . . The decorators started work on Saturday and have finished the hall and the whole of the centre well of the house. I chose the colours we agreed upon & they look lovely, I think. They are paler than what we had before – the ceiling is "pale ivory" and the walls are "pale cream" which is a shade darker. They began on the Drawing Room today. . . . I shall be glad when they have done. I am glad that you are seeing Joyce before she leaves as it will be much better. Hugh wants to use their beds so I shall put away ours in the Box Room if they will go without any fear of spoiling – (I am sure they will as the springs are all rustless being galvanised) If they won't go without risk of spoiling, I shall put away the beds in the other two rooms & put one of ours in each room. But I don't want to do that as they might get knocked about & damp. Don't you agree?

Then Hugh is sure they have their own blankets and linen. He wants us to leave enough glass and china for them and if Joyce wants their own when she comes out, he will have ours carefully put away in the glass cupboard in the Box Room. The piano question is, of course, quite OK, and I will have yours handed over to Winfred as soon as she is ready. (This was my mother's Steinway grand piano given to her by her father and autographed by Alfred Cortot. Later, my mother gave it to my sister Jen when she moved to Oxford and Jen started to give music lessons there – JMM) *Hugh says that it will be better for them to have their own rugs if they want them so I shall only leave*

*out one for the Drawing Room and have the others tinned up when they are really dry
with lots of moth balls. I shall of course put lots of mothballs in with the mattresses also,
and anything else that has to be shut up. There isn't really a great deal to do but it all
takes time and I want to be very careful that all our "Treasures" are well and carefully
put away! I think it will all be OK.*

*The weather is very much better and I think we have finished with the monsoon
except for the usual few days' real downpour which we are bound to get. But it's hot
again though dryer. I played golf on Saturday with Bill who stayed the weekend & I was
one up when we stopped. We had our usual foursomes on Sunday & Denis & I again
took a ball off Oscar (who returned from his trip on Saturday) & Kenneth. But I shall
be giving you all the detail in my letter on Thursday . . . which I shall begin tomorrow
morning, I hope. I hear Col. & Mrs Proctor are back and I shall drop in to see them
either this evening or tomorrow.*

*I am keeping well & fit, touch wood, though the sight in my right eye is not absolutely
normal yet. I hope it will get right soon and it seems to improve a bit each week. I have been
taking a bit more exercise now the bad weather looks like ending soon & I think it is doing
me good. I am being careful not to overdo it though, as it is very trying now it is definitely
drying up. But it won't be long now until we are into the cold weather & several have
predicted an early cold weather . . . I hope they're right! Cardwell returned to the office today
from leave looking very well and hearty though he was disgusted with the weather at home.*

*Well, Sweetheart, it is practically only three weeks until D.V. I shall be leaving and I
get more thrilled & impatient every week! I hope you are keeping fit & well & that our
own Bunkin is being a good "chap" – I expect you will just be moving up to town when
this arrives & I hope you have a good move. Oh, Dorkie Darling, I do so long for the
time when we shall be together again; it seems such ages since you left . . . I look forward
to the snaps next week. I wrote about our anniversary of our wedding day in my mail
letter last week and I shall only say again, I never cease to thank my lucky star & to long
for you & for us all to be together again! All my love to you, Dorkie my Darling, and
our Bunkin. Always your Geordie."*

It was very much the pattern of Calcutta life for properties to be occupied with new
tenants for the duration of six-month leaves. Some of the properties were sufficiently
roomy for more than one family to occupy. George went on leave in December 1932,
returning in May when Dorks and Jean departed almost immediately for the hills.

The arrival of Jen

The next letters are from 1933. Dorks was now expecting their second child, my second
sister, Jennifer. Dorks was again in the hills to avoid the hot weather. (The mention
of Norman's clock suggests to the author that this was Norman & Bunty Odling
in Kalimpong – they lived at "Glenrilly", a lovely house with stunning views of the
Kanchenjunga massif – their cottage, "Charitung", was to be our home from 1940-45.

"5 Alipore Park Road West, Calcutta 24.5.33

My darling Dorkiebus,
 Your letter was very welcome yesterday & as usual I loved hearing you are well & all about it up there. I spoke to Jack on the 'phone yesterday and told him about a camp bed which will be O.K. he says. I also asked him about Evian (bottled water) and he is going to take up a couple of dozen. Fin (= Finlayson – he and Pix later went to South Africa where he farmed before returning to the U.K. working in the City . . . known as "Dadda-boy". . . . Their daughter Maureen married the author's cousin Bill Perkins – JMM) *is going to get Laws to do likewise so between us all, we shall replenish the stock. I am going in today or tomorrow about Norman's clock & whenever it is ready, will send it by the next traveller . . . Laws Thursday – Jack* (Thomas) *Saturday – me Thursday next D.V. – Fin Friday next! I shall be very interested to see the banner you have got – the nice ones are most decorative in a very pleasant way I think.*

 Well, there is nothing very fresh here – I did my usual routine and left office about 5.30, went to the club & drank tea and read until about 7.45 then was hailed in for a drink downstairs by Wattie & Sylvia. Wattie was a real "birthday boy" wearing one of his new shirts and we played some of his birthday gramophone records & laughed over the riot the night before. He told me that Eric Stanton was very bruised but does not know how he got them! It was an amusing party and not so rude as some I have known. Then I came up & dined quietly & fell asleep on the verandah until about 11.00 and then to bed. It keeps comparatively cool but sticky, though there is really little to complain about. But I shall be so glad, sweetheart, to be up there with you again – this place is dreary without you, but D.V. it won't be long until I am up there, and it will not be long after that that you will be able to come down again without being stewed alive.

 Myles & Dot (Wyatt – he worked in the Calcutta Port Authority retired in the middle of the slump and eventually became manager of the airport of Croydon. He bought Airwork Services which he developed into a substantial airline. He acquired a number of businesses and became a keen yachtsman, buying "Bloodhound" now restored and moored alongside the Royal Yacht in Leith, Edinburgh. He was knighted after the war.) *have asked me to dine quietly with them which is nice of them and I am taking the projector round to show some of their cine films which Charlie Chaplin took on their leave.*

 Office matters go on in the same old way – with not too much of a rush which is a good thing. Keep meaning to get Oscar along as I never seem to see him these days; and Robin, I don't seem to have seen anything of him either. He has quite recovered from his upset . . . Charles fell off his horse the other day & has his arm in a sling with a damaged muscle. The Barrats arrive today from Murkong Salek en route for England & Charles & I are going out to lunch with them all at Firpos – a party I am not really looking forward to!

 Your letter arrived quite safely and it was so good to get. I am sorry you have had so much rain but there is usually a small burst about now in the hills I am told. Anyhow,

I hope it soon will clear. It has rained a bit here today also. All my love to you, my Darling Dorkie, and to my wee Jean, with kisses and bunny hugs. I loved her letter about which more tomorrow. Always your Geordie."

Kalimpong was beginning to open up with houses being built on the south saddle overlooking the town and with wonderful views of the mountains, particularly the Kanchenjunga Massif some 45 miles away. It was about 4,500 ft up in the foothills of the Himalayas with a temperate cool climate. We children spent the war years in the summer there in the Odling's cottage adjoining Glenrilly. Norman Odling ran the ropeway linking the town with the plains and he and Bunty acted as surrogate parents to us during these war years. She was one of three daughters of Dr Graham, a Scottish missionary and the founder of the Kalimpong Homes, an orphanage and school founded at the turn of the 19th century for Nepalese and Bhutanese children, including those of mixed parentage. This became a thriving school complex with workshops for the blind and a medical centre with a resident doctor, and it thrives and survives to this day. Jean became a lifetime supporter having been educated there until we came home in May 1945. The Chomolhari mountain on the border between Tibet and Bhutan peeped above the horizon to the northeast.

Jen was born on 14th August, at the Eden Maternity Hospital, and shortly afterwards, Dorks again left for the cool of the hills, as George's letter of 12th October reveals:

"5 Alipore Road West Calcutta

My Darling Dorkiebus,

As I knew my letter had missed the post, I sent you a wire which I hope arrived quite safely. First of all, I see in today's Statesman that Betty has a daughter. I shall send some flowers on the way to the office with a note. I do hope that they are pleased; they ought to be. I will phone John and find out how Betty is. (John and Betty Burder had two daughters, Susan and Caroline, exact contemporaries of Jean and Jen. We grew up with them in Kalimpong during the war years. Susan was a talented artist – when asked to make a Christmas card in 1944, she drew the Holy Family arriving at Nazareth in a jeep with a flat tyre – JMM).

The next news is that the X-ray result on Molly Benthall shows that it is twins. Paul is now busy doubling everything and in a quiet way, his sense of humour is tickled but I believe Molly rather dreaded twins – it was the one thing she didn't want! However, they are due in December apparently. I do hope that things go alright for them. Molly is quite alright now apparently. It will be fun seeing Paul with the twins and I'm sure nobody will be more tickled than himself!

I had a busy day yesterday with a Finance Committee meeting at the Chamber at 4.00 which went on until nearly 6.00. I then went back & finished up in the office. After that, I dropped in to the B Club for tea and a quiet read.

E.S.T. came in for a bit yesterday afternoon – much against my will but he is a most obstinate patient! He arrived soon after 3.00 and as far as possible, I kept people off.

I have not heard yet how he stood it all as I had to go out at 4.00 and he was still there then. I got back here about 8.00." (E.S. Tarleton was the eldest of three brothers within Birds. He was originally assistant to William Ironside and soon showed early promise and competence in the reorganisation of the collieries from 1906 onwards. He had become a partner in 1917 and was recognised as an innovator, bringing new ideas "to every department he touched". He retired in 1933 due to ill health.) *"Myles & Charles asked me to go to a flick with them but I chose bed instead. They are a good couple and we had a most uproarious dinner last night. Myles got on to some of his experiences and was most amusing. Afterwards, I played the gramophone to myself for a bit and so to bed. The days are still hot but the nights get a little cooler. There have been thundershowers over the last couple of days and I suppose they have helped to make the nights cooler. It must have been lovely bathing in the pool but so cold! At first, anyhow. I was amused by your description of Smudge leaping in; he is such a good little chap.*

I am very sorry to hear about John Carey; it will be dreadfully worrying for Mrs Denham until she gets to him . . . I am afraid we are all very careless about these inoculations. It is so easy to have it done every two years and it does remove the possibility of one dreadful worry anyhow. One should do it, sweetheart, & I'm glad you will be done – as soon as possible!

I long to be up there with you, Sweetheart, but it is not so long, though I am sure that it is very wise to stay there until it is reasonably cool here. I hope my Buns are still flourishing too. All my love to you, my own Darling and to our own Bun (Jean) & weenie (Jen), always your Geordie."

There is now a three-year gap in our knowledge of family events. There are photographs of Jean and Jen growing up and these suggest that the pattern of life followed

50 *Jean and Jen*

that of the early years of their marriage, with Dorks and the children spending the cold weather in Calcutta and the hot weather in the hills, with George making visits as circumstances allowed. It was considered that the plains in the hot weather and monsoon months were unhealthy for children, and later correspondence suggests that there was a syndicate sharing various properties in which Lady Brabourne was a leading organiser. She was the wife of Lord Brabourne, Governor-General 1937-39. This was certainly the pattern of our own lives during the war. The photos of traditional half-timbered houses suggest that this was Shillong during this time.

The early to mid-1930s, as already mentioned, was a period of a slump in world trade and this affected all of Birds businesses. One idea was developed and christened TUSCAL – The United Steel Company of Asia Limited – it was Tom Benthall's special "baby". Birds had all the raw materials to commence steel-making; coal from Burrakur and Karanpura, coke from Loyabad ovens, iron ore from Orissa Minerals, limestone and dolomite from Bisra, electricity from the Sijua (Jerriah) power station, refractory bricks from Kumardhubi. . . . all these provided the necessary ingredients for the production of steel. The project was put together with the participation of Cammel Laird, but it never took off due to lack of demand. It was eventually overtaken by the slump in world demand for steel in the 1930s and shelved.

1935 saw the introduction of the new India Act, which paved the way for popular responsible government to be set up in the provinces. Burma was to be separated out and also given a degree of representative government.

51 Jean and Jen with solar topies circa 1935 in Shillong

The role of the legislative councils was expanded to include more Indian representation, although the British Government still retained overall control through the presence and authority of the Viceroy and Provincial Governors and their reserved powers as a part of a diarchy. There was essentially a division of responsibilities between the Viceroy's central powers and the legislative councils which were now partially elected; the number of provinces was also expanded. The unrest was to subside after the passing of the Act, although, from the correspondence of the time of my parents, there seems to be little indication of these changes affecting the way of life in Calcutta.

One other aspect of Birds is worth mentioning. D. W. Teasdale, with whom George had shared the Harrington Gardens chummery in the 1920s, became responsible for the rapidly expanding Birds Selling Agencies in the 1930s and was then transferred to the labour operations in late 1940, working alongside James Combe. Both were made partners in 1943. This aspect of Birds business was to become of increasing importance during the war, with labour contracts with the Calcutta Port Authority and Railways loading and unloading war supplies.

George had now been appointed a Director of the Imperial Bank of India. The Imperial Bank was India's premier commercial bank. Founded in 1923 out of a merger of three provincial banks in Calcutta, Bombay and Madras, it performed many of the functions of a state Bank until the formation of the separate state bank in 1935. Both in this and in the negotiations and discussions leading up to the 1935 act, Tom Benthall played a formative role. (See Appendix 1)

Political Developments – The 1935 Government of India Act – A prelude to Independence

The review of the 1919 India Act had started early and before the agreed review date of the tenth anniversary, not least in an attempt to take some of the steam out of the independence movement and the unrest that was brewing as a result of the activities and agitation of Mahatma Gandhi and other politicians and members of the Indian National Congress.

The formal discussions leading up to the 1935 Act started with the first of three Round Table conferences in 1930. Tom had been involved in a number of the sub-committees of the Bengal and Associated Chambers of Commerce, as indeed had George within the finance committee. The Chamber was the quasi-government organisation providing an essential link between Government and business, both British and Indian-based. Tom was, after all, senior partner of one of the biggest companies in India, well respected and popular with both communities, and was the President-elect for 1932, and therefore, Vice president in 1931 as a member of Council to the Chamber: he also spoke both Bengali and Hindi. He was asked to represent the Associated Chambers at the Second Round Table Conference scheduled for the autumn of 1931, and he travelled out by sea from Bombay with the rest of the Indian delegates in the August of that year, to join Ruth at home.

The principal objective of the Chamber was to ensure a level playing field between all businesses, both Indian and British, within the provisions of the Act. A measure of agreement had already been reached at the first Conference of 1930, but it is clear from the papers that the Chamber also played a significant part in the discussions as to how any future structure of Government might affect business more generally.

The issues of British commercial rights had been agreed in principle by way of a resolution of a sub-committee of the whole conference on January 19th 1931.

"At the insistence of the British commercial community, the principle was generally agreed that there should be no discrimination between the rights of the British mercantile community, firms and companies trading in India and the rights of Indian-born subjects, and that an appropriate convention based on reciprocity should be entered into for the purpose of regulating these rights."

The outline detail supporting the resolution was fleshed out and expanded upon with two meetings, the first between Tom and Gandhi on 29th September 1931 to exchange views, and the second on 14th October, where broad agreement was reached on various points. (This second meeting was attended by Gandhi, Mr Birla, a leading Indian industrial magnate, Sir Purshotammdas, Tom and Sir Hubert Carr (British Government). The initial meeting, with Gandhi and Tom alone, was to prepare the ground for the second. The broad agreement reached at this second meeting was largely as a result of Tom's work at the first one, in getting Gandhi onside. It covered the complete equality of commercial trading rights, no differential taxation or administrative discrimination, duties to be no more than that levied on imports and exports by any other country, complete freedom for ships registered in Britain to take part in coastal trade, and complete freedom for British subjects to come and go and to acquire movable and immovable property.

Gandhi subsequently took the agreement to the minorities, the Muslims and Parsees, the latter representing the important Parsee business community in Bombay, but they disagreed with the formula agreed on 14th October. However, the subject was then taken to the Federal committee, at which Tom made a long and conciliatory speech, and the approach was agreed with the support of the Indian moderates, under the able support of the chairman Lord Sankey, and what Tom describes as the "brilliant" support

52 Waiting for a train to camp with guns and luggage and household servants l to r Dorks, Joan and Teddie Shuttleworth

of Lord Reading, a former Viceroy and now Foreign Secretary. Sufficient safeguards were agreed upon for inclusion in the Act.

It is also worth mentioning that the whole process of giving India a greater degree of self-governance was bitterly opposed by Winston Churchill and others; he had resigned over the issue and was to remain on the backbenches for ten years.

Throughout the whole of the discussions and Conference, Tom was making regular reports back to the President of the Chamber. At the conclusion of the Conference, Tom went back to India, landing in Bombay off the "Narkunda" on 1st January, and the account of his final meetings with Gandhi includes a description of his meeting and their agreement to continue discussion through a Viceroy's standing committee. Tom was to continue to take an active part in advice to the negotiations in the 3rd Round Table meeting. This third Conference led up to the White Paper and the 1935 Act itself. Despite protests to the Viceroy from the Associated Chambers and the English Association (on which George was a council member), Tom was denied representation to the 3rd Conference with the representations from the business community continued by Sir Hubert Carr. The reasons for his exclusion are given in his notes (again, see Appendix 1).

The results of the negotiations surfaced in the Government of India Act 1935, distinguished perhaps by its length as one of the longest in Parliamentary history. The eventual target of Dominion status was left inconclusive, but the Act made self-government almost inevitable as part of India's future. The principal features of the Act were firstly, the ending of diarchy enshrined in the 1919 Act, thereby limiting the overarching control of the Provincial Governors and replacing it instead with a largely elected council from an extended franchise. This new federal system of government was reinforced by the rearrangement of the provinces, with Sind now separated from Bombay, and Bihar and Orissa also given full provincial status. Burma was now completely separated from India as an independent colony, with Aden also detached from India and also given full status as a Crown colony. The act also provided for the inclusion not just of British India but also some or all of the Princely States. Membership of the assemblies was altered so that any number of Indian representatives could be elected, now able to form majorities, and be appointed to form governments. The act also established a Federal Court. The Bill, which was largely incorporated into the Act, contained 473 clauses and 16 schedules with debate consuming 4,000 pages of Hansard. The Act was given Royal assent in August 1935. The principles of non-discrimination for business, in which Tom Benthall was so closely involved, were incorporated in the Act. The Act contained a whole series of safeguards including the power of the Government to take back control of government, and to hold reserved powers, particularly in Defence and External Relations. This power was to be exercised in the early stages of the Far Eastern war when the decision was taken to imprison and intern the Congress leaders including Gandhi and Pandit Nehru. And it is interesting to note that this decision was taken by the Viceroy's Council, the only British representatives on which were the Viceroy and Tom Benthall, with all the rest Indian.

After the death of the Mahatma, Tom was to summarise and write a full account of his impressions and all his meetings with him, a paper which is full of humour and shrewd assessment and it is included in full as Appendix 1 to this book.

A separated family and the arrival of John – 1937, 38, 39 & 40 letters

George, Dorks and the two girls would have had a home leave sometime in 1934 but the timings suggest that as George was now a partner, there was some degree of flexibility over dates. John was born on Boxing Day, 1936, a longed-for son, mercifully in the middle of the cold weather, again in the Eden Maternity Hospital in Calcutta.

As both Jean and Jen had been, John was baptised in St Patrick's Catholic Church in Fort William – John's eldest daughter, Janetta, was also to be baptised there in early 1963. Dorks and the children sailed home on leave shortly afterwards; George followed them by air shortly afterwards, landing at Croydon Airport on 19th April, his first trip by air. There are photographs of the family staying at Walstead House near Lingfield in Sussex which was now the rented home in England. This was within a mile or two of East Mascles, the Elizabethan country home of Arthur and Bea MacNaught, cousins of George's mentioned in the 1914-18 wartime correspondence with Sis. It is not clear when the rental arrangement was made but it is possible that it was for the 1934 leave. There is extensive and later correspondence over the rental arrangements with Arthur MacNaught, and it is probable that he also arranged the tenancy for the family. Walstead was also the family home after the war from 1945-6.

The family were to remain in England until July 1940 during the whole time of the build-up to war and nine months after its declaration and the fall of Poland, the Low Countries and France to the Germans. George was in Calcutta for most of this time, and there is extensive correspondence between George and Dorks over this period, most of which has survived.

There is a short letter from the Butler Arms Hotel, Waterville, Co Kerry, Eire dated 15.07.37 where he had gone to fish.

"My own Darling,
It was lovely to get your letter on my return and I am glad you and the chaps are well and that the household goes smoothly. I do so hope and believe it will. Poor old Jen seems to have got it into her wee head that her chaps have to leave her for long periods – but D.V. it will not be long now that one can fly so easily.

Well, sweetheart, yesterday was a real stinker & rained all day. But I went out & fished all day. Just as well I had waders. But it was good fun and after dinner, it cleared a bit & I went out again and tried the river near here. But no salmon; only two brown trout, one so small that I threw him back – home again!

I got back here again about 10.45 & so to bed. I fairly sleep in this place; I suppose it is the air. I wish you were here, sweetheart. I think you would love it – once the rain stops! There are a lot of cheery old birds in the hotel and though it is a bit full, it doesn't seem overcrowded.

I am off to fish one of the higher lakes today & I hope it doesn't rain quite so much. Take care of your darling self. I miss you all the time and think of you and the chaps always. All my love to you, always your Geordie."

George was to return alone to India at the end of his leave leaving Dorks and the children at Walstead for Christmas, Jean now seven, Jen four and John rising one. Within the context of colonial life at the time, the decision was not unusual; families were increasingly separated as the Second World War approached and broke. As the next letter reveals, their plans were for a return to India in the spring.

"Bengal Club Calcutta 15.11.37

My own Darling,

I am glad to say it is a little cooler & less oppressive. We have had very hot heavy stinking days since I returned but I hope we may now be in for some cooler weather. I still hardly feel I am here and resent being here! I must say I have never felt quite like this before but I expect it is the sudden burst of heat which I found when I got here and the simply heavenly leave I have had, and the miserable business of leaving you and the chaps behind though I would rather you had that climate rather than this one. But I miss you all the time, sweetheart, and I miss our chaps; bless you, Darling heart, and theirs. I shall not feel really alive until we are all together again.

Well, I wrote to you last on Armistice Day. I went to the Cenotaph with Bunty and my goodness it was hot! Saw Betty and Lawrence who were full of chat and of enquiries of you and the chaps. The next day was a holiday so I did a lot of clearing up & was in the office until lunchtime. Went to a flick before dinner and after dinner went to a Cabaret entertainment given by Mackinnon Mackenzie to celebrate the centenary of the P&O. It was held at George Campbell's house and was very well done. There was a big stage up in the garden to represent the deck of a ship and people danced (and sweated!) and in the intervals, there were some excellent cabaret turns. Saw a lot of our friends – I went with Shrosbree & we sat with the Mellites – saw Helen & Manoli (of Ralli Brothers, Greek bankers and agents – particularly for jute of which they were Calcutta's largest exporters . . . Manoli was Greek, Helen American – JMM) *who sent their love to you, Jack Thomas, Charles Thomas and many others. Charles Thomas specially came over & said how sorry he was to have missed us at Southwick and how lucky they were to have chaps like you and us staying at Southwick & that his people had been so delighted – with you especially! He was in very good form and hopes to get married early next year at home. Have seen Donald Macpherson once or twice & he & his family are all well.*

Ram Lal came in to see me – his wife has died in childbirth. I told him you had said that you would like him in England & he at once salaamed & upped & said eagerly that he would go, & it would be quite easy – his wife had died and he would go!! And I believe he would go too. Anyhow, he has been with Hilda in Shillong until a few days ago and now he will wait until you return. He is a good chap, Ram Lal, and was full of searching enquiries after you and each one of the chaps. Then the mali turned up in good form too and full of grins & requests for news. I must go out soon and see the Campbells.

Talking to Ernest about the Peter Scott pictures, he told me he thought Joan was getting the two latest ones for Teddy as a present. I told him we were going to try & get them from Aldridges, Worthing, & he said that he too would very much like them so if we did get them and found that Joan has got some for Teddie – he would be very glad for an opportunity to buy them from us if we wanted to dispose of them. So, I should get them from Aldridges if you can and we shall find somebody who would appreciate them – either Joan &T or Molly & Ernest.

I went out to camp on Saturday – Teddie had invited Molly & Ernest and we had a cheery weekend. Sandy and Molly Mealing were there already and when we arrived, we found them resting in our room – I was not expected! – after a good deal of laughing and backchat! (Sandy Cameron – wife of Ronnie and mother of Diana and Mickey, and her sister, Molly Mealing, wife of Kenneth – later Sir Kenneth – parents of Shirley and Lois, all good friends and contemporaries of us children. Ronnie was to die, tragically murdered in the Calcutta riots of 1948 – his emergency replacement was Sir Paul Benthall, younger brother of Tom. Teddie is Teddie Shuttleworth. He and his wife Joan were very good friends; his son Barney was to marry my sister Jean, and Gilly, their daughter, married Bertie Sinclair of Balmer Lawrie. Joan was to look after us children in early 1938 while Dorkie was in Calcutta, having spent Christmas at Walstead.). *We went up to Bojoola and got 16 ½ couple – should have got many more – the guns were Teddie, Ronnie, Ernest, Molly and me. Teddie was right off his shooting & so was Ronnie. I wasn't up to the best form by any means but I got 8 couple out of the 16 ½ – we didn't return to camp & got a train which arrived back in Calcutta before 8.00. A good weekend and it was definitely cooler.*

I told Teddie that if you were feeling depressed, to send an S.O.S. to Joan and he said that Joan would be delighted to get one and be able to find a reason to get away from her people as she sounded "fed up" and had had enough! So here you are, Sweetheart, if you are feeling the need for any moral support!

I do hope that you have found some domestics, Sweetheart. I did so hate leaving you with all that before you – I am afraid I haven't been much use over that and I feel that in many ways I am to blame for persuading you to try and meet the Harmans when they complained on our return from Scotland. I see now that they were hoping that we should make a change – it would in many ways have been better to have done it then. But it can't be helped, sweetheart, and I expect that I will hear that you have got somebody good. I love you for your resolution over this, Sweetheart, and I believe now that it doesn't pay to be too "nice" to them – they don't understand it and only take advantage. If one is fair and reasonable and not a "nagger", I honestly believe now that they like it better. When they are well established, it may be different but as you have often said lately, it is no use trying to treat everyone the same and be too kind. The more I think of the Harmers, the more foolish I feel over it for the part I played in getting you to go to such lengths to satisfy

53 *Dorks at the camp fire Shimmerally Camp*

them. *But I always thought it might make them settle down and be more reasonable. However, don't worry your Darling self as I know you will find somebody good who will settle down and stay . . . All the time I long to hear from you. I do so much want you to be able to take it easy and enjoy it all to the full and get really strong and healthy.*

Tuesday. *The Air mail timings have been changed and we now post on Tuesdays and Thursdays. The mails come in on Wednesday nights and Friday nights – delivered on Thursdays and Saturdays. So, D.V., I should get a letter from you on Thursday. Yesterday I dined with Ernest and a lady. I seem to have seen them a lot since I got back! Tom and Heath Longfield were there too and Teddie was to have been but he has a Calcutta throat – not too bad I believe but he thought he would not go out. Heath is having a baby in March or April – all in very good form. Bog was so glad to see me, and Lear too. They did roly poly and sat up and cried and did all the tricks at dinner. Bog is as greedy as ever too! The pups are a grand couple, sturdy rough little tykes!*

The cook came in to see me in the office yesterday asking all about you and the chaps. He seems happy but wants you to come back so that he can be our cook again. He too will go to England if required! They are a good lot. Dil hasn't appeared yet but no doubt he will. (Dil Bahadur, George's Nepali driver and a good friend to us all – Bahadur means "brave heart" in Nepali – He used to drive us up the hill to Kalimpong and down again to the stations. His younger brother Ransingh became my bearer in 1962 and retaught me Hindustani as a *Munchi* (= teacher – in 1962 – JMM).

I hope that Jean's head was safely dealt with at the small bad spot – what a relief it will be to have it over and dealt with. She has been a little brick about it all. And Jen too, I hope that she is fit and cheery and my little son John with his fat smiles & laughs. I long to hear about them – I wonder if John's teeth have begun to arrive yet. I suppose the gate is finished and looks nice. There is still a trug full of bulbs which Kent should plant in the front garden below the steps beyond the flagged path.

I wonder if Hammy has got his small table and the fire dogs yet. I think it would be safe to let him send the fire dogs without first seeing them or at anyhow saying we will have them. It is going to be more difficult to see the table as I don't suppose you will want to go right over there. But I don't think he will sell it without letting us see it first and he may bring it over or perhaps Kent could bring it – just to have a look at. He would be careful, I think. But I shouldn't worry until you are more or less settled again and feel a strong chap. In case you want it, Hammy's name and address is E Hamilton, Tigne, Frimley Road, Ash Vale, Nr Aldershot; phone Ash Vale 3230. I forgot to get dog licences for our two dogbies – I hope they are fit and healthy.

I long to be with you again my sweetheart, and, D.V., it will not be long. Three months will soon pass. I miss you and our wee chaps all the time and if it is possible more than ever. All my love to you, my own Darling, and our wee chaps – always your own Geordie."

This letter is one of the longest of the whole series. George's letters were written from the Bengal Club, where he was staying, as the Campbells were looking after the Alipore house. The Bengal Club was the senior club in Calcutta with membership from the leaders of commerce and government. It was located at the southern end of Chowringhee, opposite St Paul's Cathedral, where my grandparents were married in 1901.

The servants were turning up now that George had returned, with the bush telephone working overtime, generally sourced from overheard table talk. Events were to overtake Dork's plans with the family in the spring as the following letters reveal. Having spent Christmas at Walstead, with, apart from others, her parents, Dork's mother Mabel became ill and suddenly died around 5th January 1938.

"Bengal Club Calcutta Tuesday 11.1.38

My own darling Dorkie,

All your letters have arrived up to date now and your last was written after Mum became ill when Jean went off with Joan and party to Kitzbuhal & you remained behind. I have never before wanted to be with you just as much as I have since last Tuesday, sweetheart. This has been a very sad time for you and I have been powerless to help you and comfort you ever since I got your cable. I expect poor Dad is simply lost without Mum and I shall be glad to have your next few letters, especially to hear how he is bearing up and what plans are for the future. I don't expect the poor chap has been able to think much yet, & I am sure a lot will fall upon you to decide & do. I know that you will bear up, my darling one, and try not to worry too much and keep your heart up. I just long to have you with me and take you right away while the next few weeks are passing . . . I hate not being with you, Sweetheart.

I am just going to write about your letters and what I have been doing, for last week I got your two letters written at Christmas. What a thrill for all the chaps, bless their little hearts, but it must have been exhausting for you & Joan and I can just see you both sinking down utterly exhausted! But what a joy for all the others and I am glad to hear that Barney has been out with King and seen a woodcock. What a thrill for him, lucky young rascal. I honestly don't know how you got through it all and you must have worked like a black – also Joan. But as I say, it must have been so good to see everyone enjoying themselves so – and my little John too. I must say I would have loved to have heard him when the conjurer was performing at Bea's party! How the little funnies must have simply loved her Christmas and how Mum and Dad & Jim must have loved being there too with you all. I do hope it didn't leave you too exhausted. Golly, it would have been marvellous to have been able to be with you, Sweetheart. It is amusing to hear how wee John is growing and fitting clothes for a child of two! I hope he is going to be a real husky! Bless him. What a blessing to have such good and happy staff and how you must have blessed the day the old Harmers lightened our doors. The more I read your letters about Christmas, the more I marvel that you weren't more exhausted than you actually seemed to be! It is so good to hear all about it from you, Sweetheart. I can't tell you how much I love getting your letters; it is next best thing to being there myself. Bea's party

54 *Jean and Dorks in the surf at Puri with like savers wearing conical hats made of straw*

sounded simply grand and it is good to hear that Arthur is better – I only hope he goes on being better for it is miserable for everyone when he is in such dreadful form.

I am glad you saw Dorrie Beves – a very cheery soul she used to be, very kind and happy & naughty! How Vi used to hate her (because Arthur liked her!). I wonder who it was staying with Bea and Arthur over Christmas, Mabel Stevens? I haven't seen her for twenty years but I wonder if it was she. Being out here makes it impossible to keep in touch with people.

I am sorry about the drive and I wonder if it is the bit between the gate (front) and the stables, for the drive bends a bit there and gets more wear from cars that come in too fast as most of the tradesmen runs seem to do – but am sure Dunkerleys will put it right and next summer it might be worth having it tarred and more stones rolled into the top. It is important to keep it in good order as you say.

Don't worry about finances, Sweetheart. I think you are managing it all very well and the Firm had a good year last year so we should get a good share! I do so wish you could have got to Kitzbuhel but it was of course quite out of the question. But do take care of your sweet self, my Darling one. You are everything in the world to me, my darling one. I want you to be well and fit. So do take care of your darling self and spare yourself as much as you can. I was inoculated against enteric on Friday and so didn't go to camp. The Stewards of the Turf Club asked me to lunch on Saturday & I came away before tea. The Meath Home concert was a terrific success and I believe they have made a little more than last year's one which was also a great success of course. Young Pilkington & Molly did it all between them and I am glad that it turned out so well. (David Pilkington, later senior partner of Birds and President of the Bengal Chamber. – JMM) *Shrosbree told me that it was a record house for the concerts and he particularly congratulated the Meath Homes on the result. Lady Reed wrote and suggested that she should resign from the Presidentship as it was obviously better to have somebody from Bengal. She agreed, however, to remain as Chairman (woman!) of the Shillong committee which is of course ideal as it keeps Assam interested in the Home. Lady Brabourne has agreed to become President* (wife of the Governor-General of Bengal – JMM). *Molly got a three-minute interview with her at a G.H.* (Government House – JMM) *dinner and told her about it and she agreed. So that is a very good thing and it should make a great deal of difference to the Meath Home. Molly feels happy about it and feels that she can go home on leave! On Sunday, I went out & saw her and Paul & the twins and sat and talked until lunchtime – I wanted to find out if there was anything I could do about the concert.*

I see that Fergus has been made a judge and I am so very glad as this is a great step forward for him in his profession and one which I know he will very happy to have won. (Fergus Morton was George's first cousin. A distinguished Chancery lawyer and now KC, he was to become Lord Morton of Henryton, a Lord of Appeal – JMM). *I must write to him today. I have done nothing else worth mentioning though I still seem to have more engagements than I should like.*

I shall finish this in the office, Sweetheart. It has been raining the last few days which is rapidly cooling it down I'm glad to say.

Later. Well, I am just packing up for the day and there is nothing fresh to tell you, Sweetheart. It has been cloudy all day and there is more rain about.

Take all care of your sweet self and our wee chaps. God bless your darling self and them. All my love to you, my own Darling, and to them. Always your own Geordie."

The next letter also dwells on Mabel's death.

"Bengal Club Calcutta 18.01.38

My own Darling,

I got your last letter yesterday morning as the mail was late. It was wise to have the memorial service as soon as possible. I think that it is so wrong when people wait for a week or more. I do so hate not being there with you, my Darling. There is so much I could do for you all but I am very glad you have got Jim to undertake a definite job. It is the only way and I am sure he will buckle to and help. What a good thing it would be if Uncle Reggie would stay on at 18 Queen Anne Street for the problem is going to be to keep poor Dad going. If only Jim would, he could easily run things for the household instead of staying on in the office long after office hours, especially if Jenny the cook is willing to help. I should try and get him to take it on and get Uncle Reggie to stay on too – but no doubt you have settled on some plan for keeping things going. It is a good thing, Sweetheart, that you will be home at regular intervals for Dad needs both you and Jim to depend upon and even if you are out here most of the time, it will be a comfort to him to know you are going to be home frequently too.

I am glad that Uncle Charles is doing what is necessary to settle up Mum's financial affairs and I am glad he has had a look at the executors of Dad's will. (Uncle Charles was Mabel's brother and a solicitor). *I entirely agree with you, sweetheart, about the advisability of getting Dad to appoint his Bank as an additional Trustee to act with Uncle Charles. Uncle Charles is the one to advise Dad that he has only one surviving Trustee and it is necessary to appoint another. It is quite a simple thing to arrange and I'm sure Uncle Charles could very easily fix it all up without fussing Dad. The Bank could do it also if Dad wishes. In an emergency, don't hesitate to ask Fergus to advise you for he could give you the name of a reliable solicitor who could help you but I am sure that will not be necessary.*

Bless you, my darling, for being so determined to come out here as arranged. I do so appreciate you, my own Darling one, and I'm only half alive when you are not with me. I long all the time for us to be together again and I only hope everything will be satisfactorily settled so that you can do as we plan. But I want you to know that if things are not satisfactory and you should postpone sailing, I shall understand, Sweetheart, though D.V., all should be well.

Well, since writing last Thursday, I don't seem to have done very much. On Saturday evening I went to a sherry party at Burdwans but the rest of the weekend I spent in the Club doing odd jobs of work, etc. Ted Tarleton arrived on Saturday with Mrs T on a trip. He will be here about three weeks and is staying at the Great Eastern. He came to see me on Sunday morning and we sat here in my rooms bucking for over an hour. He has a little lumbago but is in great form.

On Sunday, I made a list of our silver & plate out here and soon I hope all lists both of our things here and at home will be finished. I packed up the chest again carefully and will keep it until you arrive out again. It is of course all insured in the meantime but I have promised the underwriters fresh lists.

I hope to go to camp next weekend – weekends spent in Calcutta are wasted at this time of year but I couldn't get out of Burdwan's show and also, I expected to have my second inoculation on Friday and thought it best to stay here, but Frank McCay advised me to wait until today for the second shot as I had a good reaction last time and he didn't want to rush it. Teddie sent me a snap of Joan & Jean & Barney on skis – it was the only one he had so I had to return it but it was such a jolly snap and they looked so happy and well. I am glad you have heard from Joan that they are all going strong. I bet the children are all loving it.

I do hope that things are settling themselves satisfactorily, Sweetheart, and that you are able to take things more easily and that you are not worrying too much about anything. But I am sure that you have found there is such a lot to do. I do so wish you could have been spared all this, my Darling one, though I am sure that you are glad you are there. I should feel better about it all if only I could have been with you.

Take care of your Darling Self and of our wee chaps. God bless you and them, always your own Geordie."

In the next letter, things have settled down a bit at home.

"Bengal Club Calcutta Tuesday 25 01 38

My own Darling,

I got both your letters quite safely last week and it was so good to get them and to hear that things are slowly getting straight. It is going to be very difficult to know what is best for poor Dad but the arrangements you are making seem to me by far the best and if Uncle Reggi (another of Mabel's brothers – JMM) *will spend a part of each week at Queen Anne Street and Jim will take on a bit and be with Dad as much as he can, and if one or two friends will make a point of coming to see Dad and asking him to see them, it will keep him occupied and give him a chance of settling down again – but it is going to very hard for him, poor chap, without Mum. I am sure it is best, Sweetheart, to do as you suggest and come out as arranged. It will also give you a break and if you go back again a bit earlier than intended, you will not have been away long and it will give Dad a chance to know what he really feels about the house.*

Of course, it depends on how he feels for some would like to stay in the same house whilst others would want to move – it all depends on the wishes of the individual. Also, as you say, it depends upon whether he can dispose of the remainder of the lease. But if he really wants to leave it and can dispose of the lease, which should be quite possible, it might be much easier for him and Jim to have a nice service flat somewhere, where they would have no trouble with servants and other problems. But only Dad and Jim can decide that and it depends on so many circumstances which change almost daily. Actually, if Dad settles down again and the maids stay on, there doesn't seem any hurry about it and it could easily wait until your return I should think. However, it is not a question which can be settled all at once Sweetheart and time will help to decide it. I got Dad's letter too with your last one on Saturday. Poor Dad; I'm so terribly sorry for him. I greatly appreciate getting a letter from him. I will of course do anything necessary to settle up Mum's estate in India and I will get right on to it as soon as I hear from Uncle Charles. It shouldn't be very difficult and I will look into Dad's holdings too just to make sure they are all right. From what he told me some time ago, I gathered that most of his holdings are held jointly with Mum. But I can find that out. With such holdings, only a death certificate is required to have them transferred to the survivor and death duties are avoided. Sometimes, however, the Probate authorities – if they know of such holdings, ask for proof that the joint holdings were the property of the survivor, when it may be difficult to prove. But that shouldn't arise here. Where any securities or shares were in Mum's name only, they will have to come into Mum's estate. But there is no need to worry about it, Sweetheart, and I will do all that is necessary as soon as I hear from Uncle Charles and the lawyers. Being a Director of the Imperial Bank may make it easier as I think the accounts are here. I also wrote to Bennett by last sea mail and sent him your papers in connection with your war loan. I had a letter all signed and ready, sending the papers to your Bank for safe custody on your account when I got your letter late on Thursday saying that Bennett was kindly doing the necessary. I had the letter changed & retyped and addressed to Bennett – it is much better to let IS & Co London keep the War Loan papers in the meantime. Later on, when Mum's estate is all cleared up, you might be wise to keep everything at your London Bank, but there is no hurry about that. I have written thanking Bennett for all he is doing. He is a brick.

But all the time, my darling one, I hate not being with you to help with all this. Do take care of yourself and don't do too much. Golly, I shall be glad to have you with me again and, apart from anything else, it will take you away from it all for a while and when you get home again you will find things far easier, I believe. If nothing stops you coming out as arranged, as I pray nothing does, I should certainly go back again earlier than intended, for then you can feel happier in your mind about Dad. But don't worry too much, my Darling one – everything will turn out for the best and you have been marvellous about it all.

Well, last Thursday, I went to the Knights of Caledonia dance – dined with the Richardsons where Molly and Paul and the Colsons were also dining – we joined up with Peter and Bunty Roberts when we got to the dance – it was a real good dance as usual and I quite enjoyed it. I had a dance with Molly Smythe and Lenore and couldn't get one with Mrs Colson (which was bad luck!) I went out to Naihali on Saturday morning early, leaving here at 5.00 a.m. and after lunching here at the club, went up to camp. There was an enormous party – Sandy and Ronnie, Teddie, Geoff and me, the

55 "Bogie 39" from nose to tail

Mealings, Stephen Lyttleton & Mary Gascoigne (one of the girls staying with Stephen, a cheery person) and Inez Peg (Dick Peg didn't come). On Sunday, just before lunch, Helen and George came up. Teddie, Geoff & I and Molly Mealing went up by launch to Balaghur and had a good day – got 35 couple – all the rest stayed at camp. (Helen and George Gemmell were also close family friends – Helen, a Froebel-trained teacher, taught me mathematics in Kalimpong – Mike and Ian – their sons – latter my father's godson. After the war, they settled in Stonehouse, Gloucestershire, and were regular visitors). *We got back soon after 6.00 to find Helen & George there and Stephen and Mary Gascoigne departed on the 5.45 train as they were due in Calcutta for dinner. Teddie & I left on the 7.50 train after tea & a bath and I was in bed before 10.00. It was a good weekend and everyone seems to have enjoyed it. I saw Pitts at the club at lunchtime yesterday looking very fit and cheery – I shall try and get him to a meal here soon.*

I am glad that Ruth is installed in her London house as it ought to make a great difference to her as she has such lovely things to put into them. I am glad you went to lunch with her. Tom is due out here on 12ᵗʰ February unless he sails later than intended. Still plenty of work here, though things aren't so bad.

Dorrie writes that Rowley Pegs and she expect to arrive here early in Feb and stay about a month so I hope they may still be here when you arrive – they propose to visit Darjeeling which is wise of them, I think. I'm sure Rowley would enjoy seeing the snows. They will stay at the Great Eastern and I shall get them up to stay a weekend at

Monty's bungalow at Kinnison or else Camp – but I'm sure they will enjoy it and going to Darjeeling will give them a break.

I long to be with you, my sweetheart. Take all care of your Darling self and don't worry. I loved Jean's letter – the wee funny will be home again by now. All my love to you, my own Darling and to our wee chaps. God bless you and them – always your own Geordie."

The final letter in this series concentrates on Dork's pending return to Calcutta and Rowley and Dorrie's visit.

"Bengal Club Calcutta 15.02.38

My own Darling,

It was lovely getting your letter on Saturday. It was delivered to me early before I had got up. And on Sunday early, I got your cable for my birthday which was also so good to get. I do hope that it wasn't too hectic a time before you left and that you have been able to take it easy on the ship and that you have a good cabin. Golly, how good it will be when we are together again and D.V. it will not be long now. I shall send you a cable on Wednesday or Thursday just to send you my love and wish you bon voyage . . . I am glad Dad stayed at Walstead and I am sure he loved being with you and all the chaps. A fortnight in Kitzbuhel should have put Jim right and I expect he will be able to keep Dad going with Uncle Reggie's help. Soon you will be with them again and by then I am sure they will be far more settled.

It must have been fun going back to Eastbourne – that is one of the things I wanted to do before I left, but I hope that we may do it next time. It is so good, Sweetheart, to hear about the little dogbies & the garden and most of all, of course, about what you and the chaps are doing at Walstead. I do hope Joan will be happy there whilst you are away. I hope Bennett fixes up all finances for you – as I'm sure he did. Don't worry about it, Sweetheart. We are doing fine and it is worth untold gold to know you and the chaps are happy at Walstead . . .

Well, last Thursday I lunched in the guest room here at a farewell to James Donald. He was in good form. After office, I went out to Tolly to collect Dorrie & Rowley – Dorrie had been playing Mollie Smythe & Rowley had played Harry Harrison. (Game of golf at Tolly – JMM) I dined quietly here and went early to bed. Friday was a holiday and I was in the office until 1.00 clearing up accumulations. Played squash in the evening & then dined out with Betty and Pip Price. I went to see Rowley and Dorrie on the way to office & they were spending a quiet day writing letters & Rowley played a few holes of golf in the afternoon. The Stokes & Pitts were dining with Betty & Pip and were taken to the New Empire. On Saturday, being another holiday, I played Rowley at golf starting at 8.00 and had a most enjoyable game getting to office at about 12.00. Then I lunched with Rowley and D & we went to the Races. We dined together at their hotel & I took them to a flick & then on to a quick beer at the Saturday Club – quite a busy day! On Sunday, being my birthday, I got your lovely cable. Then D & R & I went on the Lillian for the day. We had a most restful day & got up as far as Naihali, getting back to Outram Ghat long before 11.00. I dined quietly with them at the Great Eastern when Rowley insisted on giving me champagne and I was in bed and asleep before 11.00. I think they are enjoying themselves and I am trying to keep them amused without overdoing it. I didn't see them yesterday but today I am lunching with them. I think their boat goes about a week after you arrive so I am very glad they will see you before they leave. Needless to say, they very much want to have a few days with you. Yesterday it began to get hot and the temperature was a few degrees above normal but I hope that we may yet get hail storms to cool it down before you arrive.

Tom arrived in Bombay last week and is now in Delhi. We expect him here at the end of the week when we shall get all the news. I don't know when he proposed to go home to see Ruth but I expect that it will be May or June. Paul hasn't been too well and went to Puri last weekend which seems to have done him good. He is ready for his leave, I think. Well, Sweetheart, I must shave I suppose- will finish this in the office later.

Office. *Nothing fresh, Sweetheart. I have a streaming cold in the head but nothing really to complain about! I lunched at the Great Eastern with D & R today and am hoping to get away at about 4.00 & play a few holes of golf with Rowley. I am thinking of you all the time, Sweetheart. It will be heavenly having you here again. Take care of your Darling self. All my love to you, my own Darling one. Always your own Geordie."*

One other character appears in the letters . . . Pitts Squarey. He was my godfather and an old friend of my parents. A confirmed bachelor, he eventually succumbed to marriage after he retired, and I met him and fiancée Francis in Scotland in the summer of 1954. He always referred to my father as "Failed Jubilee Medal", an award that Pitts received in 1935/6 and which my father did not.

Dorks arrived in Calcutta at the beginning of March . . . it was the last time they were to be together until Christmas 1939, during which time war loomed and was declared on September 3rd 1939. She stayed until June and then booked a flight home, the first time that she had flown out or back to India, as George's letter of 16th June reveals:

"My own Darling,

It is Saturday and I have just changed for golf as in about half an hour I am playing Bunty. When I got to the golf shoes, Bog came to life and rushed at me and licked and licked as she knows it's golf! (This was Bogie, one of their four dachshunds . . . the others were Biscuit, Bessie and Binny; Bogie was a particularly long dog, the dominating member of the pack, measuring 39" from nose tip to tail end. The sequence of ' B'-named dachshunds was followed after our return to the UK with Bulger, a greedy dog, and Bonum, who was not quite so good as his name might suggest.) *But alas, it's still races at Tolly so I can't take them. They are little funnies & they miss their golf as I haven't taken them out since you left. But I will take them out for ordinary walkies now they are all invulnerable again. I didn't really answer your last letter, Sweetheart, as it arrived the day I wrote. It must have been great fun seeing Liz and Maurice* (Maurice Foght, Ruth's doctor and his daughter – JMM) *and I should have so much liked to see them. It will be good if you can get on the same ship coming out. Interesting about old Bill. He is a funny old brush and I can understand his feelings with no job at all but I think he has been very drastic & silly as I'm sure he could have got a job at home & so enabled himself to marry his lady if he had really gone flat out to do it. But he is a funny old bird & does seem to have made an awful mess of all his greatest problems. But it is not too late if only he had somebody who would advise him sensibly so I hope he may go off home someday soon and really settle down at home and marry & not be an old goof. I will write the old stinker soon but will not mention about his Peggy. Poor old Bill – I do wish things would start going right again for him.*

I am glad that you are going to try and get Joan a dressing-case. She has been such a brick. I shall probably write her tomorrow. It would just be heavenly to be at home for a while with you and the chaps, but there it is & D.V. it won't be long.

I expect you are feeling alright again after the trip. Yes, it certainly is tiring especially the first time when it is all strange, but it is a wonderful way of travelling and I am glad you have done it. Golly, it must have been good arriving at Croydon! And I bet the little ones were thrilled. (Croydon was the airport for Imperial Airlines for land-based operations. Around that time, they were flying Handley Page land-based aircraft as well as Short flying boats for water landings, so Dorkie would have probably been flying on a Handley Page aircraft, possibly either the Hannibal or Heracles class. Myles Wyatt had, by that stage, left India and was the manager of the Croydon Airport. The journey would have taken about six days, with overnight stays on route. They would have carried airmail cargo, plus up to twenty passengers in wicker seats. Food and refreshments would have been provided in flight. – JMM)

Molly Smythe 'phoned yesterday and told me that the Waif had died. Poor little fellow had some rather drastic treatment for his hookworm and it was too much for him. But in many ways, I expect it is better that way. I am dining with Ernest and Molly tonight.

Well, yesterday I went to a flick after dinner with Manoli & Jack Thomas. Jack is off on Monday. I think I told you Robin flew home on Thursday as Enid has been so seedy. Valcari & Fitzpatrick were also dining with Manoli & we had a quiet evening.

Later. *Well, I played Bunty at golf and we had a pleasant game though I seem to get worse and worse! But it is good fun and good for the bella. This is the last day's racing so next week I hope to take the dogbies. I think Bins has clicked "for a family" though I am not certain yet. Anyhow, they are all in good form.*

Well, Sweetheart, I will stop. I hope to get a letter from you tonight or tomorrow early D.V. Take all care of your Darling Self and of our wee chaps. God bless you and them. All my love to you, my own Darling & to them. Always your own Geordie."

There is now a gap of just over a year in the correspondence from June 1938 to August 1939. Although George refers earlier to a return of the family to India, it is clear that we actually did not go back; subsequent correspondence from August to December 1939 confirms that we were in England throughout the rest of 1938 into 1939 until mid-1940. (There are, however, two nursing certificates, issued 15.2.39 and 29.04.39 by St John's Indian Nursing Association, which suggests that Dorks was in Calcutta then and this may account for part of the gap in correspondence . . . we just don't know.) George, though, remained working in Calcutta throughout but they were separated until George managed to get home for a short break over Christmas 1939, when, no doubt, future plans were discussed. It seems, therefore, that the 12-month gap in correspondence means that it continued but has not survived.

War looms and breaks – the family move to Lindridge in Devon July 1939

This period was also one of real difficulty and uncertainty for George and Dorks against the ever-increasing prospect of war with Germany. Jean was now eight and ready for school, and the family had settled at Walstead. Grandfather Fred was in failing health following the sudden death of Mabel earlier in the year. Dorks was the mainstay of events here too. So, there were many reasons for the family to stay put at Walstead, although this was to change in the middle of 1939, with war then imminent.

Since 1934/5, Germany had been rearming. In 1936, Germany reoccupied the Rhineland to the enthusiastic reception of the local population but in direct contravention of the post-First World War Treaty of Versailles. The French were outraged and sought the support of their allies, particularly Britain, which was not forthcoming. Germany was now emboldened and accelerated rearmament, progressively overtaking Britain and France in parity of arms throughout 1938 and 1939. In February 1938, Hitler annexed Austria and this was quickly followed by the proposal to annex the Sudetenland, the German-speaking part of Czechoslovakia. Meanwhile, the other Fascist state of Europe, Italy, had invaded Ethiopia and the two countries, Germany and Italy, concluded a Naval Treaty in 1939 – the "ring of steel" – which secured Germany's southern flank with the Italian fleet. Chamberlain secured an agreement with Germany at the end of August 1938 ("peace in our time") that she would confine her actions in Czechoslovakia to the Sudetenland but this was never honoured. In 1938, Britain started to rearm when, at long last, the danger of war became increasingly apparent. But at least the Chamberlain agreement bought time for British rearmament to intensify.

These were the key events that informed the decisions of George and Doreen to remain with the family in England while George continued to work in Calcutta. This was not unusual in the context of Indian family life as children grew up and went to school in England while husbands remained working in India. Contracts of employment progressively included the extra cost of family travel back, including children, to India at least once a year, generally by sea but later, increasingly by air, which became more relevant as flight times shortened and costs reduced after the war. However, the

European war made travel out and back increasingly difficult. Doreen was familiar with all this through her own childhood growing up and schooling in England while her father continued to work as Superintendent of the Presidency General Hospital in Calcutta throughout the First World War. Another factor was the building of the new home at 5 Alipore Road, during this period, while George stayed at the Bengal Club for much of the time. Earlier in the summer, the family had moved down to stay at Lindridge at the kind invitation of Ruth and Tom Benthall (Sir Edward but always known as Tom – JMM). Doreen's father Frederick had now moved out of London to Ilfracombe to be closer to her and his grandchildren. Later, as war developed, he was to move to Torquay, which was even closer to Lindridge.

The concerns about their painful separation against the background of the development of war and the progressive closure of both air and sea routes were evident from the intensity and frequency of correspondence from the end of August 1939 onwards, and as war breaks out on 3rd September.

> *"Calcutta 30.08.39.*
>
> *I think the news is better today in that it has been arrested in its deterioration. Anyhow, Hitler seems to be pausing and I hope the hesitation means he will not plunge his country into utter ruin. Meanwhile, our preparations here go quietly but resolutely on – one can do no more, no less. Incoming mail is a day late we are told so I may not hear from you until tomorrow. I haven't yet shown the lovely coloured photographs to Humphrey, but I will do so soon. I will ask him to lunch one day.*
>
> *Today, I took Oscar and one of Tata's Directors to lunch after two hours' talk about coal contracts. I expect to go up to Jamshedpur with Oscar next week to continue the negotiation.*
>
> *Last night, I had my tea sent down to Charles when I got home & we sat and talked until Joan came home. We all went up and listened to the wireless news later – and then I dined alone & read & so to bed! Nothing fresh to report today but, as they say, the news has a better tone about it.*
>
> *The house progresses and they have already fitted a number of doors, whilst the floors are practically finished except for the final polish. The pelmets are being made and should be very nice. I expect to get in by October with any luck, but I don't think we should hurry in until it is all absolutely ready. There are certain to be small delays yet, but it all looks so nice, Sweetheart. I shall be glad when we know the international verdict but my booking for the K.L.M. leaving Calcutta on 2nd December stands! I have also booked an alternative on 21st December but I intend coming by the 2nd D.V. Golly, it will be good to be up and away, all being well.*
>
> *Nothing more now, Sweetheart. I miss you all the time; take all care of your darling self and of our chaps. All my love to you, my own darling, with kisses and bunny hugs to our chaps. God bless you & them. Always your own Geordie."*

The next letter is written the next day as the crisis intensifies and a declaration of war is imminent.

"Saturday 2.9.39

I got two letters just before I left office today, yours and one from Jean and it was so good to get them and to hear that you and the chaps are well, though naturally, you are hating all the dreadful news. But I do hope, Sweetheart, that you are not worrying about it too much! There will be so much to do probably that you will have your hands full. Since writing yesterday, there have been all sorts of news about German attacks on Poland but so far today there is nothing to add to last night's broadcast. But everyone here, naturally enough as we are so far away, seems to be taking it all very calmly & resolutely, and everyone seems to expect the next news will be an ultimatum to Germany – It is all so senseless and wicked and not at all inevitable but with the present monstrous system in Germany, one feels that only renewed suffering will make the people of Germany realise that their only hope is to overthrow the monster which seems to have got hold of them again. I am sure you are right, Sweetheart, when you say it is better to face it & get it right before it gets so bad that it may be too late. Now, it may only take a comparatively short time. Later on, it may take much longer to be finished with it. But don't worry your darling self too much about it all – it will end and all the things that matter will go on. Soon, D.V. we may be together again and so long as I know you and our own wee chaps are all right, then I shall be alright here. One can't make more plans than we have already done and I am glad that you are staying down there until you know how things are going. I shouldn't be in a hurry to move back to Walstead, though it should be safe there, but you can see how things develop. I should try and get someone to stay with you if you have a house down there or if you move back to Walstead. But I expect that you are getting it all arranged, Sweetheart, though how I hate not being with you.

Last night, Molly and Ernest kindly asked me round for a drink & "pot luck" & I was glad as I didn't want to stay in. We had a good buck about all sorts of things & then when I got home, Charles called me in downstairs where I found Jack had been dining with them.

I played squash this morning and now it is after lunch and I am catching the 4.10 to Shim. I think Joan and Teddie are coming but Teddie, being a special constable, may be wanted! Anyhow, I am going and I hope they will be coming too. I am very well, Sweetheart – touching wood. If only we were together, Sweetheart, all would be well. But I have endless faith in the future, my darling one, and one must and can just go on hoping and believing. I know you feel this too. Take care of your darling self and of our wee chaps. God bless you and them. All my love to you, my own darling, with kisses and bunny hugs to our wee chaps. Always and always your own Geordie."

This was the day that Germany invaded Poland at 5.30 a.m. The ultimatum to Hitler to withdraw within 24 hours was ignored and Chamberlain announced on 3rd September that Britain was at war with Germany. The rest of 1939 was to be a period of "phoney war", the main actions being at sea.

"Tuesday 05.09 39

My own Darling,

I expect mails will start to be a bit irregular but I hope they will still go twice a week anyhow and arrangements have been made for a surcharge which should reduce the quantity of mail sent. I have to go to Tatanagar to conclude (I hope) a coal contract and Oscar and I leave after office tonight. Tomorrow is a holiday and we are due back on the day after tomorrow so there should be no dislocation of work in the office. Yesterday I played squash in the morning and, in the evening, got back pretty late & then took myself off to a cinema after dinner. Betty and Lawrence asked me to go to one with them but they had seen the one that I wanted to see and I didn't want to see the one that they were going to see so we postponed it until later in the week! If delays in mails seem likely, I shall send you an occasional cable. I listened to Roosevelt's broadcast last night which seemed eminently sane and reasonable. But there seems to be very little news yet. I expect that we shall get more as time goes on. I still can't believe that war is actually on but there it is. I shall not say more than I can help about all its madness in my letters to you, Sweetheart – it is bad enough to know that is all going on and I hate the thought of my letters to you being full of war and gloom. As time goes on, things will become more settled both here and everywhere, and one will know what can be done and will be able to arrange for the future. It is no use worrying about it all yet and later on one should know better, Sweetheart. But don't worry, my Darling, we shall be together again before long and the old world will go on. I went to see "Nazi Spy" at the Lighthouse last night; a terrific thriller and all American, based on the big spy organisation which the Americas discovered a short time ago.

The dogbies are well although they don't think much of this squash business in the mornings! They prefer golf and I must take them out again soon. The Dhurzi has begun on the curtains for the new house where they are getting on well still. But I don't expect they will have it finished until the middle of October. But I keep on dikking them. I am very well, touching wood, and so are Oscar and Paul. We are expecting men on leave to be returned to India soon but once that has been done and the sea routes cleared a bit, it should make it all much easier.

You are always in my thoughts, my own darling one. take all care of your own sweet self & of our own wee chaps. All my love to you, my own darling, with kisses and bunny hugs to our own wee chaps. Always your own Geordie."

These letters are full of reassurance, concern and love. Clearly, the separation was not easy for either of them, but us children were happy and blissfully unaware of the events that were unfolding. Doreen and George were torn between the concern for her father, her wish for the family to be reunited, the risk in any travel back and from India and the conflicting demands of children's education. The Mediterranean was quickly closed and all sea traffic routed around the Cape. Air travel was rerouted for the moment via Capetown with aircraft making their way up Africa to Marseilles and then on to England. Jean and Jen were due to start school at the Notre Dame convent in Teignmouth. Other families were in the same situation, and a popular halfway house destination was to become South Africa, with children going to school there, and travelling back and forth by air on safer routes to India for holidays.

"Calcutta Friday 8th September

My own Darling,

Since writing to you on Tuesday, I seem to have kept my nose to the grindstone! First of all, we have been notified that there will be two air mails a week but it is not known on what days so we are asked to post whenever ready – there is to be an extra charge so all ordinary mail will go by sea. So, I shall write you more or less as usual and just post so they will get the next plane home. I was talking to Robin and he says people went on leave & came back almost as usual in the last war so as soon as there are more settled conditions, I expect that it will be possible to get home – anyhow for short spells. So D.V. it won't be long until I may be with you again, Sweetheart. Anyhow, that is what I shall presume will be possible and I know the K.L.M. still fly, though they do stop for a few days and now, of course, they go by the winter route – but I am sure that there will be plane services as soon as conditions settle down. We ought to get more settled here soon too, though apart from excited & slightly mad markets, we are more or less normal – anyhow outwardly.

On Tuesday, I left office and rushed home for a hurried bath & change and Oscar & I caught the 6.24 to Tatas. We were at the Director's bungalow before 12.00 & spent a full day on the Wednesday which was a holiday here. We talked all the morning and went round the works all the afternoon. We caught a night train after dinner and arrived early on Thursday. I had a bank meeting (the Imperial Bank of which he was a Director – JMM) *and a Tolly meeting* (Tollygunge Club – JMM) *in the evening so I didn't need rocking to sleep. This morning I had a D.C.S. meeting and today seems to have been hectic. I have just come in from a game of squash after office and Dil will post this when ready! I am dining with Joan and Charles this evening quietly & I think we are going to a flick.*

I still feel it is so unreal and dreadful but one can only hope and pray it may be over sooner than expected. I do not believe the great majority of the German people want this war and the end may come from internal dissension. But we are far stronger than we were in 1914. So, one takes comfort from that and I always believe in the future, as most people are sane. We shall be alright, Sweetheart, if we keep stout hearts & I know we shall do that. I am thinking of you all the time, my Darling one, & of our wee chaps. God willing, it won't be long until I can get home to you. Take all care of your Darling self & of our wee chaps. All my love to you, my own darling, with kisses and bunny hugs to our wee chaps. Always your own Geordie."

The next letter is dated August but it seems clear that it was written in September.

"Calcutta 11.8 39

My own Darling,

I hope we may soon begin to get air mail letters again, and I understand that having stopped them for a day or so they began again on a restricted basis of two a week. Anyhow, I shall write three times a week and just post as finished, hoping there will be a minimum of delay. I believe the KLM are flying again almost as usual, but are going by the winter route, though I don't know how they manage it when they get close to the war area. But I expect they take no risks. Since writing to you on Friday, I dined quietly with Joan and Charles on Friday. We were to have gone to a flick but Joan had been inoculated and had a high temperature so we didn't go out. I went up to camp on the 4.10 on Saturday with Joan, Noel, and Mrs Brandt. The latter is, of course, under observation, like all other German women here, but only the men have been interned as yet. I think the poor woman was delighted to be away from Calcutta even for a few hours. Teddie arrived later as usual and drank his usual! It rained heavily from the time we arrived until about nine, so we had a pleasantly cool night, and this week we didn't get called at 2.30 a.m., I am glad to say! I bought an alarm clock as a safeguard and it seemed to do the trick; the light was most difficult and the birds most wild and we got only seven and a half couple, but it was, as usual, great fun, though I couldn't hit the little rascals! After a good nap, I called for Ernest and Molly and we went to the New Empire where we picked up Pitts, and they all dined here afterwards, to the enormous delight of Bogie and Bik! Their own sweeper returned on Saturday and what a scene it was! I typed the previous page before breakfast and it is now after lunch so I shall write some more!

Just before lunch, I got two lovely letters from you which I was so glad to get – one dated 30th and the other dated 31st August enclosing some lovely snaps of all the chaps. I am very glad they are all so well & I must say they look most happy in all the snaps, bless them. With any luck, the mails will begin to come regularly again though one mustn't complain as it is only eight days since I got your last letter – dated 28th August. I do hope mine have been arriving regularly.

I wish you could have seen the dogbies greeting the sweeper when he returned after a month's leave! They licked his face & hands & slobbered all over him & cried and generally gave vent to their feelings – they do like him & he seems very fond of them & grinned and talked to them. They do amuse me. I haven't taken them out golfing lately & I must do so soon, but I don't seem to have much time these days, & only seem to have long enough for a quick game of squash occasionally! But touching wood, I am very well, & so are we all. Oscar is up at the coalfields until tomorrow. The rains still go on and have been very stormy over the weekend and already we have had over sixty inches of rain this year and in Calcutta, we are nearly ten inches over normal. Let us hope we may have an early cold weather.

The house slowly approaches completion and most of the floor polishing is finished and most of the window frames and doors have been fitted and the bathrooms are slowly being fitted out. Yours is going to be very nice in its marble green fittings. They have

56 *Shimmerally shooting including l to r Dorks sitting Sandy Cameron Ronnie Cameron & others, seated Pitts Squarey Joan and Teddie Shuttleworth*

started lopping the branches of the overhanging trees which is a great improvement and the road in is almost finished. It certainly should be ready for occupation by the middle of October, all being well.

I am longing to be with you again, my Darling, and it is just possible that I may be able to get home soonish if things go well. But it so largely depends on how we are placed here for men and whether I can go off and leave it. But the next few weeks will decide it and I shall not miss a chance of being with you and our wee chaps if I can manage it without upsetting things. Anyhow, Sweetheart, we shall know more of all the possibilities in the next few months and I don't give up hope of nipping home even if it is only for a short visit.

I am sure Dad is wise to stay in Ilfracombe for the meantime.

Take all care of your Darling self and of our wee chaps. I am thinking of you all the time, my Sweetheart. All my love to you, my own Darling, with kisses and bunny hugs to our wee chaps. Always your own Geordie."

His next letter reports progress on the house and further comment on the developing international situation.

"Calcutta 15.09.39

Since writing to you on Wednesday, I don't seem to have done very much except work, though I am not overworking, but there seems to have been rather a lot to do and markets have been quite mad. *Marwari speculators have been in control and there has been no rhyme or reason for their views which has made it so difficult. Touching wood, we haven't done so badly though goodness knows why! What annoys me about it all is that the war to the Marwari merely means something to be exploited for personal gain, and his only hope is that it will not finish too soon. Oscar took me out to lunch yesterday, but apart from that, I don't seem to have anything to report. The Dhurzi has finished most of the curtains for the new house, but that does not, of course, include those from downstairs, which must wait until we move in. The trees have been trimmed which vastly improves it all, making it much lighter in the downstairs rooms. They are beginning the painting next week and then it shouldn't be long before we get in. I only wish you were here, Sweetheart, but D.V. it will not be so long until we are together again. I just live for that day. It is a great comfort to know that you and the chaps are at Lindridge and I hope Walstead has been let, for I hate the thought of your being there all alone. It would be hopeless for anyone to attempt to stay there in such circumstances, and I am most relieved that you are not attempting it. We have had a lot of rain again and yesterday it was flooded outside the gate. We are now over eleven inches over normal, but I suppose it will abate one day, and then for the sticky!* (All this is typed – JMM) *I am writing this in the office, Sweetheart, after lunch, as there seems to be a lull.*

"Percy" of Shimerali has just been in and he has two or three "juggers" (= places – JMM) *for us to shoot over the weekend though I doubt we shall manage more than one! War news is still scanty and it is difficult to see yet what conditions here will be when it all settles down. I only pray that it may all be successfully ended soon, though the only way it is likely to end quickly is by internal disruption in Germany. But everything that can be done seems to be "in train" now so one must just go on & hope for the best. I hate not being with you, Sweetheart, but I try not to worry as I know it is no use. I am full of and have also hope for freer movement between here and the U.K. in a few weeks or months, when the German submarines ought to have been dealt with, and then life will begin to look better. But in the meantime, we have much to be thankful for, Darling, so I don't complain and just hope on, as I know you do too.*

Take care of your darling self and of our wee chaps. I think of you all the time. Bless your sweet self and them. All my love to you, my own sweet Darling one, with kisses and bunny hugs to our wee chaps. Always your own Geordie."

And again . . .

"Calcutta 18.09.1939

My own Darling,
Since writing you last Friday, I seem to have kept myself busy – which is a good thing! I dined quietly with Joan and Charles on Friday and Lut was also there & we sat and talked after dinner and Lut played his eucalalagli (spelling!) and sang choruses. Fairly early bed. On Saturday, after lunching at home, I went up to the Shim, on the 4.10

as usual, and Joan and Noel joined up and we all had tea on the way. Teddie arrived on his usual train. The monsoon still goes on and it was frightfully muddy in the road from Shim to the bungalow. I have seldom seen it worse. The garden at Shim has been improved out of all knowledge and it really is going to be very trim and pleasant. We had a fairly strenuous day on Sunday and we had to walk about four miles to the shooting – Noel stopped on the way and went on by the Rly line to Madampur while we went on to the jheil. We got 11 ½ couple but it was frightfully hot and we only just caught the train at about 11.00 at Madampur having left Shim about 6.15 a.m. We changed on the train & I got home to lunch, as usual, having just looked in at the new house where they are still "finishing". They make quite good progress, but there are so many small jobs which all take time and often one job has to wait until another is finished. They are busy fitting the sliding doors and finishing the polishing of the marble everywhere. The wooden pelmets are finished except for the curved ones in the bays but I believe they will be ready in a day or two. I went into the A&N this morning about chicks and have also arranged to get an estimate for the fittings to go inside the pelmet boxes. They are going out to the house tomorrow so that the arrangements can be made to make the necessary holes etc. so that the chicks can be transferred straight away when the time comes and the actual making of the holes etc. can be done tidily by the proper workmen beforehand. I have fixed up for the various light fittings from Oslers and the concealed lighting boxes are now being fitted. They have got on quite well with clearing and levelling the garden though there is a lot to do there yet before the malis (= gardeners – JMM) can get to work. But we should get in before the end of October.

Then I had a good nap & Joan and Charles & Betty and Lawrence came with me to a flick & back to dinner with me. Betty & Lawrence can't get on leave now and of course they don't know when they will be able to get away. The K.L.M. have suspended their service in the meantime, which is a blow. But I don't know how they could have gone on when one realises the difficulties which have arisen over neutrality. But I haven't by any means given up hope of getting home sometime on a flying visit and the Imperial Airways still go, of course. Soon, with any luck, the seas will be comparatively safe again, and then it will be possible to consider it all again, Sweetheart, and as I say, in the meantime, I just hope we will be together again soon.

Ram Lal is a proud father of a son! He particularly wanted me to tell you & Jean Baba. He is very bucked about it naturally! I have had deputations from Cook and from Dil – both of whom wanted to know where you were and whether you were alright and where the Babas were. They have all been so good and both Cook and Dil sent salaams to you. They asked to see me separately, and then proceeded to ask all about you and the chaps. Some time ago, the bearer enquired too. They all asked when you were coming back and whether the chaps were coming too. Cook was very worried about you being in London and persisted until I had made him understand you had gone down to the West Country! They are a good lot and have tried to help in every way. (Ram Lal was the Kitmagar – a sort of butler – Cook the cook – the bearer waited at table and looked after George's clothes – and Dil Bahadur was George's Nepali driver.)

This morning I played squash before breakfast as I woke very early & felt I must go out & take some exercise! Touching wood, I am very well and am taking care not to overdo it. It will be good when we know more about the possibilities of movement but so far, we have not had time to get any office people back. Soon they should begin to arrive & once the first rush of travellers is over, we can then see how we are placed. Some, of course, will be joining up, but it shouldn't be many weeks until we know how we are placed for leave, etc. Golly, how heavenly it will be, Sweetheart, to be all together again . . .

The news again is full of problems & Russia once more seems to have set a problem, but whatever happens, we are going to win and that is all about it! But it is no use my writing about the news of War, Sweetheart, as it changes daily and one can't possibly know what the real truth is. I am thinking of you all the time, my Darling one, wishing I was there to help you & get everything settled – I do so hope you are not letting Walstead or anything else worry you unduly, Sweetheart. I hate to think of you having it all to cope with but I am sure you are doing it all.

Take care of your Darling self and of our wee chaps. God bless you and them. All my love to you, my own Darling – with kisses and bunny hugs to our own wee chaps – always your own Geordie."

The problem of shortages of men in the various businesses was to be permanent and to last throughout the war and increased especially when the war with the Japanese appeared above the horizon and became a reality. Many joined Indian regiments, with their knowledge of languages being especially relevant. Many left families behind and never returned. This occurred to two of my good friends who grew up without fathers, not knowing for a long time what had happened.

"Calcutta 22.9.39

My own Darling,

I can't tell you how good it was to get your letter today and hear how you all were. I am glad you have been to Walstead and packed it all up and I am most relieved that you have done so as I should have hated the thought of you being all alone there with a war on. Apart from the fact that it is too much in the London area, it would have been a grim thought that you were more or less alone. The longer Ruth and Tom and the chaps are at Lindridge the better, and, if has to be turned into a hospital or convalescent home, I feel sure you would be able to find accommodation somewhere with people you know who will join you. I think you have done the wisest & best thing, Sweetheart, and I do not think that it will be at all difficult to let Walstead. I think you have been most wise to pay maids a "retainer" as this should ensure your getting them back again when you want them which may be most valuable later on. It is good to know they will be here until it is let. I am sure too it is much the best for the children; it wouldn't be the same for them with the air raid warnings & refugees, etc. No, from all points of view, you have been most wise. I am sorry Sis is finding things so difficult. I wish I could help but it is impossible to see what one could do. I hope things will settle down for her and I shall write her soon. Perhaps Jan will get some job to do and Bill will be going back to school. You are such a Darling, my Dorkiebus, to go shooting off here to see Sis & I am so grateful to you. Please take care and don't overdo it and above all, don't worry, sweetheart, more than you can help. I don't think there is any doubt we should have been in for a far greater misery if we had allowed Hitler to go without trying to stop him. We shall stop him and we shall preserve our own system & what we have built up through the centuries – and it is worth it, I believe. Anyhow, it is far better than Nazism or Bolshevism which seem to be their alternatives. But as you say, we must, & I hope will, profit from our mistakes when it comes to settlement – already we are showing clearly that we have profited from our experiences in the last war. Long may it continue. I am glad that Dad will be at Bishopsteignton as it will be far better for him and incidentally the winter should be much milder there.

I am glad Tom has got something to do as he will feel far better about it and have no doubt he will find they will want him soon enough on important work organising something or other. The temporary job he has got sounds interesting and important too. I spoke to Van Aken (the Dutch consul & agent for K.L.M.) today in the club and he told me the K.L.M. are keeping up a service from Batavia to Naples. Imperial Airlines are also keeping on, of course, so later on, it may be possible to get home even if it is only for a short visit. But one must see how things go here as it is clearly my job to keep things going in the firm, and in a state of war with so many key industries, one feels it more than ever one's duty. But every chap must have leave! So I hope on. A regulation has been published prohibiting Europeans between 18 and 50 from leaving India so anyone wishing to go has to apply, with detailed reasons, to the District Commander. But when things settle down, I hope it may get a bit easier. One can only hope it will.

I shall be thinking of you, my Darling one, on 26th and I shall send you a cable. I don't know when air mails go out so it is not possible to post so as to get to you in time. Nobody could have been happier than I have these ten years & they have simply flown – thanks to you, Sweetheart. I just can't believe it is ten years ago – thank God for you, my Dorkiebus. Life is so full of everything worthwhile with you to share it with! Bless you, Darling heart. (It was their 10th wedding anniversary on the 26th – JMM)

I hear that Rowley has gone back to work in the Bank which is a good effort. Harry Harrison has just returned & brought all sorts of messages from Rowley. On Monday, I dined with Joan and Teddie very quietly – Mrs Brandt & Connie & Jack were also there – Mrs B was very pleased as she has heard that she can be naturalised though she is not eligible until the end of September. She says she always intended to apply for the last year or two. On Tuesday, I dined with Molly and Ken and Joan and Teddie & Laws were there. We played a football game with keys at each end which worked flaps & knocked a celluloid ball about. It was great fun and they were in good form. I took the dogbies out for golf on Wednesday & last night I played Laws at squash. Tonight, I am dining quietly with Gordon Brandon. I seem to live in one long rush in the office but, touching wood, am very fit and things seem to be going on quite well. But I can't work all the time – it would be mad to try it, and I am getting some recreation. But we are all very fit, touching wood, and soon I expect Bunty will be back and that should make matters much easier. I am writing this at home after office as it has been a difficult today starting before breakfast with a D.C.S meeting.

I am not going to sell the Rover now as nothing will be lost by keeping it – prices of cars must rise – especially of second-hand ones, so I think it better to keep it for the time being, anyhow.

I think of you all the time, Sweetheart, and of our little chaps – God bless you and them. Take all care of your sweet self & them. All my love to you, my own Darling, with kisses and bunny hugs to our wee chaps. Always your own Geordie."

In the next letter, George meets Gordon Brandon, Governor of Bengal, for dinner, and discusses the overall family situation and particularly the issues of separation of those continuing to work in Calcutta with families in England, and they compare notes. George, by now, would of course have known that he would be Vice President of the Bengal Chamber the following year (1940), leading in all probability to the Presidency in 1941. Although under 50, George would have been exempt from call up because of his wounds from the First World War, and subsequent medical discharge.

"Calcutta Monday 25ᵗʰ Sept.

My own Darling,

I am writing this before breakfast as I am not going out exercising and some work I have to do can wait a bit. Well, I dined with Gordon Brandon, just our own two selves, on Friday and he took me on to the "Metro". We discussed many things but chiefly the situation with our chaps at home. I told Gordon that having got our family settled and acclimatised at home, we were reluctant to uproot them and he agreed, although I think what he feels is that if Elsa is not with their children, he wants to be quite sure they are in safekeeping and not only with one person who might go sick causing a serious situation for the children. I told him that was exactly how we felt and that first of all, Joan and then Nancy had asked for you despite having a very reliable Nanny. (Nanny Bishop who travelled out with us to India in 1940 and stayed and looked after us while we were in Kalimpong throughout the war – she was in charge – JMM).

He said that was reasonable, he thought, and it did not mean too great a strain on one person. Then he asked me what I should do if I couldn't get home anyhow for a time, and we agreed that if and when the seas are reasonably safe, it might be reasonable to get wives to come out provided families are well settled and cared for at home. He, of course, is over fifty so he can, if he wishes, just carry out his original plan of going home next year and possibly retiring. But with me, it is not quite the same though I feel fairly certain that I shall anyhow be able to get home for a short visit before very long. The K.L.M. go to Naples only, so I should try to go by Imperial Airways which shouldn't take very long. If I only took a short leave, it would probably be best for the firm & then I

57 Steam launch down river to Barrackpore jetty

should try and take another short leave fairly soon and if you were out here by then and home leave was difficult, we could go on a trip to Ladakh or Baltistan or New Zealand or Tibet or somewhere similar. But we shall arrange something, Sweetheart, though I should hate it to be thought I was deserting the firm etc. in such a time of emergency. But I don't see why that should be thought, especially when Bunty comes back, so long as I am not away too long. Soon I shall write Tom and see what he thinks when things settle down a bit more.

I think that I shall try and book Deosri for a week or fortnight in November; there are some good Pujas and it would be very nice if I'm not going to get long leave for a time. I asked Joan and Teddie yesterday what they thought of it and they said they would come anyhow for a week, if it was at all possible. It won't be the same without you, Sweetheart, but D.V. it will not be long until we are together again. There was no racing on Saturday so Teddie was able to come up early and we left on the 2.46 & got there for tea. We had an early dinner and I was in bed by 9.00! Chota hazri (literally "little breakfast" – generally tea and a biscuit – JMM) at 5.00 and we left sharp at 6.00 walking and T & I about 6.30 on bicycles. We went to the Pippal Gatch & had boiled eggs & ham sandwiches & coffee on the roadside before we began shooting. We got 24 couple (& one couple of snippets by accident – Teddie swore his was a most remarkably good shot!) which wasn't so bad. We got the 12.15 train & were back in Calcutta by 2.00.

I did my usual and then picked up Molly & Ernest & met Pitts at the New Empire, who was our host (Pitts!) We dined afterwards with Molly and Ernest and altogether it was a pleasant evening. Both Molly and Ernest have had a sort of 'flu but they have recovered and had been shooting yesterday. I shall send you a cable today wishing you many happy returns of tomorrow. How I wish we were all together, my darling one, but I couldn't bear the thought of your setting out all alone to come out here until it is safe to travel. We shall fix something, never fear. I never cease to thank God for you, Sweetheart.

The house gets on well now and they have been very active the last few days, I'm glad to say. I have fixed up for the A&N to do the chicks & to fit the curtain rails in the curtain boxes. They have submitted a proper estimate and, after certain alterations & a reduction of 5%, I have accepted it. The only thing to do now is to get the Gas Company to lay on the gas. Cook and I visited the house last week & decided the exact location for the cooker so that shouldn't be difficult now. The Dhurzi has finished the curtains except for those downstairs which we are using. So as far as I can see, we are getting on. I will finish this later in the office.

Well, Sweetheart, there is nothing fresh today. Oscar is away at Kumardhubi but is due back tonight so will be in the office tomorrow, I hope. We are all well I'm glad to say, touching wood! God bless you and them. Take care of your sweet self and of our wee chaps.

All my love to you, my own Darling, and kisses and bunny hugs to our chaps; always your own Geordie."

This early war correspondence continues but is now dominated by thoughts of how to get home (and back). It reflects the pain of separation and worries about the developing war situation but is cheered up by news of the new house, the children, the social scene and snipe shooting. These things really were the lifeblood in keeping them both going. George had his work too, as he was now senior partner of Birds, and had a growing responsibility in the other wider aspects of commercial and community life in Calcutta as well.

"Calcutta 29.09.39

I realised last night that if I had posted this yesterday – Thursday, it would have left by the plane at daybreak today. I was in the Bengal Cub getting books and was on my way to a Tolly Committee meeting at the Turf Club so I couldn't do anything about it. But in future, I will write on Mondays and Thursdays in the hope of avoiding delays though there is no fixed time or day when the mail leaves.

It is now hot & sticky in the daytime but mornings and evenings are not so bad. I am writing this before breakfast & the dogbies have left for their walk. I haven't taken them out since last week but they never give up hope! They are all well and Biscuit has a terrific bulge now and gets more like father every day!

It was lovely getting your cable on Tuesday 26th and I hope mine duly arrived also. I was thinking about you more than ever if that is possible and that night, I kept thinking you were on your way out! That was because of Gordon's and my talk the previous week, I suppose, and my letter of the previous day discussing the various possibilities. It is early yet, Sweetheart, to make plans but I still hope to do a quick trip home before very long though I have not taken any steps beyond getting a new passport. I had to get a new photograph and I enclose a copy! I thought of getting one or two for the chaps if they would like that? I have some postcards ready to send them and I must do so!

It is good to hear how the wee funnies like their own house and it certainly has been worthwhile for them – and for us. Had it not been for Arthur's troublesomeness, it would have been even better for you and me but as it is, I have very happy thoughts of it always – I did have such a lovely leave there last time and the wee chaps are always happy there. So, when this war is over, we shall I hope all be glad to go back there anyhow until the next break in the lease. But we can think of all that later on when one can see ahead more clearly. I shall hope to hear that it has been let soon – it shouldn't be difficult if Arthur tries and doesn't just flatten out everything. It certainly is a good thing from an income tax point of view, Sweetheart, and it lets us out from the point of view of having a residence at home because we now have no residence. Later on, you may have to make an income tax return, but I doubt if even that is necessary – anyhow, I doubt if it is necessary yet. But later on, you may be able to ask Bennett. I shouldn't worry about it meantime.

Well, I haven't much to say about my doings (no rudery intended!) since I wrote you on Monday. I played squash on Tuesday & Thursday mornings and apart from a committee meeting last night which lasted until dinner time, and one the night before – Meath – which only lasted about an hour, I have come home and loafed & read & listened to the wireless here. Molly Benthall is still down but I believe she goes up to Darjeeling again on Sunday. Things go well in the office – touching wood, and markets are again settling down which is all good. People are beginning to arrive back and it shouldn't be long before we have most of them back again which will make it easier for those with military or other outside duties.

The house progresses and yesterday the Electric Supply Coy was connecting up the electricity – that only leaves the gas and I have arranged for that to be laid on, and am taking Cook down today to see about a cooker. They say they haven't got one similar to the one we have at present and unfortunately, that belongs to the landlord. But no doubt we shall find something. I forgot to tell you – the new landlord here has taken over all the fittings we wanted to sell and I got his cheque for Rs300 yesterday – so that is good!

Later – Well, Sweetheart, it was so good to get your letter when I got to office and hear that you are well and also our wee chaps. I took Cook to the Gas Coy's showroom & we chose a gas cooker very slightly smaller than our own to have on hire and they will let me know what it will cost to order one out. I expect the hired one will be alright although it is slightly smaller – anyhow, the difference is negligible.

I shouldn't have any feelings about not returning to Walstead, Sweetheart, for I simply hate the thought of your being all alone there as you know. I shall be far happier if you stay in Devon, and if Ruth has to turn Lindridge into a hospital or nursing home, I am sure you will be able to make some arrangement so that you avoid the London area or areas where there are war activities. Also, I am sure that it is best, however much we may hate being separated, and we do, to stay out in the meantime and see how things develop. I shall never lose faith that we shall be together again – even if it is only for a short time, before very long. As you say, we are very lucky to be so well placed so one does not complain. But how I wish I could get home just for a short time with you and the chaps. D.V. I shall sometime, not too far distant. God bless you.

I will not answer the remainder of your letter in this one as I must send this off. Lunched out today with Oscar & Alan Coombe who has just got back. He was on a ship with only men returning to India but seems to have had quite a good trip. I am sorry, my Sweetheart, that my letters are arriving irregularly but I have written two or three letters every week so I expect there are delays. I hope they all arrive safely. Some I wrote to Mortehoe before I knew you had gone to Lindridge so I expect you left your address there and they sent them on. I hope things will settle down to greater regularity as I know how I hate it when your letters are delayed.

Take all care of your Darling self and of our own wee chaps. I think of you all the time. All my love to you, my own Darling, with kisses and bunny hugs to our own wee chaps. God bless you and them. Always your own Geordie."

And again . . .

"Calcutta 2ⁿᵈ October 1939

My own Darling,

As I said in my letter of last Friday, it was so good to get your letter on Friday and to hear that you and the chaps are flourishing. I do hope all of my letters have now arrived. I was not sure where you would be after the end of August so I continued to write c/o Mrs Holwill, Alontehoe, thinking that you would be somewhere fairly close, until I got

58 *A fishing expedition – boys with marseer*

your cable saying that you had moved to Lindridge after which I wrote there of course. I expect Mrs Holwill sent on any letters which came, but no doubt there would be delays immediately after the outbreak of war and probably that explains the long delay. I'm sorry, sweetheart, but I hope you have got them all by now.

I am very glad you have fixed up a school for the chaps in the district and I expect they will be very happy there, bless them! Yes, loving the P.N.E.U. so much I expect Jean will make comparisons at first but no doubt she will settle down soon. I told Joan on Saturday all you said about Gilly and Barney & schools and Joan says she has heard nothing since war broke out, but she expects that they have gone back to their schools! Poor Joan, but she hopes to hear soon and says that as soon as she knows what is happening, she will let me know. She does so appreciate anything you do for Gilly and Barney, though she seems to think that Mrs Montgomery will have arranged for them to return to the schools that they were at previously.

I am glad that you have seen Liz and Maurice and that they flourish. I should so like to see them again. Give them my love when you see them again. I should think Liz might find it difficult later on to move backwards and forwards between Essex and Plymouth but no doubt she will manage it.

Well, I did nothing particular on Friday except take myself off to the Pictures before dinner. On Saturday, I went to camp as usual on the 4.10 and Joan and Noel were also on the train. We took up cases of beer, whisky, gin, etc., stocking up the drink cellar! It was lovely and cool on Saturday night and having got there just before dark, we loafed until Teddie arrived.

We started off early again and got 21½ couple in about three hours' shooting which was good fun and we caught the train back which lands us back in Calcutta at 2.00. I went by myself to the 6.00 Pictures afterwards and so home and early to bed! The rains are not yet over and yesterday evening and again, this morning it has rained. It is about 7.30 a.m. now and it is raining hard! I suppose that it will finish one day. It was pretty hot shooting yesterday but was very good fun.

The house progresses and there really isn't a great deal more to do inside except painting & whitewashing. The Chinamen have fixed one set of sliding doors and have practically finished two more so they shouldn't be long now. Our paint people advise that it is best to leave the painting as long as possible while the rains continue but it has all got to be finished in time for us to move in by the end of this month and I think it will. The bathrooms are now more or less fitted and really look very nice, especially yours, I'm glad to say. The green fittings are a very nice shade. There is still a certain amount to be done in the way of fitting shelves in the kitchen and bottle khana & the store cupboard but that will not take long once it is started. When I went in yesterday afternoon, they were testing all the electrical points, so it progresses. We have begun on the garden & the mali has a gang of chaps digging the lawn. He and I went there early on Friday and looked it over and measured it all out and there is going to be masses of room for a tennis court. It was all levelled out some time ago and now it has to be dug fairly deep before the grass is planted, I shall be very glad when the move over is finished.

I am finishing this in the office where I seem to have had a busy day. No fresh news, Sweetheart, except a few lines about Winston's statement which seems to have been very much to the point. Someday, the German people will realise that we have no quarrel with them and I hope they will realise that it is now in their own hands to have leaders who can be trusted internationally. But I am afraid it is going to take a long time and a lot of courage on their part.

I went to a Bank meeting this morning & John Burder was also on the committee. He tells me Betty is waiting for a bit & later on may fly out if she can manage it. When things have settled, it may be easier and I still hope I may get home on a brief trip. I shall write Tom as soon as we know how things are likely to go here. But I long to be with you, Sweetheart, just for a time at least, & I think of you all the time and of our wee chaps. Someday D.V. we shall be all together again. Take all care of your sweet self and of our wee chaps. All my love to you, my own Darling, with kisses and bunny hugs to Jean, Jen and John. God bless you & them. Always your own Geordie".

In this letter, there is enclosed one from Joan Shuttleworth as Doreen had written her with news of Gilly and Barney. Joan's people lived on the Devon coast within easy reach of Lindridge, but subject, of course, to the availability of petrol. She had gone to see them with Jean. (Jean and Barney were to marry in 1956). The letter is full of Joan's typical good humour and good sense of fun.

"Flat 12 a 60a Chowringhee Calcutta. 4.10.39

My Dear Doreen,

It was sweet of you to write and tell me about the children – & to take the trouble to go down to Morthoe via Lyme Regis. My people were very thrilled to see you again & both Gilly and Barney wrote and told me about you and Jean. I don't know what's exactly happened to them at the moment as our last news of them is in a letter from Dot Whitien when they were with her on August 22nd!! I think everyone in Lyme must have failed to realise the new Air Mail regulations and rates – or else, as Molly Mealing says, "They don't think we're worth 1/3d" There must be quite a lot of sea mail somewhere or other & doubtless it will roll up sometime. In the meantime, we don't really worry as between the Pitmans & their respective school authorities (who in both cases are personal friends), some arrangement will be made. I expect Gilly at any rate is back at Cobham. I see one of the "Big 5" Banks has moved to Cobham from London so it must be considered a safe spot. If Winchester is at Leallhy, the entire school will move elsewhere, I feel sure, as the Frys have their bread and butter to earn out of "Eastacre". We see quite a lot of George and we all go to Shimmers every weekend. He is looking very well indeed, but he misses you tremendously. I think he hopes very much that you'll be able to get out here next year for a little while anyway – though he is trying not to count on it too much. These separations are bad enough anyway but still worse in wartime. Anyway, even if there are 300,000 Russians in Chinese Turkistan – which is doubtful!! I think India is as safe & safer than most places. I still hope to get home sometime next year – I do so want to see the children – travelling may be easier by then – if more expensive! Teddie is fairly well – he is letting Burke see if he can cure his B Coli having tried most other things! We plan to go to Deosri for the November holidays but I don't know if it will really come off. George says he is going anyway & it would certainly do them both good. Dick Peg may abandon Inez once the child has been successfully "hatched" & join us – we all feel very mean indeed to even think of going without you.

Teddie won't get leave next year now, of course, or in '41 if the war is still going on – in that case, I think I shall have a crack at bringing both children to Kashmir so that Teddie could get local leave to see them there. We could do a mild "trek" to get some fishing. Barnes would probably insist on trailing black bears armed with an air gun! It would be fun if you could all come too. George's trews would probably just fit John by that time! How are all the chaps? – I expect they're lovely – I'd give a lot to see them. I hear the Cameron family, with the exception of Michael, have actually sailed – we've let their flat for them until Jan 15th & there is a brand-new baby in it! Still, I expect we'd be able to find them something else. Moles could fit in Doodles and Bee-Bee – or perhaps the Scott-Kerrs could take the lot. I haven't seen your house yet but George says it's very nearly finished – by the way, the old stink-wallah has a bride coming to stay with him for next weekend – I don't expect he's told you anything about this – the old snake-in-the-grass – however, I cannot conceive at immorality even among the Mortons – so there you are!

This place is billowing with pregnancy – I've never seen anything like it. I'm not complaining as the sales in Babywear etc. are just about keeping the "Good Companions" afloat! I hear Maris Kerr is on her way out with Stan Peg. I think that I shall put the chairmanship in her capable hands & join a soup kitchen canteen or one of the humbler forms of war work.

Yours with much love – aye – Joan."

Accompanying this was George's letter:

"Calcutta 05 10 39

My own Darling,

It was good getting a letter from you yesterday- earlier in the week than usual, written on our anniversary. It has been a wonderfully happy ten years, Sweetheart, and D.V. before long we shall be together again. Things may clarify a bit sooner than we expect; anyhow, I hope so. Golly, how I wish I could be with you, Sweetheart, and our wee chaps. I am so sorry to hear about John's teething fit and convulsions and I do hope the poor wee chap is quite alright again. I used to get them when I was very small and we used to have a very old Scottish hand-woven blanket which had a faint stain of oil on it which was poured on me once when I had been put into too hot water during a convulsion. My mother used to show it to me sometimes when I was bigger. So, I do hope the wee chap is alright again, bless him. What a pity you have had to alter the children's school but you may have more luck over petrol if you have applied again. If it isn't too far away, I should go & see the Controller of Petrol – if that is possible, – for a personal visit sometimes succeeds when letters fail – but I'm sure you will have managed to fix up something.

I am glad you are finding plenty to do and it is always a blessing but don't overdo it, Darling – Ruth and Tom are certainly bricks to be so good to us all and I can't say how much I appreciate it. I am glad too that Mr McJames is having a spot of leave as it will give him a much-needed change I've no doubt. By the way, I heard about a fortnight ago that Begg Dunlops has got the new tea in (Margaret's Hope) and has sent ten lbs to Dad as requested some time previously so I hope it arrives all right. I expect Dad is happy down in Devon and no doubt it will be doing him a lot of good. Give him my love.

59 John at the seaside 1937

I'm sorry the effect of photographing the little chaps has the effect of causing the shop to be burnt down! They must be "red hot"! Bless their little darling hearts. It will be so good to see the photographs in due course. I will certainly ask Joan to give Anina Brandt your love – she is much happier about things now I understand & has put in the naturalisation papers.

It is good news that Arthur has let the house and that will be a relief. Also, being on a monthly basis makes it so much easier if you want to return – which I don't expect will happen until hostilities are over. But all the same, it is a good arrangement. I can well imagine you being homesick at times, Sweetheart, but you are in the meantime much better where you are. We can consider it all again later on if there is any change. I listened to the early morning wireless this morning (6.30 a.m.) before beginning this letter but there seemed to be little fresh. I haven't taken out the dogbies for some time but Tolly races are on and there are so many horses exercising that it is a bit difficult. But I shall take them out one day soon – they hang about every morning full of hope and are clearly asking to be taken out – they are such little funnies.

I have dined out for the last three nights. On Monday, with Geoffrey Dew which was fun – just he and his stable companion, a very nice chap, and we listened to his gramophone afterwards. He gave me an excellent dinner thanks to Monica Lideardale, I suppose. They seem to be very comfortable there. On Tuesday, I dined with Neville of the Imperial Bank and he showed me coloured Leica films on a small projector which were simply exquisite. I've never seen such beautiful colour pictures & the detail and colouring were exquisite. We were just our two selves. Then last night, I dined with Molly

& Ernest who were in their usual good form and we ate some green pigeon they had shot last Sunday. Very good they were too! Ernest is a brick. He has been making sketches for a formal garden at the new house. He went round one morning & had a good look and has been working it all out since. Had a very pleasant evening and was home before 11.00. On Tuesday, I went in and had a drink with Betty and Lawrence before dining with Neville. Jan was there and was leaving the next day to join Mat in Colombo. She seemed quite cheery but it must be a wrench to leave here now. Pitts is staying temporarily with Molly and Ernest but was out last night. He is going in with Hudson later on. Hudson is a very nice one-armed man (who I think you have met) and that should suit Pitts very well. It is high time the old stoat married & set up house for himself.

Later in office. I had to break off before breakfast and it is now nearly time to leave the office so I will close this. Take all care of your sweet self, my Darling one, and of our wee chaps. God bless you and them. All my love to you, my own Darling, with kisses and bunny hugs to our wee chaps. I think of you all the time. Always your own Geordie."

George was to write a further ten letters to Dorks over the next seven weeks before getting away and flying home for Christmas in December just after his O.B.E. award and ceremony.

"Monday 9ᵗʰ October '39

My own Darling,

I can't remember if I mentioned in my last letter that I got your letter written on 2ⁿᵈ September and needless to say I loved getting it last Thursday or Friday, I forget which. But anyhow, Sweetheart, it was good to get it. Then when I got back from camp yesterday afternoon, I got your letter of 29ᵗʰ with some lovely snaps which was waiting for me here. I do so love the snaps of all the wee chaps and they do look so well and happy. I do hope John is better, poor little chap, and also Jen. It would be so good to see them again bless their little hearts. I am sure you are right to keep Jen in bed when she gets these colds and no doubt she will throw off her "chestiness" in time. Jean looks so grown up too. I will send them postcards soon.

About Walstead, Sweetheart – I should leave things as they are for a few months as you suggest. We should be alright for income tax unless I visit England whilst you have established a residence there and even then it will not be so bad if I take care not to remit. But from many points of view, it might help & give us a breathing space if there is a fairly substantial break in the continuity of our residence at Walstead. But I should leave it in the meantime, Sweetheart & we shall consider it again from time to time.

I am glad the weather has been so good there – it does make so much difference when the weather is good. The autumn is so heavenly too. We still have the monsoon with us and over 70 inches has fallen this year and, in Calcutta, we are plus about 12 inches.

I did nothing special on Thursday & Friday except that they were particularly busy days. I don't think you met Ian Craig – a very nice lad in our Jute Mills dept. – especially recruited to grow up to be a senior if he shows the capacity. He is getting married and in a weak moment, I promised Monty to get his bride put up when she arrives! Well, I decided it was best to let her stay here so she arrives on the mail on Saturday and is getting married today. Joan Thomas has been a brick about it all. I went off on the earlier train to Shim after lunching with her with young Craig & his bride & they seem to have been all right. Joan, Noel & Cecily Bland were on the train and it was a lovely cool night as there had been a lot of rain. We found the birds a bit difficult; at least I did! But we got 22½ couple – Teddie was shooting marvellously & I was rather bad but it was good fun. I got back about 3.00 yesterday & later on, Suzanne Dodswell (bride!) & I, having changed, went out to the New Empire – Joan, Noel, Teddie, Monica & Eric Lidderdale, Ian Craig, & David Pilkington (best man today) also came and we dined here afterwards. It was good fun and they all seemed very cheery. Monica and Joan Thomas are lunching with the bride today and will help her with all she has to do. They are being married his afternoon at 4.30 at St John's & then having a small reception at 37. It all seems to have worked out very well and Suzanne is a nice cheery soul full of fun. Monty was in a blue funk in case he had to do anything about it all. Anyhow, he has consented to attend the party which is something of an achievement! Molly Benthall would have done it all had she been here but she is in Darjeeling of course. But everything seems to be set & David is most efficient.

The house progresses and they are now busy painting so it really shouldn't be so very long now. But how I have had to drive them! We have had the tennis lawn dug down about three feet all over & the mali has supervised it all. I was afraid the monsoon was

60 *Some members of the syndicate l to r Ronnie Cameron, George, Teddie Shuttleworth, Jack Thomas, seated Joan Shuttleworth, Helen Thomas, Doreen*

over & that we should never get it consolidated but the Mali said it would be all right and the late rains have been most providential for it has all settled down most beautifully and we shall have a lawn in no time all being well. The inside is practically finished except for electric fittings which will only take a very few days to fix. It is, I think, going to be such a nice house and how I wish you were going to be here, Sweetheart. But D.V. you will be later on when we can see more of the various possibilities.

I must shave now I suppose. I will finish this later in the office. I miss you all the time, Sweetheart, but we must just be patient I suppose & hope things will clarify soon. We are very lucky too and I can never be sufficiently grateful to Ruth and Tom for being so good to you and the chaps.

Later in office. Well, Sweetheart, there doesn't seem to be anything fresh here and soon I shall be leaving to attend this wedding. We are all well & have heard of somebody who applied to the authorities here for permission to leave the country on leave and it was readily granted and the General said they were really most concerned about keeping people under 34 in India in case they went home and enlisted! So later on, when things settle down, it may be possible to get a short leave home – but we will see. I long to be with you, Sweetheart. All my love to you, my own Darling, with kisses and bunny hugs to our own wee chaps. Take care of your Darling self and our chaps. God bless you and them. Always your own Geordie."

Again:

"Thursday 12.10.39

My Own Darling,

It was lovely getting your letter a short time ago when I came too after an after-lunch nap – today being a holiday! I am sorry John is so pulled down but it is good he is beginning to get up again and soon I hope he will be himself. It is bad luck on the little chap but I do hope he soon perks up again – I am glad the chaps like their school which certainly is a good thing and no doubt it keeps them busy. I can understand Dad wanting to have you there every day – he is a lucky chap! I am glad he is happy and comfortable and I am sure it is far better for him than trying to stay at 18 Queen Anne Street. I will show Oscar your bit about Mrs Benthall and Tom. I thought it was lovely! Ruth always says how Mrs Benthall spoilt him as a boy!

Well, we carry on here much as usual. John Stanley Kerr arrived back last Saturday and is continuing his leave in Ceylon & India – he came and had lunch in the office. He tells me he & Miris met you in Bond Street soon after you got back.

I have written for permission to go to Deosri in November but so far, haven't heard. It is over a fortnight since I wrote but perhaps Bhadran is on tour or has been transferred. I shall send a reminder as I should like to get a week or ten days away before the cold weather really sets in. It is going to be very difficult to get away from here yet for very long but later on, when things are clearer, it may be possible. Anyhow, I shall try to get some leave even if it is only a month.

Well, after finishing my letter to you on Monday, I came home & changed into a tailcoat & though it was comparatively cool owing to rain, it was hot! And did I sweat! Joan Thomas & Monica Lidderdale were getting the bride ready and, in due course, I took the lady off in Monty Thomas's car – an enormous Buick. The wedding was at St John's & my friend Archdeacon Young performed the ceremony – David Pilkington was best man & I gave away the bride. There were only about twenty-five people there – including Monty, which was something of a triumph! We gave them a reception at 37 and it was a most cheery affair. They are a very nice couple and I have had cheery letters of thanks from them both in Darjeeling. Since then, I seem to have done very little except the usual routine with a hot game of squash on Tuesday evening.

I continue to keep up steady pressure to get the house finished before the end of the month and I am very hopeful that we shall be able to move in the last week of October. We must anyhow as I have given final notice here though I'm sure I could get a week or a fortnight's extension if it was really necessary. But I refuse to consider it. In the meantime, I am taking the line that it must be ready by then and, barring bad accidents, I feel pretty sure it will be ready this month. But how they have dallied & delayed; they don't seem to want to finish! Today, all the wiring was being finally fixed as there is a full test with the electric supply coy tomorrow. The fittings won't be put up until the whitewashing and painting are finished but that shouldn't take more than a week now. There are some pujas this month & I hope to be able to get a good deal done then as they are near the end of the month & if I can't go to Deosri until later in November, there are more pujas fairly early in November so I should be able to find plenty of time to get it all done quite comfortably.

I long to be with you all the time, Sweetheart. Take all care of your Darling self and of our wee chaps. All my love to you, my own Darling, with kisses and bunny hugs to our wee chaps. Always your own Geordie".

These letters are full of news of the developments of the new house, the aches of separation and uncertainties about the future and emphasise the importance of the support of friends at the beginning of the Calcutta cold-weather season.

"Tuesday 17ᵗʰ Oct

My Own Darling,

I got a letter from you last Saturday and as usual I loved getting it. I am sorry John is being so pushed down poor wee chap and I do hope he soon picks up again. No wonder the wee chap was upset with all those teeth but no doubt he will soon put on condition again. I was glad Jen has gone back to school & I do hope Jen keeps well now. What good news about the petrol ration! It will make such a difference, Sweetheart, & you will feel you at least have a margin now! I showed Oscar your notes about Tom and Mrs Benthall in your car & Tom walking home & we laughed a lot. I quite agree about Walstead land and farm buildings and I only hope some use is made of them. It certainly would have been good to have been home and using that land and buildings to best advantage. It would have been very much worthwhile. Never mind, sweetheart, we may yet have some land to cultivate & keep up to scratch. In the meantime, all seems to go fairly well here – I had a very rushed day yesterday and started very early with papers and files and was hard at it all day until nearly 7.00 – But we haven't been having such busy days ordinarily – though now and again one seems to get a real "beezer"! I have heard about Deosri and we can go up and shoot and fish in November – the Governor is going there for Christmas so we are lucky, I think. Bhedran wrote a very nice letter and was most helpful. I hope Joan and Teddie will come and we may get one more but I think that I shall go in any event all being well as I think it would be good for me to get away for a bit. Paul goes this week for ten days or a fortnight in Darjeeling which will be good for him.

The dogbies are well and though I haven't taken them out golfing lately, they bear no resentment! Bogie & Bin are interesting and you can imagine what a lot of little lesbians they are! Only a short time ago, it was Bik & Bess, so we had a difficult time! As soon as they are all well again, I shall take them up to camp. They are such a good lot, though Bog is not so sprightly!

I don't seem to have done very much except at the weekend. There was a long Tolly meeting on Thursday evening & I didn't get there until late. On Saturday, Joan and I went up to Shim on the 2.44 & I just loafed in peace until Teddie arrived. It's so peaceful up there and it makes me long more than ever for us all to be together again, Sweetheart. It was a cool night & we didn't get up quite so early (tea at 5.00 usually!). We walked miles and miles and saw very few birds but we got 14 couple after shooting for about three hours. Then home & a late lunch & a nap for an hour. I dined with Joan and Teddie on Sunday after going to the New Empire – Pitts and George Gemmell were there. I was glad to see George and he was in good form. Pitts was also his usual cheery red-faced self. Early to bed!

The house gets on a bit better I am glad to say and it should be ready by the end of the month. I shall be very glad when we are all settled in and it is all fixed up. I got the lease, or rather, a draft of the lease yesterday and am returning it today so that will be on its way to completion. We have had so much rain and yesterday we again had a terrific storm and it is still flooded outside our gate this morning, – though it looks as if it won't be long until it runs off. This all makes it difficult to get the new house finished though it has helped enormously in the garden and it has practically all been dug down over two feet and levelled and the rain has consolidated it. The tennis court has been levelled and he should be putting in the grass this week – so it's an ill wind! We must be over 14 inches in excess now as I think the total is 74 ½ inches since 1ˢᵗ Jan. Thursday, Friday and Saturday are holidays & I hope to spend some of them at Shim. Joan & T have asked Ernest & Molly up which should be fun & Pitts may come up for a day whilst George may come up in his launch on Saturday so we may be quite a party. I expect there will be plenty of shooting but it won't matter terribly if there isn't. I think we are just getting on to a very good time so I hope we shall have some good days whilst the chaps are up there.

I do so wish you were going to Deosri Sweetheart. It won't be anything like the same without you – nothing is – but I do love that place & I know you do and it can never be

197

the same if you aren't there. I hope to be away ten or twelve days though I doubt if the others will be able to stay as long because of Teddie's racing.

But someday, D.V. we shall be there together again. I must now shave and will continue later. Well, Sweetheart, I have had a busy day (little man!) but at last, I have broken off to write to you again. I got your cable about Gilly and Barnes and at once 'phoned Joan who was delighted to know and was most grateful to you. I showed it later to Teddie when he called. Both are very thrilled at the thought of going to Deosri again and I hope nothing happens to stop us; I don't see why anything should. It has rained again today, all most peculiar but it's keeping down the temperature which is a good thing. I long to be with you again, my Darling one. Take all care of your sweet self and of our wee chaps. God bless you and them. Always your own Geordie."

This next letter contains an evocative description of Shimarali, the camp often referred to in these letters. It was about 30 miles upriver from the bustle, heat and noise of Calcutta on the bank of the river Hooghly. In the winter months, it was an oasis of peace and fun with good company. I remember meals around the campfire with swinging hurricane lamps – we children used to make clay animals and bake them in the embers. A shooting syndicate organised the shooting of snipe and green pigeon, which we sometimes ate in camp.

"Shimarali 19.10.39

My own Darling,

It is lovely up here. I am writing this after breakfast on Friday as Teddie and I are cycling to Chakdaha and the others are going by train. I am not sure whether Molly is going by train or not.

Joan and Noel & Teddie and I came up on Wednesday night, Teddie and I on the 5.20 and Joan & Noel on the 6.20. Yesterday we shot at Harringhatta and in order to get there, we trained to Kanchrapara & from there reserved one of the regular buses which run on that road. It was most amusing all packing into a bus! The driver & conductor quite entered into the spirit of it. We turned off the road which goes past the Pipul Gatch and went two or three miles along that road which is improved as they are now metalling it. One bridge was a bit tricky & we had to put bricks on a very muddy place to get the old bus over it. But we managed it alright. Had quite a good day & got 28 couple. Then, at Kanchrapara, we caught the train on which Molly & Ernest were arriving – very clean and tidy & us very muddy and untidy. However, we got back here for tea. Today we are all going to Chakdaha & I am going to Calcutta afterwards & coming out again tomorrow afternoon. Hiring the bus was most amusing & amazingly cheap, less than two bund gharries (horse-drawn bank carts – JMM) *would have cost & we went far further! It is getting simply lovely up here and the garden is just beautiful. Dhoab grass everywhere and lots of flowering shrubs out in bloom. Colour everywhere and so tidy. The bearers have just come back with a couple of good looking hilsa* (a firm oily river fish large as a salmon – delicious eating – JMM) *I wonder if it was the one that left before 4.00 a.m. amid much noise and singing. They are a cheerful lot, these fishermen. It's going to be hot today unless the breeze comes up which I suspect it will before long.*

I had a most busy day on Wednesday before I came up, but managed to get through it all quite happily – Paul went off to Darjeeling that night so I don't want to be away leaving Oscar alone for too long. Not that it makes any difference but something might turn up to defeat him and it's hardly fair.

How I wish you were here, Sweetheart, but there it is, and it is better as it is until things get clearer and I know whether I can get home on a flying visit, but I miss you all the time and I should like to be going home as arranged. However, we must just carry on as arranged and hope for the best. I feel that it is my war work to stick to things out here anyhow for the present. I do hope some adequate job has been found for Tom. As time goes on, I'm certain he will be wanted, so, however hard it may be to have to wait – and it is very hard – I'm sure he will get fixed up with some real job if he continues patiently. I will finish this later, Sweetheart, & will post it when I get back to Calcutta.

Soon it will be your birthday (28ᵗʰ October – JMM) and I shall send you a cable, Sweetheart. I can't think what to give you as a birthday present but I shall let it accumulate if I don't think of anything in the meantime. Anyhow, here's wishing you many happy returns & may we always be together, my darling one. Teddie has just called out, "Give Doreen my love, please" & Molly, who is cycling after all, says, "and mine please". I will finish this later.

Later in camp. Well, we had a good day & got 32 ½ couple & six golden plover. I was not so accurate but enjoyed it a lot. Shooting was not too easy in places as they were getting up a long way off but all things considered, it wasn't so bad as far as shooting is concerned. I only got seven couple but didn't get as much shooting as Teddie & Ernest. I haven't been shooting as well this year. I think I have been a bit erratic but I shall get on to it again I expect. Anyhow, it is so good to get out like this only I wish you were here too, Sweetheart. I shall post this in Calcutta as I am going in & returning tomorrow. Take all care of your darling self & of our wee chaps. All my love to you, my own Darling, with hugs and kisses to our wee chaps. God bless you and them. Always your own Geordie."

His next letter continues the weekend shooting theme and commentary about the house . . .

"Monday 23ʳᵈ October

It was so good to get two letters from you last night, including one from Jean, when I got back from camp. I came in on Friday from camp and, having posted your letter, I went off home and after dinner, I took myself to the pictures. I spent Saturday morning in the office and caught the 12.45 back to Shim, lunching in the train off bacon sandwiches & oranges! George Gemmel arrived up about 9.00 on his launch and after a somewhat late dinner, we all went off to bed. Yesterday, Joan, Teddie & George went off to a jheil at Chakdaha as they were all going back to Calcutta on George's boat. Molly, Ernest and I went to Arranghatter, beyond Ranighat, where we saw lots of birds, a bit wild owing to it being a dull cloudy day but we got 24 ½ couple including two golden plover.

We caught a train soon after 9.00 a.m. & the only return train is the one at about 5.30 p.m. so we had a long day & finished by having tea in Arranghatta station made in the kettle! We came straight back to Calcutta & got in about 8.00 p.m. & I went round & had pot luck with Molly and Ernest after reading all my lovely mail. There is nothing fresh here and, as the various exchanges are closed, we are not as busy as we have been. Paul is away of course and will not be back for a bit. He has been very fit I'm glad to say but a little rest from this will buck him up again.

They continue to make progress with the house I'm glad to say and unless something most unusual happens, we ought to be in there by the end of the month. I went round this morning to see how it was getting on and they have made progress during the holidays even though it is slow progress. We have had most of the garden dug down & thanks to the late monsoon, it has all settled down & consolidated nicely. We are getting a proper level given today & then the mali can finish levelling the tennis court.

I am very glad John and Jen are better & I do hope they make steady progress now. I think it is an excellent scheme to arrange for Jen to rest a bit at school. It is all a bit strenuous for a little chap at first. I am glad Mr McJames is back and that he has had a good holiday. What is Jim's new job? I didn't know he had left the Merchant Trading. Anyhow, I am glad he is happy in it. Was it this new voluntary fire brigade? If it is, I didn't know it was a full-time job. I will write James some day.

I agree with you about the future of Europe. I do hope a better order will emerge. But whatever happens, Sweetheart, I hope it won't be too long before we are all together again. I do miss you so terribly, and I'm sure it is right to stay as we are for a bit to see what is going to happen. But whatever happens, the world will go on and the worthwhile things will go on too in some form or another so one can only pray for good health and keep working on. I have been such a healthy chap these years we have been together & nothing can ever take away that and we will not fear the future, will we, Sweetheart? I shall be most interested in the Blue Book; thank you very much for sending it. It will arrive in due course I expect. It was lovely getting your passport photograph though it doesn't begin to do you justice. I will send mine to the wee chaps. I will tell Joan what you say about Gilly and Barney & will let you know what she says.

I am glad that you are helping the ration office – I wish I could peep in & see you all at it!! Mr W.C. Urine sounds a bit of a squirt to me! But it's good to have something to do. People continue to trickle back & Bunty Nicholson arrived a few days ago looking very fit. I enclose a poem written about a trip out on the "Duchess of Bedford" which brought several of our people back.

Take all care of your sweet self – I miss you all the time, my Darling one. All my love to you, my own Darling. With kisses and bunny hugs to our wee chaps – God bless you and them. Always your own Geordie."

The next two letters confirm the completion of the house before George's holiday in Deosri and the resumption of Imperial Airways' flights both home and back; now a very crowded schedule but he is hopeful of getting a booking shortly. The letters stop

61 The new house at no 5 Alipore road (lately Rajasantosh Rd)

around the second half of November indicating a successful break for a short leave home. There is an amusing account of the house being blessed, a five-day affair with the priest in residence in the cupboard next to the bottle store!

"*Calcutta Thursday 26.10.39*

My own Darling,

Nothing particular seems to have happened since I wrote on Monday. Holidays begin again tomorrow and these last few days have not been very busy except in rushes, as it is between two holiday spells and a number of people seem to be away. On Monday, I went and dined with Molly and Ernest and Niccy as we were to have gone to a flick on Sunday but parted early instead. All were in good form though we didn't think much

201

of the film! Ernest now tells me that Norrie thinks Molly should have her tonsils out as they are probably responsible for most of the poisoning. Sounds reasonable but Molly doesn't want it done, anyhow yet, & they are quite funny about it all. Ernest has joined the Light Horse (This was the Calcutta Light Horse, a volunteer regiment of cavalry, trained by full-time NCOs. It was the successor regiment to Gardiner's Horse and had a mess just off Park Street. The young bloods of Calcutta were members and it was noted and renowned for the organised paper-chases at weekends that used to take place in the open countryside beyond Tollygunge in south Calcutta. – JMM) *& says that when he was presented with a Union Jack last Christmas, little did anyone think that he would be a soldier before the year was out. On Tuesday, I went out with Molly and Ken* (Mealing – JMM) *to a flick & dined quietly afterwards. Ernest and Molly were also there & we played their table football after dinner though I managed to get away & home by 11.00.*

Molly Mealing's nurse has resigned & Molly is worried about getting another one. She has been in touch with the Janvirm's nurse who was with them some years ago and I told Molly I would ask you about her. I don't know if she was the same one they had in Shillong who used to shut that poor little child in the bedroom in "solitary confinement" for whole days at a time but if she is, I hope Molly won't take her on. I told her that there was a governor's nurse who used to do that to the Janvirm's child but I didn't know if this was the same one. Molly asked me if I would write and ask you about it. Do you remember the woman's name? Also, what do you think? Ines Pegg had a son a few days ago, and I had a note from her yesterday thanking us for some snipe so I gather she is getting on well. I haven't heard yet if Dick Pegg is coming up to Deosri; it was suggested that he might like to. I shall be glad to get away for a short time as I am feeling a bit stale & though we aren't rushed now, we have had a pretty busy and worrying time. But it should be alright if I can get ten days up at Deosri. Last night I played squash after office and dined early and had an early bed. I am going up to camp this evening & shall come back for Saturday. Lawrence Foster is coming up with Joan and Teddie and Pitts may come up for one day.

The landlord of the new house 'phoned up early this morning and said he was sending a priest to bless the new house before we go in. Apparently, it takes five days, and later, when I went in after breakfast, I saw the old gent established in the store cupboard off the bottle khana! I doubt if it will be all ready by the end of October but it should only be a matter of a few days. Oslers and the A&N are doing the work expeditiously & well but the builders are still "mucking about". But they swear that it will all be ready and I think they are really trying to have it ready by 31ˢᵗ October. But what a game it is! Anyhow, it is all going to be very nice I think & I only wish you were going to be here when we go in.

People still keep arriving from home and I saw Petre of Martins this morning who came by air and yesterday I saw Henry Birkmyre in the distance where Oscar and I were lunching the club. I hear that Cecily is down in Puri with Helen. Stewart Gray and Gordon Brandon are also there; what a party! Wally Baird was there but returned a few days ago. I haven't seen Cecily yet but I hear that she is in good form though her shadow grows no less.

I will finish this later, Sweetheart. I am very well but just a bit tired – though a short trip to Deosri will put that right. The monsoon still goes on & we are 16 weeks over normal & it is raining here now. But it has kept wonderfully cool and we have had hardly any of that dreadfully hot sticky end to the monsoon weather so we have been very lucky & we may just pass into the cold weather without any very unpleasant month or so. I hope so anyhow. Altogether we have been very lucky in the weather. More later, Sweetheart.

Well, here we are again but with nothing fresh! Soon I am going off to catch the Shim train 5.20 – these weekends have been such a blessing. It is still raining and has been raining for four or five hours, but it is nice and cool though somewhat depressing!

I think of you all the time, Sweetheart, & long for the time we shall be together again. I hope it won't be so long. There seems to be an absolute jam on Imp. Airways so it would be impossible to get home now even if I could get away. But later, it may improve & then if it is clear here, I may be able to get a very short spell home; we will just have to wait and hope for the best I suppose.

Take all care of your Darling self and of our wee chaps. All my love to you, my own Darling, with kisses and bunny hugs to our chaps. God bless you and them. Always your own Geordie."

George's next letter is full of thoughts on travel possibilities . . .

"Tuesday 31ˢᵗ Oct

My own Darling,

Thank you for your letter which I loved getting last Saturday. I am sorry you haven't been sleeping, Sweetheart – it is miserable when one has these restless nights but I do hope you are alright and are not getting overtired or letting things worry you too much. There is no need to worry, my Darling one. We shall be together again before too long D.V. – and in the meantime, I am sure it is far better to have let Walstead & for you and the chaps to have stayed on in Devon. I should have hated the thought of you being alone for any length of time now and I'm sure it is best as it is – better for you & the chaps, so don't worry, sweetheart. We shall all be back again at Walstead before we know where we are. It is not yet possible to book by air to return to India but it may get better as there is talk of reverting to three services each way a week. If one could book for the return journey, it would change the whole aspect but until one can do that, it wouldn't be right to go home as it might be months before one could get back. But I firmly believe that it is only a question of time before it will be possible. I hate the thought of your travelling out by sea whilst these raiders are about at sea but later on, sea travel will, I hope, improve & then we can think again. What I should like is first of all to get home for a couple of months early next year and then to be able to fix up for somebody to look after the chaps whilst you came up here for a few months- by air if you would like, but I can't bear the thought of you going by sea whilst things are as they are, Sweetheart.

But don't worry, Sweetheart, we shall fix something up. If Lindridge is wanted for some war purpose, I'm sure you will be able to find other quarters in the west of England, with somebody you know. I do so hate you having to cope with all this war worry & my not being with you but D.V. it won't be for long. I am writing this before breakfast & for the first time, it really has the feel of the cold weather. The Sweeper was very worried about half an hour ago as he couldn't find Biscuit to go for a walk. He searched everywhere & finally she was run to earth in her old place in your bathroom under the bath! They are such little funnies and are in very good form, I'm glad to say, though Binnie is a bit thin.

Last Thursday, I went to camp after the office just for the Friday & Teddie, Lawrence Foster and & I got about 36 couple. I came in early on Saturday and I'm glad I did as just as I arrived at the office, we got news of an enormous sandbag order for five hundred million bags and this had upset markets considerably. But we got things more or less sorted out ready to tackle hard on Monday. I got back to camp on Saturday and Teddie, Joan and I got 37 couple on Sunday, arriving back for dinner in Calcutta on Sunday night – Oscar went away on Sunday & Paul didn't return from Darjeeling as he has got a boil on his seat! But I told Molly on the phone not to worry but keep him there until he is fit. Oscar will be back on Thursday and I can manage things without them for a few days without bursting myself. More of Darjeeling will do Paul good and it would be a pity for him to come back until he is well. Yesterday there were talks & meetings & general comings and goings – Tom Thomas and I began early as we met at Tolly at 7.30 a.m. on a committee meeting, & talked jute afterwards. This was a useful exchange of views as Tom is on the Jute Mills Association Committee. I think all the plans which have been made should get the situation in hand again. I hope so anyway as these Marwari speculators would ruin anything. I started yesterday with a meeting at Tolly at 7.30 and afterwards, as I say, Tom Thomas & I discussed Jute Mills – then I had a busy day in the office without being too busy and then I had another committee meeting at 6.30 p.m. I dined quietly downstairs with Joan and Charles; the Col. of Johnny Dalgleish's Regiment – one Galloway – was also there and the Craigs who recently got married. He has been away for a few days on military duty & she has been staying with Joan & Charles and occupying our spare room. I have hardly seen her as I always seem to be away or leave too early! But she is great fun & made us all laugh a lot with Yorkshire stories.

I saw in the Statesman that Mr Justice Morton, presumably Fergus, has been made Vice-Chairman of the Contraband Committee for which I am glad – that should keep him busy. I do so hope Tom gets a suitable job and I believe, with you, that it is only a question of time as he is bound to be wanted and will fill a pretty big job fairly easily. (Tom was to join the Ministry of Economic Warfare and the Board of Trade – he and Ruth moved back to their London home in 1940, before taking a house at 30 Ashley Road, Walton-on-Thames – believed to be safer and quieter than London during the Blitz. He worked a twelve-hour day commuting by train up and down to London, including most weekends. In 1942, he was to return to India at the invitation of Lord Linlithgow, Viceroy, joining the Viceroy's council in Delhi with special responsibility for war transport and railways, at the onset of war with Japan and the Burma campaign. See appendix 2 – Lady Ruth Benthall wartime letters to Doreen – JMM) *Ruth and Tom have been such bricks to you all & I do so appreciate it . . . I'm glad Michael has been fixed in a unit – it doesn't matter what it is really and wherever a chap happens to get posted there is work to be done. I do hope they won't send all the youngsters out – anyhow for a good time. Poor Ruth and Tom, they must feel it all so much. I am so glad you have seen Betts and Joan & I hope I may see old Philip out here* (Ironside . . . Betty was Doreen's bridesmaid at their wedding. – JMM) *Is he back with the Carabineers? I was very angry at the thought of their trying to bomb the St. Old but I was glad they didn't get there and I found comfort in the thought of what the chief officers' comments would be. I bet they were lurid! Do you remember him – a stout tough who looked as though he was weaned on whisky?*

I told Joan what you say about Barnes and Gilly but did not mention the question of safety as you suggested, Joan is most grateful to you, Sweetheart. I shall write to Sis & I'm sorry she has so much worry with Bill. He isn't strong, poor chap and has to be taken care of. I will finish this later, Sweetheart. I think of you all the time & I do hope are not worrying too much my Darling one. Later. It is now time to leave the office, Sweetheart, & so I will end this letter. There is little fresh but I seem to have had a pretty busy day – However! Take all care of your own sweet self and of our own wee chaps. All my love to you, my Darling one, with kisses and bunny hugs to our wee chaps. Always your own Geordie."

This is a masterly and reassuring letter. It reassures Doreen with the now firmer prospect of a leave home when they would be able to reassess the whole situation. It reflects their pain of separation, emphasising what George was doing and his loyalty to the continuity and management of Birds in a rapidly changing situation. They had now been separated for eighteen months, and the uncertainties of the changed travel situation brought about by the European war was foremost in both their minds. The sickening thought lurking behind these letters is that the separation might become almost permanent, certainly for the duration of war . . . Great resilience and courage would be needed, and the letters are full of hope and encouragement. George is obviously very busy, working long hours but with weekend breaks at camp, and this letter almost for the first time contains good detail of what was going on workwise.

Ever since the 1935 Government of India Act and the development of the trade union movement in India, there had been increasing representation for the improvement of workers' pay and conditions of employment. Birds had been at the forefront of providing medical facilities for workers at all their factories but had, nevertheless, suffered strikes, notably at Titagur, in the jute mills, collieries and labour cadres which needed much high-level management time to resolve. The Bengal Chamber also had an increasing role in mediation and negotiation so as to provide something of a level playing field across businesses. The sensitive handling of the Loyabad disaster had won the admiration of all and the medical facilities there were amongst the most up-to-date in India.

This regular correspondence was the lifeblood of their relationship, despite the separation, while they maintained as parents their concern for the safety and well-being of us children. As a child, I certainly was blissfully unaware of the wider aspects of this dialogue, although my elder sisters may have had a better understanding and perception, being older. Such is the emotional pain and suffering brought about by war. The letters continue . . .

"Thursday 2ⁿᵈ Nov '39

My own Darling,

For the last two mornings the cold weather seems to have arrived and last night I slept under a blanket for the first time! It is reflected in increased activity by the dogbies in the mornings and this morning they were so bobbery that they just didn't know what to do with themselves. They are now out for their walk. Soon, I shall take them out golfing again as Tolly races are now finished. It was lovely getting a letter from you yesterday and I am glad all goes well though I am sorry Jen has a cold again. I do hope the wee chap will keep fitter this winter, and she will gradually throw off this inclination to colds.

I had a letter from Tom yesterday in which he says he is going to have another try to get fixed up in a job at home and if he doesn't manage to get anything soon, he may come out for a short visit. He is clearly chafing at the bit at having little to do but these things move slowly & I'm sure he will be given something if he is patient. I must say I sympathise with his desire to be doing something – but if I were he, I should hesitate to come out here in case of getting involved in some outside job here & finding he couldn't get home again when Michael goes overseas. But no doubt he could keep clear of commitments here if he did come and it would certainly enable me to get home on a short leave with any luck. But we shall see & in the meantime, I hope he doesn't act hastily & so perhaps miss something at home. It isn't like him to act hastily though! Anyhow, it would make a short leave for me much easier. I do feel full of sympathy for Tom's feelings and for Ruth & Michael's sake, I hope he is given a job at home.

On Monday night I dined downstairs with Joan & Charles; a most hilarious evening – but I told you this in my last letter. On Tuesday I dined quietly here by myself after a fairly busy day. Yesterday I played squash before breakfast and after a pretty rushed day, I went with Joan and Teddie to a 6.00 picture & back to dinner with them. We saw "Jamaica Inn" with Charles Laughton, a most excellent film & I got home and in bed by about 10.30. They were looking after Minnie who was Pat's daughter, a bull terrier. I forget if you knew Minnie but I expect you do. But she died yesterday of distemper & double pneumonia; poor Minnie- she was such a good dog and Joan and Teddie are very upset. Sandy and Ronnie are due back at the end of this week and Molly Mealing asked if I could put them all up – they can go to the Carmichaels but Molly thought they would prefer to come here. But as we expect to be moving house then, and as Cook will be going off to Deosri next week, it couldn't be done, I'm sorry to say. It will be good to see them again.

The house is still not finished and the entrance drive cannot be finished as they ordered too little road metalling & cars can't yet get in & out! Also, the painting is not yet quite finished. So, it looks as if it will not be possible to move in until just before I leave for Deosri, and if it looks like being too much of a rush, then I may leave it until I get back & so give the paint a real chance to dry properly & to be sure everything is properly finished. It is certainly looking very, very nice & I do hope it will be a good house – as I believe it will. But it won't be right until you are there, Sweetheart. I will take some photographs soon.

Tom Mortimer arrived back yesterday & is looking very well. He & his wife came by Lloyds Tristino & apparently had no trouble anywhere. Several others have got back this week & I am glad to see them! Will finish this later.

Friday . . . *Well, Sweetheart, yesterday was the father and mother of a day! I was hard at it all day & in the evening, first of all, I had a Tolly Club meeting & then a Golightly one at Bunty Nicholson. I got home after 8.00 so I thought I would finish this letter today. I had a Tollygunge Homes meeting before breakfast today so am now writing after lunch in the office. Oscar got back last night and is in the office today. Paul won't be here until next week as this carbuncle on his bum won't clear up – most painful! At the Golightly meeting last night we decided not to have a dance, for which I am glad, and instead, we are subscribing Rs 200 each & the money will be devoted to some war charity. I don't think I could bear a dance this year & I think most of the others feel likewise.*

It is really quite cold now & we have been most lucky as there has been hardly any of the beastly September/October drying up.

I had a cable from Norman who was in Hong Kong on his way back via America & he is staying with me on his way through – he is due here on Monday next. It will be fun seeing him again. Bunty is still at home I suppose. Well, sweetheart, I suppose I must stop. Take all care of your Darling self and of our wee chaps and don't worry too much. All my love to you, my own sweet Darling, with kisses and bunny hugs to our wee chaps. God bless you and them. Always your own Geordie."

The issue of Walstead keeps coming back . . . the view was that with war, Lindridge would be less vulnerable than Walstead and therefore safer; paradoxically, however, it was Lindridge that was bombed in late 1940 after we had all left for India, while Walstead remained unscathed throughout the war.

"06.11.39

My own Darling,

It was so good to get your letter yesterday evening when I arrived back from camp enclosing one from Arthur. I entirely agree with all you say about A.R. And I'm afraid I too feel that he is a sort of dark shadow over that district. He can be so good and helpful too but he seems to have become thoroughly disgruntled with life and everything in it. I love Walstead and we will D.V. be all there together someday not too far off I hope – but I hate the idea of you being there in war-time, more or less alone, and I think it is far better to stay as you are if Ruth and Tom are willing and if you & the chaps are happy there as I know you are. After all, there is company there always and it is as peaceful a spot as we can find. When I can get home for a proper leave, we can tackle the whole Walstead problem (& taxation) & we will get it all in our own names and then we shall feel that we don't need to worry Arthur and we can deal with it all ourselves and be independent – which is the only really satisfactory way, I quite agree. Until I get home it is far better just to leave things as they are, Sweetheart, as things seem quite settled for the time being – I agree the tenants have got it at an absolute give-away price but it suits us and so doesn't really matter. Arthur is bound to whine about all he is doing, etc; it's the nature of the poor old chap, but that doesn't make it any less tiresome! I shall write to Bea one day soon. She is such a dear and has always been so helpful & understanding. I should certainly assume that you will not be going back to Walstead for some time (unless you want to, of course – even if I get a short leave home as I really think it would be better to wait awhile to & see what chances there are of more settled times. Ultimately, we will get it all settled up in our own names and then we shall feel better about it & you will feel free of any influences of A.R. But this must wait until I can get home & really get time to get it all fixed up. In the meantime, it will remain well let, so don't worry about it all, Sweetheart, & I should just hope that you can all stay on at Lindridge. D.V. We shall be able to talk it all through some time not too far distant.

Well, after writing you on Friday, it was when I finished, I went to Stanley Nairn's wedding reception. They invited hardly anyone to the church but had a big reception at Frank McKay's house which was a very good idea. (Dr Stanley Nairn was George's doctor and also became the author's doctor when I returned to Calcutta in 1961. He retired shortly after and Frank McKay took over. They were known affectionately as the Middleton Street Butchers. Maurice Shellim, one of the partners, had distinguished himself as the Doctor to the raid on Marmagau harbour in Goa, mounted by the Calcutta Light Horse and the Calcutta Scottish, which sank the Ehrenfels a German quasi merchantman/cruiser. He became a good friend. The film made of the episode was called *The Sea Wolves* – JMM)

I saw Helen Thomas there, the first time for weeks, and also Cecily who was in her usual rude health. I also saw George Gemmel & lots of the chaps. It was quite fun seeing everybody. Mrs Nairn looks charming and is most attractive, I think. I had a quiet dinner by myself. On Saturday, I was late in the office & got the 5.20 to camp, picking up Joan and Teddie at Barrackpore. We shot yesterday at Harringhalta & again went by bus from Kanchrapara. We got 32 couple & one duck and thoroughly enjoyed it all & went straight into Calcutta afterwards, getting there about 6.30. After an early dinner by myself, I went to the New Empire & saw a pretty dud film but it helped to pass the time. I was busy round the flat this morning getting things ready for Deosri as Dil & Cook leave tomorrow evening. I hope to go at the end of the week on the 10th or 11th. I hope Dick and Peggy and Joan and Teddie are coming up the following Friday. I hope to be away a fortnight – Paul returned today. I really had an awful rush last week and today has been the devil. It is now 6.30 so I shall have to stop soon as Norman Odling is supposed to have arrived. His bearer arrived from Kalimpong this morning and I sent him and Dil to meet the plane at Willingdon Reach. Golly how I wish you were here,

Sweetheart. It seems so wrong to be going to Deosri & you not being there too . . . But D.V. we will go there again sometime.

The house is practically ready though the drive isn't yet completed. I may get most of the furniture moved over before I go and then I shall be able to start clear when I get back. Joan and Charles will be able to stay on at 15a until I get back and it would be so much easier, but I will see how things go this week. It really is going to be nice I think and now the light fittings are all up it really does look nice. But it is not right without you, Sweetheart.

Take all care of your Darling self and of our wee chaps. I long for us to be together again. God bless you and them. All my love to you, my own darling, with kisses and bunny hugs to our own wee chaps. Always your own Geordie."

George's next letter has some more hopeful news about a possible short leave home, written just before he leaves for his holiday to Deosri.

"Friday 10.11.39

My own Darling,

First of all, thank you for a lovely letter received on Tuesday.

I do so wish I could get home for a short visit, Sweetheart, and I have already written to Tom, last week, I think, asking what he feels about my coming home for a quick leave as soon as I can be reasonably sure of a return passage by air. I have not had time to hear from him in reply – also Oscar has written to Pinkhorn who is the senior Imperial Airways' man in India to find out whether they can book me a return passage. There is of course K.L.M. And if I fail to get anything by Imperial, I shall make enquiries from K.L.M. if Tom thinks it is a fair reasonable thing to do. I must say I see no objection to a quick trip once Bunty is back. We had two mills on strike this week but all is quiet again and they have settled down again happily, so I hope they will stay quiet. We are doing all we can to keep them happy without jeopardising the future by granting increases we can't keep up once the war is over. I am considering a scheme of profit-sharing for labour but it takes time and it has been a dreadful rush this week – However!

I hate these separations, Sweetheart, and I long for us all to be together again – which we will D.V. before long. Before long, I hope the rush of people returning to their war stations will be over and their ordinary comings and goings may be possible. I am very glad Jean likes the convent. I do so wish I could be with the little funnies just for a time, bless their little hearts. But one can only keep determined to do so as soon as it is both reasonable & possible & I am certainly determined! Today is a holiday & also tomorrow and I might have gone to Deosri but I thought I would get cleared up here & in the new house before leaving.

I came into the new house yesterday evening & slept here last night & dined here too. I have a temporary cook – one we used to take to camp, as ours has gone to Deosri. Joan and Charles are staying on in the lower flat for a bit as they have gone to Puri this weekend & I wanted to get in here by myself before they came in. I am writing this in our new bedroom after an afternoon nap! It is looking so nice but it is still not finished – but I am sure this is the only way to make them finish it. They have been simply dreadful about the last few things and we still can't get into the drive or park a car or get into the garage, & one enters the 'grounds' through the unfinished gap in the wall! But it is practically finished inside except for one or two very minor things such as door handles on the cupboards in the bathroom. The dogbies have been most upset – firstly, they simply hated seeing all their furniture walking off & going by lorry to an unknown destination! Then, when I appeared at the old house in the evening, they were so glad to see me! The little sweeper has been their rock by which they have stood! When they were finally brought here & found me, they were simply delighted but barked at every mistry and coolie (= worker and labourer – JMM). *When I came down to dinner, they barked at me from the hall. I suppose they couldn't see any legs on the stairs and thought I was trying to be funny! They do amuse me. I got back from the office lateish & have rested for an hour. Soon I am taking myself out to a flick. All our lighting here is most effective I think & I have got all the various experts to move the piano, fridgidaire & wireless. The telephone is installed and things seem to be all right though there is still a certain amount of clearing up of small oddments to do. The preparation of the garden goes on well; in a week, it should be dug all over & grassed. The tennis court has already been done. I had no idea that we had so many pots in the garden at 15A! There is only one thing not as I would have it & that is that you aren't here, Sweetheart. But it is best as it is for the meantime until we know more about getting backwards & forwards. I quite agree D.V. that it won't be long until we know more & I can get home for a short trip – I am so glad to have got the move over before going away & there is practically nothing left for when I return, though there is still much to be done in the garden.*

I shall be leaving for Deosri tomorrow night, so there may be a little delay in sending off my next letter but I hope not by more than a couple of days. How I wish you were going to be with me at Deosri, Sweetheart.

Well, Norman arrived on Monday evening in excellent form having flown the Atlantic & the Pacific in the clippers. It must have been a most wonderful experience. We didn't do much in the evenings but on Monday went down & spent an hour with Joan and Teddie as Mr Grell was coming there to talk about Deosri – he was most helpful and showed us some most interesting photographs.

Pitts was there in his usual good form & young Eadie from Teddie's firm. Norman left on Wednesday and Joan Thomas & Bunty Nicholson & I watched him have his dinner at 7.30.! It was so nice to see him again & he seems to have had a wonderful time. I gather Bunty is still at home.

I had an early meeting at the D.C.S. this morning and here we are! I expect to be alone for the first few days at Deosri & then Dick Pegg may come & Joan & Teddie but none of them are certain so I might be there on my own for the whole two weeks. There are two holidays in the second week so it won't be too bad from an office point of view & they can always get me back in an emergency – I feel I must get away for a week or fortnight & it will do me all the good in the world with any luck. We have had a very difficult and worrying time off & on & the last two years have been pretty strenuous – but, touching wood, I am very well & shall be completely refreshed after a fortnight away – but still ready for a couple of months at home!!

Take all care of your darling self and of our wee chaps – I think of you all the time, my Sweetheart, & long to be with you. All my love to you, my own Darling, with kisses and bunny hugs to our wee chaps – God bless you and them. Always your own Geordie."

Deosri is now a tourist centre in the Bongaigaon district of Assam. It is situated close to the Bhutanese border in the middle of a forest bloc with views to the beautiful blue mountains of Bhutan in the North and the snows peeping above the horizon. Clearly a magical spot with fishing, probably for char in the mountain streams. It is situated in the Duars, one of the big tea-growing centres. At the time of this visit, it would have been largely unspoilt by tourism, with the indigenous and colourful hill people around. A comfortable bungalow provided accommodation.

"Deosri Monday 13th Nov

My own Darling,

I am sitting in the little mosquito-proof room at the above bungalow and the Aie is flowing with its usual pleasant sound in the distance. Gosh, this is a grand spot. It only lacks one essential – yourself. I have loved every minute of it up to now and already I am feeling better. I have had a very busy couple of years and the last few months haven't been easy, say what one will. But when I left, all seemed peaceful. The strikes we have had in the jute mills were over and there seemed no reason why I shouldn't go off. So off I went!

But even this wasn't all easy. First of all, after the car and Dil and Cook had all left, I got a wire from Bhadran the forest officer saying the road from Kohraghar was closed, or rather, not yet opened as the bridge wasn't repaired and asking me to send the car to Basugarda, the next station to Kohraghar about ten miles further on which doesn't depend on the bridge or the ferry. When I got the wire, the car should have arrived & I pictured it unloaded & the railway carriage sent off & Dil sitting beside a foaming torrent unable to cross! So, I got busy and sent wires to Dil, the station master at Kohraghar – also, I sent the bearer off with fifty Rupees in case. The next day, Saturday, a holiday, I got a wire from the bearer saying the car had arrived safely & had sent on to Basingaon but owing to engine trouble, Dil had been unable to start it! Friday and Saturday were holidays but I had decided to spend them in Calcutta clearing up and doing various jobs in the office & at the house. The bearer also said in a wire, "Please send mechanic". Well, I felt quite happy and determined about it all and was quite prepared to lose a day or two so long as I got there. So, having left the Rover at the French Motor Car Coy that morning – Saturday, & seen the works manager, I phoned him and explained matters & asked for a mistry to go with me on Saturday night. Sadigne collected the mistry – a very nice chap, & we set off! When we arrived at Kohraghar, I was met by the forest ranger who got in the train & came to Basingaon & as we steamed into the station, Dil, driving the car, appeared out of a cloud of dust from the other direction! He had fixed the car – it was a wad of jute waste in the petrol pipe & had taken the Cook & all baggage out here & was there to meet me with his usual round innocent face! This place is just as ever with the blue mountains of Bhutan not so very far away & the sound of the river in one's ears all the time and oh so peaceful. I got here for lunch yesterday & caught my first fish at about 4.00, too small to keep though, so I threw it back. Then another, also too small to keep, & then, in your pool, I got another which broke the gut trace. I like to think it was an enormous fish but I suspect that it was merely rather an old trace, weak in parts & probably quite a moderate fish! Anyhow it was a short thrill then nothing! By then, it was nearly time to stop & I got no more & so back here in the darkness to a late tea. Dil is being his usual cheery & efficient self & Cook has been a brick; he grins broadly at everything & is doing misalchi work (washing up – JMM) *as well as his own. Dil & he bathed in the river today whilst I was up at Hattishai – where the Governor's pool used to be. I went on an elephant this morning as the road was not quite ready for the car. It will be in a couple of days at most.*

I only got three fish today – each about a pound, not less anyhow, but there are not many really good pools up there rather like last year. I had a couple of shots at pea-fowl on the way home but they were out of range I'm afraid. I got back at dusk & here I am after dinner. It is so good here, Sweetheart, & can only wish and wish that we shall be here together again before long. I simply long for you all the time, my Darling one, & getting away like this does help to clear one's head of all the rush & mass of detail which seems to beset one in Calcutta. I left the new house already getting clear & thoroughly cleared up & Ram Lal is having a real rustle round whilst I'm away. All details should be finished before I return & Joan & Charles may have moved in. If they have, so much the better as one can settle with no further worries. I had a carpenter there before I left & shelves & things should be finished by the time I return. Anyhow, most of it will be done. The house really is very nice & I am sure you will love it when you see it. The dogbies have quickly settled down though they didn't like it much when I left. But they have their friend the sweeper who really is a most wonderful friend to them.

Dil will take this letter tomorrow to Rainikletter where the forest runners will take it to Kolraghar – I do hope it won't be unduly delayed, Sweetheart.

I think of you up here more than ever if that is possible and long to be with you. I hope Oscar may get some news for me about flying. Take all care of your Darling self and of our wee chaps. God bless you and them. All my love to you, my own Darling, with kisses & bunny hugs to our own wee chaps Always your own Geordie."

A Short Home leave by air through the war; his O.B.E., Grandfather Fred's death. A "nightmare" journey back to India dodging the bombs

This is the final letter in this series and according to his holiday programme, he returned to Calcutta around the weekend of 24th/25th November, no doubt to hear the results of Oscar's investigation into return flights. Oscar's efforts were obviously successful and with clearance now from Tom Benthall, he was on his way home on leave arriving at Croydon on an Imperial Airways flight in early December, and reunited with his beloved wife "Dorks" and us three very excited children. We don't know where they all spent Christmas but photographs in the snow suggest that it was at Lindridge. Subsequent letters from Calcutta restart on 23rd March so it was a short leave of just three months. He attended the presentation ceremony of his O.B.E. on 4th December before he left for England.

Britain had been at war now for the previous three months although rearmament and preparations had been going on for far longer. Churchill had returned to office in September 1939 to the Admiralty . . . "Winston is back" was the message to the fleet. As part of an expansion of warships, he ordered the construction of further battleships of the George 5th class as well as a number of cruisers, aircraft carriers, destroyers and corvettes for convoy duty as well as mine-sweepers.

Poland had now been completely overrun. Many Poles escaped to Britain, their military and airmen making an important contribution to the war effort. An expeditionary force had been sent to North-Eastern France with the strategic expectation that a German invasion of France would commence with an attack on the Low Countries, Holland followed by Belgium, rather than on the strongly fortified southern Maginot line. This assessment was to prove fatally flawed.

The peacetime Army was now being swelled with volunteers and conscription troops under training. Many young executives employed in Calcutta, particularly those on leave, enlisted in the armed forces. George, now rising 47, was too old, and had anyway been medically discharged following World War 1. Birds were to experience severe shortages of executive staff throughout both the European and Far Eastern wars. Rationing had been introduced although Lindridge, with its 1400 acres of farmland, was well provided for with fresh milk and butter. Dorks had invested in egg-laying hens, and other fresh vegetables and fruit were provided for with the house's extensive kitchen gardens. Fruit was stored and bottled and extensive jam making was underway.

It was the shooting season, with seasonal game, pheasants, partridges, hares and occasional wild duck available. Rabbits were plentiful most of the year and ferreting and snaring provided a plentiful supply to supplement the meat ration. There might also have been the occasional roe deer from the woodlands of the estate. George's diaries list a number of days' shooting with Tom on the Lindridge estate throughout January. But Britain had always been dependent on imported foodstuffs, particularly cereals for both human and animal consumption, as well as oil. The Atlantic shipping lifeline, just as in the First World War, was critically important. Petrol rationing was introduced affecting the school run.

Two of Germany's three pocket battleships, the *Deutschland* and the *Graf Spee,* had slipped anchor before the declaration of war, the *Deutschland* thought to be off the coast of Greenland, the *Graf Spee* loose in the South Atlantic; both ships were accompanied by auxiliary supply vessels. The *Deutschland* crept back unnoticed to Germany but the *Graf Spee* continued to raid shipping around the coasts of Latin America. She was

Programme of the Durbar
to be held by
His Excellency the Governor of Bengal
at Government House, Calcutta
on the 4th December 1939

HIS EXCELLENCY THE GOVERNOR will hold a Durbar at Government House, Calcutta, on Monday, the 4th December 1939, at 5 p.m., for the purpose of investing Mr. Edmond Nicolas Blandy, C.S.I., C.I.E., I.C.S., with the badge of Companionship of the Most Exalted Order of the Star of India; Lieutenant-Colonel Ernest William O'Gorman Kirwan, C.I.E., I.M.S., and Mr. Jnanankur De, C.I.E., I.C.S., with badges of Companionship of the Most Eminent Order of the Indian Empire; Captain James Forsyth, O.B.E., Mr. Joshua Forbes Russell, O.B.E., Mr. George Henry Welford, O.B.E., Major Bijeta Chaudhuri, O.B.E., I.M.S., Mr. George Bond Morton, O.B.E., Rai Moti Lal Basu Bahadur, M.B.E., Mr. Dines Chandra Chakravarti, M.B.E., Mr. Robert Thomas Mansfield Hayter, M.B.E., Mr. Eric John Hart Jacobson, M.B.E., Mr. Alexander Keay Thoms, M.B.E., Mr. Antony Furtado, M.B.E., Mr. Kasi Sankar Mitra, M.B.E., and Khan Bahadur Saiyid Moshfique Saleheen, M.B.E., with the badges of an Officer and a Member, respectively, of the Most Excellent Order of the British Empire, and the gentlemen

62 Georges O.B.E. 4th December 1939

eventually bottled up in Montevideo on the River Plate after a brisk action with three British cruisers and scuttled in the river just before Christmas 1939.

The U-boat battle had intensified with the sinking of the battleship *Royal Oak* in Scapa Flow by *U47* on 14th October 1939. *U47* crept into the bay through an unprotected gap in the defences and attacked the ship with torpedoes. The German cruisers *Scharnhorst* and *Gneisenau* also escaped into the north Atlantic before the declaration of war, and on November 23rd, the armed merchant ship *Rawalpindi* was sunk after a gallant but one-sided fight. Both cruisers returned to Germany and were then damaged and finally bottled up by the Navy in the Baltic after the actions in the North Sea following the German invasion of Norway in April and May.

George returned to Calcutta in mid-March 1940, by air. His first letter to Dorks is accompanied by confirmation of the arrangement with Arthur MacNaught transferring the head lease of Walstead to George and Dorks and it suggests that the meeting took place just before he flew off back to India from Croydon Airport.

"5 Raja Santosh Road, Calcutta Friday 29.3.40

My own Darling,

It was so good getting a letter from you yesterday enclosing one from Jean (aged 9) & one from Jen (aged 6) and John (aged 3) and one from Buff – and I am glad that you and the chaps are well though I hope that Nanny is getting over having her teeth out. I went round yesterday evening & saw Helen and George. Helen seemed well and cheery. Their small dog (Binnie's son) has fathered a family & one is exactly like Bins and is such a nice wee chap & simply full of beans, about eight weeks old. Helen talked about nurses, & said she was going to have some Anglo- Indian nurse to begin with & hoped later on to be able to get someone more senior & European. I said that you had wondered if, later on, our Nanny mightn't like a job in India but it was so uncertain & far ahead that you had thought Helen would have got someone, & probably our Nanny would not be fit until next year sometime, & even then, mightn't like to leave England again. Helen said even more than a year hence might interest her if she hadn't been able to get someone good in the meantime – later on, next year or so, it might still be possible to fix Nanny up if she wanted to sometime. Anyhow – go East again & you decided to change. I wondered afterwards if I oughtn't to have mentioned it as it is so long ahead & we may not want Nanny to go even then, but Helen understood that, even if there was a chance at all it wouldn't be until next year sometime any-how – in the meantime, I expect she will get somebody good. But it does show that it will probably not be difficult to fix Nanny up when the time comes – possibly with Helen.

I am glad Joan Treble has been down there. It must have been nice having her there & I'm sure it will do her lots of good. It must be lovely there now with the spring flowers all out. The weather here is simply incredible & is still cool except at mid-day. I dined with Lenore & Johnny on Tuesday, (Johnny Johnston – JMM) a nice quiet evening with Stewart Gray & the Gladstones. It was an early evening, thank goodness, & I enjoyed it. Johnny has arranged temporarily to work again at

Place Siddons in addition to his work at Tolly, which is giving him a pretty strenuous time but I am glad for his sake as he may be enabled to make a bit more. Helen told me this yesterday evening and said that Johnny was regarding it as war work owing to P. Siddons having lost several of their younger men who have joined up. Quite a number of young men have joined up & more seem to be going so later on, if this war goes on for long, it may become difficult to find people – young people anyhow. People here are subscribing freely to the E. India Fund which goes home for War Charities in the UK & big lists are published in the Statesman of Donations & monthly subscriptions – Rs100- to Rs 300- a month are quite ordinary amounts for most of the senior people here & even Pitts gives either Rs100 or Rs150 a month, I forget which, (not that Pitts is mean but this will give you a line on it!). Although people do meet for cocktails etc. there is certainly an underlying feeling of resolution amongst Europeans here & far less than usual is being spent on entertainment & drinking especially. The war feeling is not of course present here to the same extent it is at home, but there is certainly not the free spending of money here that there has been. It is difficult to define but although there is undoubtedly relatively "no war" here, yet underneath it all, people are the same or would be the same if it were possible to be in as close touch with war conditions as people are at home. The wireless gives very little compared with home broadcasts so it is difficult. I am glad I have been home, Sweetheart, not only to have the heavenly time I have had with you and our wee chaps, but to see England & home & the people at this time. Few Indians one meets seem to realise what this war might mean to them & most seem to regard it as a heaven-sent opportunity either to get more politically or financially or both. Such an attitude, permeating business & govt. circles as it does, must have its effect. But, as more people visit home, the better it will be, though some will (& do) only complain of the lack of facilities to carry on the mode of life they have become used to when they visit the UK! But whoever they are, Europeans are just as resolute I think, though entertaining in a costly way might well be reduced further. Tommy Lamb asked me to cocktails as Lady Lamb is out & he wanted her to meet all his friends. I saw him the day after he arrived & he sent an invitation by hand that afternoon with a personal letter. So I went, on Wednesday, & I compromised with my conscience by having one drink only – a gimlet, which I should have had at home if I hadn't had it with Tommy – I did not have one at home! A.D. Brown of McKinnon's – a good friend of mine, is retiring & is giving a farewell party – cocktail party, to which I shall go too, all being well, and again, I shall have one drink only – at A.D.'s expense instead of my own! Last night at Helen and George's, I had my one drink & none at home – as far as I can see there is no difference. All the same, I hope people will continue to cut down unnecessary expense! They undoubtedly have already done so & one sportsman gave Rs 750- to the War fund "anonymous, the cost of a cocktail party I didn't give". It is most interesting to sense the difference between home and here.

I have written to Arthur in just the usual way & have sent him a copy of my letter of 30th October '37 recording our arrangement. I will send you a copy with this. I hope we can arrange something with the Nortons but don't let it worry you. Well, Sweetheart,

I suppose I must stop. Take care of your sweet self & of our own wee chaps. God bless you and them. All my love to you, my own Darling, with kisses and bunny hugs to our own wee chaps. Always your own Geordie."

In later letters from home, especially those to Doreen from Ruth Benthall, there is a strong suggestion that she should initiate a group of leading hostesses to set an example of cutting down on lavish entertaining in view of the contrast between wartime Britain with its stringent rationing, and the comparative land of plenty in Calcutta.

"5 Raja Santosh Road, Calcutta Friday 05 04 40.

My Own Darling,

Thank you very much for a lovely letter yesterday enclosing one from Jen & one each from Arthur and Bea. In my letter posted last Tuesday, I expressed the same views about Oliver as you express in your letter which I got yesterday so we are thinking absolutely alike and I am very glad you have taken the line you have.

It is only right, and we both hate even remotely letting down the people who work for us – even though they may not always appreciate it. So let anyone who cares to think what they like and we will still do as we think right and proper. I am sending back Bea's and A.R.'s letters and I have kept copies.

The six months' break clause gives us all the safeguards we want, I think. I suppose the outside paintwork of the stables and buildings should be done soon. It might be wise to get this done this spring but I expect you have it in mind. I can't think of anything else. Later on, we can think again and decide on what to do but we can always get back, if we want to, on six months' notice.

Well, Sweetheart, it is such a lovely thought that you may be able to come out in July. But even if you can't get out so soon, it will be the cold weather for a few months and whichever it is, it will be simply lovely. We will see how things go and hope for the best – there is nothing else to do I suppose while the war lasts. Oscar goes on the 9ᵗʰ which is Tuesday and he is taking your gloves and stockings and Ruth's gloves and I do hope they are all right. I am off to Bombay tonight for a meeting on Monday and do not expect to be back until Wednesday, so I shall not be there when Oscar leaves and can truthfully say I can't see him off (at 4.00 a.m.!) He has been so very fit, I'm glad to say, and I am glad he is going off for the next few months as that should ensure his keeping fit with any ordinary luck. The rest of us are very well – touching wood – and I am feeling fitter and am settling down. There always seems such a lot to do here but I am on top of it all at last and with any luck, will remain so. It is hotter but dry, and it really has been such good weather. My only trouble in the week has been that I can't get time for exercise but that should improve and there are always weekends.

I dined quietly with the Coopers on Tuesday. They had about eight others including the Boltons from Shillong (capital of Assam – JMM) *– who wanted to know all about you and the chaps, and who seemed very fit. Jack Graham was also there, just the same as ever and in good heart. Got away about 11.30. On Wednesday, I dined with Betty* *and John,* (John Burder of Jardine Skinner, a fellow member of Council of the Bengal Chamber – their two daughters, Susan and Caroline, were in Kalimpong with us and came home with us in May 1945 – JMM) *both flourishing and we went to see Ballalaica again which I enjoyed. Maria and Vyvian and Kay and Tom were also there and we had a very pleasant evening – Maria & Vyvian seemed very well and I gather Vyvian's business is good for which I am very glad. It was good seeing them and Maria tells me she is going to Darjeeling very soon. Betty is not going home this summer and hopes to get Susan out for a time in the autumn. I believe someone coming out has promised to bring Susan with her – I'm not sure it wasn't Mignon but I didn't hear properly.* (Mignon Nicholson, wife of Bunty and sister of Teddie Shuttleworth. Their two children, Priscilla and Tim, were again neighbours in Kalimpong and cousins of my brother-in-law Barney Shuttleworth. – JMM) *Betty was very nice and I thought was looking very well. Last night, Clara came to dinner. He is going on leave soon & proposes to go to South Africa & then home to England for a short time only. He was in crashing form and we had a most amusing evening except he wouldn't go home! At last, I have written to Ruth. I should have done so long ago but it hasn't been easy though suppose I could have done so. It wasn't a very good letter but I hope Ruth won't mind. We haven't yet heard of Tom's arrival but we are assuming he got home quite safely & happily. We thought of cabling but didn't want to fuss unnecessarily though I wanted to cable to Bennett. We are going to decide today if we don't hear.*

I am sorry that you and Tiger didn't get your trip to Dartmoor but perhaps you will later on. How I should have loved being with you at Easter, Sweetheart, and our chaps. It sounded so lovely & the trip to Buckfast especially. D.V. we will do that together sometime. I wonder what Eileen and Humphrey will do. It of course depends upon what job Humphrey finds to do, but if Eileen & Rosalind can stay on at Lindridge I expect they will until everything is more settled, and I agree with you it is impossible to make definite plans very far ahead. I wonder what Dad has decided to do but I expect that I shall hear. I will finish this later, Sweetheart. I expect Ruth and Tom are at Lindridge which will be fun. Give them my love.

Well, another day's work done! Nothing new, Sweetheart, and I am leaving for Bombay tonight. I will write you from there and I will return Bea's and A.R.'s letter next week when I return. Take all care of your sweet self and of our wee chaps. God bless you and them. All my love to you, my own Darling, with kisses & bunny hugs to our own wee chaps. Always your own Geordie."

This letter suggests a return to India possibly in July or maybe later in 1940. In fact, events overtook the family with the death of Grandfather Frederick in June and we left as a family for India in the second half of July.

In George's next letter, written from Bombay, he describes various goings-on during his visit. He was now a Director of the Imperial Bank and he was attending a meeting at the Bank's headquarters in Bombay. He had also taken a post as the Vice-President of the Bengal Chamber and Associated Chambers of Commerce in anticipation of his election as President in 1941, for which he was to be knighted in 1942. By tradition, the Presidency was largely rotated amongst the leading firms of Calcutta.

"Bombay Monday 8th April

My Own Darling,

    I arrived here yesterday after a peaceful and pleasant journey by the air-conditioned coach. Neville was on the same train and Burn had arrived on the previous day. I am staying with Lamond and we had a lazy day yesterday sitting in the garden until lunchtime, then a nap, & then after tea, was sat on the lawn of the Yacht Club and watched the sea until it was time to change for dinner – about 25 of us with Sir Byramjee Jeejeabhoy (and his little boy! Not quite) and then an early home to bed. We have the Bank meeting (the Imperial Bank – JMM) this morning then a large lunch party & then tea and I suppose a garden party with J.B. Taylor who is the Governor of the Reserve Bank, and so to the train for Calcutta. I was very amused at Bryamjee – who is an amazing bird, as he has been sued for libel – as you know there is prohibition here and the anti-prohibitionists, Parsees, held a meeting and asked a bloke who had been 16 or 17 years in America to speak. Later, having found out a bit about the lecturer and discovered that he had seven convictions in America with nine years spent in prison for various crimes, including rape, Byramjee, in a speech to discredit the lecturer, said he was a "jailbird" who had spent ten years in jug and that although he called himself a Colonel, he, Bryamjee, thought he was better described as a Vice-Admiral with emphasis on the Vice. As the injured (!), trouble followed & now a libel action is threatened as the injured (!) party claims he is not a jailbird being no longer in jail and that he only spent nine years in jail and not ten! Can you beat it? But it all gave us a good laugh.

    Bombay is quite pleasant and not at all hot though I should have liked some exercise and at one time I hoped we might get out to Jyou yesterday for a bathe. But Bobby thought a drink at the Yacht Club & a view of the sea would be easier!

    Well, Sweetheart, I suppose I must get up and shave. It must be lovely in Devonshire now and I can imagine what the spring flowers must be like. I think of you all the time in that lovely place with our own wee chaps, and I only hope you are not trying to do too much. I am sorry Elsa has had such a rotten time. It obviously doesn't suit her there and being enervating, she never gets the same chance to pick up. If only it were more bracing, what a heavenly place it would be. North Devon is so different and I wonder if Gordon will take them all up there when he gets home. I am going to get Gordon to dinner before he goes but I don't seem to get a free few minutes these days and have had nobody to a meal since I got back, which is disgraceful (but very peaceful!)

    I wonder what the dogbies think of me going off again & leaving them. They have been in such good form and seem very happy & are always pleased to see one & seem to love having the garden just down a few steps. – they have tremendous fun in the garden trying to catch crows and the crows seem to enter into it too & stay on the ground squawking until the last second! Our cook is trying to get a temporary job and he may have got one. I told him I would make his pay up to Rs 45 – (what we pay him) if he can get a job and he is quite happy though he has said, over and over again, whenever I know you are coming out or whenever Joan and Charles move, I am to let him know immediately so that he can come back without delay – he is most keen to come back but realises he ought to try & find a temporary job until he is wanted. He is a good chap. RL is a most excellent bearer, touching wood, and soon I shall let the bearer go. He comes each day but only in case he is wanted. I think RL knows all about it now & I shall probably let him go soon after I return. I am having the "Rover" stored at the French motor Car Coy, where the office car usually stays, and am having the office car at the house. It will save about 9 miles a day for the office car & the office will pay the cost of garaging. I shall pay for any mileage I do privately on the office car and altogether it seems much the best arrangement as I use the Rover so little that we can't even keep the battery charged. Anyhow, I shall try it for a bit and see how it works out.

I will finish after breakfast, Sweetheart.

Well, it's nearly time to go to the Bank so I will close. It is pleasant here though damper than Calcutta & I miss my air-conditioned rooms! Take all care of your sweet self and of our chaps. God bless you and them. All my love to you, my own Darling – with kisses and bunny hugs to our wee chaps. Always your own Geordie."

The next letter is written after George's return to Calcutta but details the social events after the Bank meeting. There is also more comment too on the German invasion of Denmark and Norway.

"5 Raja Santosh Road 11ᵗʰ April

My own Darling,

It was lovely yesterday when I got to the office to find a letter from you. It was hot here when I arrived & I went straight away along to the office and found everyone except Tom Mortimer who has enteric, I am sorry to say. Denham (Dr Denham White – JMM) *is looking after him and I am so very glad I told Tom's little wife when she phoned that he must have a good Doctor. That was last week & fortunately, when she phoned & said Tom had some Portuguese doctor but he hadn't been that day as he was looking after some Raja! I then said how important it was in this country to have a quick diagnosis & that I hoped she would insist on one of our best doctors at once. Apparently, she did and Denham has put off leave to stay and look after Tom. I haven't had time to go along and enquire but he has nurses there day and night and is in his own flat as Denham thinks he is as well off there as anywhere else. Today I am going to make sure that everything is being done, but I am sure it is.*

Well, after writing you in Bombay, I went off to the Bank meeting & then we had a luncheon party at the Taj, (The Taj Hotel which is next to the Gateway to India – JMM) *then I had a lie back for an hour and then we went to a garden party at J.B. Taylor's house. He is reserve Bank Governor and has the most beautiful house. Sat me down at a table where Peg Mulloch was sitting amongst six or eight Indians – very nice ones, mostly Parsees. Dennis Mulloch has gone home as he has such bad footrot and Peggy*

& the two children are going up to Kashmir. She is nice I think and asked all about you and sent her love. They are staying with J.B. which is nice for them. J.B. had thrown this party as there was a meeting of the Drs of the Reserve Bank in addition to the Imperial. I must say I was tremendously impressed with the sunken garden where we all had tea. Then we just had time to go back to Bill Lamond's house for a quick drink & I went off to catch the train. Bobby Burn is staying on in Bombay for another week or ten days and it will do him good as he has been very tired. We had a pleasant return journey in the air-conditioned coach & I went straight to the office where I seemed to keep busy until about six. Then Paul and I went to Stanley Nairn for our second injection against cholera.

The dogbies were very glad to see me and I changed and went out to A.O. Brown's cocktail party. It was nice and cool in his garden and I stayed about half an hour. As I had been inoculated, I didn't have a drink, but I wanted one! Then I went to Joan and Geoff for dinner and the cine "The Lion Has Wings". Very good I thought. Lenore and Johnny and Col. Tarleton were there too & it was a pleasant evening. I gave Joan your love and your present (Rs20) to your godson. Joan is going to write you. She was in great form and she tells me she is going to have another infant. Old Geoff is keeping the ball rolling – as it were!

I feel so sorry for Denmark and Norway – they have been in such a desperate position. We have not yet heard the full story and the situation in Norway and off the Danish coast still seems obscure. But there seems little doubt the Bosch has once more "walked in" or anyhow is trying to in Norway – and presumably, Sweden will be next. I don't feel that Sweden can expect anything else but I did think Norway would be left out of it. But I'm pretty sure our Navy is busy and the R.A.F. too and one can only hope they will give the Bosch hell. If this doesn't turn American opinion, nothing will, short of a bombing raid on New York. Germany will have her hands full after this and it will be interesting to see Russia's reaction. All the same, I feel that the invasion of Scandinavia is the act of a desperate man and one only hopes it means more to Hitler than perhaps we realise. What a mess it will all be to clear up.

I will finish this later, Sweetheart. I am glad you have heard from Arthur about Oliver and I feel that we have done the best thing about Walstead in all the circumstances and we must just wait and see how things turn out. But never fear, Sweetheart; we will have our little house when the time comes, either Walstead (If A.R. isn't at East Mascles!) for a time & then somewhere else, or some other place. But we will have a home somewhere when the time is ripe. It is better to be free in the meantime. And I am very glad that you are feeling better about it all so don't worry about it anymore, Sweetheart. It is quite a happy arrangement & after all, if we really want to get back to Walstead, we can do it in six months. We must just wait and see how long this war lasts & what we want to do. We may find another district that we like better but I shouldn't worry about it as you will not have time for any looking round for a time.

Later. Well, there isn't very much fresh. Tom Mortimer is a bit better today I'm glad to say. Yesterday, he was inoculated with something or other and reacted favourably to it thank goodness. I hope now he will go steadily on.

I got a lovely letter from you today which I will answer in my next.

What a heavenly time I had with you and the chaps. I only pray we may be together again soon. Take all care of your sweet self and our wee chaps. God bless you and them. All my love to you, my Darling, with kisses and bunny hugs to our wee chaps. Always your own Geordie."

The next letter introduces, for the first time, a move from Shillong to Kalimpong as a potential residential hill station for holiday/summer periods. This was to prove a providential move since the Japanese advance was to threaten Imphal, only 100 miles away from Shillong in 1943/4.

"5 Raja Santosh Road Calcutta 15.04 1940

My Own Darling,

It was lovely getting your letter last Thursday – the day I wrote to you, and I am glad you are all flourishing and that Nanny was feeling better. I think that it is an excellent plan to take Doit's house, if you can, while Lindridge is being spring-cleaned. I do hope Sis and Bill and Jan will be able to get to Huntleys as I believe they will like it especially if it isn't hot! I am sorry that Joyce has German measles. It certainly will be bad luck if any of the chaps get it though, as you say, it is often very mild so one can only hope for the best. It is so good to hear that our own wee chaps are so well – especially Jen, and I do hope she is throwing off her chestiness. She certainly seems to be. It will be good to be all together again sometime and I hope it may not be too long before I can get home – even for a short visit. But I am very well indeed, touching wood, and have quite settled down again to work though I miss you all the time, Sweetheart. But there it is, and a war is on so I don't complain and am very, very lucky. It won't be too long D.V. until we are together again . . . Richardson is due back today which will make things a bit easier over the Chamber work. It has been quite fun doing it and it hasn't taken me more than an hour a day. I have been going every morning to the Bank (George was now resident director in Calcutta of the Imperial Bank – JMM), *as Burn won't be back from Bombay for another week. This too makes little difference & in some ways, makes work at the office easier, for once one has been to the Bank, it is finished for the day and one gets to the office quite early. If one doesn't have to go to the Bank, all the papers come to the office later and have to be read so it is the same thing in the end.*

Well, there has been nothing particularly exciting here except the Navy efforts over Norway which sounds a real first-class show. We still get little news of the war and news of Norway only filters through very slowly – but it is good – what there is! On Friday evening, we had the Meath Home meeting, and things seem to be going well. They have rented one of the Kalimpong homes and it sounds an admirable arrangement; the rent is only Rs 100 a month and there were over sixty applicants for the first party! So, there is no question of its popularity. Apparently, there is an excellent Scottish Mission Dr who will look after the children up there and there are lots of people who will help if necessary. Lady Reed has said nothing, but one gathers that she pursues her petty way! She would not allow a special church collection for the homes (as they usually did) nor would she allow the usual jumble sale.

They have of course made it clear to the Shillong Committee that we have only withdrawn temporarily from Shillong until the district has been cleared up again, but if we can make a longer arrangement at Kalimpong, I believe we might be wise to sell the Shillong house while the war is on and a demand exists. But we are going into all that. After the meeting, I went round to Molly and Paul for a drink. They are very well and yesterday, Molly and the family left for Darjeeling. While I was there, Sheila Chapman Mortimer 'phoned to say she couldn't dine with Molly as Tom was not so well and had a high temperature again and was wandering in his mind. It is to be expected though and the next few days may be critical – I will tell you the latest news today when I finish this letter in the office. Saturday was a holiday and I went out with the dogbies & played golf very early. I was on the first tee at 6.20 a.m. I had a meeting at 9.30 and was in the office all morning. In the afternoon I slept (strangely enough!) and played squash after tea. Had an early bed and again played golf yesterday very early – 6.15 first tee, to the delight of the dogbies again – then worked for the morning and afternoon (– no sleep!) and went to a flick. Joan and Charles & the Frenches – Jack Thomas joined up later for dinner which was quite fun – and here I am. Oscar should have arrived home yesterday if there were no delays and I expect that he will be visiting Lindridge soon, the old rascal! He was in great form before he left but it is wise to get him out of this for a few months while he is so fit. Bunty & Paul & Molly are all very fit though we all find plenty to do. Helen Thomas was taking her family to Darjeeling by last night's train and I understand will stay there for a few days. Jack came along here for dinner after seeing Helen off. Binnie was very pleased to see him & never forgets. Well, Sweetheart, it is time to get up I suppose and as usual, I will finish this later. I like this house more and more, touching wood, and I do hope that you will approve . . . I hated leaving our old house and I shall always have a soft spot for it and all its associations but in many ways, this new one will probably suit us far better now. The taxes work out less than I expected and are only Rs25 – a month, so all in all, it only costs Rs 525 – which is very little considering what it is.

The landlord was very lucky it was all finished before prices went up. The garden really is so nice and the lawn is excellent. Charles really worked hard at it and got Clara to supply artificial manure free of charge! I haven't set out the tennis court yet but I will do it someday soon. The senior mali has been away a couple of months and has apparently got chronic Pyorrhoea but won't have his teeth out! His sons do the work quite well in the meantime. The garden is overlooked a little from the distance at the side but shrubs and trees will soon grow up and screen it. It really is very good in that way especially. More later, Darling.

Well, the end of office for another day. Richardson is back so I have more time. The news of Tom Mortimer is a little better today and he seems to have got over a bad time in the last few days. I only hope he will go steadily on improving.

I have had Arthur and Bea's letters copied and I return the originals to you. If necessary, I should have the Persian rugs specially packed up in a tin and zinc-lined box – I'm not sure if they are in the hall cupboard which has to be cleared. My fishing rods may be there too but I'm sure you will have arranged it. If necessary, the fishing rods can be sent to Hardy's for safe custody. They will look after them well.

Take all care of your sweet self. I long to be with you again and our own wee chaps. All my love to you, my own Darling, with kisses and bunny hugs to our own wee chaps. Always your own Geordie."

In the next letter, again, the issue of either George coming back home or Dorks coming out to Calcutta is foremost, and all this is against the backdrop of war and a developing situation in Norway. The following month, Germany was to mount an onslaught through the Low Countries and an armoured assault through the Ardennes forests, outflanking the Maginot line fortifications. The Chamberlain Government collapsed and Churchill was appointed Prime Minister at the head of a coalition government.

"5 Raja Santosh Road Calcutta Monday 22.4.40.

My own Darling,

It was lovely getting a letter from you last Thursday when I last wrote to you, and also one on Saturday, and I am glad you are all flourishing, though I shall be glad when Nanny is herself again. But I suppose that it will take some months yet, though her holiday should help her a lot. I told Paul about the "omphalodes verna" and he was most interested and looked it up in his book and said it was most rare to be found growing wild. He says there is another most interesting one to be found in Kingswood called Melittis Melissophyllum – the Bastard Balm, which flowers May-June. So, I expect you will find it. You really are a most clever chap at finding interesting things. What a heavenly place the country in England is. It is a good idea to collect all the wild flowers like that.

I am very sorry to hear that Alison McNaught is so ill and I do hope they have found out what it is. I am so sorry for Bea and Arthur too. They have had no luck with illness this last winter.

I think it is an excellent idea to give up on the food office now and I only hope the nice "natural" man manages to carry on without de-winding himself too noisily all day but perhaps being in the food office will cause an artificial gathering of all his natural forces connected with the digestion of food and then what fun he will have!

I am very glad Tom has got a good job, and it sounds very interesting. I am sure he will do it well and it will keep him busy and occupied which is the main thing. I had a letter from Tom by the next mail after your letter, also telling me he had got this job, and he sounds very cheerful. I am glad you have fixed up about the lease, etc., with the Nortons. I don't expect they will want an actual lease as you say but it is as well to have the various points clear, and anyhow, I don't expect that there will be any difficulties – if Arthur doesn't make any. Also, I agree it is now time to let Oliver know. As I said in a previous letter, I'm sure we are right to treat him as we ourselves would wish to be so I'm sure you were absolutely right.

About you coming out, Sweetheart. I think it would really be better if you did come out in the cold weather rather than July – though goodness knows I want you here all the time. But situated as we are, it can't be so. It would be heavenly if I could get home for another couple of months or even less, now I have already thought it might be possible in September. I should have to be back in November but if we all keep fit here and Oscar is back – as he should be in July – I don't see why I shouldn't go. After all, I was due leave this year and coming home for two short leaves suits the firm and doesn't upset anything else yet, except Paul and he thinks it is an excellent idea. If they do want me as President of the Chamber next year, it will be a strenuous time for me though I'm not worried about it. But this cold weather and next, all being well, I must do a certain amount of entertaining. So it will certainly be better if you are here too, Sweetheart. It will be better anyhow in whatever circumstances if you are here as the weather is better than July/September which is the worst time of year, I think. Then you could be home with the chaps again in the spring. My two months home did me the power of good though I felt very lost & livery the first week or ten days after I got back. Partly the effects of 'flu, & partly the strenuous work I had to put in from the start. But I have felt so fit since and able to cope with it all that I'm sure two months makes an enormous difference. Of course, it must all depend on circumstances later on but I certainly think it will be worth planning for that if it is possible. I will plan to leave here in September if Tom agrees & leave England again in November. If I can't do it when the time gets nearer then you would come out in the cold weather and leave the question of coming out in July. I do so want you to be here, Sweetheart, but I don't want you to have just the worst months. I hate it when you aren't here but I know it is better to do as we are doing situated as we are and with a war on. Anyhow, Sweetheart, let us think it over . . . but all being well, I don't see why we shouldn't do it and it will be wise from all points of view.

I am so glad you aren't trying to do too much. It's no use, Sweetheart, & I hate the thought of you working yourself out over that beastly food office.

I'm glad you sent MacInnes a present; he is such a good chap. I am glad too you have booked rooms for Dad at the Osborne and I agree it is absurd for him to worry about a few guineas a week & you must tell him he has nothing to worry about & that his health and happiness come first, even though it may cost an extra fifty chips a week. Doesn't it sound absurd when put into rupees!

I don't seem to have done very much though I am getting more regular exercise again which is good. On Friday, Gordon came to dinner and Joan and Charles invited a young couple – the Collins. We went to a flick & then a beer at the 300, the first time I have been there for ages and we only stayed there about half an hour. Gordon was in good form, and I hope that we shall lunch together one day this week before he goes. I played squash on Saturday and had an early bed. Golfed on Sunday starting at 6.15 and played a playing caddy which was good. The dogbies simply loved it. We played a few holes on Friday morning too and they do so look forward to it, and worry me every morning now! They are so much better when they get out for a run at Tolly & touching wood, are very fit. I spent a quiet day here after golf & working & sleeping & took myself to a cine before dinner. Joan and Charles were out. And here we are! Burn is back so I shall not have to go to the bank every morning and can do a bit of visiting mills. More later, my Darling one. I miss you so much all the time.

Well, Sweetheart, no more fresh. Tom Mortimer wasn't so well yesterday but it is all part of the illness we are told. It is going to be a long, long time before he is fit again, poor chap. I do hope you are taking things as easily as you can & not overdoing it. Take all care of your sweet self and of our own wee chaps. God bless you and them. All my love to you, my own Darling, with kisses and bunny hugs to our wee chaps – always your own Geordie."

In his next letter, there are more musings on future plans, as well as the developing situation in Norway, but events were to turn out quite differently for George and Dorks due to unexpected happenings both domestically and as a result of the war. At least the turn-around of letters remained at pre-war timings, i.e., delivery within 7–10 days by airmail. Grandfather O'Kinealy had now moved into care at the Osbourne in Torquay. George was now in his vice-presidential year at the Bengal Chamber and due to become president in 1941, hence the need to do a certain amount of official entertaining.

This was to be a crucial year as Britain, with her allies from the Empire, mainly Australia, South Africa, New Zealand, Canada and India, stood alone against both Germany and Italy, principally in North Africa. The jugular of the Suez Canal and the gateway to India was now threatened. Confidence in the British and European business community in Calcutta was shaken as people became jittery with depressing wartime news. While the threat of invasion to Great Britain had diminished, following the Battle of Britain, throughout the rest of 1940, nevertheless Great Britain's cities were about to take an intensive pounding, especially London, from the Blitz, as letters from home revealed.

"5 Raja Santosh Road, Calcutta Thursday 25ᵗʰ April

My own Darling,

Since writing to you on Monday, I received a letter from you which as usual I loved getting. I don't seem to have done anything particularly exciting. I had my first enteric inoculation on Monday evening and the reaction wasn't too bad but my arm was a bit stiff and sore. It will be a good thing done and I am due to have the second one on Tuesday. Played 14 holes of golf yesterday morning very early but it was a very damp still morning, though I quite enjoyed it and also did the dogbies. Tonight, Helen & Jack and the Nethersoles are dining here. Gordon Brandon leaves on Sunday, I think. He is living in the club and I see him at lunch there when I go to the club. Robin has a heavy cold but I suspect he will be ready to leave on Sunday with Gordon. I do hope Tom is better from his 'flu and that he will soon get fit again. I had a letter from him telling me he had accepted a job at the Ministry of Economic Warfare and I do hope he likes it. It should be very interesting and I suspect it will be quite hard getting in touch with it all. He also said you & the chaps were very well and seemed to be happy there which was good.

The position inside Norway seems a bit obscure but one thing seems certain, that the German Navy has taken it in the neck. I expect it is very difficult to establish bases in Norway for an expeditionary force, though we seem to have done it, and now one only hopes we shall be able to get going quickly with our mechanised forces before the Germans establish themselves at all the strategic points in the South. I feel sure we are going flat out, and the French too, for a defeat there of the Bosch might be of enormous psychological importance. I feel certain that we shall slowly mop it all up and drive them back to Oslo. Then they must attack Sweden one would think or else get out of Norway. If only we can get them out of Norway and establish air bases, and the Swedish can keep them out, what enormous advantage it will give us. But I suppose we must wait and see. It is all so dreadful one feels, but there seems only one way out of it all now and that is a definite and smashing defeat for the Germans everywhere – sea, land & air.

I am glad you have all moved to Doit's house and it must be fun there – it will be a change too. I suppose that Ruth and Tom are back in London – Tom said in one letter that he didn't expect to see much of Lindridge this summer. Does John still think it has a funny lavatory? When I got our letter mentioning John's comments, I told Paul and he was amused and said it has got a funny lavatory! I hope the boarders like their three weeks at school. I suspect they did and, as you say, it is an excellent way of getting them used to school. Jen must miss them too and I am sorry it was a little bad over the spade! I suppose John is still his funny little happy self with all his friends everywhere. It is lovely hearing their doings, the little funnies. I must say their school does sound lovely and it certainly is good to know they can stay there.

I heard about Geoff from Bennett and I hope his operation passed off all right and the removal of his gall bladder will put him right. Poor chap has had such a bad time and must be desperate to get well again. I hope to hear again this week that he is getting on after his operation.

You say in your last letter that you feel sometimes that you have made such inadequate plans for us all. You shouldn't feel like that, Sweetheart, because I think you have made just as good plans as it is possible to make. Nobody could have done more and it is not possible to have all one's plans cut and dried, as it were, like we had when there was no war on. We have aimed to give our little chaps as much stability as possible whilst keeping ourselves as free of commitments as possible and we have done it, as far as I can see, in the best & wisest possible way. Don't worry too much about it, Sweetheart. We shall D.V. be back together again before long, and I certainly think it will be better if I can get home again before long for a short spell before you come out. But I have already written about that so will not say more until you have got my letter & replied. The time will pass D.V. and the war won't last forever . . . will do my best to get home before that. I am sure that is wisest, Sweetheart, and don't worry about it, my Darling one. You have done and are doing fine & much more than many I know and I am sure that it is best to do as we are doing much as I loathe these separations.

Later – well, Sweetheart, nothing fresh here – Tom Mortimer is a little better today I'm glad to say – we are all well, touching wood. Take all care of your sweet self and of our own wee chaps. God bless you and them. All my love to you, my Darling one, with kisses and bunny hugs to our chaps. Always your own Geordie. "

The Norwegian expedition was not in fact going particularly well so far as land operations were concerned. At the beginning of April, German forces had marched into Denmark and had overtaken the whole country within 48 hours. Their next operation was mounted against Norway two days later with a seaborne landing of German troops at Oslo. A flotilla of German ships had appeared on 8th April, and, despite a spirited defence in which the German cruiser *Blucher* was sunk, the shore batteries were silenced and the capital taken. German forces quickly occupied Kristiansand, Stavanger, Bergen and Trondheim. On 9th April, Narvik was attacked by ten German destroyers each carrying 200 soldiers and supported by the German battlecruisers *Scharnhorst* and *Gneisenau,* and was captured. Narvik was of strategic importance to the Germans as it was the marine outlet for high-grade haematite ironstone from Swedish mines just across the border between Sweden and Norway. Despite Swedish neutrality, these mines were later infested by German troops thus ensuring the continuity of supplies to German steelworks essential for the manufacture of armaments.

The British battle fleet was despatched from Scapa Flow on 7th April with a cruiser squadron from Rosyth, and, in the ensuing naval battles, the German fleet suffered severe losses. The *Hipper* was rammed by the destroyer *Glowworm* and limped back to Trondheim, and the *Gneisenau* was damaged by the *Renown*. The cruiser *Karlsruhe* was sunk off Kristiansand and the pocket battleship *Lützow* was torpedoed. An air attack was mounted on German shipping in Bergen and the cruiser *Königsberg* sunk with three bombs. At least nine German transports were sunk by submarine but not without British losses of three submarines.

An attempt was made to forestall the capture of Narvik by a British squadron of five destroyers and three of them, entering the port, sank two German destroyers; the guns of the rest were smothered and merchantmen destroyed. However, as the British fleet withdrew, other German warships emerged at the mouth of the fjord seriously damaging one of the British destroyers, which was beached, and sinking another. During the withdrawal, the German ship *Rauenfels,* carrying ammunition, was engaged and blew up.

On 13th April, a second attack was made on Narvik headed by the British battleship *Warspite* accompanied by nine destroyers and by dive bombers from the aircraft carrier *Furious.* All eight German destroyers were sunk in the battle with *Warspite's* 15" guns being the deciding factor, with no corresponding British losses.

Meanwhile, expeditionary forces were assembled to retake Narvik and Trondheim – a mixed force of British regulars and French Chasseurs Alpines plus about 1000 Canadians was assembled. Preliminary landings had been successfully carried out at Namsos in the North and Andalsnes in the South. The plan developed was to attack Trondheim initially in a pincer movement from North and South. The attack faltered, however, as the British troops were ill-equipped to cope with the winter conditions.

With no air support, and despite reinforcements, by the end of April, it was clear that a withdrawal of the exhausted troops in the face of overwhelming German strength and air superiority was the only sensible outcome.

But there remained the objective of the capture of Narvik. A force of some 24,000 troops was assembled under the leadership of General Auchinleck and the port taken from the east; the Germans retreated into the mountains. But events were to overtake this success. The British expeditionary force was in full retreat in France and the threat of German invasion of England was becoming an increasingly real one. By June 8th, all the troops had been withdrawn from Norway with large quantities of stores and equipment, and sailed in four convoys back to England.

However, the aircraft carrier *Glorious,* ahead of the main convoys, was now attacked by the cruisers *Scharnhorst* and *Gneisenau* and, being hopelessly outgunned, was sunk. One British destroyer was sunk but the other, in a torpedo attack on the *Scharnhorst,* blew in her bows before herself being sunk. Both German battle cruisers now retreated to Trondheim.

The King of Norway with his government had meanwhile been evacuated to Britain on the cruiser *Devonshire.*

Despite the failures and withdrawals of the Norway expeditions, one fact remained, namely the effective destruction of the German fleet which, despite heavy British losses, was reduced by the end of June to an effective strength of one cruiser, two light cruisers and four destroyers. Thus, the German fleet was neutralised and rendered ineffective in support of a planned invasion of England and in the disruption of the Dunkirk evacuation.

Nevertheless, these events, widely reported in the press, weighed heavily on George and Dorks' minds as they struggled to find the solution to their separation and that of the family during wartime. Once again, the letters reveal their growing uncertainties and those of the British community in Calcutta against an outward appearance of normality. The next surviving letter is that of:

"Thursday 9th May 5 Raja Santosh Road Calcutta

My own Darling,

Thank you very much for a lovely letter which came yesterday. It is good to hear that you are all happy and flourishing and enjoying being in Doit's house which does sound nice and convenient too. I am very glad Sis and her chaps have been down there and have seen you all. I am sure they will have loved it even though Jan and Bill may not have caught a fish! I was amused at Jean and I sympathise with her wanting you to be at the school too. But I sincerely hope she doesn't want you to become a nun though! It would not suit me at all in any way. What a grim thought! They are little funnies, bless them! I do so miss them. I won't try to say how much I miss you, Sweetheart, though I am glad you aren't having to cope with this weather. It has been very hot with high humidity and a minimum far above normal. How I bless the air conditioning. I haven't been out golfing before breakfast yet since Sunday as I seem to have had such a lot of work to do but I am getting it down all right.

Paul returned from Darjeeling yesterday – he went to a conference with Government on jute matters on Saturday – the same one that Charles Thomas went to. There were twenty or thirty representatives from various Jute Trade Associations & other associations and it was not without humour. Walker, the chairman of the Jute Mills Association, was arguing with Suhrawardy who is the finance member & labour minister – a clever unscrupulous little barrister – the question was what was a fair price as a minimum price for raw jute? They called it the "bottom" price and each one had his own idea what the "bottom" should be but wouldn't show it to the other. Finally, Suhrawardy, in some heat said, "All right, I will let you know my bottom if you will show me yours!" A very friendly offer I must say and from what I have been told, he didn't know the risks he was running!

The news of Tom Chapman Mortimer is better I am glad to say. His temperature has been normal for over a day now – or rather it had been up to yesterday morning. So, we all hope he will go steadily on now. Ian Craig has had to go into Miss Riordan's for removal of piles which apparently, he had very badly and the operation was done yesterday. Suzanne has been sleeping on the verandah and is using Joan's room as a dressing room. She is having an infant (September I think) but is in good form and keeps us amused. As soon as Ian is fit to travel, they are going to Darjeeling which will be good for them. Charles returned here on Monday morning and he arrived in the most stinking weather to find that their air conditioning had broken down in the night which was bad luck! I knew nothing about it until Monday morning by when it had been put right. Joan and Charles have now had an offer of the house that Barbara and Herbert had in Ballygunge and they are trying to get it – from the middle or end of June. Charles expects to go to the officers' school at Belgaum in July and then I think Joan would go up & stay in Nepal with the Beathams until Charles had finished his course & then presumably return here for the cold weather. I don't know what their plans would be then; I suppose it would depend on where Charles was sent. It is all so uncertain for everybody but it just can't be helped and it all has to be gone through. I hate all the bickering that is going on in Government but even that will have been worthwhile if it spurs everyone on to a new effort. It has shaken a lot of complacency out of everyone and, to that extent, may have been justified. I wonder what Winston will have to say tonight. One thing seems certain; we must increase our effort and the Bosch must be subdued. But it is not going to be easy though I have no doubts of the result.

On Tuesday night I dined with the Barwells and never again!! It was most kind of them to ask me but I wish they wouldn't! Molly Bird, Brigadier and Mrs Maltby, and Stanley Nairn and his new wife were also there. I have never heard such continuous and utter tripe as conversation from our host, who told the most ridiculous and lying personal reminiscences which had no point, were not funny and which flowed on continuously. After dinner, the noble Brigadier was nearly as bad and everyone got sleepier and sleepier but reminiscences poured out incessantly & I took refuge in more and more beer. I didn't get a chance of a talk to Molly or the Nairns – what an evening! Apart from that, I have had a quiet time with plenty to do. More later, Sweetheart.

Well, Sweetheart, the end of another not too perfect day! Thank goodness for the air conditioning!

I had a very nice letter from Ruth a few days ago which I forgot to mention and she had got her gloves from Oscar and likes them very much for which I am glad. She is always so nice about you and our chaps. Take all care of your sweet self. Someday, not too long away, we shall D.V. be all together again. I just live for that time. All my love to you, my own Darling, with kisses and bunny hugs to our own wee chaps, always your own Geordie."

His next letter acknowledges the invasion of France;

"5 Raja Santosh Road, Calcutta 13.5.1940

My own Darling,

No letter from you yet but I expect it will be at the office when I get there as only a part of the mail has been delivered. Nothing very fresh here and we seem to go on as usual. I dined with Winsome and Harry and Laws was there too, on Friday night, which was very pleasant and we sat in the garden afterwards. I played golf on Saturday morning with Harry before breakfast but the dogbies couldn't come as they had all been very sick on Thursday and the vet had cut out food except for milk for Friday, and on Saturday, they were washed out! But they were very upset at my going off without them and nearly managed to tug the sweeper to the car! Joan and Charles had a party for "Gone with the Wind" on Saturday but as I had seen it, I didn't want to go. Suzanne Craig had also seen it. So, Joan and Charles, the Frenches & Laws had hors d'oeuvres at 7.30 & went off to the show which started at 8.30 and I took Suzanne to another flick and we all met at the 300 for a drink afterwards. Suzanne is an amazing child and kept us all laughing. She is having an infant in September I think and has been feeling pretty ill, so Joan tells me, though she is beginning to feel better now. Ian Craig has had a pretty rotten time after his operation for piles and is still in Miss Riordan's. They hope to get away to Darjeeling at the end of this week if Ian has no setbacks. On Sunday morning, I was out at Tolly by 6.15 and played a round with a playing caddy which I enjoyed as I was playing rather well – all the way round! I got back here for breakfast and read in my room the various office papers I always seem to have for the weekend. So, I didn't see any of the household until lunchtime. The rest of the household were going to a flick before dinner so I didn't see them as I was dining out with the Hinds. Just as I left there was the most terrific storm beginning and it simply poured. Mr Justice Ameer Ali & Miss Coutts (la Martiniere) were there too and we had a pleasant evening. Mrs Hinds was in quite good form and particularly sent her love to you. Everyone does and all our friends always want to know all about you and the chaps. It was so nice and cool after the storm and I was back here soon after 11.00.

I took the dogbies to golf yesterday which they enjoyed and I think the couple of days' reduced diet has done them good. Bogie and Biscuit certainly bulge less! They do love the air conditioning partly because they can keep an eye on me and partly because they like the cool. They are on my rug now in various postures, pretending to be asleep but ready to leap up at the first sign of a golf shoe!

Well, Sweetheart, the storm over Europe has broken, and it is a relief. They have done what I think was expected they would do and gone for Holland and Belgium. I feel very sorry for Mr Chamberlain but once more, he has shown himself equal to the occasion. Whatever his critics may say, he has proved himself a great man & a great patriot. I believe Winston is the man for this moment and he has the whole country behind him. It was fortunate perhaps that the change was made when it was and if anyone was in doubt about our resolution they know now. It is dreadful to have to sit here and know what a death grapple we are in and yet just to have to carry on as usual. But there it is and I can only do what seems to be my job in this war and do it as well as I can. I only hope and pray it may soon be over and the madness of it all may end. But it has to be gone through now. . . . One feels so horribly far away, living in such an artificial atmosphere, and yet one would go potty if one couldn't keep occupied all the time. I do so wish I could be with you, Sweetheart, and our wee chaps but we are doing what is best I know. D.V. I may yet be with you and them before many months are past. I shall try to anyhow if it seems a reasonable chance. I think this battle may be the decisive one even though the war may drag on long afterwards. One can't make plans any more than one could before, but can only have "possibilities" before one and in the meantime, one must just pray that all goes well for us over there in France & Belgium & Holland as I firmly believe it will. I think all the time of you and our wee chaps, Sweetheart, hoping you and they are well and not worrying. More later.

Well, Sweetheart, soon it will be time to pack up for the day so I will finish this. The news doesn't take us much further but the Germans are not having it all their own way. It may take days or even weeks for the battle to develop but I am sure our chaps and the French & the Dutch are a pretty tough proposition.

I hear Tom Chapman Mortimer continues to make progress which is good but he must be terribly weak. Soon, I hope, he will be able to see people. Take all care of your sweet self and of our wee chaps. God bless you and them. All my love to you, my own Darling, with kisses and bunny hugs to all our chaps. Always your own Geordie."

The next letter is written as the fighting in Northern France intensifies, and follows the collapse of the Chamberlain Government and the appointment of Churchill to lead a coalition government to prosecute the war with Germany.

"5 Raja Santosh Road, Calcutta. May 16th

My own Darling,

It is so very difficult to form any conclusions yet from the fighting in the North but the French & British seem to be in action now and I hope the Bosch are liking it. It looks as if this battle will go on for weeks and nobody can know how it is going, for so much depends on resources both of men and material. It is simply desperate for everyone but anyhow it has come at last, and however much we may hate & loathe it all, it has to be gone through with now. I feel so sorry for the Dutch having to give in but at least they resisted long enough to give us time to get into Belgium – though one did hope they would hold out longer. Here more and more people are clamouring to join up – that is the effect on most I think, but there are others, I'm ashamed to say, who just jitter, and I have several to cope with in this office. But they will be the first to shout later on, I'm sure!

But enough about war – there is nothing more that one can do but carry on and hope that it may be over before long. I do hope you aren't worrying too much, sweetheart, & I do so hate not being with you at a time like this. But it may not be so very long before we are together again. I hope and pray so anyhow.

I don't seem to have done anything since writing you last Monday. I went to see Ian Craig at the nursing home on Monday evening and found him quite cheerful but still pretty down and out really. An operation like that takes much longer to get over than people think though I haven't said anything to Suzanne. They hope to go to Darjeeling early next week and he should pick up pretty quickly once he gets out of this heat. Joan and Charles are in good form though I have not heard when they move into their new house or whether they have in fact taken it. I expect they have. Cook came in to see me in the office a couple of days ago and wanted to know about you & the chaps. He was most anxious to know when you were coming back to India and I told him I hoped in the cold weather. He also wanted to know all about the war. There always seems to be something to do in the office – wanting special attention, and it is a good thing as one just keeps busy all the time. Monty has gone to Kashmir with Dr Spencer and I expect they will be a bright couple! I am very glad they have gone off together as it will be very good for them both I hope! Tom Chapman Mortimer continues to make progress I'm glad to say and I believe Denham (Dr Denham White -mentioned frequently in my grandfather Frederick O'Kinealy's diaries in 1921) *is now going away for the holiday he delayed on Tom's account. He is a brick that man. I am afraid Tom will be months before he is fit again. It will do him and Sheila a power of good to be away for a few months even if they don't actually get home. That, of course, would be best of all but I don't know what they propose. Soon I hope he will be allowed to see people but I hear that he has great pain in his legs from neuritis poor chap. I am finishing this in the office, Sweetheart, but there seems to be little fresh news. I got a lovely long letter from you today which was good. Of course I know, my darling, that you would come out here in the hot weather or any other time but I am sure it will be better from all points of view to come later as I should love to get home again if I can. The fact of the weather being better in October and November is only incidental and I know you wouldn't even consider it if we thought it better so don't worry, my Sweetheart, I am sure we are doing the right thing and I just long for the time we shall be together again . . . D.V. it won't be so very long. It is after 7.00 p.m. so I will answer the rest of your lovely long letter by next mail.*

I am well – even though I do seem never to be done with work! Take all care of your sweet self and of our chaps. God bless you and them – I miss you all the time. All my love to you, my own Darling, with kisses and bunny hugs to our own wee chaps – always your own Geordie."

In his next letter, George describes the feeling of helplessness in Calcutta with the news of the setbacks in France and the comfort he feels in knowing that the family are safe and away from it all in Devon, and not far from the west country ports, although most sailings to India went from Liverpool. A new effort was being made to capture Narvik, as described earlier. George and the Calcutta community immersed themselves in work which, for George, seemed never-ending.

His next letter is full of acknowledgements of Dorks' visits to Uncle Tom and news of the rest of the Morton family from her. The breakthrough by German forces crossing the Meuse River had occurred by the date of the letter, but news was lagging well behind events. By now, the French resistance to the German advance had almost collapsed, with the British engaged in a fighting retreat which was now increasingly to be centred on the port of Dunkirk.

"5 Raja Santosh Road, Calcutta Thursday 23.5.40

My own Darling,

It almost seems as if the monsoon has broken here as it has rained every day since Monday and made it very nice and cool. It is very difficult to know how things are going in France but however uncertain the situation is, I feel confident that the next few days will see an improvement for us. It is heartening to know how the Bosch managed to break through and cross the Meuse and I think that M. Reynaud was so wise to let the world know that it was due to the failure to blow up bridges and failure of the French to be in position. Looks like dirty work & as if the Bosch had arranged it through his agents, but it will avail him little D.V. – for our armies seem to be intact though there must be bitter fighting yet. But it is the only way now – more than ever I pray that we may all be together soon, my Darling one. D.V. it will not be so long but if only I could be there with you, I should be happy. It is a great comfort to me to know that you are in the West Country with friends, as I said in my last letter, and I am not complaining. I seem to find lots to do here and so many seem to need heartening, many most unexpectedly. But we are doing our best.

I don't seem to have done very much since last week. I forget if I told you that Joan and Charles have definitely taken the house that Barbara & Herbert had and I think they expect to move in towards the end of June. Suzanne and Ian Craig left last night for Kalimpong where they are staying with Norman until 30th and then going to Darjeeling. Ian came out of hospital on Monday & they went back to Kinneston that evening. Norman tells me Bunty & possibly all their children are expected out about the end of May but I don't know if they are flying or coming by sea. I hope to see him when he comes down to meet them.

Joan Shuttle 'phoned me a few days ago to tell me that she was trying to fly home earlier and may go next week. In view of the uncertainties, I think she felt she wanted to be there and having got there would decide whether to stay on as planned or bring her chaps out here for a few months – she doesn't know what she will do but she and Teddie are dining here quietly to-morrow and I shall hear more no doubt. Teddie is well and just the same as ever.

Tom Chapman Mortimer is not quite so well and Trebedi's reports seemed to indicate he had "B" Coli and his Portuguese Dr indicated that he thought he still had the typhoid germ. So, Sheila arranged for Dick Pegg to come in consultation – as arranged with me, and Dick was reassuring and said that he thought that it was only "B" Coli & that it would soon be cured if it was. He also said that Tom was very well considering everything and that there was no need to ask Denham to come down, and that his Portuguese Dr was doing all that was required at present. He is going along to see Tom in a few days. Sheila has been so good about it all but I think that the poor kid has had about enough and I shall be glad when we can get them both away out of this climate for a bit.

The dogbies are disgusted with me as I haven't taken them out to Tolly since last Saturday. Nevertheless, they are always glad to see me and after their meal, they always clamour to get into my air-conditioned room, where they sleep on my rug all huddled together.

The news is better I think but it will be days before we can get the situation clarified I would say. Take all care of your Darling self. I do so long to be with you again and our own wee chaps. God bless you and them. All my love to you, my own sweet Darling, and bunny hugs to our own wee chaps. Always your own Geordie."

George's next letter reflects the deteriorating situation in France and the uncertainties of war and the difficulties of making family decisions against the background of war. There was a feeling of remoteness in Calcutta, with individuals anxious to make their own personal contribution to the war effort, as well as a feeling of hopelessness in the inexorable events that were unfolding, and a consequently jittery attitude sapping confidence in the future. Business was beginning to gear up to support the war effort, particularly in the jute mills with gunny bags, and production of textiles for a multitude of uses, and curiously, leather goods including boots and shoes. The ammunition centres at, for instance, Dum Dum were also gearing up to support the Indian Army increasingly involved in North Africa and the Middle East. George was also now Vice-president of the Bengal Chamber and Associated Chambers of Commerce, with an increased workload as businesses geared up for war. The stress is reflected in his next letter home.

"5 Raja Santosh Road, Calcutta Thursday 30.05.40

My own Darling,

It was so good getting your letter yesterday and one from Jean. I shall write to our little chaps today & I do so love getting their letters. Your letter was written after your trip to London to take Hilda to Lindridge and I am very glad you saw a good number of friends in London – including Joannie. I forwarded a letter for you from Betty Ironside and sent her a few lines to the address she wrote on the back of the envelope. I hope Jean has thrown off her temperature and that she is back at school. She said in her letter that she preferred being at Lindridge! I can't tell you how thankful I am that you are all down there in Devonshire, my Sweetheart, and I just long for the time I can be with you all again. I just exist when I am away from you and thank God I have more than enough to do here. I think of you all the time and pray that you may not be having too worrying a time. . . . I know what a brave chap you are, my Darling one, and will keep the chaps' tails up and it is so good to get your courageous letters. Here I find people get their tails down so desperately easily, and I have been ashamed for some of the Europeans in the city. Times are terribly grim and I am not underestimating that but nor am I being foolishly optimistic – I am just confident that we can and shall win this war – come what may, and bad news just stiffens one's resolution and makes one more resolute than ever. All the same, I do hate being so far away from you and the chaps at a time like this but D.V. I hope I may yet get home for a short trip in the autumn. I have been so terribly happy the last ten or twelve years, Sweetheart, thanks to you, and I have faith in the future like you have too – this is just like a bad nightmare and if we just keep looking to the future, we shall be alright D.V. even though changes may come . . . Teddie Shuttle told me yesterday that Joan, who was due to leave yesterday morning by K.L.M., is now going Air France as there is considerable uncertainty for the K.L.M. beyond Naples. I gather that Joan is now going next Sunday, and I think she was lucky to get a berth on the plane. By the way, I wonder if you have sent your return-half ticket for cancellation or refund? I expect you have.

Tom Chapman Mortimer has had a relapse and is running temperatures again. They say there is no doubt it is a relapse but they hope it won't be long before they can get the germs under again. I was allowed to see him for a few minutes last night as they think it will help him to see somebody every day just for a short time It is nearly two months since he got it and the poor chap is woefully thin but keeps up his spirits wonderfully. He doesn't know that he hasn't yet shaken it right off again – poor chap – as he mustn't know, but they are trying to let him see one outside person a day. Sheila has been so good and seems to keep him going. But it will be months before he will be himself again – poor chap. (Tom was a close friend and colleague of George's and his concern, evidenced from the regular reports to Dorks and his support for Tom and Sheila, was a good example as to how the top firms looked after their people – JMM)

We are all well and I am so thankful for Bunty Roberts. He has booked to fly home in July when Oscar is due back. I wonder if you have seen anything of Osk? I expect he will come down to Devonshire before he goes. Kick him in the pants for me when you see him! Paul goes to Darjeeling today and I hope he will stay up there for a week or ten days. He tells me Molly and the twins are flourishing. Monty is away in Kashmir as he is taking his six-month leave in India. (As the war developed, local leaves were to be increasingly the pattern – JMM) *Well, Sweetheart, it is Bank morning so I must go and shave. I will write more later in the day.*

Later. *I have written to the chaps and have sent Jean some stamps & have told Jen I will ask you to get her something small from me! I hope this is alright, Sweetheart, & will you give wee John something small too? Then they have all got something! All a little difficult but I won't try & send them anything from here except stamps which I hope will go all right. I am glad you have joined the Red Cross Detachment, Sweetheart – so long as you don't overdo it. It is far better to have something to do I agree.*

I went in after the office on Monday to see Helen and George & found them in the garden. Helen seemed very well and happy and sent her love to you. We sat on in the garden and talked until quite late – their little dogs are such fun too & the little liver one is so full of beans and his black father romps with him all the time! Their daughter is well but I didn't see her and they seem very happy to have a daughter which is right and proper. George was in great form. (Very sadly, they were to lose their daughter not long afterwards. They later had a son, Ian, younger brother to Mike Gemmell. George was Ian's godfather. – JMM)

Well, sweetheart, I must close. Take all care of your Darling self and of our own wee chaps. God bless you and them. All my love to you, my own Darling, with kisses and bunny hugs to our wee chaps, your own Geordie."

By the time this letter arrived, the drama of Dunkirk would for all practical purposes have been played out. Just at the time that Churchill, newly appointed Prime Minister, was organising the administrative and military structures to prosecute the war, the Germans had invaded Holland over the night of 9th-10th May with overwhelming forces. They were opposed by almost equal forces of French, British, Dutch and Belgian divisions. However, these were opposed by formidable panzer divisions who smashed their way through the forests of the Ardennes, thought to be impenetrable to tanks. These outflanked the French heavily fortified Maginot line, and opened a 50-mile gap in the southern French defences, leaving substantial French forces on the Germans' southern flank.

To the North, the Germans swiftly captured the key points on the Dutch waterway system before they could be flooded, and key bridge crossing points over the Meuse River and Albert canal were similarly captured intact. As the panzers swung North, so the Allied defence lines had to be brought back to counter the German northerly advance increasingly encircling the port of Dunkirk. A brilliantly fought fighting retreat began . . . the war news was indeed "grim". The British expeditionary force, numbering some 200,000 troops, was under the command of their French counterparts and communications between the two were poor. An attempt to cut the German advance in half between the Northern and Southern Allied troops failed and so the British and French forces were caught in a classic pincer movement of German advances from the South and East, and then also from the West as the flank was rapidly turned. The door to the complete conquest of France was now open.

It was not as if the Allies were unprepared. The pre-prepared battle plan had been executed with advances into Belgium by the British and French 1st Group of armies, but they were overwhelmed by superior forces both in terms of equipment, firepower, the air force, particularly dive-bombers, and heavy tanks. The defensive perimeter around Dunkirk was held while a desperate operation was mounted to evacuate troops from the beaches. While most of the equipment was lost, close on 100,000 French troops and 200,000 British were evacuated from the beaches and the port to England by flotillas of Naval and other boats of all kinds and sizes. France had been ripped apart and while a gallant rear-guard was mounted along the Seine by French and British forces, the whole of the French Western seaboard was under German control by the end of the month. The vital lifeline of the Atlantic was now opened to U-boat attack from under the sea from Brest and Lorient, and to air attack above it from airports along the Western coast. It was publicly known that the Germans planned to invade England, and as a preliminary to this, the Germans needed air superiority, and so the bombing of London and air defences began in earnest at the end of June with the start of what became known as the Battle of Britain. Desperate times indeed but at least the British Navy had more or less complete control of the seas following the naval battles around Norway.

In George's letters, he mentions Joan's flight home to review the family situation, as their children Gilly and Barney were there being looked after by Joan's parents. In the event, they decided to settle them in South Africa with Pix and Fin Findlayson. Fin had been a Jute Broker in Calcutta but had resigned his firm and moved to the Orange Free State to farm. They were joined by the children of Ronnie and Sandy Cameron, and while Micky, their son, stayed in South Africa, Diana, their daughter, joined us children in Kalimpong. Barney and Micky were educated in Michaelhouse public school, and the boys and Gilly visited their parents in India from time to time during the school holidays.

The uncertainty and plans being made by other close friends to leave England against the background of a possible invasion must have had their effect on George and Dorks. But then quite unexpectedly, Frederick, Dorks' father died on 6th June. He had been in a nursing home in Torquay for a little time beforehand and he and Dorks were particularly close. Curiously, there is no reference to James, Dork's brother, in any of the correspondence around this time. He was working in London and living in the family home. Later, during the London Blitz and although profoundly deaf, he fought his war with the London Fire Brigade before retiring to Ogbourne St George near Marlborough, and setting up house there with cousins Rita and Teddie Perkins and their twin children, Bill and Liz. Although this was initially planned as a holiday of six weeks, it became his home, and he was to stay there until he died in 1977. Uncle Jim was an eccentric bachelor much loved by everyone.

George's next surviving letter is full of support for Dorks, but interestingly, it raised the issue for the first time of what the chances were of "getting out here".

"5 Raja Santosh Road Calcutta Monday 10.6.40

My own Darling Dorkie,

Your cable about Dad arrived yesterday morning and I am very sad for you, my Sweetheart, and more than ever want to be with you. I replied to you by cable at once and I hope it arrived safely. I will have the necessary notification sent to the Statesman. (This was the leading newspaper of the time – JMM) *I am very glad I was home this year and saw Dad and I am very glad you have been at home too, Sweetheart, as you must have been a constant help and comfort to him as I well know from his talks to me.*

He will be with Mum now so do not grieve, my Darling one. It is better so and he had a long happy life full of incident and work for others, and it is given to few to have so many who will remember his name with gratitude and affection. "Many more remember Tom fool than Tom fool remembers" as we have heard from him so often . . . (a favourite saying of his – JMM).

You will have a good deal to settle up, I'm afraid, and I do hope you don't have it all to do. MacInnes will be a great help I expect. If you want a firm of Solicitors, why not ask Harold Mitchelmore, but no doubt Uncle Charles will fix it. I do so want you not to have a lot of bother, my Dorkie, and I hope Jim is not tied up too closely with his work so that he will be able to fix things up in London. God how I wish I was there with you now – more than ever. One can't tell at this distance how things are there or what the chances are of getting out here so I must just wait and see and if you decide not to try and come out until later then I hope I may get home in September even if it is only for a month. But don't let it worry you, Sweetheart – we shall manage. The Bosch seems to be throwing all he has got into this battle and if only he can be held up and constantly punished now, he will slow down soon I believe. But the news doesn't tell one much except that a terrific battle is going on and that the French Armies are intact and fighting back all along the line. I shall never lose faith that we shall defeat them.

Sheila Chapman Mortimer came to dinner on Saturday and we went to the cinema just the four of us. Tom is still running a temperature but all tests have been taken with negative results. He seems better in himself and sees one person every day which appears to do him good. I played golf with Harry Townsend on Saturday morning early – nine holes. Then played tennis in the afternoon with Connie and Jack Willis. It was fun, but not having played for over a year, I was worse than usual. But I had warned them beforehand! On Sunday morning, I played golf with James Coombe starting at 6.30 which I enjoyed. The dogbies came too and chased five or six pigs along the nullah (= ditch – JMM) *from the third tee to the seventh green which seemed to give them great satisfaction, the little bads. I spent the rest of the day working and sleeping and went to church in the evening – Joan and Charles are busy with mistries* (= workmen/carpenters – JMM) *and arrangements to get their house ready. I doubt if they get in before the end of the month. Charles expects to be called up to go to this officers' training course soon and then presumably will come back here to Calcutta for the cold weather. I expect Joan Shuttle will have got home by now after many adventures by Air France and I am sure she will phone you as soon as she arrives. I haven't seen much of them – but then I don't seem to have seen much of anyone. I see Teddie more often, of course. Well, Sweetheart, I will finish later. You are always in my thoughts, my Darling one.*

It has been so hot and sticky today and I have been so rushed all day. On Friday and Saturday, our air conditioning was off and I nearly blew up! Today it is on, I'm glad to say, but I have had to go out once or twice. There seems to be little news except the Bosch is making a little progress here and there which is inevitable in view of the weight of his onslaught. But he must be getting desperate. Paul is back looking much better as the result of his ten days' holiday – I only hope he now keeps fit and steady – he does try so desperately hard but has been sleeping so badly, poor chap, and that plays the devil with nerves.

Take all care of your sweet self. God Bless you, my Darling one, and our own wee chaps. I am always thinking of you and them. All my love to you, my own Darling, with kisses and bunny hugs to our own wee chaps. Always your own Geordie."

The next letter is the last to survive and is dated 13th June and it went by airmail. The Dunkirk evacuation was complete but there were still British Expeditionary Forces fighting alongside the southern French armies which had assembled a line along the Seine. To protect their formation, the 51st British Highland Division was left in place fighting a desperate rear-guard action against the German westward advance. The Channel ports were progressively captured but remnants of the 51st were able to make their way to Le Havre from where they were evacuated. And now the final stages of the battle for France commenced. A decision was taken to withdraw the rest of the BEF, which was evacuated from Cherbourg and Brest in a second Dunkirk. Some 136,000 British and 20,000 Polish troops, together with some artillery, were taken back to home shores from Cherbourg and Brest. The French Government, now in Bordeaux, now sought an armistice from the Germans and effectively surrendered on 18th June.

"5 Raja Santosh Road Calcutta Thursday 13.06.40

Yesterday I got two lovely letters from you – one had been opened by censor -the first since war began which is good! Well, Italy has come in and we now know what we are up against. Also, it has virtually brought in America. It must be a grim fight in France, and the French and our own chaps seem to be doing simply magnificently. In every succeeding generation, people are apt to say it is effete, etc., but our own race will never be that and the most unlikely people become absolute tigers when emergency arises, thank God. Here, lots seem to get jittery but it isn't the very young; it is usually the older ones who should know better.

But even they, if they had action, would fight like devils; it is only the grim inaction which wears some out. But we are doing our utmost and I think things are better here in that way. In this fight, which as you say is a fight against an evil thing, every nerve has to be strained and every nerve will be strained. People here are agitating to go off and fight or to be allowed to do something and there is general activity all around.

The weather is at its very worst now. The monsoon won't quite break and it is so hot and the humidity is very high! But, touching wood, I have been very fit and seem to get through a lot of work and still get an occasional game of golf! Today is a holiday so I played Teddie – starting at 6.30 & he just won. Then home for breakfast & office until 1.30 and then home to lunch. I got a lot done in the office as I wasn't much disturbed. Richardson is in Simla so I have had all the Chamber work for several days. (George was now vice-president of the Bengal Chamber and Associated Chambers of Commerce to Sir (John) Henry Richardson, President, also of Andrew Yule & Co Calcutta, where he was Senior Deputy Chairman. He was also a Director of the Chartered

Bank of India, Australia and China. Birds and Heilgers shared offices with them in Clive Street, and the Bengal Chamber offices were in the Exchange Building offices next door. – JMM). *Teddie hasn't yet heard from Joan that she has arrived, though I suspect she has. Apparently, they have been across Africa and I think Teddie heard a few days ago from Algiers. I suspect Joan has arrived but that cables are delayed. Mignon Nicholson also went home a few days ago but Bunty doesn't seem to have heard of her arrival anywhere yet.*

I have had messages of sympathy from so many people since I got the Statesman to notify Dad's death. Dr Basu called in here on the evening the announcement was made. "Capital" put in a paragraph & I will send you a cutting. I will keep a note of those who send messages – but almost everyone I meet asks me to say how terribly sorry they are – Sirem Mookerjee, Weir Patterson, Arthur Hinds, Tom Elverton, Bobby Burn and a host of others. I am afraid you will have so much to do, Sweetheart, and I only hope you aren't trying to do it all yourself. I will certainly write Arthur as you suggest, Sweetheart, and tell him to do what is required, if anything, at my expense. I must also write Sis but I don't seem to be able to do it. I always seem to have something that has to be done! But I will do it. I will get up earlier tomorrow and do it before I go to the D.C.S. meeting. It can be done.

I am glad wee John and Gordon are together a lot. Gordon is such a brick, especially to children, and John is so very, very nice. I feel envious of Gordon being there but I had my time & what a heavenly time it was. And I haven't slacked since I have been back but thank God for lots to do.

Hilia too – what an angel she is, my darling one, and our own wee chaps. I can just see her cheering you all up! Give her my love – I am glad that Jean and Jen are liking school and are well. I am always thinking of you. Someday not very long distant D.V. we shall all be together again. I hear Air mails have been stopped but I hope this may go.

Take all care of your Darling self and of our wee chaps. God bless you and them. All my love to you, my own Darling, with kisses and bunny hugs to our own wee chaps. Always your own Geordie."

This is the last letter of the series, the date of which is the day that Italy declared war on Britain . . . so Naples was closed as part of the air route leaving only the Africa route . . . hence Joan's message from Algiers. France was to surrender on the 18th of June with the Luftwaffe controlling the skies above and over the West coast and out to sea. From now on, mail went by sea, taking two to three months, and the only route out was by sea down the Western seaboard of Africa to Capetown and across the Indian Ocean to Karachi and Bombay.

The obituary from "Capital" reads as follows.

"News has been received in Calcutta of the death of Lt-Col Frederick O'Kinealy C.I.E. C.V.O. who retired from the I.M.S. in 1922 after a distinguished career, quite a large part of which was spent in Calcutta. From 1910 to 1912, he was Surgeon to the Viceroy, and in the latter years was appointed Surgeon-Superintendent of the Presidency General

Hospital, which he filled for a further nine years. It was in this period that the P.G.H., as it is familiarly known, was enlarged and developed to its present size. After Colonel O'Kinealy had seen several new and important schemes to fruition, he was elevated to the rank of Surgeon General, and on the eve of his retirement, he was appointed Chief Medical Officer to the Prince of Wales during his Indian tour in the cold weather of 1922. For many years he was a fellow of Calcutta University, and he sat in the first Bengal Legislative Council under the Montagu-Chelmsford Reforms. He was well known to a previous generation of Ditchers and many men who are now serving in India as senior I.M.S. Officers remember the mentor of earlier days, whose own professional life carried the impress of great traditions. At one time, Calcutta bore an international reputation in the fields of medicine and science – an inheritance that is not yet entirely extinct. It flourished in the days of O'Kinealy and his contemporaries, and it is in this context that his work for this city will be remembered."

There were many other tributes in the Indian and British press. He was buried in Torquay and a Requiem Mass was held in St. James', Spanish Place, London shortly afterwards. Perhaps the tribute in his obituary in the *British Medical Journal* sums it up best. . . . ". . . *he was a first-rate specimen of the best type of Southern Irishman."*

Events in France moved on rapidly in June and early July. What became known as the Vichy Government was established in the unoccupied territories in Southern France. Concern grew that the powerful French battle fleet would fall into German hands, and be a considerable threat to the British fleet's supremacy. Despite assurances from Admiral Darlan, the key French admiral, that the fleet would never fall into German hands, he, after being appointed Minister of Marine in the Petain Government, announced that he had changed his mind. Two battleships, four light cruisers, some submarines including the large *Surcouf,* and eight destroyers plus about 200 minesweepers and other smaller craft located in Plymouth and Portsmouth were quickly seized with most later being incorporated into the British fleet. A French aircraft carrier and two light cruisers in the French West Indies were immobilised after protracted negotiations with the American Government.

However, the most powerful French naval forces were concentrated in the Algerian ports. A considerable naval force, codenamed force H, was assembled under Vice-Admiral Somerville, consisting of the battle-cruiser *Hood*, battleships *Valliant* and *Resolution,* the aircraft carrier *Ark Royal,* two cruisers and eleven destroyers, sailed to Oman where an ultimatum was delivered to the French Admiral offering several options including joining the British fleet to continue the fight or sailing to a British port or to the French West Indies under escort. Refusal required the French to sink their ships within six hours. After protracted and fruitless negotiations, orders were issued to sink the French fleet. The battleship *Bretagne* blew up, the *Dunkerque* ran aground and the *Provence* was beached. The *Strasbourg* escaped but was attacked by torpedoes from the aircraft of the carrier Ark *Royal* and reached Toulon, with the two cruisers. The battleship *Richelieu* was seriously damaged in an air attack in Dakar from the carrier

Hermes and other ships were disabled. This resolute and ruthless action against former close allies, and in which many French sailors perished, left a powerful impression that the British meant business. At the beginning of July, Hitler launched his daylight air attack on London and the Battle of Britain began as a prelude to the German invasion of Britain.

All of these events were powerful influences on Dorks who saw the situation of intensifying war as a very significant danger, with the possibility of a German invasion of Britain. Besides, after the death of her father, she needed more than ever to be in India with George. Joan & Teddie Shuttleworth had made that decision, as had Teddie's sister Mignon Nicholson with her husband Bunty, and Sandy and Ronnie Cameron also with children of comparable age. Despite contrary advice, not least from Ruth Benthall, Dorks, with considerable courage, decide to gather all of us children up and sail for India with Nanny Bishop. And so, we packed up, with cabin luggage separated from luggage in the hold for the voyage out.

We sailed for India after the end of my two sisters' summer term towards the end of July on the P&O 21,000-ton liner SS Strathnaver out of Liverpool with a complement of 1200 passengers. These ships often called at Falmouth and it is possible we embarked there.

This was the last unescorted sailing to India; all subsequent ones were a part of the new convoy system, with ships escorted by warships, principally destroyers and corvettes, which gave both anti-aircraft and U-boat cover. Despite being a civilian passenger ship, we were bombed in the Bay of Biscay, although the ship was clearly identified as a passenger vessel. Now aged three and a half, I remember rolling out my bottom bunk and then rolling back under it as the ship turned and twisted, and subsequently putting on a life jacket . . . fortunately, the bombs missed. Both sisters had birthdays on board in August and another memory is of the great disappointment of losing a precious balloon overboard in the wind. Rounding the coast at Capetown, and crossing the Indian Ocean, the boat eventually docked at Colombo on Monday 19th August. We were met by George who had travelled by rail for four days down to Ceylon from Calcutta. He stayed with us for three weeks and we stayed on for a further month. It is likely that we were in the hills, out of the monsoon heat and humidity of the coastal regions, possible in spare accommodation at one of the many plantations above Kandi. The Bay of Bengal was now considered unsafe because of German submarines in the waters, hence the stop-over in Ceylon where there was a large British Naval base. And so, it was not until the first week in October, at the end of the hot weather, that we left for Calcutta.

And so began the journey by rail all the way up the East coast of India. Nanny Bishop fell mounting the train on the train ferry at the Straights of Coromandel and cut her head, and so Dorks was left with three young children, and a wounded Nanny, to complete the 1500-mile four-day train journey up the coast to Calcutta. With the arrival in Calcutta on Saturday 5th October, it was just short of three months since leaving England. George took the whole of the next week as a holiday, and then the Tuesday and Wednesday the following week too. Exactly a month later, on 5th November, we departed for Kalimpong, having spent Doreen's 35th birthday on 28th October in Calcutta. In later correspondence, the journey out was described as a "nightmare". But we were all together again at last with George in Calcutta.

We were to remain in India for the rest of the European War, mainly in the hills to escape the summer heat in Calcutta.

63 George's armorial scroll given by the College of Arms 1944

64 His medals including his Military Cross, O.B.E., Coronation medal and WW1 campaign medals

65 *A view of Kinchenjunga from Kalimpong*

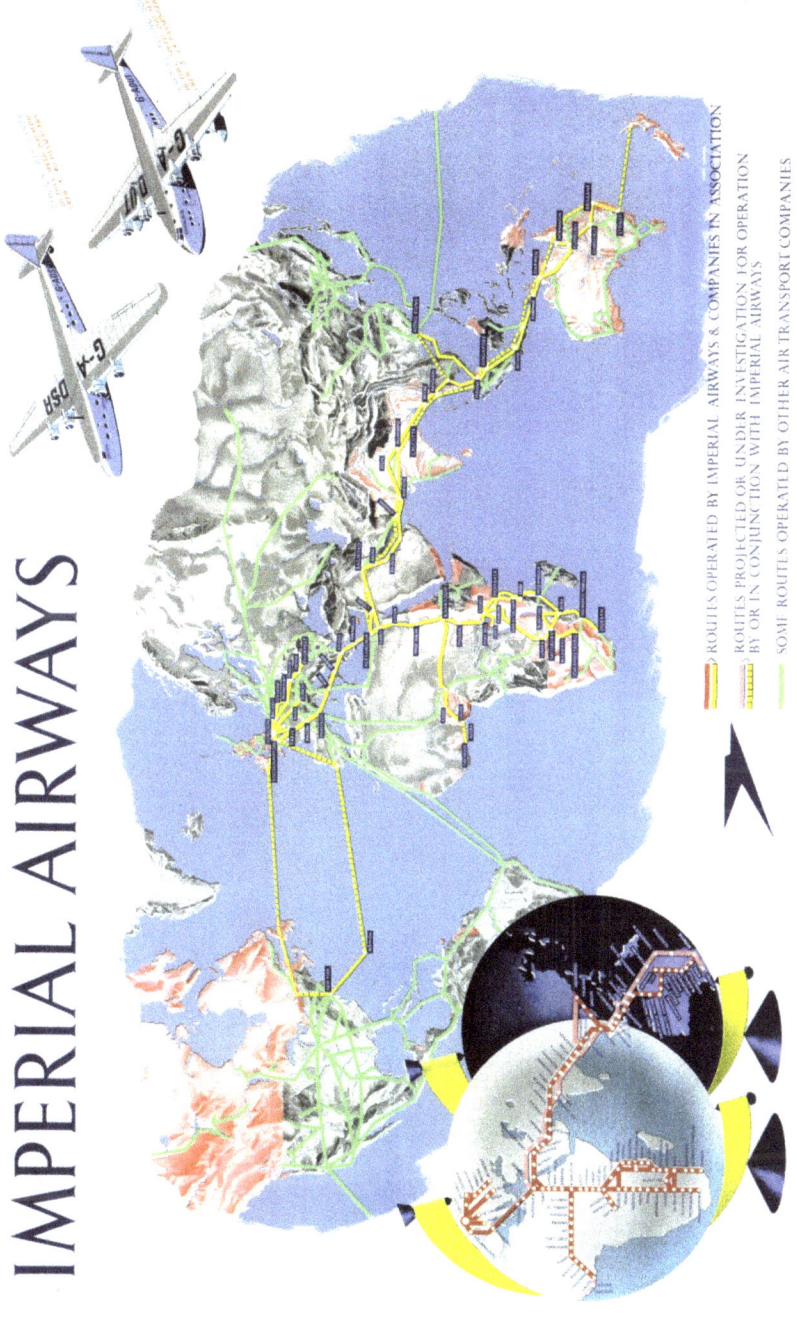

IMPERIAL AIRWAYS

ROUTES OPERATED BY IMPERIAL AIRWAYS & COMPANIES IN ASSOCIATION

ROUTES PROJECTED OR UNDER INVESTIGATION FOR OPERATION
BY OR IN CONJUNCTION WITH IMPERIAL AIRWAYS

SOME ROUTES OPERATED BY OTHER AIR TRANSPORT COMPANIES

66 *The Imperial airways international air routes of the 1930s*

67 Kinchenjunga massif from Tiger Hill in Darjeeling

*68 Chomolhari from Kalimpong showing the Homes and the Macpharlain
Memorial Church in the foreground*

69 Close up of Chomolhari from Tuna in the Chumbi valley

*70 The winding roadway below the Jelap la pass descending from 14,600 ft to Yatung
10,000 ft. This was the main trade route from Tibet into India in the 1940s.
The construction uses stone walls to support the trackway on the steep mountain side;
this was the common engineering approach to create tracks in the foothills*

Author's note: Doreen was a keen and knowledgeable ornothologist and in this she was encouraged by Sir Paul Benthall, who lived just a few yards away from us in Calcutta. Sir Paul himself was a well respected botanist and ornothologist after the tradition of Kingdom Ward and George Sheriff. Doreens bird notebooks have survived and contain two illustrations by Sir Paul as well as many others by Doreen, mainly of Himalayan species. A selection of these paintings from her birdbooks is therefore included and grouped together.

71 *Sketch of Himalayan Tree Pie by Sir Paul Benthall*

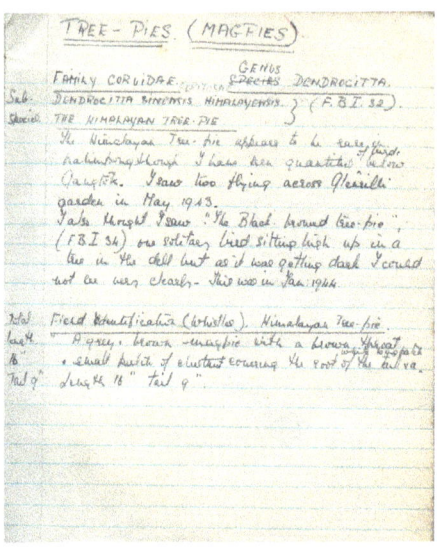

72 *Doreen's associated notes*

73 *Sketch of Himalayan Green Backed Tit by Sir Paul Benthall*

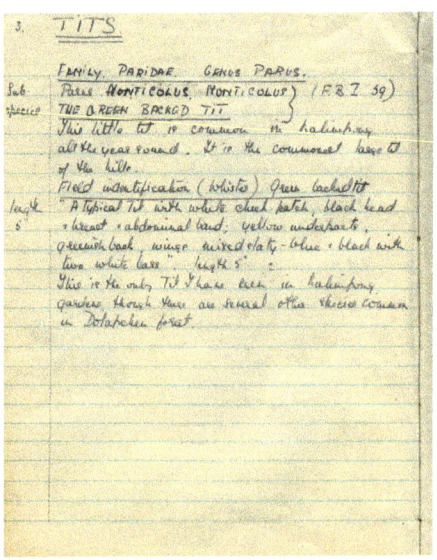

74 *Doreen's associated notes*

75 Doreens sketch of bulbuls

76 Doreens sketch of Common Babbler, Balck headed Sibia, and common Lora

---

Author's note: The next set of illustrations are from a collection of Christmas cards block printed on locally made paper by the Kalimpong Industries. This organisation was managed by Norman and Bunty Odling. George was a director and arranged the annual audit. The Kalimpong Homes London Association held a Christmas Bazaar every November in the crypt of St Columba's Church, Pont Street to raise funds for the School. My sister Jean a former pupil was a member of the committee until her death in 2000 and this family tradition has been carried on by her daughter Caroline.

Paper originated with the Chinese 2000 years ago who made it from the finest fibres of jute stalks and examples still survive, however jute does not grow on the high Tibetan plateau and so the Tibetans used the fibrous root of the Rijac plant instead which was boiled in water, pulped and the fibres filtered out and used to make paper. These techniques were also used by the Nepalese. This rare set of cards are block printed in colour on this fine fibrous light tan paper, as paper was rationed during the war due to the high military demand. The scenes depicted are of the life of the hill people and are probably from 1944. In the writer's conversations with the late Sir David Goodall he remembered, as High Comissioner to India, visiting the school to present the prizes. The late Bob Wright was for many years chairman of Trustees of the school, which is a thriving and highly rated school in the hills.

77 Bhuddist Gompa (monastery) couryard scene

78 Hillman with coracle and a saddled shoat (a cross between a sheep and a goat) for a child

79 Mountain railway

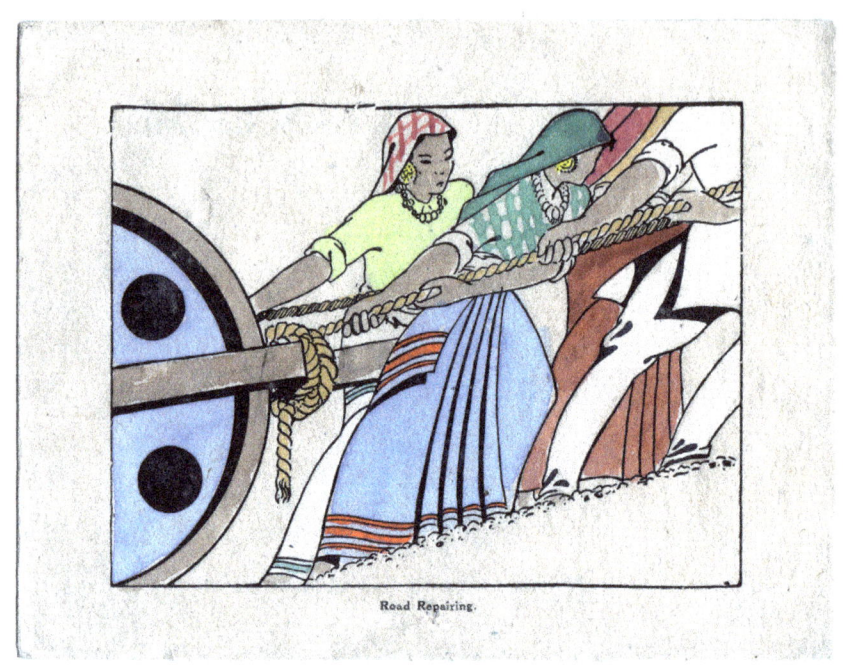

80 Road repairers

81 The Kalimpong Industries canteen during the war with rest and recuperation soldiers – probably Chindits from the 1944 second Chindit operation

82 Wool being carried by mules from Tibet

83 Games played at the autumn festival of Dessura

84 George with children Jean, Jen and parents Frederick and Mabel and Dorks autumn leave 1934

85 Jean, Jen and John at Lindridge Christmas 1939

86 Sketch of the Victoria Memorial (painted by the late Sir David Goodall GCMG High Commissioner to India 1984-7, by kind permission of his family)

87 Rectory House painted by cousin Bill Perkins

88 *George and Doreen's grave in the peaceful churchyard at Ogbourne St George Wiltshire*

German storm troopers on a counter offensive (illustrated by Robert Morton)

89 *Preparing to counter attack*

90 *Going over the top . . .*

91 . . . into battle

PART FOUR

Our New Home in Kalimpong.
George's leadership roles in an unlovely and forgotten
war (October 6th 1940 – June 1945)

Photographs indicate that Christmas was spent at the new house at No 5 Alipore Road
– (lately Raja Santosh Road – JMM) in Calcutta. George and Dorks had taken the
decision to locate us children with Nanny Bishop in Kalimpong. A newly built cottage,
called Charitung, alongside the driveway at Glenrilly, the home of Norman and Bunty
Odling, was available and this was to be our home for the next four and a half years.
We moved in in early November 1940.

The main house, Glenrilly, was built on the South Rinkingpong hill above Kalimpong
town facing North with magnificent and uninterrupted views to the Kanchenjunga
massif some 45 miles away. The mountain itself, the second-highest in the Himalayas
and third highest in the world was surrounded by four lesser 8000-metre peaks and
sixteen 7000-metre peaks covering some 2,500 square miles. To the East, peeping

92 Charitung our home in Kalimpong

above the horizon, was the peak of the holy mountain Chomolhari, with a stretch of other Himalayan mountains on the Bhutanese border at the south-eastern edge of the Chumbi Valley, and the track to Gyantse and Lhasa in Tibet.

To the North lay the Kingdom of Sikkim and to the East, Bhutan. About 35 miles West was Darjeeling and beyond that Nepal. In the valley between Darjeeling and Kalimpong was the Teesta River, a wide wicked-looking torrent, carrying the meltwater from the mountains. Along the river valley was a branch line of the mountain railway from Siliguri to Darjeeling and the road to Gangtok in the kingdom of Sikkim, off which was the road up the hill to Kalimpong. Above Gangtok, the Sikkim capital, lay the Natu La pass to the Chumbi Valley. The corresponding road track north from Kalimpong led to the Jelap La pass, also the gateway into the Chumbi Valley, and the main trade route between Tibet and India. George and Dorks used to visit us children in Kalimpong, and take local leaves trekking into Tibet in the hot summer months.

Bunty Odling was one of three daughters of Dr Graham, founder of the Kalimpong homes, a school for orphaned children, established on traditional public-school lines; Betty, a second daughter, was married to George Sheriff, a political officer in the British Residency in Sikkim and a noted botanist. The third daughter, always known as Jiggy, was married to an Irishman, Dr Coffee; she was trapped in Denmark after the German occupation and made a remarkable escape in a fishing smack across the North Sea. Norman was a veteran of the First World War in which he had lost a leg; he and Bunty acted as surrogate parents to us children.

Jean, now ten and a half, went to the school at the Homes, while Jen initially, and I went to St Joseph's Convent School, run by Belgian nuns and next door to the parish church. We were just three or four European children amongst Nepali, Hindu, and Bhutanese children. We spoke and quickly learned fluent Nepalese and Hindustani, riding on ponies to school with a syce (= *groom* – JMM) carrying our lunch in a tiffin box the four miles there and back every day. Such was our life in the hills; it was an idyllic childhood.

The journey up and down from Calcutta in the spring and autumn was on a night train to Siliguri where we caught the little mountain train up the Teesta valley. The railway line was cut into the hill above the river with bridge crossings over the many gorges carrying tributaries to the river below; in places, the railway was cut into the rock and one looked down from the carriage onto the fast-flowing waters below. There was jungle to the water's edge, and butterflies and birds flew up as the train passed along the gorge. At a suspension bridge over the river, we would be met by Dil Bahadur, the family driver, in a car. The luggage would be carried across the bridge before the car gingerly crossed, the reloaded car carrying us the nine miles up the hill to Kalimpong; frequent stops were needed to fill and refresh the car with water on the way up. And gradually, it got cooler as we climbed the 4,500 ft to the town. (Author's note . . . "*Teesta*" – *this is the modern spelling; it is spelt "Tista" on the 1930 maps.*)

President of The Bengal Chamber and Associated Chambers of Commerce – Calcutta – 1941

Meanwhile, George and Doreen were in Calcutta. This was to be a busy year for them as George was appointed President of the Bengal Chamber, one of the most senior Commercial appointments in India.

The Bengal Chamber was officially formed in 1853, replacing the Calcutta Chamber. Its principal function was to represent the interests of commerce and industry to government, but it also had separate functions such as the maintenance and governance of weights and measures as well as an arbitration role in settling disputes. As the trade union movement developed, it also became involved in the negotiation of wages and conditions of employment including safety standards. It was an active organisation sometimes described as an extension of Government. Traditionally, its membership and particularly governance was largely in the hands of the merchant and managing agency firms and the presidency was informally rotated amongst them. During the Second World War, and particularly during the Far Eastern war, many firms' activities were turned over to war production, and the closely knit business community of Calcutta, and indeed in the rest of India, depended on the closely integrated business relationships sponsored by the Chamber to foster the close working relationships between Government war procurement and business. The Bengal Chamber also included the member-associated chambers in Bombay and Madras.

93 Bunty Odling, with daughters Jeany, Shirley, and Norman Odling, all garlanded

Successive senior partners of Birds had been presidents, for example, Sir Edward Benthall in 1932 amid the crucial negotiations in the run-up to the Government of India Act 1935, and again in 1936, and Ernest Cable in 1903. Sir Paul Benthall, his younger brother, was to follow George after the war, and Sir Paul's time included taking over the Presidency in mid-term following Partition and the murder of Ronnie Cameron in early 1948, during the riots, and then again in 1950.

The activities of the Chamber were reported in an extensive annual report, and this, for the year of George's presidency, was presented at the Annual General Meeting on 26th February 1942. By this stage, of course, the Japanese had attacked the American fleet at Pearl Harbour, and had attacked and invaded Hong Kong, Malaya, Singapore and Burma.

George was in the chair (referred to as Sir George now) and presented the report to the members on 26th February 1942. Members of council present were N.C. Grant, Balmer Lawrie (his twin sons were to form Alex Lawrie, specialists in invoice discounting), A.P. Benthall (later Sir Paul and younger brother of Sir Edward), Sir Guy Cooper M.C., D.S.M., of Burma Shell, Sir Bernard Pratt. I.C.I., John Burder, Jardine Skinner (later President 1943 and knighted), Kenneth Mealing, Andrew Yule (later President and knighted 1944), A.H.D Cumberbatch (President 1947 and later knighted) and A.D. Siddiqui – (Muslim Chamber of Commerce).

It had been a turbulent year with the European war and shipping losses due to the U-boat activities. Post was taking up to three months to arrive. All was gloom and despondency. Calcutta was nervous.

Much of the peacetime production of India was gearing up for war. For example, Birds Kumardhubi Engineering works was turned over to the production of shell casings. There was a massive demand for jute gunny bags for sandbag emplacements around gun and trench emplacements, and civilian uses. India became the major source of boot and clothing production for the armed forces. Ammunition production (e.g. from the Dum Dum factory outside of Calcutta) was stepped up. The traditional work of the Chamber was therefore overlaid with coordinating war production, and this was to intensify as the Japanese war developed.

There was no immediate shortage of foodstuffs as the annual 1941/42 rice crops had been a record at just under 10 million tons in Bengal. Fortunately, imports were still available from Burma in 1941, the traditional source of rice, to make up any shortfall. However, George's report noted that in future, India would have to rely on "home-grown food"; also, that "India was unable to live only on home-produced food grains . . ." and it was "preferable in an emergency for employers to provide the necessities of life at a reasonable price level and as far as possible pay the difference themselves". This is exactly what happened during the 1942/43 famine with Birds setting an example. The Bengal production of rice had been steadily dropping throughout the ten years before 1941/42 against the background of a rising population, and so there was an increasing deficit in home-grown rice which had to be met from imports from the neighbouring rice bowl of Burma; this was averaging several hundred thousand tons a year. But this

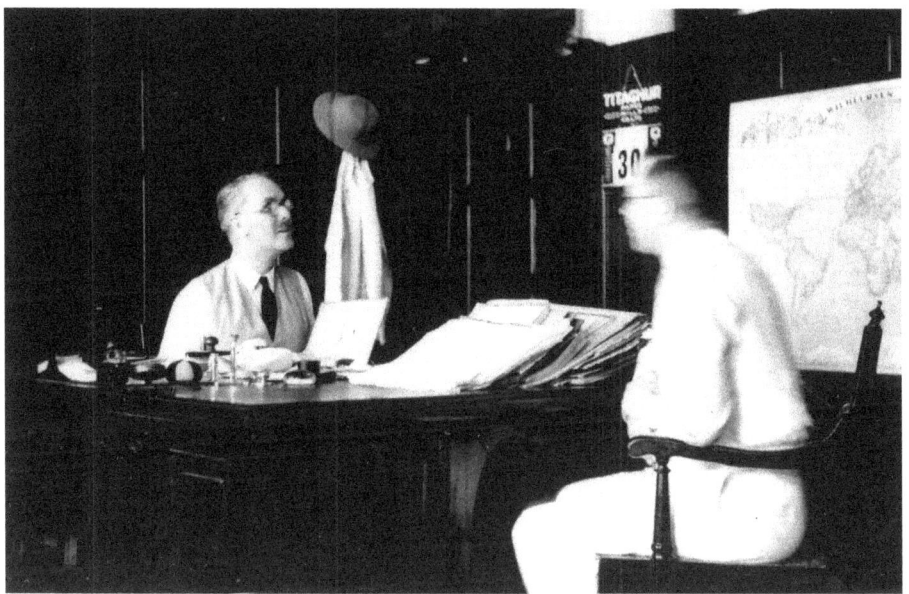

94 George at his desk in office

had now stopped with the invasion by the Japanese . . . and hence George's comments to the Chamber members. But luckily, 1941/2 was a record production year at just under 10 million tons; however, disaster was to strike in the autumn of 1942 when the bulk of the autumn crop in Orissa was destroyed by a cyclone, and with production shortages elsewhere, this led to what became known as the Bengal famine.

The Chamber report also noted that there was no avoidable delay in India acquiring full Dominion status but "we must preserve full liberty to state a case in favour of whatever safeguards we may adjudge necessary and appropriate in the circumstances of a new or revised constitution." This was the nub of Tom Benthall's work in the early 1930s by creating a level playing field for all businesses whether Indian or European. Although rejected in 1935 by Congress, Dominion status was adopted at Partition in August 1947 for both India and Pakistan.

281 arbitration cases were dealt with in 1941 from tribunals in all sorts of goods viz aluminium, barley, tax, elevating jacks, etc., etc. The Chamber also resolved such issues as the questions of lost bills of lading and the reissue of duplicates, since these gave title to goods shipped to or received from abroad.

Amongst other duties, George was on the Munitions Production Advisory Committee, and Vice-Chairman of the Provincial Advisory Committee for War Supplies. He was also a member of the executive of the Victoria War Memorial. He was on the National Defence Council of India from 1941-45, the ex-Services Association General Council and Sheriff of Calcutta 1941-2. The Defence Council alone required attendance at two to three days' meetings monthly in Delhi with the Viceroy.

1941 was a period of acute anxiety in Calcutta. The war was not going well; Britain was alone in confronting the Germans. The situation in North Africa was not going well either and the Japanese war was imminent. George was known as a steady pair of hands and probably, according to the Birds history, did more than anyone else to steady opinion in Bengal during this jittery period.

At the end of 1941, George handed over the Presidency to Sir (Robert) Henry Haddow with now John Burder elected Vice-President. George remained a member of the Council.

Letters from home 1940-42

After Dorks' arrival back in Calcutta in October 1940, she kept up a lively correspondence with friends and relatives at home. Her mother Mabel was one of nine children, the only girl with eight brothers, so there were plenty of Trevor cousins. Ruth Benthall was a regular correspondent and her letters also give a graphic account of conditions at home. These letters were taking up to three months to arrive by sea. Rationing and shortages of food were now commonplace even for those such as Tom and Ruth with substantial country estates. Dorks' food parcels, for example, small chests of tea, were particularly welcome. All of Ruth's letters to her are reproduced in Appendix II.

Many of these letters have survived . . . there is a series of five letters from Ruth and about a dozen others as well, all descriptive of events and news at home. One of these is from Rowley, an old friend of George's, and now a senior executive of Lloyds Bank. It is written on Lloyds Bank paper, Cox and Kings branch, now at

"Avon Court Bournemouth. 1 Feb 1941

My dear Doreen,

It was very nice of you to pass along a chit of good wishes for 1941 which I heartily reciprocate. I expect so far as old England is concerned it will be a fairly hectic one. I am a great optimist perhaps, but I have no doubt that we shall come through it with flying colours. As you rightly surmise, it is very difficult to fully appreciate the devastating effect of a real "Blitz" unless you have been through one or pass the result afterwards & then you cannot help patting yourself on the back and saying thank God I am English. The way the rank and file have stood up to these ghastly murderous visits from A.H.is really marvellous & to realise the heroism shown one has only to visit some of the bombed towns.

I am pleased to say Melton has so far escaped damage altho' we have had shaves very adjacent – less than 50 yards away but no 51 was not touched. A number of flats in the wings on both sides had their windows blown in by blast but we in the centre block escaped. Nos 6, 9, & 11 have also escaped so far, barring many broken windows, but Norfolk House where we had moved a sample of sections got badly damaged in Nov. Pleased to say no-one hurt but we had to find a new home.

The powers that be decided to separate Army pay from Banking & with the help of the office of works commandeered three hotels down here & moved the Pay Dept. to

this salubrious spot at the end of Nov. As it meant transferring a staff of 3/400 – since increased to a few less than 500 – it was thought desirable to send with the "Boys and Girls" a staid old gentleman to supervise & control the show. They asked me to take on the job where I have been for the last two months.

It is all very graceful altho' we get air raid warnings & occasionally a stray bomb or two but most nights our slumber is undisturbed. I must admit it is very restful after 14 months of London raids but I am afraid I rather hanker after the excitement of the metropolis & shall try to get back one of these days. The Melton Court family are going strong. Charles is still very busy, & Dorrie, running the accountancy side of the Duchess of N's fund in great style. They came down here for Xmas. Dorrie stayed on for a week or two which did her good. She had a wretched cold & was generally rather run down & the change & rest bucked her up. Nothing very recent from Pegs, but the last news to hand reported all is well. Duncan and she are now in Hyderabad but I suspect you know that. Cecil is now in the Equipment Section of the R.A.F. and, having done his bit of training, is now attached to the Air Ministry which enables him to live at his home. Much to Pat's delight, you may be sure that a nursery will be required in a few months' time. I have not seen anything of the Remenham folks (Sis, Tonge, Bill and Jan – JMM) *but we exchanged greetings at Xmas. With my love to you all, Yours ever, Rowley."*

Back Row :—Mr. R. A. Gopalaswami, I.C.S. (Secretary). G. B. Morton, O.B.E., M.C. Mr. Jamnadas Mehta. Sir Jwala Prasad Srivastava. Lt. Col. Sir Henry Gidney. Sir Gilbert Laithwaite, K.C.I.E., C.S.I.
(Standing) Lt. Col. B. M. Mahon, D.S.O., M.C. Mr. Bimu Mookerjee. Dr. B. R. Ambedkar. Capt. Sardar Naunihal Singh Man, M.B.E. Prof. E. Ahmad Shah. Rao Bahadur M. C. Rajah.
2nd Row :—Nawab Sir Mohd. Ahmad Said Khan, K.C.S.I., K.C.I.E., M.B.E. H. H. The Maharaja of Cooch Behar. H. H. The Nawab of Rampur. H. H. The Maharaja of Patiala. H. H. The Maharaja of Jodhpur. Sir Cowasjee Jehangir Bart, K.C.I.E., O.B.E. Raja Bahadur Mardaraja Deo of Khallikote. The Hon. Malik Khuda Baksh Khan. Kumararajah Sir Muthia Chettiyar. Mr. R. M. Deshmukh.
Front Row :—H. H. The Nawab of Bhopal. H. H. The Maharaja Scindia of Gwalior. H. H. The Maharaja of Bikaner, H. H. The Maharaja Jam Sahib of Nawanagar H. E. The Viceroy. Hon. Khan Bahadur Allah Buksh. Khan Bahadur Sir Muhd. Usman, K.C.I.E. The Hon. Maharajadhiraja of Dharbhanga, K.C.I.E. Begum Shah Nawaz.

95 *The National Defence Council (George back row second from Left)*

After Christmas, Dorrie also wrote, and her letter is an interesting insight into the adjustments people were making with the onset of war.

"51 Melton Court, S.W.7 30.1.41

I was so glad to get your letter of 10th Nov which arrived two days ago. It is so good to think of you all together & happy. I am so glad you decided to go; I was so afraid you wouldn't at one time. I wrote you earlier an incoherent letter just before Xmas. I was nearly at breaking point, my chest being stupid again, & as I had been in London since the beginning of the war except for short weekends, I was a little overtired & overwrought, I think. Rowley, as you know, I expect, went to Bournemouth with 500 of his staff in November, so on 22nd December, I decided to go there for a holiday for three weeks, which I did, Charles also going for a very short leave on the 26th. I felt much better when I returned & had to do three weeks' work in one to make up! Bournemouth seemed a new world – no raids or anything & only two warnings despite it being so near Southampton.

I would rather not be on the 7th floor if I could choose but having stuck so many months now, I can't be bothered to move unless I am bombed out! There is a nasty raid on at the moment & the guns are heavy. Pat is in the gardens giving Rufus her dog a turn & I wish she would come back; shrapnel is no joke. Here she is, thanks be!

To resume! Pat is having an infant in early May, hence my anxiety. It was she that had to duck behind sandbags, & when Cecil knew in the evening, he was furious with her being in the gardens at that time! However, he had been away for 5 days' duty & as he had a day off, they decided to stay up for the night & have a day in town. Cecil is in the R.A.F.V.R. in case my other letter has gone astray! Les, my brother, who is a W.6 & a Captain, had a week's leave & came along with Betty to the office whom I had not seen for months, as she is a F.A.N.Y. A.T.S. with two pips (Company Commander I think is the title). I was glad to see them and brought them here. We had had warnings from 9.30 a.m.- 4 p.m. but one gets used to things & we only put the shutters up if the gunfire is really heavy or planes overhead. Anyhow, all was well & is so far and I hope to have a good night's sleep!

We all have the win or die feeling, I think. London looks much the same really & we get a lot of praise and sympathy which I know we don't deserve. The real trouble has not yet started to my mind but that won't break us either! We must do one or the other!!

Helen Tobin W.A.A.F. has now won her pip and is doing coding in Scotland. I do wish I had been young enough to join one of the services but 51 is too much of a good thing to start a new job. Anyhow, I like my own and got lots of bouquets from the Committee last Wednesday. The auditors arrive next week, their first visitation tell George. I wonder what they will say at my bookkeeping. I like the cash ledgers but how I loathe the stock; my stock keeper is a dear but has not yet grasped that "received", "in hand" & "issued" must balance, however, she is learning! I managed to take out the year's stock Dec 39 – Dec 40 despite a rine cap – ½ d of cretonne! This must seem sneek to you, dear, but we are a comforts fund for the A.T.S. & deal in everything from carpets, deck chairs and pianos to soap and face cloths!

No news from Pegs for 4 weeks & I did expect a letter this evening. We send a cable once a month so perhaps I will get one early in February. To my mind, having a divided family & the long time between news is the worst part of this bloody war. I can't even buy things & send them out but have to ask Pegs to get them out there at the A & N stores. It makes me furious. Will continue tomorrow. I write all day & get so tired after a few sheets.

1.2.41. Thank heaven we have started another month! Betty has to go back to her Barracks this morning & as Les has another day's leave, he is coming along here and we are lunching at the club and doing a flick. Did you know that the poor old N&M (Naval and Military Club) had a real grilling? All our nice quarters are no more & we lunch in a portion of the men's dining room, screened from the holy of holies of course, & use the card room as our one and only sitting room. We enter by the servants' door & the food is as good as ever! I haven't seen Sis for months and months. I think she did ask me to lunch one day when she was up but it could not be done then. She wrote me at Xmas and told me about Bill & Pembroke; also I am doing V.A.D. work. It is a pity Sis can't get a cook or anything – it is a big house to run alone. I am glad I haven't to do it; I loathe cooking & housework – it bores me stiff. I would rather tackle the stocks sheets! Bill is on patrol work and is very fit. (Les's son) It seems strange without Rowley after all these years, but one has to get used to anything and live day by day. I wonder where in the hills you will take the children. Peg loved the places they went to but I can't spell it! I suppose there are lots of children of Jean's age in India now and that schooling will be simple. So sorry you have had a dose of illness but glad you were fit again in November. This is a meandering screed, poor you! It does seem such ages since we bought things at Harrods together. I suppose this war will end one day. I am damned sick of it! My love to George & to you, my dear. I hope Pegs & you meet one day – she is lonely, poor kid. I know she hates being so far away from her family tho' of course would rather be with Duncan wherever he is. Yours ever affectionately, Dorrie."

Melton Court where Dorrie and Rowley lived still stands towards the end of the Old Brompton Road SW7; theirs was a lifetime friendship with George and Sis as the correspondence of the First World War gives witness, so these letters are quoted in full. They give an insight into life in the Capital during the Blitz as well as the way in which ordinary people were adapting their lives to the needs of the war. There are two letters from Uncle Reggie, (Trevor) another of Mabel's brothers, full of graphic descriptions. I remember him bicycling from Bath to Ogbourne St. George to visit after the war, lean and fit, now well into his seventies. In the first he describes the illness of brother Charles, suffering from a stroke; Charles was a solicitor and the legal advisor to the family who had wound up Dorks' mother Mabel's estate. He was also attending to Frederick's estate of which Dorks was a significant beneficiary. Another two letters from Uncle Reggie:

"6 Baldock Road, Letchworth Herts 10 Dec 1940.

Dear Doreen,

I fear this will not reach you by Christmas – by many days – First I think you ought to know that your Uncle Charles is gravely ill. He & Violet moved themselves to Harrogate – to get out of London. While there, he had another stroke which has affected the movement of both legs & has paralysed partly his right arm. He was moved to a nursing home. I had a letter from Violet ten days ago saying that the doctor gave him a fortnight. Since then, he has rallied but it can be assured that it is only a matter of weeks. I volunteered to go to Harrogate but Violet said it would be no good & there was no room in the hotel, which I can quite imagine.

London had the worst raid she has yet suffered two months ago. My cousin, Mrs Tate, aged 88, was blown out of her bed at Ashtead near Leatherhead by a bomb which fell the other side of the road & her mattress fell on top of her. She hit her head against some furniture & suffered a severe shock. She has moved to her husband's sister's house in Norfolk. We have been lucky to have no damage so far. Bombs have fallen in fields in the neighbourhood but there has been no damage and no casualties. I daresay we shall get a visit one day. When Liverpool got it so badly a fortnight or so ago, we heard Jerry go overhead in waves for three hours. I took Alice to town by road – the first time I had been to town since your father's Requiem. A fair amount of damage in Willesden & 50 yards from Alice's house a house had been demolished. An incendiary fell in the churchyard here 10 yards from the church a month ago & burnt itself out. I have got nothing beyond two buckets of sand. No dugouts or anything of that sort. If Jerry means business, he won't wait till I get inside it. Living here as I do, I know no more about any damage in London beyond what I read in the papers. Hammersmith with Fulham have got it worst in the west end. Rosie Trevor still lives in her flat at Putney; they got it badly the other night after a week of quiet when she said the peacefulness was almost uncanny. The best wishes of the season – belated I fear – to you and George and the family. Your affectionate R.A. Trevor."

In his next letter, Uncle Reggie describes the landing of Rudolph Hess in Scotland (Churchill had fielded an excited call from the Duke of Hamilton reporting the event) and the bombing of the House of Commons and main line London stations.

"16th May 1941.

Dear Doreen,

I was very glad to get your letter – but I am amazed at the time taken by air mail – 6 weeks! Your comments on the situation would be amusing at this length of time were things not so tragic. What a change since you wrote – and as I just write now, we are hearing on the wireless of the entry of the Germans by air into Syria – I wonder what the developments will be when you are reading this. I take the view that the possession of all these countries will turn to dead sea fruit to the Germans. The sensation here has been the arrival of Hess in Scotland, which seems to bear out the statement that truth is stranger than fiction. It is no good my theorising for you with unknown facts long before you read this . . ."

Later he continues with news of brother Jim and the cold spring weather.

"We are rejoicing in an extra hour of summer time – that is we are now 2 hours ahead of the sun which means that we sit down to tea at 2.30 or on Greenwich time, 5 am is 7 am GMT. Black out time is ¾ hours after sunset which means that in the middle of June this will not take place until 11.40 p.m.& even now, 9.10, it is broad daylight.

Jim is still at Marlboro' as far as I know. I think he is very happy there – & so he should be for I have always thought it one of the most charming little towns in England. We have had a normal winter but a very cold spring; no nice spring days yet when one can see things grow but week after week of very cold east and north-east winds with sharp white frosts at nights – a fair amount of sun though in the day time but now cold in the mornings when at 10 a.m. it is only 8 am by the sun. We have been very lucky here. There is not a broken window in this town. One or two bombs have been dropped within a mile or so of my place in good Hertfordshire clay without casualties and on two occasions they dropped flares & incendiaries – about the extensive damage in London – though you may not have heard that the pro-Cathedral in Kensington is just a shell and I rather think that Farm Street has been either damaged or destroyed some months ago. The House of Commons destroyed & damage to Westminster Abbey – all ancient history by the time you get this. I don't know whether I told you that my cousin Clare Tate at Ashtead near Leatherhead was blown out of her bed some months ago by a bomb which exploded the other side of the room, with her mattress on top of her – she struck her head against some furniture on her way- she is 88. She went to Norfolk after that but found herself so traumatised that she is back there now – but sleeps on the ground floor.

Violet after Charles' death stayed with friends at Cambridge, then went on to Moor Park at a house of quite old friends of hers – Moor Park is near Rickmansworth. I ramble on and am reminded of the letters I wrote your mother when I was a humble private at Yarmouth & in France but now in more comfortable conditions and with a pair of warm hands – Rosie, Arthur's widow – is still at Putney & very cheerful. There are plenty of bombs in that neighbourhood but she tells me that an evening without a visit from the Hun is very flat & unexciting. It only shows to what one can get used. Violet tells me she will take a smaller flat somewhere in town – 26 Sussex Mansions is too big – she has the lease for another year but being beneath the roof she cannot live there. She couldn't get a staff – but everything is much in the air.

By the way, a Captain Alford has come to live here – he was with the Royal Indian Marines, now as you know the R.I.M. and remembers your father quite well. He is now a man about 70, retired and a bachelor- he lives with his nephew and his wife, the former being an inspector of taxes in Hitchin. But he finds this place very cold. He has been living in Bournemouth, that place is not healthy in these days. Jerry pays it a visit. Farne is in Wiltshire & there have been bombs there. Just before Easter, I spent three days at Hereford – they have had no bombs there though at Gloucester there have been plenty though I do not think the damage has been great. Five days ago, King's Cross was hit and St. Pancras was shut altogether. Paddington got it a month or two ago. I am glad George is well & that the children are flourishing. Yours affect., Reggie."

Great Uncle Reggie's chilling description in his letter of 10th December of the squadrons of German aircraft, pregnant with the instruments of death and destruction and their passing overhead for three hours on their way to bomb Liverpool is a grim reminder not only of the menacing effect on the civilian population as they went on their way but also of the devastation these raids caused. These letters and the ones that follow are from friends and relatives, many the unknown ghosts of the past; these nevertheless present a first-hand historical account of their own individual experiences as civilians in war. The major themes of these letters are food and bombs, coupled with notes of defiance against the enemy.

Two of these letters come from a Katie Scott, who signs herself as "your old friend", and is in rooms at the Blenheim Hotel in Brighton. She was living before in a boarding house at 5 Chesham Place in Belgravia, not far from Pont Street and Harrods where she had rooms, when, as she says,

"On 18th September, Hitler decided to visit us, visiting hours 2.30 p.m. I was sitting about two yards from the window . . . when the room turned red, a terrific explosion. I shut my eyes and put my hand around the back of my neck then opened my eyes, but could see little. The room was quite dark with dust & I suppose some smoke & the most disgusting smell. I was first plastered in bits of broken glass – I could hear Jill calling – so got up & shook myself free of fragments & behold, all three windows and the surrounding woodwork scattered over the room, the door blown clean out & the lintels landed in the middle of the room; not a particle of glass or mirror left except in fragments on the floor . . . I snatched up my despatch case & made for the aperture where once there had been a door – it was a bit difficult walking on glass in the semi-darkness, but getting downstairs was worse as the place was a shambles and the bannisters broken loose. However, I met Jill halfway & we managed to get into the road . . . no doors or windows left in most of the homes. An A.R.P. ambulance & all kinds of helpers were there, as if by magic. We were sent to a house minus doors and windows & given hot tea; after a while, old J turned up & drove us to his place where we had more tea, then drove us around to find another place to live in but none to be had so we 'phoned here for two rooms, scrambled through the ruins for a few necessary garments, then drove up in grand style in a council lorry, sitting beside a big dirt driver but such a nice fellow who had been on rescue work for 48 hours. The hall porter's face was a sight to remember. Jill's room had a little damage done, mine and the ground floor & basement were the worst. The bomb landed in the area & Mrs McCaib & two children were partly trapped but out of the 12 or 13 inhabitants of the house, only one maid had her leg slightly cut – it was a miracle.

The resident of the first-floor room was lying on the sofa, which was blown upside down with her underneath – this saved her life as the room was perforated with shrapnel, also the wardrobe & clothes inside ruined. It was all as I said a wonderful miracle –

the house is boarded up and I believe condemned; it is a gruesome sight. Jill was so good helping me retrieve my goods; we went up every day and collected and packed, in darkness except for two candles – in the end, I saved nearly everything – & beyond being rather tired & I so deaf – none the worse. I was so afraid it would affect Jill's nerves, but on the whole, she has come through wonderfully. For some time, Brighton fared badly, but for over a week we have had a restful time and really Brighton is quite as safe as any place. There is no place left in England where you can guarantee freedom from bombs – I hope this will not bore you, dear." She continues. . . . "This is a large and quite comfortable hotel, rather empty at the moment, but full up at Xmas which I spent in bed with pleurisy and congestion & am still swathed in thermogene – if this ever reaches you and you can spend time, do send me a line and tell me of yourself, my darling – with much love always, your long faithful old friend Katie Scott."

There is also a graphically descriptive letter of Aug 21st '41 from her in which she tells of her joy of getting a letter back from Doreen . . . but it takes six months, a turnaround of three months both ways. The letter is full of hope for the future, despite the widening nature of the war in the Balkans, Middle East and North Africa. Part of her family have gone to America, sons are at war, and she is lonely without regular news of them with letters lost as a result of hostilities. She is still at the Blenheim in Brighton and in reflective mood . . . she tells of wartime food rationing and of trips through the countryside to visit friends by bus.

"My dearest Doreen,

Dear, it was such a joy to get your nice long letter, quite an event for me as neither Mac's, Bruce's nor Doris' letters are coming through. . . . of course, Don does not write now & has not now for the last eight months. I believe he is now stationed at Amritsar (scene of the 1919 massacre in the Punjab in North India, religious centre for the Sikhs and location of the Golden Temple – JMM) *but only heard in a roundabout way. Mac writes regularly, as a rule, every week, but since Jan no letters are coming through -probably sunk or otherwise lost – I cabled in March & got a reply "all well" & he had written as usual in May but have had no reply . . . I had a cable from Bruce – promoted Major, several moves on to Tungoo – he was moved from Mungayo to Tannygyi about last April* (all in Burma – JMM); *he was terribly ill in the winter of a complicated state of health, had a month's sick leave and then went down with a high fever that same week so they had to return from their trip & declared a bad case of measles; to add to these trials came news from America that young Colin had broken his leg skiing – however, I believe their luck has changed and things are brighter. I am expecting the gong for lunch to go so I am scribbling as fast as I can.* (And her writing is almost illegible!!! – JMM) *The boys are very happy at their various schools, and Mrs Prentice Porter with whom they stay is kindness itself – I cannot believe that Kenneth is 17 – I hear of them through their other granny – Bruce and Liam are very pleased with the way the schools are run and, in some ways, think it a great improvement on the English methods. Nothing seems to have been arranged as to their future careers, but I suppose that it is impossible to plan with the world in such chaos. Kenneth would like the navy . . . I had your lovely Christmas card but no tea has arrived – but Mac sent me a small packet which did turn up – tea grown in Malaya – nice but not like Margaret Hope. I have no gas fire in my room, it is electric so I brought the electric kettle & so make my morning tea. I was ill most of the winter, congestion, pleurisy, these awful internal attacks, in fact, quite an assortment of ills, but am normal now. I dread these winters – but I've a very nice little Dr woman who looks after me – she is such a dear. We have had quite a nice two or three weeks now – no alerts – & our nerves are all the better for the rest – nevertheless, we are warned to be prepared for more to come. I think our people are just wonderful; conditions, as well as those in the services; as a matter of fact, I think our men look better. They have more strength and determination in their faces and move and look as if they had a real absorbing object in life – I am sure that this war will be good for the world in the long run – men will find that they must ask for help from a Higher power, not imagine their brains and inventions can rule the Universe – & since the magnificent way the poor and workers have shown up. Will forbid the rather scornful opinion that some held – for the lower classes – you see them by scores going back after hard work – looking so tired but joking & so good natured and taking it all in their stride, probably going home for an hour & then off as a fire watcher or some home defence service. This hotel faces one of the entrances to the Dome Art Gallery – it has an air raid shelter for 1,000 people. There are evidently many who go in regularly every night, they arrive with old perambulators piled with bundles of bedding – it is very tragic and rather like animals running into their burrows & holes – this place must have hundreds of troops billeted for miles around & in all the villages. The front is no longer a promenade – this area being a banned area, no visitors allowed so the hotel is very empty. Strange men in uniform come in for a few days & then disappear – most of the staff have been called up but they manage very well – the food is as good as can be expected – one spoonful of jam for breakfast, just enough for you to wish for more – one egg a week, plenty of tea, coffee and bread – each person has a little jar on her table and the weekly portion of butter and margarine is put in every Monday – also a small portion of lump sugar & about a ¼ of a cupful of granulated, no honey, jam, treacle or sweet stuff – no fruit of any kind, a certain amount of fresh vegetables – no sweets or chocolate. Meat but you must take what the butcher has to send. No choice in the matter but we do well. Sweetbread, fish !! horrid, I think. Bacon, 2 tomatoes . . . for breakfast. Soup (of sorts) & disguised offal – cold gelatine toad in the hole & a milk pudding or date roll for lunch – after a tiring hunt I found two dates – soup and tripe sometimes or fish – very good salmon – once a week a cut from a joint – (& sometimes what we would call in India a spatchcock chicken) a tiny fowl, stewed not roast, no fat for frying or cooking, ices or blancmange disguised – & coffee for dinner – it really is quite good, considering the difficulties. The clothes rationing is amusing – I think quite good for us to once more sew & mend as our great-grannies had to do. I am wearing out bombed dresses, etc.; we can do a lot of knitting. Jill has gone off to Edinburgh for three weeks to stay with Mary (Dr Pickford) and she returns on Friday. At times her nerves are very bad, but on the whole better & her general state of health very good . . . dear children, how I would love to see them. Jean must be quite a big girl now – have you a governess for them? It does sound as though Jean was taking after her mother a little – you were not too keen on being tidy; has she learnt to darn yet? Why was Jennifer so long away from her lessons? John is like Colin, who found a smile could work wonders – those Indians who have come into the war have done splendidly, haven't they! Will they ever co-operate does George think? I went to see my sister Mrs Carruthers. She is staying with friends . . . I left here by coach and had lunch with her at Reigate. The drive was so lovely it made me ache – once more to see fields & wild flowers & such green fields & hedges – the country was at its best. I had a lovely day and got back at 8 pm laden with flowers from their garden. Dear- I can't tell you how much joy your letter gave me. It is grand to be remembered with love – the sons are so good & write so regularly I miss their letters.*

Very, very much love, dear & pass some on to George. I so often think of you both. God bless & keep you and your dear ones. Your loving old friend Katie Scott."

A principal activity of the war in the first half of 1941 was the demolition of the Italian African Empire. Troops from India and South Africa engaged and drove out Italian troops from Abyssinia and then moved into Somalia and the Italians were now in full retreat along the Libyan coast . . . Tripoli had fallen and Benghazi taken with over 130,000 Italian prisoners captured.

Another letter, dated 25.01.1941, is from Nora, a former domestic in the O'Kinealy household, though in what capacity is not clear. She is obviously very fond of Dorks and the family. The letter is written in the train to York, she having just said goodbye to her mother-in-law, and after three days embarkation leave in London. This is a phlegmatic and stoic account; she tells of seeing Col Frederick, of being shelled out of their little house in Dover, of husband Cleb arriving back from Dunkirk tired and thin. She is now about to say goodbye to him again, posted to the Middle East. It is written in pencil.

"My dear Doreen,

Your letter was so thankfully received. I was so dreadfully out of date with your doings & had been imagining you still with Newton Abbot rural, & I had no idea about Col. O. Kinealy having died. I do so wonder when it was & if you were there. It was a very quick illness, I hope? Did I ever tell you I looked in to see him one day, can't remember when, perhaps a year ago & he looked just the same but seemed quite different & I came away feeling quite sad about him. I'm glad he didn't live for ages & ages without your mother. He was very valiant & managed to ask me all the right things but one felt it was a terrible mental effort. Jim must be thankful really not to have such a huge responsibility as an ongoing parent these days. I do so hope he wasn't badly ill for long. Do tell me next time you write.

It is good news you are in India all together. What a journey – from mid-July to October. Did you have an awful time of indecision trying to make up your mind whether to go or stay? Deciding doubtful things for other people is the worst of worries in my opinion, & at specially bad moments of the war, such as having Cleb in Dunkirk.

I tried to cheer myself up with the thought that I could do nothing about it whatsoever. Neither poor comfort, but still he got back safe, only very thin & worn out, and we've had 8 months together in York and been so happy in the narrow sense, that I often feel ashamed of being so little touched by the war. But now he has been ordered to the Middle East where letters take months to reach so the old continual anxiety will start again. We are now on the train back from saying goodbye to his mother and three nights in London on embarkation leave. Our poor little house in Dover got badly damaged by one of the September shellings. Lornie stuck it out till December living in the cellar & doing Fwd Control, then the intense cold (no windows, no gas) decided her to abandon Dover & she took up her abode with friends in Somerset. She and Anthony came to our little house for Christmas. It is a tiny council house, very easy to run. With a daily girl, even I feel capable of it.

Jim must be having his fill of firefighting. Bits of London look horrible, but worse, I think, are the rows of people sleeping in the Tubes. The majority haven't got bunks, they just lie on newspaper on the cold platforms. It seems scandalous that a better arrangement can't be made after all this time.

I've told Cleb I won't go back to work in Hoxton & really haven't the courage. Marjorie Poresty is still there. Miss Starbridge writes to me sometimes, but although she still clings to Finsbury Park, she doesn't venture into Hoxton; a good thing too. . . . Let's send pcs and not get too thoroughly separated. Much love & to George from Nora."

Other letters have survived, one from Helen Tombazi, the American wife of Manoli, head of Ralli Brothers in Calcutta, but now temporarily in London, congratulating Doreen on her brave decision and safe return to India. Most of these concentrate on the bombs, food and the difficulties of managing without servants. Most were learning to cook and clean for the first time, a pattern of home life that was to become commonplace after the war.

Ruth Benthall carried on the most regular correspondence of all, full of references to Tom's work in London with the Department of Economic Warfare – part of the Board of Trade. They had taken a house in Walton–on–Thames to get out of the Blitz, commuting daily to London, with Ruth doing various war jobs and helping Maurice Foght, her doctor, now working as a broadcaster for the Free French Radio. The particular worry was the petrol ration. Food was a problem, particularly sugar for jam-making, but they relied on Doreen's colony of hens for a good supply of eggs, plus vegetables and fruit from the extensive kitchen garden at Lindridge, as well as rabbits, pheasants, and other game in season from the estate. Ruth's letters are reproduced in full in Appendix 2, and a copy of them has been deposited in the Benthall archive at the Cambridge Institute for South Asiatic Studies.

Apart from their news of wartime conditions, these letters are also an example of the widespread personal comment and news of events from home received by the Calcutta community, contributing to the jittery atmosphere amongst business, and speculation of a possible German invasion of India, via Afghanistan, and a collapse in the face of air attack and the growing U-boat threat to the Atlantic lifeline. George is credited in the Birds history with doing more than anyone else in North East India to steady opinion during 1941, with a reputation as a steady pair of hands during his tenure of the Presidency of the Bengal Chamber. There was also the increasing threat throughout the year of an invasion of India via Burma by the Japanese.

Tom was to return to India in early 1942 taking a post as a member of the Viceroy's (Lord Linlithgow) council in Delhi, and specifically responsible for the crucial national transport arrangements and networks during the Far Eastern War.

1942 "Annus horribilis", but George is knighted – his various leadership roles

This was the year when George was knighted for his work in the Bengal Chamber, the year of the rapid development of war in Burma, and the year the Indian "Quit India" movement started, led by Mahatma Gandhi. This was the year too when George worked tirelessly as Chair of the Calcutta Evacuees Committee, organising the housing, feeding and rehabilitation of the flood of refugees fleeing from the Japanese; most of them had walked out across the dense jungle in the monsoon with just the clothes they stood up in. 1942 was also the year that the Bengal famine started, the initial reversals of the Burma campaign, and the failure of the Cripps mission to attempt a political settlement of the agitation for independence. It was the year too when the Congress leaders were placed under house arrest in the Aga Khan's summer palace in Poona.

George's knighthood was gazetted on New Year's Day and created at an investiture in New Delhi on 21st February. Ruth Benthall's letter to Dorks of 1st January records the event and recalls the memories of her father, Baron Cable's, knighthood at the turn of the century.

> *"Dear Doreen,*
>
> *It would have been a very great disappointment if we had not found your name in the papers this morning at breakfast & now you will be swimming about in a thousand wires & letters – and your bearers expecting buckshees (= tips JMM) – and I expect forming up on the stairs & have now to give your new title – it is another honour for the old firm who always seem in our thoughts at the right moment & all so very merited. I was 10 years old when my father was knighted & I remember writing to congratulate his mother – we had a happy day and you must be spending it together in spite of the Japanese and all the horrors which have crept so near to you all. I did hope that Tom for once would be wrong in his prophesy so many months ago but I know you are full of courage and perhaps a little glad you are in it too! But I am so worried about all you mothers."*

Amongst his many responsibilities, George was primarily accountable for the conduct of Birds businesses as the Senior Partner of the Bird Heilger group of companies, but he was also Sheriff of Calcutta during 1942. Originally, this office performed the duties of summoning prisoners for trial within the offices in the original Supreme Court in Fort William but the offices were transferred to the new high court building on its completion in 1872. By 1940, the office was largely an honorary post but a prestigious one with many distinguished Nawabs, maharajas, industrialists, merchants, historians, doctors, architects and other persons holding the title over the years. The emblem carried by the Sheriff at the beginning of the court sessions or term was a silver mace, which, during the British Empire period, displayed the British Crown at the head of the mace. This was changed after independence to the Indian lion and Asoka Chakra. The original offices, prisoners' cells, and deputy sheriff offices are believed to still exist in the high court building – the last records researched are from 2014.

George was also a Director of the Imperial Bank of India from 1936-45 and President of the Calcutta Local Board from 1942-5. He was also on the Munitions Production Advisory Committee for War Supplies,1940-5, and Vice-Chairman of their Provincial committee during the same period. He was a member of the Defence Council of India from 1941-45, attending regular meetings with the Viceroy in Delhi and Chairman of the Bengal Telephone Corporation. He became a director of a number of companies and banks both during and after the war.

In 1942, he became Chairman of the newly formed Calcutta Evacuees Committee, responsible for handling the settlement and care of refugees from Burma, most of whom arrived in Calcutta.

All of this left little time for family life, but somehow, he managed to get involved with us children when we were in Calcutta for the winter months as well as visiting us in Kalimpong. He managed his work so that it did not become obsessive or overwhelming. He left time for exercise and family life. Both he and Doreen took extra leave to organise treks into Sikkim, Tibet, and particularly the Chumbi Valley, taking after Tom and Ruth Benthall; the Benthall archive is full of close written diary notes in Tom's neat handwriting of similar and earlier visits to Sikkim, Gangtok and the Jelap La and Natu La passes. The family legacy of this contains some magnificent albums of photos of the hills and mountains and a few diary, birdwatching notes, and bird paintings of Dorks'. There are also George's briefly annotated pocket diaries of 1942-45.

Forgotten aspects of a forgotten war – the refugees walk out of Burma

This dramatic story is one that has largely been ignored in all the history books of the Burmese war. Disappointingly, neither was it even mentioned in the celebrations of the 75th anniversary of the end of the war in August 2020. But hopefully, this account will tell something of what happened, and of the extraordinary courage and suffering, not just of the evacuees, but also of those many people, particularly the civilian tea planters and their labourers of the Indian Tea Association, who went out to the Burmese border to help rescue the refugees, construct camps, improve roads and tracks, and provide food and medical support and shelter for those walking out.

96 George as special constable

Another section will also outline the work of the Calcutta Evacuation Committee of which George was Chairman, and their sub-committees, in their inter-community work through the Calcutta business communities and charities of resourcing, receiving, providing food, medical support and settling upwards of 400,000 refugees in the first nine months of 1942.

To understand the Burmese war of 1942-5 and its consequences, and particularly the evacuation of refugees in 1942, one needs to gain an insight into the topography and climate of the country. The coast runs from South-East to North-West, but the grain of the country runs North to South. The coastal and largely agricultural region is fed by four massive rivers also running North-South, into the Eastern end of the Bay of Bengal. From East to West, these are: the Salween, exiting into the sea at Moulmein, the city at the head of that strip of Burma running North to South alongside the border with modern Thailand (Siam in 1942), the Sittang, exiting to the east of Rangoon and Pegu, the Irrawaddy, into which the Chindwin flows 400 miles north of Rangoon, and the Kaladan, running from the Kachin hills to the port on the island of Akyab. For

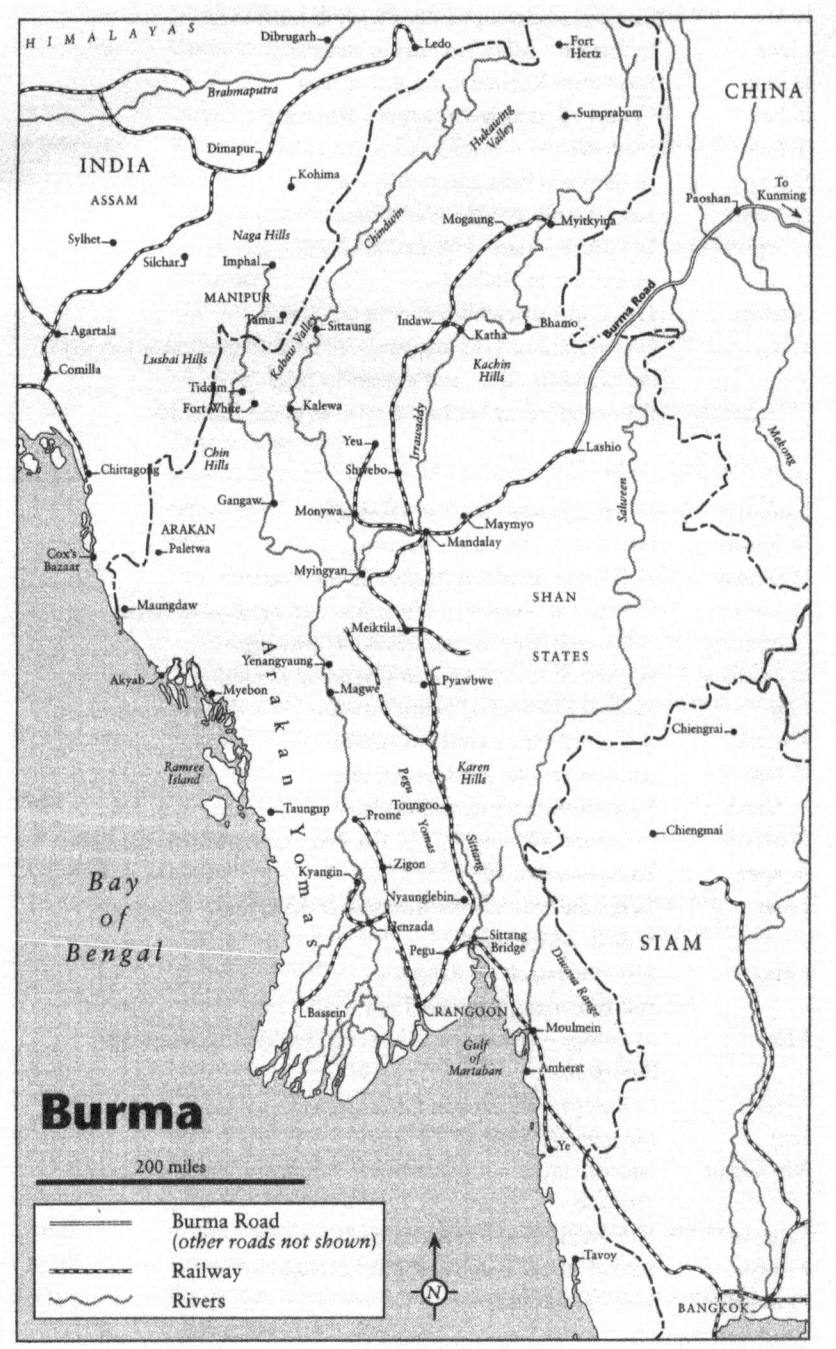

97 *Contemporary map of Burma showing the evacuation routes.*

the last hundred miles or so, the Irrawaddy opens out into a vast delta, which, at its mouth, is around a hundred miles wide. These huge rivers carry the melt water from the mountains of the Tibetan plateau as well as the rains of the monsoon falling on the Burmese jungle down to the Bay of Bengal.

Historically, the country was Asia's rice bowl, exporting large quantities of rice not just to India but with a big global export trade as well. The principal rice-growing areas of the coastal region were fed by the waters from the hills; these rivers flowed through the waterways or *chaungs*. Two principal crops were grown each year – the spring crop from the autumn plantings and the autumn crop planted in the spring. The waters from these northern hills carry a rich alluvial silt fertilising the paddy fields. The lines of hills are up to 6000 ft. high, rising in height above this height the further north they stretch, with steep escarpments rising from and falling into the valleys below. These valleys carried their own streams and rivers, some formidably in spate during the monsoon months from May to September.

Covering the slopes was thick jungle, abundant with wild animals including tiger, elephants, monkeys, leopards, snakes and other predatory animals. Sand fly, mosquitoes and leeches presented a constant menace to the traveller . . . leeches, in particular, attached themselves in hundreds, sucking blood until removed either with salt, a cigarette end, or a hot match end. Theirs was an insidious attack, their bite camouflaged by a natural anaesthetic which desensitised it; finding so many of these blood suckers on the skin was a shock (as I remember as a child having ventured into the jungle in Kalimpong). The leeches, black creepy crawlies, sometimes used in medical treatments as a substitute for bleeding up to the 19th century, caused a significant loss of blood and physical weakness, inserting themselves into the remoter parts of the human body.

Those few roads running east were rough and became seas of mud in the monsoon, the streams crossed by bamboo ropeway bridges, often swept away by the spate waters below during the monsoon. Monsoon rains soaked travellers to the skin within seconds; on occasions, a hand held in front of the face was obscured by the force of the deluge. Leech and sandfly bites went septic; malaria, dysentery, typhoid, cholera and beriberi were rife.

These then were the conditions faced both by the retreating troops and by a civilian population walking out of Burma to escape the Japanese.

Their reputation for brutality towards captives and prisoners had gone before them. They had form; the Nanking massacre of December 1937 had been widely reported in the British press when some quarter of a million civilians were killed and many women raped. In March 1942 came the atrocity in Hong Kong as hospital patients were bayonetted in their beds and nurses raped by the invading Japanese, which was widely reported in the international press. The old samurai code of respect and honour for a captive enemy had been replaced by a culture of supremacy in which prisoners were despised . . . Japan, whilst acknowledging and signing the Geneva Convention, had refused to ratify it and so it was open season on all prisoners as Japan refused, on the Emperor's instructions, to agree the protocols regarding their treatment. The wounded were bayonetted to death and prisoners either executed or used as slave labour, the women used as "comfort women" for the Japanese military. During the war there were very few prisoners taken, the Japanese preferring death to capture; the officers disembowelled themselves and other ranks crowded around an exploding grenade. Having said this, there were reports of some Japanese helping evacuees on their way out of Burma, not least because they wanted the British gone.

Originally a province of India following the annexation of the country after three wars in the nineteenth century, Burma had been separated from India as a colony under the 1935 Government of India Act, and this legislation took effect after elections in 1937. There was a growing pre-war independence movement, just as in India, and a stand-off between the colonial government and the members of the movement who were regarded as terrorists. The Burmese disliked the British and the Indians, but the tribes to the North, particularly the Christian Karens, were more favourably disposed. Hence the Japanese were, on the whole, politically welcomed initially as being more likely to grant Burmese autonomy.

The Japanese invasion of Burma commenced with a two-pronged attack. Japanese intentions had been made clear through rapidly developing events in December; the attack on Pearl Harbour on December 7th – the landing of Japanese troops in Malaya also on the 7th and the capture of airports and the landing of Japanese troops on Victoria Point to the south of Rangoon on the 14th. This was followed by the attack on Hong Kong on 18th/19th and the fall of Hong Kong Island on Christmas Day 1941. A major event was the sinking of two of Britain's most modern capital ships, HMS Prince of Wales and the battle cruiser HMS Repulse off the East coast of Malaysia on 10th December. Singapore surrendered on 15th February. The USA had declared war on Japan following Pearl Harbour, then Germany declared war on the USA in sympathy with the Japanese and so the Allies were now united together in the war against both.

The invasion of Burma was long-anticipated and the Japanese came through Siam on 15th January 1942 with the 15th Army advancing to the Sittang river. It was hotly defended with the bridge blown on 23rd February cutting off many of the Baluch and Ghurkha soldiers on the wrong side of the bridge. On 31st January, Moulmein was captured and then finally Rangoon fell on 7th March with the British forces now in full retreat to the North and North-West. Some of the British and Indian civilians had escaped by sea, but others were cut off and walked out, many perishing on the way. Bird's business in Rangoon had commenced with the merger with Heilgers in 1919. On 17th February 1942, the manager of Bird's Rangoon office was given only a few hours to dismiss the staff, collect the most important records, and organise the evacuation of some 5,000 skilled workers from the oil refineries at Syriam. All outstanding accounts had been paid and the only loss was the office furniture and a motor car. A cashier, with the books balanced overnight, walked out of Burma with them and reported to Birds Calcutta with his records. A number of staff perished on the way out. Many Indian businesses, closely associated with their Burmese counterparts, also suffered. George, as senior partner of Birds, was closely in touch with events and as a part of his more public responsibilities and now Chairman of the newly formed Calcutta Evacuees Reception Committee, was to be increasingly involved in the resettlement and community support of the many thousands of refugees from Burma, both British and Indian. Numerous British and Asians had also fled the arrival of the Japanese in Hong Kong, Malaysia, and Singapore. Those Indians left behind were given the opportunity to join the Indian National Liberation Army or alternatively to work as slave labour. Many were shot or beheaded out of hand. Other Indian military were tortured to make them break their oath. Others, notably Australians and British, were put to work in the jungle camps on the Burma railways. Many of those who dropped out of the line of the forced marches through exhaustion were shot out of hand by the Japanese soldiers.

In the early days of late 1941 and early 1942, before the closing off of river access to the sea, refugees arrived from Rangoon and Moulmein by sea at the Indian ports of Calcutta, Chittagong, Coxes Bazaar, and Atyab in Burma. And so, the seaborne refugees were the first to arrive, the British with boxes of possessions and luggage, Indians and others travelling as deck cargo.

According to the official reports, some 67,000 refugees arrived by sea. Others walked out and many perished on the way. The routes they took followed the progress of the war. Many of these refugees were known and associated with British and Indian firms in Calcutta; up to 1935, Burma had been a province of India and there remained strong links with Calcutta businesses. The Bengal food deficits, particularly of rice, were traditionally made up with imports from Burma through Indian merchant firms who made a fortune out of it – timber for pulping for paper-making and structural works provided other business links with Calcutta. Burma Oil also had oilfields and a refinery at Syriam. The Calcutta business firms' communities and charities turned out in force to receive and resettle many of these refugees into their homes.

The Japanese pinned the British down around the Sittang Bridge which was unfortunately blown before a significant part of the 17th Indian Division was able to cross. Boats were commandeered and some managed to cross in them while others swam. Part of the Gurkha battalions within the 48th Gurkha Brigade, as well as the 7/10 Baluch Regiment, could not swim . . . training was later introduced to teach them how to swim. Many soldiers attempting to cross were drowned while others were killed or captured.

The river at this point is around 800 yards wide and a formidable obstacle. From this moment on, the Japanese advance was up the Irrawaddy River and also up the coastal region towards the border at Coxes Bazaar and Chittagong. These southern routes wound westwards over the hills and plains of the Arakan. It is thought that over 200,000 escaped along these routes through the **Taungup Pass** or alternatively over the **An Pass** heading to the island and port of **Atyab** or direct to **Chittagong.** This involved a journey on foot of around 160 to 200 miles as the crow flies. depending on the exit point, and across the hills known as the **Arakan Yomas** with successive ranges up to 3000 ft and thick jungle obstructing the jungle paths. Many died here from exhaustion and disease, particularly the elderly and the women and children, possibly 30-40,000.

Unlike the Assam routes, there were no rest camps or feeding stations, the refugees relying on what they carried or the local villagers for food. Ships went from Atyab to the Indian ports, but then the Japanese arrived and closed Atyab down. It was at this point that part of the 5th and 7th Chinese armies retreated up the rail link to the rail head at **Lashio**, and then up the Burma Road into China; the rest of the Chinese soldiers came out to Assam. General Alexander had by now arrived and taken control of British and Chinese forces retreating back to India. He had been in charge of the Dunkirk retreat after Lord Gort relinquished command on Churchill's instructions, (and to avoid Gort's capture by the Germans). Part of the Chinese 5th Army also marched out into Assam with British forces and refugees.

It is clear from the details above that the movement of the evacuees was progressively moving North as the Japanese advanced up the Irrawaddy River, and that routes to the coastal ports to the North-West were also being progressively cut as the Japanese advanced into the Arakan.

In one sense, the evacuees were now being driven forward ahead of the Japanese advance into Northern Burma. From here, the escape routes reached towards the Assam border, and into Northern India. Thousands of refugees were moving northwards by steamer, road and rail.

A convoy was spotted by an American reporter of an armoured car with police outriders with flashing lights heading North . . . "There goes the Burmese Government," someone remarked; inside was Sir Reginald Dorman-Smith, the Governor, on his way to Mandalay. Tall good-looking and Sandhurst-educated, he was the epitome of the British colonial officer. He was later to write a comprehensive report on the evacuation (on which some of this account has been based), and to set up a government in exile in Simla.

Mandalay was bombed twice; the main raid on the night of 3rd April killed 2000 people and set fire to the town and the fort and wooden houses burned out of control as the fire station had been put out of action. A giant refugee camp had been set up outside the city, where cholera had broken out. The only way out now was to take the rail link **North-West to Yeu** and walk north to **Sittaung**, and then walk the 200 miles or so through the jungle hill ranges up to and along the **Ledo** road to **Imphal**, and then on to the holding camp at **Dinapore** in Assam or to travel up to the railhead at **Myitkyna,** about 230 miles north of **Mandalay**, where there was a road North and an airstrip. Sir Reginald now took advantage of the flights out, travelling up to the railhead there, and flew out to Assam with key members of the Government using Douglas Transports. And so the story now moves further North to the routes taken by the refugees into Assam.

The **air strip at Myitkyna** was serviced by the R.A.F., the U.S. Air Corps, and Chinese National Airways Co; between them, by the beginning of May 1942, they had evacuated 8,616 persons of whom most were civilians, including 2,000 army casualties, 3500 Eurasians and Burmese, 2,200 Indian and 300 British. Some 45,000 refugees were in camps around the town, and they would come to the airstrip when their flight was due.

This all stopped on 6th May when two aircraft were loading. The first had already closed its doors leaving beside the airstrip two girls of the Fuller family who had become separated from their parents . . . there was no real concern since they would catch the next aircraft. At that moment, three Japanese Zero fighter planes appeared and machine-gunned the plane waiting to take off and destroyed the other . . . 35 people were killed and the girls were left orphaned and stranded on the airstrip. They joined up with another family, the Wilbys, and attempted the trek through the notorious **Hukawng Valley,** christened the "valley of death". Mrs Wilby and the two younger girls died early on . . . the eight remaining children struggled on and were last seen in a dying condition somewhere along the road. Mr Wilby walked out thinking that his family were following, only to learn of the terrible fate of his loved ones. This heartrending story is typical of many of the families walking out.

Most of the refugees from Myitkyna now set out across the burning plains of central Burma and the jungle that lay beyond to the town of **Timu** to the west on the Assam border. They had to cross eight hill ranges before getting there and then faced a two-hundred-mile trek to **Dinapore** via **Imphal.** The monsoon was approaching and mist covered the hills with a wide variation of temperature on the chilly hilltops, and sometimes tropical conditions and burning heat in the jungle-covered valleys below.

There were four main routes out to Assam. The first of these, the Southern route, ran from the border town of **Timu to Imphal** and ended at the holding camp at **Dinapore** which has already been mentioned. The Indian Tea Association had gathered teams of labourers led by tea planters to establish camps with shelters, medical facilities and food every few miles along the road. The road itself was being widened to take transport by gangs of labourers supervised by officers of the military and from the Assam frontier government organisation. These road improvement operations were as much to facilitate troop withdrawal as to provide improved facilities for the civilians. Some 200,000 made it out but at least 10% and probably a lot more died on the way. Many of the labourers died and half of the refugees were racked with dysentery. At its peak, the holding camp **Dinapore** catered for 150,000 refugees. Access to this route on the Burmese side of the border was from **Monya** on the Western branch of the railway from **Mandalay,** from **Indaw** on the northern railroad, or from **Myitkyna,** the railhead or even from **Subambrum** to the north.

One of these was Ritchie Gardiner. A timber executive trained in jungle survival and speaking Karen and other local languages, he had escaped from Rangoon after helping with the destruction of key facilities in the port and elsewhere. He was listed as a Captain in the Burma Levies. He had made his way up the 800 miles or so of the Irrawaddy River, keeping ahead of the Japanese, to **Myitkyna** before walking out from **Subambrum** over **the 8500 ft. Chukan Pass** in the middle of the rains through the jungle.

Imphal was to become a major British wartime base storing food, ammunition, transport, and armaments of all types, as well as acting as a base for troop reserves. It was to become the main focus of Japanese attack and British defence in late 1943 and 1944. **Dinapore** was the main railhead, and the refugee camp established here fed the rail link to **Calcutta. Imphal** itself was bombed on 10th May 1942 with a reported 60,000 deaths as a direct or indirect result of the air raid. Shortly afterwards, this road was closed to refugees and the priority was given to retreating troops. Imphal itself was only 100 miles East of Shillong, the capital of Assam.

The refugee exodus then intensified along the **Pangsan and Hukawng Valleys,** the second main Northern evacuation route. It started just the other side of **Timu,** a right turn into what was named the 'valley of death'. It is estimated that around 20,000 refugees attempted this route of which 5,000 died on the way. This route passed through **Naga** country and ended at **Margarita** where a camp was established on the golf course.

The most Northern route out was **over the 15,000-ft Diphu La pass** into Tibet. It had been taken by the well-known explorer, botanist and naturalist, Kingdom Ward. He appears to have started by **entering** Burma via Timu and travelling to Myitkyna with Millar, a tea planter from Assam, but they split up and Kingdom Ward turned North to **Putao.** Ward passed through **Rima** on the Tibet border arriving at Sadiya in Northern Assam after covering nearly 400 miles on foot in two months.

The one route not recommended was that over the **Chaukan Pass**, largely because the 200-mile journey on the other side, through the jungle and along the **Noa Dehing river**, was considered impassable, especially during the monsoon. Ritchie Gardiner, who had been trained in jungle survival, now made his way up the **Irrawaddy** River, with the final 120 miles to **Subambrum** in a battered Ford van with three others.

It was the Chaukan Pass route that was chosen by Ritchie Gardiner's party alongside mixed groups totalling around 250 refugees. These included a group led by Sir John Rowland, Chief Railway Commissioner of Burma. He was 60 years old and the top railway official in the country. He had been offered a place on the plane out but refused it, writing, "I had a seat on a plane which I refused . . . having brought all these women and children to Myitkyna, and as they are forced to walk out, so will I." Two early evacuees, with the help of Mishmi tribesmen, had made it out to safety – Millar, the tea planter mentioned above, and Leyden, Assistant Superintendent of Railways. They brought the news of Sir John's party on its way, and a rescue party was organised to be led by a tea planter and expert in elephant management named Gyles Mackrell.

The story of their escape and rescue reads like an adventure story. Mackrell and 20 elephants set out on 5th June, having loaded up a wide range of stores and food, and headed up the **Noa Dehing** river. A major obstacle was the **Dapha river** flowing North to South into the Noa Dehing. He established a camp on the **Dapha**, and various rescue parties made a whole series of sorties over the river in the next three months and managed to extract and save Ritchie Gardiner and his colleagues as well as the whole of the 200 or so refugees including Sir John. Food was dropped by Dakota airdrop. As part of the rescue, Gardiner was brought out by elephant, fording the swollen rivers. One of the party, a Captain Fraser, was swept away in the river and lodged against a rock. Gardiner, at considerable risk to his own life, entered the river and rescued him. For this action, he was later awarded the George Cross.

Emaciated and starving, he arrived in Assam and was taken to Calcutta. He later became Lieut–Col Gardiner, responsible for the Burma section of Force 136. In the family archive is an annotated copy of his personal diary of the escape across the Chaukan presented to George in 1946. George and Dorks took him into our home at 5 Raja Santosh Road, (then Alipore Road) as part of the programme of recuperation, rehabilitation and support. This is the only copy of the diary known to the author apart from the one in the Imperial War Museum. The dedication of his diary says it all:

DEDICATED

to

GYLES MACKRELL

**In the hope that he will accept it
as a small tribute to the efforts
he made for us all. Without these
efforts there would most probably
have been no diary.**

These sentiments were to be echoed by all the 200 or so Indian, Burmese and European souls Mackrell rescued.

Forgotten Aspects of a forgotten war –
The Calcutta Evacuees Committee

This Committee was initially established as an informal group to organise and coordinate the reception of the refugees, but as the problems intensified, its scope was widened to incorporate sub-committees established on ethnic, religious and cultural lines to handle the growing and diverse number of refugees arriving from Burma and Malaya. These came in by sea largely from Chittagong, but also by train from the dispersal camps in Assam. The largest of these camps was at *Dinapur* next to the railway station, with a rapidly expanding cemetery next to the sidings.

At its peak, the Dinapur camp held 150,000 refugees. It was run by a tea planter, Alexander Beattie, with the HQ being the school building, a bamboo and thatched complex, which housed a hospital and food store. Beattie brought in fresh vegetables and milk from his own and adjoining tea gardens. From here, refugees went by train in rough and crowded goods wagons; there were no lavatories . . . ropes were hung from the outside of the wagons so that passengers could defecate over the side hanging onto the ropes, and as a significant number had dysentery, it must have been a very rough journey to Calcutta.

Vast numbers were provided for. It was a truly remarkable example of inter-faith and inter-community cooperation with everyone working together, regardless of faith or creed, to support the often-desperate needs of the refugees.

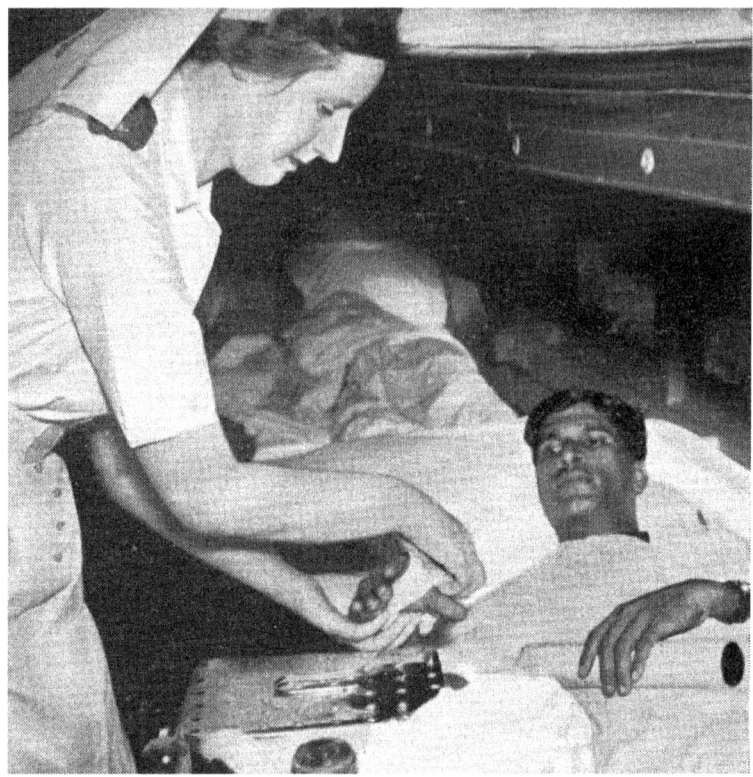

98 *Ambulance trains carrying the sick and wounded – a nurse dressing the wounds of an Indian being evcuated from Burma.*

On arrival at Howrah Station, the refugees filed past a series of trestle tables where members of each welcoming committee recorded their details and made arrangements for them to be housed. George was chairman of the main overarching Calcutta Evacuees Reception Committee. There were sub-committees for Hindus, Muslims, Indian Christians, Europeans and Anglo-Indians which coordinated the work of many associations which helped in the onerous and often expensive tasks that had to be done. The Hindu committee had to deal with the largest numbers and they were helped by the Marwari Society with medical relief, who provided medical help to 200,000 people. The Muslim sub-committee provided for some 113,000 and served about 460,000 meals. Over 14,000 patients were treated by Muslim doctors.

There were a number of camps outside the city, where refugees were fed, clothed and sheltered until they could be found jobs. Six camps were provided by the Indian Christian sub-committee alone. The committees also provided assistance in changing money and help with the Calcutta customs. Many refugees were ex-Burmese government employees, and there was a growing need for their skills in various expanding departments as a result of the war. There were a large number of labourers to cater for an expanding need in the docks and railways to load and trans-ship a rapidly growing quantity of war stores and equipment. At its peak, Howrah Station was handling 15,000 refugees a day. The author can remember piles and piles of wooden boxes on the Maidan next to our house at 5 Alipore Road; there was also an airstrip on the Maidan. It is difficult to put numbers on the evacuation because very little information is available on the largely unknown numbers who died on the way; the reports give the numbers who were recorded as arrivals but not those who left. Many slipped over the porous border and were not recorded.

Sir Reginald Dorman-Smith's very comprehensive report on the "Burma Campaign 1941-2", finalised in 1943 and initially published as a secret document (Appendix V of the report covers the civil evacuation), and Major General E Wood's report as Administrator General of Eastern Frontier, "Report of Refugees from Burma to India (Assam)", both attempt to quantify this. Paragraphs 34 & 35 of General Wood's report quote figures for the Assam arrivals;

Through Dinapur	150,533
Through Silchar	40,150
Through Ledo & Dinjan	27,772
Total	218,455

To this must be added the numbers evacuating by sea of 67,000 and those going on the Southern routes through the Arakan, possibly another 160/170,000 (although no formal statistics seem to be available). General Wood estimates 4,268 deaths amongst those going through the Northern routes but another source estimates 5000 deaths in the Hukawng Valley alone, quite apart from the other Assam routes. One source puts the total number of deaths en route at 80,000. Sir Reginald quotes the total numbers of evacuees at 364,000, but when a figure of deaths on the way is added, then the numbers are probably somewhere between 400-450,000. Most of the survivors transited through Calcutta. A majority of the deaths occurred through dysentery, malaria or both, and exhaustion. Many more died in the cholera outbreaks at Prome and Mandalay, and others along the Chindwin between Monya and Kalewa. About 800 died at the transit camp at Dinapur and many more at the golf course camp at Margarita.

General Wood's report (paragraph 12) also gives an account of the resource objectives provided to the Assam evacuees, of which 70% was achieved, mostly by the Indian Tea Association volunteers.

200 elephants
750 pack mules
1,000 pack ponies
6,000 porters

The European and Anglo-Indian sub-committee arranged accommodation in private houses, schools and the Salvation Army hostels, and later set up a special 500-capacity hostel . . . over 9,000 refugees passed through this hostel.

Of those arriving in Calcutta, 226,655 were from South India and were sent home on the Bengal – Nagpur railway with medical staff provided at Howrah Station by the Marwari Association.

Altogether this harrowing story is largely untold, and tribute must be paid to the many untold heroes who helped in the evacuation, above all, it is a tribute to a multi-ethnic and multi-faith cooperative effort by the various committees and voluntary organisations involved.

Sir Reginald pays generous tribute to the members of the Indian Tea Association and "the gentlemen of Calcutta."

Rumer Godden, the author, was commissioned to write a pamphlet about the work of the Women's Voluntary Service; this she developed into an extensive book called Bengal Journey, published in 1945. In it, she describes the events of 1942 and the role played by the women of India throughout the events of the world war from 1939 to 1945. She gives an account of their work carried out in twenty-two of the principal centres of Bengal . . . hence the title . . . as she travels from Kalimpong through Darjeeling around Bengal ending up in Cox's Bazaar. She devotes several pages to the events of 1942 and writes in moving and graphic detail about the plight of the refugees and retreating soldiers and wounded. I quote . . .

"1942 . . . was a terrible year for India. In February Singapore fell; on the shock of that came the retreat from Burma, with the exhausted men struggling back; before them, with them and after them, came the refugees, by steamer, by train, by air, on foot; wounded, sick, dying, lost, insane. They overwhelmed hospitals, camps, private houses; choked the trains, lay on the railway platforms, were lost in the jungle or in hostile border villages. Once more human endurance told its story. An Anglo-Burman soldier came in on the train from Assam, a train that had picked him up on a wayside platform; he walked on a crutch made of a cleft-headed branch. His left leg was swollen four times its size to a column of stretched flesh and gangrene; he had been shot, outside Monia, in four places in the leg and cut himself a crutch and walked out of Burma with it, begging petrol from the lorries to wash out his wounds; he lived and did not lose his leg. Five others, Yorkshiremen, had been nailed by their hands to a roadblock, so that Allied troops, coming up and seeing them standing at the barricades, would walk into an ambush; these five tore themselves free and also walked out, but they left most of their hands behind them. With the soldiers came the civilians, equally pitiable, and many of them were children. A boy of seven was found by missionaries, walking back to Burma. They tell how they brought him back with them and, passing a spot where dead bodies lay, he pointed out to them a man and a woman whom they took to be his parents; he could not tell them, nor what his name was, because his powers of speech and hearing had left him through shock. He is in a home in Calcutta, cared for by a woman's organisation and they hope that one day he will speak again. An Indian doctor, his wife and seven children and a maidservant started trekking from Minbu. The mother died first; then, one by one, six of the children, and finally the father. Before he died, he strapped his

documents and remaining jewellery to the remaining child, a little girl, tying them round her waist and thighs. The servant stole the jewellery, mutilating the child, and then left her alone at a Rest Camp and disappeared.

Ambulance Sisters of the St. John Nursing Division were to the fore in undertaking the terrible resulting work. They met trains, ships, planes; in Chittagong under the leadership of the Commissioners wife, who was also a St John Sister, the club was turned into an evacuees' hostel and she worked there with the remaining women of the station and the Sisters of the Holy Cross until an order came ordering all women to leave; she and the Mother Superior were the last to go and only left after the last refugees had gone . . .

Firms, Banks and families had sent their valuables away; as many children as possible had been sent out of the area; now at first sight of the returning troops, and of the refugees, panic had set in in Calcutta and there was a wild rush among many of the Indian community to get away. Women, with their houses full of refugees, themselves nursing, or driving, or working in other ways, found themselves servantless, with the food shops closed. Many lived four or five miles from the food markets – which on any day might, or might not open, and there was no extra petrol for cars. (Query Bicycles? Answer . . . Of course they used bicycles but have you ever bicycled eight miles daily in a temperature of 110 F?)"

Dorks had obtained her two St John's Nursing Certificates and also her commercial driving licence, (both of which have survived in the family archive) enabling her to drive ambulances and canteens . . . the author can remember as a small boy going with her. Rumer Godden continues by describing the famine which set in, in the autumn of 1942.

"The ordinary woman had perhaps been so busy that the veiled newspaper warnings of famine had not penetrated to her; but perhaps that was natural when the authorities kept repeating "there is plenty of rice". Perhaps there was plenty of rice, but in that case, who, women were beginning to ask, who were these people flocking into the towns and the city? Men and women and unclothed children, all with scarecrow legs and arms and ribs, and strange sunk eyes and swollen stomachs?

Why did they settle in swarms on the pavements, round the rubbish bins, sleeping there through the nights, covering

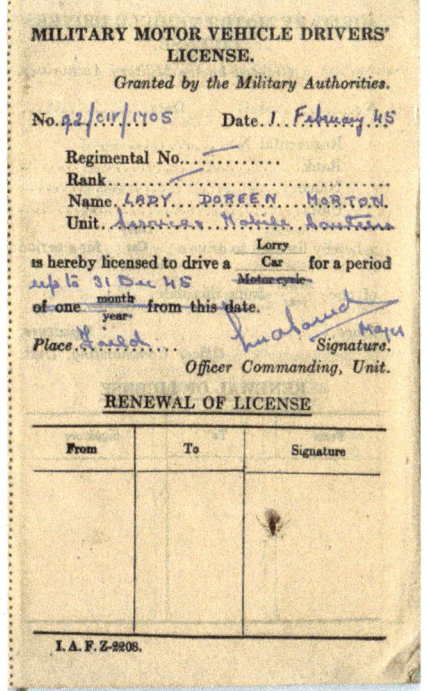

99 *Doreen' commercial driving licence*

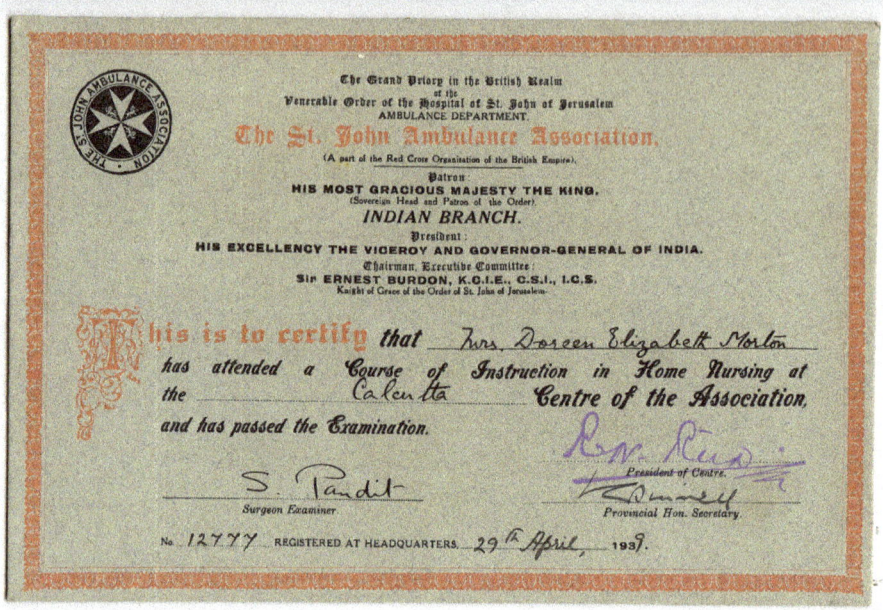

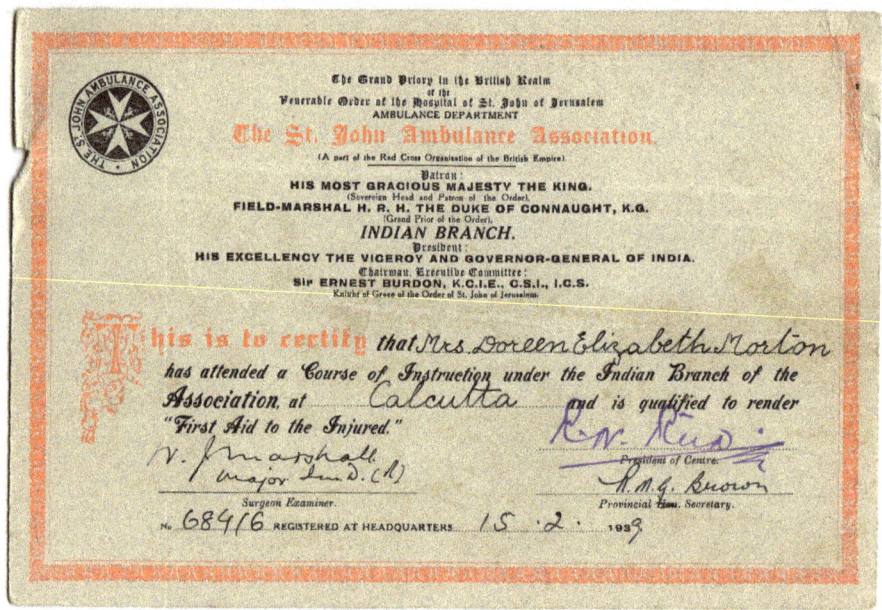

100 *Doreen's St John's ambulance certificates – home nursing and first aid, issued in Calcutta*

the streets with filth and cess? Why did no one come to move them away? Why rather did more come every day? Why did children die with that word on their lips – Rice: rice: rice?

By August the situation was quite out of hand. The destitute dead lay in the streets, newcomers were stoned off the food queues, brothels flourished as never before in the cities and towns, mothers abandoned their children, sold them; cholera, smallpox, measles appeared in epidemic form.

It was more utterly bewildering than anything that had gone before. No one could discover the truth or the remedy, and what could the women do? Some did nothing, but voluntary effort was magnificent. Hundreds of food kitchens opened at private expense; the Red Cross donated milk, stores, hospital supplies, blankets, clothes; the Salvation army sent their workers through the city and out into the districts with relief; the A.R.P. offered their help; women served in food kitchens, First Aid Posts, in hospitals; the Sisterhoods and Missions did endless, selfless work. All the time there were other women, women who were doing important war work, who simply had to continue doing it, through the heartbreak of misery and suffering and lies and shifts and blame-throwing. There was still that other, greater danger, that could, even under circumstances like these, not be forgotten. The war was close. The work went on."

It is perhaps worth quoting further descriptions from the Bengal Journey, the account of the refugee arrivals by train and by sea. She describes the work of *Mrs X* in a chapter entitled the *Eight-Pointed Star*, the emblem of the St John Ambulance Brigade.

"Call her Mrs X. Her name does not matter because she works in the anonymity of the St John Ambulance Brigade, that is, in its own words, "The Ambulance Department of the Grand Priory, in the British Realm, of the Venerable Order of the Hospital of St. John of Jerusalem, which Hospital was founded in the time of the Crusades of the Knight Hospitallers."

There then follows a description of her training, of going through two courses of lectures, a month's training at the Presidency General Hospital, a month in Operations in the P.G.H. followed by a fortnight in an Indian hospital. This must have been similar to the training that Dorks had, the only difference being that the accommodation between the two wings of the P.G.H., as it was then known, had been her home when her father Col Frederick O'Kinealy IMS CVO CIE was Surgeon Superintendent of the P.G.H. from 1912 to 1920.

"In January 1942 came her first real experience of war, when the first evacuees from Burma, 100 patients on a hospital train, were met at Howrah Station in transit by S.J.A.B Ambulance Sisters. Then everything began to happen at once"

She continues . . .

"Then began the vast and arduous work, the most heartrending of the war for the Nursing Divisions, the arrival of the Burma evacuees. Train after train came in. Patients were laid out in rows on the platform; some had emergency dressings; some theatre marks of

101 *Doreen's St John's ambulance members record book and the award of her nursing medallion; her records include working in the British Military Hospital, passing all examinations, and meeting evacuee ships from Burma in 1942*

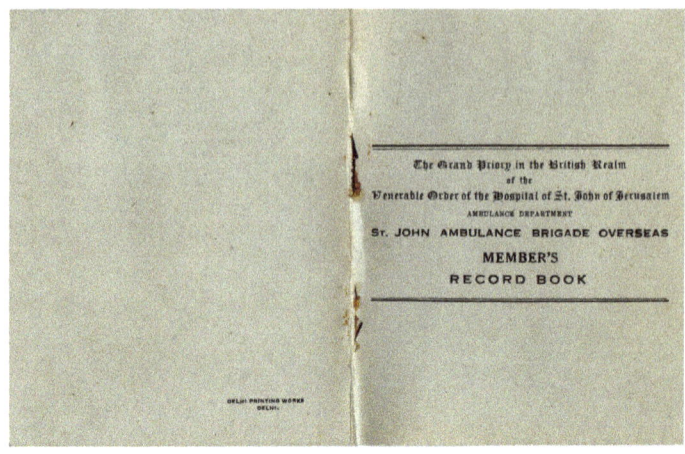

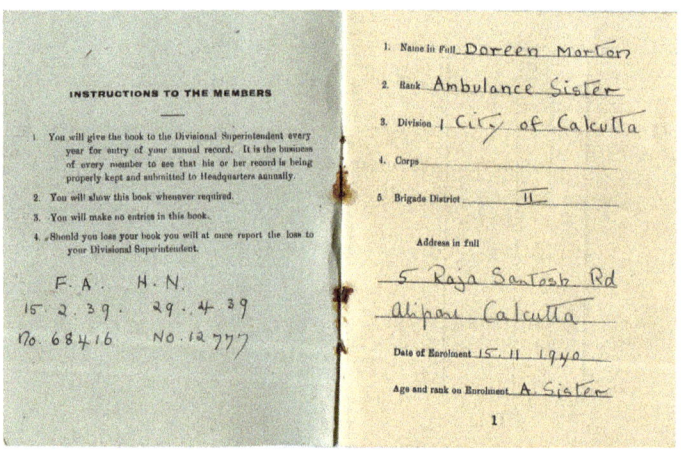

operations; some had not been attended to at all; there was gangrene, enormous poisonous swellings from bamboo splinters, limbs roughly amputated, hack knife wounds, shrapnel wounds with mortifying flesh; the septic smell was ghastly; there was disease, cholera, malaria, dysentery; there were deaths from exhaustion; Mrs X was glad now that she had worked in a free hospital. Members of the B.&A. (Bengal and Assam Railways – JMM) *Rly division helped to deliver babies on railway platforms.*

"After meeting trains all night, lying down in the waiting-room between trains, we used to rush home for a change of clothes as we were soaked in sweat and blood; then we would come on again for our shift in the day," said their Lady Divisional Superintendent.

Early in February Mrs X was one of the Ambulance Sisters who were asked to stay on call for the meeting of evacuee ships. When the calls came, they had to get themselves to the docks as there was no transport. Mrs X herself went in her small car to Headquarters for First Aid bags, one for each Sister, for stretchers and stores. They were first on board each time after the police. There might be three or four ships a day. This went on until the 6ᵗʰ of May when the last ship came in.

The heat on the docks, the heat in the ships was unbelievable. The evacuees had to be herded between decks for the voyage, and to go down among them was like facing an inferno of panic and pain and fear and noise and smell. On one hot evening, when Mrs X and two Ambulance Sisters had been on duty since 4 p.m., the ship came alongside the berth at 8.30 p.m. but lay just off, too far for food even to be thrown to the people who crowded the rail. The heat that night was overpowering and many of the evacuees died of heatstroke. The crowd on the dock, thinking that the Sisters were officials, began to be hostile and threaten them, but they stayed there until 9.45 p.m. when the ship finally berthed. "We were glad we stayed," said Mrs X. "There were 1800 evacuees on board, mostly in a very exhausted state, and ten stretcher cases, one of whom died before we could get him into the Ambulance". That night, the Sisters came off duty at 11 p.m., but Mrs X took a cholera case to the hospital in her car. She finally left the hospital at midnight."

Dorks, now Lady Morton, as a St John's Ambulance Sister and driver, was involved in all of this work; driving ambulances, working in the British Army Hospital and meeting the refugee ships in the fierce and damp heat of the Calcutta summer – she was to obtain her medallion in recognition of this work in 1944. Ritchie Gardiner, one of the refugees who crossed from Burma into Assam via the 8,500 Chaukan Pass, stayed at our home in 5 Alipore Road on arrival in Calcutta to recuperate and there may have been others as well. He later joined Force 136 as head of the Burma 'behind the lines' operation, an account of which follows.

Forgotten activities of a forgotten war; Ritchie Gardiner and S.O.E activities behind the lines; Force 136

Force 136 was established as a 'behind the lines' operation to support Allied operations in the Far East. The earlier units were formed in Malaysia as "stay-behind" groups in 1942. Because of George and Dorks' work with the refugees from the Japanese and in light of the family friendship that developed with Ritchie Gardiner, an account of these operations in Burma has been included; this again is a little-charted part of the war.

Force 136 was a part of the Special Operations Executive. Formed early in the European war, S.O.E., as it became known, was formally set up by the Cabinet on 22nd July 1940 "to coordinate all action, by way of subversion and sabotage, against the enemy". Highly trained executive military officers, both men and women operatives, were dropped behind enemy lines to coordinate local militias, and initiate specific operations to disrupt enemy infrastructure, personnel and installations. Early examples included the destruction of the Norsk Hydro heavy water plant at Rjukan in Norway, the kidnapping of General Kreipe on Crete, and the assassination of Reinhard Heydrich in Prague. All three operations were celebrated in successful films after the war. Churchill took a keen interest in their formation and personally received regular reports of their operations.

A Far Eastern example of an S.O.E member is Spencer Chapman, the author of many books and a noted explorer and mountaineer. He was a part of an expedition to Greenland while at Cambridge University, later spending a winter amongst the Innuit there. During this time, he completed a notorious feat, a combined climb of 30,000 ft of several mountains and a walk of 70 miles which he completed in 25 hours. He also completed an unsupported crossing of the Greenland icecap, losing some of his finger and toenails in the process. During a climbing expedition to the Himalayas, he met the British representative, Basil Gould, a member of the Gangtok Mission in Sikkim, and was invited to join the 1936/7 diplomatic mission to Lhasa in Tibet later in the year as secretary. He observed on the way a possible route to the summit of the holy mountain Chomolhari between Phari and Gyantse, located on the Bhutanese border. As children, we could see this peak peeping above the Kalimpong hill to the North-East. He achieved the first ascent of this 24,035 ft mountain from the Thimpu district of Bhutan in 1937, accompanied by a single porter. While a schoolmaster at Gordonstoun in 1937, he wrote an account of the mission called "Lhasa: The Holy City" full of descriptions of Tibet; he also taught Prince Philip, then a teenager in the school.

He was commissioned into the Seaforth Highlanders at the outset of war in 1939 and then selected to train New Zealand and Australian forces in guerrilla warfare. He trained in jungle warfare at Kandy in Ceylon (alongside Brigadier "Mad Mitch" Mitchell of Chindit fame) and then spent three years operating behind the lines in Malaysia. At one stage, he escaped capture by the Japanese in his bare feet surviving in the jungle for a fortnight before joining up again with the Chinese guerrillas. He was reinforced in late 1943 by two Force 136 operators and was eventually extracted in early 1945 by submarine. After debriefing in Kandy, he came up to Kalimpong to recuperate staying with Bunty and Norman Odling at Glenrilly, next door to our childhood home, Charitung, in their grounds; this was just before we left Kalimpong and India after the end of the European war in May 1945. He later wrote his classic "The Jungle is Neutral" about his wartime experiences.

As early as 1941, Karens from the North of Burma and Shans from the North-East had been formed into militias, and then instructed to hide their arms and await the initiative of the British as the Japanese invaded. The Shan tribes negotiated a settlement with the Japanese, agreeing to support their political initiatives in return for being left alone. The Karens were always under suspicion for their British sympathies – many were Christians, as incidentally were the Naga head-hunters. Within S.O.E.'s "Oriental mission", a Major Hugh Seagrim had volunteered to remain behind and was hidden by the Karens. An attempt was made to contact him in 1943 by two officers, Major Nimmo, and Captain McCrindle, dropped by parachute near Toungoo. Both Nimmo and McCrindle were captured and executed; Seagrim escaped but later surrendered to prevent reprisals against the Karens, and was also executed. McCrindle was a former colleague of Gardiner's and a part of the "commando" group that had escaped over the Chaukan pass. Hugh Seagram was an officer in the Kumaon Rifles and an account of his bravery, for which he was awarded a posthumous George Medal, is given in an appendix of the History of the regiment, published in 1988. My late father-in-law, Lt. Col. Robert Lawder, also served in the same regiment and knew him; it was he who insisted that an account of his award and the citation for it was given in the History. A copy of this is in the British Army Museum, just off Sloane Square in London.

S.O.E. Operations were to expand significantly in Europe over the D-Day landings. Over a hundred units were dropped by parachute in support of Free French resistance operations to coordinate the disruption of German Army movements, cutting railway lines and communications, liaising with the Maquis in ambushing troop movements and destroying installations. Each unit had its own radio operator to report progress and call in supplies of arms and explosives which were dropped by parachute at night. The units consisted of at least three operatives; a leader, a French-speaking liaison officer and a radio operator, often supported by one or two others. Units were generally code-named with male Christian names. These units were known as the Jedburghs, or "Jeds" for short. One of their key tasks was to train irregular local units in the use of firearms, tactics and explosives. One of these units, code-named Basil, was led by a Captain Carew and was dropped into Granges-Maillot in the Bensançon district in Eastern France on 26th August 1944.

Tom Carew was born in Dublin in 1919, the product of a roll in the hay between a lady member of the British/Irish aristocracy and her groom. Shortly after the outbreak of war, he was selected to join S.O.E. and went through and passed the selection and rigorous training process. He was an eccentric capable of thinking "outside the box" in the pursuit of objectives. Part of the job was to be able to handle difficult political situations and rivalry between the irregular forces, who often had their own long-term objectives, and in this, he excelled.

After several delays, Carew, Raincourt, and John Stoyka had boarded the Liberator which lumbered into the air bound for eastern France. After five hours in the air and several circles around the drop zone, they parachuted from 600 ft and landed, together with several containers of arms, explosives and munitions. The reception party collected everything, and they moved off to the rendezvous with the Maquis. Within a few days, they were planning an ambush.

The ambush was mounted on a German group of soldiers with the bulk killed and eleven prisoners taken. The Germans threatened reprisals but a meeting with the Germans resulted in the retention of the prisoners and the supplies, and no reprisals. Two days later, two battalions of Cossacks, used as forced labour by the Germans, joined the Maquis.

He reports," *3-4,000 ready in 6 days, 1,000 men already instructed, but less than 300 armed"*, requesting an arms drop. Two days later, a massive drop of sixty containers provided for the arming of hundreds of the Maquis. Meanwhile, thousands of Allied forces landed on the south coast and began to fight their way north against little resistance. Further operations were mounted to cut railway lines and communications and disrupt and delay the German retreat.

There then arrived a message for Carew to travel north and to make contact and liaise with another S.O.E. officer, George Millar.

George Millar was born at Baldernock, Stirling, the son of Thomas Millar, a self-made architect & builder. He studied architecture at Cambridge and later became a journalist. He was working for the Daily Express in Paris when war broke out but managed to get back to the UK before also joining the Seaforth Highlanders and being commissioned in the Rifle Brigade. He was captured in North Africa and interned by the Italians at the notorious high security Campo 5. After the surrender of the Italians, he was on his way to internment in Germany, when he jumped the train and escaped. He arrived in Munich and made his way to Strasburg. He continued to Paris and then Lyon where he made contact with the Resistance. After three months on the run, he eventually crossed the Pyrenees to Barcelona in Dec 1943, before being shipped back to England. He was awarded the M.C. for his escape, and. joined the S.O.E. shortly afterwards.

He was a cousin of George's through his mother, May Millar, the sister of Fergus Morton. George Millar was later also dropped in the Besançon district just before D-Day to help organise operations – trains were derailed, the Germans attacked in Besançon, and the mayhem created by the Maquis continued. The whole area was stiff with retreating Germans, but after several escapes and actions against German forces and installations and the liberation of the area, Tom Carew was ordered out. There was a hairy moment when the Jeds were caught between the American troops and the Germans, but after the area was cleared and liberated, George Millar and the Jeds left. Tom Carew drove to Paris in a shiny new car with Stoyka, and as his daughter and

102 *The Mobile Canteen service, visiting amongst others the troops in Barrackpore*

biographer Keggie Carew has it, with "the taste of the farewell still on their lips". He handed over the keys of the car to a Parisian fruit seller and arrived back in London. If it wasn't all true, you couldn't possibly invent it!

Tom Carew barely had time to unpack and get married before he was off again to join the clandestine operation Force 136 in the Far East. After a five-week trip out by sea around the Cape, arriving in Bombay, they were flown to Kandy (in Sri-Lanka), the HQ of the Force in the middle of a coconut and rubber plantation.

His team, code-named Camel, was now scheduled to be the first team to be dropped into the North-Western corner of the Arakan in Japanese-occupied Burma during the next moon phase. His immediate boss was the now Lieut-Colonel Ritchie Gardiner, who was in charge of the Burma section. Colonel Mackenzie, a one-legged veteran of the First World War, was the overall commander of Force 136. Originally, the Force was directly responsible (as in England) to the political arm of Government in the person of the Viceroy, Lord Linlithgow, but on the appointment of Mountbatten as Supreme Commander South East Asia Command (S.E.A.C), responsibility was transferred to him. After the bitter fighting in the defence of Kohima and Imphal, the tide of the war turned and General Slim's 14th army were now advancing into Burma as 1944 progressed.

Preparatory work had already been done for the drop. The initial overtures to local militias had been made as early as 1943. Before the war, the Burmese national movement had gathered force mirroring the independence movement in India. A group of Thakins, a highly politicised group of students, had got together to agitate for independence. The British dubbed them an illegal organisation in 1940, and soon they fled to China with their leader, Aung San. They allied themselves with the Japanese who promised them independence, and around 30 of them returned with the initial Japanese assault on Rangoon to recruit – 10,000 locals joined up within days to fight alongside the Japanese against the British, but they soon found the Japanese far from pleasant invaders. Aung San kept up the appearance of support for the new Japanese administration, with its pretence of independence and brutality from beheadings and torture. Initially called the Burmese Independence Army, it was renamed the Burmese National Army.

Force136 had been anxious for intelligence about the resistance as the Japanese advanced throughout Burma, and eventually, two Thakins managed to escape to Calcutta where they were put in touch with Force 136 representatives. After some time persuading the British that they were not traitors, they received training and code names and were given the mission to make contact with the now anti-Japanese Burmese National Army led by Aung San. Two months later, one of the original Thakins, Tin Shwe, brought back to Calcutta the Arakanese political leader Nyo Tun.

Nyo Tun now became the senior Burmese member of Carew's group, called "Camel" and was code-named Galahad. He was vitally important to the British through his contacts. A deception plan was devised to cover him and a strong rumour put about that he was dead. A separate local group had been formed – "The Arakan Defence Force" or ADF. The plan was to convert this small army, now 3,000 strong, into a guerrilla force, in support of the Allies. Some members had already been smuggled into India for training and arms and explosives were dropped by air. The pattern of Jedburgh operations in France was adapted to the Burma situation, and the Camel team was selected to be Tom Carew (now Major), John Cox his no 2, and John Sharp radio operator, plus Nyo Tun (alias Hla Maung) and four Arakanese described as "other ranks". Their job was to prepare the ADF and train them for guerrilla operations – an arms drop was planned for January.

Political complications existed between the operations of Force 136 and the ousted Government of Burma with its former Governor, Sir Reginald Dorman-Smith, now resident in Simla, who had formed a government in exile, waiting for the completion of war and their return to Burma. They had long experience of the independence movement and regarded Aung San and Nyo Tun as traitors and subject to trial and the death penalty for treason. They had set up a military wing to their administration, the Civil Affairs Service (Burma) or CAS(B). Often acting in direct opposition to the Jedburgh operations, they made life increasingly difficult for Force 136 as the advance into Burma progressed. At one stage they interfered and nearly completed the failure and cessation of essential operations, which required the intervention of Mountbatten to resolve. Both the Government-in-waiting of Dorman-Smith, and the guerrillas, wanted the defeat of the Japanese but for diametrically opposite reasons. The British wanted their Colony back, but the guerrillas wanted their country back without the British. So, it became a marriage of uneasy convenience which finished as soon as the war ended.

The Dakota with the eight members of the Camel team arrived over the drop zone. It was dangerous flying over unmapped mountain terrain with no radar, altimeters or weather avoidance radar. They all got down safely and the Burmese reception group, code-named Hound, collected the packages and they set off for a hideout two miles away through the bamboo forest. A decision was taken to split up. Carew moved off with Nyo Tun to meet the leader of the ADF some 40 miles distant, while the remainder of the party moved off into the hills to set up camp. Under their leaders, orders were issued for the ADF to rise up. Camel radioed the position of Japanese troops and 30 Thunderbolt fighters strafed and bombed a Japanese battalion as they crossed the Kaladan river. At this show of strength, recruits started to arrive. A large night-drop of arms, ammunition and explosives followed. That night they sabotaged two boatloads of Japanese troops and Camel's guerrilla army began to take shape.

By January 1st there were sixty men under arms, by the 5th a hundred and fifty. On 8th January the key island of Akyab was back in British hands and a landing strip was prepared. Soon the guerrilla army was numbered in hundreds as they were trained in small arms and handling explosives. Drops of equipment continued and again the group split into individual groups, with coordinated attacks. A confrontation occurred with the CAS(B) working with a West African Division who started shooting the guerrillas, and Carew hot-footed it to the front line and heated exchanges ensued. An amnesty was negotiated whereby Carew agreed to keep his guerrillas under control while CAS(B) agreed not to interfere. The XV Corps commander, General Christison, agreed the proposal which involved the Guerrillas returning all arms at the conclusion of hostilities. Eventually, this row escalated to Mountbatten, the Supreme Commander, and instructions were issued to General Leese not to interfere. Once the Arakan had been cleared, the Burmese guerrillas not only returned the agreed arms but also a second stack of the same amount indicating their strength.

Carew was flown back to Ceylon to report. The initial operation had been an outstanding success, with over 4,000 Japanese killed and a further 248 prisoners taken with Camel casualties astonishingly numbering only one man. The success is attributed to "the personal courage, coolness and resourcefulness of Major Carew" and he is recommended for the DSO.

Plans were now developed for the next stage of the operation. Intelligence had come in that Aung San, the leader of the Burmese National Army, was planning to turn his Army against the Japanese. To facilitate this, Carew and his team were appointed "controlling Jed", with the code name Weasel. The Japanese armies were now being pushed back both in the North and in the South. The Akyab airstrip now came into its own, flying in supplies, and by the time the army had moved into central Burma, the pilots were flying in five sorties a day. Again, a row broke out with General Sir Oliver Leese C-I-C land forces SE Asia, who banned the issue of weapons to the AFO overturning previous agreements. The case was taken up by Ritchie Gardiner and Col Mackenzie and again reached the desk of Mountbatten who countermands Leese's instructions. The language between Mackenzie and Leese turned blue and Leese was formally instructed not to interfere with the proposed operations of Weasel. Mandalay was now taken after bitter fighting in March. After further political manoeuvrings by the guerrillas, it was agreed that the rising up of the National Army was to be set to begin at the end of March regardless of Allied strategy.

The uprising became nationwide and there was much political concern about the now armed BNA, but the Jed units took the view that there was a war to be won. Aung San's soldiers now fanned out into the jungle and Carew coordinated their activities with their leaders. Amongst other actions, he personally led an operation to rescue a Jed officer from a group of rebel Indian National Liberation Army soldiers.

There was now a race to take Rangoon before the rains set in. The guerrillas assisted in essential operations to delay the Japanese retreat and Rangoon fell on 1st May 1945. But it was not over yet. Large groups of Japanese were trying to retreat to the Siam border. The mopping up continued with the guerrillas now playing an important role in rounding up the Japanese. Towards the end of operations, Aung San was invited to meet General Slim and promised safe conduct but he was immediately imprisoned. Carew went and saw Mountbatten to obtain his release. The situation was eventually resolved at a meeting between Mountbatten and the two guerrilla leaders, Aung San and Than Tun, and temporary peace ensued. But civil war was subsequently to break out, as a prelude to Burmese independence, and Aung San was assassinated.

As a foot-note, Aung San's wife gave birth to a baby daughter on 19th June 1945 who they named Suu Kyi – she became a distinguished pianist and, after years of house arrest, became the President of Burma, although at the time of writing, is under arrest again.

The "Quit India" Movement 1942-Gandhi and Congress leaders interned and India erupts

Elections to the new India State Legislative Assemblies were held in 1937 and despite the official rejection of the 1935 Government of India Act by the Indian National Congress party, many members took part and were elected. By and large, the new assemblies were a success, with the wider franchise resulting in an improvement of Government. Muslims, on the whole, had not done well and consequently, there was a polarisation of the minority Muslim population towards Muhammad Jinnah's Muslim League. This split was to deepen and lead eventually to the partition of India.

Meanwhile, the European war had started, and in late 1940 and 1941, Indian troops were increasingly involved against the Italian troops occupying Abyssinia, Somalia, Libya and North Africa. The Cambridge-educated Netaji Subhas Chandra Bose was a rising figure in the Congress party; as chairman in 1939, he saw the Munich crisis as the opportunity to put pressure on a weakened Britain for a commitment to Indian independence. In late 1940, Gandhi launched his new satyagraha but despite this, thousands joined up to fight. Many Indians in support of satyagraha were imprisoned but were released in December 1941.

However, the pressure on the British government increased, despite Churchill's objection to any commitment to the Indian nationalists, as the Japanese invaded Burma and raced towards the Indian border. Churchill was at last persuaded to offer independence in return for support for the war, and in March 1942, Sir Stafford Cripps was despatched to India to negotiate a settlement. Cripps was deeply sympathetic towards India and was a vegetarian like Gandhi; he seemed the right man to bring together the differing views of Indians in the fight against fascism in exchange for independence. Churchill was also under pressure from the anti-colonialist sentiments of the Americans, and especially Roosevelt. In a famous exchange about the Indians, Churchill was to say, "We have millions of Indians prospering under British rule, but you seem to have got rid of most of yours".

Cripps arrived by air on 22nd March with the British proposal to grant India immediate independence after the war and the freedom to draw up their own constitution in exchange for commitment to the war effort. The day after his arrival, the Japanese attacked and took the Andaman Islands. Then, on April 5th, five Japanese aircraft carriers arrived off the coast of Ceylon and sank the heavy cruisers *Dorsetshire* and *Cornwall* and the next day sank the carrier *Hermes*.

But Cripps found that he could not make any headway with the British proposals. On April 9th Cripps and Congress negotiators managed to cobble together some sort of deal which involved circumstances whereby native ministers could take office as part of the Viceroy's council, only for the deal the next day to be repudiated. Gandhi was reportedly behind this rejection describing the deal as *"a post-dated cheque on a failing bank."* On 12th April Cripps left India, his relationships with his Congress friends in tatters. Churchill was neither surprised nor disappointed.

Gandhi, however, dreamed up an alternative plan, which involved forcing the British to leave India. Gandhi had convinced himself that the Japanese would never wish to take over India so he made a concession to allow British forces to remain in India during hostilities. But Churchill would now never agree. On 7th August Congress agreed to Gandhi's proposals and sought a meeting with the Viceroy before they launched their "Quit India" plan. This was refused and Viscount Linlithgow decided to act.

Tom Benthall, who had now returned to India as a member of the Viceroy's council, made a revealing comment about the late-night meeting at which the internment of Gandhi and the other Congress leaders was discussed and agreed. *"In 1942, I was the sole British member of the Viceroy's Council, except for Lord Linlithgow himself when the formal decision was made, late at night, to arrest Gandhi and the rest of the Congress leaders."*

The police moved quickly and Gandhi, Nehru and the rest of the Congress leaders were arrested the following morning, awakened from their beds at 4.00 a.m. They were interned in some comfort at the Aga Khan's summer palace at Poona, which was surrounded with barbed wire, and guarded by soldiers with machine guns. Gandhi, his wife Kasturba, Murabehn his *chuli* (= disciple – follower – JMM), and his secretary were all accommodated in comfort at the palace, but Gandhi was shocked, literally, into silence – he spoke to no-one for six days. India erupted at the news of the internment with *hartals* (= strikes – JMM) and riots in Delhi and most of the other major cities. Over 200 police stations were sacked, but there were no civilian casualties although two Canadian pilots were murdered. Linlithgow reported to Churchill at the end of August that the mood was ugly and that he feared a second mutiny, but the army remained loyal. The protests subsided within six weeks, and India was back to normality towards the end of September but obviously within wartime conditions.

Gandhi's rejoinder to his confinement was to make various direct and indirect approaches to Linlithgow, all of which received barely an acknowledgement from a secretary. He was desperate to open a dialogue, but none was forthcoming unless he abandoned his Quit India plans.

Two further events affected Gandhi profoundly – the first of these was the sudden death of his secretary, Mahadev Desai, who had been arrested with Gandhi and the others. Six days after the arrests, he had died; he was Gandhi's right-hand man and the calming influence on him. Worrying stories now emerged of the maltreatment of prisoners after wide-scale arrests for violence. In sympathy, a well-known detainee, Professor Bhansali, launched a hunger strike in protest against the beatings at Chimur prison. Gandhi's request to visit him was refused by Linlithgow unless he abandoned his Quit India protest.

On New Year's Eve, Gandhi announced to Linlithgow that he was going to start a 21-day fast in protest; in the past, these hunger strikes had resulted in his release, but not this time. Tom Benthall's comments are interesting – *"Gandhi decided to fast unto death."* (In fact, the fast was limited to 21 days but, nevertheless, dangerous; Gandhi was not in the best of health with a weak heart and high blood pressure – JMM) *"His daily weight was recorded in all the newspapers and was watched with breathless interest by the whole Hindu population and indeed by the world. To none was his slow loss of weight more interesting than to me, who had weighed him personally more than ten years before, which perhaps made his gesture slightly less alarming to me than to others. He was not, I think, in any real danger and Lord Linlithgow had made a particular study of such fasting, but it was an anxious time, when even the most westernised Hindu friends were moved to a pitch of emotion."* Gandhi, after all, was the *"Mahatma"* ("the holy one" – JMM) revered as a living saint by Hindus, an accolade perhaps not fully appreciated certainly by Churchill and others of the British Government. Surviving on water, his kidneys began to fail after thirteen days, and it seems generally recognised that his sustenance of *nimbu pani* (water flavoured with limes – JMM) was dosed with glucose by his British and Indian doctors. Now weak with a loss of 20 lbs in weight, his fast ended on the 21st day with a drink of orange juice, and the whole world breathed a sigh of relief.

Nevertheless, the failure of the Cripps mission with its offer of independence, and the launch of the Quit India campaign, made the issue of Indian Independence almost inevitable after the Far Eastern war. Perhaps the steadying influence of leaders like Tom Benthall and others such as George, with respect for the highest standards of ethical business dealings, meant that the British business interests were treated well and fairly for the next 17 years or so after independence. The end of the Raj was now almost inevitable but the war had to be won first.

The Bengal Famine of 1943

In mid-October 1942, a massive cyclone, which had been brewing in the Bay of Bengal, struck the coast of Orissa destroying a large proportion of the autumn rice crop. These cyclones are a feature of the weather patterns of the Bay of Bengal creating periodic wide-spread destruction of lives, housing, animals and crops upon which the farming populations of the then East and West Bengal depended.

Further North, the confluence of the majestic Brahmaputra and Ganges rivers created a twelve-mile-wide river which descended into the main rice-growing areas of the delta of Orissa around Calcutta and Chittagong, before exiting into the sea. Both rivers provided the necessary waters for local crops of rice, as did other rivers, gathering waters from the monsoon and meltwaters from the Himalayas, such as the Teesta River from the 2500-square-mile Kanchenjunga massif, and bringing alluvial silts into Bihar, Bengal and Orissa states so necessary for the fertilisation of the rice crops. The combination of an aggressive monsoon and cyclones could devastate the autumn rice crops and seriously disrupt the autumn planting of the second spring crop. The historical consequence of this was that India made up the differences between production and consumption by importing rice from Burma.

In his report to the Bengal Chamber of 26th February 1942, George had warned they would have to rely now upon home production of food. In the Eastern states and the Deccan, this meant rice. In the northern states of the Punjab, the main staple food was wheat-based with breads based upon *atta* (wheat flour – JMM). However, the Bengali will not eat wheat-based foods, and even the addition of atta to bulk out a rice-based meal was unpalatable.

In fact, the divergence between Bengal's population growth and the production of rice throughout the 1930s had been masked by the convenient availability of imports from Burma, which had only relatively recently been elevated to separate colonial status after the elections of 1937. Burma had previously been administered from Bengal. Imports of rice had now ceased with the invasion of Burma by the Japanese, who commandeered the crops to feed their own army.

The numbers illustrate the scale of the problem. At the time of the author's grandfather's medical reports of 1921 for the year 1920 as Surgeon General of Bengal, Bengal's population had increased from just over 46.5 million to 60.3 million according to the 1941 census, an increase of around 14 million over 21 years. The corresponding rice production figures showed a drop from the average annual production of rice over the five years to 1937/8 of 8,600,000 tons to an average of 7,764,000 tons for the

5 years to 1942/3. In the Deccan (South India – JMM), a tidal wave in the Western Goldani district of Madras State destroyed 400,000 tons of rice and a corresponding drought in the Cauvery delta North of Madras led to a further 150,000-ton shortfall of rice production. So, the nub of the problem was a dropping rice production against an increase in population, balanced by imports from Burma which were now no longer available as a result of the Japanese occupation.

The problem was deferred thanks to a Bengal bumper rice crop of 9,821,000 tons in 1941/2, but due to the climatic problems in October 1942, production dropped to 6,043,000 tons in 1942/3. An increasingly starving population started to eat the rice grain reserves planned to support the spring 1943 planting. The production of wheat in the Punjab region more or less covered consumption with a small surplus, but instructions by the Governor were reportedly given to hang on to the wheat surplus rather than transfer it to Bengal to support the worsening situation. Apart from the native population of Bengal, there was an increasing additional problem created by the Burma evacuation with upwards of 400,000 extra mouths to feed in the first nine months of 1942 around Calcutta. Facing the Japanese, there was also a growing Indian army to be fed, many of whom ate rice rather than breads made from wheat.

In late 1943, Wavell had replaced Linlithgow as Viceroy; Wavell had considerable military experience as a young officer in the Indian Army and had become C.I.G.S. of the Indian army in 1942, relinquishing his command of Middle East forces in favour of General Auchinleck, who transferred from his post as C.I.G.S. India – so it was a straight swap. As Ruth Benthall's letters reveal, George and Doreen had entertained Wavell at a dinner given by them for him at 5 Raja Santosh Road in late 1941 during George's Presidential year of the Bengal Chamber. Wavell's initial assessment was that India needed 1.5 million tons of food grains, and he made an appeal to Churchill for supply.

The problem was not just a shortage of rice production but also difficulties of distribution, and so Wavell immediately ordered the Indian military to assist in the distribution of rice, an increasingly contributary problem to the growing famine particularly in the rural areas of Bengal. There is no doubt that there was hoarding of rice amongst the merchants but most of the more reputable firms refused to get involved. Suhrawardy, now the chief Minister, came under suspicion of being involved in profiteering . . . he had been minister in charge of labour following the 1937 elections and was a clever Cambridge-educated barrister in charge of labour negotiations in the late 1930s, known well to Birds.

Churchill has come under considerable criticism from modern historians for ignoring the problem, but the correspondence revealed recently in Andrew Robert's biography shows that this is far from the truth. He appealed to Roosevelt for supplies and transport, and while supplies of wheat were available from Canada, there was no transport available. The battle of the Atlantic was in full swing, and England was on very short rations and dependent on the Atlantic route for supplies of food and munitions. Eventually, supplies of around 150,000 tons of wheat were shipped from

Australia to India but it was too little too late, and hardly contributed to the shortage of rice. Churchill has also come under some criticism for diverting much-needed supplies of food grains to the Indian army units fighting the Italians in Ethiopia and Somalia, and later, on the North African coast against the Italians and Rommel's Africa Corps.

Starving Bengalis now arrived in Calcutta in search of food. Initially, food kitchens were set up on the Maidan but such was the scale of the problem and the congestion in the city centre that these were moved to the outskirts of the city.

The writer has witnessed the effect of the mighty Brahmaputra in flood during a visit to the Assam oilfields in mid-1962, and particularly being tossed about in a Fokker Friendship aircraft during the monsoon with towering storm clouds, and the Brahmaputra River below like an inland sea, flooded from horizon to horizon when viewed from 12,000 feet. Such is the awesome power of nature. He wrote to Doreen describing the scene and predicting the failure of the Autumn rice crop. Starving Bengalis from the country crowded onto the Maidan in the middle of the city that winter, almost too weak to beg.

Rationing was introduced with a ration of 16oz of rice per working man and this persisted until well after the war. Price controls were introduced. The Bengal Chamber introduced its own food programme making available through member firms food grains at subsidised prices. Birds also introduced a similar programme for employees, especially welcome to its considerable workforce servicing the Calcutta docks and railways.

The official statistics show that 1.5 million people died as a result of the Bengal famine but the unofficial figures of deaths are significantly higher than the official estimates. One source quotes 3.0 million. There is some evidence that significant numbers of deaths were caused by Mycotoxicosis, a poison present in mouldy rice causing fatal food poisoning. This was identified in the transit camps in Assam where stores of rice in godowns were affected by damp, and, although boiled and cooked, they still caused deaths amongst refugees weakened by the privations of their escape. This is based on evidence within the Mackell records in papers written in 1981, now in the Cambridge Centre of South Asiatic Studies. The evidence is not conclusive, but nevertheless, exists.

George, now a council member and retired President of the Bengal Chamber and senior partner of Birds, was deeply involved in these food programmes throughout 1942-44.

Bird Heilgers Group adapts to Wartime

One of the key factors affecting wartime trading was the introduction of an excess profits tax. Business margins were set at the level achieved in the year before war broke out; in the case of Birds, there were over forty trading companies within the group; this diversity meant that strong profitability was maintained throughout the war period. Prices were controlled and dividends were taxed at penal rates. The effect of these measures on Birds was that reserves increased significantly, although it was deemed necessary in some cases to spend reserves to increase protective shareholdings.

Demand for most products increased significantly, with mining and mineral processing factories and service facilities geared up to meet wartime demand. All the business departments remained in Calcutta, except the share department, which was moved to Kurseong in the foothills of the Himalayas south of Darjeeling for better security, where it remained throughout the war under the leadership of A.K. Sen. 'Ashu', as he was known, was immensely popular. He became partner's secretary after the war. Serious staff shortages resulted from men being called up for military service and many also took up additional voluntary work to help with the war effort.

George had extensive responsibilities outside of his role as senior partner of Birds but he was strongly supported by his partners, particularly Paul Benthall, and former flatmate David Teasdale who had moved from the Agency department in Delhi to the labour departments to help handle, as a new partner alongside James Coombe, the varying demands of unloading and loading goods on the docks and the railways. Alan Carpenter played a leading role in the mineral and engineering departments.

Many of the firm's business products were essential anyway to the war effort, particularly coal, paper, gunny bags, and the various materials essential for steel production; other companies, such as Kumardhubi Engineering, switched to the production of munitions. Shortages of materials caused major problems but the production of jute and paper continued throughout the war due to the foresight of 'Old' Bennett in London who had brought in big stocks of machinery and stores for the jute mills and wood pulp for the paper mills shipped to Calcutta at the onset of war in 1939.

Labour

From 1940 onwards the labour department expanded rapidly handling enormous quantities of war materials. The work came in rushes as convoys of materials arrived in the docks, with periods of slack in between. Several flats and steamers were removed for service in Iraq, causing a bottleneck of stores in Calcutta, due to the shortage of onward transport to the war zones. A daily wage system was introduced to help iron out the peak and slack periods, with rates raised temporarily during peak periods. A camp was provided outside the dock to provide accommodation and air raid shelters inside the dock area itself. Special shops were established to provide food at subsidised rates and food grains obtained through the Bengal Chamber scheme, with *atta* flour used to persuade the traditional Bengali rice eater to consume it as a complement to the rice diet. A malaria epidemic broke out with the vast numbers of East Bengalis returning to Chittagong, Noakali and Tippera, and the huge influx of civilians arriving from Burma.

Materials from the lease-lend operation were also transhipped to China via Calcutta, and Birds also acquired the handling of the contract from the Army at Outram Ghat, where sheds had been built on the foreshore. The first air raid came in the Christmas week of 1942, with just one bomb on the labour lines causing little damage, but the daylight raid a year later was more serious. Not only was this Calcutta's worst, but also Birds' labour lines were hit and 46 men were killed, principally because they had not taken to the shelters.

In March 1944, Union Jute at Chandpur were appointed storage contractors to the Civil Supplies Department, with Union employing the labour department for handling. Further contracts were secured from the US Army, first at the King George's Dock and then in the Dalhousie, Northbrook, and other jute mills in the Budge Budge area. At this time there was a rapid build-up of supplies destined for the war areas, with the labour department now employing 30,000 men. Payment of the men required a major logistical operation, and through its efficiency, Birds was virtually responsible for holding steady the cost of unskilled labour in the port area generally. The war brought with it a significant rise in living standards, together with this recognition shaping the future afterwards.

Coal

Coal production within Birds had been affected by the underground disaster at Loyabad and the enormous cost of the recovery operations of the casualties and the mine. It had been caused by a fire which precipitated a fall blocking the egress from the mine. After a year, air samples revealed that the fire was out, but it took many months to reopen the mine and recover the bodies of the miners – an exercise which was carried out by European employees to spare Indian sensibilities. After two years, the mine, which was by far Bird's largest, was brought back into production.

As a result, profitability was affected, and this, combined with low demand for coal in the immediate pre-war years, meant that the effects of the excess profits tax bore heavily on coal operations, but demand for coal picked up dramatically after 1942, and coal prices improved as well. Coal was being shipped abroad to South Africa, Brazil and other countries, as well as Britain where there was a shortage. 1943 was the critical year with floods affecting the railways caused by the aggressive monsoon. Demand, particularly from the steelworks and Birds, own Loyabad coking plants for coking quality coal, increased dramatically, while at the same time, there was a labour shortage. For the first time, women were recruited to work the mines.

Many improvements were made; important amongst these were the company-sponsored hospitals and schools within the mining communities. In 1945, the government set up the Coal Mines Labour Welfare Fund, funded by a cess of four annas per ton of coal despatched.

Birds pioneered the practice of hydraulic sand stowing which involved filling the voids left by coal extraction with sand mixed with water and pumped in under pressure. Apart from the obvious advantage of reducing falls, the capacity for further extraction was significantly improved, extending the life of each mine.

By 1945, India's total raisings of coal had increased to 26.25 million tons of coal, with Birds production now 1.7 million tons – an increase of 440,000 tons over 1939.

Jute

The products required by the war were varied and included a wide range of items. Principle amongst these were gunny bags for supplies and materials as well as millions of sandbags used as reinforcement for gun emplacements, shelters and trenches. George, in one of his 1940 letters, mentions just one order for five million sandbags. But other products included canvas for tents and stretchers and the development of parachutes, scrim for camouflage, and a host of other items. Jute was grown in Bengal and so the supply of raw jute was readily available and not really affected by the invasion. The mill workshops were used to provide training for a number of trades, and the manufacture of transit plugs for shells.

Jute is made from cut stalks immersed in water to soften them and enable the fibres to be separated out before being baled into raw jute. It is then processed and woven into fabrics of different types. The finest fibres can be used to make paper, a process developed by the Chinese thousands of years ago. As mentioned above, the company's godowns were taken over for the support of various Government programmes during the war, including the secure storage of food.

The company was responsible for the development of a parachute manufactured from jute, called a "parajute", and these were to play a massive part in the war. This was a joint development between the Ordinance Department of the 14th army and Birds; manufacture was of a light single-warp hessian canvas, with parajutes of three sizes- four, six and eight feet. Birds developed and submitted samples within three weeks, and after trials, an order was placed shortly afterwards for fifty thousand parajutes with delivery within a month. It was too big for Birds to handle on their own so with the help of the Jute Mills Association, the work was split up among a number of mills managed by Birds and five other managing agents. Parajutes played a major part in the air supply drops to the troops in the jungles of Burma during the war.

As with other companies, Birds suffered from a reduced pre-wartime baseline of profitability, and wartime profits of jute manufacture were hit by the excess profit taxes, rising to just under 75%.

Paper

Titaghur's pre-war development of using bamboo pulp to manufacture paper paid off when the timber trade with Burma collapsed due to the war. Production increased steadily during the war years and the company was relatively unaffected by the excess profits tax, due to relatively strong profits in the immediate pre-war year. Thanks to the foresight of H.P. Bennett, substantial stocks of wood pulp were built up and available at the onset of war, however, the use of bamboo pulp was increased to conserve wood pulp stock, which was topped up from time to time and a number of old digesters were brought back into production. At one stage, the Government requisitioned 90% of output, and customers had to be rationed, the problems of allocation being particularly difficult. Prices, particularly for student exercise books, became exorbitant, so the company started an exercise book coupon scheme enabling each student to buy three books at a fixed price.

Between 1939 and 1945, Titaghur supplied 89,500 tons of paper to the government including 9,000 tons of special map printing paper and millions of coils of teleprinter tape.

Minerals

Steel production, excepting scrap-based special electrical arc and induction processes, starts with a blast furnace producing iron. The ingredients are iron ore with preferably the highest possible % of iron, plus coke made from coking quality coal, and limestone to act as a flux. The steelworks of Tatas and the Indian Iron and Steel Co were flat out throughout the war. Once the iron-making process is started and the blast furnace lit, the chemical reaction between the ingredients becomes a continuous process, with ingredients fed to the top of the furnace through a double bell system and iron and slag periodically tapped from the bottom. Slag is used for roadmaking, and the molten iron goes to the various steel-making furnaces, carried in large ladles. Both the blast furnace and steel-making furnaces are lined with special refractory bricks. Manganese is an essential ingredient for high-grade steels. Birds mined or produced all these elements for the Indian steel industry, and had a significant but varying export trade as well, some of which continued during the war. Before the war, Bird's Orissa Minerals were supplying IISCO with 150,000 tons of iron ore a year but this jumped in 1940 to 375,000 tons, which was kept up for the next three years. Output from the Thakurani mine touched 452,000 tons during the war and this included supplies to Tata. Bisra's despatches of limestone and dolomite rose from 640,000 tons a year in 1939 to 840,000 tons a year for the war years. Manganese ore was exported at varying times to Great Britain, South Africa and the USA, while shipments to Japan and Europe were suspended. All internal shipments were affected by a shortage of rail capacity due to the transport needs for war materials and food during the famine.

The Kumardhubis

As mentioned above, refractory bricks are essential not just for steel-making, but also in the manufacture of glass and cement; Kumardhubi Fireclay and Silica Works Ltd (KFS for short) was easily the largest producer in India, not just for refractories but also for the special magnesite bricks used in the open-hearth steelmaking processes; these had to be capable of withstanding the very high temperatures generated by reversing burners at each end of the furnaces. Demand exceeded capacity, but because of the war, it was just not possible to bring in the equipment needed. Birds worked out a scheme, which was implemented in 1941, using the small amount of imported equipment needed, combined with all the existing equipment, to increase output from 32,000 tons (the best pre-war figure) to 48,000 tons. It also increased the output of sillimanite and high alumina bricks for the glass and cement industries. Kumardhubi engineering works, with its scrap-based induction crucible and electric arc furnaces turning out specialist steels, made its production over to the manufacture of 3" cast steel mortar bombs, with equipment designed in-house. Eagle Rolling Mills, the re-roller brought in from Madras in the 1930s, worked three shifts to increase output of bars, rods and various light steel sections.

With the increase in activity, Bird's Sijua (Jherria) power station was worked to capacity, but still managed to increase output from 34 million units in 1938 to 54 million in 1944. The plant was kept going through the outstanding work of the largely Indian engineering and maintenance staff. A scheme was worked out to interconnect all of the power plants in the area as a safeguard against possible breakdown. The only two Europeans working the plant were the chief engineer and his deputy, who had joined up at the outbreak of war; he was captured and spent three years in a Japanese prisoner of war camp. The maintenance of electrical supply was critical to the coal-mining pumping operations to prevent flooding of the mines particularly during the monsoon.

The Selling Agencies – Distribution

The agency dept of Birds played a crucial wartime role in distributing products on behalf of other manufacturers, using their marketing strengths and widespread connections. The operations were centred on Chartered Bank Buildings with three offices at Kanpur, Delhi and Lahore. The operation shifted from a peacetime emphasis on selling to balancing the wartime needs of the Government and military with other civilian demand. Much time was spent assisting and advising Government.

India's cement industries were vital to wartime construction – Birds were the agents for the Associated Cement Companies mainly in the Northern States. A control system was introduced to balance demand between the military and civilian demands with a quota system, with Birds now Regional Honorary Cement Advisers. Birds were also sole selling agents for Asbestos Cement Ltd.; almost all of their output went for Government use of this more specialised product.

Vegetable oils were used as a substitute for real *ghee* – oils and fats – and the Delhi and Lahore offices handled the agency for the Hindu Vanaspati Manufacturing Company of Bombay. Sugar was another product handled pre-war which continued, however, again, controls were introduced following a poor sugar cane crop in 1942, and the British Government appointed Birds sole purchasing agent for any surplus over and above Indian Government needs. This was a trade worth Rs1.25 crores or over £1 million. At one stage, Birds redeemed a damaged cargo of bristles from China which was treated and reshipped to Britain in good condition.

The Rangoon office representing both Birds and Heilgers continued to operate until 17th February 1942 when it closed in the face of the Japanese invasion.

The overall account above is just an indication of the widely diverse nature of Bird's operations, whose management was in George's hands, and it says much for the way in which the Company was both managed and controlled, in spite of staff shortages, that it did not just remain afloat and strong, but that it was able to contribute in so many ways to the war effort. George remained well informed and influential through his membership of the Security Council Committee, and various wartime supplies activities and committees. As a member of the Viceroy's Council throughout the war, Tom Benthall was also closely in touch as not just a close friend but also a major shareholder in Birds and still a partner until his resignation in 1961.

Netaji Subhas Chandra Bose and the Indian National Liberation Army

Netaji Subhas Chandra Bose was one of the most outspoken pre-war advocates for independence. He had been imprisoned many times and had been chairman of the Indian Congress Party in 1939. The story of the formation of the INLA is quite an extraordinary one.

Germany, of course, had "form" from the First World War in encouraging revolt in India. Indirectly, this had been a contributory factor to the third Afghan War in the spring of 1919. The whole affair had achieved momentum during the First World War with the desertion of some 23 Afridi's tribesmen of 58th Vaughan's rifles, a regiment of frontiersmen from the Tirah region of the Northwest Frontier. The Germans had established a special camp for Indian POWs outside Berlin called Camp Crescent Moon, and deserters had also been encouraged by leaflets from the Germans appealing to them to join the Jihad against the British with an offer of sanctuary. In the camp, there was a mosque and the religious differences between Hindu and Moslem were recognised and respected. The camp accommodation was comfortable with facilities for the separate preparation of food. Lectures and propaganda classes were held – one of the lecturers was Maharaja Mahendra Pratap.

The objective was to create a small force to enter Afghanistan to foment the Jihad declared on 14th November 1914 by the Sultan of Turkey against the British. His Imam's published terms of the Jihad were to "kill British Christians" – those who did so and died would be guaranteed a place in paradise while those who did not would be despatched to the eternal fires of hell.

The Tirah region of Afghanistan had been a trouble spot for years with a major campaign against tribesmen threatening Peshawar and the closure of the Khyber Pass just 20 years previously. However, distinguished regiments of Afridi had been raised under the British flag, notably the Guides. Pratap became an advisor to the Berlin Foreign Office and quickly developed the idea of a mission to Kabul to the Emir Hasbullah. The initial idea was to take sufficient Indians to form the nucleus of an army to raise rebellion against the British. Only the Pashtun Afridi volunteered.

The group split into three entering Afghanistan via Turkey and Baghdad and two surviving groups arrived there on 19th August 1915. Initially, their reception by the Emir was warm, but he later declared Afghan neutrality and the German plan for a grand alliance foundered, much to the relief of Viceroy Hardinge, who had been aware of the conspiracy since its inception. Pratab had declared himself President of the movement. So, the idea of an Indian Liberation army was not a new one and Bose initiated moves to resurrect it.

Bose had escaped from house arrest in Calcutta in mid-1941 and, travelling across India in disguise, entered Afghanistan, and making contact with the Germans, entered Berlin. The Germans had offered money and support for Bose's *Azad Hind* (Free India Legion – JMM). However, his call for volunteers only resulted in a potential army of about 2000 and, despite a personal appeal to Hitler, the Germans lost interest. But having heard of the Japanese plans to raise an Indian National Army, Bose expressed enthusiastic interest and arrangements were made with the Japanese to ship him to Singapore.

It was on April 23rd 1943 that the German submarine *U-180* carrying Bose surfaced some 400 miles south-south-west of Madagascar having sailed down the East coast of Africa and around the Cape, to rendezvous with the Japanese submarine *I-29*. There was a heavy swell but *I-29* launched a small motor-powered dinghy and the German submarine's hatch opened and a small bespectacled individual stepped out onto the deck. The Japanese unloaded their cargo – fifty forty-one-kilogram bars of gold (worth just over £70 million in today's terms) and the gold was stowed while Bose and Captain Werner Musenberg watched. Bose then stepped into the dinghy and was taken back to *I-29,* then both submarines disappeared.

Ten days later, *I-29* landed on the coast of Sumatra where Bose was greeted by Colonel Satoshi, of Hikari Kikan, a specialist unit set up to recruit Indians and South Asians into the INA. The Japanese hoped that Bose would be able to unite the various factions amongst captured Indian servicemen and breathe new life into its new INA formation. Like Hitler, Bose wore uniform throughout the war and, as head of the formation, delivered a series of speeches rallying the troops.

He entered Singapore alongside General Hideki Tojo on 2nd July 1943, declaring total war to the finish. But he was only able to recruit some 40,000 volunteers, many of whom saw this as their opportunity to desert and return to India. Of these, only some 6000 actually fought alongside the Japanese, who regarded them as little better than coolies. 400 later died as battle casualties, a further 1500 died of disease, and a further 1500 deserted, of which 800 surrendered to the British. Indian army units fighting in Burma regarded them with contempt. George, as a member of the Security Council of India, would have been aware of Bose's INA activities from briefings.

After the end of the war in early August 1945, the problem of what to do with the INA, most of whom were now prisoners, remained. Some 20,000 were technically deserters. Tom Benthall, amongst others, made an impassioned speech advocating an amnesty against prosecution.

Independence for India was now looming. But the Government saw it differently and decided on prosecution of the INA officers. The other ranks were granted an amnesty and treated with "mercy and generosity.". Officers were graded according to their complicity with the Japanese. The first category, "white," included those who co-operated with the British forces; many of these had actually deserted the INA. The second category, "grey", were those who had supported the INA under duress and the third, "black", those guilty of actually helping the enemy. It was decided to prosecute those officers of the "black" category prima facie guilty of heinous offences by courts-martial and seven officers were indicted for desertion and other offences. It was decided that the trials should be held in public. The first three were sent for trial in the Red Fort Delhi, itself an inflammatory and insensitive decision because of its association with the uprising of 1857, and again, serious civil unrest began.

The defence produced evidence of torture of the men involved and of executions of those who refused to break their oath and, therefore, the defence of joining the INA under duress was made, of which there were significant accounts. Major General C.M. Maltby's report (C-in-C Hong Kong and captured) which was carried in the Times of India on 3rd September 1945, about the fall of Hong Kong, gave an account of a young Punjabi Muslim soldier being hung upside down for 48 hours by his heels in an attempt to persuade him to break his oath and join the INA, and the subsequent Japanese admiration for his bravery when he still refused to do so. Eventually, the trial against two of the initial three collapsed, and the prosecution of the rest was abandoned. But the trial itself did little to enhance the reputation of the British against the growing clamour for Indian Independence.

Bose's death remains a mystery with various accounts of him dying in an air crash in the jungle. One of these, reported in the Times of India on 23rd August 1945 from a release put out by the Japanese News Agency, reported him dead from injuries received in an air crash at Taihoku Airport on August 18th, having left Rangoon on the last day of the evacuation, the 17th – he had also reportedly transferred his government in exile to Bangkok. All of his entourage had also died in the crash, with Bose dying at around midnight. But this hardly seems credible since Rangoon had actually fallen on 1st May, and the date and time reported of his death was midnight on the 17th / 18th August, the actual day of Japan's formal surrender. These coincidences seem remarkable and so the precise details of his death remain something of a mystery.

Bose's INA was a military failure but his influence on the Indian national movement towards independence was profound, and he is regarded as a great patriot in modern India. Clive Street in Calcutta was named after him in honour of his memory.

Kalimpong Life; George and Dorks' treks in Sikkim and Tibet

Arrangements were made for Jean, Jen and myself, with Nanny Bishop in charge, to take Norman and Bunty Odling's cottage *"Charitung"* in the grounds of their home

103 John playing football with Jonghi on the Glenrilly tennis court

"*Glenrilly*". We travelled up by car and train on 5th November 1940 to Kalimpong before the cold weather. Situated 32 miles due East of Darjeeling, this was an increasingly popular hill station about 4,500 ft up in the foothills of the Himalayas, 30 miles south of Gangtok, the capital of the kingdom of Sikkim. It was to be increasingly the home for a number of children with parents in Calcutta during the hot summer months. Our nanny, Nanny Bishop, was in charge. In reality, this became our home, while we travelled back to 5 Alipore Road (now Raja Santosh Road) for Christmas and the winter and spring school holiday months.

Jean, now rising eleven, was immediately enrolled in the school at Dr Graham's Homes, and Jen also at St. Joseph's convent school run by Belgian nuns next to the Catholic church, about three miles down the hill on a spur of the nine-mile road up from the River Teesta to the town; I followed her there very shortly afterwards. We all rode to school on little mountain ponies accompanied by a Syce carrying our tiffin boxes. Mine was a 32-year-old white pony, optimistically called Dynamite.

Bunty Odling was Dr Graham's daughter. Norman, her husband, had lost a leg in the First World War and ran and owned the ropeway from the railhead at Siliguri to the hill above the town at Rinkingpong. This carried essential food and other supplies, such as rice, up to the town. They became surrogate parents to us children. Dr Graham, a Church of Scotland pastor, had founded the Homes as an orphanage for children of mixed parentage on Scottish public-school lines, and it had become an important school in North India with an excellent academic reputation providing education to a wide ethnic grouping of children. As a child, I remember meeting him walking up the hill to visit Bunty and Norman and tapping me on the head with his walking stick, telling me to be good.

Bunty and Norman had three daughters. The eldest, Diana, had studied music and was a member of the Covent Garden Opera Company, singing soprano in the chorus, and occasional minor solo roles. Next came Jeany and then Shirley, both spending the war in Kalimpong. Jeany and Shirley both married afterwards. Jeany became president of the London-based Kalimpong Homes Association. Bunty's sister Betty was married to George Sherriff, a senior political officer in the British station in Gangtok. I remember his wonderful films in colour of Tibetan fetes in Lhasa and the swirling ceremonial dances and the Potala Palace. The Chumbi Valley was the main route from Kalimpong to Lhasa via Gyantse and this was one of the principal trekking routes taken by Doreen and George during their trekking holidays into the hills. Bunty's second sister, Esme Coffee, was married to an Irish doctor. She was always known as Jiggy and was trapped by the advancing Germans during the Scandinavian occupation in the spring of 1940, making a miraculous escape across the North Sea in a fishing smack.

Kalimpong town was in the middle of two hills. On the Southern hill, facing North with views of the Kanchenjunga massif, there was a collection of houses, including *Glenrilly*, with magnificent uninterrupted views to the North and the snow-capped Himalayas. *Kanchenjunga* dominated this landscape. The complex, 45 miles away and covering 2500 sq miles, had four main 8000-metre plus peaks surrounded by a further sixteen 7000-metre ones. The meltwater from this complex became the Teesta River valley to the west between Kalimpong and Darjeeling; above the rickety suspension bridge was the junction between the Ranjit and Teesta rivers, the Ranjit flowing eastwards into the Teesta.

On the Northern hill, facing South, there were the Kalimpong Homes and the MacPharlain Memorial Church, the complex accommodating some 600 Anglo-Indian children in 20 cottages. The children had their own chapel, school buildings, farm, swimming pool, gymnasium, bakery and stores, and ropeway. In the nearby mission, there was a medical centre staffed by British doctors/surgeons, again run by the Church of Scotland, with a dispensary, surgery, and leper hospitals. The complex also included the Kalimpong Arts and Crafts workshop, making furniture and household articles such as blankets, using local woods, and wool and silks brought in from Tibet. Norman and Bunty Odling were responsible for the running of this small factory and shop. My eldest sister Jean and later Jen were pupils in the Girls' school. Jean, for many years, was on the committee of the Kalimpong Homes Association in London, and her daughter Caroline now carries on this family tradition seventy-five years after we left as a family in 1945.

Above the central bazaar in the middle of the saddle was the Macfarlane Memorial Church, built in memory of a former missionary and associated with the Young Men's Guild of the Church of Scotland which started in Kalimpong in 1873.

To the east was a *maidan*, a flat open space where the yak trains from Tibet gathered descending to the town from the Chumbi Valley over the Jelap La pass bringing wool, carpets, woollen articles, jewellery, copperware and a host of other items to trade mainly for rice and other necessities. The roadway northeast above the town with its series of *Dak* bungalows led to the Jelap La pass into the Chumbi Valley, the main trading route with Tibet. It was on this road just two miles outside the town that the house of the late Raja Ugyen Dorje, Prime Minister to the Bhutan Durbar, stood. It was in this house that the Dalai Lama stayed for a time on his journey from Lhasa to Darjeeling in around 1913 following an early Chinese invasion of Tibet. Rooms were set aside and furnished as a shrine in honour of the visit of His Holiness. Jigme Dorje, later prime minister of Bhutan, was a pupil at St Joseph's Convent School. To the Northeast, peeping above the horizon was *Chomolhari,* the holy mountain, on the border of Tibet and Bhutan.

The *Dak (=post – JMM)* bungalows right across the northern hills were originally rest houses for travellers during the Raj and originated from the postal systems with ponies carrying mail and despatches across the mountains. They supplemented the telegraph system initiated in the mid-19th Century. Generally, they were spaced about 8-10 miles apart on a variety of routes giving an easy march between overnight stops. Many of them have survived and today offer accommodation for tourists trekking in the hills. The Indian postal system was extraordinarily efficient . . . my "Beano" comic, posted from England during the war, arrived regularly in Kalimpong surviving the sea voyage, admittedly a few months late, but nevertheless, a real treat and a cause of great excitement.

104 Nepalese ladies knitting socks – altogether Kalimpong ladies contributed 15,000 pairs of hand knitted thick woolen socks made from Tibetan wool for the war effort, particularly welcomed by our seamen

This important frontier trading town then was our home for four years and gave me an idyllic childhood with its totally fresh freedoms amongst the most friendly people in the world. I became fluent in both Nepali and Hindustani, with some Tibetan, and the Hindustani was invaluable when I returned to India to work for the Tata organisation in November 1961. I have a kaleidoscope of Shangri-La-type childhood memories of one of the happiest times of my long life.

The journeys up in the spring and down again in the autumn were adventures in themselves. Leaving Calcutta early in the new year generally meant an overnight journey to Siliguri, the railhead of the broad-gauge line to the hills. From here, the narrow-gauge mountain railway climbed (and still climbs) up 7,000 ft to Darjeeling. A branch line ran up the gorge of the Teesta River to a suspension bridge and the nine-mile road beyond up the hill to Kalimpong. A substantial concrete bridge had been built by Birds (the Anderson Bridge) in the mid-thirties but it had been swept away by the river in a particularly heavy monsoon. The valley was known as the "valley of the winds" in Nepali. The railway passed through jungle, initially through the Terai, that mosquito and fever-infested strip of jungle running all along the Himalayas. Hot and humid with the heat of the plains, the jungle on either side of the river was teeming with hidden life and the buzz of insects. Clouds of butterflies and brightly coloured birds would fly up as the train puffed its way through. Monkeys screeched their warning cries.

The river was a swirling and wide boiling brown torrent pouring down the gorge swollen with the meltwater from the Kanchenjunga massif, the mountain peeping above the hills as the train wound its way up the gorge. A road crisscrossed the railway line over bridges and ravines in the hillside. In places, one looked down directly into the river from ledges cut into the rock carrying the railway line. The train made a screeching whine as it turned a corner, rather like a wet finger on the rim of a wine glass.

At the Gielle Khola station halt beyond the bridge, we would be met by Dil Bahadur, a Nepali Gurkha and George's driver, in an Austin car; the luggage would be loaded and we would set off for the bridge. Here the luggage would be unloaded and we would walk with it over the suspension bridge, the car following to be reloaded at the other side. Gradually, it got cooler as we climbed up to Kalimpong, periodically stopping to refresh the car with water added to the radiator.

The household at Charitung consisted of us three children, Nanny Bishop, a Nepali ayah called *Rutemayer,* a bearer called *Kancha,* a cook/ masalchi (a cook who did the washing up – JMM) and a sweeper. There were also two syces (grooms – JMM) who looked after the three ponies. The house, cut into the hillside, faced East, the sweep of the hill descending to another river gorge and the blue hills of Bhutan beyond. Sheer magic. The Rinkingpong roadway immediately below the house carried a constant flow of folk carrying baskets on their backs held by a head strap coming and going on the hill road, most with a *kukri* (hill knife – JMM) hanging from a belt. Rutemayer's son Jongi and I would play football together on the hard tennis court in bare feet just off the drive to Glenrilly.

105 View of Darjeeling and the mountain by air. This photo is particularly interesting because of its perspective from the air showing the hills leading up to the sweep of the mountains beyond. The Darjeeling houses face South overlooking the plains below. The hills inbetween include to the North West the Singalila ridge and Nepal beyond with Everest Makalu and Lhotse in the left background

There were a group of us children in Kalimpong following the same routine of coming up from Calcutta in the hot weather and spending it in KP. There were Priscilla and Tim Nicholson, children of Bunty and Mignon, often referred to in George's letters. Mignon was Teddy Shuttleworth's sister, and so became cousins of my sister Jean after her marriage to Barney in 1956. Priscilla married John Jardine Patterson, who later became president of the Bengal Chamber, and CEO of Mackinnon Mackenzie, part of the Hong Kong-based Jardine empire. Then there were John and Betty Burder's daughters, Susan and Caroline, both almost exact contemporaries of Jean and Jen. John Burder had followed George as president of the Bengal Chamber in 1944. Susan was a talented artist; when asked to draw a nativity scene, she drew Joseph and Mary arriving in Bethlehem in a jeep with a flat tyre. Susan travelled back to England after the war with my mother and Jean, and Caroline with Jen, myself and Nanny Bishop. Sandy and Ronny Cameron's daughter Diana, together with Helen and George Gemmell's son Michael, another contemporary of sister Jean's. were also there. Helen Gemmell was a Froebel-trained teacher and gave me mathematics lessons using coloured bundles and sticks. There were also the Morgan family just up the Rinkingpong road living next to a pineapple farm.

106 John with syce on his pony called Dynamite

107 John and Jen on the steps leading to the Glenrilly driveway

In 1944, all these children put on a performance of *Shakespeare's Mid-summer Night's Dream* in the gardens of Glenrilly. I had a walk-on part as Mustard Seed. There was a cinema close by the Homes, and showings of *Walt Disney's Pinocchio, Snow White and the Seven Dwarfs, and Dumbo the Flying Elephant* were particularly popular.

Our parents made regular visits to see us and spend holidays trekking; leave home to England was prevented by the dangers of travel, and so they had extended local holidays during the year constrained by the workload, staff shortages, and the extra wartime and often voluntary war tasks undertaken. Just one letter survives, written perhaps when Doreen came up to KP to take over looking after us when Nanny had a holiday. She went to Kashmir, coming back with postcards and photos of her trip. There are interesting reflections from Ruth Benthall in this letter on the pressures of the workload during the war and the effects on married life.

"5 Alipore Rd West, Calcutta. Friday 28th April. (1942)

My Darling Dorkiebus,

Yesterday was much more peaceful and I cleared up a lot of outstanding matters in the office. Ruth and Tom must be arriving in Bombay now and I expect they will be thankful to see "the best view in India." I got a chit from Ebbo yesterday asking me if I would care to join up with Stephen & him whilst you are away which is very nice of him. I should have liked nothing better if I hadn't got this flat of ours, but as it is, it would cost a good deal extra to go & stay with them apart from the fact that I like this place of ours v. much and don't want to leave it, certainly not unless I could get someone to take care of it – so I think I must decline – but it is very nice of them to have offered and if I had been contemplating the Bengal Club I should have jumped at Ebbo's offer . . .

It was good to get your letter and hear that you are all going strong. I was most amused at the conversation between John and Jen. They are a sweet couple. I suppose Maureen isn't quite big enough to join in properly with them yet. I am glad that you are arranging for the Bun to have a pony on the odd days and it will give her a nice gentle cruise without tiring her or Nanny, and it's good to hear she likes ponies . . . I hope we shall be able to keep one for her when she gets a bit bigger. I quite agree that the Odlings are bricks and if you think of any way of our doing something for them let me know if I can do anything here . . .

Well, I left about 6.00 last night & read at the club and got home in time for Din. The tum is lub and I got home in time for Din & early bed. It is still much the same. Sticky in the day but not so bad at night. . . . only a week, sweetheart, and D.V. I shall be off to Kalimpong. I am due on this jury on Monday so it is impossible to say how I shall be fixed for getting away on Thursday next. But I shall go if it is at . . . . only all possible. The Tum is still better today so I think one can call it all right! It was a slight liver chill I'm convinced now.

The Dhurzi is working away on my pyjamas & has finished one suit as a pattern and I think he has finished the second. Everything else seems to be working smoothly here.

*The gold Mohurs and other flowering trees are out and it does look lovely. We still have carnations and few antimors in the garden and it looks very trim and nice. The new bearer – touch wood – seems excellent & am having an absolute minimum of trouble at present. Long may it last. All the time I miss you sweetheart but the time slips past & soon I shall be with you again D.V. Ruth said to me the other evening when I went to see her that Tom's & her souls were not their own and went on, **"you are going the same way, Batcha (George's nickname = baby – JMM) & very soon you will think of nothing else and will only live for work and office and politics & Doreen will have to spend her whole life over this blasted social business!"** She was quite bitter about it, poor Ruth . . . but I assured her that I would watch my step & see that it didn't drain me body and soul even if it wanted to! And I shall see to it too, sweetheart . . . Golly, won't it be good to be home again!*

Well, it is near the end of the day again – it has been a busy day & I have had Directors' meetings all the afternoon & still have a table full. Your letter was most welcome and I loved it. I will answer it tomorrow. Keep well, Sweetheart. All my love to you and our Buns. Always your Geordie."

This letter highlights the stress they were all under brought about by the war and truly, George's new family motto, to be registered with the College of Arms in 1945 following his knighthood, "Toil Endure Believe", was being lived out to the full. As children, we all thought this a bit of a joke, little realising then, perhaps, what our parents were going through. Their holidays took the form of visits to us children and treks into the hills and mountains beyond.

Kalimpong and Gangtok had been the assembly points for the 1904 Younghusband expedition to Tibet which resulted in a new treaty between the two countries. Telegraph communication was established between Kalimpong and Gyantse as a part of this expedition, and it was later extended to Lhasa in 1921. An English school was established in Gyantse in 1925, and there was an increasing appetite amongst Tibetan and Sikkimese high officials for attending English schools in both Kalimpong and particularly Darjeeling to learn English. Frank Ludlow ran the school. He was a noted botanist and a good friend of George Sherriff who retired to Scotland bringing with him several new Himalayan plants which are named after him and are now in the Glasgow Botanical Gardens. The writer met Ludlow after the war in the British Museum where, now in his seventies, he was working in the basement.

Kalimpong was also the assembly point for the 1933 Ruttledge expedition to Everest. My late father-in-law Col Robert Lawder of the Kumaon Rifles, (and the subject of the author's next book) a noted climber in the Hindu Kutch on the North-West frontier, was asked to go on a later expedition but could not make himself available. Spencer Chapman, the explorer and distinguished "stay-behind" soldier in Malaya, had been a member of the 1936 diplomatic mission to Lhasa as secretary, with a special assignment to collect plant specimens and provide a commentary on the abundant wildlife that flourishes under the benign Buddhist tradition with its respect for all forms of life.

He was a keen ornithologist and his book *Lhasa: The Holy City* is, unusually, full of colour photographs whose printing and development techniques were in their infancy at that time. Many of these expeditions entered Tibet over the Jelap La pass and into the Chumbi Valley from Kalimpong, which was also a main trade route to and from Tibet. From Sikkim and its capital Gangtok, the route to the valley lay over the Natu La pass and both roads joined up in the valley itself. As the 1936 Mission started at the British Residency in Gangtok, this was the route taken. These two passes into Tibet are in fact only 3 miles apart as the crow flies but separated by a mountain in between.

There are photographs of an earlier trek than the three wartime treks described below. From this album of photos, the writer has identified this trek that marched alongside and close to the Nepalese border in the North-East direction from Darjeeling. Separate to these photos is a collection of photos annotated on the back showing the pathways up to Phalut, a mountain top on the Singalila Ridge to Sandakphu. In an album are some magnificent photos of the Himalayan mountain range stretching westwards from Kanchenjunga to Everest itself, as well as the bungalow at Sandacphu. Everest can also be seen on a clear day from the top of Tiger Hill at around 8000ft above Darjeeling, a pimple just over a hundred miles away, but the view from Phalut is significantly closer at around 70 miles. The date is uncertain but it was possibly 1941, although this was a busy year for George as President of the Bengal Chamber. It was, however, a much shorter trek (just over 30 miles) than the later ones – possibly of no more than a fortnight's duration. There is now a branch mountain line to Jalpaiguri and a metalled roadway up to Sandacphu mountain, about 30 miles from Darjeeling on the Singalila Ridge – the whole area is now a part of a tourist attraction incorporating the Singalila National Forest, with stunning views of the mountains.

From the album, it appears that Dorks and George may have been with Jack and Helen Thomas, and this provided them with a short "taster" for the later and much longer treks that followed, which are described below.

Dork's birdwatching notes and the 1942 Oct-Nov trek to Sikkim via Jelap La pass, Gangtok and return to Kalimpong

A trekking holiday would take a fair amount of organisation. A *sidar* (= headman – JMM) would be appointed together with porters for the baggage and stores and food for everybody including the porters. Fresh vegetables and meat, mainly mutton or chicken, could be bought from vendors en-route. Bungalows would be selected and booked in advance along the chosen route. George and Doreen would have had all the necessary contacts. Ponies would need to be selected for them with a syce each, together with maybe a spare pony or two which could be available as pack animals, and mules for the heavier loads. From conversations with my parents, the furthest and highest they went was up the Chumbi Valley beyond Phari, and so I have written an account of this to give the reader a taste of their likely experiences. They did at least two other treks through Sikkim, with its wonderful wildlife, flowers, and scenery. They also took us children on shorter local treks to Dolopchen, Gangtok, and elsewhere.

From Kalimpong, the 40/50-mile route to the Jelap La went through the village of Rang Po and then past the Changu lake at 12,600 ft. up to the pass itself at 14,600 ft.

The Changu lake is described in the book *"Tours in Sikkim"* by *Percy Brown* as a *"weird and silent sheet of water about a mile long and might well be the haunt of the loos or water sprites of the lake"*. He adds, *"the bungalow is beautifully situated overlooking the lake, and to rest here is one of the most exquisite pleasures of touring . . ."* Rhododendrons would have been abundant on the march, growing as small trees and particularly beautiful when in flower in the spring.

Bungalows had been built from local wood and stone mainly by the engineers of the 1904 Younghusband Expedition all along the various routes, and there were rest houses also in the villages and towns in Tibet itself. So, there was a string of accommodation for the traveller, all of which George and Dorks used.

It is impossible to underestimate the immensity of the country. The Jelap La pass was around 10,000 ft higher than Kalimpong at 14,500 ft and the Chumbi Valley plain averaged around 12,000 ft rising to 17,500 ft. And yet this was only about half the height of Kanchenjunga to the North-West. Looming to the East was the peak of Chomolhari, effortlessly rising above the plain, a mere 24,000 ft., with a range of mountains beyond. Spencer Chapman was to climb this mountain in 1937, a first ascent, with just himself accompanied by a Sherpa, summitting below the actual peak in respect for the Bhutanese deities. By comparison, Mont Blanc is only 15000 ft and the Andes not much higher. The furthest that George and Doreen reached in the valley was beyond the fort (Dzong in Tibetan – JMM) of *Phari*, at 14,600 ft. and then several miles further on to *Dorchen* before turning back.

I returned to Kalimpong in August 1962. I stayed at the Himalayan Hotel run by David MacDonald's daughters; he was a much loved and legendary figure in Kalimpong. He was at that time just short of his ninetieth birthday. He is described as an old man by Spencer Chapman in 1936 when he joined the mission in his early sixties. His father was a Scot, his mother Sikkimese, and his wife a Nepali, and he was described as having a wider knowledge of the Tibetans than any other Englishman. As a young man in his early thirties, he was the official interpreter to the Younghusband expedition of 1904. He showed me his treasures, fine *thankas* and jade Buddhas. My photo of this legendary figure shows him with all his medals, which included the rare Order of Merit. He died six weeks after I saw him.

Doreen was a keen and knowledgeable ornithologist, and her bird book notes are contained in an exercise book and two hardback books which she illustrated. The exercise book also describes in outline two of their treks. Paper was, of course, very short during the war and costly . . . The front cover lists "Subject" which she has filled in "birds" and continues "Name . . . Doreen Morton", "College/School . . . St Pauls" *(St. Pauls was a substantial school in Darjeeling – the author's sister Jennifer taught music and French there in 1962/3 – JMM) . . .* and finally, "Class"– which she enters as "bottom"!!!! The flavour of her birdwatching is captured in her diary notes . . .

"September Kalimpong (1943)

13th Saw some grey-backed shrikes for the first time. We also thought we heard a laughing thrush of sorts very early in the morning.

15th A grey-backed shrike was sitting in a bush with a flock of red-vested bulbuls. We hear them calling in the mornings. They have only I think just come. This evening a yellow horned warbler was very excited about something sitting in the tree outside Charitung & chattering with green-backed tits and bulbuls.

16th Saw a magpie robin on the road by the Dak bungalow, though there have been none in Glenrilly garden since the last fortnight of August. The weather is much more settled & mornings & evenings quite chilly.

17th Saw some bush chats on the hill with the shrikes & bulbuls. Also, a female, the colouring quite different from the male.

19th Saw a couple of magpie robins in Glenrilly garden today, the first I have seen this month. Also, the grey-backed shrike again.

21st The Burders say they saw a Hoopoe in their garden today; the last time I saw one here was mid-April. Helen Gemmell thought she saw one in Darjeeling about then but we were doubtful if they ever went as high as this.

24th Continue to see an increasing number of grey-backed shrikes about & bush chats. Last night I heard an owl, but am not able to identify which species.

25th Saw some Indian Grey Drongos today flying over the trees in Rinkingpong forest.

26th Heard for the first time this autumn a bird we also heard frequently last year. It has a plaintive song of five notes on a descending scale. I have never yet seen it . . . Bush chat?

30th The white wagtails are here again. I saw a lot in Glenrilly garden two days ago. There are a lot of magpie robins back again too. For three weeks I saw none but perhaps it was because there was so much rain. The weather is lovely now & it seems as if the Monsoon is nearly finished. Here continue to be many bush-chats. Do we sometimes see the Japanese bush chat here or is it the female of the Pied Bush Chat or Tibetan Bush Chat?

October. Continue to see green-backed tits and magpie robins, grey-backed shrikes, bush chats, wagtails, as well as all the resident birds.

13th Saw a hoopoe today.

14th In Darjeeling noticed a small bird sitting on top of a tree – general impression grey/ black & white with appearance and habits of a small flycatcher.

15ᵗʰ Saw a flock of cinnamon sparrows in the bushes round the Rinkingpong hill. There are also several hawks about. I have noticed them for some time & I think one at least must be the Crested Hawk Eagle. The Brahminy Kite is quite common."

George's small pocket diary confirms the first recorded trek as 1942, and Dorks' trek diary supplements this and records another one in 1944. His 1943 diary also simply records the dates of their notable trek in May and June over the Jelap La and into the Chumbi Valley in Tibet up to Phari Dzong and beyond. His 1944 diary notes a longer trek of around three weeks to the source of the Teesta River in Oct/Nov.

Arriving in Kalimpong on 13ᵗʰ October '42 with a fortnight's leave, they started their trek on the second day of the Durga Puja holidays on Saturday 17ᵗʰ October with its first leg from **Kalimpong** to **Rississum**, a march of about 8 miles. Known to the Lepcha people in Sikkim as Marikit, it is situated atop the summit of a small hill rising out of the forest and commands magnificent views of the snows to the North and to Darjeeling to the South-West.

"Oct 17ᵗʰ Trekked from Kalimpong to Rississum . . . 6700 ft – cloudy day snows not visible but the hills startlingly clear . . . saw a small hawk of sorts (sparrow hawk) between the Homes and Algarah (described as a level walk and about 2½ miles short of Rississum – JMM). *It was hovering above something; was unable to see the correct colour but it was light in colouring. Masses of Black-headed Silicas & flycatchers at Rississum; it was a misty evening which made birdwatching difficult but there were some very active small birds about the size of Algarah (green-back tits – olive green above and yellow below with orange breasts – could not see them properly – the leviculia was in full bloom & the scent was lovely."*

Oct 18ᵗʰ Rississum to Ari . . . 4700 ft. The road is described as passing through lovely woodland scenery down to the Rishi Chu River at Pedong, which was the crossing from India to Sikkim, then through Rhenok, and a further 3 miles to the bungalow at Ari. Dork's diary continues. . . .

"Pouring rain like a very wet day in the rains we feel aggrieved at this as the previous fortnight has been so perfect. Not the sort of day for bird-watching, though it cleared up slightly towards the middle of the morning as we got going. Just before we reached the Rishi, heard and saw a flock of Laughing Thrushes (white-crested L T). There were also a good many other birds but could not stop long enough to see them. Riding up from the Rushi to Rhenok we saw many Tree Pies (Himalayan T P) also two woodpeckers, one with a gold crest, but it was raining by this time could not use my glasses.

It cleared in the evening though there is a lot of low cloud about still. The hills were magnificent and looked like velvet. We saw a woodpecker which we wondered if it was Tickell's Golden-Backed Woodpecker."

The rest house is described as an old-fashioned building overlooking the ridge of Maria Busti, the home of the settlement of Société des Missions Étrangères at that time.

Oct 19th Ari to Sedonchen . . . 6500 ft. This is a march of some 13 miles, described as an initial descent to the river Rongli, and then through the gorge of the river past the Rongli rest house, followed by a steep climb up to the Sedonchen rest house, a queer little building, set in a bowl of mountains. The river itself is said to contain snow trout, and the scenery spectacular.

"Fine day but didn't do much bird watching -saw a yellow wagtail by the Rongli, a couple of enormous vultures (Himalayan Griffin?) sitting in the trees near Sedonchen – the view from Sedonchen in the morning was lovely though clouds were over the snows."

Oct 20th Sedonchen to Guatong . . . 12,300 ft. The road is described as steadily ascending, rising in zig-zags above the village of Jeyluk through a rhododendron-covered mountainside with magnificent views with glimpses of the plains, up to the village of Lingtu, and views of the Kanchenjunga range and Kabru and Siniolchu outlined from the East before the road descends to Guatong. From here, the mountain of Gipmochi can be seen, marking the border of India, Sikkim and Bhutan, before passing a cemetery with some British casualties from the 1888 and 1903/4 "missions" to Tibet buried there. During the 1903/4 Younghusband expedition, Guatong was a military base – the stream was dammed and the lake was used in the winter for skating. It is the last village of any size before the Jelap La Pass; here there was a telegraph office.

"Thick mist & some rain all the way – we were very cold when we got to the top of the "staircase" but soon thawed out in a herdsman's hut at the top. Whilst we were having lunch, we saw some small birds which I have so far failed to identify. They were quite bold & didn't seem to mind us. The sun came out occasionally on the way to Guatong."

Oct 21st. Guatong to Kapup. 13,000 ft. This is a short march of 4 miles to the glacial lake at Bidang at the far end of which is the dak bungalow, the lakeside surrounded by gentians and edelweiss. From here, there is a further 3-mile march up a zigzag path to the Jelap La pass (14,390 ft). The summit of the pass overlooks the descent into the Chumbi Valley, and marks the border into Tibet.

"Thick mist, rain and sleet. However, after lunch, we went up the Jelap in a blizzard. It froze hard in the night & was a perfect morning. It was 29 degrees F in my bedroom."

Oct 22nd Kapup to Changu . . . 12,600 ft. This bungalow and lake on the direct route to the Jelap La have already been identified and described above.

"Lovely day until 10.45, after that thick mist. Saw a Plumbeous Redstart, a wren of sorts, and several flocks of small birds too far away to see properly. We had a glimpse of Tibet from the top of the Natu. On our way to Changu we saw a Lammergeier, also a small falcon or hawk chasing a small bird. The birds of prey are difficult to identify. I also saw a small robin-like bird, olive coloured with orange sides, sitting on a bush on the way up to the Jelap."

108 Dorks with the Changu Lake behind and the snow covered route up to the Jelap La Pass

Oct 23ʳᵈ Changu to Karponang . . . Pussum 9500 ft. A march of about 10 miles. The road is described as spectacular with part of the roadway a ledge in a vertical cliff protected by a rough wooden railing over a precipice. An impressive stand of timber lines the road with several waterfalls and magnificent scenery. The bungalow is on the mountainside.

> *"Fine early morning but clouded over by 9.45. We saw some hawks above Changu with a cry like a sea-gull, one of them dived quite 100 ft. & seemed to have some difficulty in landing. We saw a chestnut-backed Nitalia and then just above Karponang a Rose Finch (Red mantled) & Hume's willow warbler or a green willow wren. There were a number of these. Also many Blue-throated Redstarts & several Grey-Backed Tits."*

Oct 24ᵗʰ Karponang to Gangtok . . . 5800 ft. This is the capital of Sikkim, the seat of Government with, in those days, close links with both India and Tibet. Many of the high officials were related to their counterparts in Tibet. The ruling Maharaja lived in the Palace, which had a monastery in the palace grounds. Close to the palace was the Dak Bungalow where Dorks and George stayed. There was also a British Residency, and a motor road along the Teesta Valley. It was from the British Residency that most of the diplomatic initiatives with Tibet were mounted, and George and Betty Sherriff spent some time in Lhasa during the war. After the war, they mounted an expedition to Eastern Tibet to collect plants, birds and animals for the British Museum, from whence a letter from Betty to Doreen survives.

The diary continues:

"Lovely morning and we could see Kalimpong in the distance; there were many birds but as we wanted to get in easily, we did not stop a great deal. However, we saw a striated bulbul & heard many whistling laughing thrushes. Also saw a Blue Rock Thrush."

Oct 25th Gangtok to Pakyong. . . . 7400 ft . . . A march of about 11 miles. Some three miles into the journey, the path drops down steeply to a bridge over the river Roro near its junction with the Rongni river and then crosses the Rongni and climbs steeply through forest to Ahugaon and again up through beautiful woods with tree ferns and orchids, brilliantly coloured butterflies and birds. Further on, the pathway opens out along a cliff face, before rising through cultivated land to the bungalow. Located a mile below the monastery at Kartok, it is described as charming and covered with climbing roses.

"Lovely day; a lovely march. There were masses of birds. We saw a mass of male & female Himalayan tree pies, green magpies, tits (grey, redheaded?), woodpeckers (yellow-necked?) white-crested laughing thrushes, spotted forktail drongos (Unable as yet to identify the species) and heard several birds. Also, many small birds; wren warblers of sorts no doubt."

Oct 26th Pakyong to Pedong . . . 4,900 ft . . . thence to Algarrah and Kalimpong. This is a long march initially down to the river Roro, across the bridge at Rorathang and then up the hill through forest to Tarpini and Rhenok, across the Sikkimese border at the Rishi and Rongli rivers and back up the hill to Pedong. From there, a short 3.5-mile march took them past the Kalimpong Homes and up the Rinkingpong road to Glenrilly. Dork's diary continues on this, the last day of the trek.

"Lovely day. We started early & spent some time trying to see some birds in the trees on our way down to the valley of the Rongli. They were laughing thrushes of sorts, I think. I saw one solitary laughing thrush (white-crested) on a tree on the way to Rhenok and some woodpeckers but they were too far off to identify. Any number of drongos down by the Rishi at about 3,000 ft on the way to Pedong, a pair of Rollers (broad-billed?) one sitting characteristically on the telegraph wire, the other perched on the top of a tree not too far distant."

George spent the night at Charitung, returning to Calcutta the following day, 27th October. He would have caught an afternoon mountain train from Gielle Khola in the Teesta valley to Siliguri, then an overnight train to Calcutta to arrive in time for the office the next day. Dorks stayed on with us children until the following week before returning to Calcutta and then accompanying George on his business trip to Delhi.

They left Calcutta on the evening of the 9th November for Delhi arriving the morning of the 11th. George's diary noted that they shot on Sunday 15th with Tom Benthall and Pitts Squarey with a bag of 6 black and 10 grey partridges, 3 quail, 3 green pigeon and 3 hares (the author has fond memories of a tandoori partridge with a fresh roti nan eaten on the open rooftop of the Moti Mahal restaurant in Delhi on a hot summer evening in 1962).

Tom was by this time resident in Delhi as a member of the Viceroy's Council. Dorks' bird diary notes some 53 different bird species seen during the Delhi visit from 11th – 15th November. George's diary also notes that Dorks left for Kalimpong on the evening of 21st December.

Also, on the same day and in very tiny writing, the diary records "air raids 3.25/5.45 am." This was the first of two air raids typically arranged to cause panic early on a Monday morning just before Christmas. Only one bomb fell on the labour lines in the docks, but George would almost certainly have had to evaluate the situation in his position not just in Birds but also in his role as a member of the National Defence Council. It is not clear from the 1942 diary entries how this affected Christmas, and whether we all spent Christmas together in Calcutta or in Kalimpong, but George seems to have been in Calcutta, as he had lunch on Christmas Eve with Tom Benthall, and there are no further entries for the year. However, an entry on 5th January suggests that we all spent Christmas in Calcutta, returning to Kalimpong on that date by train from Sealdah station on the East side of the river Hooghly. The National Defence Council was taking up much of his time with regular trips to Delhi by train from Howrah Station and three-day meetings there, in Viceregal Lodge with the Viceroy present, in view of the seriousness of the situation in Burma, and the contingency planning for a potential Japanese invasion of India. A photograph shows the wide

109 Tea for breakfast overlooking Changu lake

composition of the members including many of the members of the Prince's Council who held field rank in the British army in their own right.

May – June 1943. Trek from Kalimpong over Jelap La pass to Tibet through the Chumbi Valley to Phari Dzong past Chomolhari to Dorchen and return

In 1943, Dorks and George embarked on their most ambitious trek yet into Tibet and they spent over three weeks in the mountains with a five-week holiday from 17th May to 26th June. Paul Benthall had returned to Calcutta from Darjeeling. George was of course overdue his UK leave, which was impossible to take because of the war. They would have had to have had special permissions for the Tibet trek and it would have taken a good deal of planning. They left **Kalimpong** on 24th May spending that night at **Pedong**, then to **Ari** on 25th, and then trekking to **Sedonchen** and **Kapup**. All these places are already described above. From **Kapup,** they crossed the **Jelap La** pass into Tibet, and then down to the rest house at **Yatung**. The account of Spencer Chapman's journey of the same route in 1936 describes what they experienced.

At the approach to **Yatung:** *"we crossed a bridge and passed a number of chortens surrounded by fluttering prayer-flags on enormous poles* (chortens are monuments of stone usually erected above the ashes or remains of a holy man – JMM). . . . *I saw several bronze-winged turtle doves in a field of pink buckwheat. A pair of hoopoes crossed the river and a white wagtail. Many crows too and orange-billed choughs".*

Yatung is in the middle of a bowl surrounded by 15,000 ft mountains. Here there was a British agent with an agency bungalow overlooking the village. His description continues. . . . *"a lovely long low red bungalow with a glass verandah in front. It possesses a most heavenly garden; the drive bordered by riotous masses of nasturtiums, green lawns, a pergola of rambling roses in full bloom, a paved garden with huge pansies, lupins, antirrhinums, eschscholzias and petunias – all you could wish for. There are bharal in the hills and many bears which come down from the hills and raid the crops."* Doreen and George spent four nights here from Wednesday 26th of May leaving to Gautsa on the Sunday. Yatung is given as 10,000 ft and **Gautsa** as 12,400 ft., and the march between the two some 15 miles. Yatung is described by Spencer Chapman as a sizable village with a British Agent there and a garrison of Indian troops. It is probable that they needed to rest, acclimatise and enjoy the spectacular scenery and explore. George had, after all, climbed up from the hot plains of Calcutta up to over 10,000 ft within the space of a week, and they were shortly heading for **Phari** at 14, 600 ft and beyond.

Not far away on the spur of a hill overlooking the Chumbi Valley on the border with Sikkim is the monastery of Kargyu, the name itself given to a special sect of Buddhism prominent in Bhutan. This tradition of monastic Buddhism traces its origin directly to the Buddha himself using specialist meditation techniques.

Musicians greeted the 1936 party which *"followed them through a most attractive wooden gateway into a large cobbled courtyard where a crowd of monks welcomed us.*

Behind carved pillars there was an ambulatory right round the yard with ancient-looking frescoes on the walls, depicting fierce Gods embracing, meditating Buddhas, multi-headed Buddhas, Buddhas with blue, green, or red skins – hundreds of Buddhas, and all different; also the wheel of life depicting man's vicissitudes through endless cycles of existence. We climbed a rickety wooden stair, up and up until we reached the Abbot's room. Here we were presented with blue, instead of the customary white scarves of greeting, which were collected again before we left. The Abbot (he has held that position for twenty-seven years) is an aged man with a benign yet lively face; unlike other monks we met, he wore a grey robe and had a great mass of hair tied in a bundle on top of his head. We were told that never in his life had he cut his hair. He wore flat discs of spiral curled ivory in his ears and rings on his fingers – surely unusual for a monk. He also wore steel-rimmed glasses. A very striking figure, but that of a man of the world rather than that of an ascetic. When we asked him if it was going to be fine, he replied that it was bound to rain for the next three days as the Holy pig had just risen from Mansorawar lake (near Mount Kailas) and that three days of rain were necessary to consecrate it."

Leaving **Yatung**, George and Doreen would have followed an eastern tributary of the **Amo Chu river**, and passing through **Lingmatang**, they entered the wild country on the approach to **Gautsa** with rushing rivers, gorges and crags between mountains 15000 ft high. The village of **Gautsa** contained the bungalow – *"a tiny village of wooden houses roofed with shingles".* After spending the night here, the 23-mile march next day passed along the open plains leading up to the fort of Phari which they reached on the 31st May 1943.

Spencer Chapman's graphical and beautifully written descriptions give us something of an insight into their experiences.

"August 5th 1936. We have entered another world. A world of immense distances; the dun plateau slopes up to meet the rounded sienna -scarred hills, and behind them the far snows are dominated by the ethereal spire of Chomolhari rising alone into the clouds. In the distance, the flat-roofed village of Phari looks like an excrescence on the barren plain. Around it there seems to be a lake of blue water several miles in extent, though we know that this is not so. As we approach, we find to our amazement that certain parts of the plain are thickly carpeted with blue forget-me-nots and darker aconite. One of the most beautiful things I have ever seen in my life – the sober olives and browns of the plain, then suddenly these exuberant splashes of cerulean blue running up to the massive keep of the Phari fort and the mud boundary-walls of the village. The plateau, austere and lifeless at a casual glance, is actually full of life. Tiny blue gentians and a minute yellow flower like a celandine smile up at one.

I saw several kinds of snow and mountain finches, and Elwes' black-horned lark with its black and white face like a ringed plover. Soaring above are many birds of prey – lammergeiers, Himalayan vultures, kites and a solitary harrier. Hundreds of mouse-hares, attractive little rodents sit up and watch us, only scuttling into their burrows at the very last moment."

Most commentators describe **Phari** as a filthy and desolate spot. Lying at 14,600 ft above sea level, it is one of the highest inhabited villages in the world, bleak and frozen in the winter months. The Tibetan rarely washes, and the combination of piled dung in the roadways of the fort made it a particularly uninviting spot only relieved by the spectacular scenery and wildlife.

As the crow flies, the Jelap La is thirty miles northeast of Kalimpong, and **Phari Dzong** another thirty-five miles further on – allowing for the ups and downs and the contours of the road, probably a march of over a hundred miles or two hundred out and back. The journey, allowing for stops, would take 3-4 weeks. It is not hard to understand the attraction of this magical land, the wildlife, (Dorks a keen ornithologist), with its magnificent scenery, after the stresses of wartime life in the hot and humid climate of Calcutta. The open spaces of the huge countryside and the combination of fresh air and exercise created an almost spiritual and peaceful hold on the visitor.

From **Phari** they travelled on to **Tuna,** at 10,000ft, through the village of **Chu-gya** at 15000 ft (which means frozen stream – JMM) *and* over the flat summit pass of **Tang la**, and down to **Tuna,** a march of 21 miles. To the south, the magnificent mountain of **Chomolhari** rises effortlessly from the plain to just under 24,000 ft. (7,314 M), with its associated range of mountains stretching to the South and East. As noted earlier, Spencer Chapman was to climb this mountain in 1937. It would have been in constant and close view to George and Dorks from Phari.

At Tuna, a road branches West heading towards Everest and the Northern approaches to the North face favoured by the early expeditions, including the Ruttledge expedition of 1933. This expedition also commenced its journey to Everest following the exact same route from Kalimpong as that taken by George and Dorks, and starting earlier in March of that year. The author's late father-in-law, then a young officer in the Kumaon Rifles and a noted climber, was invited by Hugh Ruttledge to join a later expedition to Everest but could neither afford the time nor the cost.

Spencer Chapman describes his view of **Chomolhari** from **Tuna.**

"An incredible mountain – for impression of sheer height and grandeur it surpasses any I have ever seen, except the Matterhorn. Put on gym-shoes and ran up the rounded hill to the North-East with the idea of examining its approaches. Heard a marmot whistling in the valley behind and put up a couple of blue hares and a fox. I had a good view of the long Southern snowface of Chomolhari. It is not very steep, and though it is cut by several ice falls, it looks possible if one could cross the intervening valleys and get on to it. The north and east faces look quite unclimbable . . . I think the southern arete might "go". Across the other side of the plain rises the great snowy mass of Pauhunri with no very striking peaks. Got back to photograph our yaks being loaded up. They don't like the smell of Europeans but are most placid with their own drivers. Their horns and shaggy coats resemble those of Highland cattle, but they are much larger and have long thin faces."

It is perhaps worth recording here that the first serious skirmish that took place between the sizable Younghusband "mission" and the Tibetan forces occurred near

Guru about 10 miles beyond **Tuna** on the **Dorchen** road. An attempt to disarm a Tibetan army of around 1500 swordsmen failed and firing broke out. Around 700 Tibetans were killed, caught in rifle and machine-gun fire from the Maxim guns of the Sikh troops. The 168 wounded expected to be slaughtered, but were humanely treated by the mission doctors, and all except 20 survived to be released. This created a very good impression with the Tibetans, as it was an encounter that nobody wanted. The Daily Mail correspondent, Candler, was cut down by Tibetan swordsmen and received seventeen wounds including the loss of a hand, but survived.

George and Dorks made their final eastwards march to **Dorchen,** a distance of 13 miles on 2nd June 1943. Spencer Chapman describes his experiences:

> *"Got up at 5 and ran up the hill behind the bungalow. I seem to be fairly well acclimatized as I climbed a thousand feet in 40 minutes and took seven to get down again. The pyramid of Chomolhari is clear but does not stand out, for from here it is no longer isolated but forms the western peak of a magnificent line of mountains. Dorchen Lake, the Hram Tso or Otter Lake can be seen running up to the foot of them. . . . the track led around a corner of the Tuna hills and away across a wide level plain. There were tufts of vetch, occasional thistles and a sedum-like plant otherwise it was barren and stony. Still no wild asses, only Tibetan gazelle seen dimly in the far heat haze. There are solidly built square milestones along the track, but many have been raised, and the mileage is only written in Tibetan . . .* (hardly surprising!! – JMM)

The road skirts the lake before the bungalow at **Dorchen,** described as built around a courtyard. From here, Doreen and George turned around after spending the night and retraced their steps back to **Kalimpong** staying at exactly the same locations. However, at Yatung, they branched off to go to **Chumbitang**, a bungalow 5 miles below the Jelap La, and spent the night there, possibly reconnoitring it as a possible alternative venue for a future trek, before returning to **Yatung** and crossing back over the **Jelap La** pass. They arrived back in **Kalimpong** on 10th June.

Later on, us children were allowed to accompany our parents on trek. This started with Jean as the eldest and I can remember being really miffed at not being allowed to go too. These were short treks and one is recorded in George's diary over a weekend in May 1944 to **Dolopchen** and **Gangtok.**

This May one involved Doreen and George, Jean and Betty Burder. Her husband John of Jardine Skinner was President of the Bengal Chamber in this year, and their daughters Susan and Caroline, exact contemporaries of Jean and Jen, were in Kalimpong with us. Leaving on Friday 19th May, they spent the next two nights at the bungalow at *Dolepchen*, about 6 miles north of *Kalimpong*. They returned on the Sunday, the short trek causing the least disruption for Jean and Susan's schooling. George had taken a fortnight's leave and left for Calcutta on Monday 22nd June on the 4.20 train arriving the next morning at 10.40 at Sealdah station before going into the office.

October – November 1944 trek to Northern Sikkim, the source of the Teesta River and beyond

The October trek was a part of an extended leave from Monday 23rd October to Wednesday 22nd November 1944. It was to take them up to the furthest Bungalow in Sikkim to the source of the Teesta River through Gangtok to Lachen and the Lachen valley. They left on 31st October for **Pedong,** and then went on to **Pakyong** (1st Nov) and **Gangto**k (2nd Nov). From here they went to **Singhik (3rd Nov).** This is a long march of some 23 miles. It passes the ancient capital of Sikkim of **Tumlong,** where there is a monastery, then it descends to the **Dikchu** bungalow, at 2,150 ft where they were to stay on their way back. Continuing along the bank of the Teesta, they then crossed a suspension bridge some 250 ft long and hanging 250 ft above the river; here, the river Rongrong pours into it, before trekking up into the hills to the **Singhik** bungalow, **at 4600 ft**, where they spent the night. Here there is a wonderful and close view of the sheer walls of the **Kanchenjunga** massif above the Tumlung valley. The country is cradled by the snows above; the next day, Saturday 4th November, crossing the Teesta again just beyond the bungalow at **Toong,** they climbed up to the bungalow at **Chungthang** . . . **5,350 ft.** This lies between the angle made by the Lachen and Lachung rivers which unite to form the Teesta River itself. George and Doreen then climbed up to the bungalow at **Lachen at 8,800 ft.** This is described as one of the finest marches in Sikkim, with wonderful views of the cascading river below. A place to stay and savour. They stayed three nights walking and birdwatching, evidenced by the many birds noted in Doreen's notebook. It was here also that a Finnish mission was located, making woollen articles including blankets and rugs using local vegetable dyes. On 8th November, they climbed up to the **Thangu bungalow at 12,800 ft** at the head of the austere and cold Thangu valley with a rough path leading over the Donkhya La to Tibet, with the fluted columns of **Kanchenjunga, 28,100ft,** towering above to the South-East, Chomo **Yummo, 22,400 ft,** and **Khangchengyao at 22,700ft,** dominated the North and North-West. Returning to **Lachen** on 9th November after a night at **Thangu,** they returned to **Chungthang,** the head of the Teesta, where there was a monastery and the bungalow nearby, and then back via **Dicchu** to **Kalimpong.**

Other Wartime memories

Our 1940, 1941, and 1942 Christmases were spent in Calcutta. In 1943 and 1944, our parents joined us in Kalimpong for Christmas with the Odlings. Gradually, depending on the season, the weather would start to cool down from September onwards when the monsoon rains would be tailing off. Initially, the nights would become cooler, and then the days, and by October there would be a noticeable drop in daytime temperatures.

No 5 Raja Santosh Road was a second home. I have childhood memories of weekends in Shimmerally, North of Calcutta alongside the Hooghly River, one of three weekend camps sponsored by Birds and taken by syndicates for shooting snipe, duck and green pigeon, and of going upriver and back by launch or by train . . . and the evening campfires around which we gathered. We made clay animals which we fired in the embers. Tollygunge Club was a venue for tea and lunch as was the Calcutta Swimming Club. I can remember panicking in the swimming pool there. (Returning to Calcutta, I became a member in 1962 and turned up for lunch wearing my Brigade of Guards tie. A member came up to me saying "so very glad to see you have decided to join the club"! Another similar experience occurred when I was returning from Barcelona after a business trip there in 1973, again wearing the tie. I was rather surprised to be given VIP treatment at the airport and on enquiry was told . . . "that we like to look after members of the Barcelona Football Club"– such can be the unforeseen international advantages of membership of the Brigade of Guards!) _

Calcutta itself was the transit hub of the war – vast piles of wooden boxes and stores on the maidan, and an R.A.F. Centre next door where there was a Spitfire training simulator. I can remember the great excitement of being invited next door and sitting in the simulator itself. Most of the troops, in transit either from or to the

110 Bedtime Christmas 1940 John left, Jean next to Doreen, Jen patting one of the dachunds on the sofa, Bogie under Doreens feet

*111 Chindits on rest and recuperation in Kalimpong with Jean,
Shirley, Jeany John and Jen*

*112 Christmas 1944 in Klimpong; on the steps of Glenrilly l to r back row Dorks,
Bunty Odling, George, Norman Odling, Shirley, Jean, seated Jeany, Jen, John*

war zone, transited the city through camps outside the city. Dorks, with her commercial driving licence, also drove a canteen to the camps at Barrackpore and I went with her. I remember falling into a *bund (water pool – JMM) at* one of the camps and climbing out covered and stinking with mud and being hosed down. Another memory of passing a troop train with my father and the troops, burnt brown, lining the windows, and one soldier with an enormous boil in the middle of his back. And another of looking at the garden wall at breakfast on the verandah and seeing the astonishing sight of a grand piano apparently moving along the top of the wall, but in practice being carried by a troop of labourers with cloths wound on their heads, swaying in unison and in step, trotting along the road past the house.

Kalimpong was largely free of the influence of the war until 1944. I can remember seeing a Japanese aircraft circling the town with its distinctive red roundel, but that was the last Japanese visit. In mid-1944, the second Chindit operation returned from Burma to India. Most of the casualties were from disease, and few fit men returned. The civilian population turned out to organise Rest and Recuperation centres, and Kalimpong was one of these. Spare bungalows were made available, with one of these just down the hill from Charitung housing a group of British soldiers.

They warmed to us British and especially us children giving us Chindit cap badges and shoulder flashes. These browned and emaciated men, yellow with mepacrine and far away from home, were real heroes surviving harsh conditions behind the lines in Burma.

In 1944 also, a construction group of American engineers arrived to build a military barracks at Rinkingpong. A small bulldozer got to work levelling the ground and we could never quite work out how it had been transported up the mountain railway . . . we could only assume it had been brought up in sections and assembled on site. The Americans travelled around in Jeeps giving us children rides and sweets. The project was later abandoned at the favourable turn in the fortunes of the Burma campaign.

Towards the end of the year, the outcome of both the European and Far Eastern wars was becoming clearer. Following the D-Day landings and the Allied advance into France and across the Rhine, it was becoming clearer that the European war might end in 1945. Progress was also being made in Burma, with the defence of Kohima and Imphal, and the advance into Burma itself. And so, we again spent Christmas in Kalimpong at the invitation of Bunty and Norman Odling. Jeany always remembered my comment "let's all eat too much" at the sight of their Christmas table.

By the spring, it was time to pack up and say goodbye to Charitung and the Odlings who had done so much for us. I was horrified at being told that when we got to England, I would have to make my own bed. In late April, we decamped down to Calcutta to prepare for the journey home. My mother, Jean, and Susan Burder travelled home first, leaving for Colombo on 11th March to avoid Japanese warships in the Bay of Bengal, and now that the Mediterranean was cleared, to prepare Walstead for the family arrival. Jen, Nanny, Caroline Burder and myself followed.

Two letters survive, one from Jen, the other from the author written and posted from Calcutta and dated 09.05.1945

"Dear Mummy, we will be very soon which will be super. We had a lovely journey down & saw kingfishers (2 kinds) and a blue jay. The view was lovely just as dusk fell. I got into a coupe with Sandy who had a coupe all to herself, and John and Nanny were in another one. We were met at the station by Daddy and I don't think we will be long in seeing you. The parting from Kalimpong was very sad and pussy was more like a dog than a cat. The Industries canteen was absolutely super & must do a whacking trade. I think Bogy missed you rather a lot but is still the same old battleship. I will say goodbye now. Lots of love and kisses, Jen."

And the one from John

"We left Kalimpong yesterday and had a very comfortable journey down. I think that it is rather hot down here but it is not too bad. Mummy, we saw a blue jay coming down in the car to Siliguri. It was very sad parting and a little bit muddling but we got off alright in the end. I am sitting in Daddy's study listening to the wireless and it is rather nice. Someone is playing a piece on the piano that you used to play. It will be lovely to see you again. With love from John."

We left shortly afterwards on a P&O cargo ship, travelling around the coast through the straits of Coromandel to Cochin where we took on a cargo of tea. We passed the battleship George Vth in the Gulf of Aden on her way to join General MacArthur's battle fleet preparing for the invasion of Japan, and transited the Mediterranean, arriving in Falmouth on a sunlit evening with the sun dipping below the horizon before docking in Liverpool. I remember the gaunt ruins of the city, staying in a B&B, and catching the train to London, to be met by Jean and my mother.

And so ended our childhood in Kalimpong.

113 *Looking back down the approach to the Jelap La pass to lake Changu*
with a snow storm in the background

114 Dorks at altitude in the snow

115 A halt taking in the view

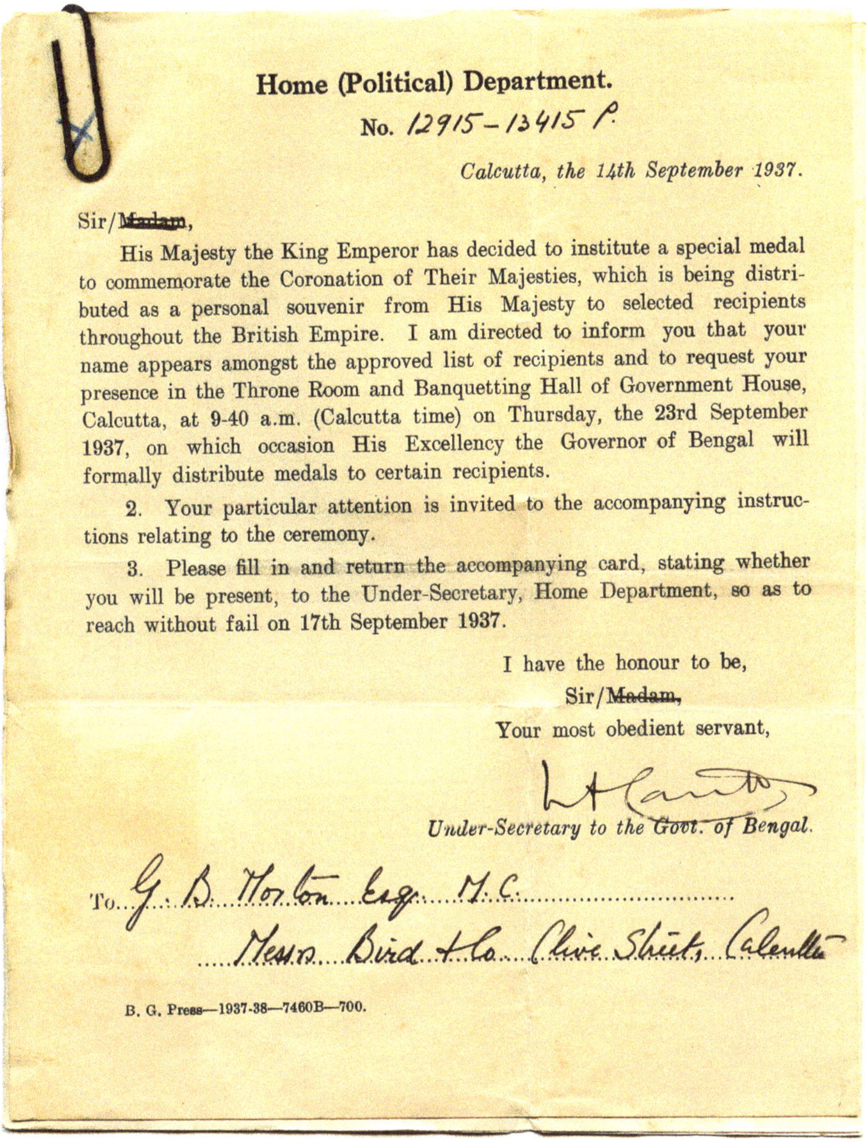

Home (Political) Department.

No. *12915–13415 P.*

Calcutta, the 14th September 1937.

Sir/~~Madam~~,

His Majesty the King Emperor has decided to institute a special medal to commemorate the Coronation of Their Majesties, which is being distributed as a personal souvenir from His Majesty to selected recipients throughout the British Empire. I am directed to inform you that your name appears amongst the approved list of recipients and to request your presence in the Throne Room and Banquetting Hall of Government House, Calcutta, at 9-40 a.m. (Calcutta time) on Thursday, the 23rd September 1937, on which occasion His Excellency the Governor of Bengal will formally distribute medals to certain recipients.

2. Your particular attention is invited to the accompanying instructions relating to the ceremony.

3. Please fill in and return the accompanying card, stating whether you will be present, to the Under-Secretary, Home Department, so as to reach without fail on 17th September 1937.

I have the honour to be,

Sir/~~Madam,~~

Your most obedient servant,

Under-Secretary to the Govt. of Bengal.

To *G. B. Morton esq. M.C.*
Messrs. Bird & Co. Clive Street, Calcutta

B. G. Press—1937-38—7460B—700.

116 The award of George's C.I.E. (Commander of the Indian Empire)

117 Upper reaches of the Teesta gorge with the roadway supported on timber tree trunks

118 On trek with the baggage train

119 A mule train carrying wool from Tibet

120 Assorted packages bedding rolls and kit being carried as part of the trekking baggage

121 *A Tibetan lady with her temple dog on her lap and child*

122 *Chorten with flags – a chorten is a stone monument generally over a burial place for a Bhuddist saint*

123 Jean Dorks Precilla Nicholson and Susan Burder on the march

124 Jean Precilla (behind Jean) and Susan paddling in a cold mountain stream

125 Jean Precilla Dorks and Susan at the bungalow at the end of Changu lake

126 Jean and Dorks on mountain ponies

PART FIVE

George retires, purchases Rectory House, packs up India spring 1946, joins Economic Mission to Greece (winter 1946/47) and realises his farming dream

George had already indicated his retirement from Birds in 1945 and came home shortly afterwards to spend the summer with us. Memories of hot sunny summer days with cheerful Italian prisoners of war working the fields and me learning to ride a bicycle – and rabbits streaming out of the cut corn and rationing with Dorks learning to cook for the family. All of us children were off to school in the autumn, myself to Avisford, a prep school near Arundel, and Jean and Jen to St. Mary's Convent School, Ascot. Christmas was spent at Walstead. Our parents had settled on the purchase of Rectory House, a lovely old Georgian rectory in the village of Ogbourne St George about four miles west of Marlborough and not far from the GWR stations in Swindon and Hungerford. Here also lived Dorks' brother, Uncle Jim, her cousins Rita and Teddie Perkins and their twin children, Bill and Liz.

Goodbye to India winter 1946

George returned to India early in 1946 to pack up. His letters are full of nostalgic references as he says goodbye, visiting the Odlings in Kalimpong for a last board meeting of the Homes Industries, and also full of practical references as to what might be useful in Rectory House. Particularly painful was the farewell to the dogs. The first surviving letter is from Shimmerali of Sunday 24th February 1946, suggesting perhaps that George had left for Calcutta in January.

"My own Darling,
I am sitting on "the point" after tea, with a strong breeze blowing and it is so lovely. The bougainvillaea has never been more beautiful, I'm sure. The Finneys couldn't come so the party consists of George, (Gemmell – JMM), Teddie, (Shuttleworth – JMM), and I, and Noel and Paul Van der Gucht. It has all been good fun. We went to Sona in George's car & got 17 1/2 couple & finished lunch after a bath (& the usual gins!) at about 4.00. I sat in the middle and the others twice round the jheil. It was very pleasant. It is so nice seeing Noel again; what a nice person she is, and Paul too. They have gone off with Teddie to shoot Jaity and George has gone to the Railway Station to see about trains. So, I am left in possession here. We nearly didn't come up yesterday as

325

the A.B. Rly suddenly went on strike yesterday morning & having left Kal at Sealdah at 9.00 he 'phoned at 10.30 and said that no trains were running. So, when Teddie and I left at 11.00, we went to Sealdah to find the cook and all his bandobast & the servants all stuck there. So, after various telephonings, we arranged that George & us would go "in convoy" in the afternoon and that the lunch Teddie and I were to have eaten when we got here would be eaten in Teddie's flat. So, it all went as arranged, and bar meeting one or two processions, we got here without incident at about 5.15. It may be our last visit this season & it's all very sad, and lovely too. It is just possible we may get up again, but unlikely. Teddie has had notice to give up Shimmers so I don't know what they will do after that. So, 47/48 may be the last season here. If we come out that cold weather it will still be going & they may get it extended. I do hope so as it is such a haven. But Teddie intends to retire that season anyhow, & I suppose that George is more likely to have gone by then as not. Ronnie & Sandy, I presume, will still be here. Went to a drinks party at Jack Thomas on Friday & saw lots of friends there. Mervyn Thomas and his new wife Christine (Hermione's sister, next to Noel) were there but I didn't happen to meet her. . . . The tension goes on though more and more it is clear that it is purely & simply the work of labour & political agitators. It has all been thoroughly organised by Congress plus Communist parties and the more violent part of it is, I think, purely left-wing Congress & Communist aided by men like Suhrawardy who is anything really dirty, violent, or extreme. (Husseyn Shaheed Suhrawardy, a Bengali Muslim, and Oxford-trained barrister, was a prominent member of the Muslim League, and a long-serving member of the Bengal Legislative Assembly, becoming Minister of Labour and Commerce in 1937 . . . as a result, he had extensive dealings with the Bengal Chamber of Commerce and Sir Paul Benthall and George both on account of Birds and the Bengal Chamber itself. Lord Wavell, Viceroy from October 1943, believed he was behind many of the excesses and deaths during the 1943-44 Bengal famine, and he was certainly behind the bloody Calcutta riots of August 1946, and was known by all, Indian and European alike, as "the king of the Gondas". He later became the 5th Prime Minister of Pakistan in 1956. – JMM) *The scum of Calcutta are taking part, inflaming all and sundry when possible and forcing "incidents" on the authorities, in fact, the work of trained and skilful revolt canaries backed by large funds. The Navy Mutiny is undoubtedly the work of a single disruptive party & where there is genuine labour unrest – and there is bound to be with the unwinding of the war effort, the agitators get to work and make the unrest into something really violent by skilled exploitation. All our information confirms that the men themselves don't want these upsets and one of our Mills last week refused to be coerced into striking and insisted on working. The Railway upset is only a strike from Calcutta to Naihati and trains outside that area are running. The Railways have of course given notice of a general strike to begin on 11th March unless their demands are conceded and, in the meantime, negotiations are going on. If negotiations break down then there will be a railway strike on 11th March, and there may also be other strikes, though great efforts will be made to prevent them and I believe they will be successful. The authorities seem to be determined to keep order and I'm sure they will, but with so many disruptive elements at large and in the face of years of inflammatory newspaper propaganda – aided by that arch rag the "Statesman", there is bound to be unrest. But my bet is that it will all settle down if firmly handled as the Naval Mutiny has been . . . the light has gone, Sweetheart, so I will suspend operations until the lamp comes! Light again! I hope you will be able to read all this, written in the fading light. Bro George just back from the Station to say that trains have been running to and from Calcutta all day so all should be well & it is a great relief. The Naval Mutiny has been really well handled, I think, but it is a miserable business and has undoubtedly been handled on a political basis from a central control. There are signs of the Congress party becoming uneasy at this juggernaut they have built up over the years and which now shows signs of getting out of control. The R.A.F. strikes have set an unfortunate example in this country, led by the Americans who held protest meetings. This happened first & then the R.A.F. had their sit-down strikes & then the Navy, or rather the Indian Navy. The I.N.A. Trials and then their bungling gave an excuse for agitation & so it goes on. But it will peter out, I'm sure, & soon they will be in the throes of constitution-making. Noel as she went off said please give Doreen my love & say how I wish she could have been here & how too I wish that, Sweetheart, or better still, how I wish I could have been there. But not long now D.V.*

Monday. *It was so cool and lovely this morning, Sweetheart, & Teddie and I got back at 9.00 and found everything normal & peaceful. Have a real "busting" day – out all morning at the Chamber discussing with Tyson, Griffiths (central group leader) and Owen (British Trade Commission) "Sterling Balmers". What a real question it all is . . . Anyhow, I had to do a lot of talking & then we went out to a special lunch with speeches (Not by me!) and all most interesting – But I am afraid my desk is piled high with things waiting to be done. But they will be cleared by tomorrow, I hope!*

How I long to be up and off – not long now D.V. Take all care of your sweet self. All my love to you, my own Darling, with hugs and kisses to our J's when you see them – God bless you, your own Geordie."

It was after all only just over six months after the cessation of hostilities and the surrender of Japan when this letter was written. The shambles of the failed prosecution of the selected officers of the Indian National Army has already been referred to earlier; this prosecution had been bitterly and publicly opposed by Tom Benthall, as well as other senior members of the British community, anticipating that it would lead to trouble. Nevertheless, the Army authorities had gone ahead with the courts martial in the Delhi Fort showing little sensitivity to the issues or location of the trial proceedings, nor to the duress the accused had been placed under by their Japanese captors to break their oath. As a former senior member of the Calcutta business community as well as the National Defence Council, George would have been uniquely well-informed.

The strike by the R.A.F. was a comparatively short-lived but more widely supported affair. It arose from slow demobilisation and poor conditions of service and involved over 50,000 men all over India extending to the Middle East and Singapore. The protests were peaceful and short-lived, varying from three to eleven days. Americans were notoriously anti-imperialist, while Britain at war was motivated to protect India and recover its Burmese, Malayan and Singapore colonies.

The Indian Navy mutiny which followed was a more serious affair but firmly handled; it started on 18th February just before this letter was written. Again, the pretexts were the general poor living conditions. By now, the Royal Indian Navy had expanded to 78 vessels, but the strike was not supported by Congress which feared that it would affect the move to independence; it was a largely Communist-inspired affair. Mahatma Gandhi also condemned it as did the Muslim League. Eventually, after an ultimatum to the ratings on board the *Hindustan,* fire was opened by guns of the Royal Artillery; the ship surrendered and elsewhere the mutiny petered out after most of the demands were met . . . there were casualties on both sides. But the event was significant in that it led to a British fear of a more general mutiny and accelerated the move to the grant of independence. This combined with the Calcutta riots of August 1946 was to lead to Mountbatten being quietly approached to initiate independence by Attlee in the December and Wavell's resignation at the beginning of 1947. Of the members of the Shimmerali syndicate, all were to retire before independence with the exception of Ronnie Cameron, who was murdered during the Calcutta riots in March 1948, while Sandy and their children, Mickey and Diana, were at home.

George's next letter was written from Kalimpong . . .

"Sunday 3rd March.

My own Darling,

Arrived here for breakfast yesterday and it is so lovely to be here. Bunty and Norman & Jeanie and Shirley all flourishing & Bun looking so much better. It really is quite cold and I was really cold when I got here but some hot tea and breakfast soon put me right. Had a coupe to myself and a lovely new Plymouth car to meet me. After breakfast, Bun and I went shopping, and got Jean a Tibetan hat and then went searching for Bhutan silk & got some for pyjamas. I think I shall bring some home too as it will be useful for something, I'm sure. Betty and George came in before dinner yesterday and Betty has got some green parachute silk for a couple of nighties which are being made for you at the Industries. The other two are nearly ready so there will be four for you which will be good! It may be a long time before we can get them again. Your overalls are also being made & may be ready for me to take down when I leave on Tuesday. Also, I'm bringing you some hanks so we are getting on! I have arranged for one of our departments to ask the American Agents to send you three pairs of stockings from America as a present from America and a debit to me here. So, if they turn up, you will know how they came to be sent. I do hope they will manage to do it for me. If I can get some in Calcutta before I go, I will do so but I have had no luck though they do come in from time to time & I still hope to get some. Blankets are available here and I shall get two for Nannie tomorrow. No Tibetan drum for Jean yet but I may find one before I go! I brought Dil up with me and he seems to enjoy being here. How I wish you were here too, Sweetheart . . . I haven't visited our little Charitung but I shall do so before I leave again. What lovely happy times we have had up here. . . . Norman seems to grow more and more keen to settle at home & plans to visit home this year & perhaps settle at home after '47. Everywhere here seems to hold so many happy memories.

Well, the old chaps held their dance on 28ᵗʰ and the fates were kind on the morning as we had a very heavy rainstorm which made it delightfully cool. Went to cocktails at the club first as Doris and Henry gave a party. Then Willie and I dined together at the club (Bengal) and went out to Tolly at about 9.30. Guests began to arrive at 10.00 & I don't know how many we had but it seemed just right – not too many but quite enough! I left about 3.15 with Willie & two tables were still eating eggs and bacon in the marquee which had been set up on the tea lawn. One could see into it from the south verandah steps but it was about 30 yards from the house. Everyone seemed to enjoy it and I had a number of letters on Friday. The hard cases like Donald McPherson & Tom Longfield & Bill Brodie seemed to enjoy the bars most. Others danced a bit and supped & drank & gossiped a bit. I did a few dances and talked & lounged about the bars a bit and generally enjoyed it all. But how I wished all the time that you could have been there with me, Sweetheart. Anyhow, it has returned some of the hospitality I had last cold weather. There have been masses of cocktail parties but few dances so it was all the more appreciated. . . . When I get back to Calcutta I shall try and get away the boxes etc., which have been packed up. Names and addresses are to be painted on before I get back so there shouldn't be a great deal left to do. The drawing-room curtains are now being washed and I will have them packed when they are ready. I got a second sluggards joy as it will be useful, I'm sure. The ordinary light line will take one sluggard & possibly two at the same time in one room but it would be safer to use a power plug if two are in the room at the same time. It shouldn't be difficult to have a power plug put in at Rectory House in the dining room for them and then we should be certain. Much more convenient than meth., and a 10" plate will take quite a lot."

The rest of this letter, probably a farewell back page, is missing but George's next letter covers quite a lot more about his farewell visit to Kalimpong.

"Calcutta Thursday 7.3.46.

My own Darling,

Thank you so much for a letter which met me at Sealdah when I arrived back from K'p yesterday morning. Needless to say, I loved getting it and there were also letters from Jean and Jen, who sound well and happy. The train was up to time & I had a cool & comfortable journey with a coupe to my self. Trains are not nearly as crowded nowadays and I also had a coupe to myself on the way up. I did so enjoy my short visit and the views were magnificent after the first day. There is such an air of infiniteness & peace up there with the great misty sleepy mountains and the cheerfully serious little friendly people on the hillsides and the countless things that go to make it such a restful friendly place. There was only one other guest at Glenrilly, a girl from the W.V.S. recuperating after illness & it was so happy and peaceful there. Bun and Norman and the two girls are all in very good form and moving steadily (mentally) towards going to England for good with periodic visits to K'p. I saw Jongi who talked in English to me and got John's address. Also, Rutmeyer Kancha and the masalchi – all very glad to talk about you and the chaps. . . . (These were the close Nepalese family retainers who looked after us; Jonghi was my special friend; Rutmeyer our Nepalese ayah and Jonghi her son; I used to play football with him on the hard tennis court next to the drive in bare feet in order to harden them, and the relationship helped me to learn and speak fluent Nepalese. Kancha was our bearer/cook looking after the household. The masalchi owned the prize cockerel which I shot with my catapult – it was he who killed a baby cobra that came onto the verandah – JMM) *I went through Charitung, empty but bright and sunny & the same very happy feeling about it. No ghosts, but all the time I felt that some one of my own chaps might be just thereabouts! The garden at Glenrilly is lovely and lots of little birds. The dell silent and peaceful and nothing even remotely sinister in the deepest shade there. I don't know what I did but it seemed to flit by. Bun had waited back for my arrival & after bacon and eggs & a bath, we went down to the Bazaar for Assam silk for pyjamas, then to the Industries to collect the rest. Betty has got you some green silk (parachute) and with what I have sent there will be 4 nighties. Bun has got your overalls nearly ready and I got 6 as doubtless Jean would like one or two. Got two blankets for Nannie and they are putting aside some hanks for you hoping better material may be available before I leave in which case the better will be substituted. (I have also got some hanks from Pyne for you) Got a Tibetan hat for Jean and Dil got a small (not very nice) drum for her.* (The Tibetan hand-held drum had toggles attached to the rim, the knotted ends of the toggles making a rapid drumming as the drum was shaken). *It was the best that we could do. I have still to get Jen's things & something for John . . . Bet and George have greatly improved Tashiding layout – a wall has been built between them and the Morgans & a few trees removed whilst the hill there up to the road has been cleared and sloped beautifully in undulations – Morgans gave up some land and the whole of that end has been opened up & nicely laid out. A garage and workshop are being built at that end and above are to be a double bedroom with bathroom, and a dressing room with bathroom joining the house by the passage upstairs. The downstairs bedroom and bathroom have been knocked into one & it makes a lovely little room with fireplace. Outside, and in extension of the existing loggia, there is to be a big loggia where they can have meals & really extend themselves! The garden too which was lovely is being improved under Bet's and George's planning. It always was lovely but it is going to be far lovelier when it is finished. The rest of my time I spent walking down to the village in the mornings in time to get a lift back for lunch! Had an Industries Board meeting on Monday afternoon, before which Norman and I visited the Homes. I said goodbye to the Duncan rb P.B . . . dear old P.B. He is writing you and was so pleased to get your Christmas card. Then, on Tuesday, I left . . . nothing like leaving when you and the chaps were there. What a haven it has been, and still is with its lovely setting & the indefinable smells of the trees & the wood smoke & all the many and varied oddities! Not the least of these the hill people and greatest of all the friends & the spirit of Dr Graham which will go on. Well, well. It was good and someday we shall revisit it all.* (And yes, that happened . . . first of all, I went back in the autumn of 1962, staying at the Himalayan Hotel and visited Charitung which was occupied by a Nepalese army officer and his family . . . we played carrom together, the Nepalese board game with counters. Jen taught for some time in St Paul's School Darjeeling in 1963, and Doreen went back in the spring of 1964. Kalimpong is now much changed with a big rise in population. And yes, Bunty and Norman retired to Stonehouse close to the Gemmell family at Standish Park Farm. And my eldest daughter Janetta stayed at Crookerty, a Balmer Lawrie rest home just up the hill from Glenrilly in 1992. But George never returned. – JMM) *Had the usual terrific welcome from the Bs* (Binnie, Biscuit, Bogie and Bessie – the dachshunds – JMM) *on my return. How they hate those boxes which half fill the hall. I think everything else goes to plan . . . and with any luck, I shall virtually finish it this weekend. Poor old John, I was so struck by his remark about "better spacing" in seeing you!!* (This was my second term at Avisford and I had written to my parents saying, "I hate this place; please take me away from here" . . . I too was missing the freedom and peace of Kalimpong – JMM) *Jeanie Odling got your letter to her whilst I was there and wrote to John. Passages to Australia seem even more difficult than to the UK. And she doesn't know when she will get away. Nice seeing Jim Reilly & I too feel so sorry for such chaps, but he will find something if he persists, I feel. I can't think of anything here which would suit him – even if he wanted to come, which I doubt. Extra training should be available for such chaps. It's far more important than the purely manual. I did so appreciate the snaps of the Rectory House & garden. It is so lovely there. About carpets. I believe duty is only 33 1/3% but even if it is more, Sweetheart, it is worth it to get the carpets and to be more or less fixed with the essentials in the house. The final cost will still be less than they would cost at home even if they were available there – which I understand they aren't, so I'm sure it is right to get it all fixed. Jack Graham wrote to Bun asking her to get him carpets too so it seems pretty general. They should look very nice & with our rugs, it all should look lovely, Sweetheart. If we have too many rugs, we can find homes for them, I'm sure! Yes, I ordered carpet for the landings and only hope that there will be enough. I expect there will be. It will be interesting to hear more about public schools and we will certainly visit Downside when I get home. It is another excellent school and between them all, I'm sure we shall get him happily fixed up where he will definitely benefit from it all. Eton, Marlborough, Ampleforth, Downside; any one of them should be good, I'm sure & I'm sure we shall get where it will be best for him, the old funny. I do hope you have shaken off your cold, Sweetheart. It is beastly the way they hang on. With any luck, it is only about a month now until I'm off though I haven't heard when . . . As soon as I do, I shall cable you. Must now go and shave.*

Later in office. Another lovely letter has just come, Sweetheart, & I will refer to it in my next. After lunch and am feeling lazy but can't be lazy! All goes well, touching wood, and am rapidly finishing off the last things. Longing to be with you, my Darling. Take all care of your sweet self. All my love to you, my own Darling, with hugs and kisses to the chaps when you see them. God bless you and them. Always your own Geordie."

This is a poignant letter . . . All of us had a great affection for Kalimpong and our life there. My eldest sister Jean became a lifelong member of the Kalimpong London Association, raising funds for the Homes, a family tradition carried on now by my niece, Caroline. Our life there had a special magic, with deep friendships built on the tradition of hospitality. It was an oasis of peace, with the infinite timeless presence of the hills and snows; Doreen and George had made three extensive treks, two into Sikkim, and one into Tibet during the war years. I was able to go back in 1962 when, fortunately, little had changed. Glenrilly was bought by a wealthy Marwari family but is now expanded into a luxurious hotel. By the early 1990s, Charitung had been pulled down.

Even if it were possible, there are mixed feelings now about going back. The old town has grown from a thousand or two to fifty thousand and is called a city; Sikkim is now a flourishing province of India. Much further East is the disputed border along the old McMahon line, never ratified after the Simla conference of 1913, although seemingly accepted since as a line of control. It is the direct route South down the East border of Bhutan into Assam from Lhasa to Tezpur and is constantly threatened by the Chinese. This was the traditional southern direct route to India, the one followed by the present and fourteenth Dalai Lama when he escaped as a young man from Tibet in 1959 (and followed by the Chinese when they invaded in 1962). Now an old man of 85, there are serious doubts as to whether he would wish to be reincarnated; if he did choose to do so, it is likely that his successor would be found amongst one of the many Tibetan settlements outside of Tibet itself. The worry is that the Chinese might claim a separate finding leading to a disputed succession with serious political implications.

So perhaps it's better now to live with the wonderful memories, rather than have them spoilt by going back. But the lure of the hills, the mountains and the people, and its life and its long hold over me, is still very strong 76 years later.

George's next letter is from Calcutta – the house is almost packed up and there is "an end of term" feeling about it all, the old guard about to retire, anxieties about the changes that are coming up, and nervousness about the simmering violence beneath the buzz of everyday life; this violence was set to explode in Calcutta in the communal rioting of August. This is the last letter written from Alipore Road before George moved out of the house into the Bengal Club. . . . his nephew, Bill Tonge, is about to arrive to stay for a few days on his way to Burma with his regiment.

"5 Raja Santosh Road, Calcutta 21.3.46.

My own Darling,
Thank you for your letter which I got on Monday and which I loved getting as usual. I am glad all goes well. It is a good thing to have arranged for the sale of the washing

machine and the oak chest contraption, etc.! I expect we may have other things for sale too when we come to fit into the house, but much of it will be useful for furnishing the cottage if necessary – or maybe another cottage if we get the chance of one in the village for domestic help when we can get it. I feel sure we shall get domestics, maybe sooner than we expect. But there is time to consider furniture when we go in. How I am looking forward to getting settled in, Sweetheart. I am sure it is going to be so lovely & pleasant there and I can't tell you how I am longing to be there with you, bless your Darling heart.

Well, 29 packages have gone off to Mackinnon Mackenzie to be shipped when all the packages are ready. There are 16 packages at Hall Anderson and I have another 6 or 7. I suppose we will get them unpacked in time! The dogbies go off today to Lawrence but I shall see them before I go, all being well. Bill Tonge turned up a short time ago and is staying with me for a couple of nights. When I say a short time ago, I mean about an hour! I am writing this in office as I couldn't get at it this morning being in the throes of last clearings up! Bill looks well and is en route to Burma. I have a room at the club from today but shall move in finally on Saturday which is the day Bill leaves. More of my things will be moved tomorrow. Went to a "reception" at G. H. on Tuesday which was quite good fun – it was really a cocktail party. The new Governor seems a very decent chap & I hope everyone supports him. I am sure they will and he looks as if he could get tough if the necessity arises. Tonight, Brother George has a colossal cocktail party at 41 to which I shall take Bill.

I have arranged to go up to Delhi next week for a couple of days to see Tom. He can't put me up so I'm staying at the Imperial. I had heard he was overflowing at his house and I expected to stay at the Imperial where Jack has fixed me up. If my passage isn't fixed before then, I hope to get it finally fixed when I am up there. Jack has recently been active on my behalf over passages so I hope it will be fixed soon. "The Calcutta Girls' Club lunch party" sounded grand and I bet you made a noise, all of you! I hear Ronnie is expected back here soon. It will be good to see the old scout again. I am sorry that Oscar is depressed and I hope he is all right – I haven't heard from him lately but I wrote him from K'p. Shall be glad to see him when I get home D.V. My office bearer is going on pension after I, and I have given him an extra Rs5 a month out of my own pockets. He is so pleased & has sent me a letter which I will bring home. Yes, I gave them your salaams – the office bearers, and they were very pleased. What a business it is this going off, but D.V. it will not be long now until I begin to slip back home into the limbo of forgotten things! I would not have it otherwise.

I had a letter from Eileen about her stored things and I will take it up as soon as I get a chance – probably tomorrow.

Soon D.V. I shall be cabling an approximate date of leaving – unless the rules are changed!! Longing to be home with you. Take all care of your sweet self. All my love to you, my own darling, with hugs and kisses to our chaps when you see them. I had letters from Jean and Jen a few days ago. God bless you and the three J's.

Always your own Geordie."

The next letter, a longer follow-up and written on the eve of his departure to Delhi, and after Bill departs on his way to Burma, describes saying goodbye to the house, the dogbies and the final packing up.

"Bengal Club Sunday 24ᵗʰ March

Here I am back at the club having left our house yesterday after tea. Bill left this morning. It was pleasant having him with me the last few days and I stayed on at our house an extra day – everything with little numbers stuck on! My teapot was no 13 which was lucky! Eventually, I left – not liking much & Bill &I went to the cinema. He came back here to dinner and was due to leave for Burma this morning, so slept at his transit camp. Kali and Dil moved me into here & I have spent this morning getting it all cleared up & ready for the final packing. Not much to do now. I won't try to tell you, Sweetheart, how I felt leaving our house & the servants and it all. I have been busy working out what to give each one & I am basing it on 3 months full pay as leave plus a month's pay for every year of service . . .

The dogbies went off to Lawrence on Thursday & by mistake got off at Clive! (The location of his statue at Barrackpore, one of the very few now still left. – JMM). *So the Cammil (50 odd ft long with a crew of five) was sent up the following morning to take them down. Hendry tells me they have got a really large godown and access so should be all right. Paul is away in K'p but will be back again on Tuesday when I go off to Delhi for a couple of days.*

George Gem had an enormous cocktail party at 41 on Thursday and I took Bill. Audrey and Patsy brought their new son & parked him in the darkened drawing-room where he lay & kicked as good as gold! I went and saw him & when I met Patsy, I told him his son resented being brought to a cocktail party and not being offered a drink – Patsy said, "He doesn't want one; he had one before he came out; I saw him!" He is so droll! On Friday, I had to go to a meeting of the Victoria Memorial Trustees with the new Gov: in the chair – he was excellent & made a very good impression on the Indian Trustees. On from there to a cocktail party here by Gentle & so home. Then on Friday, we had a final clear up at the house. It was looking so fresh and clean & friendly and nice, as though one saw it again for the first time.

A ship is going on Thursday or Friday from here & our packages, or as many as I can get away, are to go on her, which will be good. George Gem is booked to leave on 11ᵗʰ April & Bunty Nic on 16ᵗʰ (Bunty Nicholson, father of Priscilla and Tim – JMM) *but Bunty hopes to be given an earlier one. I have asked for 5ᵗʰ and I only hope I get it. I can hardly bear to wait but there it is! I ought to get news in Delhi this week. We have had rows here and there. The Auxiliary Fire Brigade, as a protest against demobilisation, lit huge fires in the streets and all over the place & indulged in some mild rioting! We had strikes in Mills in one area where the Communists are strong. The labour is peaceful but are protesting against the reduction in rations. I only wish it could have been avoided but what is to be done? They would have been quite quiet had agitators not worked on them – even so, they are behaving reasonably. It is well after lunch, so Sweetheart, I think that I shall have a little think. It will be so good to be with you again.*

Monday. Not much fresh, Sweetheart. Went out to Tolly yesterday after tea & went up to Barbara & Bill Poole's flat (Secretary's) for a drink which was pleasant. We had a heavy rainstorm in the evening which has cooled it down – it was very oppressive until then. Will continue in office.

Office . . . Got a lovely letter from you, Sweetheart, this morning. Thank you very much. I do hope the carpet permit is granted as otherwise, it will be necessary to leave them here until the regulations are released or until we can persuade them. But I hope all will be well. Better send the permit to Miss Stoddart Sweetheart if it arrives after I leave. I will make arrangements here before I go. Take care of your sweet self. All my love to you my own Darling with hugs and kisses to our own J's. Always your own Geordie."

George's next letter is from Delhi. The journey of 800 miles or so from Calcutta took approximately 20 hours at an average 40 mph so it was possible to lose only a day with two overnights on the train by catching the night sleeper. Normal first class would have been in a coupee, with a bearer accompanying and air conditioning. He describes his meeting with Tom Benthall, then a member of the Viceroy's (General Wavell) Council looking after the massive portfolio of Indian transport, but still involved with Birds as a Director and major shareholder. George, now retiring, is anxious not to discuss business and colour the impressions that Tom might himself form in his impending visit to Calcutta. Birds faced serious problems with Independence looming and particularly the establishment of the then East Pakistan where most of the jute was grown and shipped as raw jute for processing in the Birds mills on the Hooghly River above Calcutta. Burma was also just opening up . . . Titaghur Paper had developed pre-war papermaking from bamboo pulp which had helped it to maintain wartime production when supplies of timber pulp from Burma had been cut off, thanks to the foresight of establishing large pre-war stocks of timber for pulping during 1941. The post-war slump in steel demand had also led to a downturn in the demand for ores, coke and refractory materials and other activities converted to wartime production were returning back to their previous activities. Paul Benthall had now succeeded George as CEO of the Birds companies and, in 1946, was in his Vice-Presidential year of the Bengal Chamber. And so, it was the beginning of a period of great impending change, needing the continuity of strong management in the face of rising agitation and labour unrest. . . . and so also a good time for George, now just aged 53, to retire.

"Imperial New Delhi, Thursday 28th March.

My own Darling,

Arrived here on Tuesday evening in time for a latish dinner. Tyson was in the hotel all by himself & we had a grill together which was good. Have just got in from a call from Jack at the office and the priority board met this morning and I am one of the lucky ones with a priority berth leaving Calcutta by Sunderland flying boat on Saturday 6th April. I don't know when it is due at Poole but I should say on the 9th. I shall cable you today, Sweetheart, and when I get back, I will cable the office so that they can let you know the actual arrival date. I will phone you just as soon after I arrive as possible. I just can't believe it; I'm so thrilled & thankful! Everyone has been very kind and helpful . . . Tom is so weary with all the politics that I have tried not to talk shop to him. I dined out with him last night & we had a short talk but I wish he hadn't as he is so very weary & there is nothing he needs to worry about until he is clear of the session and has more time. He hopes to get down to Calcutta sometime soon, he says, and I do hope he just reads the papers that I have brought and saves up the talk until he sees Paul and the others. He wants to come along about 6.00 this evening & stay on to dinner and I do hope he just takes it easy and doesn't try and talk about office things. He is in good form and has his house overflowing as usual! I lunched there yesterday but no shop, I'm glad to say. Tom Mortimer came in here & had a drink about 7.00, in good form and off home by air very shortly. Then Joan and Jack picked me up & we went out for drinks to Alan's house, one of Jack's assistants. Then to dinner with Tom. Did a little shopping earlier in the day & gave Jack & Joan & Jill & David coffee & ice creams. Joan and the two children are off to Bombay next week & Jack flies home at the beginning of July.

Went to a cocktail party on Monday given by the Cumberbatches as a farewell for Molly and Ken (Molly and Ken Mealing . . . Ken Mealing, former Bengal Chamber Chairman and head of Yule Catto. Molly was a sister of Sandy Cameron. – JMM) *Saw Ronnie* (Cameron – JMM) *there looking very well I thought & having only recently arrived. I heard at that party that our sale must have gone well but as I left after lunch on Tuesday, I hadn't time to find out definitely. I shall hear when I get back tomorrow, I hope. My bearer Kali was at the house on Sunday, the "on view" day, &*

127 *Jen with Gwinks*

he shook his head sadly and disapprovingly and said there were lots of sahib log and memsahib log all over the house, upstairs and down, in every room – so the servants dislike it all too! But I'm glad friends bought our very nice furniture, or some of it . . .

Our packages, 52, were finished on Thursday morning and I signed the necessary papers so that ought to be all right. There now only remains the piano and a "last-minute" box which shouldn't be difficult. Your K'p hanks arrived down on Tuesday – not the colours I would have chosen for you, Sweetheart, but very nice and they will be useful, I'm sure. Paul Benthall got back from a visit to Betty and George & he brought the hanks.

It is much cooler here than in Calcutta & I have been sleeping under a blanket without a fan. But it is warming up, they tell me.

It was lovely getting your letter on Monday, thank you, Sweetheart. I do hope we get the permit for the carpets but if we don't, we must just wait until we can ship them. I'm sure we shall get them & one can only hope they do give the permit. I mentioned in my last letter that the permit number should be cabled to Miss Stoddart – she will pass it on to the right quarters. Glad you found Johnny Morton flourishing. I had a letter from him on Monday, quite a good one! The wee chap seems happy. It will be good to be home with you, Sweetheart, I just can't believe it, & with the chaps. . . . You do seem to have been gay, bless you, and I'm very glad. The shows sound lovely.

Not much for me to do before I leave but doubtless things will turn up until I go! I shall have just over a week after I get back to Calcutta and that should give me lots of time – If only I could go to sleep & wake up at home! However! Take all care of your sweet self. God bless you & our chaps & may we soon all be together again. All my love to you, my own Darling, with hugs and kisses to our J's. Always your own Geordie".

George was clearly delighted to be allocated a berth on a Sunderland flying boat home. The journey time had been halved to just over three days thanks to the wartime development of lengthening the range of the aircraft in its naval reconnaissance and attack role, one that continued until 1959. Capable of mounting 14-hour patrols, the post-war civilian version had up to 24 berths or 16 sleeping berths, with overnight stops on the India route in Karachi, Cairo or Alexandria, and Marseilles, with a terminal at Poole. The following year, Mountbatten, returning for urgent discussions on the progress of Indian Independence, flew home non-stop in his Viscount with his entourage in just 24 hours.

This is the last surviving letter from India. Returning home, the first task was the furnishing of Rectory House before saying goodbye to Walstead. George was a regular visitor to London with directorships in Grindlay's Bank and the Army and Navy Stores, to be followed by the Imperial Bank in 1947, intensifying his time in London to at least one day a week. He joined the Lansdowne Club in Berkeley Square, attracted by its sporting facilities – squash courts – and an underground swimming pool, to supplement his membership of the Oriental Club, then a little further North in Hanover Square. But his initial retirement was to be short-lived as he was recruited later in 1946 by the Foreign Office to join the British Economic Mission to Greece.

The story of the liberation of Greece and subsequent British Economic Mission 1944 -7

The background to the severe economic conditions in Greece did not just emerge as a result of the German occupation after their withdrawal in late 1944, but was in part attributable to a laissez -faire attitude to economic affairs in the pre-war period as well; action in 1944 was not just deemed necessary on economic grounds, but also from the political fears of a communist take-over of the country after the Germans left. Britain, although exhausted and financially drained from the war effort itself, drew the short international straw to head up the economic rescue attempt. This was partly as a result of Churchill's direct intervention, but also from a strong position of trust built up over the years since the British military intervention in the spring of 1941 when the Germans invaded, and Britain's strong relationships with the Greek government and Royal family in exile.

A whole series of interwoven events had created the overwhelming danger of a Communist take-over of the country just before Christmas 1944, after the withdrawal of the German occupiers from Athens, At the heart of this was the country's economic collapse caused primarily by severe hyper-inflation. This was an endemic problem resulting from a failure over many years to act to contain consumer demand for goods and services as well as a policy failure to tackle successive Government budget deficits. The rapid increase in the money supply led to hyper-inflation and an accelerating decline in the value of the drachma, echoing similar problems in 1923 in Germany itself with the Deutschmark. The dramatic pictures of German workers carrying home their pay in wheelbarrows full of banknotes illustrate the problem. A whole series of international loans, ostensibly provided for infrastructure projects to Greece, gave some temporary relief from the debt crisis, but this money was largely used for debt relief which only added to the country's spiralling debt repayments and servicing costs.

Britain had had direct experience of similar potential emerging problems at the beginning of the war. The wage bill of the armed services, the rapid increase in production of war materials and munitions, all of which had to be paid for, coupled with shortages of imported foodstuffs, led to serious budget deficits and inflationary pressures on prices. The British Government brought in the distinguished economist John Maynard Keynes who took a holistic approach to the problems working at the Treasury. Income tax was increased to 50% with surtax at 19s 6d in the pound (97.5 %) and this was to last to 1947. George, a true Scot, commented then that, "he would far rather pay the tax than lose the income." A tax was introduced on all firms producing war supplies and attractive Government-sponsored savings schemes were introduced. Food was rationed and price controls introduced. The effect of these painful measures was to raise tax revenues, reduce consumer demand for goods and services, and head off inflationary pressures and stabilise prices. A similar exercise was mounted in Egypt, the hub of Allied Middle East operations, in order to protect the Egyptian economy and the strategically vital Suez Canal, through the actions of the Middle East Supply Centre (M.E.S.C.).

In 1936, Greece once again became a constitutional monarchy with the arrival back in the country of the King and his family. At the onset of WW2 and at the end of October 1940, the Italians invaded Greece via Albania, and although initially repulsed by the Greek army, Germany invaded both Yugoslavia and Greece at the beginning of April the following year. Crete was also captured and Greece occupied and divided up into occupied zones, controlled respectively by the Germans, the Bulgarians and the Italians. The King and Government initially fled to England and then later settled in Egypt forming a government in exile in Cairo.

128 *A political map of Greece circa 1946*

A resistance movement started in 1942 and large tracts of mountainous country in northern Greece were recaptured by the largely Communist-led National Liberation Front movement (E.A.M.) and its guerrilla army, the National People's Liberation Army (E.L.A.S.). It was now increasingly in control of large tracts of country tying down Axis troops. In 1943, E.A.M. called a political conference which declared Greece a republic again. The Greek Mountain Brigade, which had fought alongside Allied troops in North Africa, mutinied as a result of republican sympathies, as did one of the Greek Naval ships. Both mutinies were put down without bloodshed, and Greek forces purged of the agitators. But there remained a strong political suspicion of anyone associated with the pre-war right-wing Metaxas dictatorship in which, rightly or wrongly, the Monarchy was implicated. By mid-1944, the German Army was in retreat from the Russian onslaught to the North and German forces were being progressively withdrawn from Italy, the Balkans and Greece to prop up the Russian front.

In August 1944, Churchill ordered the preparation of an emergency plan for the swift occupation of Athens and the re-establishment of the Greek Government in order to avoid a political vacuum in which elements of the guerrilla armies could exploit the German withdrawal, and establish a Communist-led Government. Senior British representatives, with supporting officers from S.O.E., had already been dropped in both Yugoslavia (Brigadier Fitzroy MacLean) and Greece (Colonel Woodhouse),

129 The Occupation areas of Germany, Italy and Bulgaria. After the collapse of Italy the Italian area was taken over by Germany

as well as Crete, liaising directly with London via S.O.E. and were reinforced with arms and explosives and instructors to support guerrilla activities. As a direct result of this and a new political alliance between the Greek Government in exile, led by the newly appointed Prime Minister Papandreou, and representatives from E.A.M., plans were now laid for the reoccupation of Greece. This was at best a fragile situation needing the presence and support of British troops.

The liberation started in October 1944 with the landing and capture of the Margara airport outside Athens by the 2nd British Parachute Brigade. Athens was occupied, with 23rd Armoured Brigade operating as infantry, supported by Greek forces, and the 15th Cruiser squadron led by the battle cruiser HMS Ajax (of the Battle of the River Plate fame). Food was short and British troops went on half rations to help out. However, the arrangement was still a fragile one and the 4th Indian Division was also sent in to stabilise the growing crisis. The Communist guerrillas had now advanced into Athens and taken over the police stations, and so British troops went on to the offensive. The 4th British Division reinforced the situation and Athens was held with fierce street fighting between Greek guerrillas and British forces.

Churchill, together with Anthony Eden, left for Athens by air on Christmas Eve 1944. Archbishop Damaskinos, the head of the Greek Orthodox Church, was persuaded to be appointed Regent with the reluctant agreement of the King, and both supported new arrangements for the establishment of the new Government, with a plebiscite promised on the future of the monarchy. (This, incidentally, took place in 1947 and endorsed a reinstatement of the King). The immediate political crisis was averted. Greece was temporarily freed from the threat of Communist government, thanks in no small measure to the personal intervention and foresight of Winston Churchill.

However, in spite of this, the fighting continued in Athens and while the situation was gradually stabilised and reversed by British forces under General Scobie, the Papandreou Government fell in the first week of the new year, and yet another new government was formed under General Plastiras.

The British again presented their economic recommendations to the Minister of Finance, and it was clear that they were losing patience with the whole situation. Arguments had led to the adoption of a basis of valuation of the Drachma, and a Professor Zolotas was appointed joint Governor of the National Bank, whereupon the existing Governor, Professor Varvaressos, resigned, only to be reinstated by General Plastiros, whereupon Zolotas resigned.

Varvaressos's views on the economic direction to be followed were much more in line with British views on the austere economic measures needed, including price controls, wage restraints, and measures to raise tax. The cost of government was swelled by a policy of taking onto the Government wage and pensions roll those who had lost their jobs through a series of corporate bankruptcies. The civil service terms of employment reflected a 25-hour working week and many government employees took advantage of this with second jobs. A large element in successive Greek budgets relied on the sale of free foodstuffs temporarily provided under UN aid. Anthony Eden, returning from the Tehran Conference, reflected the impatience of the British, who were footing much of the bills for aid including the wage bill for a new Greek army, and he addressed the situation with the Greek Government in what was described as "less than diplomatic language"

Yet another Government was formed under Admiral Voulgaris and a comprehensive plan to stabilise the economic chaos prepared by Varvaressos was adopted with British support and implemented in mid-1945. Initially, these reforms showed welcome progress, but opposition to them rapidly grew and a stand-off between the draconian enforcement measures introduced and opposition to them led to Varvaressos being completely isolated and the reforms largely abandoned.

Winter 1946-7. George joins the British Economic Mission and Lieutenant-General John Clarke in Athens. A collection of family letters

By the autumn of 1945, it was becoming increasingly apparent in Whitehall that the British Government needed to take a more proactive approach to stabilise the Greek economy, and a plan to form an Economic Mission to Greece gradually took shape. This was to form the basis of the London Agreement. Throughout this period, Reginald Leeper, British Ambassador to both Greece and Egypt, and his commercial attaché Hill played a prominent role in representing the British position to the Greek government. Two bodies were formed; the British Economic Mission (BEM) and the Currency Committee, and both were incorporated in what became known as the London Agreement.

Greece was in a relatively strong overall position, with no internal debt, with substantial foreign exchange reserves of approximately £40 million in sterling, dollars, and gold; for the time being, it was also receiving massive foreign aid particularly in the form of free supplies of food and commodities. The country was therefore in a favourable position for recovery and reconstruction, provided the budget could be balanced. Again, the Government associated with the Varvaressos reforms collapsed to be succeeded by yet another under PM Kanellopoulos, with a new finance minister Kasimatis. One of the planks of his proposals was the continuation of government sales of gold through exchanging gold reserves for British gold sovereigns, a policy resisted by the Bank of England as a temporary economic palliative, but reluctantly acceded to as crisis followed crisis. This was designed to mop up purchasing power through sales of gold, but with the downside of further weakening the drachma. In July 1945, the British general election introduced a new Government under Clement Attlee, and plans for the Mission, an initiative from Foreign Secretary Ernest Bevin, were formulated.

Under proposals from the Bank of England, a currency commission with executive powers was formed with one British and one American representative, with statutory powers of management of the note issue. The proposals included waiving the repayment of sterling wartime loans of £46 million provided that the Greek Government adhered to the plan. A loan of £5 million, later increased to £10 million, would be given to top up a Greek deposit of £15 million from reserves into a special note cover account to support the new drachma currency. Provided the Greek Government agreed to the drachma stabilisation plan. Britain would waive the repayment of the £46 million war loan. The Mission was to last 18 months with the possibility of a further six months extension.

The Mission consisted of six strands – Cooperative Movement, Supply and Distribution, Labour, Transport, Finance and Industry. Great pains were taken to secure the purely advisory nature of the Mission. It was headed by Lieutenant-General John Clarke, with Sir Vyvian Board, a senior British industrialist with wartime experience at the Ministry of Supply and an impressive range of directorships in British companies, leading the industry section, and with Edward Grove as head of the finance section. Its work started in January 1946 in Athens and advisors were senior British members with a wide range of relevant experience.

George, with extensive relevant overseas experience in India in Banking and Trade, joined the Mission later and left home in the November of 1946.

The political, economic, and military background, problems and challenges that the British Economic Mission to Greece faced led to an unstable country riven with political rivalries, devastated by war, with bands of guerrillas controlling the countryside, unable to feed itself, and suffering from rampant hyperinflation – obviously no picnic.

By now, Britain was shouldering the bulk of the cost of the Greek armed forces and a significant proportion of the police costs as well, while Greece was receiving massive support in foreign aid, particularly foodstuffs made available for sale by the Government at profit. But up to the time of the Mission, there had been no less than five different Governments, each with its own budget, none of which had either been met or had shown a surplus. Successive chronic budget deficits continued with the outcome of continuing rampant inflation.

Mantzavinosa, the finance minister, had produced yet another budget, which completely ignored the British advice on taxation. Mantzavinosa was succeeded by Kasimatis under the new Kanellopoulos government, and yet more new budgetary proposals were introduced which were greeted with scepticism by both the Treasury and the Bank of England – the latter worried about yet more proposals to sell gold. And so, yet another Government was sworn in and the political merry-go-round continued.

Meanwhile, back in England, the search for a family home so that we could move out of the rented Walstead House in Sussex had resulted in the purchase of a lovely Georgian rectory in Ogbourne St George near Marlborough in Wiltshire. This was the same village where Uncle Jim O'Kinealy had set up home during the war with cousins Rita and Teddie Perkins and their twin children, Bill and Liz, at Applegarth at

130 John, Bill and Liz Perkins, & Jean and Jen at the garden door of Rectory House

the bottom of the hill in the village just 300 yards away. Bill had been at Marlborough College and had just entered Dartmouth Naval College. Jen and Doreen and myself went over in the holidays and stayed at the Castle and Ball in Marlborough to meet up with the Perkins and Uncle Jim to have a look at Rectory House. Teddie had lost a leg in the First World War and had just given up running the Marlborough Times, the weekly local newspaper. Rita was my mother's second cousin. This was to be our home for the next ten years.

The house had three attic bedrooms and a bathroom, (one my own) and two rooms for Mr and Mrs Curtis who "did" for us. There were also four second-floor bedrooms with two bathrooms (for Jean, Jen and parents, plus dressing room), and a ground floor kitchen, scullery, study, dining room and drawing room plus downstairs lobby and loo, cellar, garden and large kitchen garden. A "ha-ha" separated the garden from the field below the house. It became a home from home and we loved it. We moved in in 1946 having said a tearful goodbye to Nanny Bishop, and Walstead House.

George was to come home on leave from Greece, bringing with him tins of delicious Greek honey, food unobtainable or rationed at home. Doreen was home for the school holidays, but flew out to Greece for a local leave in Spring 1947. Particularly generous during this time were Helen and Manoli Tombazi with their hospitality at their Greek island home. George's secretary during this time was Irene Sterling, the sister of the wartime founder of the SAS, David Sterling.

At the outset of the discussions leading to the Mission, the Greeks had emphasised the need for reconstruction backed by foreign aid, while the British were clear that the stabilisation of the currency was of equal importance and that reconstruction could not be wholly dependent on allied aid. In view of the needs of other countries, aid was not unlimited. Both sides recognised that the matter was vitally important in order to avoid bloodshed and famine. It was against this background that the Mission proceeded, but the essential weakness was that its main function was only advisory.

The revised budget estimates of June 1946, almost for the first time, proved reasonably accurate. However, unbudgeted increases in wages and other remuneration measures began to creep in to placate the unions, including the free distribution of UNNRA foodstuffs, but even so, strikes broke out increasingly frequently towards the end of 1946. The Bank of Greece began to make huge agricultural loans to farmers, with the consequential increase in note circulation. Despite significant improvements in budget management and the raising of revenue, the financial situation remained precarious due to lack of control over expenditure. 1946 saw a massive increase in retail gold sales to stabilise the budget deficit and currency. But as the end of 1946 approached, it was becoming increasingly clear that in spite of endless meetings between the British and Greek officials, only slow progress was being made. In response to union pressure, extra remuneration was being provided in the form of free foodstuffs to supplement the government wage bill, and other unbudgeted expenditure had crept in. Despite this, union-sponsored strikes began to affect increasingly the economy. The UNNRA aid was due to end in January 1947, and it was clear that Greece would not survive economically without massive foreign aid, the provision of which was well beyond the capability of war-torn Britain. Greece's problems were simply too large. Hitherto, the USA had been reluctant to get involved but only they had the economic muscle that could provide the massive support needed. In March 1947, a decision was taken by Ernest Bevan to withdraw the mission. The USA then stepped up to the plate, as Harold Truman began to recognise the potential strategic dangers of a Communist presence in the Eastern Mediterranean as the Russians began to dominate the Balkans.

Back home, the winter of 1946/47 was one of the coldest on record. The correspondence that survives is a collection of Doreen and George's letters to each other (all the others in this book are from George to Doreen), sometimes enclosing letters from Jean, Jen and John. His keeping of them was indicative perhaps of how much he was missing home and the family growing up. It was bitterly cold with snow and ice covering the whole country. The letters start in November 1946 when George went to Greece to join the mission, and end in February 1947 when Doreen left to spend a few weeks in Athens with him. They provide a fascinating insight into post-war Britain and school life and are supplemented by his photographs of Greece put together in albums in the Spring of 1954 while he was in the West Middlesex Hospital in the last few weeks of his life.

The first letter is written from the Welbeck Hotel by Doreen after seeing George off on his flight to Greece on 21st November.

"My own Darling,

I do hope you didn't have an awful journey yesterday. It was a foul day here – pouring rain, thunder & hail and a gale! It was such fun seeing Bee & we wandered round, looked at the King's pictures again & I got Jean an evening dress. In the evening, I took Jan to see a rather rotten play but we quite enjoyed it! I do miss you and do take care of yourself. I hope you don't find it all too difficult and frustrating.

Bee looked tired & her problems are just the same. She says that Margaret has put on 3 stone but as her bodily health has improved, her mental condition has deteriorated & she isn't nearly as cheerful now as she was when she was so desperately ill. She is to have her eyes operated upon, I gather.

I am going to see Aunt Ethel today. I enclose a letter which I can't deal for you. I thought of sending it straight to Oscar but you had better do that! No word yet from Sandy. I will ring up Molly I think this evening. I wonder how Sandy's lunch went yesterday.

I thought I would go and see Helen T today – my cold has disappeared. Much love, darling. Take care of yourself, Your own Dorkie."

The next letter from Dorks is written from "Helen's" (Helen Gemmell) after seeing George off. . . .

"November 25th Rectory House

My own darling, was very glad to get your wire on Saturday to say that you had arrived safely & I do hope you are comfortable & that all goes well. I took John & one friend called Jeremy (rather a shy boy) out on Saturday. It wasn't a very nice day but we took a bus after lunch into Bognor & fiddled about in that Fun Fair place & then came back to the hotel in Littlehampton & had tea there; a very nice hotel and the food not bad there.

Yesterday I came out here & am writing this before leaving. Helen is well and so is Jan except for a cold. We have between 60 – 70 people coming to our party. I do wish you were going to be there. I am going down to see the Rembrandt this evening. Sandy is going to spend Tuesday night with me; she had lunch with the owner of the house who she said was charming. They only want 3 gns a week for it & will put what furniture she likes in – three months on either side & she's to be out in 1949 – I don't think she could do better & she is coming over to see it.

The weather has been foul – high winds & pouring rain. John had a cold when I saw him on Saturday & seemed a little pale but it is the time of year. I enclose a letter which came after you left. I am catching the 5.5 today. I hope Gwinks is alright. Now do take care of yourself – I hope it is all being interesting. All love, your loving Dorkie."

The funfair at Bognor was a favourite for a day out when parents visited, and one was allowed to take a friend. Avisford, the school, was not far from Arundel on the Chichester road near the village of Slindon. It had relocated to Ampleforth for the duration of the war and so it was natural that Ampleforth became the main school for the boys from Avisford. The house had belonged to the Henty family; G.A. Henty was the author of boy's adventure stories and a prominent writer in Victorian times. Michael Jennings was the new headmaster, following on from his father, affectionately known as "C.J." Michael had been severely burnt as a result of his tank being brewed up when he had gallantly gone back to rescue his driver and his hands were particularly badly scarred.

Gwinks was a newly acquired Welsh Corgi dog, somewhat scatty in nature. We believed that he had been dropped as a puppy, which explained his erratic temperament. He was quickly joined by a dachshund called Bonum following the Bs of the Calcutta dogs; Bonum was followed by Bulger, aptly named as a scavenging and greedy dog. George then acquired a golden labrador called Lee after the American boxer Lee Savold. He was a real friend and after the sale of the farm and house in 1957, retired to Standish Park Farm owned by George and Helen Gemmell.

George's first letter confirms his safe arrival after an earlier telegram.

"British Economic Mission to Greece 6th floor 23rd Nov 1946

My own Darling,

Hope you got my telegram letting you know I had arrived safely. The journey was most comfortable, very smooth and all well organised. First stop Marseilles for lunch & next stop Rome for the night. I had no time for sight-seeing as it was dark when we landed, but when I come back for Christmas, I hope to see a bit more and do some shopping. I believe there is a lot of unemployment in Italy but I gather food is not so difficult and we certainly fed very well at the Hotel. One of the passengers on the plane was Lord Louis's elder sister (I think) who is married to an uncle of the King of Greece. She seemed a very pleasant kindly person. Nobody knew who she was until we left Rome.

I am staying in the Grande Bretagne and although it is only a shadow of what it was inside, it is not so bad though everyone complains of the food. So far, my first impressions of this Mission are not good but I hope I'm wrong and will not say more until I have had a better chance of judging. I am still vague as to what I shall be expected to do though it is clear that there is plenty waiting to be done. It will take a lot of time to get the hang of it all but of its importance and urgency there can be no doubt so I hope to be able to help. But I will have more to tell you about it later. The air is so clear & there is a transparency or luminous quality about the sky which makes it all so lovely . . . .

Leaving England was all so familiar – and, I'm afraid, so distasteful, sweetheart, and I shall be glad when the time comes for my Christmas holiday! I hate being away from you and I do hope all goes well. You will be with Johnnie now and I hope he is well. I wonder if you will be watching him play football this afternoon!

I have done no sight-seeing here but there is so much I want to see and all being well I shall begin soon as I do not intend to burst myself! Take all care of your sweet self. All my love to you, my own Darling. Always your own Geordie."

His comments about leaving England reflect perhaps his misery at leaving home . . . as a couple, they had had so many separations but this one was made more poignant and painful as they had just settled into a life together with the children at home. For the first time, he kept all of Dork's letters, enlivened as well by letters from us children which they shared; we were all away at school, and no doubt he read and re-read them all in some of his more lonely moments.

George next writes three days later after a busy weekend and describes a lunch party on the Saturday given by the deputy head of the Mission and a supper on the Sunday given by General John Clarke, the head of the Mission.

"British Economic Mission to Greece Tuesday 26th Nov

My own Darling,

It seems an age since I left & I am getting down to it though it is all very confusing and not a little confused here generally! Going back, the authorities did not take my ration book when I left and I still have it so it will be available on my return. D.V. I shall bring chocolate and other things of which the shops here are full. Yesterday I sent you a box of currants and sultanas which they say will take three weeks to get to you. Today I shall send Rita and Teddy & Sis some. I also sent you a box of Turkish Delight. I will also try and bring some oranges & lemons. What about gloves and stockings? There seem to be plenty here but should like to know your sizes again. As far as I can see, my luggage will consist of presents & foodstuffs, & why not! It is lovely here in many ways, sweetheart, & the sun shines but I prefer home. I do hope that I am going to find enough to do, and I think I will. On Saturday, the deputy head of the Mission, a very nice chap in the Foreign Service, asked me to lunch with five or six of the Mission including Gregory, which was very pleasant. He and his wife have a house with their own furniture as he was to have been our Ambassador in Albania if relations had not been broken off. Then Gregory and I dined out on Saturday. On Sunday I went for a walk after breakfast & Gregory and I motored out some way along the coast road and lunched at a small restaurant on the sea. In the evening I went to supper with Gen Clark, the Mission Head, which I enjoyed. The General and I talked whilst the others played noisy card games which looked fun. The General's wife is off home this week. They have a lovely house just outside Athens, provided by the Mission, and his PA & secretary have their quarters here. He is a wealthy man I gather and does the job on the same basis as I do, i.e. – expenses and keep.

On my walk on Sunday, I saw a sort of Remembrance Parade in memory of the Albanian War. Also saw a platoon of Greek Guards in national dress looking grand in their funny clothes and marching excellently.

Oranges are on the trees growing at the sides of some streets & though I believe not edible, they look very nice! I believe Jan & Feb are the coldest months. An application has gone in for my berth home in December so I hope all will be well but I will let you know when it is all fixed. I do miss you so much, sweetheart, and I hope all goes well & that Johnnie was well and hearty on Saturday. Most things are very expensive here but everything seems to be available though I doubt if stocks are very large. Food and clothing are rationed but everything seems to be available – at a price – but it's not a black market being quite open and above board!

I am still in a bit of a daze as it is quite a big change though I am gradually getting to understand the set-up & some of the problems.

How is little Gwingo? I miss the funny wee chap. I haven't got used to the posts yet but this is meant to catch tomorrow's plane & I hope it does.

I am thinking about you, sweetheart, at all times and hoping all goes well. Take all care of your wee self. All my love to you, my own Darling. God Bless. Always your own Geordie. Our office hours are 9-1 and 5.30-7.30 so I get a nap after lunch!"

George's letter, dated 28th November, refers to these two earlier letters above which he sent using the Army post bag. Dorks' letter of 2nd December speaks of their arrival. Subsequent letters appear to have been sent via the reliable and regular Foreign Service bag. There was also at that time a courier service by the King's Messenger Service operated by retired military service officers.

"British Economic Mission to Greece, 6th Floor HQ L.F (G) 28.11.1946.

My own Darling,

Just a week since I left! Time is going fast and I'm finding more to do, thank goodness, and think I shall really be able to help. Yesterday before tea, Gregory and I went to the Acropolis, and although it was a dull day, it was lovely to see it again. I hadn't realised that in the 15th Century the Turks had made it into a Mosque. I am reading a short history of Greece in my spare time! Also, I have got an excellent book about recent happenings called "SIMEOMATA" which I think that you would like – I will bring it home anyhow. What I would really like is a "Baedeker" – even though it is a second-hand one – perhaps fifty years ago! I will write to Hatchards today, or to Foyles, but it may have to wait until I get home.

Yesterday morning I was taken to see two Greek Ministers. We have a good deal of "seeing Ministers" to do and much of the work seems likely to be interviewing and discussing to unstick the wheels of trade and commerce & get them to get on with it again. They have been cut off from the outside world for so long under occupation (& even before they were cut off by occupation they were cut off, virtually ever since the outbreak of war), so under rehabilitation they can't realise that a new technique has to be learned – more's the pity as it is full of frustrations & difficulties, but there it is. All of their economic recovery is being retarded by Politics, Frontier troubles – caused entirely by Communists, & other sources of uncertainty making for instability. But they get on and if only they can go on without a major upset for another year, all should be well on its way to recovery. But it seems to be a touchy situation.

I hope you have received my two previous letters, Sweetheart? There are two ways of getting letters home – one by the Foreign Office bag and one by the Army Post Office – I am told that there is nothing in it & if anything, the Army way is better. Anyhow, I sent the first two the Army way and shall send this the F.O. way so that you can see. I hope to hear from you soon but doubt that there has been time yet. We rank as if we were in the Army and get Army Post Office facilities which they say are good. The way to address me would be

A.P.O. 1 ½ p stamp
Sir George . . .
British Economic Mission
H.Q.L.F Greece, Athens . . . & it all comes by air.

When I am home, I will make sure you can send things to me by the F.O. Bag but in the meantime, I'm told the A.P.O is just as quick as "the Bag", & it all comes by air & is comparatively inexpensive so that's all good (especially when it comes to heavy papers)!

I'm going to write to our chaps soon and try and tell them a little about what goes on. Already there seem to be things to discuss when I'm at home so if discussions are numerous, I may be able to stay a bit longer. I hope so and I shall certainly try! It is going to be most interesting here I feel and I can see that one will have to be firm about the amount of work one undertakes! I wish you were here, Sweetheart, as I'm sure you will love it – we can arrange some jaunts with any luck. Take all care of your Darling self. God bless you. All my love to you, my own Darling. Always your own Geordie."

George's next letter follows, a long one, just three days later, and he has now received Dorks' first one.

"British Economic Mission to Greece 6th Floor HQ LF (G) Sunday 1st December 1946

My Own Darling,
Your first letter arrived on Thursday 28th which is good so that is only 4 days including day of posting.

I was so glad to get it and to hear how things are going. I expect the cocktail party will be good fun & I only wish I could have been there too! Anyhow, I hope all goes well & nobody has to be carried out hiccupping(?)! I do hope Sandy finds the house suitable and takes it. I must say it seems a most exceptionally suitable arrangement, just what she has been seeking & provided it looks reasonably comfortable, she will be wise to take it. It would be good to have Sandy so close too. I wonder how you and Jan enjoyed your evening the night I left?

Well, I am gradually getting a grip of the work here and it really is most interesting. I felt so lost for the first few days with new problems in a new country, new currency & new names and government "set-up" – all very confusing; also, new weights and measures and in fact, a great deal to pick up but I am slowly getting the hang of it and can see much that has to be done where I may be able to help. It is a curious situation here, so unlike anything I have ever known. The shops are full of imported things, clothing of all kinds, lovely shoes, stockings, dresses, watches, clocks, (Cartier and all the best makes) and men's things too, of all kinds. Also, sweets, chocolates, cakes, cigarettes and in fact all the things we can't get in England – the country's foreign exchange has been partly used to buy these things but one wonders why they bought such expensive luxury items when they will be hard put to find the necessary exchange to buy the food needed to keep the country from very serious food shortages. So far, the United Nations have supplied food and other necessaries but that is gradually ceasing and soon Greece will have to depend for her imports on her exports and that is where we hope to come in. They can export such things as minerals, tobacco, dried fruits, olive oil, etc and they will have to increase their home-grown supplies of food grains. But it is so difficult to get things going again as the partisans, the Germans, and our own Air Force between them have wrought such havoc with all communications and installations, including the Corinth Canal and the Port of Piraeus. Cattle and livestock have been decimated so you can imagine some of the troubles – added to this there is the brigand activity, in the North especially, which is undoubtedly inspired, financed and supported in all ways by the European Communist boys. Many of them are the forces trained & led by allied officers in the war to harass the Germans. The Government itself is really and truly unrepresentative and none too firmly established with simply colossal tasks of rehabilitation. So, all round, it is a difficult task though not without hope. Anyway, I am finding plenty to do.

The first night was spent in a noisy badly furnished room but the next day I was moved into a quiet and well-furnished one where I am very comfortable. I have no sitting room but I don't really need one for this first month. But when I get back, I have arranged either to have a sitting room here or to be put up in a flat. So that should be alright. One Brigadier Ritchie looks after these things and he will arrange whatever I want. But I am quite comfortable for this first trip anyhow. The food here is adequate but not very good as it is mainly Army Rations. So, we dine out fairly often and there are small inexpensive restaurants where one can get good food for a change.

It is a wet day today so I doubt if Gregory will motor out to Corinth as planned – the climate is of course delightful. It is cold but not very cold yet. I believe January and February are the coldest months here. I am hoping to send you a couple of parcels of fruit, nuts, etc for the Christmas holidays though they may not get there before Christmas. It is being done through the office but I don't know if they have been packed up and sent. I will find out tomorrow before this is sent, Sweetheart.

I hope that the carpets have now all been laid and that the logs have come in from Gale and that all goes well and that the weather has improved. How I miss you, Sweetheart. It is only a fortnight on Wednesday that I have asked for a passage so should be in London and it will be so heavenly to be with you again, Sweetheart. I see that we are due at Victoria House at 5.22 so if we are up to time, I should be able to catch the 6.00 – that will be Thursday 19th. D.V. Anyhow, I will let you know more details later but even if I don't catch the 6.00, I should probably get the 7.55 or one to Swindon. I expect chaps will be arriving about then too so you will be pretty busy and will not want to come up to London unless we all get here the same day . . . what a party that would be! Simply lovely – more later, Sweetheart.

Monday morning. *Had a quiet day yesterday as it was not a very nice day – Gregory and I dined out quietly in the evening. So, I was able to do a lot of reading & I also wrote a bit. It is still dull and cold but looks as if it will clear – a parcel goes off today containing lemons, figs, walnuts (shelled), raisins and dates. It may be two pounds, I'm not sure. Another parcel is being put in a box containing olive oil (tin). I do hope they*

*all arrive safely before Christmas! Take care of your sweet self – all my love to you, my
own Darling – Always your own Geordie."*

England, heavily dependent on imported food supplies, was of course in the throes of
rationing and, for the next twenty years or so, the balance of payments was to be a key
economic factor in the value of sterling which was then controlled by fixed rates. Sweets
and chocolate were rationed, as was sugar, meat, flour, and other essential food supplies.
Very few of the luxury items mentioned in George's letter were available in England
because of the shortage of foreign exchange. The amount of sterling that could normally
be taken abroad was strictly controlled. I can remember eating my first banana around
this time – extraordinary for us children recently home from India where there was an
abundance of bananas. Nevertheless, despite this, we remained well-fed and healthy
with eggs from our own hens and game, particularly rabbits, reasonably available. We
grew our own turkeys in the garage . . . a black and gold variety called "broad-breasted
mammoth bronzes", which always raised a smile. They were stupid suicidal birds kept
in deep straw to keep their feet from getting wet.

Doreen's next letter to arrive describes a visit to Sandy Cameron's proposed house
at Lyddington:

*"Rectory House 27th November My own darling, I hope I shall get a letter soon from you.
I enclose the children's letters. The weather today has been appalling. I think we must
have had a cloud burst here as it has simply pelted down & I imagine that it is only
because we are 400 feet up that we aren't flooded out.*

*Sandy stayed last night here & this morning we went over to see the house at
Lyddington – I think she will take it. It has everything & is rather charming with a
lovely view – the bedrooms are small & actually quite a lot of money could be spent on
it if it was a question of purchase – but it looked very clean & will be v. easy to run
& I think it could be simply sweet. I don't think Sandy could do better given all the
circumstances & the rent & I think with a little trouble she could make it quite charming
– it is exactly five miles from us, about a mile from our bus & about ¼ mile from the
Swindon – Hungerford bus – so she says she will write to Mrs Whitworth tonight. I only
hope Ronnie won't hate it!! Actually, at 3 gns a week and with three-monthly notice on
either side, she can't go far wrong. The drawing room is charming.*

*David and Gillian Pilkington came over yesterday, both looking well though Gillian
was thin I thought. David says that work is difficult as the babus are erratic about
coming in – it does look now as if things are working up to a crisis. Nehru has started
his old song again. I feel very sorry for Wavell.*

*Gwingo was I think quite pleased to see me – Mr and Mrs Curtis have gone off today
& will be back on Monday – Rita seems alright again and Jim has a cold. I am going
down there tonight for supper. I do hope that you are alright & things are going well.
I will leave this open until tomorrow in case there are any more enclosures.*

Much love darling – take care of yourself – Your own Dorkie."

The house was indeed charming . . . and home to Micky and Diana. Micky was about to start training as a doctor and surgeon, later becoming a leading gynaecologist at St Thomas's Hospital, London. Diana, a good friend and exact contemporary of mine, was at Westonbirt School with her cousins, Lois and Shirley Mealing. Ronnie Cameron was in his Vice-presidential year at the Bengal Chamber – tragically, he was murdered during the Calcutta riots in early 1948 having just been elected president.

Lyddington was on the back road to the Swindon-Aldbourne-Hungerford road heading over the downs past the historic iron age fort of Berkeley Castle . . . I used to bicycle over to see Diana and Sandy during the holidays. David Pilkington was a colleague of George's in Birds, a good friend and partner, later becoming senior partner during a particularly difficult time for Birds in the mid-1960s. 1947/8 was the period of Mountbatten's appointment by Attlee as Viceroy in succession to Wavell which was to lead to the declaration of Indian independence on August 15th 1947.

George's next letter describes his meetings, and particularly, meeting Manoli Tombazi's two sisters in the evening at a dinner with Princess Alice, elder sister of Lord Louis Mountbatten; Doreen had been a part of Edwina Mountbatten's work with the troops in Calcutta and George's work on the Defence Council of India had also involved meetings with both Viceroys Lord Linlithgow and General Wavell. So, there were elements in common, particularly as Lord Louis had been Commander-in-Chief South East Asia. At long last, letters from home have also arrived.

"British Economic Mission to Greece 6th floor HQ LF (G)

My own Darling,

Yesterday morning I got two letters from you which was so good. They were the first you wrote and the third, just after Sandy had been down to see the house. Your second letter got here first so one must expect a certain irregularity I'm afraid! But anyhow, I can't tell you how good it was to get your letters and the letters from the chaps. I'm sorry that Johnny was "poor" in the eyes of the headmaster but doubtless he will "recover"! Bless him. What lovely chatty letters from Jean and Jen too. Greedies! I'm very glad Sandy plans to take the house near us as really, I don't think she could have chosen better even if there had been a "pre-war" choice, as it were. Anyhow, it gives her a breathing space and at three guineas a week and with an option of three months' notice, she is hardly committed to any serious financial obligation. It will be fun to have Sandy so close to us . . . Glad you and Bea (MacNaught from East Mascals – cousins of George's – JMM) *and Jan enjoyed the evening* (Janet Tonge, George's niece and a doctor, later married another doctor David Archibald – JMM)

I hope the Curtis's had a good few days' holiday and got back safely. You would be pretty busy in their absence & I do hope all went well, Sweetheart. I hate you being all alone there even for a short time – in spite of the little Gwinks! I wish I could have seen him when you got back – of course he was glad to see you! Well, it is only a fortnight now when, all being well, I shall be on my way home – I shan't know until quite near the time when I go, so shall have to wire you. I see Jean and Jen break up on the 18th and

19ᵗʰ and I suspect they will be home on the 18ᵗʰ but hope to hear definitely later before I leave. We will make a plan nearer the time & if you aren't going to be in London I can always phone up on arrival & say what train I'm catching though it will certainly be the 6.00 p.m. or a later one.

Well, the work gets more interesting as I get deeper into it, and there always seems to be something fresh. I had a terrific day yesterday, at it all the time. Went round the Piraeus Port in the morning and was taken in a very comfortable launch. It was a lovely day and sunny so everything was looking its best. Then a conference at the Bank of Greece which lasted until 2.00, then lunch & as I was going out to tea, I worked from 3-4.30, then went out to tea with Manoli's sisters – simply delightful & one of them particularly like Manoli. A charming chap to whom Manoli had also given a letter was also there with his elderly sister. They all spoke English just as we do & it was so very pleasant. There were also two other people there including a lady who interprets for the Mission, a very nice person. Then office again until 7.30 with just time to change and dine out with the G.O.C., and the Princess, who was on the 'plane coming out, and her Lady-in-Waiting were also dining. A pleasant evening. The Princess is Princess Alice (or Andrew of Greece), sister of Lord Louis & aunt by marriage of the King of Greece. A nice pleasant person about 20 years older than Lord Louis, I should say. I need scarcely say that yesterday is not a sample day! Gregory has had a slight go of 'flu but is better again & has taken a small flat. I am very glad as he was hating it in the hotel. I shall try and get one on my return & it can all be arranged. Then all will be set for your visit. We must get on to booking your passage, & Jean's if she is coming, as soon as possible after my return as sometimes, there is a rush I'm told. I don't expect the F.O. will arrange it & we shall have to go to the B.E.A but I will also find that out – here if possible. I wonder what date in March we ought to try & get? Early March I suppose, & hope. It would be very nice if you and Jean came with Helen if she plans to come out at a date which is suitable. I am laying careful plans (!) to see that my baggage contains the right things for the "Morton" tummies at Christmas! Take all care of your Darling self – I miss you so. All my love to you, my own Darling,

Always your own Geordie. PS have sent off two boxes each containing one doz oranges."

Doreen's next letter of 2ⁿᵈ December anticipates Christmas, asking for stockings for Jean and Jen. Nylons were the ladies fashion item of the 40s and 50s – almost impossible to get in England, glamorised by the likes of Jane Russell and Marilyn Monroe and other American movie stars.

"My own darling,

Many thanks for two letters which I was very glad to get. I am glad you are getting the hang of things – it must take a bit of getting used to. It all sounds rather lonely. It will be grand if you can bring a few things home! I am alright for stockings but Jean and Jen might have a pair each, size 10 and 9 ½ & if you can get black gloves, I take 6 3/4 but don't get them if they are very expensive as one can get them here. Any fats are really what are useful but not if these are difficult there – but anything that you can bring easily & that you feel there is plenty of is welcome!! I went over to see Jean and Jen on Saturday – Jen looked a bit peaky and had a nasty cold, Jean was alright. I had a talk with Mother Ignatius about Jean's prospects of getting into a university & she says she thinks she should manage it but that she shouldn't take the entrance exam before she is 18 & that she must do a lot of wide general reading . . . she was most helpful. Molly and Ken joined us at lunch. Molly looks so much better. I hear the Finlaysons are home. Sandy has decided to take the house but I haven't heard from her since she went & she has been very busy as Wendy isn't alright yet. Yesterday I went over to Sally's confirmation at Calne. The address was very good I thought, given by the Bishop of Salisbury – Teddy had meals with me yesterday as Rita and Jim are away until today – I haven't written since last Wed. as I have been busy with the Curtis's away – they come back today.

I think Gwingo quite likely has worms again & I must worm him this week sometime. He is very bobbery at times & at other times simply won't come & finds life very bewildering! The weather has been simply appalling; we have had only one fine day since you left & even then there was the odd shower. I can't ever remember such heavy continuous rain & gales in the country. Scurays are ready for the car, so I must ring up to take it in.

I had better go and find some lunch I suppose. All love, darling, I miss you very much.

Nothing of importance has come for you – I enclose John's letter and a scribble from Aunt Ethel. Take care of yourself. All love, Your own Dorkie.

John's letter:

"Dear Mummy and Daddy,

After such monsoon weather we have got a sunny day. Last week we had a lecture by Father Tak, all about old printing and writing. We have got a lecture on the Prushen wars. I can still skate if I do my skates with string.

I have got a good report this week. There is not much news so Love from John". . . .

demonstrating perhaps an early inability to spell as well as brevity. A popular activity was to skate in the yard by the classrooms on roller skates.

Aunt Ethel's letter which follows is almost indecipherable in pencil:

"St Joseph's 16 Church Street, Edmonton N9 Friday 29th 1946 My dear George, I feel I must send you a few lines for Xmas & the dear Jean and Doreen came to see me not so long ago & heard you're in Greece, & that you were coming home for Xmas. You will be home soon & then you will have a very nice time all together. I wish I could be with you instead of this horrible place. The children will keep you from being bored. Doreen came and had tea with me the other day which was very nice & I meant to ask her a lot & I never did . . . hope she (Doreen) took the best of my things in my room . . . a good carton of . . . for their breakfast. What they will do for their Xmas I don't know. I want to keep out of it all, altho' I may go to see the Xmas tree. I am getting on with my walking, the Drs tell me to walk for an hour every day so as to help my knees . . . I suppose before and after my lunch. God bless you all and best wishes . . . mind you wish

before eating the plum pudding!!!" There follows an indecipherable reference to a Miss S taking things and the letter ends with love.

Ethel was the third child of Justice James O. Kinealy and was born in 1875; she died in May 1948, the last of his children to do so. From her legacy, Doreen funded the building of a hard tennis court for all of us at Rectory House.

Doreen's next letter outlines preparations for Christmas

"Rectory House 06 12 46

My own Darling,

Herewith two enclosures for you. Have had quite decent weather the last three days & a hard frost – the first of the winter – the night before last. Great flap the other evening just as I was going off to the W.I. Meeting . . . Gwingo was lost. The gate had been left open and Jean Godfrey found him in the middle of the road outside Applegarth! He is a funny little dog & I try to take him for a walk most days.

Last night Helen Stibbart and Frank Poole (Brother and sister and next-door neighbours -JMM) *came to supper here & they took me to the cinema which was fun – Lenore comes here for the weekend & the Wyatts for 24 hours. I am trying to get the Christmas presents tied up etc.! I took the car into Skurays & they fitted a really quite comfortable seat in the back. I also went to see Tomliers & ordered more fuel which they are going to send. Rufus has had his shoes removed but I haven't yet seen Burden to ask him about the new pony. The children and you will be home in just under a fortnight which will be lovely.*

Meryl Edwards has got whooping cough & Ivor (contemporary children on the next-door farm – JMM) *has got measles which is very bad luck. No more news at the moment. I will write after the weekend. I hope all goes well. Take care of yourself. All love, your own Dorkie."*

Helen and Harry Stibbart, together with Helen's brother Frank Poole, had a farming business with land around the village and another farm at Baydon, in the downs above Aldbourne. They were good friends living just 200 yards away towards the main Swindon road. Susan, their daughter, was my age and a son, Peter, was younger and eventually took on the farming business. The Godfreys were the owners of Skurays, a firm of motoring agents with repair workshops in Swindon. They supplied my first proper car, an Austin A35 when I was working with Stewarts and Lloyds in 1960. The Edwards family lived at Hallam Farm about a mile away across the fields towards Marlborough. Angela Edwards, their mother, was a widow, and later, when the children were grown up, she married again and moved to Scotland, living in a lovely house, Rozelle, by Ayr. She died but her husband John Hamilton was most kind to me when I moved to Glasgow working in the export department of Stewarts and Lloyds at 41 Oswald Street. Ivor and his wife Judy put me up on arrival in Calcutta at the end of 1961 before I moved into the Dover Street chummery. I had been an usher at Ivor's wedding.

George's next two letters are full of his excitement at the imminent prospect of Christmas at home and his travel plans.

"British Economic Mission to Greece Sunday 8th Dec

My own Darling,

It is now evening and I have just got back from a day's outing to Corinth which is about 50-60 miles from here – or perhaps less. We had lunch at Corinth & wandered about for about an hour. On the way, we left the car and walked for a bit which was good for us. For most of the way, the road runs beside the sea (of the Gulf of Saranikos). The Corinth Canal has been blocked though the work of clearing it has begun. On the far end of the Corinth Canal, which is a few miles long – 4 or 5 I think, there is the Gulf of Corinth and the small town of Corinth. The sea & the islands and the colour and everything was so lovely and I can't tell you the joy it was to get out into the countryside. Here and there were clumps of Cyprus trees & for a lot of the way we went through fields with some winter crops growing, possibly wheat, and olive trees everywhere. The country is stony and scrubbly but it is so lovely in parts. At almost every bridge or steep embankment there were rusting wrecks of bridges and trains wrecked either by the Germans or by the civil war which followed the evacuation. Bridges & track have been repaired but the wreckage remains like a festering sore to remind one of past agonies . . . but some day, it will be cleared up. . . . Everywhere the people look well-fed and clothed. It was particularly striking, however, that everyone was well-clothed and shod, which is good. After a rather trying week for Gregory and rather a long monotonous one for me (except for the rush of last Wednesday), it has been a great rest to get away into the country for a day. I have planned a visit to the olive district further west next weekend and a visit to two Bauxite mines in some interesting country and I hope to leave here on Friday and get back on Sunday – then only a few days later, I hope to leave for home & you & the chaps, bless you and them. It will be so good to be with you, sweetheart. I wonder how all goes at home & I hope all is well – that the little Gwingo is hearty – I expect that he will have grown a lot, the little funny. I am hoping to send home some lard soon and some honey and rice if I can. Golly, how well we shall be greased over the Christmas holidays, which will be good! I shall try & send a regular weekly food parcel home so that the D.D.C. can be built up high and heavy! I hope the first parcels have got there by the time you get this letter but they may not do so until just before Christmas but I hope they will arrive by then. When I get home, we will talk of gift parcels or anything else you may want to send, all of which can go duty-free into the UK as we rank the same as services abroad in regards to duty-free gifts. The work is beginning to "take shape" though it is still a bit obscure but I will tell you more about it when I am there again. It is so difficult to achieve anything positive here. But it won't be for the want of the effort anyhow. More tomorrow, sweetheart, when I shall post this as it can't go today and I may get a letter from you tomorrow. God bless you.

__Monday__ . . . Your letter of 2nd arrived today quite safely and I was so very glad to hear again. I do hope Jen's cold will soon clear up – poor old Jen does seem to get all the *colds going though I suppose she gets fewer than she did. I will write more fully by next letter sweetheart. Have really had a good and busy day today & we get on – I think! I am going out into the olive oil districts next weekend I hope but more later. Hope the weather is better – it has been really stormy here off and on but lovely in between. Take all care of your darling self. All my love to you my own Darling – longing to be with you. Always your own Geordie."*

The trip to Corinth skirting the northern shore of the Gulf of Saranikos across the narrow neck of the isthmus of the Peloponnese and into the city of Corinth is almost biblical in its description. To the south, just off the eastern shore, lie the Greek islands, amongst them the southernmost island of Poros. It was here that Helen and Manoli Tombazi had their villa home on the seashore, where George and Doreen stayed in their March holiday the following year, 1947. Dorks fell in love with Greece and stayed there frequently after George died in 1954, sometimes with Sandy Cameron who was also widowed. A photograph album of photos taken by George survives in the family archive. George's final pre-Christmas letter details his travel arrangements back home.

"British Economic Mission to Greece Thursday 12th Dec

My own Darling,

Home in another week D.V.! I can hardly believe it but although time has hung heavily at weekends sometimes, the rest of the time has flown. I hope this gets to you quickly as otherwise I may get there first! I hope to get my reservation for Wednesday next week and we should be due at the Victoria Airways Terminus at 5.22 on 19ᵗʰ which will just enable me to catch the 6.00 if I can get a taxi to Paddington. If I don't get a letter from you on arrival telling me what to do otherwise, I shall make for the 6.00 & if I can telephone I will. If I miss the 6.00, I shall almost certainly have time to 'phone and let you know how I am coming. I expect you may be up in London meeting Johnnie in which case all should be well. But anyhow, Sweetheart, don't worry as I can always phone from Hungerford and wait to be collected! There may be no time to 'phone if I get the 6.00 but as I say, I can always 'phone from Hungerford. It will be so good to be home with you again, Sweetheart – I got a letter written just after the Curtiss had returned, which I loved getting and I'm glad you will have had a bit more time to do other than cook! I also had a letter from Jean which was good. She sounds very happy, bless her. They haven't got my letters but will have by now. I am bringing them home some stamps.

I plan to go away tomorrow to visit Delphi & visit some Bauxite mines but should be back on Sunday evening if all goes well. (Delphi is inland off the north coast of the Gulf of Corinth so George would have repeated the journey of the previous weekend – JMM)

As soon as I know about leaving here, I will wire you – I hope my suitcase will be full of "good grub". All my love to you, my own Darling. Take all care of your sweet self. God bless you. All my love to you. Always your own Geordie."

George now came back for Christmas bringing tins of honey and butter and all sorts of other unobtainable goodies; we children broke up from school to celebrate our first Christmas all together at Rectory House with our Perkins cousins and Uncle Jim. Bill had now left Dartmoor College and was a second lieutenant on a frigate. I was to visit him and be shown around his ship.

Being in a country village, our meals were supplemented from an extensive kitchen garden, and pheasants, partridge, rabbits, wild duck, and hares from local shoots, and the game was hung up in the cellar below the main entrance hall, with its door under the front staircase. Doreen kept hens from which there was a good supply of eggs. Summer egg surpluses were

***131** Jim in the garden at Applegarth*

stored and sealed with water glass. In spite of rationing, we never went short. I learnt at an early age how to gut, skin and dress a wild rabbit, of which there were countless numbers in the fields and woods.

Sadly, the holidays went by far too quickly and George flew back to Greece in the second week of January. His letter of 12th January describes the journey. This is written on Rectory House notepaper and dated Sunday 12th January.

"My own Darling,

Well, we are here after two days' hold up in Rome. We left Northolt more than an hour late as the wireless went wrong and we had to be transferred to another plane. We got to Rome late but I just had time to go out and got a two-way & a few BBs for you! Next morning, we left Rome on schedule but after a fairly bumpy journey through bad weather for about 1 1/2 hours, we had to turn back as the weather ahead was apparently too bad. The next day we were told that we couldn't leave as the weather was still too bad. When we got back to the hotel, I met a Colonel friend just off to Northern Italy and he put his car at our disposal after he had left. Another man and I shopped in the morning & I got more things for you & the chaps and a pair of gloves for myself. After lunch, we went on a tour in the Colonel's car with a very nice English-speaking Italian driver who looked after us well. The hotel had failed to get us two tickets for the opera that night but our Italian driver came with us to the ticket office & we got two seats in a box which was great luck as it was simply packed out. So, after a quick tea, we left for the opera at 5.30 – La Traviata, which was simply excellently done. The orchestra was between 75 & 80 and the artists were superb, I thought, a lovely evening only spoilt by your not being there too, Sweetheart. Well, we dined after 9.00 and so to bed. This morning we made an early start & allowing for the one hour's difference between Rome and Athens, we got here about 12.40 & lunched between 2 & 3. I shall send a wire first thing in the morning as apparently there are difficulties on Sundays though goodness knows why.

They have given me a nice bedroom & bath with a sitting room adjoining where I am writing this. It is all comfortable & when you arrive in March we shall not need to move over to another room. After giving Gregory dinner last Wednesday, I wrote you a few hurried lines, Sweetheart, and also wrote to Salmon at the F.O. about your passage out. If there are any difficulties, I shall write to the higher chaps and ask them to make a special effort. It should be easier by then but nobody seems to know anything definite yet. (The Mission was about to be wound up with the Americans taking over – JMM) *Saw Helen and Manoli before dinner and after seeing you off that evening. Helen looked far from well but was so nice & kindness as ever, both she and Manoli, and it was very good to see them, especially as I wasn't liking anything much just having left you on the train. I suppose it is childish of me but I do so hate it when I have to leave you, Sweetheart. I'm always so happy when I am with you . . . just can't tell you, and the chaps too, bless them. They have been in such good form. You are much too sweet to us all, bless you, Darling heart, and it will be heavenly to be with you in March D.V. I may be able to get over to Rome to meet you but we must have a few days in Rome together either going or returning and we will see how things work out. Apparently, Helen has booked by sea from Marseilles just as a safeguard in case the passages are still short in March and April. An airways official was on board and though he could not be definite, he seemed to think that services would be back to normal fairly soon. But I shall keep at it and let you know how things go. Everything here seems well according to Brig Ritchie who met us, very kindly. Rapp the deputy here 'phoned this morning which was kind of him . . . will finish this tomorrow morning. I do miss you so.*

Monday *Sent off a telegram this morning & hope it gets there without delay. Will write again soon, Sweetheart. Have been busy seeing all the chaps & hearing all the "grip". It has been lovely weather but I gather it has not been very good until yesterday. Take all care of yourself, Darling, & the chaps. God Bless you and them. I hate it without you, Sweetheart. All my love to you, my own Darling, and hugs to the J's. Always your own Geordie."*

Doreen was now planning the trip to join George on holiday in March. Doreen's letter of 10th January (misdated & probably 15th) sets out the plan. . . . she acknowledges the letter from Rome which has not survived.

"Rectory House 10th January

My own darling,

Very many thanks for your letter. I will post my passport to Mr Salmon. I do hate you going but it will be lovely to come out if possible in March – I am sending off some letters which came for you. Yesterday was a lovely day so hope you had a good journey.

All went according to plan. We had lunch in Bath & I met Christopher alright. We all very much enjoyed the pantomime. John roared with laughter at all the rather coarse comedians, really just his cup of tea. I wish you could have seen his beaming face. After, we had tea with Cara and Sally and so home.

Today we are going to visit the hunt kennels at Sunninghill & have tea in Marlborough & I suppose the Camerons arrive in a body tomorrow.

It is a grey day today & there was a hard frost this morning but it has thawed. The children have gone riding & John & Chris have gone for a bicycle ride. I don't think there is any more news. All Love, darling – take care of yourself. Your own Dorkie." (Avisford had a number of Polish boys as did Ampleforth, establishing a separate house for them, and Christopher Balinski, an orphaned Polish count, became a good friend and spent a number of school holidays with us – JMM)

George's next letter describes his meeting George Millar, his cousin and former S.O.E. agent in France – a very modest man and war hero (and mentioned earlier in this book).

"British Economic Mission to Greece, 6ᵗʰ floor HQ LF (G), Athens 15ᵗʰ January 47

My own Darling,

It is colder today but very pleasant. I dined quietly at the General's house last night and first of all one of his P.A.s told me it was quite easy to get down to Rome now by train from London. So, if air all the way is difficult, I might be able to fix it from Rome if you came by train. I would be in Rome to meet you anyhow. If you have heard from Salmon, I hope to hear about it soon and I can then take what further action from this end that seems necessary. Also, George Millar's name was mentioned so I laid low a bit and then asked which one they were talking about and it was "our" George Millar! They were seeing him today so I said, "Ask him if he has heard of George Morton" – This morning, he & his wife walked in! He has not changed a great deal and looks incredibly young. We had a talk & they go off by air on Friday morning. They are looking for a house or cottage somewhere in our area & I asked them to look you up, as you may be able to help & in any event, you will, I'm sure, like to see them both. It was nice to meet him again after so long & his many adventures. Also, his wife seems so very nice. George Millar said his mother was to have come out here and has a friend at the Prestwick Air Base who has influence and would, he is sure, fix you up for passages if the worst came to the worst. So do ask him if they call. I don't know his mother's address but Fergus would. (She was May Millar, Fergus Morton's sister and George's first cousin – JMM).

I got the enclosed letter from Jean which I haven't answered. I have written at the top the address which was on the outside of the envelope. It is good to think that she has come through that grim time they must have had.

We had an amusing evening at the General's – just a homely party with only a very young RAF officer & me from outside.

I have been busy fitting myself out with the requisite for tea-making in my bedroom & made some tea this morning which was good. There is plenty of tea here so all's well. We are working up a parcel for you consisting (1) a similar tin of butter to the one I brought (2) A small tin to show you the size (3) two large tins of honey (4) a few small tins of Nescafé. I have also got for a later parcel a tin of rose leaf jam and will build up a bit more! The undies I have got so far will also go this week when I have got them properly packed. Got two two-way stretches, one for you and one for Jean if you think it is the right sort for her – three Bbs similar to your pattern & three a little smaller for Jean. Three cotton stretchy pants for you as indicated & I hope they are the right size. Three vests for John. I will complete the list soon. I also got you some Chanel no 5 & nail polish. I must get it all carefully packed. Have got well into it again & it hasn't taken long.

When I got here, the chap who was sending off the lard said he had thought it better to send Australian butter as a consignment had come in not tinned, for Christmas & he had it tinned up and sent, I think 15 lbs or it may have been 5. The point is, Sweetheart, I don't know how airtight the tins will be and it may not keep long so I should watch it and open straight away – might be better to distribute it to our friends if there is any doubt and if there is enough. So many would be glad to have it, I feel, especially if its keeping capacity is doubtful. Have just seen my friend. He tells me the tins were only sealed with tape but that the butter is especially made for the east so that it will keep for the maximum time possible. I expect it's like the New Zealand that used to come to Calcutta. Apparently, it is in 1 lb pats – there are three tins with 5lbs in each. If kept in a fridge, it should be alright for some time, I expect. Anyhow, Sweetheart, you will know what is best.

Gregory got back on Monday very depressed about everything. I am dining with him tomorrow evening & shall hear more I expect. I may go out to see old Corinth at the weekend. One can do that in one day if one starts early enough. Take all care of your Sweet Self & of our chaps. I'm always thinking of you. God Bless. All my love to you, my own Darling, with hugs to the savages. Always your own Geordie."

Dorks' next letter describes the arrival of The Cameron family and a visit to the circus, and acknowledges George's telegram confirming his safe arrival.

"Rectory House 14. 01. 47

I was very relieved to get a telegram this morning to say you had arrived safely. I guessed you had been held up with bad weather but as usual, the papers were full of reports of crashes all over the world & the weather in Eastern Europe does sound pretty awful. I hope you aren't frozen.

We had a pretty hectic weekend with the Cameron family here. Diana and John and Chris nearly rose the roof & played rowdy games – sardines & football. However, they seemed to enjoy themselves & all got on very well. Sandy isn't really fit – she has a rotten cough – however, she says she is going to stay in bed & deal with it next weekend. She is pleased about the house & the daily woman can cook & has a son who can probably do a bit of distempering for her. She is probably coming down for a night next week to see about odd things. Micky is such a nice boy – we had a lovely day yesterday at the

Circus though all feel a bit part-worn today! It was a wonderful show, and well worth seeing & we all enjoyed it, even Jan! Matt Watty & Sylvia (Smythe – JMM) *& family were there too – everything went according to plan, rather to my surprise – we hired a car so did the thing in style & got back to Paddington in time for some tea before the train left.*

John & Christopher have gone to Marlborough by bus this morning. It is a beastly morning & this will at least keep them quiet. We are going over to the Burder's tomorrow afternoon.

I enclose some letters. Skurays bill has come to £22 but this does not include the new seat. I will pay it. I do hate you going away – I sent my passport & a covering letter asking for a priority passage but haven't heard anything yet. All love, darling – take care of yourself. Your own Dorkie."

Doreen's next letter is written towards the end of the school holidays.

"Rectory House 17ᵗʰ 01 47

My own darling,

I expect that I shall get a letter soon from you. I forgot to tell you in my last letter that the glasses have arrived from Ross. They are lovely – John and I went for a walk on the Downs this morning & tested them out – they have such a big vision & are so light.

Jennifer says Meryll says thank you very much for the Turkish Delight – also, I put John's purse on your desk one day; can you tell me what became of it? My passport has come back from the F.O. & they have put in for a priority passage for me for Monday March 3ʳᵈ but I shan't know until a day or so beforehand. What if any cash shall I bring out with me? And how much weight am I allowed – I suppose I ought to bring one evening dress. We have had two Spring-like days, but decided to go to the Races tomorrow only as there seemed a lot to do & I felt two days racing might be exhausting. So, we are going tomorrow & Rita and Teddy are coming with us. The McNaughts couldn't manage it. John has been a pest. I think really it is because he doesn't want to go back to school & is making the most of the end of the holidays by drawing as much attention to himself as possible! Christopher's visit was a great success. He went on Wednesday & Jean and John and I saw him off. I took the material in to have Jean's coat and skirt made up. Jan is coming to the theatre with me next Tuesday and the old dame is giving me a bed so all is well. I shall go and see Aunt Ethel on Wednesday. Jean and I cleaned the car yesterday & Fisher says he will do it whilst you are away. Tom has sent us a lovely book called Georgian Cabinet Makers. Most interesting and has a lot of illustrations.

I hope all goes well & that you are not very cold. It will only be about six weeks before I leave to see you. Much love, darling, Your own Dorkie."

George's next letter describes a supper at the General's house for the King and his sister, and also the arrival of the US Porter Mission which was now taking over the work of the British Mission – it was to be wound down by the beginning of March, an initiative of Ernest Bevan, the Foreign Secretary.

"British Economic Mission to Greece 5th floor HQ LF (G) Athens 21.1.47

My own Darling,

Nothing much fresh since last I wrote except that I have been moving in high society! The King and his sister were supping with the General last Sunday and it was the most delightful informal supper party of about fifteen or sixteen. We helped ourselves at a buffet supper and afterwards talked or watched the chaps & girls dance eightsomes! The General had got along a Scottish piper who made excellent Scottish music on an accordion and they danced Scottish reels. The King didn't join in! (Nor did I!) I had quite a chat with him and we talked about India and the Willingdons (Viceroy to India 1931-36 during the second and third round table conferences leading up to the 1935 Government of India Act – See Tom Benthall's reflections of his meetings with Mahatma Gandhi in Appendix 1 – JMM) & *all who were there when he visited India. He seemed most cheerful & happy to talk about it all & joke about some of the personalities. He is very worried just now about outside things. He has a great sense of fun – I should think he needs it, poor chap. His sister was also very charming & cheerful & seemed to enjoy herself also . . . then yesterday was a busy day in office. I should have been very glad of a quiet evening by myself. But I dined out with the Rapps – a quiet dinner with only six of us. This evening I dine alone & go early to bed. Am just having my tea after a nap after a late lunch – discussions all morning lasting until nearly 2.00. Gregory has retired to bed with a feverish cold and a tummy. Very wise of him to take a day off. The Porter Mission has arrived & we are busy getting together all the material we think may be of use to them. So we go on, but all good fun. It is a cold dull day today, very cold and raw but it will clear up. I believe flying conditions have been bad in patches. Greece seems to have bad flying weather at times but usually planes are grounded as they are very careful, thank goodness. I expect the chaps will be back at school by the time you get this. I am writing them today. How is little Gwing? I miss him, the little chap! A dull letter, Sweetheart, but there seems so little to tell . . . I miss you so much. Take all care of your sweet self. God Bless. All my love to you, my own Darling. Always your own Geordie."*

George's letter, despite him suffering from a bout of the blues, records a most interesting social encounter with the King. After the summer 1946 elections, during which an overwhelmingly right-wing government was elected, the plebiscite which had been promised had taken place on September 1st with an overwhelming vote in favour of Greece returning to a constitutional monarchy. A subsequent investigation found significant fraud but confirmed the overwhelming support for the result because the fraud would not have affected the overall result! It must have been hard to avoid a feeling of failure on the arrival and take-over by the US Porter Mission, tempered perhaps by some relief that the frustrations of the prevarications of the Greek Government in accepting advice were finally coming to an end. George's next letter describes his move out of the hotel to stay in the General's house.

"British Economic Mission to Greece, Athens 23.1 47.

My own Darling,

It was lovely getting a letter from you this morning and also one from Johnnie, sending me his snaps and advising me not to lose them, bless him! I am so very glad you have heard from the F.O. about a passage and I only hope all goes well and that you get one on 3rd March. It will be lovely when you get here and I'm sure you will love it. This morning I got a message from the General asking if I would like to stay with him and I think I shall have to do so as it is a most comfortable house more or less in the country and it is very comfortably run and there should be no bother. Another chap from the Mission and his two lady secretaries also stay there and it seems a happy household. If only I could be there when you get here, it would be lovely as I'm sure you would infinitely prefer it to the Grand Bretagne. Anyhow, let's hope for the best. The General is a very cheery chap whom I'm sure you would like a lot. The Ministerial "crisis" is over (one of the regular occurrences) and the Govt. is being reshuffled to include more parties which will we hope be a good thing. They are in for a very difficult year but it will, with luck, all come well in the end though there will doubtless be many critical times . . . John said in his letter, as you did too, Sweetheart, that you were going to Cheltenham which sounded good! I wonder how the gambling went! Very glad the field glasses have come and that you approve. I must say I was very impressed with them, and their being rather larger is not much of a disadvantage, especially as they aren't too heavy. We are well set up now. I will write and get them insured. I do hope my letters are arriving regularly now – I expect they are though flying weather hasn't been too good. Glad the Turkish Delight arrived for Meryl. I forgot about John's purse but it may be in the third drawer of our bedside chest of drawers right at the back. I hope that is where I put it. About bringing out cash when you come, Sweetheart. I think that one can bring twenty pounds without any restriction and without affecting one's ability to spend seventy-five pounds in one year abroad. If that is so then bring twenty pounds in one-pound notes (no fivers). Actually, I can get all the money we shall need without affecting our ability to go abroad next winter and getting the maximum then. So, the less you bring the better and I can get all we shall need; 'nuff said'.! If you find that you are not allowed even twenty pounds without it going against the seventy-five, then I should bring ten pounds only. I shall do my utmost to be in Rome when you arrive but, in any event, you should not want more and I will let you know what I manage about getting over to Rome when I have had a scout! I am determined either to be there to meet you or to go over when you leave or both! It should not be difficult. You are allowed 44 lbs free & up to 66 lbs by paying extra, I think, but I should enquire there about it & in any case should bring the 66 lbs. Yes, an evening dress would be wise – you will probably want to get some day things here & I believe they are very good.

Hope you and Jan enjoyed the theatre. Wish I could have been with you. How very nice of Sheila and Tom to send us a book.

Take all care of your sweet self. God Bless. I do miss you so but D.V. it will not be long before you get here. All my love to you, my own Darling. Always your own Geordie."

Amidst some relief at hearing from George, in the next letter is the acknowledgement of George's meeting with his cousin George Millar; he was a retired member of SOE, very modest about his war exploits in France, and a keen sailor about which he wrote a number of books. He died in 1998 after a long life and retirement in Dorset.

"Rectory House 23.01.47.

My own darling,

Lovely to get two letters from you & to know that all was well. I am interested that you met George Millar & hope that they turn up here. I will answer Jeannie's letter. You sound as if you had a good time in Rome.

The chaps went off to school on Tuesday & I came back last night. The house is so quiet without them and funny little Gwingo misses them all so much! John was really very good though a bit tearful at the end.

Jan & I went to see "Grand National Night" which was very good & well-acted & I spent the night at her digs – very nice of the old dame to have me. She wouldn't let me pay anything so I shall have to find something to send her. Bets and Joannie had lunch with me yesterday, both really very well. Lady I (Ironside – JMM) has settled some of her own money which is nice of her as Betts can use it to help the Trebles. They seem to be managing alright. Paddy still has nothing – apparently, he has had his name down at the local labour exchange since before the war!! I went to see Aunt Ethel yesterday afternoon – she was well but full of grumbles; however, it must be very dull for her. Nannie came and spent the day & helped do a few last-minute things for the children.

On Saturday we went to the races & took Jean Godfrey with us. (The Godfreys were neighbours and owned Skurays in Swindon – JMM) It was a lovely day but we had no luck & lost 14/- between us all! Rita and Teddy came too. Helen is picking me up tomorrow and I am spending the weekend in Stroud & returning on Monday – I have to be in London on Feb 13th (your birthday) & thought I would go & see Mr Salmon at the F.O. & find out what chance there is of getting a priority passage on March 3rd Such a lovely day today though cold.

Your hat has come back. Also your maps of Greece. I presume you don't want them with you? There are lots of odd jobs to do clearing up, etc., after the children. The hens are starting to lay – 3 eggs on Tuesday & 4 yesterday!

All love, darling – longing to be with you. Your own Dorkie."

Jan, at this time, was studying medicine. News too of Betty Ironside and the Trebles . . . Joan Treble, another cousin. We were to become regular visitors to Helen and George Gemmell and their two sons Michael and Ian at what was to become Standish Park Farm. In the summer of 1947, we spent a holiday with them at Milton Damerel near Barnstable in Devon; there we met Bill and Edna Stone, farmers, who later made their home at Standish. Bill became foreman of the farm; Edna used to make delicious scones and Devonshire clotted cream.

132 *Helen Gemmell, Dorks, Sandy Cameron, and George Gemmell*
at Standish Park Farm – 1947

Meanwhile, George had moved out of the hotel into the General's accommodation. The Mission is beginning to wind up and hand over to the Americans.

"British Economic Mission to Greece 6th Floor HQ LF (G) Sunday 26ᵗʰ Jan '47

My Own Darling,

Here I am at the General's House having moved in this morning. Very comfortable in a nice room with my own bathroom. The hotel was comfortable & the food good but one gets so tired of hotel life so I am grateful to them for thinking of asking me to come and stay here. They are a very happy and cheery household and I have asked the General to chuck me out when they want the room. The hotel was very nice & told me they would again give me good quarters there when I wanted them so all should be well.

***1st Olives!** I am told that when decanted, the olives should be kept covered with the liquid from the tin & if so, will last a year or more. The liquid is salt and water & a little olive oil but plain salt and water will do. I have been sampling all the varieties & have chosen what I think you will agree is the best and am getting a few small tins to be sent home.*

***2nd Olive oil.** This is best taken out of the tin and kept in bottle. It keeps for years in bottle and actually improves, they say. I am getting another tin to send home.*

***3rd Shopping** I have now had another shopping and have got two dress lengths for Jen which I hope you will approve of. I have also got vests and pants for Jen & pants* *for John as instructed. I do hope the sizes will be right. They look small but I am told that cotton stretches and after washing is bigger. I hope this is right but I am assured that it is. I got vests for John in Rome so they should be all set up. I shall be anxious to hear if they are reasonably near a fit. If not, somebody will be glad of them & I will try again if you let me know. When you come out, Sweetheart, you will find lots of things you can do with, I'm sure. I have discovered the street for these things!*

When the first parcel comes, it will contain the Rome shoppings with pink cotton next-the-skin pants you wanted. Here again, I hope the sizes are right. The two-way marked JAVA is the better one but you will know. There are 7 BBs of various kinds some smaller than others, but you will see them & hope the lady hasn't let me down & that they will be the right size!

It will be so lovely if you do manage to get out by the plane of 3rd March, Sweetheart. When is the latest you ought to be home? I hate the thought of you leaving again but perhaps one ought to plan early. I have got together some food for the next parcel: some small tins of Danish butter. Tins of honey. Tins of Rose Leaf jam. It is marked "orange peel" but I'm assured it is rose leaf. Rice. I shall make up the weight with any oddments I have including sweet ration with chewing gum for John Morton! Must get the D.D.C. well-furnished for April. I shall send Sis some stockings later & will try to get gloves for our Js later too. Also, perhaps stockings for Jen. I haven't seen any lisle ones for you yet, Sweetheart, but will try again. Am so very glad the new field glasses are nice. They have the new coated lenses which cut down reflections and are supposed to make everything much brighter & clearer.

I hope all went well with the chaps' return to school. I expect it did and by now "Operation Sandy" should be successfully over! I bet it was fun & it will be so nice having Sandy so near. The old girl will miss her car but perhaps it will be repaired reasonably soon? I hope so anyhow.

I seem to have done nothing special. I have been fairly busy with the work and by 5.00, have been getting back to the hotel & having a bath; it has been nearly 9.00 & then dining by myself & to bed by 10.0. It is a comfort to have my own utensils for making early morning tea & I'm awake early. I have been having it quite early! Here I expect it will be brought to me but I can always make it here too!

Weather has been so cold & raw. One morning, I'm told, there was ice in the streets but I didn't see it. I certainly believe it, however! Will finish this tomorrow, Sweetheart, and send it off.

Monday *A dull morning but not too cold. I wonder if you have been getting my letters fairly regularly? Flying conditions haven't been too good and maybe there are delays at both ends. I wrote to Johnnie today in reply to his priceless effort enclosing his photos. Take all care of your sweet self. All my love to you, my own Darling. God Bless. Always your own Geordie."*

Clothing and food were a big problem due to rationing. We had allowances of coupons, which never seemed to go far enough. And so, it is not surprising that these letters are dominated by both. Doreen's next letter describes the onset of winter, one of the hardest in living memory.

"Rectory House 27.01.47

My own darling,

I have just come home from spending the weekend with Helen at Stroud – it was great except that it snowed practically the whole time so that it was a bit difficult to get about and we stayed at a v nice hotel called the Bear Inn on the common above Stroud and did quite a lot of walking round. Polly and her mother were there also. (Polly Newth who lived at Painswick was Helen's sister – the Bear Inn is still there! JMM). Needed to have the brakes adjusted so came back today by train to Swindon & then bus. I hope the car will be ready tomorrow as I want to go into Marlborough. Sandy is due to come down for 2 nights but with skiddy roads, she may not risk it as she has only just got her car again. There has not been much snow here but it is bitterly cold, freezing hard and seems likely to continue for a bit.

Mr Salmon rang up from the F.O. on Friday & said that the chances of my getting a passage weren't too good but the situation might change in a month's time & towards the middle of February he is going to let me know how things stand. He says that I can only pay the single fare from here – will this make the cash position difficult for you if you have to pay for the return journey in Athens & how much cash ought I to bring? I would much prefer to fly the whole way if possible but if passages are difficult then I will see if I can get by train to Rome. This will be more complicated as trains, I gather, are a bit uncertain & I think one has to take one's own food which means of course more luggage, and I suppose that I might be overnight to fly from Rome to Athens but none of this is insurmountable. I have to be in London on Feb 13th (your birthday) & I thought I would probably go and see Mr Salmon then.

I wrote to Audrey Geidt to come and stay & I hope she is coming – she sounds very tired having had no help since December. Helen is coming on Thursday for a few days & Sandy I think will probably make her head-quarters here on and off after Monday next. I won't seal this letter down until tomorrow morning in case there is a letter to answer from you. I had a p.c. from Mother Ignatius to say that Jen was in bed with mild bronchitis & John seems to be in bed with a cold – very tiresome as they were all so well but I suppose it is this weather.

All love, my own darling, Your own Dorkie."

Our sister Jen had a chronic chest condition and was advised in India to stand on her head in order to release congestion, strange but effective medical advice. The letters of this time have several messages from school saying she was in bed with an infection. Helen Gemmell's Stroud location was close to her sister Polly Newth, as she had bought Standish Park Farm. The farmhouse itself needed almost a complete renovation. I can remember an umbrella over the kitchen sink while rebuilding was going on and the magnificent "cheese" room converted to a drawing room with a huge open fireplace and an upstairs gallery at the other end of the room. Potential travel arrangements and the dreadful weather continue to dominate the correspondence.

"Rectory House 30.01.47

My own darling,

I haven't heard from you for a week but I expect that all the planes are held up with this awful weather. It is just as cold as it was in January 1940 only worse because there has been so much snow. There are terrific drifts up on the Downs and the roads are hopeless without chains. I haven't used the car so haven't put mine on. We had 22 degrees of frost the night before last & 18 degrees last night and yesterday morning all the pipes in the pump house were frozen – however, Fisher got them clear – the house is beautifully warm but it has been very hard on people with no central heating or dependent on electricity because there have been so many cuts. There is a lot of 'flu about too but I think Jen and John are both alright again. The Curtisses went off yesterday in a blizzard! They had to go by train to Swindon because the buses weren't running though I think they are running today but are very erratic as Rita and I waited half an hour for one this morning & then gave it up! Gwingo loves the snow & I can't get him to come in when I call him. Helen is going to come tomorrow if she can get along from Stroud but Sandy, who was coming for two nights, has changed her plans & is coming tomorrow or Sunday. I have told her that it is all her fault for saying she wouldn't move in a blizzard. I do hope you haven't been frozen down in Athens. Jean and Jen break up on March 29th so unless I can get away on March 2nd, I think I shall have to leave it until after the Easter holidays & come out at the beginning of May – what do you think? Otherwise, I shall have so little time with you – I do want to come. I went down to dinner with Rita last night and am going again tonight – Jim came up yesterday and took away a pair of skis but the bindings are rusted so he can't use them. A Mr and Mrs Pinkerton called here last weekend & wrote a very nice letter – is that the nice old chap who is a friend of the Thomases? I must answer the letter.

I must go and feed the hens. In spite of the weather, they aren't laying too badly which seems very odd! All love darling, Your own Dorkie."

Letters from Jean, Jen and John were also sent to George. . . . Jen's. . . .

"St Marys Convent Ascot 02.02.47,

Darling Mummy,

Hope you aren't snowed in! We have had about 6" at most, but I haven't been allowed out in it. Such a shame! It's not much fun going out in it though, because we aren't allowed to throw snowballs at one another. I had to come out of mass today because I went green. I was made to lie down until the end of mass, but just as I was dropping off to sleep, one of the sisters came to empty our buckets, and she got me a cup of tea, jolly decent of her. I still feel a little bit wonky in the knees when I go downstairs, but I think it is wearing off now. We had candle mass this morning, and each got a blessed candle – I think it was the incense used for blessing the candles that made me feel queer. We have two completely new form captains, one (our one) is one of the best swimmers in the school, and the other one is the sort of girl who never does anything that she oughtn't. It is Shrove Tuesday, and we have to go to the fancy dress in pairs. I am going with a girl called Mary MacDowell; she is rather nice. I am going to get some photos of the Nativity Play, so I will show them to you when you come up and see us. I expect John is having a lovely time in all this snow. I wish we were at home with the snow; school is such a dull place when it snows. This term is a very short one, thank goodness, but I expect next term will be a very long one, however, it won't be so bad next term because there are all the nice games, including tennis and swimming. I shall have to get a tennis racquet next holidays. It is snowing again now. I think the snow has thawed quite a lot. One of the nuns put two games of progressive ping pong in the gym, a jolly noble undertaking. Our form and the form below us had the proper ping pong table and net, and then third form had a table with 3 blackboards on it and it made a jolly good ping pong table. It was great fun once a few people were out, because we weren't all like sardines, but so many people forgot to drop the bat that people went out almost every time. We must try and put up ours next holidays – ping pong is such fun. The calamity came when we carried the table back into the novices' room, because there was ink in one of the drawers and it tipped out all over the polished floor!!! If Ig had come down just then, we would have all been blowed high sky, never to land again in the right place in her books! I hope Gwingo grows out of his running away habit; it must be quite alarming at times. I expect the roads are pretty trecherous now, and that you have got the chains on the car; my goodness it must be a job driving in this weather. Well, I must stop now as there isn't any more news. Lots of love and kisses from Jen."

There follows two lines of Xs!

Jean's and John's letters were a lot shorter. . . . Jean's. . . .

"St Mary's Convent.

Thank you for your letter. We haven't had quite as much snow as you have, but it's jolly deep & yesterday when we went up on the golf course, we saw marks of someone who had been skiing.

Jen is better now and is doing lessons as usual.

Our weekend is from Friday Feb 21ˢᵗ at 11.30 to Monday Feb 24ᵗʰ at 11 am. which is quite soon. It's going to be quite hectic for the next few weeks what with the History prize & exams in a week & Shrove Tuesday the following week. Please will you send the jewellery if it is safe because we want it as soon as poss so we know what we've got? Only the Nepalese rather large things because the smaller ones may get lost or something. I wish we'd been at home for the snow – it seems to be thawing a bit now. I hope all the pipes are allright now & that the ponys had some food & shelter from the snow.

We got letters from Daddy the other day & he said he'd sent a store for the D.D.C. Nothing has happened this week except snow and work. Please come and see us soon & I will tell you about Shrove Tuesday. Must do my French. With lots of love, your loving Jean xxxx"

Jean was now rising seventeen. George was a stickler for correct English and particularly spelling. Mine was also not very good but I was excused on age . . . Jen's was very good but Jean's should have been better. I can remember being taken to buy shoes with him and the attendant came up to us and said "Are you both together?" to which George replied, "Yes, both of us" . . . the subtlety of the reply escaping him. He once sent Jean a letter completely miss-spelt from beginning to end and Jean noticed nothing! Jen was very musical like Doreen and went on to gain entry to the Guildhall School of Music for piano, cello and singing.

John's letter was even shorter;

"Avisford (undated)

Dear Mummy,

I hope you are very well. It has been raining a lot and all the snow has turned to slush. This morning we all had candles given to us (this was in chaple . . .) (as spelt – JMM) *two boys came round and lighted them.* (Feast of St Blaise – JMM) *Then we had high mass. Thank you very much for your letter. I have had two letters from Daddy so I must write to him. I have still got all the photos. When you sent me my photos there were lots of Diana and Chris missing. They did not come with the letter you sent with the photos. We have got a film show tonight at about 6 pm. Please will you send me some caps? Love from John."*

He had a cap pistol . . . and enclosed with the letter is a listing of all the pupils at Avisford – all 62 of them. George's next letter crossed with Dorks' letter of the same date and both identified delays due to the increasingly harsh winter. There is now mention of the various American Missions and preparation for the take-over by the Porter Mission, the initiative of US President Harry Truman.

"British Economic Mission to Greece. 6ᵗʰ Floor HQ LF (G) Thursday 30.1.47

My own Darling,

They tell me no less than three planes which had been held up are either arriving today or actually arrived yesterday so D.V. I should get some letters today or tomorrow. It seems ages since I got any mail but I don't suppose it is very long actually! Well, the weather has been fairly foul the last few days. We had one beautifully clear bight day but since then, rain and cold. However. it isn't so bad. I haven't seen a paper for days but I gather there has been snow and frost at home. I do hope all goes well, Sweetheart. We have been busy on reports to help the Porter Mission and it has all been most interesting to me (and instructive) especially as Rapp (the deputy head) has had the editing to do & has pushed most of it along to me for comment and help. These F.O. Chaps really are so very thorough and efficient which is more than one can say of some of the members of the sections of this Mission. However, they all contribute something even though on paper they may be (and are!) terrible. All interesting but what with the Porter Mission (the American economic one) and the U.N.O. Enquiry commission into the Frontier incidents, we are getting rather thick on the ground! The General had a cocktail party for the Americans and our own missions which was good and unstuck people a lot and dispelled any feelings that the Americans may have had that the British Mission was not out to give them every possible help. All seems to be going well. It's so very much nicer staying at the General's house and peaceful. It is such a pleasant and homely atmosphere & he is so full of fun and good cheer. I always have coffee & toast & butter & fruit in my room for breakfast; in fact, I have tea at 7.00 and breakfast at 7.30 & then shave & am ready for the car by 8.30 or so. We then go into the office. We leave at 1.00 & lunch at the house & then I retire to my room for an hour or so until tea downstairs. We again leave for the office at 4.45 & finish at 7.00. I usually have my bath then before dinner. All very pleasant! Apparently, "my" car is actually in the port & as soon as the strikes are over, I should get it which I hope may be in a few days. I shall then be independent which will be good. The General's two P.A.'s are very cheery and efficient young women who keep everything going well and are very kind and helpful. Last night there was a supper party at the house. I counted 23 all told! The party dissolved into two liar dice groups in two parts of the room, one of which took to the floor! I sat and watched one party, all very amusing.

I wonder how all goes with you, Sweetheart – I expect Operation Sandy is now over & that the old girl is safely installed I hope so, anyhow. Helen will have been down and you will have visited Gloucestershire with her. I last heard from you the day before you and the chaps went to Cheltenham so I am hoping for lots of news when the mail is delivered. I wonder how Gwingo is, the little funny. Also, I wonder if George Millar and his wife turned up? I should have written him yesterday, Sweetheart, but I hoped I might get the mail.

Take all care of your sweet self. It will be good so good when you get out here & I do hope there is no hitch over priorities. I do miss you so, Sweetheart. All my love to you, my own Darling, with hugs and kisses to the chaps when you see them. God bless. Always your own Geordie."

A postscript . . . *"In the end, all the underclothes and the two dress lengths went in one parcel. I am sending the Chanel separately. A food parcel also went. Hope it all arrives safely. I have some olive oil & two tins of olives to be packed up. All love G."*

At long last, George has a letter from Dorks and so he replies to her at the weekend.

"British Economic Mission to Greece HQ LF (G) 2nd Feb '47

My own Darling,

Thank you for a most welcome letter which came later in the day on which I last sent you a letter. I had a whole packet of delayed Times and several letters from the office. What a nice letter from Sheila. I saw that Tom had passed in two of his exams; it was in the "Times" a short while ago. I must write them. Also, a nice friendly letter from Meriel (never seen this spelling, have you?) Soon hope to hear from the chaps & am writing to them today. I had a long chatty letter from John which I told you about. He really has come on well with his letter-writing a lot. I hope the little Gwingo is going strong. Yes, I am sure he will miss the chaps. He's a good chap himself! I ought to have known that Paddy would have had himself down for a job at the Labour Exchange. I can't imagine his doing otherwise when I think it all over quietly & realise the quality of his whole family. I just can't think what niche he will fit into. It is difficult but it should not be insurmountable somehow. One can only hope that some solution will emerge, maybe quite a simple one if any kind of a job does become possible. If only he were qualified for some kind of research work – working with or for some professor . . . his disability would matter so little in such a job.

I am so glad, and relieved, oddly enough, that Lady I (Ironside – Philip and Betty, her children and Dork's cousins, were Usher and Bridesmaid at George and Doreen's wedding in Sept 1939 – JMM) has settled something on Bets. It was a stroke of genius by somebody; I wonder if it was Philip, as it solves so many problems, both practical and psychological. I am very fond of Philip but I do so dread the growth of that devastating, defeatist, bitterness which seems to have poisoned his every thought on the last few occasions when I have seen him. As an occasional mood, it can be dealt with but it must not be allowed to colour everything. Perhaps I am not good for him or my attitude merely makes him worse, I don't know, but I have felt that only by removing his "bogies" or showing him them in a better perspective can one hope that he will make the most of things both for himself & all concerned. If only he would try and learn instead of merely resenting his inability to understand & blaming everyone else but himself. . . . but he will D.V. He has got so much of the good things of life that a greater contentment ought to be possible – anyhow, I hope so. I so wish I could be better with him. I will try harder when I see him again.

Glad you and Jan enjoyed your night out. I hope to write whiskers (Bill Tonge – JMM) and Jan soon. I have been writing quite a lot of private letters but still have a lot to answer. There is so much, at times, here to read & study quickly that one can't get at one's correspondence. Having a Steno-typist does help a lot with some of it.

I nearly forgot!! I had a most welcome invitation from the Chairman of the National Bank of India asking me to be a Director of the Bank. He knows I am here for a few more months and have asked me if my answer is "yes" when I can join. This is of course Tom's doing and I am so very bucked. It means one regular meeting a week and one casual visit a week – two days a week. It is quite near the office & fits in excellently with a Directorate at Birds London. Fees are about a thousand a year, too, so that's good especially as it will be earned income for taxation purposes which carries some small tax concession. Please don't mention it to anybody until it is an accomplished fact, Sweetheart, but it will help. Make the old chap work a bit too which is good and for some years, with any luck, we can keep busy and have some plans for both of us to stay in London from time to time if we want to! Hope you approve, Sweetheart.

It is so very comfortable and pleasant here. The General is such a very cheerful pleasant kindly soul and there are two girls who look after him and are so helpful and nice. They rag him so much & he does love it so! When he says "that reminds me" they *look at one another and then discuss whether they have heard it or not and whether he may tell it again! When he has related it (only personal reminiscences – no vulgarity at all!) they often say, "That's not what you said last time," etc. It is very amusing and he revels in it. The father of one of the girls stayed recently. He is a Major General & was at the Staff College when our General was an instructor there. He too was so very nice & is a serving soldier. He gave a small farewell party to which I was invited which was good fun and we went to a Cabaret show – my first here – afterwards. It will be so lovely when you get out here. I'm sure the F.O. will do all they can. I am trying to make a plan for some trips which really will be lovely if all goes as planned, & and it will D.V.*

One hears of snow and ice everywhere at home and I do hope all goes well and that the fuel situation at Rectory House is satisfactory! Also, I hope that Fisher is well & the Curtis's. The work here continues to be interesting and so far, we haven't got to the point of the future resulting from the Porter Mission. So much depends upon the American attitude, and the country's future will depend upon outside help which is going to be difficult to get. I am pretty sure that I shall have finished most of what I came for by end April – that is my plan, anyhow, as I come home not later than the beginning of May. My work here should by then be possible for a junior to continue and one might always advise from London or later in the year even slip out for a week if wanted. But I doubt if it will be wanted. More tomorrow, Sweetheart.

***Monday.** Nothing fresh except it is a heavenly day today; much too nice to work. However! Take care of your Darling self. All my love to you, my own Darling. God Bless. Always your own Geordie."* Having established the date of the start of the Easter holidays, Dorks sends George a telegram: *"have written you twice weekly hope letters reaching you girls holiday start 29th March if unable to get passage 2nd March, suggest I come in May, all well here, love Doreen."*

In George's next letter, he makes arrangements for a flight home for Dorks at the end of March in the hope that she will get a flight out at the beginning of the month, and how this might all fit with his joining the Board of the National Bank of India also the alternatives if their holiday together is delayed to May (in fact the British Mission was to be largely wound up and handed over to the US Porter Mission by the end of March and George returned home in early April in time for the Easter holidays).

"British Economic Mission to Greece 6th floor HQ LF (G) Thursday 6th February

My own Darling,

It was lovely to get two letters and a telegram from you this morning. I agree that if you can't get out leaving on 2nd March, it will be better to make it May. I have said to the Nat. Bank that I shall be back in England at the beginning of May, but I do not think that will cause any difficulty as I'm sure there will be an easy way of getting over that. As soon as I hear from the Bank, I will let you know, as the best alternative might be for me to come home for a week or ten days in April & for both of us to come out for May. We could then come out and go back together which would be so much nicer. The

General would agree to that I know. I might then join the Board of the Bank while I am there and then get leave of absence from the Bank for May. I am half hoping the Bank may suggest my joining the Board before I get home anyhow & then getting leave of absence which would make everything quite easy. So, if passages look difficult for 2ⁿᵈ March, it might be better in every way to make it May. I will find out the latest position from the Air people today & add it to this letter which I am writing before tea – having had my half-hour's nap after lunch! Of course, the Bank may say "join us when you get home & we don't mind whether it is the beginning or end of May" – that is most likely I feel & then there would be no difficulty as far as I can see. It was nice of Mr & Mrs Pinkerton to call. Yes, he is the elderly lame chap who travels between Hungerford and Town and he is a Director of the National Bank of India and a great friend of Jack Thomas's family – Very kind of them to get in touch and very friendly – all the more so as I am to be a "new boy" on his Board. I hope! I will wire you today anyhow, I think, but will first contact the Air people.

What a time it must have been with all the snow and ice! We have been having really bitter weather here – one morning I was told there had been ice on the roads in Athens. Mails have been held up all round and I do hope you have got my letters all right. I have now got yours written up to the one written on 30ᵗʰ. Thank you, Sweetheart. It really is bad luck on John and Jen going down with colds so soon after their return to school & I am very relieved to know from your telegram that all was well again. I do hope all continue to keep fit. Am very glad you have been keeping fairly busy & it will be good fun having Sandy making Rectory House her headquarters. I must say I would have liked to have seen "Operation Sandy" in full blast! I do hope all went well and that you didn't try to do too much.

Nice letter from Doris & I'm interested in what she says about the cook! He certainly was a good cook and always brought good things and I am glad others besides ourselves thought so too and are willing to pay his bills!! Things here go along quite well & very pleasantly. The General has been so good and kind. The weather has improved and is simply lovely. I only hope it is better with you too.

***Friday** I am finishing this today, Sweetheart. I went myself yesterday evening to the Air booking centre to make sure about passages. They told me that the passages from London are still, they think, all on priority but from Athens, some are still reserved for non-priority civilians. They suggested that I book you provisionally & if we want to swap later or a cancellation, it can be done. So, I have booked a berth provisionally for 25ᵗʰ March, which should get you back in good time for the chaps' holidays and provided you leave on 2ⁿᵈ March from there it will give you about 3 weeks clear here. It will be so lovely to get you here, Sweetheart, but if March should prove difficult or impractical then we might begin to plan for May but the first thing is to know the chances for 2ⁿᵈ March. If we do decide May, then I'm sure we can get all the uncertainties resolved so that we do manage May. I will let you know as soon as I hear more from the Bank. About money, I can draw here on my London Bank. I mentioned funds in an earlier letter which I hope* *you will have got by now and if you bring about ten pounds English money, that will see you through. I think you are only allowed to bring £20 maximum so it doesn't matter much & anything up to £20 would be O.K. We can buy English pounds here for the return journey & I can easily fix the return journey in local currency. How are you off for funds, Sweetheart? I have arranged to draw Indian income in London now so all is well! I will pay some into your a/c whenever you want it. I will go into this when I next write & will answer your two letters properly. If you don't get out in March, Sweetheart, I shall visit home in April D.V. Take all care of your Sweet Self. God Bless you. All my love to you, my own Darling. Always your own Geordie."*

George's letter emphasises the very strict controls on taking British currency abroad, which was limited to £20, which made overseas travel almost impossible but George's diplomatic status as part of the Foreign Office enabled him to fund Doreen's visit out to Greece.

Doreen's next letter is full of home news . . . and her impending visit to Greece. But the winter has the whole country in its icy grip.

"Rectory House 7.2.47

Very many thanks for your reply to my wire. I will write & see what the position is & go and see Mr Sandler when I am in London next week. Actually, we have had quite a hectic time – not so much doing things as there has been frost and snow & we have not been able to get out much. Sandy and Molly arrived on Monday & at last, on Wed. the furniture remover got some of his furniture in, but the roads are like glass and they have not returned since. Driving has been beastly; the road from Swindon was completely blocked, but the snowplough got one-way traffic going fairly quickly & yesterday completely cleared the road, however, as it then froze on the already beaten-down snow, the result was beastly. Sandy won't be able to move into the house until there is a thaw as she has had a burst pipe which stops her from using the immersion heater & the boiler needs extensive repair. Also, she can get no coal or wood till next week & with the roads as they are, she can't get back to Little Marsh to collect the rest of her belongings. Tiger isn't coming on account of the roads. Then just as I was sitting down to write to you, Fisher came in to say the central heating boiler had burst; nothing really to do with the cold but I suppose heavy firing had strained it & there was a big leak. This sounded really serious however Ray Hawkins, who is trumps in a crisis, removed the offending part and has welded and patched it & says it should last us this winter. So, with buckets of water, we filled the tank up (the lead to the tank in John's room is so slow). We had to get the tank full to get the water circulating to all the radiators & Fisher got the boiler going again. So, we were only eight hours or so without central heating. It is still freezing with more snow to come but we are promised a slow thaw after that! Helen is here & I am going back with her for a couple of nights if we can make it. We went and helped Sandy yesterday. I must go and get the rations which I haven't done this week yet. I must say we have had some very good laughs & it has been great fun having the girls here!

I have so many letters to write but don't seem to get them done. All love darling . . . take care of yourself. Your own Dorkie.

P.S. I am going to write to Beff about boiler. What about a dual-purpose one so that we can go straight into oil? I believe one needs a permit & it takes ages to get a boiler so I shall start in straight away."

Fisher was the gardener and a brilliant handyman – I remember him as a slightly lugubrious character.

George's next letter is full of excitement at the thought of Dorks coming out either at the beginning of March or early May after the school holidays, depending upon flights.

"Athens Sunday 9.2.47

My Own Darling,

Have been out for a pleasant walk up one of the stony local hills, along the ridge a short way and so home. It took about an hour and a half and I went very easily. The old ticker behaved quite reasonably. The General left yesterday for a holiday in Switzerland and expects to be away two or three weeks so the house seems a bit deserted. One of his P.A.s is down with either a liver chill or jaundice, the Doctor hasn't decided which. There seems to be a certain amount of jaundice about but I hope she hasn't got it as it is such an unpleasant thing. Otherwise, all well.

Yesterday and the day before I got letters from Jean, Jen, Sis & Jan! Great luck as first of all I got two from you. The weather has been very bad and there have been long delays but all seems well. It is good hearing from the chaps and I enjoyed Johnnies two letters which you forwarded with yours. I do hope they all keep fit now. Jen sounded cheerful in spite of the two bronchitis attacks & Jean was in good form. They all loved their holidays & Jen was hoping term would pass quickly.

I hope my last letter was intelligible? I also wired in case things looked hopeless for 2ⁿᵈ March. If you do manage March, Sweetheart, then I might finish here end April; if you can't manage March, then I shall stay on until mid-May. As far as one can see now, the Mission will go until then at least. Also, all should be well as far as Nat. Bank is concerned and I should hear more about it fairly soon now. It will be lovely when you do get out here, Sweetheart. The weather is beginning to be good and it is so good. The work goes on, a bit fitfully, but usually there is plenty to do though sometimes we seem to be "marking time". Occasionally a Communist newspaper will attack the Mission but that is usually a compliment though never meant that way!

As I have been told I can cash cheques here (I have written to my bank to fix it up definitely) by applying to the Bank of England, all will be well about funds while you are here & for the passage home etc. Also, I have quite a lot of traveller's cheques which I am keeping. So, all should be well. I would bring with you in £1- notes between £10 & £20. If I can get over to Rome to meet you on our way out, I shall be able to fix any funds needed there. If I don't manage to get over to meet you on your way out, I shall go back to Rome when you leave again so that any shopping can be done then. It will be heavenly to have you with me again, Sweetheart. I rather agree about getting to Rome by train & it will be better to fly.

I wonder if Audrey did manage to get over to stay with you. I hope she did. Glad you put the car in for brake adjustment. They were beginning to need it when I was home. What a time it must have been with all the frozen pipes! We have been lucky, Sweetheart . . .what a godsend central heating is. Sis seems to have had a hectic time with several fires going to keep the frost out. Jan got home and retired to bed with a feverish cold they say, poor old Jan, but she sounded quite cheerful as there was a fire in the old day nursery to which she retired! I hope the Curtis's have a good holiday & are in good form. Jen was amusing about Gwingo who, she says, ran off up to the lime quarries where Jean used to take him for walks. What a little funny he is! I was interested to hear from Doris and bought such excellent food always. He charged a lot but it was worth it. I am amused at Paul paying P1's letter that they were with Paul and that our cook was there too. Well, they are jolly lucky as he was as good a cook as anyone could have. I am amused at Paul paying up! Nevertheless, he is wise, I think. I hate the thought of a Burman at our house . . . more tomorrow, Sweetheart.

Monday *Nothing very fresh, Sweetheart, except that I went out to drinks before dinner last night at the house of one of our Mission where I met the wife of another member of the Mission who I had met before & who knew Evelyn & May Morton. I discovered last night who she was! She was one Elsie Taylor whom Sis would remember. Her father was a doctor who had been at school with my father; all very complicated! We were to know the children quite well from having him for holidays to Lamlash (Arran) at the same time. Also, they lived near us in London when we were very young. It raised all kinds of ghosts and half-forgotten happy days & the old pains when my father died and all the rest which lies so far in the past. But it was good to know who she was & talk of old days. I should never have recognised her. My brother was rather a boyfriend of hers – both older than me! You will meet her when you come out.*

Well, Sweetheart, I will close. Take all care of your Sweet Self. I long to be with you. God Bless All my love to you, my own darling – Always your own Geordie."

The next of Doreen's letters enclose letters from the children and descriptions of the harsh winter. This undated letter would have been written either 12th or 13th February.

My own Darling,

Thank you so much for your last letter & for your wire – I expect that the weather has held a lot of letters up. I sent you a wire today to wish you many happy returns of the day – I wish we were spending your birthday together – well, the weather continues to be vile here and Operation Sandy continues to be in abeyance more or less in consequence. We are not in one of the areas affected by this compulsory electric cut. There was a very stormy debate in the house yesterday but I suppose this government have got too big a majority for anyone to oppose them effectively. Our only hope is that the already serious position isn't much worse than they have let on. There was a partial thaw yesterday but it is freezing again today & though the main roads where the snow has melted away aren't too bad, the side roads are like glass today. Sandy's second load of furniture arrives today. She and Molly are planning to go back to Ascot on Thursday and will come back sometime next week. She really can't move in until it thaws properly as she daren't turn the water on in case she has got to have extensive repairs done to the boiler, though this won't stop her using the immersion heater. Helen and I are trying to get to Northwood tomorrow where I am going to spend two nights. I am going to see Mr Salmon about my passage on Thursday. I don't know whether the weather has made a big hold-up in Air passages. I suppose it may have. I also want to try and get down to see the children this weekend & may spend Saturday night with Molly at Ascot.

There was more snow on Saturday night and on Sunday afternoon we went skiing & tobogganing. I felt my bones creak a bit when I tried to ski! Gwingo is the only one who really likes this weather. He loves the snow and likes being taken out for walkies in it.

Fisher has been awfully good & I don't know what we would have done without him. Various people have had tea from India & have asked me to thank you – Cara Newman, Jock Cumberledge & the Godfreys. The children sound alright so I hope they are warm. The Marlborough boys look pretty cold walking about the town. I have had a grand tidy up in my room which Sandy says is swank! All my love, darling, Your own Dorkie."

George's next letter is written on his birthday.

"Athens 13.2.47

My Own Darling,

Thank you so much for your greetings telegram which I loved getting this morning. Also, for the three letters which came a day or so ago. It was so very good to get them and to hear how things were going. One contained letters from the chaps which it was also good to get. I think I mentioned I had a lovely bunch of letters from the chaps and Jan & Sis all of which I hope to answer in the next day or so. Also, it was good to get Helen's amusing letter written on 2nd. She sounded very cheerful & happy and you all seemed to be having an amusing & cheerful, if busy time in spite of the weather and all the upsets. It certainly must have been a bit of a problem at times! How very fortunate Ray Hawkins was able to fix the boiler & the pipes. It will be most interesting to hear what he says. Doubtless we could improve on the fuel consumption though it is most important of all to be sure of efficient heating! Our old one certainly gave the necessary heat. Also, it would be interesting to hear what the experts say about the smell of oil burning. One would be wise to get Buff to send down a central heating expert to measure the whole installation so as to be sure we get the required efficiency. Did you think of getting one to burn coal for the present and then later to convert it to oil if we decided to? I expect one can get the convertible type – but if they have dual-purpose ones which would either burn coal or oil with a small alteration, that would probably be best of all. Shall be most interested to hear what Buff says. Most wise to get on to it now, Sweetheart, as you suggest. Driving

*on these roads must have been beastly & I have been thinking so much about that &
do hope all has gone well, Sweetheart. . . . I can't make out who the Pinkneys are unless
that is the name of our lame friend! It doesn't strike any other chord in my rather poor
memory for names! I wonder if the Frosts know how our lame friend does spell his name?*

*Very little fresh here, Sweetheart – it is a trifle less cold(!) but still not warm. I have
bought a large Danish ham – about 10lbs or so – also a couple of very nice Army blankets
(Australian) at fifteen bob each! Am having a very quiet life reading a lot & going out
very little which is quite pleasant. I shall try and send the Chanel in the next day or so
but packing materials are the chief difficulty. Also, it is time I sent off another food parcel.
I have all the stuff ready to go when a suitable box can be found – Miss Holland is very
good and helpful about that & she said this morning she hoped to get one for me soon.*

*No news of the General but he should have arrived safely at his destination and be
busy curling or winter sporting, lucky chap! With any luck, I ought to hear soon about
the chances of your getting off on 2nd March. You will be in London today and though I
doubt if they can be very definite, they may be able to give you an indication. As soon as
I hear, I can begin to lay plans! It will be lovely when you get here, Sweetheart. We have
had some nice sunny weather but for the last two or three days, it has been cloudy again.
Doubtless it will clear up again soon and it can be so good when it is fine.*

*I went out to tea on Monday to a friend of Manoli's sister's who kindly asked me.
They came too & also an American newspaperman & his wife who were most interesting
on Balkan politics. Miss Tombazi says Helen has been seedy again, poor Helen, what a
rotten time she has had. Do give them my love when you see them.*

*Take all care of our Darling self – God Bless. All my love to you, my own Darling.
Always your own Geordie."*

Doreen's next letter confirms a provisional flight out on 2nd March.

"Northwood 14.2.47

*I am staying here with Helen & was going back home today & down to the children
tomorrow but am spending another night here & going by train to Ascot tomorrow,
spending the night with Molly & going home by train on Sunday as the roads are still
pretty frightful & there is a risk of more snow.*

*First of all, I went to see M. Salmon yesterday and there is a very good chance that I
may get away on March 2nd as so far, only one other person wants to go on that date – so
that is good & I shall I expect to wire you – & will you from your end see if you can get
me onto a plane to arrive home before March 29th when the holidays start? If I don't get
away on March 2nd I may still get away on Thursday 6th but shall not come if I can't
get on either of these two dates & of course shan't know until 3 days beforehand when
I will wire you.*

*Helen and I came back here on Thursday & didn't have too bad a drive. The road
through the forest was like a skating rink (Savernake Forest on the A4, long before
the M4 opened – JMM) but once we were through, the thaw we had last weekend had*

washed the road clean & we had no more trouble. It is still freezing hard but we have had no more snow in the South since Sunday. This bitter weather looks like going on for another week & Londoners look so cold & miserable; everything is wrapped in gloom with no lights or heating between 9 & 12 and again between 2 & 4 with the knowledge that unless we all pull our socks up, things will be worse next winter & we may end up completely in the soup – occasionally, we have an uninspiring wobbly little speech from Atlee – if only we had Churchill to breathe a little blood & thunder into us, but the rank and file don't want it & think that it is anyone's fault but their own. Someone said yesterday in the House of Lords that we were suffering not from an Act of God but from the inaction of Emmanuel; what an awful mess it is.

Helen had a wretched cold & is in bed today – I am going to have tea with Bets presently. Molly and Sandy got home alright but Sandy won't be able to live in her house until there is a thaw. Helen tells me that I am to tell you the story about the absent-minded butcher who hung his wife on a hook instead of a carcass of beef & pinned a notice on her with "Registered Customers only" printed on it.

I am only allowed to take 44 lbs of luggage so I shall have to think out carefully what to bring – I suppose it will still be cold. Will write again in a day or so. All love, my own darling, your Dorkie."

Again, this is an example of Dorks trying to keep things going in the face of adversity. It was something that had been bred of wartime, keeping going and helping others. She was just 41! Funny to reflect that the 20-kilo restriction on luggage is still largely in force amongst airlines 73 years later.

"Rectory House 18.2.47

My own darling,

Lovely to find two letters from you when I got back on Sunday. I haven't yet sent you a wire but will do so today but shall not be able to send you a final wire saying whether I am coming or not until a few days before the actual date of flying as I shan't know – but I hope you will book me to come back provisionally as you say in your letter. I had tea with Philip and Bets (Ironside – she – Betty Treble – was Doreen's cousin – JMM), *both well I thought – Bets has given up working and looks better for it. The Treble finances seem to be working out a little better than they thought which is a good thing. On Saturday I took Jean and Jen out and we had lunch at the Berested & tea at Molly's after. Jean was well but Jen looked wretched with a heavy cold & a cough & so I asked them at school to keep her in bed for a short while until she had got rid of it. She had no temperature but it is the aftermath of the bronchitis & it is difficult to throw anything off this awful weather.*

Molly, Ken, Sandy (Mealing – Molly and Sandy were sisters – JMM) *& I returned here by train on Sunday, a very easy journey really & Copplestone met me. Audrey Geidt arrived yesterday; it is very nice of her to come in this awful weather – she looks tired. She says she thinks Ruth is better but things are short in the South of France* (Ruth Benthall would have been with her doctor Maurice Fogt – JMM). *There is no sign of any break in the weather & it remained freezing with grey skies – it has been like this for a month now. How long these electricity cuts are going on for one doesn't know but if we can't start our industries soon, the outlook is pretty grim. One can't blame this Government for the general fuel situation but this immediate crisis should never have arisen if they'd bothered to have some sort of plan – it is so typical . . . let's use up everything until there is no more left & then what? We have enough fuel here to last for the central heating boiler & hot water boiler for a month. I went to Toomers and told them this yesterday and they said they'd let us have what they could early in March – as soon as there is a proper thaw & decent weather, we shall have to let the central heating boiler out & I have been trying to find out about a new one from "Bays" in Swindon. They don't recommend oil-firing but something which burns coal dust – I don't quite know what it is – they are coming out to have a look sometime. It will be heavenly if I can get out to Greece. All love, darling, Your own Dorkie. PS. no parcels have arrived from you – have you sent any?"*

Two undated letters from John and one from Jean were also enclosed . . .

"Avisford Arundel Sussex. Dear Mummy, I hope you are well. Nearly all the snow has melted now except the piles of snow and the remains of the forts. We have had a little rugger practice but I only went up to the field once and then I was not allowed out. It froze last night and the yard was covered in brown ice, so we had some fun sliding mostly on our botams . . .(!)

This term has gone very quickly. I am going to work hard this term, because our Latin master said that if all the masters agreed that we had worked hard this term, we could move up into form 3 and then in the Autumn be in form 4. And I think it is worth it, because you're paying a lot of money to have me in the school and I don't see why I shouldn't work hard so I am going to try and get into form 3 and then into form 4, love from John"

The letter had two racing cars drawn in pencil at the bottom!

John's next letter was longer . . .

"Dear Mummy, I hope you are very well. Thank you for The Children's Newspaper. Have you stopped my Rover? If you have, it does not matter. It was snowing on Saturday evening. Yesterday morning we spent all the morning making two forts. Then in the afternoon, we were not allowed out. Anyway, I wasn't very cross because we were allowed to play in the gym. In the gym, we had cockfighting, that is fighting with a person on your back, only they do the fighting, not you. When I had somebody (I wasn't carried because I was too heavy) on my back, we went charging into the attack, bumped into each other (I had an opponent) and of course . . .(!) landed on the floor. When I looked up, somebody had a nose-bleed and the other two were crying. I was the only one that dident . . .(!) land a bump, at least I did, but it wasn't very hard. It has been very mild and all-most as soon as the snow landed it melted. As we werent . . .(!) alowed out yesterday we were alowed . . .(!) today in what you might call iced snow. Any body who wanted to snowball

had to put on football clothes, and those who dident . . .(!) want to snow-ball just put on foot ball stockings and boots or gumboots. I have not got into my other foot ball boots yet and I don't think I will this term. Anyway my feet might shoot out suddenly and then I shall need them, so that's why I am not sending them home.

Thank you very much for my sweet ration which I got today in a parcel. It is rather nice because our Chaplain is very nice and lends us comics called Topics. He calls them pri. Last evening Major Jennings had us all in his study and he read to us. We had a latin test and I came second top with 94 out of 100.

We are having a film show on March 2nd, a Sunday. We have not had rugger from the beginning of this term but I think that we are going to break the record and have it on Wednesday Thursday and Friday if we don't have any more snow. There is one boy who is very nice called Martin Wells and gave me some birthday so I think it would be nice to take him out. Sorry I have not sent you very long letter. Love from John."

The letter ends with a long line of xs! Finally, this collection ends with a letter from Jean – *"St Marys Convent Feb 16th* (but posted direct on 20th – funnily, the stamp seems to have been steamed off).

Dear Daddy,

Mummy came to see us yesterday and we went to tea with the Mealings & then Mummy came & saw the dress rehearsal of our 6th form Shrove Tuesday opening scene. We are doing a sort of Arabian Nights only it's Persia, but it's very effective & colourful so no-one notices the mixture of Eastern ideas. I am a dancer with 3 others & we dance in front of the Emperor. My turban is great fun, & I wand a huge red scarf round & round my head only I hardly ever get it as neat as the bearer's pugri used to be!!

The 6th form weekend next week which is fun, only poor Jen has to stay at school. Its freezing cold here & everyone says it hasn't been so cold for so long for over 50 years & the electricity is cut 3 hours a day because of coal & there is very little coal for other uses, and so that what with ice & snow & dim or no lights & what not you are jolly lucky to be in Greece & it's a good thing that Mummy is going out there too, because at school they do try to keep the pipes going even if the lights are hopeless but at home Mummy's getting worried about coal etc.

We have had exams all this week & now thank goodness there over . . . (!) . . . I don't know what the History Prize results are yet, because they have to be sent away to be corrected so we won't know for a week or so & about why others were fairly good except for Latin in which I only got 35% (anyway I wasnt bottom someone got 13%) & I redeemed myself with 90% for French. John wriote me a lovely letter which Mummy took so I hope she remembers to send it on to you. Jen hasnt been too fit with this beastly weather & her nasty cold but now exams are over & she needn't work so hard she may pick up again & we'll feed her up on Shrove Tuesday. I must go now & there's no more news. Please write soon. I will tell you all about Shrove Tuesday next week it's going to be super fun & we've got hold of some balloons!! With lots of love and kisses from your loving Jean."

St Mary's was partially self-sufficient with its own farm producing dairy products, milk, butter, cheese, and vegetables, eggs, and other foodstuffs, all managed, worked and run by the nuns, the Mary Ward Sisters, especially welcome during rationing . . .

The next letter from George is a short one . . .

"British Economic Mission to Greece 6ᵗʰ Floor HQ LF (Q) Monday 17. 2. 47

My own Darling,

I meant to write you yesterday evening when I got back from a trip to Sumion but I had a bit of a throat and felt a little mouldy so didn't write. Throat is better today and in any event is not very bad. Well, I went out to Cape Sumion which is about two hours' motor drive with one of the General's P.A.s and her mother who is staying at the house occupying the General's quarters in his absence. They are both very nice & Lady Dowler, the mother, is a most pleasant cheerful body who has been having a bit of a holiday out of England. It was such a lovely day and the place is so beautifully situated with one of the Temples of Athena on the tip of the headland (some say it is the temple of Poseidon but I don't know). We took a picnic lunch and got back to a late tea. I spent most of my time loafing in the sun enjoying it all. It was good and the road not so bad though patches were very bad.

Last week, I inspected a margarine factory which had a boiler fired either by oil or coal, whichever they chose. Apparently, they were readily convertible from oil to coal and vice-versa so it can be done & doubtless Buff will have more to say as to its practicality for a central heating installation. It will be lovely, Sweetheart, when I hear about your coming out. I am so longing for you to be here. By the way, I am writing to Fullerton today asking him to pay £300 into your a/c, OK? I wrote Sis and Jan early yesterday morning & have the chaps to write soon. I had good letters from them last week bless them. I still can't find a suitable box for your Chanel but am still trying! I shall get something soon. Also, it's time another parcel went off. I do hope the weather there has been a bit better and I also hope all goes well, Sweetheart. Take all care of your sweet self; longing to be with you. All my love to you, my own darling. God Bless. Always your own Geordie.

Hope Gwingo is well, the little funny."

George's final surviving letter concentrates on the arrival of Dorks.

"Athens Thursday 20.2.47

My own Darling,

Several letters from you in the last few days which as usual I loved getting. I was most amused by the "communal" epistle from the girls! You all sounded in good heart which was good. What a time it must have been there and still is, I gather. And how the Govt. has mucked it, tactically chiefly perhaps, but in every other way too. It has been difficult, and, in the financial position we're in, we have to take risks but why not have the courage to tell people so? Churchill would have told the country at the beginning of winter of the jam we might be in & would have prepared everyone for the possibilities. But this lot haven't the knowledge or the guts to risk public odium. Anyhow, they haven't got away with their inefficiency this time. I was thrilled to get your telegram saying the chances were good for you leaving on the 2nd. Things are slackening so much here now and if you do leave on 2nd, I shall with any luck be home again before the end of April, possibly before the chaps return to school. I have been thinking about where to stay when you get here, Sweetheart. The hotel is all right but it is so much nicer at the General's house. We shall be out on tour quite a lot of the time so if we can stay with the General for the short spells we shall be in Athens, it will be so much more pleasant and convenient. I shall wire to the General and sound him. He won't be back after 5th March according to his present plans so in any event, we could stay until then and if he has people coming to stay, we could move into the hotel. Anyhow, Sweetheart, I will do what seems best. It will be so heavenly to get you here & there are so many lovely places to visit. I have been trying to fix up to be in Rome when you get there but it is turning to be most awkward as the last plane I can get lands 3 days before you are due to arrive. If, by any chance, you were delayed, it might be a bit of a business so I might not meet you there on your arrival. You will have very little time there ordinarily & if we want to, I can fix it that we leave together a few days earlier and spend the time in Rome. But we can see when you get here, Sweetheart. There are all sorts of possibilities & we needn't decide yet. Anyhow, I will wire you before you leave.

Have heard from the Nat. Bank that they are pleased I am joining them and will do the actual election nearer the time when I can be at home & attend meetings. They say May is quite OK. All's well & whenever I know I am leaving here, I shall let them know so that I can be elected. So, if you don't get here until May, all will be well as far as the Bank is concerned. Having had a few cold, dull and & miserable days, it is lovely today. If only it keeps like this for your visit, Sweetheart, how you will love it. My sore throat is practically better, touching wood, & I feel better all round. There seems to have been a lot of sickness here, including these throats, with a mild 'flu. Anyhow, mine is OK, I'm glad to say. I hope Jen is alright again. She was still having a bit of a cold when I last heard but doubtless all is well again. I hope so. Had a letter from John recently full of snow fights! They must have enjoyed it all. Well, Sweetheart, I will stop. Take all care of your sweet self. I long to be with you. All my love to you, my own Darling. God Bless. Always your own Geordie."

Doreen's letters are now also focusing increasingly on her travel plans to Greece.

"Rectory House Sunday 28.2.47

My own darling,

Thank you very much for your letter & for a lovely parcel which arrived on Thursday with a lovely tin of butter and a small one, honey etc: all went straight into the D.D.C. Except for the small tin of butter which I gave to Audrey for Jeremy. I shan't know until Wed or Thurs. whether I shall get away next Sunday or not & wondering if this last heavy fall of snow will have so dislocated bookings & traffic that I shan't get away. It still goes on & we had about another 6" to 8" of snow here yesterday & on Friday & there seems to be no prospect of a break. People say gloomily that it will continue now for another fortnight or even a month as it didn't change with the new moon. However, this afternoon the sun shone (the first time for 3 weeks) so we sallied forth with the skis & had great fun. Jean is home for her long weekend & she got on very well on skis. Audrey departed in a blizzard on Friday, however, we got into Swindon alright but I got Copplestone to meet Jean in the evening & he is taking her to Hungerford tomorrow morning early. I have chains now on the car though the main roads aren't too bad beyond being very skiddy – alright if you go slow enough & don't get stuck on a hill. It was fun having Audrey here; I think she had a rest though she really wanted longer than three days.

We went into Bath on Wednesday – it was freezing but was before the fall of snow & the roads were quite clear. I got a wedding present for Anne Morton who is being married in March. I got a Regency paper holder – it cost £21-0-0 but I simply couldn't see anything – any other piece of small furniture was prohibitive or not very nice. I felt it would be useful in a small flat. Jennifer has spent this week in bed, but Jean says she is much better & I expect will be up again soon. I enclose her letter. John will be annoyed with me because I haven't been to see him but the weather has been impossible for long-distance motoring & I haven't been able to fix to go by train & anyhow it would have been too cold to do anything but sit in a hotel. If I don't get away next Sunday, I will go and see him.

I enclose your vouchers for the National Hunt Meetings. Please will you sign them and send them to Rita if I get away on 2nd or if I don't, send them to me. I will ask Rita not to fill them up for anyone we don't know.

The Government plan for India sounds pretty awful to me. I can't see how there will be anything but chaos and perhaps there will be that anyhow – I wonder what I can bring as I am only allowed 44lbs.

Poor Sandy – really there seems no hope of her getting into the new house yet – I suppose she is still at Ascot – it is maddening for her.

Gwingo loves going for walks now. Jen's pony looks a bit thin & tucked up, though Rufus is flourishing. I suppose it is this bitter weather, – Burden gives them lots of hay but I fancy Rufus has more than his fair share. Must take carrots down to them more often. How I wish it would thaw & we are warm & comfortable – must be hell for some people. All love darling. Your own Dorkie."

Jen's letter is full of news of her wretched chest infection, undated and written from the infirmary . . .

"St Mary's Convent

Darling Mummy,

Thank you very very much indeed for the parcel you sent us. I am so sorry for not writing, but I have been in the infirmary and the nuns have not had time to get me paper or pencil. The parcel was super, lots of good things came out of it, some of which (dates and sweets) I have here. I was sent to bed on Sunday night after supper and stayed in bed all the next day Monday; in the evening, I had a temperature, & believe only very slight, so I was removed here. It's a single room and is pretty bare and the pipes are hardly ever hot. On Tuesday night my temperature went up again and on Wednesday morning the nun told me it was because I coughed too much and told me not to cough! However, knowing that if I didn't cough, I would never get any flem up, I coughed whenever I felt like it and brought up a lot of stuff. I had a temp again that night so Thursday, yesterday she dosed me with some funny yellow cough mixture and pills called phensin or something. It is suppose to kill 'flu germs and certainly seems to have had some effect because my temp was normal all yesterday and if it stays normal today without these pills, she says I can get up, and she thinks I will stay normal. My chest was as tight as a drum and ached as it did when I had bronchitis on my both sides, left and right, and all down my back to my left leg which was worse than my right – it used to hurt at night most, I don't know why, and it used to tighten up in the evening and loosen in the morning. It is much better now and does not at all except sometimes although I am still bringing up an awful lot. Jean is lucky going home. However it is only 5 weeks today until we go HOME. What a shame Daddy won't be there any part of the holidays at all. It has been snowing again here, such a beastly bore, though not much, but I should think it's pretty dangerous because underneath the sprinkling of snow, it is just one solid mass of ice, also the thick clouds make it terribly dark and I am honestly writing by torchlight it is so dark. Incidently, the Shrove Tuesday went off very well indeed. Mother Ignatius came to see me after the actual day and said it was far better than the dress rehearsal. They did have a carpet and everyone was much more majestic etc. Two Irish girls won the prize in middle school – they were in our form, and they went as the Farmers' Friend and Joe, a crow and a scarecrow! Marvellously original. The people in bed got the same food as the others which was meat sausage, green peas, mashed potatoes, but no beetroot and half a hard-boiled egg surrounded by breadcrumbly stuff only much nicer, then we had jelly with two blobs of cream on top and a piece or orange inside half of a scooped out orange then we had jolly good fruit salad (I believe Jean did fruit salad) and little sorts of cakes and things; it was super. The dancer girl had on a blue dress with tinsel on; it was shorter and 100 times nicer & better. After the feast which was supper, a nun, the English mistress, Mother Bridget, came round and gave all the people in bed a balloon; there were quite a few of us and I had a green balloon, but I bust it yesterday by prodding it, but it certainly was cheering. I am so sorry my writing is so deplorable, but I can hardly see. I got your letter this morning thank you very much for it and the books you are going to send, it will be super to have something decent to read, I finished Kim yesterday (Rudyard Kipling's classic). I started it on Tuesday. It is a super book. I was made to inhale this morning for the 1st time since I have been in bed. Well, I must stop as there isn't any more. Sorry for the deplorable letter give my love to all. Longing for the holidays. Lots of love from Jen."

Poor Jen; with her almost chronic chest condition, she had had a rotten time in the bitter winter.

Meanwhile, Doreen was preparing for her departure to Greece and cabled on the 18th *"679 MARLBOROUGH 23 18 1200 APO SIR GEORGE MORTON BRITISH ECONOMIC MISSION TO GREECE ATHENS STAND GOOD CHANCE LEAVE MARCH 2ND WILL WIRE DEFINITELY END NEXT WEEK LOVE DOREEN"*. The final letter of this series is dated Friday 28th February, written on 5 Raja Santosh Road, Calcutta airmail paper in pencil!

"My own darling,

Just a line which I will post tomorrow & hope it reaches you before me. I wired you today first saying that I was leaving on Sunday. This is because I went into the F.O. on Wed and they said that as far as they knew I would get away on Sunday. I left it until today hoping they would confirm it but as nothing had happened at 2.30, I rang them up and they said they had a definite booking for me for Tuesday 4th, & hoped I wouldn't be "off-loaded". So do I!! I had to send you a second wire. As I am all packed up & have made all arrangements, I rang up Betty & will stay with her three nights instead of one & try and slip down and see Johnny on Sunday if the Sunday trains are reasonable – am most disappointed at not getting away on Sunday as I was all tied up but there it is and as long as I am not thrown off at the last minute. Tonight, we are going to the Hunt Ball – I don't want awfully to go & would sooner go to bed but am taking my own car & shan't stay late. It will be heavenly to see you, darling, Your own Dorkie."

Hunt Balls normally were held at the old Aylesbury Hotel in Marlborough High Street; Doreen sent wires from the post office in Ogbourne confirming her travel status. . . . *"B 1973/UK816 OGBOURNESTGEORGE 16 28 1524 SIR GEORGE MORTON BRITISH ECONOMIC MISSION TO GREECE HQLFAPO ATHENS LEAVING SUNDAY MORNING LOVE DOREEN"* . . . *and then the revised plan – "MY PASSAGE CANCELLED NOW LEAVING TUESDAY STAYING FROM TOMORROW IRONSIDE WILL WIRE MONDAY LOVE DOREEN".*

And so, she was off to Greece at last.

Photographs show them visiting the Acropolis in Athens and Delphi as well as staying with Manoli and Helen Tombazi at their island home on Poros, and sunny days away from the harsh winter at home. Passports reveal that Doreen flew home on the 27th of the month in good time for the holidays. George followed on the 1st of April, at the closure of the British Mission and the handover to the Americans. And so, unexpectedly, he was home for the children's holidays.

Final years. A dream realised.
Farming and a country life

1947 was to be the year of the partition of India. Mountbatten had been quietly approached at the end of 1946 by Clement Atlee to take on the process with a view to Independence in 1948. Wavell resigned but communal bloodshed reached such a level with the Muslim League and Jinnah insistent on a separate Muslim state that the date was advanced to August 1947. The assassination of Mahatma Gandhi shocked the world, including the writer; I can remember thinking that India as we knew it was "finished"; this the reaction of a ten-year-old.

A few letters from friends still in India survive, including one from Joan Shuttleworth describing Gill's wedding to Bertie Sinclair and another from Betty Sherriff who was accompanying her husband George and colleague Ludlow on an expedition to Eastern Tibet to collect flowers and birds for the British Museum. Astonishingly, this letter travelled up to Lhasa where the pre-printed 6 anna stamp was franked on the airmail letter at the post office six weeks later and then travelled across Tibet to India and then to Rectory House. It is addressed from:

"Camp Layoting, Tongyuk Chu, Province of Pome, S.E. Tibet, 12ᵗʰ March 1947

Doreen Darling,

I don't know when this letter will reach you but I'm writing on the chance that it will roll up one day. We had a lad who is supposed to be bringing our mail from Gyantse (about six weeks journey) but he is now a month overdue – we are wondering if he has been beaten up and robbed – anyhow, poor soul, if he doesn't turn up, we will try and get hold of someone going to Lhasa who will take our letters up there to be posted. We got our last mail nearly 4 ½ months ago and are now longing for news. We have a wireless so are kept in touch with world news & have heard of the ghastly winter you are having and the fuel shortage. Poor lambs, life must be very difficult & very uncomfortable for you. I do hope things improve soon & also that George and you and the family keep well in spite of everything. I hope too that the new house is a great success and that you are all happily installed in it. Well, here we are in the promised land of Pome and the scene of our summer labours. We travelled for 68 days after leaving K'Pong along the Lhasa route until we reached the Tsangpo river two days from Lhasa and then turned eastwards along the valley for about 350 miles as the river winds itself through gorges where no road is passable, & up side valleys & over passes . . . the roads are just tracks of course & sometimes up stone staircases and along built-up wooden balconies on the cliff face with the Tsangpo roaring hundreds of feet sheer below us – how the ponies and little donkeys and men who carried our kit managed it all never ceased to make me wonder. The scenery was very fine & it was interesting how the bare dark brown hills gradually became covered with scrub, & then juniper and pine trees etc. as we got further east. We had good weather on the whole – 'tho we froze at nights (temp down to 36 degrees of frost). We usually thawed out during the days & we didn't have too appalling winds. We left the Tsangpo valley at Tsela Dzong and climbed up over our last pass (the 14,000 ft Temo La and down to Pome – here we are in glorious country, thick forests and rushing snow-fed rivers, quite unlike the plateau country. We stayed at Tongyup Dzong over Xmas & the new year and then came on down the Yigrong where we have been doing short expeditions to spy out the land for our summer activities. It has been disappointing for flowers, for we thought that by coming to these low altitudes, 5-9000 ft, we should find winter-flowering Rhodos and Primulas – we have found some but nothing like as many as we hoped for – birds, however, have been interesting – so far, G & L have taken about 300 specimens. I often think of you and how you would love to see the birds – I don't like to see them being shot but it has to be & I am glad of the chance of learning about them. George and I had a lovely trip down the Tsangpo Gorge to Gompa he (Kingdom Ward writes of this area in "The Riddle of the Tsangpo Gorge" and of the area that we're in, in "Assam Adventure"). We had the most amazing views of Namcha Barma & Gyala Peri – so close that you felt that you could almost stretch out and take the snow off them (not quite) and now we are on our way back to Tonyul. Ludlow and Henry Elliot go back over the Temola to have a look at the Konglio Tsampo gorge & there they spend the month collecting on the Yigrong range – G and I do a month and then come back to the Yprong and make SHOWA our headquarters – we all plan to meet at Tzela Dzong at the end of September and then make for K'Pong probably through Bhutan – hope to be back there at about the end or middle of November – we are all very fit and rather dirty as we have sadly underestimated the amount of soap we would need. However, we don't show up too badly amongst the locals. We are managing to get local supplies of flour, millet, mutton, chickens, eggs (mostly bad!), milk, butter and honey, and also shot for the pot pheasants, duck, geese, snipe, woodcock, and our Sidar shot 3 Takin. They taste rather like tough beef but are fine-looking creatures. Hope you will see the skins set up in the British Museum one day. The people are friendly and hospitable on the whole. Some are terrified when they see us. One party threw their

133 *George pheasant shooting*

loads and then themselves down a 200ft slope into the jungle rather than meet us. We certainly do look European. I have cut my hair short and look like Miss Shirras!! Masses of love to you all, Betsy."

This amazing letter is postmarked 7th May 1947 Lhasa and the gap between the date of the letter, and Lhasa's posting of six weeks suggests that it would have taken up to six weeks to get to Lhasa. From here it would have travelled by postal pony to either Kalimpong or Gangtok and onwards to Siliguri by road or mountain railway. Then rail to Calcutta for sorting, airmail to England and delivery to Rectory House by GPO.

The plant and bird collections that they gathered were indeed for the British Museum; as mentioned earlier, I can remember visiting there and meeting George Sherriff and Ludlow in the basement of the Museum, where they were sorting the collection. This must have been spring or summer 1948. George and Betty retired to near Blairgowrie in Scotland and a number of their Himalayan plants are in the Glasgow Botanical Gardens and named after them.

The last seven years of George's life were spent in Ogbourne. We children were growing up and generally away for nine months of the year at boarding school, so these notes are largely from memory, supplemented from a motley collection of farm records and photographs. Jean would have left school just eighteen at the end of the summer term in 1948. She passed the entrance exam to Trinity College Dublin where she read Social Sciences. Here she made contact with the Coffee family and their three boys, Timothy, (who became a doctor like his father), David, who became an engineer, and Cheema. Jiggy, their mother, was a daughter of Dr Graham of the Kalimpong Homes, and, as mentioned earlier, escaped in a fishing smack across the North Sea shortly after the Germans invaded Scandinavia. All three Coffee boys visited us at Rectory House and David was a regular visitor helping with the harvest during the summer months. Meat was of course rationed in England, but not so in Ireland and so Jean brought back hunks of beef for the holidays. Jen stayed on at St Mary's and then went to the Villa Beata in Fribourg, Switzerland to be "finished", learning and speaking fluent French. There are pictures of her skiing in Wengen. The climate suited her health. Jen was musical and clever and graduated to the Guildhall School of Music, studying piano, cello and singing. Her studies were interrupted by my father's

***134** Jen skiing at Wengen*

392

135 The Rectory farm farmyard

death in 1954. Both sisters did secretarial courses. Jean, Jen and Janet Tonge shared a maisonette at No 22 Montagu Street to the North of Marble Arch. Janet was by this stage studying medicine at the North Middlesex and continued with the flat into 1956, after which she and David Archibald, who was also an intern at the North Middlesex, got married. Jean helped run the farm during the last two years of George's life until she too married Barney Shuttleworth from Rectory House and the farm was sold. John continued at prep school at Avisford where he became head boy and played rugby, cricket and soccer, before passing common entrance to Ampleforth College.

The opportunity occurred after George retired to purchase the adjoining farm, consisting of about 220 acres, of which around 45 acres stretched south of the house and village down to the river Og. There were farm buildings opposite Rectory House which George completely rebuilt incorporating a milking parlour with automatic milking with an Alfa Laval milking assembly, calving pens and a bullpen and bulling pen. To the rear was a large barn storing grain in two-hundredweight sacks, and feed. There were also pig pens. Behind the barn were two cottages, one for Fisher, the other for Fred Wiltshire. The farm manager, Forsyth, lived in the farmhouse next door where there was a large chicken house. Chickens used to free-range across the field below the house as well as straying into the garden, much to the irritation of Fisher. At one stage, we had a few guinea fowl to which Fisher used to refer as "them damned birds" until George relented and shot them from the middle-upper window of the house.

Milk was cooled into tanks and taken away for pasteurising in milk churns. Ayrshire milk was rich in butterfat and we made our own butter and cream. Four further farm cottages in the village housed the farmworkers. The rest of the land was to the East and beyond the village on the south of the Aldbourne road leading up the hill. The land around the house was put to grass, the rest being used to grow grain, particularly malting barley, and other crops. Initially, the corn was cut and stooked in bundles and after drying out, stacked and thatched, before being thrashed in a special thrasher towed and belt-driven by a steam tractor. Later George bought a small combine harvester. The farm tractor was a single-piston Marshall machine which was started with a cartridge. It had a large flywheel which could be used for belt-driving static machinery.

And so, George achieved his dream of a country life with the farm. As mentioned earlier, Jigme Djorge and his prime minister came to see the farm and stayed . . . he made the delightful comment that in his next reincarnation, he would like to be a dog in an English family!

George continued to be in demand as a company director; amongst his directorships were the Army and Navy Stores and Grindlay's Bank, as well as Bird and Co., London and National Bank of India. He fulfilled his commitment spending "duty time" with them most weeks as well, travelling to London from Hungerford for meetings, staying overnight at the Oriental Club on occasions.

Despite failing health, he continued with these working commitments until October 1953. There is a short diary entry in December of that year referring to the exploratory operation which confirmed a diagnosis of liver cancer as well as a note of Sir Paul Benthall's visit to him in the West Middlesex Hospital shortly after and just before Christmas. He kept up his interest in rugby with the Varsity match and the internationals using the match arrangements of the Oriental Club. These were the days when the Club was in Hanover Square.

136 John on the Marshall tractor

George was a keen fisherman and shot, and a member of two pheasant and other game shooting syndicates, one run by Gerry Waterfield at the top of the Aldbourne hill incorporating his own woods and other farmland, the other near Hungerford with duck shooting on flooded ground by the Kennet River. Salmon fishing was taken on the Test, generally a beat on the Mountbatten estate. He taught me to shoot, and, in his final winter of 1953/4, asked me to take his gun when he was unable to shoot himself.

Holidays involved trips to Scotland; particularly popular were Skye and Scourie. The latter involved an overnight train through the Highlands to Lairg, and then by bus to the town. Handa Island was very near . . . sea fishing for pollock and shooting rabbits on the island itself are particular memories. We used to walk to hill lochs to fish for trout which were eaten for breakfast. Another memory is being taught how to play bridge by my mother in the evenings.

One year, the bus broke down and there was a slight panic to catch the train. The bus conductor lay on the front mudguard pouring petrol from a whisky bottle into the carburettor and we made the station in time. Another summer holiday was taken in Milton Damerel in Devon with the Gemmell family. These last years were very happy ones.

The Cameron family, Sandy's son Micky, and daughter Diana, had settled just five miles away in the village of Liddington, just under the downs above the Swindon

137 *House party at Rectory House l to r Mike, Ian and Helen Gemmell, Jean, George Gemmell, Jen, Diana and Sandy Cameron, Dorks and Helen Tombazi, and Lee the labarador.*

road and Chisledon. Ronnie was still in Calcutta in his early months as President of the Bengal Chamber. Amongst his personal charitable work was his support for an orphanage north of Calcutta not far from Barrackpore. One Saturday in March 1948, he had personally organised and paid for a tea party for the children to celebrate their Easter prize-giving and had gone up by car to be with them. He had decided to spend the night at Shimerali camp and so driven by car to the Barrackpore jetty on the Hooghly, he went by launch upriver to camp spending the night there. The next day, the Sunday, he travelled back by launch with Teddie Shuttleworth's kitmagar, a Muslim, to be met at the Barrackpore jetty by his car and driver, a Hindu. It was a time of serious rioting in Calcutta with the Muslim population under threat and trains leaving with Muslim refugees for East Pakistan from Sealdah Station being intercepted by Hindu mobs and passengers being massacred. The railway policy was not

RECTORY AYRSHIRES

CATLINS URSULA 46406 (Lot 7).
Dam of Lot 43. G. Dam of Lots 41 & 43.

Dispersal Sale
at
OGBOURNE ST. GEORGE,
MARLBOROUGH, WILTS.
on
Wednesday, July 27th, 1955
Commencing at 12 noon.

Vendor :	Auctioneers :
LADY MORTON, Rectory Farm, Ogbourne St. George, Marlborough, Wilts.	THIMBLEBY & SHORLAND, Reading, and DENNIS POCOCK, Marlborough, Wilts.

138 Sale of Rectory Farm Ayrshires
July 27th 1955

to stop, resulting in deaths and injuries to the rioters lying on the railway line. Such an event was occurring just as Ronnie's car approached the level crossing with the DumDum road. The crowd stopped the car, opened the driver's door and stripped the driver naked, and then seeing from his birthmark that he was a Hindu, set him free. The kitmagar, a Muslim, was similarly treated and hacked to pieces. Ronnie stepped out of the car to defend him and was also hacked to pieces. His dead body was tended to by a haridan woman (the lowest caste who tend the bodies of the dead) and then recovered and buried in Calcutta. The crowd, realising what they had done, dispersed and at the news, Calcutta quietened down. Nehru's comment on this terrible incident was that Ronnie Cameron was a severe loss and he was "a great friend of India". At home, we were all so very sad.

George's health began to fail across the winter of 1952/3 when he developed jaundice which took him time to shake off. He had had hookworm in India which was thought to be a contributory cause. Later in 1953, the symptoms returned, and liver cancer was diagnosed. He came home for Christmas and returning, never came out of hospital. There is a diary entry "Kitzbuhel" in early January but it is not clear whether he went. Doreen then stayed in London to be with him . . . Jean ran the farm with Forsyth. I knew nothing of this having returned to Ampleforth, until I had the news broken to me by Fr Sebastian in early March that he had a short time to live, and I was released from school and driven to York Station by Fr Bernard and met off the train by my mother to see him. I had a little birthday present for him; he was sitting up in bed, pale but cheerful, surrounded by photographs of Greece which he was carefully arranging in an album. He had developed a great love of Greece and he and Dorks had returned again on holiday staying with the Tombazis in May 1951.

And so that was the last time I saw him.

Jean and Jen were at Rectory House, where Joan Shuttleworth was staying and looking after us. Doreen was in London spending the last few days with him. And so came the news that he had died. His funeral was at St. Columba's Pont Street, with Dr Scott of the Church of Scotland presiding and conducting the funeral. He was buried in the Putney Vale Churchyard off the A3 in Wimbledon.

Doreen was just 48, devastated, and never went to a funeral again.

EPILOGUE

Rectory House was sold in 1957 and Doreen moved to a rented flat in Albany Terrace, by Regents Park, accompanied by Jen. Jean and Barney had gone out to India, to the hills around Vandiperiyar in Kerala where Barney was working, tea planting for the Travancore Tea Estates. John had done national service and was reading law at Trinity College Oxford. One of the farm cottages had been kept, Beechlea Cottage, initially as a second home for the family. A small plot of land had also been kept at the bottom of the hill as a potential building plot and Jean and Barney eventually built a house, Fawn Close, there as a U.K. base. Jen started working for an interior decorating firm in Knightsbridge. She went back to India in 1963 and taught at St Paul's School in Darjeeling before returning to teach music to disadvantaged children in the East End of London. She later moved to Oxford, took a late degree in music at Somerville College and became the assistant librarian in the Bodleian Music Library before retiring while continuing to teach music. She never married and died in 2009. Jean and Barney came home for good in 1969 and Barney established a tea business near Harwich . . . it was he who developed the round tea bag for British Rail. He sold the business . . . Jean died in 2000, Barney in 2010.

Doreen bought a house at 55 Limerston Street which became the family home, but moved to Beechlea in the mid-1960s where she lived until she moved into a retirement home in Marlborough. She died in April 1989. John married Jane and moved to Somerset in 1980 raising a family. Jane died in 2017, shortly after John retired. Now aged 84, he still lives there with his four children and their families nearby and continues to write.

Footnote

Following Doreen's funeral, the family decided, if possible, to arrange for George to be transferred from the Putney Vale Cemetery to the Ogbourne St George churchyard, so that both parents could be together. Accordingly, the author arranged for an exhumation order from the Home Office. He travelled up in the undertaker's van arriving at Putney Vale with a large coffin in the back, to find the exhumation already nearly completed as the exhumation party had started very early that morning. One coffin was placed in the other, and we started back for Marlborough. We were all in need of breakfast, so we pulled into the Heston Service Station, leaving George in the back of the van, with the party enjoying a hot breakfast, before arriving in Marlborough late morning. How the parents would have laughed! And so, they are now together again, after a simple service in the Ogbourne churchyard. Theirs was a short but loving marriage of great strength; George died just before their silver wedding.

In 2004, at the beginning of April, on my return from a client appointment in Marlborough, I decided, on the spur of the moment, to visit their grave. Looking at their gravestone, it was the exact day 13th April, of the 50th anniversary of George's death.

July 2021

APPENDIX 1

Sir Edward Benthall K.C.S.I. Reflections on Mahatma Gandhi. (Source – Benthall papers in The Centre for South Asia Studies, Cambridge – C.S.A.S.C. – (Box 2)

The first time I saw Gandhi was when he came to London for the First Round Table Conference. *(1930 – JMM)* Amongst his first engagements, he attended a meeting of admirers at the Friends House presided over by, I think, Laurence Houseman. *(Laurence Houseman was a younger brother of A.E. Houseman, the classical scholar and poet. Lawrence was a noted playwright, writer and illustrator – JMM)* At once he created a very great impression. A little gnomish figure in white surrounded by fidgeting Westerners, he sat motionless amongst them, his very stillness creating an impression of great dignity. Ruth and I sat at the back of the hall, trying to sum up the personality who was going so much to affect our destinies in India.

It was not the first time she had seen him for she had sat beside James Roxburgh, the chief Presidency Magistrate, in Calcutta when he was trying Gandhi for having placed illegally a few rags of British cloth upon a bonfire in the streets of Calcutta during the time of the boycott of British goods. The fine was nominal, but it was a strange commentary on the times, not only that she should be there, but that nobody thought it was at all unusual that she should be there. Yet it is paralleled by the presence on the bench at Assizes in England of friends of the Judge, the Sheriff, the Deputy Sheriff and the Chaplain. Roxborough is the only judicial authority to have conducted his cases with his eyes fixed mainly on his silent typewriter, which he tapped incessantly throughout the case.

At the second Round Table Conference, I was to get to know Gandhi fairly well and indeed felt that I had struck up almost a friendship with him. There was, I flattered myself, a certain amount of mutual esteem; or at least there was considerable esteem on my side. He possessed very great charm, a marvellous sense of humour, and wonderful manners. In spite of his political actions, he made one feel, in conversation, that he was well disposed towards Britain individually and collectively, but, being born a bania, he was as hard as nails in bargaining over matters which he considered important, or which affected his amour propre. At this conference, his speeches showed him to be a megalomaniac and it was a most bitter blow to him when the Minorities committees, other than the Hindus, joined together in the Minorities Pact and demolished his claim, honest enough in his own mind, that he represented every soul in India.

It was my role, as representative of the Associated British Chambers of Commerce in India of which I was President, together with Sir Hubert Carr *(British Government – JMM)*, Edgar Wood *(Bombay Chamber – JMM)* and Tracy Gavin Jones, to endeavour to secure for the draughtsman of the Bill authority to include in the new Government of India Act clauses to secure our interests from legal or administrative discrimination, or from expropriation without compensation. This necessitated constant meetings and at one moment we thought that we had reached agreement with him over a formula which would have been sufficient for our purpose. But, having agreed the formula, he took it away for discussion with the Hindu and Parsee business elements and it was the Parsee element, strangely enough, which took exception to it. They paid me the compliment of saying I was securing an undue influence over Gandhi in matters which he did not understand, but I think myself that he understood well enough but was trying to satisfy us in order to detach us from the Minorities. When next we met, he explained that his reading of the formula was different from mine which was not surprising because, throughout his career, he often found a metaphysical reading of words that put a different interpretation upon a sentence to that attached by the ordinary reader. The effort failed, the subject was taken to the Federal Structure Committee where I made a long and conciliatory speech which earned the approbation of moderates such as Sapru and Jayakar and under the able Chairmanship of Lord Sankey, the brilliant support of Lord Reading *(foreign secretary and a former Viceroy – JMM)*, and the tacit agreement of our friends in the Minorities Pact, sufficient agreement was reached to enable the safeguards to be included in the Act.

These meetings recall certain unforgettable pictures to my mind. I see him sitting in a Queen Anne bergere armchair in the flat which my mother-in-law had lent us in Berkeley Square, an incongruous figure in the background of antiques and brocades. I see us after a very long sitting in the apartments of G.D. Birla at the Grosvenor House Hotel, which ended at 2 a.m., and as he came to see me to the lift, we weighed each other on a machine in the corridor. I turned the scales at 18 stone 4 lbs and he at 7 stone 5lbs in two dhotis. How we laughed! *(Tom was a mountain of a man turning 6ft 4", ex-Cambridge Rugby Blue and reserve second row for England – JMM)*

There was another occasion in Sir Corvasju Jehangir's flat in St James' when the financial experts were discussing the proposed Reserve Bank and the financial clauses of the Bill while he sat on the floor incessantly operating his hand spinning wheel. It was incongruous enough but a timely reminder of India for which we were trying to legislate. His thoughts seemed to be elsewhere.

Most memorable of all was a call he made when we were in my sister-in-law's house at the corner of Deanery Street, beside the Dorchester Hotel. He came accompanied by G.D. Birla who left him for a twenty-minute talk. The maids were hanging out of the upper windows to see the arrival of the exotic dhoti-clad figure. When the butler, a one-eyed and consequently rather bleary-looking family retainer in a morning coat, opened the door, he was rather taken aback by Gandhi shaking him very warmly with both hands. After half an hour's talk in a little study downstairs, towards the end of which I was rather conscious of Birla pacing up and down the street outside, he consented to come upstairs to meet Ruth, and after a few preliminaries, the following conversation took place between them.

"Mr Gandhi, what do you do with your spare time in London?"

"You see, Mrs Benthall, with all this Round Table Conference work and many engagements, I have no spare time."

"But, Mr Gandhi, you ought to take some relaxation for the good of your health. Do you never go to the cinema?"

"No, I am too busy."

"But you ought to relax. Haven't you seen Charlie Chaplin's latest film? Oh, but you must know who he is – one of the most famous men in the world."

"No, Mrs Benthall, you see that I live like a toad in a well immersed in my own affairs." (He used the word toad though the common Indian word is "a frog in a well".)

"Then, do you dance?"

He threw his head back and laughed. Then wagging his finger and still cackling, said, "But when I was a young man, articled to a solicitor in London, I used sometimes to put on my best clothes and go to a dance hall in the evenings." And we all, himself included, laughed long at this picture of him in his black suit and top bowler hat. He really enjoyed the contrast to his present world-famous position.

Another picture. Buckingham Palace and a reception to all the delegates to the Conference. His Majesty had initially refused to allow him to come to the levee wearing other than orthodox dress, but had eventually relaxed the regulations and permitted his appearance in dhoti. Ruth and I followed immediately behind him in the queue to shake hands with their Majesties and when Gandhi's turn came, neither of them showed any distinction but shook hands with the incongruously dressed leader just as with anybody else. He seemed faintly surprised but moved on with the procession. After this formality, a space was cleared in the salon and the King had brief conversations with various delegates. Presently, Gandhi's turn came and His Majesty was seen wagging his finger at Gandhi and obviously expressing displeasure. Gandhi shifted his feet and smilingly but awkwardly answered back. More finger-wagging by King George, and eventually, the conversation appeared to go amicably. It transpired afterwards, as we learnt from another member of the Royal family a few days later, the King had said to Gandhi, "Tell me, Mr Gandhi, what have I done that you should be so hostile to me nowadays? There was a time when you led an ambulance in South Africa in support of the British troops." And the gist of Gandhi's reply was that his opposition was not to him but to his government. *(Both Majesties had made an extensive visit and tour to India almost exactly 20 years previously, a key event being the Coronation Delhi Durbar at the beginning of December 1911. They were the only ruling Monarchs ever to do so – JMM)*

The Political Society at Eton had, in a moment of rashness, invited Gandhi to address them and when, rather to their amazement, he accepted, they asked me to come down and help them through with it. He duly arrived, motoring down with Miss Slade, on his way to stay with the Master of one of the Oxford Colleges, and for half an hour or forty minutes, addressed the boys in their tailcoats in deathly silence, broken only at the end by generous applause. They could not understand the strange workings of his mind but were deeply interested in Gandhi's case. A fortnight later, I took down Mohammed Ali who had been, at one time, a noted cricketer. He talked cricket and made them laugh, but obviously made little or no impression and quite failed to put across the case for the Muslims to a youthful and intelligent audience who were to provide a fair number of the nation's political leaders in later years. *(Tom's son Michael was a pupil at the time and a member of the Political Society – JMM)*

When the Round Table Conference was over and Gandhi was about to return to India where excitement was growing and an outburst was obviously imminent, Hubert Carr and I went to see him for the last time in England in a house adjoining the Hyde Park Hotel, to appeal to him to trust His Majesty's Government and to avoid disturbances. I arrived at ten minutes past six to find that Gandhi had, for ten minutes, been having his evening meal while talking to Carr and for another hour he ate and talked, dates and celery, curds and biscuits and fruit steadily disappeared. He was tired and depressed feeling obviously that he had not been the success in London that he had hoped. He seemed at a loss, not knowing what his next step would be, but nothing that we could say would induce him to commit (which he rarely did) to a course of cooperation. When he had finished his meal, and without turning his head, he called loudly "Bowl!" and from behind came Miss Slade with a brass bowl in which he rinsed his false teeth. Soon after, it became apparent that our interview was at an end and he became fidgety. We bade him farewell, and turning, realised that the room behind us had silently become full of his British admirers who had come for the evening prayer meeting, and there were many more coming up the stairs. We realised that here, in these people, he found much consolation. It was all perfectly sincere and demonstrated where his power lay.

We left for India and I travelled out in the P & O steamer with Lord Willingdon who was taking over from Lord Irwin with instructions to stand no nonsense if civil commotion was threatened. In Bombay, after discussion with the local Europeans, Geoffrey Winterbotham and I went to see him to make one final appeal, an action incidentally which caused a certain amount of unfavourable comment in Government circles and a very great deal of hostile criticism from the British in Calcutta who were, for the most part, spoiling for drastic Government action. We found Gandhi on the rooftop of a house, surrounded by his entourage of devoted women, old and young, and in the greatest of good spirits, so different from his last days in London. Here he felt himself at home again, in an atmosphere he understood. He strode purposefully across the rooftop, full of confidence and obviously relishing a struggle with Government. Polite and friendly as ever, he soon made it clear that we were wasting our time and we left him conscious that we had failed but not necessarily completely because our persistent efforts had, I firmly believe, not been fruitless, and had, to a considerable extent, offset the feeling of hostility engendered in our joining in the Minorities Pact.

(The political gulf between Hindu and Moslem was to bedevil Indian politics for decades resulting in Partition and the hostilities that still exist today not least in Kashmir – JMM)

On returning to Calcutta, I was faced with an attack on our policy by the Royalists, a sterling body of the younger generation who felt we were going too far to meet Hindu ideas and who were not afraid to say so. They felt fundamentally that the senior businessmen were content to buy appeasement at any price which would afford peace in their time of service. I was opprobriously known as "Bengali Sahib" among certain of the die-hard elements among the British and altogether had a most uncomfortable time, though backed throughout by the responsible firms on the Bengal Associated Chambers of Commerce. Looking back, I have no doubt that the policy followed by the leaders of British business throughout this anxious time was right, for the reasonable line we took over twenty years to independence, capped of course by the willingness of His Majesty's Government to grant that independence, prepared the way for the fair manner in which the Congress Government dealt with us when they came to power. The Chambers of Commerce nominated me for the third Round Table Conference, and Lord Willingdon supported the nomination. Here, however, an unfortunate incident occurred. I had addressed the Bengal Chamber members giving an account of events at the second Conference. The meeting was of course confidential though Hindu members were present. In the course of my remarks, I had occasion to say that Gandhi, and also the Conservatives, had decided to go back on the extent of agreement reached at the first Conference and had largely changed their minds because of the stand taken by the non-official delegation. This latter was a fact. The attitude of the Liberal and Labour delegations, supported by the steady line taken by our small business delegation, ultimately resulted in an adherence to the former plan. The Royalists were impressed by this speech and asked that it might be printed and circulated to their members, to which I foolishly agreed. The upshot of that was that one of their members sold the broadsheet to the congress for a job in the Corporation and one morning, when I was attending a further reforms committee in New Delhi, I suddenly became aware of a horribly cold atmosphere from many Hindus on the committee. The broadsheet had been published in every Hindu paper under the heading "The Great Betrayal". Whether the title referred to my comments on Gandhi or to the Conservatives, I never knew, though Congress obviously resented my phraseology and Sir Samuel Hoare rejected my appointment to the third Round Table Conference, no longer regarding me as a safe man. It was a nasty setback though I re-appeared as a witness to the Joint Secret Committee of Parliament and Sir Samuel Hoare's wrath did not last long as he passed my name for recognition in the new year's honours list of 1933.

The interesting thing to me, however, was the effect on Gandhi, for he might well have taken the line that I had demonstrated a false friendship. Not at all. He was much too big a man. It was some years before I saw him again. He had come to stay in a house in Tollygunge and I went to see him. He was a sick man, sitting on a South verandah, propped up on cushions and surrounded by medicine bottles. When I arrived, he raised himself from the ground and smiling in his most welcoming way, said, "After so long a time" One could not help but have a deep affection for a political opponent who could do this and though our talk was not more fruitful than any others, I felt that there was neither personal hostility nor any ill-feeling against the British business community.

In 1942, I was the sole British member of the Viceroy's Council, except for Lord Linlithgow himself, when the formal decision was made, late at night, to arrest Gandhi and the rest of the Congress leaders. Next year, Gandhi decided to fast unto death. His daily weight was recorded in all the papers and was watched with breathless interest by the whole Hindu population and indeed by the world. To none was his slow loss of weight more interesting than me who had weighed him personally more than ten years before, which perhaps made his gesture slightly less alarming to me than to others. He was not, I think, in any real danger and Lord Linlithgow had made a peculiar study of such fasting, but it was an anxious time when even the most westernised Hindu friends were moved to a pitch of emotion such as I had never before experienced.

My last meeting with Gandhi was at Birla House, New Delhi, in 1947. I was staying with the firm's representatives at Delhi, the Stokoes, who occupied the bungalow next door, and, wishing at any rate to be present at his prayer meeting, I climbed the low garden wall and met him for a moment coming from the house to the site of the meeting. He produced his usual welcome and was in high spirits, not much changed. I attended the meeting and spoke to several friends from the Assembly, then flew on to Lahore. Next day, a bomb was exploded at his meeting but when I returned there a few days later, the meetings were going on just as before. The day after my next visit to Lahore, he was murdered.

I was not in Delhi during the remarkable scenes which followed but shall never forget the day when some of his ashes were committed to the Hooghly at that beautiful bend in the river between Serampore and Barrackpore. The Committal was to be from a barge anchored in the middle of the river. All that morning, every kind of river craft made its way to the scene, and, at a respectful distance, anchored around the barge. The Governor of Bengal, that grand old man Rajagopalachariar, friend and confidant of Gandhi, embarked amongst tens of thousands of people, and, at a respectful distance, anchored from a landing stage at Barrackpore Park, where the Gandhi memorial now stands, accompanied by a few people and by a life-saver in a loincloth in case of accidents. He climbed aboard the barge before the watching multitude and the plan was that the Committal should be followed by two minutes' silence. Rajagopalachariar was so overcome with emotion that it seemed that the services of the life-saver might well be required. Then, at the critical moment, a police launch hooted for silence. But instead of silence, pandemonium broke out. Every launch and steamer in the river, including ours, hooted also. Rajagopalachariar stood on the barge waving both hands for silence but it only had the effect of spurring the hooters to louder efforts, like a conductor extracting fortissimo noises from his orchestra. The strange thing was not that it was unseemly but that Gandhi was going to his last rest amid a paeon of glory, a sort of unpremeditated Last Post which seemed thoroughly appropriate to the occasion and even more impressive than a continuation of silence which would have had no beginning and no end. His spirit lived on and after his death, had, and has, an even more important and profound influence on the new state than during his lifetime.

APPENDIX 2

Wartime letters from Ruth Benthall to my mother

Letter 1

Following the bombing of Lindridge, sent from 30 Ashley Road, Walton-on-Thames, November 30th 1940.

"Dear Doreen, Thank you for your wire about Lindridge – I don't know if anyone has written you since to give you all the news about that or the tragic death of Humphrey – the worst thing about that is that it was his own fault – pushing his bike without lights on the wrong side of the road – I imagine with his head down so that he didn't see the oncoming car – he was killed instantaneously – it all seems so futile – if he had been bombed it wouldn't have seemed so awful would it? It must have been awful for Hugh Colvin to have ????? up Lindridge – he told Tiger & I gather she told Elsa who had to break it to Eileen, who was, I believe, wonderful in her self-control – she and Eileen motored straight away to Eileen's people in Dorset – Humphrey was cremated at Worthing – I didn't know this as I would have gone to be with Eileen – she has now gone back to Lindridge with H's sister – her desolation must be terrible. I have had one very brave letter from her – but one feels hopeless & unable to help and all – I can't have her to stay here because we get so many bombs – & she mustn't take any risk now – it would be terrible for her children if anything happened to her. Everyone at Lindridge is trying to find some work for her to do so that she has something to do all day – work is the only thing that will help her now, we all feel – only time will help with the wound & the dreadful gap in her life – it is really awful, Doreen, that it should have happened in that way – I am so awfully sorry for the driver of that car – I've learnt that it was full of his own fellow officers but why more cyclists are not killed I don't know – it is a nightmare. We have taken this villa-cottage really only to sleep in – long winter evenings in our London basement were becoming impossible – with Tom trying to work sitting on the back stairs, dining in the pantry & all of us on stretchers in the passage, so we decided to take this – we get bombs and damage just the same – but one feels here that there is some chance of survival & one can dine in a room, and sleep in another altho' even here, most people sleep on the ground floor – we have Maurice Fogt living with us – he had been bombed out of all his flats & seemed so lost and helpless without his family & ???? doing any work yet. I have been too busy otherwise & it is very tiring going up and down every day – and yet I feel that I must go up with Tom as life is so very insecure in

London now – 69 is still standing; yes, it was hard luck about Lindridge – they are all convinced it was deliberate but Tom says not – anyhow, it was a marvellous escape for the house – all the windows have now been replaced and most of the other damage repaired; it might all have been so much worse – the front that fell a few yards from your hens didn't even ruffle their feathers – altho' Tiger said they laid scrambled eggs the next day! One just prays that it never happens again. It must have been an awful shock to them all & I was glad Gordon and Humphrey were there – Tom and I went down three days later – everyone seemed much more cheerful & alive! I am glad now in a way that you left England when you did – altho' I am thankful to be here – it is something to have to share in the glorious struggle England is putting up – & the courage of people in London is still amazing – it is sad to go up every day & find some fresh wounds – there is very little that has escaped – I don't mean that most of it isn't still standing – people coming from America are amazed at the small amount of damage but the total is mounting up – everyone now has had their narrow escapes – I certainly have had one or two! Have to tell you I have greatest confidence in your ring! (This was a family cat's eye ring – a token of good luck – believed to have originated from Andrew Trevor, my mother's great-grandfather, when, as surgeon to Wellington's 33rd Regiment of Foot at the battle of Seringapatam, on 4th May 1799, he certified Tippu Sultan's death. The ring belonged to Tippu – it was given to Ruth by my mother in thanks for her kindness to all of us at Lindridge during 1939-40 – JMM.) *So very much goodness & kindness has come out of this war & one is so very proud of being British. The Greeks too are putting up an amazing show of courage – Manoli is so proud.* (Manoli Tombazi was married to Helen, an American, and CEO of Ralli Bros Calcutta, associated with Birds through their substantial export trade in jute – JMM) *If only we can get through this winter one will feel that we have turned the corner – but I am afraid now it is going to be a much longer business than poor Chamberlain predicted. Tom is terribly busy & never stops working & he is very tired but anyhow his work interests him which is the main thing – he says that we shall all be living on potatoes next year – very good food too – your hens have really been a Godsend – there are no eggs to be bought anywhere & it seems impossible to cook anything without them – onions too have disappeared – where no-one seems to know! I wonder how you are all doing – I think of you often – anyhow, you are all together which, in these days, is everything. Michael is still waiting for an O.C.T.U. I have seen very little of him since you left – Oscar left Euston at 8 a.m. a week ago – he stayed here & we got up at 5.30 a.m. in order to see him off. I hope he is enjoying his voyage. I am glad Tom wrote to George telling him that it was his fault, Doreen, that no passage could be found for him. I could see that it was Hell for him having to leave England at this time – so I do hope he will get a welcome from the office & not cold looks! I doubt that Geoff Allen will ever be fit enough to go out again – he writes very pluckily but he seems to be no better – Audrey is sleeping here for a few nights as she is packing up her home. Freddy is at Cardiff playing darts & is as she says no longer any help to her about anything. Geoffrey Garratt tried to get out of the army but failed; these old men shouldn't have joined up – they are all handling it very nationally. Gordon is giving a local Dr a hand but hopes to find something permanent. Hilda is now in his hands – if only that poor old lady had died instead of Humphrey – it seems so stupid somehow. Perhaps this will reach you about Xmas – I have no idea but if it does, you will know that we shall be thinking of you all & to the Benthalls, please show this to Molly with my love; it is awfully hard to keep in touch these days but one does in one's thoughts and prayers. With love to you all & especially to John. Ruth."*

Ruth was my godmother. This was the time of Tom's working in the Ministry of Economic Warfare and the Board of Trade. He was to return to India in 1942 at the invitation of the Viceroy, who had set up a supply secretariat at Delhi, still very much involved in Birds as a major shareholder and partner. He became a member of the Viceroy's Executive Council with specific responsibility for war transport and railways. This was to be of significant importance during the food crisis and the distribution of food grains, particularly rice, during the latter part of 1943 as the famine developed and Wavell, having taken over from Linlithgow as Viceroy, brought in the army to help with its distribution.

George was now senior partner and about to become President of the Bengal Chamber during the crucial year 1941 when the war in the Far East started as the Japanese occupied Malaysia, Hong Kong and Singapore and then invaded Burma in 1942. This was the year of the sinking of the battleship Prince of Wales and Ark Royal off the coast of Malaya, and the end of imported rice from Burma and the far East, leading to the Bengal famine of 1943.

Letter 2

No address but dated 22nd January 1941 . . . letters are taking 8/9 weeks by sea mail around the Cape.

"Dear Doreen – judging by the time that your letter took you will get this about March 22nd & one wonders what is going to happen to us by that time – all the country's neutral (?) and otherwise say Britain is 'for it' in the next few weeks or so; well so be it! – Tom was so pleased to get a letter from you but as he works from 6 am to 10.30 pm, I don't know when he will – I do as much as I can about answering his letters etc but he is a very difficult man to help. I do hate seeing a man permanently tired – the relief when one day he is slightly less tired is wonderful! Everyone at the moment is a bit tired – on edge – the weather is foul, snow – ice – otherwise, a deluge of rain & pitch-black days with no sun – England at its worst but the evenings are lighter. We still leave Walton in the blackout but we do leave London in the twilight now and generally get back before the alerts and the damage – the air raids have not been so hard except spasmodically since the end of Oct: in London . . .? – these incendiary bombs have been the latest menace – Maurice Fogt & I have volunteered to be firefighters at Walton. I can't even lift the sandbags but I suppose I can work the stirrup pumps – I am hoping that it will get warmer and finer before I have to take my turn – I shall loathe spending four hours with two strange men

at 2 a.m. – but as I am doing nothing else in the way of work, I felt I must volunteer! I have never felt so grateful to pheasant and rabbits before – just live on them with tripe and fish for a change – but eggs are better now & no-one is starving; it is only a little difficult to make meals varied & attractive! What is making me furious at the moment is Wandel Wilkie who is coming from America on a fortnight's visit to see how we are all reacting in our struggle for life and death – he & a lot of Americans seem to think that we are exhibits – he wants to spend a night in a shelter with the poor – I hope he gets bitten first and then bombed! A bomb was dropped in King's Wood just opposite Strong's Farm; it smashed three lovely old . . .? down but otherwise no damage. Tiger thinks they really do think Lindridge is a Factory or a Military objective – it happens every full moon. I don't know what to say about your suggestions about Eileen going to a . . .? I don't think she would take the risk now – it is far greater than it was when you left. I expect she will write to you about measles etc. – this is always a bad time of year for communal living – I expect they will be delighted to get the extra tea – and I will send your suggestion of sugar for jam to Tiger, but I'm not sure that Tom will oppose – he's not touched sugar or butter himself & doesn't approve of our even having our meat ration because we get rabbits! Doreen, I loved your story of the Tibetan who says his children must starve if necessary to help the British Raj – one needs all those kindly thoughts so much – we do appreciate & are very conscious of all your thoughts reaching out to us to help in the struggle – I still feel we haven't reached the bottom of our abyss yet – & we are still not humble enough to be worthy of a victory. The papers and the B.B.C. made me sick the way they bragged about the Italian Rout; it made a wonderful & tragically on our behalf of . . .? (difficult to decipher – JMM) *sounds so cheap – we seem to have lost so much of our inherent dignity – I hope we will get it back – it was lovely to go to a French Lecture at the Geographical Society & to hear the Secretary announce that a suggestion had been proposed to alter the day of their meetings to suit members who were doing war work – but as they had held these meetings always on a Monday for the last 100 years, they had turned down the suggestion – it was a lovely lecture by a commander (Free French) on archaeology in Afghanistan – Maurice Fogt hopes to get some interesting work in . . .? propaganda Dept; he has been doing some broadcasting to the French – I have instituted a monthly lunch at Simpsons now to keep in touch with friends, so very important these days I think – the Tombazis – Villiers – Jack Hodge - Tom and Maurice & strong people who can come like J & Audrey – I wished you and 'G' were listening into a discussion on the wireless on Sunday between Roman Catholic – C of E, – & Wesleyan priests – there is a great feeling that all religions should get together now – the trouble is, Doreen, that your church will go on praying that everyone in the world should become R.C's & the rest of the Christians would . . .? less disagreements and more unity – Tom thinks it would be an excellent thing if we did all revert to becoming R.C's but for heaven's sake, don't let's try to convert when we choose to all non- Christians- I think the Buddhists are wonderful. I always remember with such pleasure our mad discussions with 'G' – I always say you are the most religious person I know in the best sense – I still love wearing your ring & Manoli was so intrigued by it. Well, love to you all & to all my friends and please thank Sandy for her letter.*

(This is almost like a P.S.) *I have one suggestion to make about people in Calcutta & that is that they take this grand opportunity to lower the absurd standard of living out there – I hear that the Archdeacon of Calcutta cursed everyone for not taking the war seriously & for drinking too much – this I am sure is all wrong but I do think it would be a wonderful thing for people in Calcutta now to live more simply & more normally – couldn't you and Molly start a campaign? – Tom thinks it a good suggestion; it really only means less competition for food – simpler food – drinks ditto? It would so help to simplify the life of Chokras* (young assistants – JMM) *out there who really should be saving money and not spending it all. What do you think? Ruth."*

This has been a particularly difficult letter to transcribe. It gives the impression of being written in considerable haste but underlines the very close affection between my mother and Ruth. War had forced her to re-evaluate their lives faced with shortages and the ever-present dangers of the blitz. Maurice Fogt was a French doctor; I can remember meeting him when he called at 22 Limerston Street to take my mother out to dinner, probably in 1961. He was charming and then living in le Touquet. He was a very close friend of Tom and Ruth.

Letter 3

This is a typed letter and somewhat easier to read. It is dated April 4th 1941.

"Dear Doreen, I feel horribly guilty at not having written before to thank you for that enormous chest of tea. I do hope Lindridge has written to you about theirs. I can't tell you how grateful we all are for it, but I think that we are all feeling a little stunned and it has seemed almost hopeless to write to people in India, one feels letters will never arrive, which I know is stupid because they all do in time, but one wonders if they would get to heaven just the same. Along the same lines I wrote about some months ago, to simpler living, but I don't agree with him about not changing for dinner; it would be hell after a long hot day in the office! But what does strike one as odd to read about is that people are spending 75 Rups on going to a boxing show for three days; one feels dreadfully guilty here in spending a shilling or two on a cinema, and if one does, one doesn't really enjoy it very much! There is an outcry now about having the Easter Monday holiday and working on Good Friday. I wish I didn't always think every point of view to be the right one! I am afraid that Molly must be miserable about her father; it must be hell for her being so far away, and probably not feeling her best either. I hope by this time your family are well again, you really have had a rotten time, Lindridge is full of measles and flu, just as Tiger was going away for a few days, she really ought to go away, she is much too conscientious.

Tom is working just as hard, we don't leave London now until 7 pm which means getting back here for dinner, news, and bed, and off again at 8 am. I shall strike soon and come back by train, because there is a nice little garden here to sit in when it gets warmer. I am going to bind books for the Navy, a job I can do at my leisure and where I like, there isn't time for me to do a regular job in London now, there are so many oddments to do for this house etc. No-one need worry about the food problem so far – we have ample to eat, but it is only the question of what to get or what there is to get. The jam rationing was the biggest blow, however, Lindridge has a year's supply in hand, but I don't know how we shall be able to make any more this year as there is to be no more private jam-making; poor Tom, he has already given up so much, it was a great blow to him because he adores his Jam! However, he gets all our rations in this house and we are saving our sugar to make him some! And I expect that Eileen has told you that she is going to breed Rabbit which will be a great help next winter, when I suppose that we really will be short of food. We are in a very exhilarated frame of mind at the moment because of the wonderful victories we are having but I suppose that we mustn't get carried away and think like I do, at once, that the war is as good as won, but it would be nice to hear our church bells ringing out over England to celebrate. It is the grimness of this war that gets one down and the awful feeling of fear that all these nations are living in all of the time. We here are frightened because there is, at the moment, no awful blitz going on; instead of being thankful, we wonder what now and worse things the enemy is thinking out for us. Lindridge still misses you a lot, Doreen, Tiger specially. Perhaps you left a deep impression on that rather difficult menage; poor Eileen feels at the moment so lost, and she and Rosalind don't somehow seem to be fitting in with the rest very well. I wish she had a job which takes her out all day, and I wish Geoff Allen would marry her; he needs someone to look after him because I don't think he will ever be really fit again. Rosalind is getting very spoilt, and the other children don't like her, she misses John, I think, George is too young for her. Gordon is finding an English country practice very different to his Calcutta work, but he doesn't seem able to find what he wants elsewhere. Hilda now only gets up for dinner, Elsa is an angel to her. I hear from Oscar that your new house is lovely, I am so glad. It must be getting hot now, the loveliest time of the year, and I suppose that you will be moving the family to the hills again very shortly. We are going to spend the weekend with' J' which will be a nice change from this very monotonous life we lead. Elsbeth and Jack have taken a house here for the summer which will be nice for me. I believe the daffodils are wonderful again at Lindridge but they are being sold as soon as they come out, and Stevenson has done some miracles in the kitchen garden now that he is boss. Tom and I hope to go down for the weekend soon. I must just see all that heavenly spring blossom; we have only got a garden the size of a lavatory, but I get thrilled at the sight of one daffodil, it is all so good for us I suppose and I still don't think that we are fit to win this war. You must be so glad you went out to India when you did, and I am so glad I couldn't change your mind for you, at least one of my friends is happy, and I hope safe. Do write and tell me what you are doing, and how Molly is; please give her my love and say how dreadful I am for her.

You will doubtless realise that I have only just started typing – Maurice lets me use his – which is noble- with very much love to you all. Ruth. "

Letter 4

This letter is handwritten. 30 Ashley Road, Walton–on–Thames October 8th

"Dear Doreen – Your letter of June 23 arrived last week, also the first parcel of butter and sugar – I feel that this is very unnecessary because we really have plenty until it comes to jam-making – & God knows how this will be done at Lindridge next year when it will be a girls' school – we have quite enough butter with our Rations in this small Household – I feel it ought to go to some family with children – it is amazing how much we have to eat – it may be monotonous but we have heaps always – & the tendency is to eat less and less – I think one always wants the other to have more – everyone has got thinner in consequence – but there is really need for this; we often talk of the heavenly food you are all enjoying without any difficulty – eggs I miss more than anything – but thanks to your hens, I hope to bring back a lot for the winter – Tom & I go down this week and to meet Miss Donkins & to face a rather sulky Tiger & a tired Eileen – I am simply dreading it, Doreen – Tom has had no holiday & is awfully tired & we just long to be alone there for a few days & have nothing to do – I can't bear to see Tom so tired – we are lucky if we dine at 9 o'clock now & then he has to get up every day at 7.15 & start again – Sundays he works all morning – sleeps for an hour – then we go to some gardens – we only have enough petrol now to use the car once a week for London and our Sunday outing. Maurice is almost as bad now – but he does work here on Saturdays instead of going to London – I am so lucky to have Lisbeth Hodge living so close– we are hoping to find some local work to do together in the winter – I have been tied to London lately – as Maurice has his private office there & there are no 'chars' to be got, I have become a very good House-maid! England has become really down to earth & everyone is working, working, working; there literally are no servants to be got, poor Dawn is having an awful time – she has never had to cope with anything in her life before & is really up against it – I am terribly lucky to have two awfully nice women here and we lead a very luxurious life compared to most of my friends who are doing everything for themselves. Audrey has taken a very nice house & is going to have PGs with the help of a girl of 16 – she is really wonderfully plucky – Freddy is about to become a Major & may be sent to the North of Ireland – he has been in the Shetland Islands for months. The Brandons are still practice and house-hunting living on a farm near Guildford; they can find neither – there are no houses anywhere near London. The Glammona (?) are now with their children – he has got a job.

George & his sister are in the North somewhere. I don't know what Eileen intends doing or Tiger – will you give Molly my love & thank her for her letter – I am so glad we are having a friend of hers living at Lindridge & I do hope she and all the girls will be happy there – they are so lucky; they are going to get any amount of fuel and petrol – I think Lindridge would be impossible to run permanently this winter. Hilda is fed & comfortable near Ascot – semi-nursing home – hotel – at last she is trying to let her flat – Tom lets me see some of his Indian mail so I get some idea of what you are all doing – & I saw a photograph of you outside your shop – how Jewish it was there – it was awful not to be able to go anywhere in England even if Tom got a few days' leave – there is nowhere to go; everything everywhere is full up, London is packed with people – now I suppose the first raid will send them all flying off again – some hotels make you do your own room they are so short of staff! We are all at the moment worried about Russia – it is . . .? having a critical time – it is so strange now to go to the Films which show endless propaganda pictures of Russia – & how wonderful they are etc. etc. others are too! I think we have all settled down to a very long & grim war & we really haven't started it yet – one can't see any end to it all – & afterward the Peace will be worse – The work will never stop for any of us & I don't see any hope of us having an idle old age at Lindridge. I doubt very much our ever being able to live there again – we are in the middle of a revolution & we can never go back – but some of us have lovely memories to look back upon – & the present generation will have known nothing else – the youth of today is full of common sense & very shrewd & I think more religious in a way – I wonder when we shall all meet again – we talk so much about you all – & we love getting all your news – only do send it Air Mail! & if you want to send people here anything, Doreen – the best thing is clothes – it is going to be very difficult to get through the Year with our coupons – especially people with children like Eileen – everyone is so grateful for anything in the way of clothes now – undies – handkerchiefs – stockings – anything but hats which we can get coupon free – we don't really need them – so don't send me any more butter and sugar but send Eileen clothes instead – material to make up for Rosalind – I wish I could see John in Kalimpong – I wish I could see you all – I so often dream I am back in Calcutta – & I hate waking up to find I am not.

With love to you all & write again soon, Ruth.

PS I find this is a very gloomy letter. I am sorry but there is no colour in our life now, not much to laugh at."

Jan 1st 1942 Letter 5

"Dear Doreen,

It would have been a very great disappointment if we had not found your name in the papers this morning at breakfast & now you will be swimming about in a thousand wires & letters – & your Bearers expecting buckshees! & I expect forming up the stairs & have to give your new title – it is another honour for the old firm who always seem in our thoughts at the right moment & all so very merited – I was 10 years old when Father was knighted & I remember writing to congratulate his mother, because it seemed to me that the honour should be hers and not my mother's – we had a happy day; you must be spending together in spite of Japanese & all the horrors which have crept so near to you all – I did hope that Tom for once would be wrong in his prophesy so many months ago now but I know you are all full of courage & perhaps even a little glad that you are in it too! But I am so worried for all you mothers. Mme Fogt, Maurice's eldest daughter, has just arrived back from Canada – she worked her way across there as Mess Boy in a courageous & . . .? to join up her (?) – very sporting! She arrives in London tonight-

413

lovely for Maurice to have someone of his own in this country – we have had notice to leave our little house in Walton which is awful because I don't see any hope of getting another. London is not going to be a very good place to come back to in the spring I fancy- I think Hitler is bound to try and drag us down into Hell insane & should him – what awful things the German soldiers must be suffering – they must be almost insane & I think thankful to be shot – very ersatz clothes and no gloves, Doreen – can you imagine anything more ghastly – & we have got so much to be thankful for here in England.

Tiger is I think going to run a land girls' hostel she can keep her own car . . .? & motherly doing that altho' she played with the idea of a commission in the W.R.E.Ns. Eileen is still seething (?) light– and has spent Xmas with her widowed brother – in – law; she must marry that man, I think! The Brandons are going to Kingston to take a house and practice there – left may be Eileen, Hilda and me so we can meet her – silence from Lindridge; I expect they are all very busy getting it converted – most of the girls are going to sleep in the dining room and garden room and all classrooms in the attics! I like Miss Donkin so much so I hope she will be able to make a success of it all & get enough petrol etc. I will give Eileen the nightdress when I next see her – but it is much too cold to sleep in anything but woollies at the moment – it made me shiver to look at those lovely nighties but we shall be thankful for them in the summer – I have seen Pam & Joan Geary and tell Evelyn they both look very well – Joan has an 'Ensa' job now which exempts her – I don't know what Pam will do – Michael is just off on another course & may go abroad I am afraid – but I am very lucky to have had him here for so long but I am just dreading his going -

***Jan 7th** – my two servants now say they are going & as I can't cook, the outlook is not too bright at the moment! – how I long for two or three bearers, because there really is no chance of getting any servants anywhere and most of the Registry offices have been closed anyhow – it is sad to think of Monty leaving the Firm – I do wonder how he will do – Oscar wrote me a long account of your Wavell dinner party – I wish I had been there – he really has got a job to do now – and I hope to God that he does it as well as Auchinleck has in Libya!*

***Jan 10th** Your wire Xmas arrived yesterday thank you so much for it. I do wish I could see you all and John. The film Oscar sent home did make us feel so homesick for India – it is bitterly cold, Doreen, but we are so lucky to have warm clothes, food and fires – the suffering of the Greeks is ghastly & Manoli says they have no fuel – he hopes they have enough to eat – (his own people I mean). The people are starving, falling down in the streets from hunger- I am afraid Rommel has got away in Libya now they have the devil's luck in the way of weather. I met Eileen in Harrods yesterday looking very ill I thought & still without any plans – it is impossible for her to get a house and furnish it now – I tried to get some sheets and they asked 5 guineas a pair – I just refused so by next year we shall have none! Tiger is going to take this Land Girl's job – she has a fortnight's training in a Y.M.C.A hostel first – I do wonder if you are in Kalimpong – it must be lovely up there now – how thankful the Morgans must be to have settled up there! Please* *thank Bunty Odling very much for her card. I hear that Elsa is* (Bunty's sister, known as Jiggy, trapped in Denmark under German occupation – she later escaped back to England in a fishing smack – JMM) *hoping any day to be rescued by the commandos but is treated very well. What a nightmare world, Doreen – the honour of it all seems to grow worse and worse, doesn't it?*

My very special love to John – Tiger sent me a letter Jennifer wrote her which was wonderful. Ruth. " (Jennifer, my middle sister aged eight and a half, had a very special affection for Tiger – JMM)

July 2020

415

BIBLIOGRAPHY

The 11ᵗʰ Battalion Royal Fusiliers First World War Diaries 1915,1916,1917,1918. The Fusilier Museum, HM Tower of London, London EC3N 4AB

The Wartime Memories project 11ᵗʰ Battalion Royal Fusiliers during the Great War

Daily Telegraph Monday 25ᵗʰ February 1917 *"Boom Ravine – battle in the fog – a grim struggle from Philip Gibbs British Headquarters (France)"* – (Morton Archive)

Daily Telegraph 25ᵗʰ July *"killed in Action Lieut William Cattell Morton".* Telegraph August 16ᵗʰ 1917 – *his Military Cross.* – (Morton Archive)

The Times Wednesday April 18ᵗʰ *Temp Capt. George Bond Morton Military Cross and short citation. Invitation to investiture by H.M. the King 4ᵗʰ October 1918. (*Morton archive)

History of the 54ᵗʰ Infantry Brigade Chapter viii – (Imperial War Museum)

History of the 18ᵗʰ Division Chapter ix – (Imperial War Museum)

The battle of Boom Ravine by Trevor Pidgeon (Pen & Sword Books Limited 1998)

Theipval Somme by Michael Stedman (Pen and Sword books Limited 1995)

Trench notebook Capt. G. B. Morton – (Morton Archive).

Letters from George to his sister Alice 1915, 1916, 1917- (Morton Archive)

Letters from William to George and his sister Alice 1915, 1916, 1917 – (Morton Archive).

Letters from fellow soldiers about the Battle of Boom Ravine including Sgt Major Fritterer and others.

Letter from fellow soldiers of William Morton's service and death. – Morton Archive

Somme: Into the Breach by Hugh Sebag-Montefiore (Viking division of Penguin books)

Catastrophe – Europe goes to war by Max Hastings (William Collins – 2013)

Trench – a History of Trench Warfare on the Western Front by Stephen Bull (Osprey Publishing 2010)

Great Britain's Great War by Jeremy Paxman (Penguin books 2014)

Digging the trenches – The Archaeology of the Western Front by Andrew Robertshaw & David Kenyon (Pen and Sword Books Ltd 2008)

Artillery in the Great War by Paul Strong and Sanders Marble (Pen and Sword Books 2013)

The Young Gunner – The Royal Field Artillery in the Great War. By David Hutchinson (Troubador Publishing Ltd 2016)

Father Browne's First World War by E.E. Donnell S J (Messenger Publications 2014)

Bird and Company of Calcutta – A history to mark the firm's centenary 1864-1964. (Privately published) by Geoffrey Harrison

100 years of British Banking in Asia and Africa – a History of National and Grindlay's Bank 1863-1963 by Geoffrey Tyson C.I.E. (published by National and Grindlay's Bank Ltd of Bishopsgate London E.C.2 1963 Centenary History.)

A History of the Indian Medical Service by Lieut Col D.G. Crawford I.M.S. (published by W Thacker & Co. 1914)

Annual report on Bengal Medical Services – 1920 Col F. O'Kinealy C.I.E., C.V.O., I.M.S., Surgeon General, Bengal. (The author's grandfather. Published 1921 & now in James Hardiman Library NUI Galway Eire)

British India 1772-1947 – A survey of the nature and effects of alien rule by Michael Edwards (Sidgwick and Jackson 1967)

The British in India – Three centuries of Ambition and Experience by David Gilmour (Allen Jane – a Division of Penguin Books)

Lives of The Indian Princes by Charles Allen and Sharada Dwivedi (Century Publishing Co 1984)

The History of The Second World War by Winston Churchill Volumes 1, 2. (Cassel)

Letters from George to sister Alice 1919,1920,1921. (Morton Archive)

*Letters from George to Doreen 1929 – 1940 (*Morton Archive)

The Benthall Archive boxes 1-13 (Cambridge Institute for South Asiatic Studies)

Lindridge (from "The lost houses of Devon")

Family of the Raj by John Morton (1917 The Memoir Club)

Annual Report to members of Bengal Chambers of Commerce 1941 Presented by Sir George Morton 25th February 1942 (British Library African and Asian section)

The Second World War by Winston Churchill (Vols 3, 4, 5, 6.- Cassel to 1954)

Knights Bachelor -1949-1950 21st Edition by Gerald W. Wollaston Knight Principal

The Imperial War Museum Book of the War in Burma 1942-45: A Vital contribution to Victory in the Far East by Julian Thompson

Gandhi and Churchill – The Epic Rivalry that Destroyed our Empire and Forged Our Age by Arthur Herman (Hutchinson 2008)

*The Macrell Archive Boxes 1-4 (*Cambridge Institute for South Asiatic Studies) principal extracts from this archive included *Report on the Burma Campaign 1941-42 by H.E. Honourable Sir Reginald Dorman-Smith;* the full report was researched and is available in the British Library and includes *Appendix V Report on the Civil Evacuation.* Further extracts include an *undated despatch from London Times & New York Times* from Harrison Forman, Pneso Hostel, Chunking, China, *Race and Resistance in Burma* by Andrew Selth, *Memoirs of Maj W.H.D. Newton* – Imperial War Museum P 370, also Major General E Woods, Administrator General of Eastern Frontier India – *Report on The Evacuation of Refugees from Burma to India Jan-July 1942 dated 1-10-1942.* Full report also available and accessed in the British Library together with the *Report of The Indian Tea Association* on the evacuation. Also, paper by A. Ramsay Tainsh *Journal of International relations Vol 7 no 1 May 1981 Mouldy grain disease – Mycotoxicosis*

The Times of India reports – August 23rd 1945 reporting death of Netaji Subhas Chandra Bose and companions at midnight 17/18th. August 1945 in an air crash, also that of 3rd September 1945 – Major General C.M. Maltby's report on Japanese treatment of Indian prisoners, and that of November 6th 1945, reporting on proceedings by courts martial against INLA soldiers. (British Library fully digitised records)

Flight by Elephant – the Untold Story of World war II's Most Daring Rescue by Andrew Martin

A Matter of Honour – An Account of the Indian Army, Its Officers and Men by Philip Mason. (Jonathan Cape 1974)

The Indian Empire at War, from Jihad to Victory – the Untold Story of the Indian Army in the First World War by George Morton-Jack (Little Brown Book Company 2018)

Dadland – A Journey into Uncharted Territory by Keggie Carew (Chatto and Windus 2016)

Diary of Escape over the Chukan Pass by Ritchie Gardiner (Privately published 1946)

Tours in Sikkim and the Darjeeling District by Percy Brown and Joan Townend

Merchant Prince: Memories of India 1929-58 by Sir Owain Jenkins

The Making and Unmaking of British India by Lawrence James

Letters from Doreen to George and George to Doreen November 1946 – February 47 (Morton Archive)

Official Government files of reports correspondence from ICS civil servants Viceroys Lord Linlithgow, General Wavell and others on the 1943 Bengal Famine (Africa and Asia section of the British Library)

Churchill – Man of Destiny by Prof Andrew Roberts (Allen Lane 2018)

Lhasa: The Holy City by F. Spencer Chapman (Catto and Windus 1937)

The Jungle in Neutral by F. Spencer Chapman (1948)

Britain and the Greek Economic Crisis: a PhD Thesis 1999 by Dr Athanasios Lykogiannis

INDEX

Lightning Source UK Ltd.
Milton Keynes UK
UKHW021152031222
413275UK00008B/176/J